EMILY   DICKINSON

EMILY DICKINSON

by Cynthia Griffin Wolff

ALFRED·A·KNOPF·NEW YORK·1986

This is a Borzoi Book published by Alfred A. Knopf, Inc.

Copyright © 1986 by Cynthia Griffin Wolff

All rights reserved under International and Pan-American Copyright Conventions.

Published in the United States by Alfred A. Knopf, Inc., New York,

and simultaneously in Canada by Random House of Canada Limited, Toronto.

Distributed by Random House, Inc., New York.

Owing to limitations of space, all acknowledgments for permission

to reprint previously published material can be found on page 641.

Library of Congress Cataloging-in-Publication Data

Wolff, Cynthia Griffin.   Emily Dickinson.

Bibliography: p.   Includes index.

1. Dickinson, Emily, 1830–1886—Biography.

2. Poets, American—19th century—Biography.   I. Title.

PS1541.Z5W58   1986   811'4 [B]   86-15192

ISBN 0-394-54418-8

Manufactured in the United States of America

First Edition

FOR

TOBIAS BARRINGTON WOLFF

AND

PATRICK GIDEON WOLFF

(*in random order*)

CONTENTS

ILLUSTRATIONS

Acknowledgments

I would like to begin by thanking my former husband, Robert Paul Wolff, who was very helpful during the preparation and early stages of composition.

A number of people offered unique help during the periods of research and writing. Mrs. Kendall DeBevoise, curator of the Emily Dickinson House (where I spent many happy afternoons as a guide), was able to give me facts about its history that have been scattered among many secondary sources, for Mrs. DeBevoise has become, herself, a knowledgeable scholar of Dickinson's life and work. John Lancaster of the Frost Library was more than helpful in my assemblage of information about Dickinson's schooling—and was particularly informative about Edward Hitchcock and his work. Finally, as many Dickinson scholars know, the Jones Library in the town of Amherst has an "Emily Dickinson Room," where a vast store of secondary material has been collected. Daniel Lombardo, the curator of this collection, so graciously made its resources available that I could move my typewriter into a small study and read books and articles about the poet—all the while able to gaze out the window and look down Main Street, where the Dickinson House could be glimpsed in the distance.

Several of my colleagues at the Massachusetts Institute of Technology provided help of another sort. Professor Jay Keyser took time from his own busy schedule to discuss a number of vexingly difficult poems. Arthur Kaledin, superbly knowledgeable about American social history and letters, scrutinized the manuscript's attempts to re-create Emily Dickinson's social milieu. Claudia von Canon, musician and novelist, gave her advice and support throughout the long period of composition.

Other colleagues, more geographically scattered, were invaluable because they read what proved to be a very long manuscript—receiving chapters as I wrote them and pointing out deficiencies of exposition, organization, and analysis: Professor Katherine Henderson of the College of New Rochelle; Joseph Mazzeo, Professor Emeritus of Columbia University; Everett Emerson, Professor of American Literature at Chapel Hill; and Priscilla Hicks, Professor of English at the University of Massachusetts at Amherst.

All of these people—friends and colleagues—gave me much more than merely intellectual assistance: they gave warmth and affection and sustaining encouragement. Two in particular gave such substantive help that their literal aid and their emotional generosity were of crucial importance. Monica Kearney put the many successive versions of this book on a computer disk; she kept track of the footnotes I lost; she read each section with an interest that was an incentive to keep writing; and she reassured me when I doubted my own work. Elizabeth C. Moore was kind in so many ways that they cannot be listed: she took time from a busy life to help with the drudgery of counting lines of poetry and proofreading galleys; together with her husband, Barrington Moore, Jr., she was a constant source of comfort during a long and arduous labor. I can find no words adequate to express my thanks.

Finally, I would like to thank Robert Gottlieb, my editor at Knopf. Oddly enough, it was not his insightful and tactful comments about the manuscript that I most appreciated. What mattered had more to do with character: his honesty, compassion, and generosity. Such traits are rarer than mere intelligence—and more valuable by far.

Belmont, Massachusetts
1986

Prologue ◆ *The Oven Bird*

There is a singer everyone has heard,
Loud, a mid-summer and a mid-wood bird,
Who makes the solid tree trunks sound again.
He says that leaves are old and that for flowers
Mid-summer is to spring as one to ten.
He says the early petal-fall is past
When pear and cherry bloom went down in showers
On sunny days a moment overcast;
And comes that other fall we name the fall.
He says the highway dust is over all.
The bird would cease and be as other birds
But that he knows in singing not to sing.
The question that he frames in all but words
Is what to make of a diminished thing.

—Robert Frost, "The Oven Bird"

The Dickinson House is a spacious, center-hall brick home on Main Street about three blocks east of the Amherst village center. Built in 1813 by the poet's grandfather, it has all the grace and symmetry of the pre-Victorian American style. Yet as one of this country's landmarks, it seems to have little to make it distinctive. By contrast, the Mark Twain House in Hartford, Connecticut, is a flamboyant emanation of Twain's idiosyncratic imagination: shaped by its sweeping verandas and jaunty chimneys to look like a Mississippi steamboat, the Twain House bears the distinctive imprint of its illustrious owner everywhere—from the window centered defiantly in the sitting room's chimney on the first floor to the billiard room and study on the third. Nothing in the Dickinson House is comparably revealing. Although Emily Dickinson's bedroom has been fitted out to look very much as it did during her lifetime, with a Sheraton bureau, Franklin stove, and chaste cherry table between the two front windows—a near-duplicate of the simple stand at which she wrote—the room is unrefurbished with the lingering personality of its former occupant. It is something of a puzzle, then, that so many readers regard this House almost as a holy place, making the trek to western Massachusetts as if to a saint's shrine, seeking some ineffable truth.

Guides at the House have become accustomed to the questions. The visitors accept the poet's genius without question. They acknowledge that the verse is difficult, sometimes quite inaccessible; nonetheless, a great many of them know the poetry with exceptional intimacy. Yet what they ask about is seldom the work. They want to know about the *woman*. The well-intentioned insistence of this curiosity is something of an embarrassment, for there is little apparent substance to satisfy the pressing need. Indeed, it would be difficult to cite an American author of commensurate power whose life offers less in the way of striking occurrence. The essential narrative can be told in a few sentences.

Born on December 10, 1830, Emily Dickinson was the middle child of three: her older brother Austin had been born in April 1829, and her sister Lavinia was born in February 1833. The poet lived in Amherst for her entire life, taking no more than a dozen extended trips away from home. Even Austin and Vinnie, both of whom were fond of traveling, never settled anywhere but Amherst. The family was a tight-knit group, almost a little society unto itself, and the closeness was finally broken only by death. Emily Dickinson obtained a superb secondary-school education at the Amherst Academy right in the middle of town, and she spent most of one year at the new Mount Holyoke Female Seminary in South Hadley to finish her formal schooling. During the 1840s and 1850s, Amherst witnessed significant religious "revivals," outpourings of evangelical piety that summoned Christians to submit to faith through conversion. Alone among the members of her family, Emily Dickinson turned away from these religious injunctions, and gradually she stopped attending church altogether. During her girlhood and young womanhood, she took an enthusiastic part in all of the usual social activities—sleigh rides, excursions in the countryside, and parties. She had beaux, and from time to time she expressed a particular preference for one or another young man; however, her youth brought her no single great love. Neither she nor her sister married, and both lived all their lives in their parents' home. The single extraordinary happening in Dickinson's life was a bout of severe trouble with her vision. Everyone in the family except Father suffered from some form of eye ailment, but Emily's was by far the worst. In the fall of 1861, she experienced an episode of seriously impaired sight; she made two long journeys to Boston, one in 1864 and the other in 1865, to be treated for the illness; after 1865, the trouble seems to have subsided. For the rest, she stayed quietly at home.

The only truly remarkable thing about Emily Dickinson's existence is that she produced a very great deal of incomparable poetry. Ironically, even the way in which her work found posthumous publication is a more striking story than the external events of the author's life.

Her family and friends knew that she wrote poetry; however, none had an inkling of how much she had written (fewer than twenty poems were published during her lifetime). After Emily's death in 1886, Vinnie was given the task of sorting through her sister's effects; to her complete astonishment, she came upon a locked box that contained a vast store of verse—1,775 poems were eventually discovered, a great many neatly copied out and others in much rougher form (written on the back of a bill, for example, or inscribed on a graduation program). It was a treasure, but a treasure that presented immense problems. Emily Dickinson's handwriting is very difficult to read, so much so that some of the products of her last years seem little more than hieroglyphics to an untutored eye. Furthermore, no easy chronology could be established, for the poems bore no dates. Mercifully for subsequent generations, Vinnie decided not to consign the work to oblivion; instead, she embarked on an almost fanatic campaign to get her sister's verse into print. Eventually she achieved her goal; the first slim selection was issued in 1890. However, even Vinnie's efforts were only partially successful. In the 1890 volume and in subsequent editions as well, the poetry was "corrected" by editors who feared that the irregularities of rhythm and rhyme might offend their readers. Thus a complete and fully accurate collection of Dickinson's work was not published until Thomas Johnson's variorum edition of 1955, almost seventy years after the poet's death.*

The full details of the complicated path by which Emily Dickinson's verse was brought to the public make an interesting story, and when visitors come to the Dickinson House seeking information about the poet, this is one of the distracting narratives that can be told. Yet that fact in itself tacitly acknowledges the paucity of overt drama in the life these visitors really wish to learn about. Another somewhat more useful distraction can be given by telling something about those who constituted Dickinson's world—Austin's family, for example, and his mistress, Mabel Loomis Todd.

In July 1856, Austin married Susan Gilbert. Sue was darkly attractive—exotic or handsome rather than conventionally pretty. She had a strong character and a powerful intellect, and for a number of years she was Emily Dickinson's closest confidante. After a stormy courtship, Sue and Austin settled into what appeared to be a happy marriage; they had three children—Ned (born 1861), Mattie (born 1866), and Gilbert (born 1875). Austin was genial and easygoing, but Sue, who was witty and opinionated, made enemies among the townspeople. Still, few suspected serious trouble in the family. In 1881, David Peck Todd joined the faculty at Amherst College, and when he moved to town, he brought his twenty-six-year-old wife, Mabel Loomis Todd, and their infant daughter Millicent. The Austin Dickinsons "took up" the young couple, and for a while Sue and Mabel were good friends. However, Austin found himself more than liking this beautiful, talented newcomer, and in the fall of 1882 he and Mabel became lovers. There is little doubt that the couple was sincerely in love, but late-nineteenth-century New England mores did not sanction divorce and remarriage. Thus although both spouses knew of the affair (which did not end until Austin's

---

* A large part of Johnson's effort went into dating the poems, an exceedingly difficult business because Dickinson left so little evidence about her method of composition. Johnson used two major criteria: Dickinson's handwriting varied a good deal from year to year, and the variations in handwriting can be tracked by the letters (many of which are dated); occasionally a poem was included in a letter, and when it was, a date could be assigned if the date of the letter was known. There are many difficulties and uncertainties presented by using such evidence, but one seems of overriding significance. If a copy of a poem can be assigned a year with some certainty, the only thing we can infer is that *the poem was not written after that time:* it may have been written in the year when the copy was made, or it may have been written at any time *before* that year (the earlier draft having been lost or destroyed). Johnson's dating has never been seriously disputed; however, it locates an astonishing concentration of poems in three years, and many scholars have labored to explain this oddity. Before 1858, no year has more than one poem; the years 1858–66 offer the following array.

1858 --- 52 poems	1861 --- 86 poems	1864 --- 174 poems
1859 --- 94 poems	1862 --- 366 poems	1865 --- 85 poems
1860 --- 64 poems	1863 --- 141 poems	1866 --- 36 poems

After 1866, no single year has more than fifty poems.

death in 1895), no easy resolution was available. Professor Todd seems to have accepted things without much comment; Sue, on the other hand, was deeply hurt and profoundly angry, and the two women, once friends, became implacable enemies. Susan let it be known that she considered Mrs. Todd entirely devoid of moral scruple; for her part, Mabel intimated that Austin's marriage had never been happy, that Sue had always had an aversion to sexual relations and such a morbid fear of childbirth that she had submitted to several abortions rather than risk pregnancy and delivery. There was, then, a sordid and vicious strain at work among these unhappy people.

Such antique gossip would be entirely irrelevant save for one fact: Mabel Loomis Todd played a crucial role in getting Emily Dickinson's poems into print.

After Vinnie discovered the cache of poetry, she appealed first to Susan Dickinson. Yet Sue did not share Vinnie's passion for publication, and after a while Vinnie enlisted Mabel Loomis Todd's help. Working with a few poems at a time, Mrs. Todd made scrupulously accurate and readable copies of the verse; eventually, she transcribed 665 poems, and without her devoted labor, Emily Dickinson's work probably would never have been published. Mrs. Todd collaborated in the publication of three short volumes of Dickinson poetry (1890, 1891, and 1896) and two volumes of letters (1894) before Vinnie's death in 1899. Yet the enmity that had begun between mothers was continued by their children: after Susan Dickinson's death in 1913, her daughter Mattie began issuing her own editions of the poetry and letters (for the manuscripts had now become divided between the Dickinson and Todd families); and Millicent Todd Bingham, having been her mother's co-worker, eventually became her successor as author and editor. The ancient feud has still not been settled. Each side has its champions and its enemies, and even the legal agreement that permitted the eventual variorum edition was not reached until the era of the Second World War.

This all-too-well documented love affair between Austin and Mabel is of such vivid human interest that it occasionally threatens to obscure the cold truth: Mrs. Todd never met Emily Dickinson face to face; she did not even move to Amherst until the last five years of the poet's life; and although she played a central role in preserving Dickinson's work for future readers, neither her character nor her relationship with Austin had any bearing on his sister's poetry. Indeed, others among Emily Dickinson's circle are more worthy of attention (though they do not trail such an interesting train of gossip).

Despite the fact that her work was largely unpublished, Emily Dickinson was on close terms with three distinguished literary men: Thomas Wentworth Higginson, Samuel Bowles, and Josiah Holland. The last two, Bowles and Holland, were both connected with the Springfield *Daily Republican*. The paper had been owned by Samuel Bowles's father; when the elder Bowles died in 1851, his son became part-owner and editor, and Josiah Holland also became a part-owner, retaining his control over the "cultural and social departments" of the paper. Emily Dickinson met Josiah Holland and his wife in the early 1850s, and both Vinnie and Emily became very fond of Mrs. Holland, who was but a few years their senior. In 1853 and again in 1854, the two sisters visited the Hollands in Springfield. Throughout the poet's lifetime, Elizabeth Holland remained Emily's closest female friend outside the small family circle. It is perhaps surprising that although Josiah Holland had literary interests (he moved to New York to take over *Scribner's Monthly* in 1866), Emily Dickinson seems never to have been particularly interested in him except as the husband of her beloved friend.

Sam Bowles was a different matter. Bowles and his wife were close friends of Austin and Sue, and Emily Dickinson's friendship with them began in the late 1850s. Bowles was strikingly handsome, with a vigorous, impassioned personality; under his guidance, the *Republican* became one of the most influential papers in America. He soon attained national prominence—to a modest extent as a literary man, but more as a liberal Republican political commentator and wheeler-dealer. Dickinson valued him chiefly for his wit and his ready intelligence. More than once she attempted to engage him in a serious consideration of the concerns that informed her poetry, but each time she failed; in the end, she was content to have his friendship, for Sam Bowles was a favorite with the entire Dickinson family.

Thomas Wentworth Higginson occupies a privileged place in this group; without any personal introduction at all, Emily Dickinson initiated a correspondence with him in 1862 after having read one of his essays in *The Atlantic Monthly*. Like Bowles, Higginson was a man of national prominence (although the two occupied different ends of the political spectrum). He took a degree in divinity from Harvard in 1847 and served as a Unitarian minister until 1861. All the while a prolific essayist, he campaigned actively for women's rights and for abolition; when the Civil War broke out, he resigned his ministry to lead a Negro regiment for the Union Army. He saw Emily Dickinson in person only twice; nonetheless, he corresponded with her extensively, and more than one hundred of her poems were included in various letters to him. Although Higginson did not appreciate the quality of Dickinson's work during her lifetime, after the poet's death Mabel Loomis Todd managed to convince him of its worth, and he helped to get the verse into print.

Higginson was also instrumental in bringing Emily Dickinson together with Helen Hunt Jackson, one of America's leading women writers. Jackson, who was the same age as Dickinson, had known the poet when they were both girls growing up in Amherst; however, the two women had lost touch with each other and were not reunited until the mid-1870s. In the meantime,

Helen Hunt Jackson had won great acclaim as a writer and a crusader in behalf of American Indians; today she is perhaps best known as the author of *Ramona* (1884).

Helen Hunt Jackson, Thomas Wentworth Higginson, Samuel Bowles—even Josiah Holland—these were distinguished and influential people during their own day. It is a peculiar and ironic twist of fate, then, that as time has passed, they have become remembered primarily as the friends of Emily Dickinson. Like insects suspended in the rich amber of her poetry (preserved equally with such humble creatures as Fanny and Loo Norcross, two cousins with whom the poet conducted a long, confiding correspondence), they retain their compelling interest by virtue of the almost accidental fact that their lives came into contact with Emily Dickinson's genius. When visitors arrive at the Dickinson House with their inquiries and their often urgent desire to discover "Emily Dickinson," it is temptingly easy to deflect their interest in the direction of these nineteenth-century luminaries. Helen Hunt Jackson led an active, varied, and relatively public life; so did Higginson, Bowles, and Holland. Thus there are details, dates, statistics to give about such people. One can tell a coherent "story"—albeit not the story most of these visitors have come to hear. In order to tell *that* story, one must confront the obstinate paradoxes that attend Emily Dickinson's legend, for it is a far from simple tale.

Unlike some honored authors (Pound and Stevens, for example), Emily Dickinson wrote poetry that appeals to an unusually diverse readership: her work is taught in American grade schools and American graduate schools; her verse is treasured by modest men and women of limited education and by learned professors in distinguished universities. Few would disagree with the judgment that she is a great poet—one of America's greatest, perhaps even *the* greatest. Yet there are those among her admirers who confess not only that her work is very difficult, but also that there is a general uncertainty at the most literal or elementary level as to what some of the major poems are "about." And there is a similar confusion or disagreement concerning her poetic mission. Here are two paradoxes, then: a poet whose work defies understanding, but who readers nonetheless agree was an artist of the highest order; and an undeniably cryptic author who nonetheless addresses some deep need in a very wide variety of readers.

The relationship between life and work simply adds to these puzzles. Many readers feel that they have been in touch with Emily-Dickinson-the-woman when they have read her work; further, they have an intuitive conviction that if they could only learn the "truth" about Dickinson's life, this knowledge would allow them to understand her verse. And some such impulse surely lies behind the persistent curiosity that is expressed by visitors to the Dickinson House. The paradox here is that the need to know seems to be inversely proportional to the amount to be known: to be sure, readers are interested in the lives of authors like Herman Melville and Ralph Waldo Emerson; yet there does not seem to be the urgency in these cases (where, ironically, the author in question led an active, varied life that was full of incident) that there is in the case of Emily Dickinson. It cannot be the external life, then, that is in question—not the day-by-day round of events—but some dynamic of Dickinson's interior life that infuses her poetry with power and passes through the verse to readers, touching so many with intimate appeal. Elusive though it may be, this compelling interior drama is a story worth pursuing, for somehow it seems to have become central to American life as we understand it.

Occasionally, the intensely felt, essential concerns of one individual's life coincide with the overriding concerns of an epoch and a nation. It is difficult to estimate how often this happens, for when the conjunction occurs, none save the individual in question can know of it unless the personal flows into some larger, public role. However, in those extraordinary cases when the public and the private do intersect in significant ways and the individual is willing to accept the burden of a role that will translate the private into meaningful communal terms, such a person stands above the ordinary run of humankind. These people become our saints, our heroes, and our poets. In the first chapter of *Representative Men*, Emerson discusses this phenomenon. "We have social strengths," he argues. "I can do that by another which I cannot do alone. . . . Other men are lenses through which we read our own minds." Emily Dickinson has become the lens through which Americans can read their fate as men and women whose national identity was born out of an errand into the wilderness.

She lived in a time and place when God's grandeur still glimmered in the panorama of New England. Yet she never knew the dawning or even the noon of America's heroic age, but only the long shadows of its twilight; and later, she knew the darkness of the merely commercial, instrumental society that was to follow hard upon heroism's end, a society that led to modern times. It was the end of our glory and the beginning of our sorrow that Emily Dickinson could see in Amherst, Massachusetts, during those years surrounding our Civil War.

She did not study the issues of her time analytically, as a philosopher might—sifting evidence and testing arguments. Possessed of supreme intelligence, she was capable of such work; however, her strength lay elsewhere. For Emily Dickinson, the pressing concerns that would loom large in America's sense of communal identity were experienced internally: for Emily Dickinson, these were not public issues, but questions of existential importance. How best to "be" was the strenuous and informing concern of her life, and it is this concern—transformed and divested of the merely personal—that finds passionate expression in her poetry. Thus it is that readers quite rightly suppose themselves to be in touch with Emily Dickinson the woman when they read her work: in her case, all the art of being was invested in the verse. Many years after Dickinson's death, Robert Frost would write a sobering poem about the "Oven Bird": Frost's verse celebrates a courageous songster who can make music even as it acknowledges the fading of transcendence from the world. Emily Dickinson was America's Oven Bird, confronting the unthinkable dilemma: "what to make of a diminished thing."

Dickinson's concerns were inclusive, reaching backward to a mythic past and soaring forward toward eternity. Thus the "story" of her life and work is no quotidian chronicle that can be narrated on a summer's afternoon to patient visitors assembled in the hushed and shadowed parlor of the Dickinson House in Amherst. Still, there is an intuitive truth in the pilgrimage they have made to this unexceptional yet hallowed house, for it is here that Emily Dickinson's story begins and ends.

Part One ◆ *My Father's House*

9   *After this manner therefore pray ye:*
    Our Father which art in heaven,
    Hallowed be thy name.
10 *Thy kingdom come.*
    Thy will be done in earth, as it is in heaven.
11 *Give us this day our daily bread.*
12 *And forgive us our debts, as we forgive our debtors.*
13 *And lead us not into temptation, but deliver us from evil:*
    For thine is the kingdom, and the power, and the glory,
    for ever.
       Amen.

—*Matthew, ch. 6*

I ❖ Samuel and Edward: The Last Jerusalem

"When a little Girl," Emily Dickinson wrote in her thirty-ninth year, "I remember hearing that remarkable passage and preferring the 'Power,' not knowing at the time that 'Kingdom' and 'Glory' were included."[1] Dickinson envisioned an heroic victory to be won in those final years of New England's supremacy—and a Power commensurate with her capacity for contention. Perhaps she suffered from the sin of pride: certainly she conjured a colossal destiny for herself. Nonetheless, there is something poignantly American about her vaulting ambition, for the nation itself had been conceived out of the prodigious dreams of those first New Englanders—men and women who made the long journey west to establish a New Jerusalem, supposing that they really might be able to make God's "Kingdom" come into being here, on the shores of a New World wilderness.

The Dickinson family was of ancient and honorable stock. In the distant, fabled past of the mother country, the original English ancestor had "been cited on the battle-roll of Hastings."[2] Nathaniel, the first New World ancestor, had crossed the ocean in 1630 with John Winthrop in the Great Migration, and when Winthrop issued his call to glory in the subsequently famous address "A Model of Christian Charity," a Dickinson was among the crowd that heard it. "We must delight in each other, make others' conditions our own," Winthrop had enjoined: ". . . the Lord will be our God and delight to dwell among us, as his own people. . . . He shall make us a praise and glory, that men shall say of succeeding plantations: 'the Lord make it like that of New England.' For we must consider that we shall be as a city upon a hill, the eyes of all people are upon us."

Later, when God's people were assaulted by heathens with red skins, Nathaniel's son and grandson, Samuel and Ebenezer Dickinson, had been there to fend them off. Their descendants Nathan and Nathan, Jr., carried the tradition on into the French and Indian War and the Revolution. "Nathan, Jr., who was Emily's great-grandfather, also went so hotly into Shay's Rebellion that he was obliged to take the oath of allegiance—a stately form of being bound over to keep the peace."[3] Fighting for God, fighting for independence, fighting (in Shay's Rebellion) to save farm lands mortgaged during the Revolutionary War, the men of the Dickinson family constituted a microcosm of the American experience as it sprang from the Puritan roots of New England.

Emily Dickinson's poetry was a conclusion to that tradition, and the vision of the kingdom of God on earth that had been summoned in Winthrop's invocation of a "city upon a hill" was the precondition for her art.

The township of Amherst had its own "city upon a hill" in Emily Dickinson's day—Amherst College, located on the rise of ground at the southern end of the Common. It had been established to train missionaries and uphold the Puritan virtues in an age when old-fashioned religion was beginning to fail. Samuel Fowler Dickinson, Emily's paternal grandfather, was the moving force behind this idealistic endeavor, deliberately and self-consciously attempting to revive and reassert the fervor of John Winthrop's generation. If Grandfather had failed in his efforts to establish the College, his granddaughter would not have had the tools needed for her craft; thus, in a direct and explicit way, he played a necessary role in her development. Yet his indirect influence upon her may have been even greater. Samuel Fowler Dickinson was not an uncomplicated, straightforwardly pious man; his life was a series of heady triumphs, desperate fanaticisms, extravagant generosities, dubious schemes, and abject humiliations. The notion of a "Father" in the Dickinson household—particularly as it related to "Kingdom" and "Power" and "Glory"—was complex and fraught with conflicting emotions. The character of Samuel Fowler Dickinson's oldest son, Edward (Emily's father), was crucially shaped by his reactions to his own father's motley career. Thus despite the fact that Emily Dickinson had personal contact with Grandfather for only the first three years of her life, the reflected force of his influence extended throughout her lifetime. Perhaps no one can fully understand Dickinson's poetry without knowing something of her ambiguous inheritance from Grandfather Dickinson; certainly no one can understand the life that gave birth to that poetry without starting here—two generations before she was born.

In 1813, Samuel Fowler Dickinson built the first brick house in Amherst. The large lot on which it was set had originally contained a modest frame dwelling that was dismantled and moved three blocks away to make room for it. Many features of the new home had been included merely to satisfy the demands of taste: high ceilings, double parlors, an expansive front-to-back central hallway with the transverse hall set at a right angle to it, bed-chambers the size of sitting rooms. Indeed, the residents of Amherst would have been justified in surmising that the house was a gracious but explicit assertion of money and success.[4]

For generations, the Dickinson family had been an exceptionally hardy breed: during a period of high infant mortality and perilous childbirth, the Dickinson wives lived to grow old and their numerous children survived. Samuel Fowler Dickinson seemed the very embodiment of this vigorous heritage:

He allowed himself but four hours of sleep, studying and reading till midnight, and rising at four o'clock he often walked to Pelham or some other town before breakfast. Going to court at Northampton, he would catch up his green bag and walk the whole seven miles. *"I cannot wait to ride,"* he would say to those who suggested that many horses in his stable would be idle, and outwalked the stage, with its four-in-hand, to Northampton. Bread, cheese and coffee, apples and cold cider before breakfast were almost his sole diet. No man could outwork him, mentally or physically. He was ill but once in many years, till his last sickness of one week.[5]

For many years, whatever he did, he did with all his might. Tyler, the great chronicler of the early years of Amherst College, writes that "he was ranked among the best lawyers—perhaps he was the very best lawyer in Hampshire County, and might doubtless have had a seat on the bench, if he had continued in the practice of his profession."[6] And yet, successful as he was in his various professions, lawyering and doing business were not sufficient to contain the intensities and aspirations of this man. Long before the era of the Brick House, he had already begun to turn large portions of his energy to politics, education, and religion.

The youngest of seven children, Samuel Fowler Dickinson entered Dartmouth College at the age of sixteen and graduated at the age of twenty (the youngest graduate that year) as second scholar of the class of 1795. The family's choice of Dartmouth had almost certainly grown out of religious convictions rather than more broadly defined intellectual concerns. As the eighteenth century drew to a close, religion in New England had become increasingly polarized: the liberal Unitarian interest centered in Boston at Harvard; the conservative Trinitarians—inheritors of Jonathan Edwards's latter-day Puritanism—were gathered in the west. Harvard's defection from the faith was formalized in 1805, when a Unitarian was appointed to the Hollis Chair of Divinity. Standing against Harvard were the staunch Trinitarian bastions of Yale, Dartmouth, Williams—and, eventually, Amherst College. Though Dartmouth was not quite so conservative as Yale, deciding to send a boy to Dartmouth was nevertheless an act of religious piety. He would receive orthodox Congregationalist instruction; if he were lucky, he would undergo a conversion experience.

Samuel Fowler Dickinson was not blessed with a personal awakening during his years at Dartmouth. He left college uncertain about the direction his life would take and spent the year following graduation as a teacher in New Salem, Massachusetts. This was in 1795–96, during a period of great religious ferment. Two decades later, the president of Williams College would describe the feeling that had swept through New England at the end of the eighteenth century: "The year 1792 . . . ushered a new era into the world. . . . In that year commenced that series of revivals in America, which has never been interrupted, night or day, and which never will be until the earth is as full of the glory of the Lord as the waters cover the sea."[7] In this climate of raging evangelical piety, Samuel Fowler Dickinson fell seriously ill; when he recovered, the mortal terror that had been inspired by that illness brought him to his knees in conversion.

Almost immediately, he joined the West Church of Amherst and became, at the age of only twenty-one, deacon of the church, a position he held for nearly forty years. In the first heady rush of religious excitement, he decided to become a clergyman and began the study of theology with an older brother, the Reverend Timothy Dickinson of Holliston. But his nature was not suited to the ministry: his restless ambition chafed under the scholarly, contemplative mode of life, and he soon abandoned it to study law with Judge Strong in Amherst. Here, in due course, he set up his own office and established his practice. On March 31, 1802, he married Lucretia Gunn of Montague, and they settled down to rear a family.

If his career had continued uninterruptedly in law and in the business he conducted as a side line, Samuel Fowler Dickinson's life would be remarkable only for his monetary success: after only a few years, he had made a small fortune by local standards. But merely earning money appears not to have satisfied his complex nature. Those who have recorded his life reach for extravagant phrases to capture the convolutions of his driving ambition, and he eventually became a legend in the family. His great-granddaughter Martha Dickinson Bianchi called him "a flaming zealot for education and religion. . . . [He ached with the desire] to hasten the conversion of the whole world. His passion for the accomplishment of this audacious end burned with true missionary fire. Like some of the other early saints, 'he believed like fury,' and acted on his belief."[8] Tyler's language is more restrained, but his image of the man comports with Madame Bianchi's: "The conversion of the world often pressed heavily on his mind. . . . [In his educational and religious work he thought to] hasten that promised event; . . . he was as certainly fulfilling the command to 'preach the gospel to every creature,' as if he had himself gone in person to the heathen."[9] Unfit by nature for the ministry, he had nonetheless internalized the most radical injunctions of evangelical Puritanism. To the end he was painfully divided in his commitment to vocation: a businessman and lawyer by trade and by natural proclivities, he gradually gave his soul over to the work of Christ in this world.

At first, Samuel Fowler Dickinson's zeal was channeled into political activity. His affinity for the melodramatic element of the American heritage can be heard in even his earliest public statements. The prose of these is not yet elegant—for in the full pride of his manhood, Samuel Fowler Dickinson was celebrated as the most eloquent orator in the county, a county with more than its share of polished preachers of the gospel—however, the grandiosity of his thinking is already embedded in his language.[10] He did nothing by halves. He was town clerk continuously from 1804 (when he was only twenty-nine) until 1818; he was representative from his district to the state legislature in 1805–9, 1813, 1816–18, 1827–29; he was active in the Whig Party; he served on town committees; he gave uncounted public orations. In the beginning he was merely a lawyer who took a public-spirited interest in his community. But little by little, the tempo of his activities outside the limits imposed by his business quickened. Eventually it reached a dizzying blur, and he entirely lost the capacity for moderation and control.[11]

Nowhere is the pulsating, contradictory force of his nature more clearly articulated than in his visionary exertions in behalf of Christian education. Before 1814, the provisions for education in Amherst were dismal; the village had only a one-room school. For reasons both of piety and of prudence, the prosperous men of Amherst decided to offer "higher advantages" to their children. They wanted to be certain that their sons could make their way successfully through one of the great Trinitarian colleges; surprisingly enough, they also wanted their daughters taught the more advanced branches of education so that they could be good Christians and mothers. Several preliminary meetings were held, and in July 1812 Samuel Fowler Dickinson began the original subscription to finance the Amherst Academy. When the Academy opened its doors in December 1814, a superb religious school was available as an alternative to the township's inadequate educational facilities.[12]

Except for a few years, Amherst Academy was regularly open to both male and female students; and despite the belief of its founders and teachers that an orthodox religious education took precedence over all other learning, the range of secular learning in the curriculum was comprehensive by any standard, even at the very beginning.

In general the branches taught comprised reading, grammar, declamation, rhetoric and composition, . . . ancient and modern geography, . . . sacred geography, general history, . . . history of the United States, . . . intellectual and written arithmetic, . . . algebra, . . . conversations on natural philosophy, conversations on chymistry [*sic*], . . . moral philosophy, . . . intellectual philosophy, . . . practical mathematics—comprehending navigation, surveying, mensuration, and astronomical calculations.

After only a few years, Latin, Greek, French, and German were added to the course of study; and after the arrival of the distinguished botanist and geologist Edward Hitchcock, students taking one of the expanded number of science courses could receive instruction from him—either at the Academy or (later) at Amherst College, where they were regularly allowed to sit in on classes.[13]

Samuel Fowler Dickinson's oldest son, Edward, was nearly twelve in December 1814 when the school offered its first term, and it is probable that the father's initial interest in the Academy was quickened by his desire to have all of his own children provided with the best possible schooling. Yet whatever exclusively personal interest he had quickly fell away, and the messianic fervor that twenty years earlier had led him to suppose he might want to join the ministry soon insinuated itself into his dream of education. The beginning of this transformation was deceptively small. In November 1817, the Board of Trustees of the Amherst Academy voted to raise a fund for the "gratuitous instruction of 'indigent young men of promising talents and hopeful piety, who shall manifest a desire to obtain a liberal education with a sole view to the Christian ministry.'" In the service of this project, a committee of five men (one of them Samuel Fowler Dickinson) undertook to solicit "donations, contributions, grants and bequests" to support a professorship of languages.[14] However, once the committee members began their work, they found that they could not raise the full amount needed; they would have been obliged to report failure if they had been content to rest with the project as originally defined. Instead, they came to a paradoxical conclusion: " 'The establishment of a single professorship was *too limited* an object to induce men to subscribe. To engage public patronage, it was found necessary to form a plan for the education of young men for the ministry on a more extensive scale.' "[15] Unable to raise the money for a single professorship, they decided instead to raise the money for the establishment of yet another great Trinitarian college. Thus what they presented to the Board in August 1818 was not a statement of failure, but a lengthy and complex plan for " 'an Institution . . . for the Christian ministry.' "[16] It would be created for the purpose of training missionaries to preach among the heathens, and it would be free of cost to young men who could not afford to pay the tuition. It was to be called Amherst College.

Whether or not the audacious undertaking originated with Samuel Fowler Dickinson, as some claim, the important fact remains: here at last was a vision commensurate with his imagination, and he pledged his entire future to its success.

The Trustees responded enthusiastically. A meeting was called for the next month, and the Congregational and Presbyterian clergymen throughout New England were urged to come vote their support for the proposed college. The Trustees evidently expected little opposition and an enthusiastic endorsement of the plan. Yet as soon as word began to get around, challenges were raised to urge that the new college be located not in Amherst, but in the larger, more accessible city of nearby Northampton. There was an exceptionally large turnout for the September meeting, and the air was heavy with dissension. The hot, humid church of the West Parish in Amherst was packed with impassioned men: ministers from forty different parishes, teachers from Amherst Academy, and distinguished laity from both sides of the Connecticut River. When the first day's session adjourned in the late afternoon with the issue still unresolved, the argument was merely carried into the streets and the local inns, and even into private homes that had given over bedrooms to accommodate the crowd of visitors. The dispute raged on until well after midnight. The Amherst contingent had been relying on Squire Dickinson to stand and make their case with his usual oratorical skill; however, with the cunning of a practiced lawyer, he hung back, waiting until the most vulnerable moment. Finally, in the afternoon of the second day, he took his position in the aisle with deliberation and launched into "one of the most powerful and telling speeches" of the entire convention; as he spoke, the men who had filled the church gradually ceased talking among themselves and fell silent. He gained first their full attention and then, slowly but decisively, their support. It was the turning point of the debate. After but little further discussion, the plan was approved, and the arduous task of raising money could begin.[17]

The undertaking was of heroic proportions, and there were two initial barriers to cross. First, the complex plan that had been approved stipulated that subscribers must be found to pledge "at least *fifty thousand dollars,* as the basis of a Charity Fund for the proposed Institution," a princely sum in those days; it further stipulated that in case the sums subscribed "shall not amount to the full sum of fifty thousand dollars, then the whole, or any part, shall be void according to the will of any subscriber on giving three months' notice."[18] Thus if the backers failed to secure the entire fifty thousand, they stood to lose even the money they *had* managed to get, and the enterprise would fail entirely. Second, after the money was raised, the new college would have to obtain a charter from the Commonwealth of Massachusetts.

The Unitarians in Boston (a powerful force in the legislature) opposed every effort to preserve the old-fashioned Puritan strain in religious education. However, Trinitarians from other parts of the state were also hostile to the proposal because the newly established Williams College had discovered that its isolated situation behind the barrier of the Hoosac Mountains was a serious discouragement to prospective students. There had been talk of relocating Williams to a more central part of the state; however, if a Trinitarian college were to be established in Amherst, relocation of Williams would become impossible.[19] The little band of Trustees seems pitifully weak by contrast with their opponents. They had no wealthy backers. The list of original donations still exists: few were sizable, and many were very small; pledges on the order of fifty cents annually for five years are scattered throughout.[20]

What the backers of the new college did have was a remarkable unity of feeling within the community. The town of Amherst and the neighboring villages worked cooperatively in this enterprise as they never would again. Before the state legislature had granted a charter to the proposed institution, even before the Charity Fund had been accumulated, ground was broken for the first structure. Everyone helped, for the dream of a "city upon a hill" once again swelled New England hearts and gladdened their souls.

The stone for the foundation was brought chiefly from Pelham by gratuitous labor. . . . Donations of lime, sand, lumber materials of all kinds flowed in from every quarter. Teams for hauling and men for handling and tending, and unskilled labor of every sort, were provided in abundance. . . . The people not only contributed in kind but turned out in person and sometimes camped on the ground and labored day and night, for they had a mind to work like the Jews in building their temple, and they felt that they too were building the Lord's house.[21]

What man in old Squire Dickinson's place would not have felt that God was working His will among an inspired people and that He had chosen men like the Biblical patriarchs and prophets to lead them and give example? "The entire movement . . . looked toward the past or an imagined past, toward the so-called primitive religion of our fathers, when church and state were—or were at least said to have been—identical, when the clergy were watchmen on the towers of the New Jerusalem."[22]

Somehow the fund was raised by 1823—not all of it in actual cash dollars (for that was not yet necessary), but in a combination of cash and pledges—and the charter of the College was presented to the state legislature. At this point the Unitarians and the hostile Trinitarians from Williams used quasi-legal measures to challenge the pledges, and a crisis was at hand.[23] The committee met at Boltwood's Hotel in Amherst and began going through the list of subscriptions, one by one. The ordeal lasted for two weeks as day after day, the soundness of each promise was tested. During all of this time, the members sat around a table, often with rolls of bills literally in hand. When they discovered that a pledge had been withdrawn, one or another would say, "I will cash that." Eventually, three "of the trustees . . . drew up an obligation, assuming the amount of $15,000," and Samuel Fowler Dickinson headed the list.[24] The fund was made solvent, and the legislature granted preliminary approval for the new college.

Squire Dickinson was not solely responsible for the founding of Amherst College; several men contributed grandly to the enterprise. However, Samuel Fowler Dickinson's role was unique—not because he gave more than anyone else (though he may have done so), but because he gave in a different spirit. The other men were not willing to put their entire fortunes at the disposal of the founders. Businessmen and farmers, they were a hardheaded, prudent lot in spite of their zeal. Squire Dickinson alone seemed not able to judge where generosity left off and recklessness began. Soon the "cause" took control of his life, and things that had formerly been important to him fell by the wayside. After 1818, he served as representative to the legislature for only one two-year period (1827–29), and then it was expressly to lobby for the interests of Amherst College. His time was diverted from business and the practice of law, and although he continued to pay the salaries of those who usually farmed his land, he often sent them to work on the construction site instead.

"When there was no money to pay for the teams to draw the brick or men to drive them, his own horses were sent for days and weeks till in one season two or three of them fell by the wayside. Sometimes his own laborers were sent to drive his horses, and in an emergency he went himself, rather than that the work should cease." At the same time, he boarded more or less of the workmen, and sometimes paid their wages out of his own pocket, while his wife and daughters toiled hard to board them.

Eventually, everything, including the Brick House he had built with such pride in 1813, was consumed by the insatiable hunger of his evangelical dream. And the end came not at once, but with an excruciating protraction: " 'He became embarrassed and at length actually poor.' "[25] When he failed, his entire family was swept along with him, and no one was affected more profoundly than his oldest son.

In 1818, when it began, Edward Dickinson was fifteen and in his last year at the Amherst Academy. Ready for college in 1819, he went down to Yale—Jonathan Edwards's university, the most doctrinaire of the Trinitarian schools. The letters that the father sent to New Haven carried a mixed message. On the one hand, he worried incessantly about the state of his son's soul, and the urgency of his concern was intensified whenever some small local tragedy was reported—as, for example, when the father's close friend Jacob White died suddenly.

Death seems fast making inroads on this neighborhood—You must always be prepared to hear of it entering our doors. Mr. White when you left home was far more likely to live than I. May this remind you, & me, that our time here is short! ... If, Edward, I could hear that you were among the number who had embraced the Savior, how joyful the news![26]

Such language rang familiarly in Edward's ear: he had witnessed at first hand the pious enthusiasm out of which Amherst College had been conceived; and he had heard revival language often enough to recognize its stately cadences. Very soon, however, a second theme emerged—perhaps eventually it even dominated—this time a consideration quite unfamiliar to the heir of the most successful lawyer in Hampshire County: panic over money. "Dec. 17, 1819 ... In relation to you, I have determined to have you study in the Academy the residue of this year—I think it may be equally beneficial. ... Jan. 2, 1820 ... The bills of this quarter since exceed my expectations. ... If you can sell your furniture without much loss, I think you had better do it."[27] The January 2 letter was written the day after Edward's seventeenth birthday. It was a strange birthday message, all the more so since Edward had been doing excellent work at Yale. Amherst College had neither buildings nor faculty at this point, and the boy was being required to come home and do no more than resume secondary-school education. Nonetheless, come home he did—sometime in early February 1820—and he remained in Amherst until early June, when he returned to continue his education in New Haven.

To his credit, Edward adapted well to life at Yale, despite the uncertainty and the flood of depressing news from Amherst, despite even his own stringent living conditions. He was for all his life an enthusiastic alumnus; more than fifty years later, letters from his college friends—breezy notes from brash, optimistic boys who address him by the nickname "Dick"—were found among his papers. And throughout the taxing family ordeal he continued to be a superb student. His work merited praise from his father; yet not one of the surviving letters contains any congratulation for the boy's scholastic achievements. Indeed, Samuel Dickinson did not much play the father's role with Edward. Instead, he treated the boy as someone to lean on and confide in, someone who would give encouragement rather than seek it. Edward was left to "father" himself: Samuel Dickinson was busy founding Amherst College.

There was no relief from the burden of family worry, even after Edward took up residence in New Haven once again. His father's letters continued in the same complaining tone as before, and the boy even began to hear about the family's trouble from members of his own generation, as teen-aged sisters coped unhappily with the unfamiliar burden of boarders, whose number continued to increase. In 1821, Edward's third year at Yale, Amherst College opened its doors (the new college had begun educating students even though its charter was not granted until 1823). Once more Father's letters took on an ominously pointed tone. Why could Edward not return to Amherst to complete his schooling? Edward protested; Father backed off a bit. "As to your coming into the Institution in Amherst, I shall consider the subject fully before I make any determination—Should you come here—you will take a room in the College building, and have no connection with home, except boarding." It is true that Father sweetened his persuasion with brave talk about the new college; but in the end, there was no subterfuge to cover the real deciding force in the matter.

Sept. 4, 1821 . . . What may be my determination respecting your continuance at N[ew] H[aven], I do not know—this must be left till we see how things shall be at Amherst—One reason seems, however, almost unanswerable—necessity—inability to supply the money necessary at N.H. You may leave all as though you should return—they can be sent for afterward, if you return. . . . As to degrees [at the still-uncharted Amherst College]—there is no difficulty in obtaining them, if qualified—Some of the Williamstown seniors have taken degrees at Union & others . . . at Dartmouth.[28]

At this point the correspondence broke off; once more Edward went home to Amherst.

What can the son have made of his father's behavior? The vision of 1818 had been (or had appeared to be) a purely religious one. If such were the case, the model was clear: the Old Squire was a wealthy and powerful man who had freely chosen to turn his resources unstintingly over to God; and if God deemed it necessary for him to relinquish all, he ought to be willing (as the rich young man in the Gospel had not been) to renounce all his worldly possessions and follow Christ. Moreover, provided a man *did* give uncomplainingly and without reservation—give and give again at God's will—then he could not fail to achieve greatness, even in poverty. Yet in 1821, when Edward was again forced to quit Yale, his father's letters were not filled with a sense of honor at having served the Lord. Even a year earlier, when the querulous letters began, Father had written not as a man fulfilled in God, but as a man betrayed by Him. The letters to his son seethe with resentment at his poverty and the loss of social standing; as he sank ever deeper into rage and despair, he lost confidence even in the grandeur of his celestial dream, and he began to dwell with increasing petulance upon his own hardships.

Samuel Dickinson wanted the New Jerusalem, but he wanted to keep the Brick House on Main Street, too (he spent his last years in Amherst concocting desperate schemes to keep it). Not willing to give up all his worldly success for God, he was equally unwilling to turn all his energies to the rescue of his personal fortune. Finally, he served neither God nor Mammon. And in his irresolution he became not tragic, but pathetic. The Old Squire had more than a sufficiency of time to reflect upon his place in history. And this occupation, too, filled him with bitterness. If he could not remain wealthy and socially distinguished, at least he wanted to be congratulated on the results of his sacrifice. But he was not, and his final days in Amherst were an unrelieved nightmare of despondency and humiliation. Tyler, who is generous in his judgments throughout, nonetheless identifies the Old Squire's discomfiture with the unintentional cruelty of the unbiased historian: "In his poverty he had the additional grief of feeling that his services were forgotten, like the poor wise man in the proverb who 'by his wisdom delivered the city, yet no man remembered that same poor man.' "[29]

The second interruption of Edward's studies at Yale lasted five months: he left New Haven in September 1821 and returned in February 1822 for the second half of his junior year. During his senior year (all of which was spent at Yale) he evidently practiced the unwelcome economy of living off campus, away from his friends. In 1823 he graduated, at the age of twenty, valedictorian of his class. He was full of ambition and yearned to go to the city and study in a prestigious Boston law office. Father was thoroughly against such a plan. In fact, by the time of Edward's last term in college, Samuel Dickinson's attitudes toward both business and religion had become tangled and confused:

We may be blessed with a revival of religion, even here. There is a consistency in true religion which we find in nothing else. But we may be afraid that much now passes for piety, which will not appear so at the last day—Have you remarked, that few obtain religion after middle age—even after engaging in active business? It is true, that it is as easy for the Spirit to subdue the heart of an old sinner, as that of a young sinner: yet, the whole system of God's dealing with men, is by means—and when a man is embarrassed with disappointments—difficulties in business & the cares of a family—he seems to have no time to think of God & duty—Serious thoughts are constantly kept out of mind—as others are continually crowding in. I mention this as a serious fact for your reflection. My own experience shows the increasing difficulties in the way of being religious, as we advance in life. I would say to all my children & to every young person, *Remember thy Creator in the days of thy youth.* "Seek the Lord when he may be found." I hope you will make more time than I do, for serious reflection—There is an importance attached to these considerations, which is not to be estimated.[30]

This may have been a statement of concern for Edward's soul; however, it may have been something else as well—a sorry confession of Father's own wavering faith.

As Samuel Fowler Dickinson's spirits declined, one by one his other sons deserted him. Edward's younger brothers William and Samuel Fowler, Jr., were not willing to sacrifice the prospects of their futures to contribute to the fortunes of a failing parent. William finished Amherst Academy and left home as soon as he decently could ("at the age of fifteen 'or thereabouts' "—in 1819).[31] For ten years he roamed in search of opportunity, and in 1829, when he was twenty-five, he moved to Worcester, where he became a wealthy manufacturer of paper machinery. Of the five brothers, he was the most successful financially. He remained on excellent terms with his older brother, and their families visited back and forth during Emily Dickinson's lifetime. However, he never attempted to salvage his father (or if he did, there is no record of it). Samuel Fowler, Jr., bolted before he reached the age of twenty-one. Perhaps because he bore the name of the man whose adversity was becoming more and more public, he felt that he needed distance between himself and Amherst; he did not, for instance, attend Amherst Academy, but went instead to the Monson Academy, some fifteen or twenty miles away and lived there as a boarding student. He left New England soon after graduation, migrated to the Deep South, and settled in Macon, Georgia. In early 1831, he wrote a bitter letter back home to Edward, who had been trying to get him to return: "I think yet I am not a fool although I have been sounded deeply for one in Amherst & probably should [have] thought I was a cursed fool if I had stayed in Amherst a year or two more."[32] Edward's other two brothers were much younger than he: Timothy was born in 1816 and Frederick in 1819, after Edward was ready for college. Timothy eventually joined Samuel Fowler, Jr., in Georgia, absolutely determined never again to venture even as far north as New York City.[33]

Thus Edward was alone among Samuel Dickinson's five sons in standing by his father, whose erratic behavior increasingly failed to merit such loyalty; in fact, for many decades, he was the only one of the nine children to settle permanently in Amherst. He never did go to Boston and join a law firm there. Instead he came back home in 1823 and read law for two years in his father's office, concluding his study in 1825–26 with one year at the Northampton Law School. Life at home could not have been pleasant; his mother had always been known for her outspokenness and difficult disposition. Furthermore, once on the spot, Edward became implicated in many of Father's moneymaking schemes.

These were terrible years. The Old Squire had mortgaged everything he owned to cover the pledges on the Amherst College Charity Fund. Since he did not have the resources to pay off the mortgages, he spent days and nights on the road trying to raise money while Edward managed business at the law office. Of course, the donations he sought were begged in the name of Amherst College; however, he was really petitioning on his own behalf, for his early exuberance for the cause had degenerated into terror about his own future. In April 1825 the Amherst postmastership fell vacant. A petty office in this small village, it was a job that the Old Squire would most likely have dismissed before; now, however, he made ineffectual public efforts to acquire it for the salary it would pay. He circulated a petition and wrote a pleading, querulous letter to the Postmaster General of the United States (implicating Edward in the process): "My own claim rests on a settled habit of doing business . . . being by profession, a Lawyer, & necessarily in & about my office—having with me in the study, a son fully competent to perform the duties in my necessary absence. . . ." The final ignominy was that he failed to get the job. Yet when the post was again vacant nineteen months later, he once again schemed to obtain it—if not for himself, then for Edward (petitions were circulated for both). Once again he failed.[34]

In 1827 and 1828 Samuel Dickinson returned to the Massachusetts legislature. But when he ran for the United States Senate in 1828, he found that he had exhausted his capital of public support; never again did he hold elective office. He had not, however, depleted his energy for concocting projects to make money. In June 1828 he ran a public notice:

LAW SCHOOL

The subscriber proposes to open, at Amherst . . . a School for instruction in the science and practice of the Law. . . .

That the course may be the more interesting and useful, provision is made with the Faculty of the College in this place, for the attendance of Law-Students, without expense *to them* on all lectures there delivered. . . .

The annual charge for rooms, Library and instruction, will be *One hundred dollars.* . . .

Other expenses will be reasonable.

An extensive and well chosen Library will be furnished. . . .

This Prospectus is issued *with extreme diffidence:* in as much as it promises only the efforts of *an humble individual;* and, it may be, in competition with those of a more eminent character, already exerted, in other similar schools, in New England;— an individual too, whose attention for some time past, has been partially withdrawn from the Profession. Yet, believing that *perseverance,* united with untiring *application, and exclusive devotedness* to the object of pursuit, always possesses a redeeming spirit, as well as an overcoming power, the undersigned *is determined* to omit no exertion, and avoid no sacrifice, *to deserve,* what he humbly hopes *he may receive* a portion of the public patronage.

Amherst, Mass. June 18, 1828   SAMUEL FOWLER DICKINSON
                                      Counsellor in the
                                        Supreme Judicial Court

Perhaps nobody responded to the advertisement; the "Law School" never came into being.[35]

Edward Dickinson left a lengthy, un-self-conscious record of his response to his father's increasingly dubious schemes. In January 1826, during a business trip to Monson, he met a shy, quiet girl named Emily Norcross, the daughter of a prosperous farmer; the couple were married somewhat more than two years later. During the courtship and engagement, Edward wrote her frequent, circumstantial letters. While these are remarkably devoid of romantic sentiment, they contain a wealth of detail about Edward's ambitions for himself, ambitions that reflect the urgency of his desire to dissociate himself from the ever-increasing failures that threatened to overwhelm his father. This young man, now in his mid-twenties, had a passionate desire to make something important of himself.

"Power" is a word that occurs with remarkable frequency in Edward's courtship letters. He attached it to two separate but related questions. First, how far ought the power of his ambitions carry him—beyond Amherst, beyond Massachusetts? He had great difficulty resolving this problem, and many years passed before he even began to frame an answer; indeed, perhaps he had not fully answered it by the time of his death. The second question seemed simpler: how might a man establish his identity independent of his father? Edward Dickinson already had an "identity" for the people of Amherst: he was Samuel Fowler Dickinson's son. The children who departed from Amherst (four brothers and four sisters—eventually everybody except

Edward) could start anew and unknown. But for Edward, who was so conscious of Father's reputation (and who had become implicated in so much of Father's business), "Power" became the capacity to be "somebody" in his own right. Thus over and over again he reassured his bride-to-be that America is a country in which each individual has his own unique opportunities—that here a man can be self-made in the most fundamental way, overcoming the deficiencies of his background merely through his own exercise of will and hard work. Emily Norcross's letters to Edward have survived, and there is not the slightest evidence in them (or anywhere else) that she had raised any questions along these lines; thus the obsessively repeated reassurances in Edward's letters quite clearly address not *her* fears and anxieties at all, but only his own.

Nov. 27, 1826 . . . I am like the majority of young men who receive an education & engage in a profession: & rely upon exertion for success. My education is my inheritance. . . .

Men are unconscious of the power they possess—And when compelled by circumstances to make a desperate effort, the greatest difficulties vanish—the mightiest obstacles are removed—and the most powerful opposition disappears.

July 22, 1827 . . . I believe that the great secret of becoming eminent in any profession, or of gaining any desirable object lies more in the *unconquerable will*, than in any other power. . . . I desire not the pleasure which he feels . . . who wastes his time to spend what has been collected by his successful ancestors—I do not wish . . . distinction thro' any passage by my own exertions.

Jan. 27, 1828 . . . You have a right to expect that I shall do all in my power for you & myself—and you have a right to expect much from me—I owe it to you to try to make myself a reputation of which you will not be ashamed.[36]

Edward Dickinson had formulated an imperative for himself (part of which he construed as if it were coming from her). He would exert his power to become a success in his chosen fields of business, and the entire community would recognize his accomplishment and define him accordingly. Marriage, then, might be the beginning of a new "House": the lineage of *Edward* Dickinson.

Although he was still involved with his father's affairs at the time that he was admitted to the bar, Edward tried to think seriously of setting up practice elsewhere. "I have not yet made my determination as to a place to establish myself in business," he wrote Emily Norcross on July 13, 1826. He declared himself still undecided in August, but he may never have been fully conscious of the depth of his commitment to Amherst and his father's fate there. More and more, Samuel had come to rely on his oldest son, and the young man's letters to his fiancée offer touching glimpses of his sense of responsibility. I am still "sitting at the writing table in my father's office," he wrote wearily on September 5, 1826, late at night, "and with what business naturally presents itself." Such was often the case, and many letters were written under these conditions—Edward toiling by lamplight in his father's office, snatching a few moments to write private notes. Little by little he relinquished all fantasies of leaving: "I have this morning decided to open my office in Amherst and shall raise my sign and commence my business this afternoon." He retained at least a nominal independence, however, not joining his father in a partnership but setting up his own office across town.

EDWARD DICKINSON

ATTORNEY AT LAW

HAS TAKEN AN OFFICE IN AMHERST

IN THE NEW BRICK BUILDING

OVER "GRAVES AND FIELDS" STORE, OPPOSITE BOLTWOOD'S HOTEL

Where he will attend to any business that may be intrusted to him in his profession

Amherst, (Mass.)   *Sept., 1826*

This choice not to go into partnership with his father constituted an effort to disengage himself from Samuel's woes. However, despite such efforts, he continued to respond dutifully whenever Father called upon him. And Father called often. Thus on October 22—even though he now had his own place of business—he was still writing his personal correspondence late at night from Squire Dickinson's office where he was working on the backlog, "which the absence of my father on a journey for the last week has produced." The following year found him much the same: "Feb. 1, 1827: . . . I have not had an opportunity, as yet, to improve [my own business opportunities] as the absence of my father a great part of the time confined me closely to my office."[37] And so this theme continues unabated throughout the two-year correspondence.

Even his domestic life eventually became entangled in the web of Father's failures. When the couple married, on May 6, 1828, they set up housekeeping in the Widow Montague's home (a significant distance from the Brick House on Main Street): it was a roomy, even gracious living arrangement. Edward ceremoniously inscribed his Bible:

FAMILY RECORD

Edward Dickinson was born Jan 1, 1803
Emily Norcross was born July 3, 1804
They were married May 6, 1828

Here at last was a new beginning. He would be the head of his own family, no longer a child in his father's house. Eleven months later, he made another entry in the Bible:

> *William Austin, their first child, was*
> *born April 16, 1829 at 12 o'clock AM.*

Now, with a son of his own, Edward's sense of indenture might have ended; instead, it was this short stint of independence that was soon brought to conclusion.[38]

Squire Dickinson had grown more and more financially distressed: in the mid-1820s, while he still had hopes of raising enough money for the College to recompense him, he retained title to a good deal of land (though he had borrowed against most of it); by 1830, however, county records list virtually no land in Samuel Fowler Dickinson's name, and the mortgage on the Homestead was about to be foreclosed by Nathan Dickinson, a distant relative, and John Leland, treasurer of Amherst College and a close personal friend of Samuel Fowler Dickinson's. Neither man had any desire actually to live in the Brick House (most likely they had assumed the debt for it merely as a gesture of friendship), and neither was in any hurry to foreclose. Since Squire Dickinson's financial position was no longer strong enough to warrant their holding on to his mortgage, an arrangement was made to forestall disaster, and the terms of it drew Edward and his family into the imbroglio. Samuel Fowler Dickinson moved his wife and resident children into the eastern half of the house, and in April 1830 Edward moved his wife and son into the other half.

When he moved, Edward actually purchased the western half of the Homestead from John Leland and Nathan Dickinson. The property line was fixed down the middle of the commodious central entry hall, splitting even the front and back doors—a grotesque subdivision of the home's elegant proportions. Almost immediately, Edward sold his half-house *back* to Leland and Dickinson, but the resale had a significant provision: Edward retained an option to buy back his half if within three years he paid roughly one-half of the amount he had received and if within five years he made up the rest. Although it may seem an example of New England eccentricity, this buying and instantly selling back, it actually made perfect sense to the Dickinson men. If Samuel Fowler Dickinson was forced to declare public bankruptcy, at least Edward's half of the house would be safe from Father's creditors. If things took a turn for the better and Samuel Dickinson wanted to secure ownership, he would be able to pay off the mortgage on *his* half of the house, comfortable in the knowledge that the other half was at option to his son. Since Edward had a legally binding option to buy his half of the house, he may have had oral assurances that he would have first refusal of the other half. In the meantime, by moving his family into the Homestead, Edward relieved his father of a large portion of the interest payments. And, in a further set of related real-estate transactions, Edward retained the lot and building to the west of the Homestead, which eventually became the site of Austin and Sue's house.[39] In these close quarters, Edward's family increased: a daughter, Emily Elizabeth Dickinson, was born on December 10, 1830, and a second daughter, Lavinia Norcross Dickinson, was born February 28, 1833. With Lavinia, Edward's family was complete.

The year of Lavinia's birth, 1833, was Samuel Fowler Dickinson's last year in Amherst. None of his plans had succeeded; none of his son's efforts had been sufficient. Exhausted and despairing, he did not want to continue living in Amherst under any circumstances—not even if one of his sons could buy the Homestead back. He felt that he had been publicly and irrevocably disgraced, and he wanted exile.

Lyman Beecher, who was active in Amherst College religious affairs, had been asked to come to Cincinnati, Ohio, as the president of Lane Theological Seminary. He invited Samuel Dickinson to come with him. Some say that Squire Dickinson was in charge of supervising the manual labor that was required of all students at the seminary; some say that he went to take charge of Lane's financial concerns; his grandson Austin saw the journey westward as Samuel Fowler Dickinson's last effort to serve the Lord by devoting his energies to evangelical Trinitarianism.[40] The salient fact was this: he had been offered honorable work far away from Amherst, and he took it. The holders of his mortgages finally foreclosed: on February 27, 1833, a newspaper advertisement offered the Brick House on Main Street for public sale; and on May 22 the entire Dickinson Homestead was sold to David Mack. In the end, Edward had not exercised his option to buy the western half of the house. Perhaps he cared to own *half* a house only if his father could hope to own the other half, or perhaps he simply did not have the cash. In that same spring—sometime toward the end of May—Samuel Dickinson left with his wife and several dependent children. He never saw Amherst again.

Considering the circumstances under which his father had departed, it is perhaps surprising that Edward not only remained in Amherst, but remained as a tenant in the ancestral home. He made only one significant alteration: he removed from the western half of the house and took up residence in the eastern half, which his father had just quitted.[41] Edward had sound, practical reasons for the change: Samuel Dickinson's half of the house was a good deal roomier than his son's portion had been. Nonetheless, by making the move he was taking his father's place in a quite literal sense; and in other than symbolic ways, Edward increasingly took up what had been his father's role, relinquishing forever that treasured dream of becoming an entirely self-made man.

The most obvious legacy was the multitude of concerns that beset the newly chartered school. Amherst College was in desperate financial straits, and it had been the crowning agony of Samuel's disgrace that when he left Amherst, he was convinced that the College was about to be closed. In 1835 Edward became the treasurer of Amherst College, and he held the position continuously until 1873, the year before his death. His father had been a visionary, incompetent in the actual management of money; Edward was shrewd, practical, and hardworking, and he succeeded splendidly where his father had failed. When he took office, "the College was deeply in debt. . . . Its friends were in grave doubt as to whether the College could in fact survive. At the end of his term, the College had assets over a million dollars."[42] Any complete chronicle of Edward Dickinson's work for the institution would fill a volume. It is sufficient to say that he labored longer and more diligently for Amherst College than his father ever had, that the most time-consuming and exhausting portion of this work occurred in those early years just after Father had left to go to the Midwest, and that unlike Samuel Dickinson, Edward was in these early years spurred by no religious vision. Indeed, it is hard to reckon the motivation of this man, now no longer in the first flush of his youth. Once so hopeful and fired with ambition, once longing to launch himself into some splendid career that would make both his name and his fortune, he had settled into following the very path that had been set out by his father. Yet this course could not hold out to Edward the kind of satisfactions it had promised the Old Squire. Far from meaning the establishment of God's New Jerusalem, as it had to Samuel Dickinson, the cause of Amherst College meant no more to Edward than following the course of duty and filial piety—the confirmation of his identity as Samuel Fowler Dickinson's son.

Edward turned thirty on New Year's Day 1833, only a few months before his father left Amherst for good, and he was restless and dissatisfied. On September 7, 1835, shortly after becoming Amherst College treasurer, Edward wrote an angry, despairing letter to his wife, then visiting her sister in Boston:

Tell y^r father I wish he would speculate a little for me in "*Maine land*"—as I can't go myself, until October, at the earliest. . . . I am somehow disposed to believe that if I should go to Bangor, I should make a few thousand dollars—and I am dissatisfied that I did not go when I wanted to & was ready—in spite of every thing. . . . I must make money in some way, & if I don't speculate in the lands, at the "East," I must at the "West"—and when the fever next attacks me—nothing human shall stop me from making one desperate attempt to make my fortune—To be shut up forever "under a bushel" while hundreds of mere Jacanapes are getting their tens of thousands & hundreds of thousands, is rather too much for my spirit—I must spread myself over more ground—half a house, & a rod square for a garden, won't answer my turn—[43]

He was far from poor in the late 1830s. He had a busy law practice that kept him from home a good deal, and he was active in virtually every community project. He did invest in land, both in New England and in the Midwest, and unlike his father, he was never even tempted to sacrifice his private holdings to the needs of the College. Still, he was not happy. Perhaps he was never really happy.

In 1838 and 1839 he went to Boston as a representative to the legislature. It was the first time he had been away from the Amherst area for any extended length of time since his college days in New Haven. His primary reason for going was the "cause": still in financial difficulties, Amherst College hoped to obtain a grant of money from the state. Yet, as soon as Edward arrived in Boston, the long-dormant yearnings to achieve some splendid career returned as he met distinguished and influential men from all over New England. "I have been introduced to the Speaker, Mr. Winthrop, & the Clerk of the House, Mr. Cushing. I am making acquaintance every day. . . . We have had exciting debates, for two days past, on the subject of the Banks. One Bank has failed," he wrote during his first few weeks. Edward Dickinson's feelings were not unmixed, however: his wife, a shy and dependent woman, missed him sorely; and his own business in Amherst often required his attention. Thus his letters are poignant documents that express a counterpoint of several competing desires, reservations about spending so much time away from home often standing side by side with expressions of pleased enthusiasm at this new and busy life: "I think I shall never be so unwise as to allow myself to be a candidate for such a place again. I find many pleasant acquaintances, & am forming new ones, every day." He toyed with the idea of making a career out of such activity and bringing his family with him to ease the burden of separation, and he several times broached this proposition tentatively to his wife. However, the idea never took hold, and Edward fell back into a recurrent litany of reassurances: "I will not leave you again, for any such business. You need not face it. I can not do it."[44]

The life that Edward Dickinson saw small glimpses of in Boston and eventually in Washington—the life of national politics and high finance—excited and fascinated him. Hence, contrary to his steady stream of avowals in 1838 and 1839 never to spend long periods away from home again, he continued to stand for public office with great regularity, to run when he was nominated, and to serve whenever he was elected. When he died in June 1874, he did not die in his own bed, but in a Boston hotel, without any member of his family present. He had assumed yet one more term as representative to the legislature.[45]

Virtually every letter from him throughout his political life speaks of the intellectual stimulation he felt in a cosmopolitan setting and of his surge of pleasure at hobnobbing with men of prestige and imagination. Yet he could never consistently and unequivocally commit his energies to the affairs of the great world outside of Amherst. To some extent, he seems to have felt guilty about leaving his timid wife. But the real obstacle was most likely his own ambivalence, for whenever he was in one of the great cities, his letters reveal the hesitancies of a newcomer and an onlooker. He could observe the scene with intelligent interest, and he enjoyed mixing with men of power. But he did not seize authority. He was hardworking and reliable, but he never became a significant leader outside of Amherst. Even Vinnie had some awareness of Father's small-town awkwardness. "Father writes to us very often & I guess he is getting happy," she wrote Austin in late 1853, during Edward Dickinson's one term in Washington at the House of Representatives. "He told us in his last letter, that he had been sending out his cards to various persons of rank. He says he don't know much about etiquet [sic] but he is trying to learn."[46]

He never experienced the fervor of his father's messianic commitment to the evangelical mission of Amherst College. Although he managed their money superbly, the "cause" provided no emotional center for his life, and his dealings with the institution were purely pragmatic. He spent much of his energy in business—both practicing law and engaging successfully in other moneymaking projects, such as real estate. A very great success by small-town New England standards, he never carved out a great career for himself. And, for whatever reason, he spent very little time at home: his wife and children provided no emotional center, either. He was a lonely man, and as the years passed, he became only more lonely.

Certainly his daughter Emily was sensitive to his isolation.

My father seems to me often the oldest and the oddest sort of foreigner. Sometimes I say something and he stares in a curious sort of bewilderment though I speak a thought quite as old as his daughter. . . . Father says in fugitive moments when he forgets the barrister & lapses into the man, says that his life has been passed in a wilderness or on an island—of late he says on an island. And so it is, for in the morning I hear his voice and methinks it comes from afar & has a sea tone & there is a hum of hoarseness about [it] & a suggestion of remoteness as far as the isle of Juan Fernandez.[47]

The Sabbath was Edward's only day "at home." Yet New England Congregational churches held two lengthy services on that day, and good Christians were expected to be in attendance at both. Not surprisingly, his children felt no tremor of conviviality, even on Sunday. "'My father only reads on Sunday,'" Emily Dickinson told Higginson; "'he reads lonely & rigorous books.'"[48]

He soon drove the sleekest, fastest horses in Hampshire County; eventually, his house became a showplace. And he had an immense power with words: like his father before him, he was the most eloquent speaker in the county. On the whole, Edward nurtured a proud conviction that he was above even the superior run of local men. His daughter Emily was sympathetic to the notion that he would have to go beyond Amherst to find men whose acquaintance he would want to seek. ("He says he meets a great many old friends and acquaintances, and forms new ones," she wrote to Austin in 1852, when Father went to Baltimore as representative to the Whig convention. "He writes in very fine spirits, and says he enjoys himself very much. I think it will do him the very most good of anything in the world, and I do feel happy to have father at last among men who sympathize with him, and know what he really is.") And when he died, Emily was perhaps the only one who felt the full bitterness of the truth: he had never attained either private happiness or national acclaim; she mourned her "father's lonely Life and his lonelier Death," as she told Higginson.[49] Sadly, Edward's dry, emotionless manner precluded the possibility of comfort, even from this perceptive, compassionate daughter who loved him best.

Gradually Edward Dickinson learned to acknowledge the discipline of measuring his aspirations by the standards of a little township in western New England. He never relinquished the tie to his own father, and he was an "Amherst man," nothing more—despite the tenacious nettle of his ambition. By the time he had reached middle age, Amherst once again revered the Dickinson name, now as a result of *his* accomplishments: Samuel Dickinson was remembered chiefly because he had fathered "the Honorable Edward Dickinson."

Samuel Fowler Dickinson did not prosper in the Midwest. Whether he had been brought to the Lane Theological Seminary for the purpose of handling their money or not, he very soon got himself into a position of financial responsibility, and he made a mess of it. He was not opportunistic; he did not benefit himself by underhanded dealings. He was simply incompetent. On October 26, 1837, he resigned from his position at Lane (no one knows precisely what the circumstances were, but Lyman Beecher's diary indicates that he was grateful to see the man go). He moved once more, this time from Cincinnati to Hudson, Ohio, where the new Western Reserve College had been established. After serving less than one year as its treasurer, he died there of pneumonia on April 22, 1838. Because the family was dispersed, the burial ceremony (which had to take place in Ohio almost immediately) was modest. "William has sent us a letter he received from Professor Nutting [in Hudson, Ohio], giving us more particulars of the last days of his life than E[lisabeth Dickinson] gave—& of his funeral," Lucretia Dickinson wrote to her brother Edward; "it is a source of great comfort to us that so much respect was paid to his remains—as was done by *strangers*. I cannot realize it all, it seems like a dreadful dream."[50]

Before he left, Samuel Dickinson had spoken vehemently in town councils against separating the deceased members of a family, especially a husband

and wife: "There is a feeling in our natures, which exists strongly . . . that as they were united among the living, so they desired that their dust may mingle together in the congregation of the dead."[51] Samuel's wife, Lucretia Gunn Dickinson, returned to Massachusetts. Quarrelsome as ever, she lived with first one and then another of her children (never with Edward's family); on May 11, 1840, she died. Some time later, Samuel Fowler Dickinson's body was disinterred in Hudson, Ohio, and brought back to the little cemetery just beyond the northern ground of the Brick House on Main Street. He was buried next to his wife.

> *Samuel F. Dickinson died at Hudson, O.*
> *April 22, 1838 aged 62*
> *Lucretia G. Dickinson died at Enfield, Mass.*
> *May 11, 1840 aged 64*
> *Their remains were removed to this spot*
> *By their children*

Although Samuel Fowler Dickinson died in despair, convinced that his great sacrifice had been in vain, his dream of one last Jerusalem to bring God's message to a New World wilderness was actualized in Amherst College before the Civil War. Edward shared none of his father's extravagant religious zeal; nonetheless, it was he whose diligent work finally brought success to the enterprise. Grandfather passed out of Emily Dickinson's existence before she was three years old, and her own father presented himself to the world as a businesslike, pragmatic man who had little sympathy with enthusiasms. Yet a perceptive intelligence like Emily Dickinson's would have had little difficulty in recognizing that there was a spectral shadow-play of forces behind the surface appearances of her family's life. A mythic story of Puritan fathers and sons had been re-enacted in this nineteenth-century setting: the terms were complex and perhaps not altogether clear. Power was at stake. In many ways, the father's force had been surpassed by the son's; in one significant way, however, the Old Squire remained supreme. Nothing in Edward's life could match the emotional and spiritual vitality of Samuel Fowler Dickinson's original vision. Ultimately, Edward's life was pinched and compromised and unsatisfying: he never yielded himself entirely to any beckoning phantom of heroic grandeur, though he seems to have had many poignant glimpses of some glory that might have been; and the ghosts of this drama haunted the Dickinson family throughout the poet's lifetime.

II ✦ Mother and Father: The Fall into Language

In 1826, when Edward first began to think seriously about marriage, his father's failure had not played its final act; yet the end (which did not come for more than a decade) was by this time ineluctable, and the menacing specter of it clouded Edward's judgment. He wanted to be different from Father (he wanted harmony and happiness and palpable success), but he was ill-equipped to chart his course. More like his father than he supposed, he too pursued an idealized vision—possibly never more so than during the years of his courtship. He had concocted an image of the kind of woman that would be a fit companion for him, and he had little or no ability to deal with the complexities and shortcomings of the real woman to whom he proposed. Indeed, it is not clear that he was even able to comprehend her as a person in her own right.

Edward Dickinson met Emily Norcross in January 1826 when he was called to Monson on business, and they married two years later when he was twenty-five and she was twenty-four. Most of the courtship had to be carried on by letter because Edward was so engrossed in his work that he found few occasions to take the short jaunt down to the Norcross farm (he made only eighteen trips, most of them for but a single day, during the entire twenty-eight-month period), and their correspondence gives a quite circumstantial record of the relationship between them. Edward's push toward a firm commitment was astonishingly rapid: his first letter was written on February 8, 1826, and he made a formal proposal of marriage by letter on June 4, having seen the girl only twice during the intervening months. The haste was due to no fervor; rather, it was the brisk efficiency of a person who likes to dispatch business promptly.

Even though the young man had barely turned twenty-three when the couple met, the requirement that he remain steady in the face of the eccentric and taxing behavior of his father seems to have robbed him of all spontaneity. Having been treated as a confidant and fellow sufferer, he had never experienced any proper youth, and the price of having assumed so much duty seems to have been a form of premature middle age. Every one of the sixty-eight letters he wrote to Emily Norcross exudes an air of gravity, even pomposity. Not one is passionate or romantic. The tone is most discordant when he speaks of marriage, for he addresses this most intimate relationship as if it were a textbook exercise. Thus in his third letter to her, he sketches his notion of a model wife. She must possess "an amiable disposition—modest & unassuming manner—a thorough knowledge of every branch of domestic economy—good sense, cultivated & improved by a moderate acquaintance with a few of the most select works of taste, & an acquaintance & frequent intercourse with refined society & a happy contentment & equanimity of character, & a desire to promote the happiness of all around her."[1] The proposal he made two months later merely continues this inventorial form of address: he has come to a "satisfactory conclusion respecting [her] qualifications" and has become convinced that she possesses virtues "calculated to render yourself and your friends happy." He concludes by asking her to become his "friend for life."[2]

Nor did the two years that elapsed between his proposal and their marriage sweeten his discourse. About five weeks before the wedding, Edward sketched a prosaic picture of their future together: "I do not expect, neither do I desire a life of pleasure, as some call it—I anticipate pleasure engaging with my whole soul in my business, and passing the time which can be spared from that, in the enjoyment which arises from an unreserved exchange of sentiment with my dearest friend—May we be happy & useful & successful and each be an ornament in society and gain the respect . . . and confidence of all with whom we are in any way connected."[3] It is true that he was engaged in acquiring a wife. Nonetheless, virtually every deeply felt positive feeling that is expressed anywhere in his courtship letters pertains to his work. His reaction to Father's ongoing public failure and his need to disengage himself from its stigma dominated his imagination and such passions as were available to him. The upshot was that he had little emotion to invest in the family he was so precipitately beginning.

It is tempting to suppose that the standards for courtship and marriage were different then—prissy and prudish, perhaps, or "Victorian"—but nothing could be further from the truth. In the half-century after America's independence was declared, and to a lesser extent right up until the post–Civil War period, there was almost no supervision of courting couples. Diaries and letters indicate that young men and women were given absolute privacy in which to dally and whisper; sexual play was the norm, and parents generally kept out of the situation entirely. Like Edward Dickinson and Emily Norcross, many couples were constrained to conduct at least part of their relationship by letter, and an informal but widely observed code of intimacy evolved. Nothing short of true and ardent love was thought to justify the serious step of marriage, and courtship was the period during which a couple were meant to explore their emotional compatibility. Thus they were urged to communicate with utter candor. Ellen K. Rothman has compared the customs of this period to the customs of the Revolutionary period: "After the turn of the century, openness became almost an obsession for courting couples. The eighteenth century had demanded frankness on certain subjects

. . . but it was not necessary that one expose one's whole self. In the nine-teenth century, it was no longer enough to be sincere in one's affections; lov-ers were urged to be frank and open about everything."[4] Love letters were expected to be not merely romantic but passionate, and they were often frankly so. Men usually took the lead, and they generally pressed more insis-tently for marriage than women did (perhaps because men were not forced to endure the pain and danger of childbirth). However, women were expected to be candid and outspoken, too—even openly sensual. A woman was not censured for passion; on the contrary, she was thought unusual if she main-tained too much maidenly modesty.

Thus Edward Dickinson's attitude was far from ordinary, and any num-ber of things about his behavior ought to have alarmed Emily Norcross in June 1826, when she received his proposal. First was his inexplicable sudden-ness. If courtship was supposed to allow a couple to get to know each other intimately, to form ties of mutual sympathy and affection, what could it mean for a man who had known her for so short a time (and so superficially) to be willing to join with her for a lifetime? And there was the matter of his rhet-oric. Edward was expansive in his epistolary style, but he talked in chaste generalizations: he told her at length what qualities he thought a woman ought to possess, but he said nothing personal about *her*. There was no pleas-antly irregular feature of her face that charmed him, no idiosyncrasy of speech that had caught his ear, no mannerism of voice or gesture that he remembered with fondness. He did not reminisce about the ways they had found to amuse themselves—and there was not the slightest hint of sexual longing in his remembrances of her or of sexual anticipation in his desire to see her again. Perhaps the most telling signal (never relinquished throughout the two and a half years of their courtship) is his repeated use of the word "friend" to describe her. Men and women who married each other were sup-posed to have passed far beyond "friendship." What, then, could it mean when a prospective groom asked his lady to become a "friend for life"?

Edward wrote so many letters and such very long letters that it is possible to obtain a reasonably clear picture of him. Sanctimonious and frightened, repressed and prudish, honorable and honest, but bullying and bossy—Ed-ward reveals himself to have been all these things. However, no picture of Emily Norcross can be gleaned from his letters. If he had rhapsodized upon her appearance, subsequent generations would know what she looked like; if he had recalled tender moments they had spent alone together, we would know something of her behavior and speech. But without such reminiscences, anyone who wants to learn about Edward's future wife is forced to turn to the letters that were written by Emily Norcross herself. And here anomaly is merely compounded. The most striking fact is that she wrote so little—twenty-three notes in all, scarcely any of them covering more than one side of a letter sheet. If Edward was long-winded and impersonal, Emily was all but mute. It is sad but perhaps not surprising that Edward Dickinson managed to discover a woman who was, if anything, less emotionally forthcoming than he.

He soon became impatient with her failure to write more often, and as early as May 1826 he had begun to chastise her for it. However, this procedure brought nothing but the passive resistance of silent unresponsiveness. He fell into the habit of writing sarcastically that he *"presumed"* her silence to indicate this or that reaction, but usually this tactic, too, proved generally unsuccessful. In fact, very early in the dance of courtship, one characteristic of Emily Norcross's mode of communication emerged with startling clarity: she preferred never to speak for herself. It was not that she was pliant or unselfish or without personal wishes (although Edward imputed all of these traits to her in his more optimistic moments); she communicated her wishes indirectly, through a complex and often inefficient game of verbal hide-and-seek. Instead of laboring to speak out, she withheld communication entirely; confronted with her unchanging inarticulateness, Edward was forced to guess at her preferences. Ironically, his habit of bossy volubility was an asset to her here, for she could consistently count on him to elaborate a plan for her to follow or to "presume" what her silence might mean; he would go on with this guessing (becoming increasingly impatient) until at last he hit upon the "correct" formulation. Then, and only then, she would respond. Never her own spokesperson, she forced Edward into the role of speaking for her. When he failed, as he occasionally did, she turned to others—her father or even her much younger sister, Lavinia.

The first example of this pattern occurs after Edward's June 4 letter proposing marriage, for Emily Norcross's "response" was utter silence. He wrote again, restating and clarifying his wishes. Still silence. He wrote again, making his request even more pointed. Still silence. He wrote to ask whether she had doubts concerning his character. Silence. He wrote angrily, impatiently, sarcastically. By the time *she* finally wrote again, four months had elapsed since her last letter, and more than two months since Edward's proposal of marriage. Her letter gave no answer, but instead instructed Edward to raise the matter with her father—a patently evasive maneuver since courtship customs mandated that the couple settle matters between themselves before informing the parents of their decision. Undaunted, Edward wrote Joel Norcross in early September; he received no answer from that quarter, either. Now there was nothing but silence from *both* father and daughter.

The young man had finally reached the end of his patience by late fall. On October 22 he wrote a long letter that ventured to *"presume"* a number of things.

I have . . . hoped to have a more full account of your parents' views in relation to the subject of our intercourse, but after the length to which our correspondence has proceeded, is it not fair to me to infer that our wishes in relation to the subject of a permanent connection, are the same, and am I not right in my conclusion, that your family are not disposed to interfere with our arrangements in relation to it? . . .

I should be unwilling to think that I did not understand you. I shall, therefore, say something as to the time when it would be proper to consummate our union. We are both young, & on that account, need not be in haste.

Perhaps merely by chance, in this last sentence Edward finally hit upon the unuttered reservation, addressing here a concern that she had never explicitly raised. She responded almost at once.

Oct. 30, 1826 . . . You may rightly conclude that my feelings are in unison with yours. I am happy to learn that you are not disposed to be in haste; the reasons you have advanced correspond perfectly with my fathers [sic] views relative to this particular point.[5]

Thus did the couple become formally engaged.

The letters that passed between them make it difficult to fathom why they wanted to marry each other at all. If anything, Edward's reasons are clearer than those of his future wife. Probably Emily Norcross's diffidence seemed a considerable attraction, quite the opposite of his own mother's manner. Indeed, the entire Norcross family was agreeably different from his own. Joel Norcross, Emily's father, was one of the most prosperous men in Monson. An honest, bluff-mannered, practical farmer, he had to be judged prosaic by Dickinson standards, for he had none of Samuel Fowler's colorful enthusiasms. He wrote awkward, uncultivated letters and had little elegance in society. Yet withal he was a welcome contrast to the Old Squire, for he did have, as Edward remarked with appreciation, a "peculiar way of producing an agreeable surprise in having things prove much better than he represents."[6] His wife, Betsy Fay Norcross, had those domestic virtues that Edward Dickinson prized: she was "pious, amiable and useful, [and] her prudence, and affection, [her] regard to the happiness of all around her, appeared most conspicuous."[7] Life at the Norcross farm in Monson was soundly financed and domestically ordered, and Edward may have expected to assure the fulfillment of his dream of repose and comfort by marrying the older daughter. Sad to say, the rest of the courtship gave little reason to suppose that such hopes would be realized.

Although the evidence is all indirect (for she gave no *voice* to her dissatisfaction), Emily Norcross seems to have become increasingly unhappy with Edward. Perhaps his lecturing and patronizing air offended her; perhaps his failure to express ardent passion disappointed her. For whatever reason, after a year or so she began to taunt him—though as always, her methods were both indirect and passive. The torment took several forms; however, the principal bone of contention was his wish that she pay a visit to his family in Amherst. The rules of common courtesy demanded this, yet she demurred. Sometimes she failed to respond to his requests; sometimes she put him off with vague excuses, never offering any very precise explanation for her refusal. What is more, during the time he was so urgently petitioning her, she managed to take other trips—to Connecticut, even to New York City—but she never came to Amherst. She had made one brief visit during the commencement week in August 1826; thereafter, she never again returned until she came as Edward Dickinson's bride in May 1828. And her evasions made him nearly frantic with frustration and anger.[8]

Edward found a suitable house for them to live in after the wedding, and he urged her to take a look at it and give her approval. Instead, she asked him to dispatch measurements of the rooms and of the color scheme (which he did), and then, in late January 1828, she sent her sister Lavinia, only fifteen at the time, to inspect the premises. Edward asked her at least to tell him whether the kitchen suited her expectations, and in February she sent her father up to Amherst to make the judgment for her. Edward wanted to publish the banns in time to marry in April; she withheld her permission, and they could not be married until May. Edward asked after details of the ceremony—how many of his family and friends he could expect to be included—and she insisted (against all prevailing customs) on a private wedding with no one to "stand up" with them. The last few months of the engagement degenerated into a pitched battle of wills, and because Emily Norcross had only inertia as her weapon, it was a battle she was fated to lose. The force of Edward's anger and tenacious insistence propelled them slowly but steadily toward a union. And the young man who had never managed grace or affection in his wooing could at least be solicitous when victory was clearly in sight.

April 29, 1828 . . . I shall leave the management of the ceremony entirely with you till I meet you—and if not convenient for any company to stand on our right and & left, I am not so diffident but what I could consent to stand by the side of My Dear, for a short time—unsupported by friends—No, My Dearest Emily, I shall never fear to stand by you, *alone.*[9]

At this point, it was comparatively easy for Edward to be munificent. He writes that he will never fear to stand with her *"alone."* But it was she, not he, who would be forced to contemplate a future of solitude—"alone."

If the transactions of the courtship reveal nothing else, they demonstrate how deficient both Edward Dickinson and Emily Norcross were in those skills by which people communicate in an intimate, domestic environment— how awkwardly and inadequately each handled personal discourse. Neither party can be judged more at fault than the other, for both were tragically inept in dealing with emotions. Yet the *result* of their joint failure would inevitably fall more heavily on the wife than on the husband, for once the marriage had taken place, Edward's shortcomings in this regard could be glossed over. He could transfer all of his emotional energies into his profession (he had repeatedly avowed his intention to do so)—could be out of the house for the entire day and evening, could go out of town on business, could occupy his spare moments with work for the town or for Amherst College. He could limit most of his discourse to exchanges with colleagues and clients and men of affairs; in short, he could arrange his life so that he largely avoided situations that demanded a more intimate, feeling form of expression. And in doing so he could win the admiration and gratitude of the people around him, for who would be willing to criticize a man so industrious in business and so generous in giving himself to public works? By contrast, his wife would have none of these options. She would be limited to home and children, and Edward Dickinson held out little promise of support or comfort or love.

Emily Norcross may have understood some of this, though she did not formulate her fears clearly and did not give voice to her resentment. She was loath to depart from her family's farm when the time finally arrived. She was leaving it for a house she had never seen in a township where she had no friends; instead of spending her days with her parents and brothers and sister, she would be quite alone—alone in an empty house while her husband was away pursuing his exemplary career. When children came, it would be she alone who took care of them, for Edward Dickinson's family had no regular domestic help until 1855. Emily Norcross had possessed insufficient resources to communicate effectively with Edward even during the relatively carefree days of their courtship (when a woman's "power" was at its height). What was it going to mean for her to become his wife and the mother of his children? As the date for the marriage drew nearer, her inarticulate terrors found oblique expression. "March 22, 1828 . . . My mind is often completely confused when I allow myself to dwell upon the subject [of our marriage], but I usually lay it aside with the reflection that it will result in our happiness. . . . April 23, 1828 . . . My dear I would wish you to be gratified, but give me liberty to say that I wish the proceedings to be managed with as little noise as possible. . . . I have many friends call upon me as they say to make their farewell visit. How do you suppose this sounds in my ear. But my dear, it is to go and live with you."[10] When the couple were married on May 6, 1828, she entered upon her new life with fears and foreboding.

From the first she was desolately lonely. Her sister Lavinia wrote on May 13 and again on May 15: Father "says it is foolish for me to write so often, but I think news from home must always be desireable especially to one who is so homesick—."[11] Almost at once, Edward was drawn away by his absorption in his work. Less than a week after the wedding, Samuel Fowler

Dickinson was elected to his final term as representative to the state legislature; he would not be going to Boston to serve until January, of course, but while he was away, Edward would, as always, be obliged to look after his business. It was peculiar, then, that about one month later (on June 26, 1828), Samuel Dickinson offered his prospectus for a "School for Instruction in the science and practice of the Law," for if this venture had been successful, Edward would have had to bear the principal burden of it as well. As it was, Edward had enough to do without the overflow from his father's life. He was secretary of the Fire Society (no minor task in a village with frame houses and nothing but well water) and clerk of the parish, and he traveled as often as before in connection with his own growing legal practice. His wife was left by herself much of the time. In September, Edward wrote her from Northampton, the seat of the County Court, about the possibility of their taking in a boarder so that she would not be in the house at night without the protection of a man. Possibly the prospect of the additional income was also a considerable inducement.

The Hon. Mr. Bliss of Springfield has spoken to me to-day, about boarding his son. Says he & Henry Morris are coming to Amherst to-day, & he will try to get in, at our house. You know my opinion respecting it, and I leave it entirely with you to manage as you think best. The work, you know, comes upon you, and it is wholly immaterial with me, what you conclude. . . . I shall be at home to-morrow. Let one of my Sisters stay with you to-night, without fail.[12]

This appears to have been the entire extent of his concern to overcome her unhappiness. She was by this time pregnant with her first child.

Subsequent generations have judged Emily Norcross Dickinson harshly. "Mrs. Dickinson seems to have had one positive trait, and that was fear," Millicent Todd Bingham wrote.[13] And elsewhere, Bingham (who, after all, never met either Edward Dickinson or his wife) is even more vehement: "Their mother was a meek little thing. She didn't know what to do for them. She was not important enough to be included in the family feuds."[14] John Cody's complex psychological approach retreats from affixing "blame"; nonetheless, he diagnoses the poet as an "unsatisfied and love-starved child."[15]

Yet Emily Dickinson's own references to her mother are more positive and generous, and when she was away from her parents, she missed them both. "This week, on Wednesday," she wrote to her friend Abiah Root during her residence at Mount Holyoke in 1847, "I was at my window, when I happened to look towards the hotel & saw Father & Mother, walking over here as dignified as you please. I need not tell you that I danced & clapped my hands, & flew to meet them for you can imagine how I felt. I will only ask you do you love your parents?" Her many evocations of home conjure an image of

Mother's quiet warmth and gentle concern for the children. "Home is a holy thing," she wrote to Austin when he was teaching school in Boston; "here seems indeed to be a bit of Eden which not the sin of *any* can utterly destroy." . . . "Mother is frying Doughnuts—I will give you a little platefull to have warm for your tea!" . . . "[We sent] all your clothes in such beautiful order, and a cake of new maple sugar, and mother has with her own hand selected and polished the apples, she thought it would please you so." Later, in the letters to Susan Gilbert (Austin's wife-to-be), there is the same affectionate regard for a mother who is good-natured and well intentioned: "Mother sends her best love to you. It makes her look so happy when I give yours to her. Send it always, Susie." Later, much later—after Edward Dickinson had died and Emily Norcross Dickinson had grown elderly and been seriously disabled by a stroke—it was her daughter Emily who kept the loving vigil: "You kindly ask for Mother's health," Emily Dickinson wrote her confidante, Mrs. Holland: "It is tranquil, though trifling. She reads a little— sleeps much—chats—perhaps—most of all—about nothing momentous, but things vital to her—and reminds one of Hawthorne's blameless Ship— that forgot the Port."*[16]

Emily Dickinson spent these years as nurse (there were seven altogether) in uncomplaining service, and when Emily Norcross Dickinson passed quietly away in 1882, her daughter Emily's sorrow was deep and sincere. Such sentiments, beginning in Emily Dickinson's earliest days and lasting through her final moments with her mother, do not comport with so simplistic a diagnosis as "love-starved child." Emily Dickinson wrote a language of genuine affection that would be difficult to credit if her home had been devoid of love.

And yet those who have attempted to discover the weakness in Emily Dickinson's relationship with her parents have been correct in supposing that the family was not altogether happy. Emily Dickinson's younger sister, Lavinia, gave an unsettling description of the family: "While contributing to the maintenance of a solid front, each component part remained distinct and independent. . . . [We] all lived like friendly and absolute monarchs, each in his own domain." There is a positive tone to this—a sense of the freedom and the independence that Vinnie and Emily enjoyed—yet withal there is a tone of penetrating sadness: "You were bound to those to whom you gave loyalty and devotion, but with whom you did not share your thoughts."[17] This was a house of isolation, a house where the children's independence could be maintained only if easy intimacy and spontaneous affections were sacrificed. Vinnie describes, in the end, a fortress of terrible loneliness.

* "Hawthorne's ship" was a legendary vessel that haunted the port of Salem but never came to land. For Dickinson to be "at sea" is always to be in a state of helplessness, confusion, and unhappiness. Here, with empathetic acuity, she identifies her mother's emotional state by associating it with such moments of misery in her own life.

There are also moments when Emily Dickinson, usually the most generous of daughters, spoke with uncharacteristic cruelty about her mother. "My mother does not care for thought," she dismissively wrote to Higginson. When he came to visit her in Amherst, a note of nastiness—even of rancor—crept into her conversation: "Could you tell me what home is. I never had a mother. I suppose a mother is one to whom you hurry when you are troubled." And in a letter just after their interview, as if to reinforce her point, she reiterated the assertion to Higginson: "I always ran Home to Awe when a child, if anything befell me. He was an awful Mother, but I liked him better than none. There remained this shelter after you left me the other Day."[18]

The reality, then, is complicated and contradictory. In talking about her mother, Emily Dickinson could give voice to affection, could understand the anxious good will that characterized Mother's feelings for her children. And along with this, there was Emily Dickinson's deep bitterness, the cryptic anger that she occasionally expressed. The bitterness did not vitiate the affection, nor did the affection temper the bitterness. Rather, they coexisted, uneasy and opposite members of Emily Dickinson's affective life. "Could you tell me what home is," she asked Higginson. "Home is a holy thing," she had written to Austin. Again, although in talking to Higginson she asserted, "I never had a mother," the truth was that she *always* had a mother: unlike Father, Mother virtually never left the home. Paradoxes—all. In her life and in her letters, Emily Dickinson was more inclined to express the positive side of this polarity: fondness for Mother and acknowledgment of her innumerable efforts at kindness (Mother mending clothes, Mother polishing apples for her homesick boy); respect and great love for Father, sympathy for the ambitions so puzzlingly unfulfilled and for the terrible, hollow loneliness of his life. Yet in her art, the other side of the paradox finds voice. The story of the poet, then, must return to those early days in the marriage of Edward Dickinson and his wife. September 1828: Emily Norcross Dickinson, married only four months, is pregnant with her first child.

In 1828 it would have been difficult to find a woman in Amherst who could contemplate childbirth without fear. When men married, they took on additional financial responsibilities but few other significant trials. However, marriage catapulted women into the midst of life's most awful mysteries—pain, mutilation, and possible death. Birth control was not available during the early nineteenth century in New England, and every married woman faced the possibility of a series of unplanned pregnancies, each one of which threatened an agonizing extinction. Perhaps only young men who enter active combat during a war confront similar crises.

Childbirth had not presented so many horrors in earlier times when it was managed by midwives, whose philosophy was to offer liberal emotional support, interfere as little as possible, and let nature take its course. At the beginning of the nineteenth century, however, the care of women during pregnancy and childbirth was increasingly managed by male doctors who had received absolutely no obstetrical training of any kind. Unlike midwives, these doctors viewed pregnancy and parturition as a form of "sickness"; and they reversed the practices of midwives, offering no emotional support but a good deal of active interference. Of course, difficult birthings had always been horrific under any management. Anesthesia was not available; labor was sometimes protracted; and the possibilities for addressing problems were brutally primitive. An armamentarium of instruments had been in use for several centuries:

Blunt hooks to bring down the thighs in a breech delivery, sharp hooks (crochets) and knives and perforators to puncture the fetus's head when it was completely impacted or dead, and the ancient device of the *speculum matricis* to dilate the vagina and make it easier to cut out obstructions or reach the fetus. . . . Most often the surgeons had to kill the impacted child to save the mother's life.[19]

By the eighteenth century forceps were added to the array; and, unlike midwives, male doctors were inclined to employ them even when a birth was proceeding quite normally.

Unlike the "low" forceps used today . . . many male attendants were using "high" or even "floating" forceps, which were applied before the fetal head was engaged in the mother's pelvis, or "mid" forceps, when the head was engaged in the curve of the birth canal, but not yet visible. . . . These latter operations present extreme danger to both mother and child, the possibilities of physical damage, infection in damaged tissue, hemorrhage, and a crushed fetus head.[20]

By the early nineteenth century yet another aid began to be employed: ergot, a drug that caused the uterine muscles to contract and helped to speed the delivery.

Ergot is a fungus that grows on rye and other stored grains. It causes powerful and unremitting contractions. . . . Ergot also quickens the expulsion of the placenta and stems hemorrhage by compelling the uterus to contract. . . . There was in fact no antidote to ergot's rapid and uncontrollable effects until anesthesia became available in later decades. So if the fetus did not move as expected, the drug could cause the uterus to mold itself around the child, rupturing the uterus and killing the child. Ergot, like most new medical arts for birth, was a mix of danger and benefit.[21]

Finally, of course, there were all of the usual medical procedures that would be applied to any "sick person" (not just a woman having a baby).

The result of combining all of these could produce something like a monstrous nightmare, as an episode both temporally and geographically proximate to Emily Norcross Dickinson demonstrates.

In a famous case in Boston in 1833 a woman had convulsions a month before her expected delivery. The doctors bled her of 8 ounces and gave her a purgative. The next day she again had convulsions, and they took 22 ounces of blood, gave emetics to cause vomiting, and put ice on her head and mustard plasters on her feet. Nearly four hours later she had another convulsion, and they took 12 ounces, and soon after, 6 more. By then she had lapsed into a deep coma, so the doctors doused her with cold water but could not revive her. Soon her cervix began to dilate, so the doctors gave her ergot to induce labor. Shortly before delivery she convulsed again, and they applied ice and mustard plasters again and also gave a vomiting agent and calomel to purge her bowels. In six hours she delivered a stillborn child. After two days she regained consciousness and recovered. The doctors considered this a conservative treatment, even though they had removed two-fifths of her blood in a two-day period, for they had not artificially dilated her womb or used instruments to expedite delivery.[22]

In the face of such possibilities, fear seems a not unreasonable reaction to pregnancy.

This grim combination of birth and death had an even more personal meaning for timid Emily Norcross Dickinson than it did for most young women in Amherst at that time, for the Norcross women often bore sickly infants. "It was a local saying in Monson that the Norcrosses could not manage to raise their girls"—that is, that the Norcross female children did not survive.[23] Both Lavinia and Emily Norcross lived to marry and have children of their own, and genealogies list only one additional girl child—Nancy, born 1818, deceased 1824. Thus there is a puzzle here, for the death of only one daughter out of nine children is scarcely cause for such a reputation. However, a widespread New England custom regarding newborn children may offer some clue. Infant mortality was very high, and parents became distraught when one after another, the babies born amid such fear and anguish lived only long enough to make the losing of them painful. Thus families often did not formally acknowledge a new member's existence until he or she had weathered the dangers of the first months, sometimes not even giving the new arrival a name until he or she was a year old.[24] There may have been Norcross infants that died before being named or officially recorded. In any event, to make matters worse, all of the usual avenues of female support were closed to Emily Norcross Dickinson. There was trouble at home, so that neither her mother nor her sister could be spared; she was not on cordial terms with Edward's mother or sisters; she had no close female friends in the Amherst area; and this first baby, like the subsequent children, would be brought into the world not by a midwife but by a male, Dr. Isaac Cutler of Amherst.

By the time of his death in 1834, Dr. Cutler had assisted 1,336 cases of childbirth. That is, he was at least an experienced practitioner when Emily Norcross Dickinson had her first child.[25] Nonetheless, any woman attended during pregnancy and birth by a man in the early nineteenth century had yet one more concern added to her many fears: a complex system designed to impose "modesty" upon this unusual male-female relationship (so intimately tied to sexuality and at the same time so thoroughly and necessarily asexual). "The term 'confinement,' by which Victorians commonly described pregnancy and lying-in, expressed the shame and impropriety of exposure during pregnancy, for the expectant woman separated herself and kept to her home, indicating her need for rest and her unfitness for polite, mixed society."[26] Emily Norcross's own mother had surely gone about her work on the family farm in Monson during her pregnancies, but Emily Norcross was forced to seclude herself as soon as her "condition" became visible. Although Lavinia offered support, she had to do so by letter: "It may aggravate you—to think you cannot go to sleigh rides," she wrote in early February; "it is enough to make any-one discouraged to see what all the married folks are coming to."[27] Finally, her fears and troubles were not limited to the concomitants of her own condition. Unlike the hearty Dickinson tribe, the Norcross clan was not noted for its health: tuberculosis lingered in the family like an indelible affliction, killing randomly in every generation. In the spring of 1829, death had once again begun to walk the halls of the family's farm in Monson. Two of Emily Norcross's brothers had died before the time of her marriage, Eli (1809–11) and Austin (1802–24); now her oldest brother, Hiram, was mortally ill.

Shortly before Emily and Edward's marriage, Hiram—then twenty-eight, married, with a five-year-old son and a newborn daughter—had become very ill and resumed residence with his parents. On February 26, 1829, when his sister Emily was in the seventh month of her pregnancy, Hiram died. In March, Lavinia Norcross wrote an unsettling account of the loss:

Amanda [Hiram's widow] is well—but is very lonely—she has devoted all her time for a long time past to Hiram, but to have him taken from her & be left alone, she can hardly be reconciled—every moment was spent in administering to his wants—but how changed—he who was so lately with us a member of our family—where is he? His form we cannot see nor his voice hear—he has gone to the silent grave, his voice his forever hushed in death—but his spirit has ascended on high—& we trust he is with his Savior in glory.[28]

Nor was the season of Emily Norcross Dickinson's tribulation yet over. By the time her baby boy was born on April 16, 1829 (she called him Austin after one of the three brothers who had predeceased her), her own mother was mortally ill. Mrs. Norcross came to Amherst in late May to see her daughter and her new grandson, but after her return to Monson on May 21, her condition deteriorated rapidly. Emily Norcross Dickinson could not leave the new baby, who was still nursing, and a newborn could not safely travel. Yet as soon as the final chill of spring had departed and she did not have to fear for the infant's health, she hastened home to visit her mother, taking Austin with her.

Edward was in no way sympathetic to the trip. "I am obliged to say," he wrote, "that the warm weather affects me very much—and that my health is far from being good. . . . I am not pleased at all, with the life of a widower. . . . You can judge, probably—from your own feelings, whether I should like to see you and our little boy. . . . I receive calls, as usual, when you are at home—Shall I return them, or wait for your company?—I treat them with Lemonade—and Cider—as *you did not leave any wine!!*"[29] His wife returned to Amherst for an uneasy summer.

Lavinia continued to write anxiously, and their mother began calling out in her fevered condition to see Emily. On August 18 Lavinia wrote a piteous letter:

I can say but few words. . . . [Mother] is not able to sit up but a few minutes & not able yet to turn herself in bed. I cannot think you realize how feeble she is—should any disorder attract her, but little would bring her to the grave, you can have no idea how emaciated she is nothing but the skin covers her bones, she cannot yet take any thing to nourish her except a little water-gruel & something of that nature she is very anxious to see you wishes after commencement is over to have your husband fetch you down you must not disappoint her. . . . Emily, do come & see us—I feel as tho you must come & sympathize in our distress.

At the end of the month, Emily Norcross Dickinson was urgently summoned home; now sick herself (not from consumption, but probably from emotional exhaustion if nothing else), she took the baby and went to Monson once again. On September 5, 1829, Betsy Fay Norcross died at the age of fifty-one. William Otis Norcross, one of Emily's brothers, wrote to Edward: "The Funeral will be attended on Monday next. . . . Emily is better than when she left you—the babe is well & quiet."[30]

It is difficult to imagine Emily Norcross Dickinson's state of mind during the spring and summer of 1829. How could she have assimilated the ongoing nightmare—the dyings and the birth—what meaning, what reality did it all have for her? There is not the least sign that Edward Dickinson offered any sympathy. But his behavior was not altogether unusual. It was women and not men who were expected to deal with sickness and death. So common was this division of responsibility that it seems to have been almost a birthright of females at that time to become intimately acquainted with mortality.

Women bore the babies and nursed them and often watched them die. Whenever there was sickness in the house, the womenfolk (even if they were very young) were expected to be in attendance: seventeen-year-old Lavinia Norcross was her dying mother's principal caretaker. There were no professional nurses, and during every severe illness some woman or other kept a "night watch" to give the patient reassurance, see to his or her comfort, and respond to any crisis in the disease.[31] (Many years later, the poet Emily Dickinson would attend to her own mother much as her aunt Lavinia had tended Betsy Fay Norcross in 1828–29. The poet's sister Lavinia shared the burden, but it never occurred to anyone to ask for nursing help from Austin. His realm was the public world; comforting the sick and dying was women's work, not men's.) The tone of Edward Dickinson's letter to his wife in June 1829 seems heartless to a modern ear. However, its tenor may be no more than a reflection of the practices of the day. Those who frequent only the front rooms of a home—who have their clothes washed and their meals prepared and their children taken care of and their sicknesses assuaged—cannot be expected to comprehend the exhausting physical labor or emotional anguish that attends so many of these activities. Millicent Todd Bingham remarks with telling insight that few men during the nineteenth century understood that "the peace and harmony of a household . . . was built upon the ceaseless toil of the women of the family."[32] It was equally true that few adult women had escaped hearing the greedy rasp of a "death rattle." Herman Melville learned of bloody death and bloodier birth by shipping out to sea. Emily Dickinson was constrained to consider such issues merely by having been born female.

The letter Edward sent to his wife during her June 1829 visit to Monson has an interesting series of lines that seem to bear little relation to her behavior (and none at all to the emotional drama being enacted during her mother's final days): "Pay all the debts you contract. . . . Women must keep clear of debt."[33] Written just about one year after Samuel Fowler Dickinson's ineffectual efforts to establish a "Law School," it might best be seen not as a piece of communication for his wife, but rather as a talisman of Edward's unremitting preoccupation with his father's decline. Emily Norcross Dickinson bore three children, and with the birth of each she suffered a significant loss. In the case of the first, the blow had come from her side of the family: the death of her brother Hiram and then of her mother. With the second and the third, however, the principal trauma came from the Dickinson side, as Edward and his own family were all swept into the maelstrom of Samuel Fowler Dickinson's public disgrace.

It was early April 1830, just before Austin's first birthday, when Edward bought the western half of the Brick House on Main Street. This acquisition suggests that he was in funds, as do other events in his life then: he bought three pews in the new church, and in May he took a trip to New York City. However, he was still much away from home, and in August his wife (then five months pregnant with their second child) was again taking in boarders. Sometime in the fall of 1830, Edward, his wife, and the infant Austin made the move from their separate home to join the Samuel Fowler Dickinsons in the Brick House on Main Street.

It was not a happy time. Lucretia Gunn Dickinson was perpetually ill-humored: at a softening distance of considerable time, her nature may seem merely amusing, but during her life and at close quarters, many people found her impossible to tolerate.[34] Any retreat to Monson was out of the question: the widower, Joel Norcross, was intending to be remarried in January 1831, sixteen months after his wife's death, and neither Emily Norcross Dickinson nor her generous sister Lavinia cared for the woman he had chosen. "What shall I call her?" Lavinia wrote on December 6, 1830. "Can I say Mother. O that I could be far away from here—."[35] No longer mistress of her own home, no longer as welcome in the home of her childhood as she once had been, Emily Norcross had no support but that of a husband who was devoting himself desperately to business.

There is a legend (as Sewall observes, "it is probably little more than that but may contain a grain of truth"[36]) that throws some light on what might be called the "border disputes" between the Dickinson faction and the intruding daughter-in-law. "A painter and paper hanger in Amherst [named Lafayette Stebbins] says that at the time [her second baby was expected, Mrs. Edward Dickinson] wanted to have her bedroom painted but the Hon. Edward Dickinson would not allow her to have it done—nevertheless she went secretly to the paper hanger and asked him to come and paper her bedroom. This he did, while [the baby] was being born."[37] In truth, almost nobody cares whether a bedroom was being redecorated during Emily Dickinson's birth. The story retains currency only for the insight it gives into her mother's situation. Never outspoken by nature, now beset by many trials, Emily Norcross Dickinson gave a spasm of rebellion of the sort that had punctuated the latter days of her courtship. The little explosion of defiance signaled fear and distress, and it was the prelude to unhappy, silent acceptance.

Under these circumstances a baby entered the world on December 10, 1830, the second child of the Edward Dickinsons. A girl—Emily Elizabeth Dickinson.

The record of Emily Norcross Dickinson and her new baby becomes elusive now, and this is the point at which chroniclers of the poet's life begin to dismiss her mother with casual contempt: a "self-effacing wife," Bingham remarks, "she served chiefly as a carrier of Dickinson traits. Her three children, Austin, Emily and Lavinia, though bearing her Norcross family names, were essentially Dickinsons."[38] Yet how could this be the case? Edward was away so much of the time that his wife was virtually the sole parental figure during the early years of their children's lives. The one brief glimpse that remains of Emily Norcross Dickinson's attitude toward her daughter Emily is so touchingly tender that it belies the simplistic claim of "loveless mothering" as well. A letter written to Edward, who was visiting Boston, when the baby was about six months old, is revealing: "I have retired to my chamber for a little space to converse with you, with my little companion [the baby Emily] on the bed asleep. I have as yet had the pleasure of heareing [*sic*] from you every day which has given me much support."[39]

The puzzle remains. In the poet's infancy and early childhood, Mother was always there, and the evidence of Emily Norcross Dickinson's well-intentioned, affectionate nature is affirmed throughout her daughter's testimony; yet something went awry, for the anger at some failure remains, too, in Emily Dickinson's recollections of her mother. Love and rage coexist in uneasy companionship, and the historical record falters here, just when information is most needed to explain the dilemma. Yet if history fails here, the daughter does not: "Mother" exists most directly and vividly in her daughter's style of communication, her use of language, and her attitude toward words—their power and their limitation. Human interaction came first with Mother. Both the intimate and intuitive exchanges that precede the coming of "the word" in a baby's life and the more self-conscious and public discourse that defines verbal interaction—virtually all of Emily Dickinson's notions of communication began with Mother. Father played his part, to be sure. The most polished and powerful orator in Hampshire County, he read the Bible aloud to the family in his sonorous voice every morning of his life when he was at home. Father added another dimension to his daughter's sense of language, but this was secondary. The first and most primitive feelings about words and about communication in general derived from Emily Dickinson's relationship with her mother.

Indeed, there is panoramic evidence of this indebtedness throughout Emily Dickinson's poetry. No other American poet has understood so well the power of *withholding* communication, of remaining quiet in lieu of speaking—of being parsimonious with language and using ellipses rather than proliferations of words. Emily Dickinson challenges her reader to "hit" upon the correct meaning of her many silences. This technique is an act of filial piety: it is her mother's habit of discourse transfigured into art. Yet there is an even more powerful remnant of Mother's relationship with her poet-daughter, and ironically, this remnant (whose traces can be found in Dickinson's language throughout both letters and verse) came from the preverbal stage of life, when communication is achieved *visually* and *silently* through a complex interaction of eye contact and face-to-face play.

A newborn baby's most efficient reflex is sight—the ability to focus upon an object, to follow it, and to control receptivity by opening and closing the eyes at will. Of all the baby's initial reflexes, this is the only one that does not decline and drop away; instead, it develops with remarkable speed, so that by the end of the second month it has already assumed the form that it will keep throughout adult life. Communication begins as soon as a baby makes eye-to-eye contact with its mother, usually sometime during the first hours of life; very soon, an intricate "language" begins to evolve, allowing the baby to express the subtleties of her needs and moods. Gradually, what develops is a complex, almost balletic, often playful "gossip" of watching and being watched. Both partners can become virtuoso performers in this silent dance of "language"—locking eyes in concert and glancing elsewhere; facing each other and turning aside, only to face each other once more with joyous, flirtatious invitation; accepting the intimacy of this purely visual discourse, or refusing it for the moment by resolutely looking away.[40]

When mother and baby are able to engage successfully in nonverbal communication, the infant will derive immense emotional strengths from the process. This is the time when a person's initial sense of identity is formed: the baby learns to distinguish between her "self" and the other people who exist in her environment, comprehending with ever-increasing clarity that she is not an extension of her mother and that her mother is not an extension of herself. Furthermore, the baby is receiving her first lessons in how to interact with others. When this stage of communication is skillful and loving, the infant learns to feel good both about her mother and about her own emergent self, acquiring a fundamental sense that the universe is on the whole benign. Little by little, the baby also begins to be able to tolerate separation from her mother, because she has discovered that the partner in this "dialogue" is reliable—mother may leave, but she will always return.[41] This period of eye / face communication is a universal, crosscultural phenomenon; and "its expression in the cultural heritage of language and myth suggest[s] origins deeply rooted in common and universal experiences of humanity."[42] Thus its successes are always the same successes—a strong and confident sense of self, an ability to interact gracefully with others, and the conviction that the world is a good place. Moreover, when there is difficulty, disruption, or failure during this period of development, there are certain characteristic problems that may follow the infant through childhood and into adulthood. A sense of the integrity of self, insufficiently confirmed in this initial phase, may always remain weak. Intimate relationships with others may be difficult to sustain; separation from loved ones may always be fearsome. The world may even seem a dangerous place, governed by an indifferent or hostile God.[43] Finally (and perhaps most important in the case of a poet), the infant's initial attitude toward language may become distorted.

In cases where nonverbal communication is adequate (or better than average), speech becomes a tremendous gain; it adds immensely to an already rich "vocabulary" and opens new vistas for the child without foreclosing a return to the intimacy of that unspoken "discourse," eye / face gossip. In the opposite case, however, when the infant is forced to employ language as a necessary remedy for otherwise unsatisfactory communication—in the case, that is, where the discourse of eye and face has failed in some crucial way—then language is not a pure gain. Verbal communication is better than failed nonverbal communication, to be sure; but the move from nonverbal into verbal communication becomes, in this case, the acknowledgment of a loss that nothing can ever fully remedy. The "magic time" of mother-infant intimacy, when silent dialogue is possible, has never properly occurred. No compensation, however great, in subsequent experience can actually turn the clock backward to reclaim that magic period. The joy of this time of life is lost, and a sense of that loss may color all the life to follow. The movement from silent, eye / face dialogue to verbal communication, then, may ever after be construed as a "Fall into Language," verbal discourse seeming a second-best alternative to some other, loosely defined, transcendent intimacy: a nostalgic inclination to value the *visual* may remain in the child's personality, a tendency to express ultimate pleasure, pain, and conflict in visual terms, and the propensity to overvalue *seeing* (as opposed to saying). Yet, perversely, just because language has been forced to perform so critical a task in the early life of such an infant, verbal formulations may also seem to have unique sovereignty. No Power will compare to the Power of the Word.

The central paradox of Emily Dickinson's use of language suggests that it was precisely some disruption of this earliest form of unvoiced communication that lingered in her creative imagination: although she was a supreme craftsman of the *word,* she consistently construed verbal communication as only second best to *seeing.*

For example, when Edward Dickinson and his wife corresponded, they spoke of the letters as bridging a break in spoken exchange—that is, when either wrote the other, he or she thought of the letter as a form of conversation, of talking. Edward typically wrote, "I shall again devote the very few moments that remain before the mail closes . . . to converse with you." And Emily Norcross typically responded, "I have retired to my chamber for a little space to converse with you."⁴⁴ This is such a natural mode of construing a written correspondence that it is worth noting only because their daughter Emily deviates from it so markedly. In Emily Dickinson's letters, written exchange is used to bridge a break in *visual* exchange: in her estimation, ideal communication is an occupation for the eye and face.

In many letters, her articulation of this paradigm takes a relatively simple form: a break in communication is a disruption of "seeing" which the letter is designed to repair.

August 3, 1845 [to her friend Abiah Root] . . . I want to see you all so much, that it seems as if I could not wait. . . . Dont look at the writing and dont let any one see the letter. I want you should keep the Seal and whenever you look at it you can think that I am looking at you at the same time.

September 25, 1845 [to Abiah Root] . . . I long to see you, dear Abiah, and speak with you face to face; but so long as a bodily interview is denied us, we must make letters answer, though it is hard for friends to be separated . . . Do write me soon, for as I cannot see you, I must hear from you often, very often.

January 31, 1846 [to Abiah Root] . . . I so long to see you. It seems to me I shall be almost perfectly happy to see you again.

January 29, 1850 [to Abiah Root] . . . If you are thinking soon to go away, and to show your face no more, just inform me—will you—I would have the "long lingering look" which you cast behind—

June 22, 1851 [to Austin Dickinson] . . . I cant help wondering sometimes if you would love to see us, and come to this still home. . . . I have desires to see you now that you are gone which are really quite intelligent.

about 1851 [to her friend Emily Fowler (Ford)] . . . It has been a long week dear Emily, for I have not seen your face, but I have contrived to think of you very much indeed, which has half reconciled me to not seeing you for so long.

June 27, 1852 [to Susan Gilbert (Dickinson)] . . . I sit here by my window, and look each little while . . . and I fancy I see you coming. . . . I grow too eager to see you, I hasten to the door, and start to find me that you are not there. And very, very often when I have waked from sleep, *not quite* waked, I have been sure I saw you, and your dark eye beamed on me with such a look of tenderness. . . . Shall I indeed behold you, not "darkly, but face to face" or am I *fancying so,* and dreaming blessed dreams from which the day will wake me? I hope for you so much, and feel so eager for you. . . . I must have you . . . once more to see your face again.[45]

Really, no amount of excerption can capture the insistence of this motif, the clamoring for a kind of relationship that is primarily and essentially visual, not verbal, and which no word can ever fully satisfy. The terms "look," "see," "eye," "face," "interview," and the like beat a persistent rhythm in Dickinson's letters—from earliest to last—and this language of vision eclipses by its frequency any other verbal pattern.[46] It is used with all correspondents, and it continues throughout Dickinson's lifetime, though as she grew more mature its significance was both expanded and refined.

Death, for example, is the closing of "eyes" or the loss of "face."

late April 1860 [to her sister, Vinnie, just after the death of their beloved aunt Lavinia Norcross] . . . Blessed Aunt Lavinia now; all the world goes out, and I see nothing but her room and the angels bearing her into those great countries in the blue sky. . . . Then I sob and cry till I can hardly see my way 'round the house again; and then sit

still and wonder if she sees us now, if she sees *me,* who said that she "loved Emily!"
. . . Dear little aunt! will she look down? . . . How I wish I could comfort you! How
I wish you could comfort me, who weep at what I did not see and never can believe.

early May 1862 [to her cousin Louise Norcross] . . . I want so much to see you, and
ask you what it means, and why this young life's sacrifice should come so soon,
and not far off. I wake in the morning saying "Myra, no more Myra in this world,"
and the thought of that young face in the dark, makes the whole world so sorrowful,
I cover my face with the blanket.

late February 1870 [to her aunt Mrs. Joseph Sweetser] . . . I know we shall certainly
see what we loved the most. It is sweet to think they are safe by Death and that is all
we have to pass to obtain their face.

about 1883 [to Susan Gilbert Dickinson] . . . I sometimes remember we are to die,
and hasten toward the Heart which how could I woo in a rendezvous where there is
no Face?[47]

Similarly, the living and the dead are both recollected vividly by "eye." "Not
to see what we love, is very terrible," Dickinson wrote to Mary Bowles in
1862, while Samuel Bowles was vacationing in Europe; and in 1878, just
after Bowles had died, Dickinson remembered chiefly "the beautiful eyes."
Of both her father and Bowles, it is their eyes that linger in her memory—"I
see my father's eyes, and those of Mr. Bowles—those isolated comets." Eventually all of her lost loved ones are incorporated into this universal vision:
"gone Eyes, glowing in Paradise." Photographs of friends are "faces" ("My
sister's face," she writes of Mrs. Dwight's picture; "Thank you for the Face,"
she wrote to James Clark, who had enclosed a photograph of the Reverend
Wadsworth in his note). And even abstractions grow palpable and real in her
description by having a face assigned to them: "There's all the *future* Susie. . . . It is the brightest star in the firmament of God, and I look in it's [*sic*]
face the oftenest"; or "I think of Sun and Summer as visages unknown"; or
"is this the Hope that opens and shuts, like the eye of the Wax Doll?"[48]

In the end, Dickinson left no doubt what genuine "sight" would be. Separated from her friend Jane Humphrey, Dickinson paid an imaginary evening
visit to her correspondent: "I would whisper to you in the evening of many,
and curious things—and by the lamps eternal read your thoughts and response in your face, and find what you thought about me." Two years later,
Dickinson wrote in a similar vein to Susan Gilbert: "Oh that you were [here],
my Susie, we need not talk at all, our eyes would whisper for us, and your
hand fast in mine, we would not ask for language."[49] A true and open interplay of eyes transcends speech. To see the "face" and look in the "eye" of

another is to know that person intimately and directly, without the mediating persiflage of words.

Communication in this *wordless* manner is divine, literally so, for it is God's habitual mode of address: Dickinson engages playfully one day with an invisible "Trinity"—herself, her absent friend Abiah Root (summoned by Dickinson's vivid recollection of her), and "*God . . .* looking into my very soul to see if I think right tho'ts." As Dickinson matured in her vocation, she usurped God's role: if He can look into the human heart and know its mean-ing without a word's being uttered, then the poet / "seer" can look into the heart of nature to extract its meaning. "Should I spell all the things as they sounded to me," she assured Mrs. Holland, "and say all the facts as I see them, it would send consternation among more than the 'Fee Bees'!"[50]

The pattern that emerges is one not merely of communication, but of emotional priorities as well. Ideal communication, supremely intimate com-munication (and in its purest form, "Divine" communication), operates through the visual faculty; when it must be described in words, it is rendered in a diction of "eye" and "face" and "see." Thus the obsessive preoccupation with communication by seeing and the conviction that language is a "fallen" form of discourse combine to exhibit the traces of the problems that afflicted her earliest relationship with her mother. And only when the operations of art raise language to its highest capacity may it begin to recompense the loss—as visual and verbal become one. "Oh, Vision of Language!" the ma-ture Emily Dickinson exclaimed in wonder.[51]

No one can ascertain exactly what took place between Emily Norcross Dickinson and her infant daughter in 1830 and 1831, as tragedy followed upon tragedy—death stalking the Norcross family and disgrace hounding Samuel Fowler Dickinson. That Mrs. Edward Dickinson was often depressed and tearful is a matter of record; one can only surmise that this personal anguish interfered in her relationship with her infant. It was not a failure of love, one can speculate, but of communication; and surely Emily Norcross's courtship correspondence amply documents her more general deficiencies in communication.

Such an hypothesis does much to clarify Emily Dickinson's mixture of attitudes toward her mother. Mother polishing apples for a homesick boy, performing many solicitous tasks that appear nurturing (and which there is no evidence for believing to be other than well meant), but managing too often to misestimate her children's real needs. It was eventually easy for her children to comprehend (at an intellectual level) that her behavior was an attempt at affection; but infants are not capable of distinguishing between affection that is inadequately expressed and an absence of affection. Mature offspring may *feel* irritated by a parent's ineffectual hovering, even when they *know* the parent is trying to please. Bingham passes along an often-repeated family anecdote that, if not literally true, has accrued such authority that it must at least convey the spirit of Mrs. Dickinson's manner:

... Austin told us that her chief claim to attention had been her constant attempts to bring something to any caller which he or she could possibly require. Her continual questionings had almost exhausted their patience. "Won't you have this or that to make you more comfortable?" or "Can't I bring you another chair?" Such questions were the basis of her poor little attempts to make anyone within her circle happier, which failed sadly, as she never seemed to realize.

One day Emily was holding a very high and intellectual conversation with——— where they were quite above the mundane plane. Mrs. Dickinson had fussed in and out many times to see if they needed anything, and at last she bustled in, just at some fine climax of the talk, and asked if———'s feet were not cold, wouldn't she like to come in the kitchen and warm them? Emily gave up in despair at that. "Wouldn't you like to have the Declaration of Independence read, or the Lord's Prayer repeated," and she went on with a long list of unspeakably funny things to be done.[52]

A kindly and solicitous woman without, however, the capacity to comprehend the wants of those in her house might well be a mother who was always there but who contrived, nonetheless, to frustrate her daughter and make her *feel* as if she "never had a mother."

It took many decades for the relationship to right itself. Not surprisingly, perhaps, accord came at the end, after the roles had been reversed: tending to her stricken mother in that long last illness, Emily Dickinson had a second chance to engage in nonverbal communication, only this time it was she and not Mother whose skill at interpreting the unvoiced message was called into play. Emily Dickinson proved a wonderfully adept "mother" under these circumstances: the pain of the past which had ached for so long was at length assuaged, and appropriately enough, Dickinson describes this ultimate success as breaking the wall that had been a barrier to *seeing*. "We were never intimate Mother and Children while she was our Mother," Dickinson wrote shortly after Mrs. Dickinson's death, "but Mines in the same Ground meet by tunneling and when she became our Child, the Affection came."[53]

During these earliest years, Emily Dickinson seems never to have been separated from her mother for any length of time. Mother continued to be very close to her sister, Lavinia, who was fond of both Austin and the baby Emily, but after Mr. Norcross's remarriage there was little incentive for Emily Norcross Dickinson to visit Monson when Lavinia could as easily come to Amherst. Thus what Emily Norcross Dickinson lacked in intuitive skills to deal with her precocious daughter she made up in constancy. Her presence must have been a stabilizing force, especially given Edward's many absences from home. There were disadvantages to such a relationship between mother and child: the infant would have few opportunities to "practice" being separated from Mother (and this disadvantage would be intensified for any child whose mother found separations fearful herself). Still, for two years there was relative calm. In 1833, however, everything changed.

Emily Norcross Dickinson was seven months pregnant with her third child when the year began. Sometime in late 1832 or early 1833, Samuel Fowler Dickinson had gone alone to Cincinnati to try his hand working at Lane Theological Seminary, and on February 22, 1833, the newspaper advertisement for the Brick House on Main Street "lately owned by Samuel F. Dickinson, Esq." appeared.[54] On February 28, 1833, a third child was born to Edward and Emily Dickinson, who were still living in the western portion of the Homestead—a daughter named Lavinia—and something went badly awry during the delivery. No one recorded the details of the birth, so the exact nature of the calamity can never be known; however, both mother and child were sickly for several months. And after having produced three children in fewer than five years of marriage, Emily Norcross Dickinson never had another. The reasons for thus abruptly limiting the family must have been of life-threatening seriousness, for at that time the only really effective method of birth control available to Edward and his wife was abstinence.[55]

The result of this concatenation of catastrophes was an abrupt end to whatever calm had prevailed during the previous two years. Aunt Lavinia could not be spared to come to Amherst and lend a hand, so Edward and his wife decided to send their toddler, Emily, to visit in Monson. To the adults it appeared a sensible solution. However, from the point of view of Emily Dickinson, then little more than two years old, it must have been terrifying.

Aunt Lavinia was familiar and certainly loving; however, the rambling farm in Monson was unfamiliar, and in the spring of 1833 death was again walking its halls. Amanda Norcross, Hiram's ailing widow, was still living there, and the sickness that had taken first Hiram and then his mother still lingered in the house. During the child's visit, Lavinia's letters to her sister were meant to be reassuring: little Emily is "very affectionate & we all love her very much," Lavinia wrote on May 20, two and a half weeks after the little girl had arrived. "She dont appear at all as she does at home [she was unusually subdued, perhaps] & she does not make but very little trouble"; nine days later, Lavinia wrote further encouraging accounts: "She is well I believe & appears perfectly contented—There never was a better child."[56]

In fact, Emily Dickinson's docile demeanor may have been a response to horror, for her aunt was engaged in nursing the mortally ill. "Amanda is as well as when I wrote last—but I am afraid & do believe that she will never get well," Lavinia reported on May 20 to her sister in Amherst; "she is bled very often—for if there is any change in the weather she is immediately affected—& troubled to breathe—Her lungs are very weak—I believe, at heart she thinks it is doubtful how it will terminate. . . . [Our stepmother] is not so much discouraged as I am—I do not think she has seen so much of the consumption as I have." Although Lavinia Norcross was but twenty-one, she was a seasoned nurse to the sick and dying. For her niece, however, this was another brutal introduction. So soon after her mother had gone through a difficult birthing, Emily Dickinson was now witness to that particularly "female" occupation, "watches."

May 25 . . . When I wrote last I told you that Amanda was not as well—since last Monday she has been confined to her bed & has watches every night.

May 29 . . . Amanda is now very comfortable—tho' she does not sit but a few moments at a time—& has watches now—We don't know what to think of her.

June 11 . . . I can say nothing encouraging about Amanda, she is comfortably sick— tho' the silent destroyer is busy, her flesh wastes & her countenance for several days past looks very bad—you may depend she is no more to see health. . . . She says things look darker and darker—but she says she can give up every living thing but her children—this she told me weeping—she says to hear them speak is like a dagger through her heart—poor woman.[57]

Amanda lived just long enough to remarry before consumption claimed her. At the time of her visit, Emily Dickinson played with Amanda's children, William (then ten years old) and Emily Lavinia (then four or five); Emily Lavinia Norcross remained a good friend to her cousin Emily Dickinson, and fifteen years later the two girls roomed together at Mount Holyoke. But like her mother and father before her, Emily Lavinia eventually died of consumption (in 1852, when she was twenty-two); her brother followed two years later, and the disease continued to hound the Norcross family like some inexplicable ancient curse.

By the time Emily Dickinson returned to Amherst in early June, Grandfather and Grandmother had both departed for Cincinnati with those of their children who still lived with them, leaving only their son Frederick behind to stay with his brother Edward. Emily Dickinson had been born in the house Grandfather built and had lived there in close quarters with him and his family for all her life. Now Grandfather had mysteriously disappeared, and she never laid eyes on him again.

The child experienced many things in these months that were difficult to comprehend. Birth and sickness linked in some unformulated way: birth as intrinsically dangerous (so dangerous that Mother never had another child). Death: the fear of death at home with Mother and the new baby, and the almost palpable presence of death in Monson where another mother was sick and another little girl named Emily was fearful of losing her mother forever. Separation. This was the hardest to comprehend, for it was the ultimate mystery—the danger that lay behind all others. What was death but the final separation, and what was sickness or birth if not a cause of separation?

Could anyone explain the meaning of these things to Emily Dickinson once she had returned? Father was preoccupied with the loss of his own father, whose disgrace was to color all of Edward Dickinson's subsequent life. Mother's time was necessarily devoted to the fragile infant still nursing and to the move—most of which may already have taken place before Emily's return from Monson—from the western side of the Homestead to the eastern to take up the quarters so recently vacated by Edward's father. (Another change for the child, as mysterious as all the others.) Years later, in 1882, when Mother's death resurrected one portion of these early fears, her daughter was moved to reminisce about the horror of this period in her life. "Thank you for speaking so earnestly when our Mother died—" she wrote James Clark. "We have spoken daily of writing you, but have felt unable. . . . No Verse in the Bible has frightened me so much from a Child as 'from him that hath not, shall be taken even that he hath.' Was it because it's dark menace deepened our own Door?"[58]

By the late summer of 1833, the Edward Dickinson family had settled into its new quarters, and life became more stable and predictable. The daily crises of Grandfather's failure were no longer enacted in the Brick House; no more brothers and sisters were born; and Emily was forced to accept no further journeys away from home during times of emergency. Still, things were far from smooth. With the Old Squire gone, the full burden of the Dickinson commitment to Amherst College fell upon Edward, already more than occupied with the career in which he was determined to succeed. In 1835, when he formally became its treasurer (having worked behind the scenes for many years), the College was in the midst of the greatest crisis it was ever to experience: not a single dollar of its endowment remained, and it was running at a deficit. To make matters worse, the student body was deeply divided over the question of slavery; enrollment had begun to drop, and tuition fees had drastically dwindled as a result.[59]

These were the years during which a daughter normally and inevitably transfers her primary feelings of affection from her mother to her father. Yet in the Edward Dickinson household, Father was seldom there to receive his daughter's love. His emotional energies were all invested elsewhere, and what dominated the home was not Father's presence, but the almost palpable specter of his absence.

All her life, Edward's wife fretted whenever her husband went for even so short a trip as the drive over to the District Court in Northampton. Always recessive by nature, she never voiced powerful, unmitigated accusation; instead, she was preoccupied and sad; often she fell sick with nameless illnesses and wept with quiet resignation.[60] The letters Mrs. Dickinson wrote her husband when he began to spend so many months in Boston during the 1830s give evidence of a pattern that must always have been the norm in some manner. Whenever she expresses her own loneliness and unhappiness, the tone is qualified: for every phrase that speaks of her sadness, there is a companion phrase to nullify the complaint, a sort of epistolary embodiment of "wifely resignation." So she typically writes, "I realise your absence deeply, and sometimes feel that I cannot wait, the appointed time for your return, but I endeavor to disipate [*sic*] such feelings as much as possible, knowing that it is not right to indulge them as I have every thing provided for my comfort and I know my dear husband does not leave me except from a sense of duty."[61]

Yet if she did not speak her feelings *directly,* she made explicit, *indirect* objections to Edward's desertions. The woman who had expected her fiancé and her family to express her wishes during courtship allowed her offspring to express them now. The *children* resented his being away, she claimed; and such accusations as these almost always came without mitigation. The pattern began early.

June 1, 1831 . . . Little Austin [twenty-six months old at this time] often speaks of you. When the bell rings he thinks you are comeing and opens the door to welcome you.

During the absences after 1835, Mother construed both Emily and Austin as missing their father.

January 7, 1838 . . . The children are well. . . . They are very desirous I should say to their Father they have been good children. Emily sais she wishes I would write to you that she should be glad to see you but she hopes it is all for the best that you are away.

January 21, 1838 . . . The children are well except Emily she has not been as well as usual, for a week I think however she is much better now. I have not let her go to school more than two or three days since you left. She speaks of her Father with much affection. She sais she is tired of living without a father. The children send their love. They often exclaim how glad I shall be to see my dear Father.

March 20, 1838 . . . The children send much love and wish very much for their dear Father's return.

January 6, 1839 . . . The children talk much about their Father and wish the time would go faster. They send much love to their father and Uncle Loring and Aunt Lavinia and little cousins.

January 19, 1839 . . . I have been thinking much of your return this eve. and have felt as Austin says as though I could not have papa gone any longer.[62]

There is no way of knowing whether the children's unhappiness genuinely originated in their own feelings or whether it was prompted by Mother (or, what may be the same thing, was prompted by their sympathetic identification with her feelings of bereavement). Edward responded always as if his *wife* were the principal complainant, and his messages to the children were either admonitions or instructive comments that had scant hint of personal affection: "All you learn, when you are young, will do you a great deal of good when you are grown up. Austin, be careful, & not let the woodpile fall on you—& don't let the cattle hurt you in the yard, when you go with Catherine, after water. Take good care of Emily, when you go to school & not let her get hurt."[63]

A father who had acknowledged his daughter's affection, returned it, and at the same time *defined the limits of their feelings* might have done much to provide Emily Dickinson with help in defining "self" and achieving a finite, coherent notion of the feelings experienced by that self. A good relationship with a father who was more or less regularly at home might have helped to mend the damage of those early days. Instead, his absences merely made things worse. Mother responded to the strain of life without her husband by conflating separation and death: "I attended church all day yesterday," she wrote in 1838, during Edward's first term in the legislature; "I felt quite like a widow."[64] In addition, she commingled her own feelings with the children's in ways that denied the distinction of their separate identities. Far from being a positive force in his daughter's life, then, Father engaged in behavior that (both directly and indirectly) reinforced old problems from his children's infancy—confusion in communication, uncertain limits to the sense of "self," and an inability clearly to distinguish separation from death.[65]

There is no doubt that Emily Dickinson loved her father, loved him deeply and enduringly. Sad to say, there is little evidence that Edward Dickinson returned this affection in any commensurate measure—or even that he took serious note of it. It was a "fact" in his universe, possibly a pleasant fact, like the sun's rising or the spring's coming. He was not possessive. He did not scold her or turn his anger upon her or even reject her openly. He did, in the end, what was worse: he simply did not very much notice her.

Edward Dickinson survives everywhere in his talented daughter's language. In her everyday discourse, he survives most touchingly in her invocations of the heroic. Whatever other things she said about Father, the consistent thread throughout her letters is the conviction that he was different from other mortals, that he moved in a superior realm (and such is the case even when she portrays him humorously). It is difficult to make this image consistent with an unbiased historical portrayal of the rather pinched actual person, Edward Dickinson, so preoccupied with leading a "rational" life, so persuaded that "business" provided a suitable arena for the activities of the "soul." The heroic is not plausibly an attribute of Edward Dickinson himself. Thus "Edward Dickinson" in his elder daughter's renderings of him is principally the mirror in which her own feelings have been reflected. And yet, since such images of a father are essentially childlike, unemended into some more accurate, comprehensive, adult evaluation, the persistence of this way of perceiving him suggests that the relationship was relatively static. Her anger at his absence and his unavailability never intrudes into her letters (for unlike Mother, she does not voice even qualified unhappiness). Instead, rage is entirely separated from "my father, Edward Dickinson": it finds expression only in the poetry, directed toward a "Father" in Heaven Whose face we never see and Whose voice we never hear.

The heroic scale according to which Emily Dickinson measured Edward Dickinson's nature may have served one useful function: it allowed her to live with (and perhaps justify) his dismissive attitude toward her. By the time of his death in 1874, she had been residing in his house for nearly forty-four years, her entire life. Her recollection of their last day together is intended to convey her sorrow and her love (which it surely does), but it conveys something else as well, the heartbreaking habit of awkwardness between them.

The last Afternoon that my Father lived, though with no premonition—I preferred to be with him, and invented an absence for Mother, Vinnie being asleep. He seemed peculiarly pleased as I oftenest stayed with myself, and remarked as the Afternoon withdrew, he "would like it to not end."

His pleasure almost embarrassed me and my Brother coming—I suggested they walk. Next morning I woke him for the train—and saw him no more.

His Heart was pure and terrible and I think no other like it exists.

I am glad there is Immortality—but would have tested it myself—before entrusting him.[66]

To the outside world in the late 1830s, the Edward Dickinsons of Main Street may have appeared a family remarkable only for the father's diligent success. From the inside, however, things seemed not so peaceful. A talented housewife whose custards and baked goods would be remembered with pleasure, Mrs. Dickinson was nonetheless isolated by her tearful withdrawals and obscure maladies. Although she was undoubtedly loving and well intentioned, she did not have an intimate relationship with any of her three children. Despite her constant presence, there was an abiding sense of emotional separation. In the case of Father, his habit of emotional withdrawal was lethally reinforced by his frequent absences from home. Consequently, the children all looked principally to one another for comfort and affectionate responsiveness, and throughout their lives they were unusually close. Yet of the three, Emily had one additional, unique resource. The child who had experienced a "Fall" into language as the only way to repair the earliest failures of unspoken communication also construed language as a force that could combat the various dangers of separation.[67]

Emily Dickinson's letters to Joseph Lyman contain the most familiar allusion to words: "We used to think, Joseph, when I was an unsifted girl and you so scholarly[,] that words were cheap & weak. Now I don't know of anything so mighty. There are [those] to which I lift my hat when I see them sitting princelike among their peers on the page. Sometimes I write one, and look at his outlines till he glows as no sapphire."[68] Words can become a unique community of "people" who remain entirely within the author's control. In her second letter to Higginson (who had evidently asked about her friends), she said, "For several years, my Lexicon—was my only companion." These phrases from her young womanhood have been repeated like a litany whenever Emily Dickinson's spirit has been invoked. But there are others, many others, scattered through her later letters that assert the same thing—that for the poet, words have acquired the attributes of human beings.

August 1877 . . . You asked me if I wrote now? I have no other Playmate—

June 1878 . . . How lovely are the wiles of Words!

about 1878 . . . Tuesday is a deeply depressing Day—it is not far enough from your dear note for the embryo of another to form.

early September 1880 . . . What is it that instructs a hand lightly created, to impel shapes to eyes at a distance, which for them have the whole area of life or of death?

late 1882 . . . A letter always seemed to me like Immortality, for is it not the Mind alone, without corporeal friend?[69]

There is an extraordinary power in words: words can define a self with impregnable clarity; words can give life's many dangers a name, thereby asserting control over those dangers; words can even conquer death because although the flesh passes into dust, words remain unchanged. For Emily Dickinson, words became her refuge and her one great love.

III ✦ School: Faith and the Argument from Design

In the Amherst of Emily Dickinson's youth, it was not a difficult thing to believe that words could have magic, for this was a land where myth and legend still exalted everyday life and infused it with sublime significance. During these years before the Civil War, Amherst remained one of the last outposts of America's Puritan past, and the beliefs of our Founding Fathers enjoyed their final hours of supremacy.

Amherst was not unique: other New England towns such as Hanover, New Hampshire, and Williamstown, Massachusetts, were similar bastions of old-fashioned faith. However, such communities were not typical of the country as a whole. Elsewhere, great social changes were taking place, and with them came radically new and different ways of thinking about God and society. A nation that had been primarily rural in 1790 was becoming primarily urban by 1840. The rate of change was accelerated by two forces, the removal of many farm boys into cities, and the first massive waves of European immigration to the United States. The Second Great Revival (1815–35) occurred during this period, but as one disheartened minister reported, " 'Cities are poor places to promote Revivals.' . . . Even in the generally receptive Middle West [where Samuel Fowler Dickinson had carried his exhausted zeal to Lane Theological Seminary in Cincinnati], revival fires 'licked very close to the towns, but could not find inflammable material in them.' "[1]

The change in American life came with astonishing speed. "In the thirty years preceding the outbreak of the Civil War, the urban population increased by over 700 percent, from about 500,000 to 3.8 million. . . . In the Midwest, this development was particularly dramatic along the network of rivers, lakes, canals, and railroads. . . . First came the river cities—Pittsburgh, Cincinnati, Louisville, Memphis, Saint Louis—thrusting 'a broad wedge of urbanism' into the heart of the transappalachian wilderness. Then came the lake cities: Buffalo, Cleveland, Detroit, Milwaukee, and Chicago." Urban areas grew so rapidly that adequate housing could not be erected quickly enough; the poor were huddled together in squalid conditions, and municipal disorder was epidemic. "The 1834–1844 decade saw more than 200 major gang wars in New York alone, and in other cities the pattern was similar."[2]

Confronted with this rapid and radical reorganization of American life, people began to adjust their moral sensibilities. Personal piety was still paramount at first; it was the primary goal of the American Tractarians during their vigorous early years before 1830. These evangelical Protestants continued to regard the Bible as the ultimate repository of moral truth, and in 1816 they formed the American Bible Society to promote the study of the Scriptures. Taking advantage of the dense population in big cities, they formed a highly effective system of distribution; by 1849 they had passed out nearly six million Bibles and Testaments. Little by little, however, they lost ground and were forced to compromise their original goal. Niceties of conscience and subtleties of sin became less important than grosser forms of moral decay, and the Tractarians of a later day joined with other moral leaders—the founders of such societies as the Young Men's Christian Association, the Association for Improving the Condition of the Poor, and the Children's Aid Society—to promote those "virtues" that would at least serve to keep the public peace. By the time the century was drawing to a close, it had become necessary to add the goal of eliminating widespread institutionalized corruption.

In 1630, Winthrop could contemplate the possibility of an ideal community, the "city upon a hill," and a role for the Puritans that might serve as a model for all subsequent generations. And Winthrop could voice the prayer that whenever future generations gathered to ask God's blessing upon their society, they would formulate their hope in this way—"The Lord make it like that of New England." However, by the time the last reverberations of the Civil War had died away, New England was no longer a moral, governmental, or cultural leader. Most Americans had lost faith in man's capacity to create an ideal society, and at the same time, they had relinquished their belief in the absolute, overriding value of sternly imposed, rigorous personal piety. As early as the 1840s and 1850s, the tumult of expansion in America's cities foreshadowed the scope and nature of the changes that were to follow.

Amherst was not completely isolated from these changes. Businessmen like Edward Dickinson traveled back and forth between the village and the large metropolitan centers; the Dickinson family took several newspapers and all the best journals, and Emily Dickinson, along with her father and brother, read omnivorously. In addition, by 1847 (and possibly earlier) there were lyceum lectures in North Amherst, and well before that time a large assortment of public speakers began coming through Amherst proper to address both college students and town residents. Indeed, the exceptionally fine science faculty of Amherst College was even in close touch with the many debates that led up to Darwin's publication of *On the Origin of Species* in 1859. Yet despite these contacts with the larger world, the life of the mind for many of the residents, perhaps for most, was shaped by categories that had changed very little over the course of two centuries—categories that were dominated by the themes of death, time, and immortality.[3]

In most ways, Amherst was as primitive a community as those that had existed in the upper Connecticut valley a century earlier; only the threat of Indian massacre had been eliminated. The town's streets were unpaved— muddy in spring and fall, dusty in summer, and glistening with rutted ice during the winter. There was no public lighting; kerosene lamps and candles were the only source of indoor illumination, and on dark winter evenings an entire family generally gathered in one room and left the rest of the house in chilly darkness. There were no sewers, no sources of water save wells.

The medical profession could not offer protection from the commonest killers: antibiotics were unheard-of; surgery was performed without anesthesia or any proper form of antisepsis; typhoid, pneumonia, smallpox, cholera, and malaria were all local threats to life; consumption could be seen on the faces of neighbors and family members; and even dysentery might prove fatal—Samuel Bowles's father died of it in 1851 at the age of fifty-four. A simple sore throat could have lethal consequences, and throughout Emily Dickinson's school days both parents worried about her tendency to come down with protracted bouts of flu; often they kept her home from school, sometimes even obliging her to miss an entire term, an irregular pattern of attendance that was not at all uncommon at the time. No less than in Emily Norcross's girlhood, death continued to haunt the family. Alfred Norcross took over the farm in Monson when his father died in 1846; he was a prosperous man and owned more than a thousand acres when he died in 1888, but three of his five children died in infancy from tuberculosis. Lyman Coleman, who took charge of the Amherst Academy in 1844, had married Maria Flynt of Monson, a cousin of Mrs. Edward Dickinson's. When the Colemans moved to Amherst in 1844, they had two daughters—Olivia, then seventeen, four years older than Emily Dickinson, and Eliza, twelve. Both girls were outstandingly attractive and Olivia was a great beauty; however, both were cursed with the dry cough of consumption. The Colemans hovered over their children more protectively than any other parents in the village, but death came anyway. Olivia was claimed suddenly and without any warning in 1847 during a carriage ride. Eliza languished for years, always in fragile health; she married and had children, but consumption killed her before she reached forty.

We know there are societies that routinely personify death, construing it as a monstrous and fearful creature possessed of an almost human physical form. In such societies, death is perceived as stalking mankind like an implacable hunter, snatching us from this life and carrying us to an unknown afterworld. Twentieth-century readers may assume that such ways of thinking generally passed out of existence many centuries ago, yet such is not the case. In Amherst and in other small New England communities like it, death still retained a form and face: it was God's emissary, the Angel of Death. It moved among Emily Dickinson's family and friends with the insolent familiarity of a neighbor, and it was referred to by name. "Abby Haskel . . . is much better," Emily Dickinson wrote of a friend; "I verily believe [she] will live in spite of the 'angel of death.'"[4]

Few in Emily Dickinson's world could put death out of mind, for it was too daily and too near. Instead, there was an intricate culture that took the inevitable fact of death as its starting point and then robbed death of its horror by juxtaposing to it the promise of an everlasting life to come. This opposition—the hope of some future Heaven balanced against the fear of ineluctable death—manifested itself in every aspect of Dickinson's environment. Indeed, far from being ignored, the fact of dissolution was insistently reiterated, for unless each individual could achieve a comprehensive acceptance of death, he or she could never embrace faith ardently enough to gain Heaven. From her earliest childhood days, dating at the latest from her experiences at the Norcross farm when she was two years old, Emily Dickinson had been acquainted with the slow process of extinction. Just as early, however, she had begun to become familiar with her culture's complex and stylized ways of delineating it.

Most Amherst families taught their pre-school-aged children to read by using the *New England Primer* (the Dickinson family owned two separate versions); and the *Primer* served to initiate even the youngest into an acknowledgment of death. Bedtime prayers, for instance, taught that sleep was a metaphor for death.

> I in the burying place may see
> Graves shorter there than I:
> From death's arrest no age is free—
> Young children too may die.
>
> My God, may such an awful sight
> Awakening be to me!
> O! that by early grace I might
> For death prepared to be!

Or:

> Awake, arise, behold thou hast,
> Thy life a leaf, thy breath a blast,
> At night lay down prepar'd to have
> Thy sleep, thy death, thy bed, the grave.[5]

Even books with no avowed religious purpose stressed the same dismal message. In *Physiology for Children*, there is this dialogue concerning "The Length of Life":

Do most people live to be old?

No, one half die before they are eight years old. Only one out of three lives to fourteen, and but one in four lives to see twenty-one.

What is that general rule which tells how long a thing will live?

Whatever grows quick decays quick, or as it is worded in the old saying, "*Soon ripe, soon rotten.*"[6]

Since time was death's principal agent, propelling each of us closer to the inevitable confrontation with eternity, even the ticking of the heart within the breast might begin to seem little more than a prologue to doom.

Anyone who wanted to see what death looked like needed only to visit one of the older cemeteries, for generations of New England stonecutters had emblazoned the Angel of Death on gravestones. This stonework was often a complex pictorial ideogram designed to convey a message. There was the core icon of death, a skull or face. Symbols of time—an hourglass, a sun and moon, the grim scythe of reaping—were often associated with this icon to demonstrate the intrinsic relationship between time's passage and inevitable demise. Yet symbols of hope might be added as well—birds' wings or feathers, diamonds or hearts, suns or other markings of brightness—to convey the message of a promised resurrection from the grave. The overall configuration of the grave might also become a metaphor: there were shaped headstones called "bedbacks" and occasionally footstones as well, grim visual assurances that sleep was but a metaphor for death.[7] The gravestone's inscription itself was construed as an art—a form of naïve poetry—and collected into books. "Suddenly Death threw forth his dart, / The fatal arrow pierced my heart, / When health and vigor crown'd my day, / Alas my soul was snatch'd away."[8] The Dickinson family library contained a volume of such verse, and today the book still holds two pressed flowers, the sentimental gesture of a generation long past. This theocentric art of the grave was so integral a part of Amherst life before the Civil War that when its citizens traveled to other New England towns or cities, they toured cemeteries much as their more urbane fellow countrymen visiting Europe went on excursions to museums. "Have you ever been to Mount Auburn?" Emily Dickinson, who had recently visited Boston, inquired of Abiah Root in 1846. "If not you can form but slight conception—of the 'City of the dead.'"[9]

Amherst's remedy for death was also introduced early in Emily Dickinson's life. Whenever Father was at home, he began the day by reading ceremoniously from the Bible and then leading the family in prayer. His voice could be a ruthless weapon in the Amherst political arena when he had set himself upon an unyielding course; however, the vigorous cadences that could harrow a village crowd or swell in persuasion before distant senates submitted to the resonant cadences of the King James Bible, the book of his own father, when Edward spoke formally at home. God's promises uttered

This image from the grave of Mrs. Susanna Jayne (d. 1776) contains a fascinating collection of messages in emblem form. Many gravestones had emblems of time's passage (an hourglass that had run its course or the scythe of the grim reaper). This gravestone, which captures a number of these, suggests how firmly rooted in latter-day Puritan tradition Dickinson's own preoccupation with time was. Bats below and angels above render the opposite alternatives of the afterlife; the snake biting its own tail conveys the circle of unending eternity. And Death, grinning triumphantly, holds the sun and moon—representing the diurnal cycle of his power.

in these stately, commanding tones left an ineradicable impression upon his poet-daughter, and the precise echo of Father's sovereign voice still sounded in her ear long after Edward Dickinson's death.

When I think of his firm Light—quenched so causelessly, it fritters the worth of much that shines. "Dust unto the Dust" indeed—but the final clause of that marvelous sentence—who has rendered it?

"I say unto you," Father would read at Prayers, with a militant Accent that would startle one.[10]

Whenever his elder daughter resurrected Father's memory, it was his words and never his actions that she invoked to give it life.

The lingering reverberations of Edward Dickinson's rich speaking voice surely intensified the Bible's message for Emily Dickinson. She knew every line of the Bible intimately, quoted from it extensively, referred to it many times more often than she referred to any other work. Yet in this regard she was not unusual by Amherst's standards. A great many of the good men and women of that township had most of the Bible by heart, for it was the Bible and its promises that provided a foundation for the hope of transcending death. This hope rested upon a paradoxical fact—indeed, upon a mystery so impenetrable that it seemed a quintessential riddle. A man had brought death into the world, and a man had conquered death; Adam's sin had consigned mankind to mortality, and Christ's Death and subsequent Resurrection had released us from the curse of Adam.

. . . Christ died for our sins according to the scriptures. . . . But now is Christ risen from the dead, and become the firstfruits of them that slept. For since by man came death, by man came also the resurrection of the dead. For as in Adam all die, even so in Christ shall all be made alive. . . . For he must reign, till he hath put all enemies under his feet. The last enemy that shall be destroyed is death. . . . Behold, I show you a mystery; . . . for the trumpet shall sound, and the dead shall be raised incorruptible, and we shall be changed. For this corruptible must put on incorruption, and this mortal must put on immortality. So when this corruptible shall have put on incorruption, and this mortal shall have put on immortality, then shall be brought to pass the saying that is written, Death is swallowed up in victory. O Death, where is thy sting? O grave, where is thy victory? [I Corinthians 15:3, 20–22, 25–26, 51–55.]

This is the legacy of Christ, the God-man. And perhaps no single passage in the entire Bible had such currency in mid-nineteenth-century Amherst as I Corinthians 15, Saint Paul's account of Christ's victory over death. Every Amherst Congregationalist would have recognized an allusion, however subtle, to any portion of it. Yet every other part of the Bible was important, too, for this Holy Book had endowed latter-day American Puritans with many gifts.

One was the gift of narrative structure. The Bible offered a prototype: over and over again, God's chosen people had fallen away from the truth, pursuing false idols and vain ambitions; yet just as often God's providential care had returned them to the path of righteousness. The Congregationalists in Amherst believed that this pattern was a paradigm for all of human affairs: in an individual life, a Christian might lose faith and turn away from the Lord, yet God's loving kindness would always welcome back the child who had strayed. Even the secular history during the eras from the time of Christ until the present was believed to evince the pattern of God's providential care; properly understood, it was believed to have essentially the same narrative structure as the Bible.

A second gift, the possibility for heroism, grew out of the first. The architectonic of providential history contained many subordinate structuring elements, and one of the most significant was the pairing of "type" and
"antitype." These two terms were used to denote a prefiguring action or occurrence: that is, an event, person, or circumstance in the Old Testament was
construed as anticipating some similar event in the New Testament. Abraham's willingness to sacrifice his only son to God was the type (or prefigura-
tion) of God the Father's willingness to sacrifice His only Son for mankind;
Christ's Crucifixion was the antitype (or fulfillment) of that foreshadowing.[11]
Dickinson was perfectly familiar with these notions of "type" and "antitype," and she could employ them seriously or in a lighter vein (while she
was in school at Mount Holyoke, she wrote to Austin, "Thank Abby for her
note & tell her I consider it only a *type* of what is forthcoming"—that is,
Emily Dickinson understood the note as prelude to a visit[12]).

It was an extension of this notion of types—the doctrine of "correlative
types"—that provided the basis for defining heroism. An Old Testament hero
might be seen as anticipating not only some crucial moment in Christ's life
as described in the New Testament, but also crucial moments in any individual Christian's life. Thus these figures might become "correlative types"—
prototypical models of heroism whose superior behavior could be emulated
by the members of all subsequent generations. The notion of correlative types
was introduced into Dickinson's life as soon as she learned to read—perhaps
even before—for the *New England Primer* contains a piece of doggerel verse
listing correlative types that are suitable for children's emulation.

> I must obey my Lord's commands
> Do something with my little hands: . . .
> Young SAMUEL that little child,
> He serv'd the Lord, liv'd undefil'd;
> Him in his service God emply'd
> While Eli's wicked children dy'd: . . .
> Young King JOSIAH, that blessed youth,
> He fought the Lord and lov'd the truth: . . .
> These good examples were for me;
> Like these good children I must be.

When she grew older, the family's own library provided more elegant and
sophisticated models of the "correlative type," such as those found in John
Foster's *Miscellaneous Essays*.[13]

The implications of "correlative types" were far-reaching. *Any* New Englander might become an Abraham (patriarch and covenant maker) or a
Moses (leader in adversity and lawgiver) or a Solomon (righteous ruler and
repository of wisdom) or an Ishmael (outcast and wanderer). There was,

then, a continuum of heroic and antiheroic possibilities that extended uninterruptedly from the ancient Biblical past into mid-nineteenth-century Massachusetts. Grandeur still lay within human reach, and epic opportunity
glimmered in every human life. There were great deeds yet to be done, momentous journeys upon which to embark, and an incalculable destiny awaiting every man or woman who dared to aspire to it. So long as God's spell
was still cast upon New England, life was rich with unbounded possibility.

The Bible's third gift was a gift of language. Words had not yet lost their
mythic power among these people for whom the Holy Book was a still-living
legend. For example, "bread" signified more than merely the staple of our
diet. It conjured looming memories of a Saviour celebrating His Last Supper
on earth: "And he took bread, and gave thanks, and brake it, and gave unto
them, saying, This is my body which is given for you: this do in remembrance
of me" (Luke 22:19). And so was it with much of the language that was
employed in Dickinson's environs. When writing to Vinnie's friend, Joseph
Lyman, Emily Dickinson mused, "Father says in fugitive moments . . . that
his life has been passed in a wilderness." Edward Dickinson, his sensitive
daughter, and that daughter's correspondent Joseph Lyman *all* understood
the despondency of such an utterance: Moses had led his people for forty
years through a barren desert "wilderness," and at the bitter end he had been
denied entrance into the Promised Land. Thus Edward Dickinson was giving
voice to a deep, inconsolable, Biblical despair. In a society whose language
had such profound mythic roots, complex notions might be conveyed with
supreme economy; moreover, the resonances of a transcendent realm might
be invoked with subtlety and precision.

Just as there were gravestone renderings of the image of extinction—the
terrifying mask of the Angel of Death—so, too, were there visual renderings
of Biblical passages and more general Christian admonitions. These were
often elaborate and stylized, and they took the form of emblems. The simplest emblems were for children; found in the *New England Primer* or instructive periodicals like *Peter Parley's Magazine,* they included an illustration, a
title, and a short homily. The Dickinson family owned a copy of Frances
Quarles's *Emblems, Divine and Moral,* a collection of elegant plates illustrat-
ing such "silent parables" as a stony, hardened heart being assailed by God's
arrows of love. And in the middle of the nineteenth century, William Holmes
and John W. Barber issued *Religious Emblems* (1846) and *Religious Allegories*
(1848)—melodramatic illustrations of such Biblical passages as "For we
walk by faith, not by sight" (II Corinthians 5:7).

Emily Dickinson was aware of all these things well before she embarked
upon any serious scholastic study: a knowledge of death and of the many
elements of her culture that had evolved to characterize death and its strategies; a knowledge of the Bible's promise of a release from death and a familiarity with the emblems that had been created to illustrate Christian

commonplaces; and, most important, perhaps, a knowledge of the many he-roic possibilities (both in life and in language) that were the concomitants of a Bible-centered society. Eventually, each one of these played some part in her poetry.

In 1840 two major changes took place in her life. Late in April, Father relinquished his tenancy of the Brick House, having purchased a comfortably roomy frame house four blocks away on North Pleasant Street; and on Mon-day, September 7, Emily Dickinson began her years at the Amherst Academy, where the religious notions that suffused her world would be examined more searchingly. Now, perhaps for the first time, her intelligence had room to expand and encouragement to exercise.

A large part of school was sheer fun. Dickinson was one of a circle of lively girls, some of them Amherst College faculty children, whose friendship she continued to value long after they had all left the Academy. Writing to Abiah Root in 1846, she said, "Please do not let . . . any one see this letter. It is only for you. I carried your letter to Abby, & we read it together. I shall show it to no one else, of course, as I never show any of the letters of the 'five' to any one but Abby as she is one of them."[14] Abiah Root (who had left Amherst and moved to the Springfield area in 1844), Abby Wood, Harriet Merrill, and Sarah Tracy were probably the girls who, along with Emily Dickinson, made up the "five," an informal club. But Dickinson had other friends, too: Emily Fowler (Noah Webster's granddaughter and the acknowl-edged beauty of the village), Jane Humphrey, and (later) the Gilbert sisters, Mattie and Sue (who was to become Austin Dickinson's wife). The letters of this period have their full share of lugubrious, adolescent sentiment. Yet an impish, irreverent intelligence and a pungent sense of humor convey the emergent shape of Emily Dickinson's mind. "The Afternoon is Wednesday," she wrote Jane Humphrey,

and so of course there was Speaking and Composition—there was one young man who read a Composition[] the Subject was think twice before you speak—he was describing the reasons why any one should do so—one was—if a young gentleman— offered a young lady his arm and he had a dog who had no tail and he boarded at the tavern think twice before you speak. Another is if a young gentleman knows a young lady who he thinks nature has formed to perfection let him remember that roses conceal thorns[] he is the sillyest creature that ever lived I think[.] I told him that I thought he had better think twice before he spoke.[15]

In many ways she was a typical teen-aged girl. She developed enthusiastic crushes on some of her teachers: "I had a newspaper as large as life from Miss Adams our dear teacher," she wrote to Abiah. "She sent me a beautiful little bunch of pressed flowers which I value very much as they were from her. How happy we all were together that term we went to Miss Adams."

She gossiped with her friends about local beaux: "Sabra [Howe] has had a beautiful ring given to her by Charles you know who as well as I do," she wrote to Jane Humphrey. And to Abiah Root, "Your *beau idéal* D. I have not seen lately. I presume he was changed into a star some night while gazing at them, and placed in the constellation Orion between Bellatrix and Betelgeux. I doubt not if he was here he would wish to be kindly remembered to you." Her own future seemed both predictable and promising. "Are the teachers as pleasant as our old schoolteachers?" she asked Abiah:

I expect you have a great many prim, starched up young ladies there, who, I doubt not, are perfect models of propriety and good behavior. If they are, don't let your free spirit be chained by them. . . . I am growing handsome very fast indeed! I expect I shall be the belle of Amherst when I reach my 17th year. I don't doubt that I shall have perfect crowds of admirers at that age. Then how I shall delight to make them await my bidding, and with what delight shall I witness their suspense while I make my final decision.[16]

Altogether, she pronounced school a success.

Yet the exuberance with which she pursued her friendships was not un-touched by tragedy. By and large, the members of her immediate family re-mained in good health; however, like virtually every girl her age, she lost companions to eternity. One such occasion made an unusually vivid impres-sion upon her; three months after her fifteenth birthday, she recalled this loss when writing a note of condolence to Abiah Root.

Yesterday as I sat by the north window the funeral train entered the open gate of the church yard, following the remains of Judge Dickinson's wife to her long home. [The Amherst cemetery could be seen from the second story of the Dickinsons' house on North Pleasant Street.] His wife has borne a long sickness of two or three years with-out a murmur. She relyed wholly upon the arm of God & he did not forsake her. She is now with the redeemed in heaven & with the savior she has so long loved according to all human probability. I sincerely sympathise with you Dear A. in the loss of your friend E. Smith. Although I had never seen her, yet I loved her from your account of her & because she was your friend. I was in hopes I might at sometime meet her but God has ordained otherwise & I shall never see her except as a spirit above. . . . I have never lost but one friend near my age & with whom my thoughts & her own were the same. It was before you came to Amherst. My friend was Sophia Holland. She was too lovely for earth & she was transplanted from earth to heaven. I visited her often in sickness & watched over her bed. But at length Reason fled and the physician forbid any but the nurse to go into her room. Then it seemed to me I should die too if I could not be permitted to watch over her or even to look at her face. At length the doctor said she must die & allowed me to look at her a moment through the open door. I took off my shoes and stole softly to the sick room.

•

There she lay mild & beautiful as in health & her pale features lit up with an unearthly—smile. I looked as long as friends would permit & when they told I must look no longer I let them lead me away. I shed no tear, for my heart was too full to weep, but after she was laid in her coffin & I felt I could not call her back again I gave way to a fixed melancholy.

I told no one the cause of my grief, though it was gnawing at my very heart strings. I was not well & I went to Boston [to visit Aunt Lavinia] & stayed a month & my health improved so that my spirits were better.[17]

Sophia Holland had died on April 29, 1844, when Emily Dickinson was thirteen years old. To a twentieth-century reader, unaccustomed to the presence of death in the home, Dickinson's persistence and curiosity may seem morbid. However, the adults of her own time evidently regarded her behavior as quite understandable. At first they allowed her to help with the "watch," and during Sophia's last hours they allowed her to view the body. Lavinia Norcross had been only seventeen when her mother died, and throughout the protracted illness Aunt Lavinia had both tended the invalid during the days and sat the "watch" at night. The vigil over Sophia Holland constituted a part of Emily Dickinson's training for womanhood in mid-nineteenth-century Amherst; and if the confrontation with death inspired horror, as it seems to have done in this case, there was no adequate remedy. Dickinson's parents sent her away to Boston so that she might put the episode out of mind; however, death knew no boundaries of city or town, and she understood as much. Thus the event lingered in her imagination, crying out for redress or at least explanation.

In truth, the only remedy Amherst offered for the brutal fact of death in everyday life was the Bible's promise of a resurrection from the grave; and Dickinson's education, first at the Amherst Academy and later at the Mount Holyoke Female Seminary, was designed with the principal aim of offering a comprehensive understanding of this promise.

Academically, the Amherst Academy offered a course of study that was as strenuous as many colleges today. Dickinson was an outstanding student, and she was justly proud of the taxing curriculum she was pursuing. "We have a very fine school," she boasted to Abiah. "There are Mental Philosophy, Geology, Latin, and Botany. How large they sound, don't they? I don't believe you have such big studies."[18] With the possible exception of mental philosophy, the list of subjects sounds entirely secular, but nothing could be further from the truth. The reason the deeply religious character of instruction is not immediately obvious from Dickinson's list (which does not, for example, this term include lessons on the Bible) is that *all* disciplines were approached as extensions of religious learning.

The Amherst Academy was so thoroughly identified with Amherst College—many of the College professors gave courses there and many groups of

Academy students attended lectures at the College—that there was no difference in educational policy at the two schools. In the beginning, the Board of
Trustees of the Amherst Academy had acted as trustees of the Charity Fund
of Amherst College, and this committee appointed Zephaniah Moore as the
first president of the College. President Moore died in 1823, having served
for only two years, and was succeeded by Heman Humphrey, who remained
in office for almost a quarter of a century—until 1845. Humphrey was a
Trinitarian of the old stamp. Born in humble circumstances as one of fourteen
children on a farm in West Simsbury, Connecticut, he entered the ministry
after studying privately for only six months with the Reverend Mr. Hooker
of Goshen, Connecticut. He was no scholar, but he had tremendous strength
as a pastor and a leader of revivals, and he put his distinctive mark on
the newborn institution he had been called to lead. "He found it the Charit-
able Collegiate Institution at Amherst; he made it Amherst College," Tyler
writes:

The administration of President Humphrey . . . was our book of Genesis in which
many of our organizations, usages and characteristic traits had their origin, and at
the same time our Exodus when we went up out of Egypt and obtained our charter
and laws—when precedents were established, principles settled, habits formed, and
that character fixed, which our College still retains and doubtless will retain more or
less in all coming time.[19]

Humphrey's publications were of a typically conservative nature, harking
back to authentic Puritan practices: he authored an edition of the *New England Primer* and wrote the comprehensive *Revival: Sketches and Manual* for
the American Tract Society; but he was the last president of the College to
model himself upon the traditional Puritan ideal. When Emily Dickinson began her studies at the Amherst Academy, Humphrey was still in office; however, in 1845, toward the end of her time there, Edward Hitchcock took his
place.

If Humphrey looked to the past, Edward Hitchcock looked to the future.
He was a distinguished scientist and had been a professor at Amherst since
1825, the year the College had received its charter from the state. Hitchcock
was well aware of the changes taking place in society; he was principally
conversant with the new scientific discoveries both here and abroad, but he
was a man of wide learning, and he could see the inevitable future already
gathering in the great cities of the Eastern Seaboard—could read the inevitable demise of rigidly old-fashioned and close-minded religious attitudes in
the scientific disclosures of his research and reading. He was no social historian: he could not foresee the revolution in moral categories that urban life
would bring. He was, however, an intellectual cosmopolitan, and he earnestly believed that the truths that had been proclaimed during those periods

of "awakening" in New England were in no way refuted by the new discoveries in science. Rather, he believed that truth in every branch of learning would necessarily manifest God's nature and reinforce His will as it had been articulated in the Bible. His inaugural address, delivered in 1845, was a bold and revolutionary statement. He proposed to strengthen and extend the College's mathematics and science departments; and he claimed that the study of these branches of learning, so often viewed as the enemies of revealed religion, would only fortify a belief in God's promised resurrection. "Mathematics . . . forms the very framework of nature's harmonies, and is essential to the argument for a God. . . . [Chemistry] abounds with the most beautiful exhibitions of the Divine wisdom and benevolence. . . . The wide dominions of natural history, embracing zoology, botany, and mineralogy, the theologist has even found crowded with demonstrations of the Divine Existence and of God's Providential care and government."[20] In short, this man whose work with the prehistoric fossils of the Connecticut valley was world-famous proposed to make modern science an apologist for the doctrine of the resurrection of the body from the grave.

Hitchcock held joint appointments as professor of geology and of moral theology; during the brief decade of his presidency of Amherst College, the Puritan past was momentarily yoked to the science of the future. More or less directly as a result of his presence in Amherst, Emily Dickinson became conversant with the most sophisticated science then available in America. Religion was not diminished in importance during Hitchcock's presidency, even though the various departments of science were greatly strengthened; if anything, the power of religion was extended by Hitchcock's endeavor to make all branches of learning into forms of theology. In addition, he continued the venerable practice of revivals. The Great Revival of 1850 took place during his administration, and there were other major revival years during his presidency—1846, 1849, and 1853. This pattern was a continuation of the rhythm that had been established during earlier presidencies. For many decades—extending even through the Civil War period—it was the boast of Amherst College that no student who completed the four-year course of study failed to witness a revival. It was not just that old-fashioned religion lived on, nor that Amherst owed its peculiarly insulated quality to the relative absence of immigrants and slums. What made Amherst distinctive was persistent habits of mind and categories of thought that had begun to vanish elsewhere in the country.

Thus the world Emily Dickinson explored during the years of her education, 1840–48, was closer to the world of Grandfather's young-manhood than it was to the world of her contemporaries in Boston or New York. When Samuel Fowler Dickinson left Amherst in disgrace, he was a broken man and Amherst College was on the brink of bankruptcy; the exalted vision for which he had sacrificed everything seemed fallen and lost. He never lived to know that Amherst College would survive (in 1838, when he died, its future was still uncertain), never knew that largely through his efforts the grand-daughter who had been born under his roof would see the world as he had seen it, learn of God in the old-fashioned ways—speak the words not of an increasingly mercantile and secular society, but of her Puritan forebears. Father's voice reading the Bible each morning was a brief but regular recursion to the accents of Grandfather's day; this was the language that linked Emily Dickinson with the larger world of Amherst. She would learn it more perfectly in the Academy and later at Mount Holyoke; eventually, she would use it to write poetry.

Dickinson's years of formal schooling provided her with an astonishingly broad repertoire of humanistic and scientific knowledge. She learned several foreign languages and studied music as well, and she was superbly educated in the fields that most students still study today. Yet throughout the curriculum at both institutions, religion was held to be the most important study of all. Formal training in religion fell into two parts.

It began with a proof for the existence of God. By 1840, latter-day Trinitarians had recourse to a welter of arguments, many of them ancient in origin; at the Academy (and again at the Mount Holyoke Seminary), Dickinson was taught from the works of William Paley, who offered a classic statement of the "Argument from Design" in his *Natural Theology* (1802). There must be such a Being as God, Paley argued, because countless intricate structures in the natural world exhibit a teleological organization explainable only on the premise of a rational, purposive Maker. "In crossing a heath," he begins,

suppose I pitched my foot against a *stone,* and were asked how the stone came to be there: I might possibly answer, that for any thing I knew to the contrary, it had lain there for ever. . . . But suppose I had found a *watch* upon the ground, and it should be inquired how the watch happened to be in the place; I should hardly think of the answer which I had before given, that, for any thing I knew, the watch might have always been there. Yet why should not this answer serve for the watch as well as for the stone? . . . For this reason, and for no other, viz. that when we come to inspect the watch, we perceive (what we could not discover in the stone) that its several parts are framed and put together for a purpose, *e.g.* that they are so formed and adjusted as to produce motion, and that motion so regulated as to point out the hour of the day. . . .

Suppose, in the next place, that the person who found the watch, should after some time, discover that, in addition to all the properties which he had hitherto observed in it, it possessed the unexpected property of producing, in the course of its movement, another watch like itself. . . .

He would reflect, that though the watch before him were, *in some sense,* the maker of the watch which was fabricated in the course of its movements, yet it was in a very different sense from that in which a carpenter, for instance, is the maker of a chair; the author of its contrivance, the cause of the relation of its parts to their use. With respect to these, the first watch was no cause at all to the second. . . .

Nor is any thing gained by running the difficulty farther back. . . . A chain composed of an infinite number of links. . . . Contrivance must have had a contriver; design a designer. . . .

. . . Every indication of contrivance, every manifestation of design, which existed in the watch, exists in the works of nature; with the difference, on the side of nature, of being greater and more.[21]

Paley's first lengthy example of divine Design is the mechanism involved in the construction of the eye; he moved from that organ through "the succession of plants and animals," through the "mechanical arrangement in the human frame," through "the relation of animated bodies to inanimate nature"—indeed, through so many familiar organisms and systems that evidence of Design seemed to be scattered throughout the created world. Paley's argument focuses on the remarkable way in which organisms and even individual parts of organisms have been mechanically suited for the tasks they must perform. By his account, the existence of the human body itself—a complex arrangement of skeleton and muscle and metabolism all working in coherent, concerted order—is the most immediate and powerful argument that the world was created by a rational, purposive Being. Every individual, then, is a smoothly functioning "watch" that proves God's existence.

Hitchcock agreed wholeheartedly with Paley; however, Hitchcock saw that the Argument from Design as stated by Paley could be extended even further. Paley had found evidences for God in such striking and particular adjustments of means to end as the coherent mechanism of the human eye, and the parts and integrated functions of the human body. By contrast, Hitchcock believed that the uniform, law-governed regularity of *all* natural processes was the most persuasive argument for the existence of an intelligent, purposive Divinity. The natural phenomena of nature "teach many a moral lesson with great clearness and force," Hitchcock asserted, "and the religious man should ever desire to secure this most needed benefit from every thing beautiful and sublime in nature."[22] Particular, striking instances of ordered functions can give obvious examples of God's handiwork; but God is manifested most perfectly in *general* or *universal* laws. It would have been easy for God "to turn all nature into a chaos in the execution of vindictive justice upon the guilty"[23]—as He did in the case of Noah's flood, for example. Instead, in His bounty, He has dictated eternally consistent laws whose very regularity is of constant comfort to mankind. "No wonder that the rainbow, as well as every other circumstance connected with the deluge, should have entered so largely into the mythological systems of heathen antiquity, and that the bow should have been personified in the goddess Iris. . . . It is the token of that only covenant, which ensures the constancy of nature's operations! . . . Suppose that every time we saw the clouds rising, we were to anticipate a penal deluge; or every time the thunder and lightning played, we were to expect some signal manifestation of God's displeasure towards the guilty."[24]

Not only do universal laws of nature offer a more powerful argument for the existence of a rational Creator than that provided by the existence of any individual member of the natural world; it is also true that the consistency with which these laws are executed is man's most perfect consolation in times of fear. Reason alone can decipher the regulations that have governed all the many eons of the world's existence; by the same token, reason will necessarily infer the existence of a rational, Supreme Creator. According to Hitchcock, then, the reality of God is affirmed in the unvarying motions of the planets; it is affirmed with equal cogency in the uniformity by which plants and animals develop. The earth, through all its eons of existence—indeed, the entire cosmos—might best be characterized as a vast laboratory. Here, one after another, "experiments" are endlessly enacted. The consistency of result confirms and reconfirms the manifold laws of the created universe, and these in turn prove the existence of God.

Hitchcock embraced the theological value of science so enthusiastically that "Design" working throughout the order of *any* scientific discipline was held to confirm the existence of a God. For Paley, the doctor of divinity, the watch proved Design although the rock did not; for Hitchcock, the notable geologist, even the rock had mysteries that, once unlocked, would prove the orderly workings of God's laws. The stately and regular procession of the seasons; the unchanging and unchangeable movement of time, second by second and minute by minute; every experiment in chemistry with its predictable and calculable result; every lesson in the orders of insects and plants or even in the unvarying patterns of microscopically small creatures—all would demonstrate the presence of both Law and a Lawgiver. All scientific learning was a form of religious education.

Thus Dickinson's account of her curriculum at the Amherst Academy in 1845 is deceptive: of the four subjects she reported—"Mental Philosophy, Geology, Latin, and Botany"—only Latin might not have had an explicitly theological import.

As Dickinson grew older, more complex religious questions would be raised, but the Argument from Design came first, both because it was logically prior to subtler questions about God and because it had a powerful intuitive appeal and was thus persuasive. Yet even from the beginning of her formal education, Emily Dickinson seems to have been uncomfortable with the implications of "Design." If the seasons moved in an orderly fashion, they also moved inexorably and without regard for the individual case. In another climate, perhaps, where winters were brief and mild, "Jack Frost" might receive a merry greeting; but in flinty New England, where the first black frost of September marks the beginning of the longest season, where bleak March gives way to uncertain April, and the annual crops cannot be set until June is under way, the frost is a fearful omen. "Have you any flowers now?" Emily Dickinson wrote in September 1845. "I have had a beautiful flower-garden this summer; but they are nearly gone now. It is very cold to-night, and I mean to pick the prettiest ones before I go to bed, and cheat Jack Frost of so many of *the treasures* he calculated to rob to-night. Won't it be a capital idea to put him at defiance, for once at least, if no more?" The following fall she reiterated her dismay at the impassive and unrelenting progress of the seasons: "Does it seem as though September had come? How swiftly summer has fled & what report has it borne to heaven of misspent time & wasted hours? Eternity only will answer. The ceaseless flight of the seasons is to me a very solemn thought, & yet Why do we not strive to make a better improvement of them? . . . God has said, 'Work while the day lasts for the night is coming in which no man can work.'" Ironically, even the apparently benign interpolation of New England's regular "winter thaw" only reawakened the sorrows of September: "What delightful weather we have had for a week! . . . I have heard some sweet little birds sing, but I fear we shall have more cold weather and their little bills will be frozen up before their songs are finished. My plants look beautifully [in the greenhouse]. Old King Frost has not had the pleasure of snatching any of them in his cold embrace as yet, and I hope will not."[25]

If the regularity of the seasons in New England more often brought snow than warm and sunny days, at least the reassuring *cycle* of the seasons promised regular respite: "The older I grow," Dickinson wrote when she was seventeen, "the more do I love spring and spring flowers." By contrast, time moves in only one direction and leads always to but one destination. Death.

The notion of time seems always to have haunted Dickinson, and she almost never remarked time's passage without a tremor of fear. "Would that we might spend the year which is now fleeting so swiftly by to better advantage than the one which we have not the power to recall!" she wrote in 1845. The following year found her in much the same mood: "How sad it makes one feel to sit down quietly and think of the flight of the old year, and the unceremonious obtrusion of the new year upon our notice. . . . The New Year's day was unusually gloomy to me, I know not why, and perhaps for that reason a host of unpleasant reflections forced themselves upon me which I found not easy to throw off. But I will no longer sentimentalize upon the past, for I cannot recall it." Consistently, during these years, it was the wounding, inexorable *law* of time's passage that dominated her ruminations on the subject. "'We take no note of Time, but from its loss,'" she wrote to Abiah Root. "'T'were wise in man to give it then a tongue. Pay no moment but in just purchase of it's worth & what it's worth ask death beds. They can tell. Part with it as with life reluctantly.' Then we have higher authority than that of man for the improvement of our time. For God has said[,] 'Work while the day lasts for the night is coming in the which no man can work.' Let us strive together to part with time more reluctantly, to watch the pinions of the fleeting moment until they are dim in the distance & the new coming moment claims our attention. . . . There have been many changes in Amherst since you was there. Many who were then in their bloom have gone to their last account & 'the mourners go about the streets.' "[26]

Many years later, after Higginson had visited the poet, he reported her as having said: " 'I never knew how to tell time by the clock till I was 15. My father thought he had taught me but I did not understand & I was afraid to say I did not & afraid to ask any one else lest he should know.' "[27] Dickinson gives not the slightest hint in even her earliest letters that "clock time" was mystery to her (indeed, she gives every indication of comprehending the measurements of time's passage only too well). However, "I did not understand & I was afraid to say I did not" captures her pervasive mood. Her concern over the inability to recapture time or even to stay time's progress, her terror when contemplating the final, lethal wound of time—these are recorded from the very beginning.

Death was the most intimate mystery, insinuating itself into every home and every relationship. Youth was no protection from time's assault, and when she learned about birth, Emily Dickinson learned as well that births were the occasion for no more than tentative rejoicing. "Mrs Jones and Mrs S Mack have both of them a little *daughter*," Dickinson wrote in 1845. "Very promising *Children* I understand. I dont doubt if they live they will be ornaments to society. I think they are both to be considered as Embryos of future usefullness."[28] For Dickinson, death was always the phenomenon that most required explanation, and here the Argument from Design only proved that death was inevitable. In the end, Emily Dickinson learned more than enough science to become convinced that the universe operated in an orderly fashion. Reason convinced her that there must be such a Being as God; and as to God's *existence*, she seems never to have wavered. Yet the immutable fact of death led her to question the *nature* of this Being Who had authored our fate. And questions about God's intentions for mankind could not be answered by reason. When confronting these questions, a Christian was instructed to abandon reason and embrace hope in its place; and this process comprised the second part of a religious training in Emily Dickinson's Amherst.

It was a contradictory fact about the practice of piety in Dickinson's day that while natural theologians urged the Argument from Design to "prove" the conclusion that there existed some rational and purposive Divinity Who had created the universe—relying upon reason, seeking to appeal in endless and complex arguments to reason—all agreed that the yearning for some life after death was *intrinsically irrational*. Reason ought necessarily to infer the existence of an orderly "Author of Being" from the regular and unvarying laws of nature; however, nothing hopeful about the *disposition* of that Being toward mankind, nothing to support the yearning for continued existence after death, could be inferred from a *reasoned* inquiry into natural processes or a measured and rational examination of human history. This was a matter of hope, and for *hope,* mankind had to turn to the promises of the Scriptures, where the truths of "revealed religion" could be found. Hitchcock states the case:

The resurrection of the body is eminently a revealed doctrine. After its announcement in the Bible, philosophy does indeed point us to interesting examples of transformation in the natural world, which some have considered as evidence of this doctrine; but they are rather its symbols. When satisfied of its truth on the testimony of inspiration, these . . . afford beautiful *illustrations* of a doctrine so delightful to contemplate: But the analogies fail in some of the most important points: and, therefore, have little force in argument. . . . [The] checkered aspect of human society and individual experience, has perplexed and confounded many, who have not drunk deeply into the spirit of revelation. Aside from that fountain of truth, it is not, indeed, strange, that men should be confounded by what they witness. . . . The morning bow . . . does aptly symbolize some human hopes that extend into eternity. If not built upon the right foundation, those hopes, however confident, will never be fulfilled. . . . Every hope will thus terminate that is not founded on Jesus Christ and him crucified, every hope that does not begin with *the washing of regeneration and the renewing of the Holy Ghost* . . . the marvellous light of the Gospel.[29]

Hitchcock, Humphrey, and all the other Trinitarians of Dickinson's world agreed upon a clear relationship between reason and faith. Through reason, mankind could infer the *existence* of some purposive Divinity; however, reason would not enable one to infer the *nature* of that Being or apprehend His intentions toward mankind. In order to discern God's nature, a Christian had to acknowledge this insufficiency of reason and yield to faith. In practice, the embracing of faith entailed an acceptance of the truths of Revelation—a submission to the authority of the Bible. Nature did have a meaning; however, *nature's meaning could be discerned only after Scriptural truth had been accepted.* The Bible was the only reliable guide to the signs and emblems of the created world. The ritualized and formal occasion when men and women rejected reason and submitted themselves to faith was the "conversion experience"—and most often conversion occurred during the time of a revival.[30]

Here, then, was the terrible paradox of religious belief. The very power of intellect that had been necessarily employed to infer the existence of God from the world's "Design" had to be cast aside in conversion. In its place the pious Christian was to put nothing but blind obedience: utter, abject submission was the prerequisite for faith.

It was an incalculable price to pay; thus conversion seldom came easily.

Still, it is not difficult to comprehend faith's attractions in a world where death was so immediate and so industrious. For women especially, conversions were encouraged by intimate encounters with death. In the spring and summer of 1829, after Hiram Norcross's death and during the long, wasting, and finally fatal sickness of her mother, Lavinia Norcross wrote her sister and brother-in-law, the Edward Dickinsons, whose first child, Austin, had just been born. The spirit of revival had begun to gather in Monson:

April 27 . . . O let one tell you this evening has witnessed my tears for you & Edward I love you much—. . . . Choose Christ for your portion. Open your hearts to the influences of the Holy Spirit & may you be formed anew in Christ. . . .

August 18 . . . [Mother] is very anxious to see you wishes after commencement is over to have your husband fetch you down[] you must not disappoint her—There is now quite a revival here. . . . It is a precious time & may this revival not pass till we all shall taste and see that the Lord is good. The Bible lays open to us a kind & endearing invitation. . . . When we consider how short & uncertain our probationary state is it becomes us to secure that pearl of great price to secure to ourselves religion which will carry us through the dark valley & shadow of death & place us at the right hand of our Saviour in the day of final retribution—

On September 5, 1829, Betsy Fay Norcross died; sometime between mid-August and mid-October, Lavinia Norcross underwent a conversion experience.

October 25 . . . Yes the convert has enjoyment the world knows not of. I enjoy my mind very much & thought yesterday I was perfectly happy[] my enjoyment does not consist in the fleeting pleasures of this world but it consists in a perfect submission to the will of God, an entire trust in him & an anticipation of happiness when I have finished my course here below. There is nothing in death which appears terrifying, no gloom is affixed to the dying bed & to the soul about to take its flight. Where? To heaven—transporting thought that we shall join with our beloved friends.[31]

One year and nine months later, after continued urging from her sister, Emily Norcross Dickinson joined with her sister-in-law Lucretia and entered the First Church by "profession of faith."

A generation later, Susan Gilbert, Emily Dickinson's best friend and Austin's future wife, was striving mightily for faith. Like the Norcross sisters before her, she was profoundly influenced by the unpredictable ruthlessness with which death struck: in mid-July 1850, her older sister Mary died in childbirth, and Susan was ever thereafter morbidly fearful of bearing children. On Sunday, August 11, Susan Gilbert was admitted to the First Church of Christ by profession of faith.

The earliest records of Emily Dickinson's struggle over conversion date from her Amherst Academy days. A sensitive, serious, and meditative child, she may have begun to puzzle over the mysteries of death and the new birth in Christ much earlier, but her letters to Abiah Root on the subject begin in January 1846, when Abiah herself was going through a season of revival.

January 31 . . . I have had the same feelings myself Dear A. . . . I feel that I shall never be happy without I love Christ. . . . There is an aching void in my heart which I am convinced the world can never fill. I am far from being thoughtless upon the subject of religion. I continually hear Christ saying to me Daughter give me thine heart. . . . Perhaps you will not believe it Dear A. but I attended none of the meetings last winter. I felt that I was so easily excited that I might again be deceived and I dared not trust myself. Many conversed with me seriously and affectionately and I was almost inclined to yeild [*sic*] to the claims of He who is greater than I. . . . Does not Eternity appear dreadful to you[?] I often get thinking of it and it seems so dark to me that I almost wish there was no Eternity. To think that we must forever live and never cease to be. It seems as if Death which all so dread because it launches us upon an unknown world would be a relief to so endless a state of existense [*sic*]. . . . I cannot realize that the friends I have seen pass from my sight . . . will not again walk the streets and act their parts in the great drama of life, nor can I realize that when I again meet them it will be in another & far different world from this. I hope we shall all be acquitted at the bar of God. . . . I feel that life is short and time fleeting—and that I ought now to make my peace with my maker—I hope the golden opportunity is not far hence when my heart will willingly yeild [*sic*] itself to Christ. . . . Although I am not a christian [*sic*] still I feel deeply the importance of attending to the subject before it is too late.[32]

No quandary in life presented Emily Dickinson with such wrenching choices as the demand for conversion. In favor of faith was the fact of ultimate separation, the final inability to *see* some beloved face ("I cannot realize that the friends I have seen pass from my sight . . . will not again walk the streets"). Yet against faith was the fact that one must yield one's identity entirely to God, for the conversion experience was an obliterating relinquishment of self—a total loss of independence and autonomy wherein an individual's control over the organization of his or her experience was given over to the Lord. The integrated vision of the world that had united a unique set of memories and values and emotions into a coherent "self" was replaced by the uniform, divinely dictated vision of a world renewed in Christ's love. The emotional gain was very great. As Lavinia Norcross's letters indicate, the newly professed Christian had "enjoyment" in her confident reliance upon God so that "nothing in death . . . appears terrifying, no gloom is affixed to the dying bed & to the soul about to take its flight." This was no small prize. However, there was a commensurate emotional loss. The profession of faith carried with it a serious and binding commitment to this vision of redemption; necessarily, then, it required an abdication of the right to formulate some independent vision, and certain responses had to be renounced forever. True faith meant that a Christian would never react to the spectacle of sickness and death with horror or resentment or rage. No matter how unjust or untimely suffering and dying might be, a Christian who had submitted to God would maintain faith in divine justice and mercy. Terror was interdicted; rebellion was utterly prohibited. Above all, each Christian who passed through a successful conversion experience would relinquish the primary authority of individual reason and submit to the incomprehensible authority and will of the Deity.

The polished urbanity of Edward Hitchcock captures the mid-nineteenth-century Trinitarians in their most accommodating posture, acknowledging the discoveries of the rapidly changing natural sciences and adjusting traditional beliefs in infinitesimal ways to maintain a compatible relationship. But revivals and conversions were not susceptible of such delicate adjustments. The practice of revivals might itself be attacked (not long after the Civil War it was abolished entirely). However, so long as revivals and conversion experiences persisted, they continued to demand the absolute eradication of individual will.

Hitchcock's more rustic predecessor Heman Humphrey has left the most vivid and detailed accounts of this religious exercise. Like Lyman Beecher, Humphrey was well known for his ability to conduct revivals, for there was art to the proper management and pacing of them. A well-conducted revival, like a good sermon, had a shape, the several successive parts of which were carefully contrived to maximize the efficacy of the Holy Spirit's work among the members of a congregation. Such was Humphrey's skill in managing revivals and conversions that he wrote a manual for the Tractarians on the subject, describing these several stages clearly and citing the relevant Biblical texts. Predictably, the manual pointed to those many passages in the New Testament that stipulate the possibility for "new birth"; however, certain other Biblical texts were also seen as central—Matthew 7:13–14, "Enter ye in at the strait gate . . . because strait is the gate, and narrow is the way, which leadeth unto life"; I Kings 19:12, "and after the fire a still small voice." The lesson of these was woven into a coherent and unvarying story. Christians who hoped for a second "birth" after death were enjoined to listen for the "still small voice" that might bring the gift of faith, for only the faithful would pass through the "strait gate" into a Paradise hereafter.

The harrowing of soul and self that was necessary for conversion did, in truth, constitute a fundamental revision of one's sense of self; today we would probably term the process an "identity crisis." It is little wonder, then, that in this earlier age, where epic categories were still current, a "correlative type" became the heroic model for Christians confronting this ordeal. The core text for all revivals came from Genesis 32:24, 26—Jacob's wrestle at

Peniel. "And Jacob was left alone; and there wrestled a man with him. . . . And he said, I will not let thee go, except thou bless me." The "man" was God, and the blessing Jacob won in his striving was the promise that his sons (who were to become the patriarchs of the twelve tribes of Israel) would come into a royal estate. Thus did Jacob become the prototypical hero for these men and women who were New England's final Puritans.

Revivalists returned to this moment over and over again: each Christian was destined to "wrestle"—wrestle with God, with the Holy Ghost, with the angel of the covenant, with his or her own conscience (the story was susceptible of many slight variations)—and this agony of wrestling or striving was the very core of the conversion experience. Even a practiced minister might lead his parishioners only so far: encouragements, threats, cunning arguments—these might prepare an individual for the encounter. But when the crisis came, it came to each alone, a terrifying and wrenching junction when the solitary Christian confronted God Himself. On the side of the world, there was independence, autonomy—pride, so it was deemed. On the side of the Divinity there was submission and servitude—and along with these a release from the terrors of the flesh (disease and death) and the promise of rebirth into a life of happiness in Heaven after death. Jacob had always occupied a unique place in the Puritan tradition. Yet in mid-nineteenth-century Amherst, Jacob's encounter with the Lord at Peniel took on an intimate meaning for each Christian, and the words "wrestle," "strive," and "grapple" all carried the heroic implication of a strenuous and successful encounter with the Lord.

Nothing conveys the experience of conversion more effectively than a personal narrative: like all Trinitarians from pious families, Dickinson heard many of these from family and friends. Among the written accounts that have been preserved by Humphrey and Tyler, none is more compact or suggestive than the conversion of Nathan Fiske, Helen Hunt Jackson's father. "At the age of 15, I entered Dartmouth College," Fiske's memoir begins:

A new field was now presented to my view. For the first year, I saw little but its surface. A world in miniature was before me, variety of books, varieties of characters. . . .

. . . But at the close of the first year, the charm of being a lively boy began to break. I had always performed the tasks assigned me, and my mind consequently had gained some increment of strength. From occasional tasting, I had found the sweets of literature too delicious to be forgotten. . . . My second year, therefore, commenced with new exertions . . . the mere cravings of a mind, beginning to feel new energy in itself, and to seek gratification in exciting that energy to action. . . .

. . . I was reading in a book of sermons. I recollect nothing of the book, but that an attempt was made in one of the sermons, to show that the doctrine of election does not encourage licentiousness. I know not that I had previous to this, thought upon the doctrine, or the natural effects of a belief of its truth. But now, the objection which the author of the sermons was laboring to answer, seemed a full refutation of it. A doctrine which plainly declares to its votaries, if you are to be saved, or if you are to be damned, you will be, do what you may, could not be true. But I soon saw, that to reject this was to reject all the doctrines of grace, and I became a little giant in reasoning against them. I sometimes disputed with pious persons. They appeared abject and slavish, for they distrusted their reason and depended on scripture. I prided myself that I *reasoned*, and would not put out the infallible light within me. . . .

. . . [A revival had begun, and] it was suggested, that it could not be rationally expected, the Spirit would remain with us longer than it did at Yale, which was only one week. . . . I returned home deeply concerned for my situation. I read the sermon of President Edwards on Deut. 32:35 ["To me belongeth vengeance, and recompense; their foot shall slide in due time: for the day of their calamity is at hand, and the things that shall come upon them make haste"], and found my own state exactly described—that I was in the hands of an angry God who would take vengeance. . . . Professor Moore preached a sermon . . . that the reason all men were not saved, was their unwillingness to throw themselves at the foot of the cross and repent of their sins and plead for mercy. And thought I, the only reason why I am unreconciled to God is my own unwillingness? Yes, this proud heart will own no master; it cannot, it will not submit to the humbling terms of the Gospel. Willingly would I cut off an arm, or pluck out an eye, to obtain eternal life, but to submit to God, to confess my dependence on him and receive salvation as a free gift, how degrading. . . .

. . . Then I was shown that my whole heart was corrupt . . . that I was absolutely and entirely dependent on God for ability to accept [salvation's] terms, and yet, that my inability was inexcusable, as it originated or rather consisted entirely in the unholiness of my heart. . . . Then was I humbled. I threw myself into the arms of Jesus and pled for mercy; nor did I plead in vain. A beam of light darted into my mind. . . .

. . . On Friday, Mr. S. of B. preached from John 9:25, "Whereas I was blind, now I see." I thought I could in a measure adopt this language. . . .

. . . The morning bell, which once beat its dismal notes to call me to a tedious duty, now joyfully rings, Arise, arise and worship thy Creator.[33]

Fiske's account, lucid and artfully focused, brings together the many elements scattered through Lavinia Norcross's account of her own conversion. The sinner must humble self and reject reason utterly, forsaking autonomous activity and yielding the soul to the will of God so that a new "light" can illuminate the mind. Eventually, "vision" is altered: once the Christian is possessed of faith, he or she will be able to "see" the external world with new eyes, and it will be revealed as the visible embodiment of God's promises. Such accounts of individual transformation are full of wonder—accounts of miracles, so the authors clearly believed. The revivals that brought these conversions may indeed have witnessed the very last miracles of New England.

Although mid-nineteenth-century Congregationalists believed that a conversion experience radically altered individual identity, the change was of course not manifest in any alteration of form or face; instead, a Christian's feelings were transformed, and one of the ways this transformation might be reflected was in his or her attitude toward language. When, in her second letter to Higginson, Emily Dickinson spoke of her "Lexicon" as her "only companion," she was doing more than merely signaling her own preoccupation with words: she was alluding to a normative attitude toward the use of language that prevailed in Amherst. Joseph Lyman recollected poring over Noah Webster's monumental work, the *American Dictionary,* in the Dickinson home.[34] It is a striking fact that this lexicographer, whose work eventually became a standard for usage throughout the United States, was a devout Trinitarian of Amherst who regarded his scholarly examination of language as an essentially religious undertaking.

According to Webster, the proper use of language was an act of piety that demonstrated the ongoing willingness to abide by God's will—one aspect of the subservience of self that was the permanent remnant of a conversion experience. The virtue urged in every part of the dictionary, then, was "Quiet Christianism"—the practice of obedience. "Webster's emphasis on Quiet Christian behavior appears throughout the definitions in the *American Dictionary* itself. The reader is reminded of his divinely-directed role in life and the values by which he should live. The fear of God, absolute and rigid controller of all things, the depravity of man, and the character traits of meekness, humility, passivity, and whole-hearted submission to proper authority are celebrated in the definitions of hundreds and perhaps thousands of words."[35] Thus after defining "author" as "One who produces, creates, or brings into being," Webster goes on to add, "as God is the *author* of the Universe."[36] Definitions such as these cannot readily be distinguished from lessons in practical piety, and Webster left little doubt that moral instruction was, if not his first aim, at least the informing principle of his method. The examples in the dictionary of his orthodox Trinitarianism are far too numerous to list; however, the general message is simple, consistent, and direct. Obedience to God is man's primary moral obligation: reason must submit to faith.

Webster had not always been a latter-day Puritan; he did not come to faith until the winter of 1807–8, when he underwent a harrowing conversion experience at the age of forty-nine. Already established as an arbiter of usage in this emergent country (he had published the *American Spelling Book* in 1783–86), he then resolved to wed his interest in language to his newly won faith in the Lord. Deeply rooted in his etymological studies, then, was the conviction that words and syntax are essentially moral instruments: an extraordinarily lengthy (and ultimately misguided) preface to the dictionary traces the American tongue backward through countless transformations to the moment when language began in the Garden of Eden. In the beginning,

Webster asserted, God gave language to Adam. "Adam was not only endowed with intellect for understanding his Maker, or the significance of
words, but was furnished both with the faculty of speech and with speech
itself, or the knowledge and use of words as signs of ideas. . . . *Language* [that
is, the rules of syntax], as well as the faculty of speech, was the immediate
gift of God."[37] In short, Webster's assertions about the origins of words and
syntax constitute a primitive semiotic system that is linked to a rudimentary
moral claim. God gave us words to be the "signs of ideas," and their primary
role for Adam was in "understanding his *Maker*" (for Eve had not been
created, and discourse between humans was not yet possible). It is, therefore, always this link between man and Maker that must be the primary
focus of language: we can demonstrate obedience to God by naming the
world correctly, and we can manifest disobedience (through inattention or
through prideful rebelliousness) by bending language to merely personal
aims.

Webster lived in Amherst from 1812 to 1824, during the formative years
of both the Amherst Academy and the College, and his influence was felt
everywhere. A friend and co-worker of Samuel Fowler Dickinson, Webster
"wrote many of the early documents pertaining to both these Institutions;
and while they show the pure taste, good sense and well-balanced mind of
Mr. Webster, it is interesting to observe how fully this distinguished philolo-
gist sympathized with the most puritanical of the founders of their religious
faith and the fervor of their Christian spirit. . . . A conservative in politics, a
progressive in education, a radical reformer in language, and a Puritan in
religion, he was a power in his age and country." Tyler concludes his laudatory account of Webster's influence upon Amherst with a remark that is strikingly similar to Dickinson's claim in the letter to Higginson that her
"Lexicon" was her "only companion": Webster's "Dictionary is, perhaps,
beyond any other uninspired book, the constant companion, friend and
counselor of the educated and educating classes."[38]

In the end, Emily Dickinson's relationship with her Lexicon was immensely complex. Its most direct and lasting influence was to reinforce and
expand the conviction that Words were Power: not merely a force to be exerted in the time-bound, quotidian world, but a direct link between God and
mankind that would allow any human to reach into the transcendent. Insofar
as the dictionary's definitions eschewed explicit religious implication, they
become the standard for her usage. Yet her feelings about the "Quiet Christianism" that pervaded every page of it were subsumed into the larger issue
of her attitude toward the relinquishment of reason and the embracing of
faith that a conversion experience demanded. The notion that an individual's
command over words was necessarily given over to God as a concomitant of
faith raised fundamental problems for this girl whose "fall into language"
had proved such a source of strength.

An even more vexing problem was raised by the fact that the Congregationalists of Dickinson's world believed faith to be not only a way of *naming*, but a way of *seeing* as well. Indeed, the two concepts were linked.

Nathan Fiske's account of his conversion is replete with allusions to a change in vision. He claims that "a beam of light darted into [his] mind" when faith was fully established; he finds the text from John, "Whereas I was blind, now I see," particularly apt; in short, his view of the world has been entirely altered by faith. At one level this talk about a revised "vision" of the world after conversion is metaphorical: a Christian in faith can now "envision" Heaven as a glorious sequel to death. Yet at another level, all such talk of vision, eyesight, and the like was quite literal. Hitchcock and his colleagues all agreed that the world and its "Design" contained no *proof* of God's promises; however, once the golden link had been forged and a Christian had acquired faith, he or she would quite literally *see* the validations or confirmations of God's promise that have been scattered throughout the created world. If the existence of God can be inferred by reason, the authenticity of God's promises is reiterated metaphorically through countless signs and symbols that can be perceived throughout nature—visual tropes for the promised resurrection. Even science, when informed by authentic Christian belief, could offer telling reinforcement of God's promises.

Indeed, the Book of Nature was full of apt illustrations of moral truth. Following a long tradition (and by his own acknowledgment, following the recent example of Bishop Butler in his *Analogy of Religion: Natural & Revealed*), Hitchcock demonstrated how the Book of Nature ought to be read. Using the terms "emblem," "sign," and "analogy" loosely and more or less synonymously to refer to objects or processes in nature that represent some spiritual fact, Hitchcock pointed to the promise of rebirth embedded in such transformations as the caterpillar's metamorphosis into the butterfly. The dry bulb of autumn, seemingly so lifeless, became another emblem of resurrection, concealing the promise of lilies to rise from the earth in the spring; the return of the birds, the new life of nature after the "death" of a long New England winter, sunrise (as reprieve from night's dark portents) or sunset (a going home to God)—all these and more were "analogies" or "signs" in nature intended by God for the edification of mankind.

In short, as the Saviour met the sower going forth to sow; or saw the corn growing up, or the trees putting on their foliage and flower; as he saw the vineyards dressed, the grass waving in the field, the birds flying through the air, the chickens gathering under the wing of their mother, the burrows of the foxes, the plowmen holding the plow, the architect building houses, the soldier going to war, or a band of thieves breaking into the house;—all these events, and many others, were seized upon by him to illustrate the great moral and religious truths.

Now with such illustrious examples, is it not the part of wisdom to attempt to seize upon passing events in nature . . . and make them subservient to moral instruction?[39]

All examinations of nature, then, made secular learning "subservient to moral instruction"; and such was the assumption that informed Emily Dickinson's schooling. Students were taught to perceive God's handiwork in the pattern of human history, His presence and promises in the laws of mathematics and science; they were taught that the use of words had a moral implication: in sum, they discovered little by little that all disciplines were ultimately ways of discerning God's nature and the nature of His promises to mankind. In the end, if the aims of the teachers were accomplished, their students accepted their obligation to submit to God's will and underwent a conversion to faith.[40]

Piety, when it was sincere, became a new way of living, suffusing every action, thought, and perception. Thus a Christian would always be able to test whether he or she was truly in faith, for if an individual's conversion had been authentic, the world would be seen differently. What is more, if every glance at nature and every examination of the laws that govern nature's processes would reveal "emblems" and "signs" and "analogies" of God's promises, it followed that to *name* these "emblems" and "signs" and "analogies"—dawn, lily, butterfly, and the like—would be to identify not only the natural phenomenon but also the spiritual truth of redemption for which it stood. Thus did *seeing* and *naming* reinforce each other continuously in a Christian's daily exercise of faith.

This newly acquired capacity to *see* God's promises in the world and to *name* them using nothing more than the language of everyday discourse was generally thought to be the greatest gift of faith. Sorrow and grief would be forever interdicted: the promise of the "new birth" in Christ eliminated the reasons for resentment or rage or fear or despair in the face of suffering and death. Only the glory of the God-made-man would remain to suffuse sight and discourse with grandeur. Little wonder, then, that earnest men of God like Heman Humphrey drew upon all their rhetorical skills to persuade the wavering Christian to accept the Lord's bounty. "Summon all the energies of your awakened soul; let them be concentrated in the anguish of the sharpest pangs of an awakened conscience [a spiritual ordeal like the pangs of labor and birth]. Strive with all the agony of a broken and contrite heart. Cast yourself at once upon the mere mercy of God, through Jesus Christ, and he will save you."[41]

Such were the calls that Emily Dickinson had been hearing all her life; and the pangs of spiritual struggle that she described to Abiah Root in January 1846 were the beginnings of just such a striving and wrestling within her own soul. True faith might have done much to put the ghosts of the past to rest. Samuel Fowler Dickinson was still vividly recollected by the elders of

This lithograph, which served as frontispiece for Edward Hitchcock's Religious
Lectures on Peculiar Phenomena in the Four Seasons, *illustrates a number of
natural events that were commonly considered to be "signs" or "emblems" of
the promised resurrection: the metamorphosis of caterpillar to butterfly (and
even the butterfly alone); the metamorphosis of polliwog to frog; the newly
leafed tree; the bird that has returned after a winter's absence; the various flowers
that spring from bulbs; and, perhaps most important, dawn itself.*

Amherst College, and revivals were a part of the patrimonial legacy on Edward Dickinson's side of the family—perhaps even as much a *felt* legacy as
that other inheritance, public failure. A sincere conversion would have been
a noble continuation of the honorable portion of Grandfather's all-
consuming endeavors. What is more, true faith would have put the menacing
shades of Monson decisively to rest. Disease and death would remain: infant
death, the mortal peril of childbirth, consumption, typhoid, strep, pneumonia—all these would continue to haunt Amherst throughout Emily Dickinson's lifetime. However, Saint Paul had assured us that Jesus of Nazareth,
the God / man, had already conquered death. Thus ardent faith, actively pursued, offered so apt a solution to the problems that the Norcross-Dickinson
heritage presented to a young woman of intelligence and sensitivity that it is
no wonder Emily Dickinson accepted the challenge of revivals and the possibility of conversion so earnestly.

Even by the middle of the nineteenth century, Amherst—both college and
town—still looked upon conversion as one of the crucial events that marked
the division between carefree youth and responsible adulthood. The secular
world had begun to make some inroads: for men like the barristers Edward
Dickinson and his son, Austin, conversion was less significant than it was for
those who anticipated a life in the ministry. Nonetheless, it was a recognized
public rite of passage for all, an alteration in the nature of one's identity that
received widespread communal recognition. In fact, it was generally held that

the momentous transformation in one's sense of "self" was the most reliable sign of true faith. "Of one thing I am certain," a convert told Heman Humphrey, "a great change of some sort has taken place in my views and feelings. I do not seem to be the same man I was before. Every thing appears new. The sun shines brighter, the flowers are more beautiful, the birds sing more sweetly, the mountains lift up their heads in greater majesty, and all nature seems to be praising God."[42]

In women's lives, the act of conversion was especially important as a sign of maturity: since secular professions were closed to the women of Dickinson's world, a public declaration of faith was the only thing that endowed a woman with a socially acknowledged adult identity that was independent of both father and husband. "I presume you have heard from Abby," Emily Dickinson wrote of Abby Wood, who had recently gone through a conversion experience. "Religion makes her face quite different, calmer, but full of radiance, holy, yet, very joyful. . . . She is certainly very much changed. . . . We take different views of life, our thoughts would not dwell together as they used to when we were young—how long ago that seems! She is more of a woman than I am. . . . Abby is holier than me. . . . She will be had in memorial when I am gone and forgotten."[43]

Even Father's obsession with inheritance and honor might be readily translated into transcendent terms. There was a noble estate awaiting the redeemed, and Emily Dickinson yearned for it. "I think of the perfect happiness I experienced while I felt I was an heir of heaven as of a delightful dream," she wrote Abiah Root after a brief period when she thought she had received the gift of faith. "Perhaps you have exchanged the fleeting pleasures of time for a crown of immortality. Perhaps the shining company above have tuned their golden harps to the song of one more redeemed sinner. I hope at sometime the heavenly gates will be opened to receive me and the angels will consent to call me sister."[44] When revival sermons were preached to a congregation of young people, the certain glory of eternity was often stressed: "The silver is mine, and the gold is mine, saith the Lord of hosts" (Haggai 2:8). All the splendors of salvation were clothed in regal garments: the link forged in the chain binding the Christian to her God was of "gold"; the promise was of a "crown"; God presided over a gorgeous palace, "and the building of the wall of it was of jasper: and the city was pure gold, like unto clear glass" (Revelation 21:18). It was a glorious vision, intended as a princely enticement; and its grandiosity appealed to Dickinson's nature even as the visionary dream of a different holy city upon a hill had appealed to Grandfather Dickinson's prodigious imagination two generations earlier.[45]

But most of all (and for a young woman with Emily Dickinson's personal heritage, this promise may have been more compelling than any attainment mankind could imagine), conversion into faith offered God's perfect love and companionship. Here at last might be an adequate reparation for the loss of that intimate, unvoiced communion that Mother had failed to provide. Confidant and unwavering trust in an "unseen Divinity" was sufficient collateral to bind the covenant, and it was a compact Dickinson's deepest nature craved to establish. "The few short moments in which I loved my Saviour I would not now exchange for a thousand worlds like this," Dickinson wrote in 1846. "It was then my greatest pleasure to commune alone with the great God & feel that he would listen to my prayers."[46]

Yet if the promises of conversion spoke to her deepest desires, the risks touched her where she could least bear wounding. In her infancy, Mother's love had existed, but the hungering child could catch no glimmer of it. The "magic time" of silent mother-infant intimacy and affection had never occurred, and Emily Dickinson had never known that most primitive luxury of absolute trust. Only the fall into speech had relieved her anxiety. And later, when she had sought for Father's love, he had been too preoccupied with business to notice her need or respond to her requests for his presence. She could believe in God's existence; there seemed good reason to do so. However, she could not bring herself to trust implicitly in the goodness or generosity of a God Whose face she had never glimpsed and Whose voice she had never heard.

Thus there was an ultimate paradox for Dickinson in the value Amherst had placed upon revivals and conversion. Her earliest interactions with both parents had given her at best a diffused sense of inner self. If, during her adolescence, her society had offered acceptable roles for articulating an adult female identity, this deficiency of her emotional heritage might have been mended in some measure. But conversion demanded an utter *relinquishment* of self before the coveted adult identity could be claimed. For Dickinson, such an act of abnegation seemed beyond the realm of possibility. Her sense of failure (and for a while she perceived it as *her* failure, not God's) was voiced in a diction of "eye" and "face" and "voice" that poignantly echoes the anxieties and losses of those youngest years.

How strange is this sanctification, that works such a marvellous change, that sows in such corruption, and rises in golden glory, that brings Christ down, and shews him and lets him select his friends! In the day time it seems like Sundays, and I wait for the bell to ring, and at evening a great deal stranger, the "still small voice" grows earnest and rings, and returns, and lingers, and the faces of good men shine, and bright halos come around them; and the eyes of the disobedient look down, and become ashamed. It *certainly* comes from God—and I think to receive it is blessed— not that I know it from *me*, but from those on whom *change* has passed. They seem so very tranquil, and their voices are kind, and gentle, and the tears fill their eyes so often, I really think I envy them.[47]

She may have experienced the desire to convert as early as 1842. The fall term that year saw a major revival at the College; Edward Hitchcock's daughter Catherine declared her faith by profession, as did Emily Fowler. However, the earliest mention of Dickinson's own wrestle with the Lord is in January 1846. Edward Hitchcock had become president of Amherst College less than a year earlier and had established regular Monday-evening prayer meetings at his home; it seemed to the students "like a great family at morning or evening prayers, and in this benign, paternal atmosphere, a reverent spirit soon began to gather."[48]

During the winter term of 1845–46, a major revival began. As Reverend George E. Fisher (Amherst, 1846) recollected later, the last prayer of the evening meeting had been offered

"when this young man arose and asked us to stay for a moment. I remember distinctly just where he stood and how he appeared, when he said: 'My friends, the Spirit of God has been striving with me many days. I have resisted his strivings. I have resolved and sought to banish my convictions, but I can not succeed. I feel myself to be a sinner, most guilty and unworthy. I want your prayers that I may be brought to Christ.'"[49]

This revival touched upon the family: Emily Dickinson's cousin William Cowper Dickinson was among those who made a profession of faith in 1846.

At first Emily Dickinson did not go to the meetings (which were open to all): "I felt that I was so easily excited that I might . . . be deceived and I dared not trust myself." Yet she felt great longing for this "golden opportunity." By late March she had summoned the courage to attend several prayer meetings, and her reactions were both powerful and frighteningly conflicted: "I feel that I am sailing upon the brink of an awful precipice, from which I cannot escape & over which I fear my tiny boat will soon glide if I do not receive help from above. There is now a revival in college & many hearts have given way to the claims of God."[50] The figural rendering of the soul poised at the edge of a tumultuous waterfall is curiously balanced in its tone and implication. The usual reading for this quite conventional emblem is that only the "strong arm" of God's grace through faith can save the soul from a "fall" that is here construed in literal and horrific terms. Yet Dickinson's language suggests that grace itself, when it must be obtained through the conversion experience, is but another form of "fall": all constraints and all boundaries and all resistances to God's pressing claim must "give way." This releasing of the coherent self to God's control was an intolerable nightmare for Dickinson. Better to keep one's "I" intact, even if the promise of Paradise must be rejected.

Dickinson's health was poor throughout the latter part of the spring and the summer that year, and her parents sent her away to visit Aunt Lavinia in

Boston (as they had three years earlier after Sophia Holland's death) to get rid of her "cough & all other bad feelings."[51] The following autumn, 1847, she began her first semester at Mount Holyoke.

The shaping force of Mount Holyoke was Mary Lyon, who founded the institution in 1836. She had attended the Amherst Academy, and Tyler quotes this description of her years there:

The number of young ladies that term was ninety-two. Some had been teachers. They were all ages, from nine to thirty-two, and from all parts of Massachusetts and the adjoining States. Among these pupils was *one* whose name is now famous in history. Then uncultivated in mind and manners, of large physique, twenty-three or twenty-four years of age, and receiving her first impulse in education. She commenced with grammar and geography, and soon advanced to rhetoric and logic. Having a comprehensive mind and being very assiduous in her studies, she improved rapidly. Her name was Mary Lyon.

A protégée of Edward Hitchcock's, Mary Lyon was intense, earnest, and deeply religious. She had taught at a number of schools before founding the Mount Holyoke Seminary—at Buckland, Derry, and the Ipswich Academy. "Her regard for the Bible was so fervent, and her reverence for it so profound, that she would dwell on its beauty and sublimity with deep interest. She would also talk with great delight of the principles of natural religion; and when instructing in natural philosophy, astronomy, &c., she never omitted an opportunity of impressing on the minds of her pupils the power, wisdom, and goodness of God, as displayed in his works." By the end of September 1847, when Emily Dickinson began her studies there, the seminary had been blessed with the revival spirit and conversions by profession of faith in every year except its first. "A person might live for weeks in the seminary, during [a period of revival,] and yet see nothing unusual, save a deep solemnity and tenderness during religious exercises."[52] There were no hysterical outbursts. The influence of Mary Lyon was more subtle (and perhaps more insidious) than haranguing. When she spoke to the students in the morning exercises, her address was often a kind of "sermon."

On Emily Dickinson's first day, the subject of Miss Lyon's talk was separation: "Regard due to absent or deceased friends." On this first day at college, then, Dickinson was probed patiently, gently, and persistently about her feelings on a subject she had always found particularly painful. The Mount Holyoke "Journal Letter" recorded the events of these days.

Sept. 30 . . . [Miss Lyon] spoke in her own feeling way to the [students], who now many of them had left their parents' house for the first time; she asked what would those parents say, were they to speak this morning, what would they first be told to do by those parents, who have gone home to Heaven, what would they say to you to day? As you have entered this new year, would they not say "Respect and treat kindly your teachers" would they not say treat kindly your companions, do right in all things; but more than all would they not say, "Fear & honor God," even those parents who are not Christians, do not they want you to be. There were many tearful eyes.

Oct. 1 . . . This morning Miss L. continued the subject, by applying it to our own . . . pastor [who had recently died], what would he say to you this morning were he to speak to you, how would he say it? Those who have seen him have loved him and know how solemn would be his words & how his bright eyes would kindle. . . . It made eternity seem near. . . .

Oct. 2 . . . This morning Miss Lyon again spoke of Mr. Condit. . . . She spoke of his health so feeble at the close of last term. She then hoped he might recover, he seemed better for some time, but before the month of August was through he began to fail. . . . Miss Lyon was absent, but hearing of his feebleness, she hastened home. . . . He could only say a few words. . . . Taking her hand he said, "Miss Lyon, I am glad to see you. . . . There is another world of interest. I am going there. I have expected it though others have not. I have no great ecstasies, but I have deeper views of my own unworthiness and the danger of being deceived. . . . I think I love the government of God, which I have loved to preach. The government of God by grace, is my all. This government, I hope to love and enjoy in another world."[53]

Emily Dickinson had feared attendance at Amherst revival meetings because she was "easily excited" and might "be deceived." At Mount Holyoke the religious influence was far from coercive, but it was unremitting and inescapable. The "Journal Letter" continues: On the evening of October 2, "the names of the professors of religion [those who had 'professed faith'], those who have a hope, and those who have not were taken. I cannot tell you how solemn it was, as one after another class arose. I saw more than one weep as her name was put down *no hope*. There is a large class of this character[] will it be so at the end of the year? I think I never felt such a strong desire for an early spiritual blessing as now." On Sunday morning, October 17, Edward Hitchcock preached for the students and teachers at Mount Holyoke; the text of his sermon was "And the building of the wall of it was of jasper: and the city was pure gold, like unto clear glass" (Revelation 21:18). In the afternoon his text was "Enter ye in at the strait gate" (Matthew 7:13).

There were things Dickinson liked very much at Mount Holyoke, principally the institution's unwavering dedication to a serious education for women. "I love this Seminary," she wrote Abiah Root, "& all the teachers are bound strongly to my heart by ties of affection. . . . I am now studying 'Silliman's Chemistry' & Cutler's Physiology, in both of which I am interested."[54] However, here as at the Amherst Academy, there was no escaping the fact that the Bible and orthodox Trinitarian belief were the foundation of all study.

Dickinson's roommate was her cousin Emily Lavinia Norcross (whom she had first met in 1833 during her visit to the Norcross farm in Monson). Emily Norcross was a pious girl who began little by little to respond to the spiritual admonitions. Meetings were held for the impenitent, and Mary Lyon continued her systematic efforts to start the revival spirit. On October 11, 1847, she "read the passage 'Straight [*sic*] is the gate.' . . . Her closing remarks were very solemn; there seemed to be solemnity at least, upon every one present. Some were in tears." By Christmas week, feelings were beginning to stir. On December 20 Miss Lyon's meeting with the impenitents was "one of interest. There is attention & some awakening but little deep feeling yet." [55] On December 25 Emily Norcross wrote back to Monson that she had " 'indulged hope,' " and she added her own prayers to those of her teachers that other impenitents would also submit to the Saviour. On January 11, 1848, Emily Norcross wrote, "Emily Dickinson appears no different. I hoped I might have good news to write with regard to her." [56] Mary Lyon continued to call the unbelievers together and to put probing questions to them. On January 17, after one such meeting, Dickinson wrote Abiah Root, "There is a great deal of religious interest here and many are flocking to the ark of safety." But for Emily Dickinson, the same stubborn resistance remained: "I have not yet given up to the claims of Christ." [57] She was not unique, nor did she make any vociferous issue of her resistance; but neither did she yield to the unrelenting exhortations to relinquish reason for faith.

By early May, Mother and Father had decided that she should not continue beyond the summer term at Mount Holyoke. She had been intermittently homesick; in early spring she had spent more than a month at home, recuperating from yet another attack of severe flu; and after the comprehensive curriculum at the Amherst Academy, even the Mount Holyoke Seminary did not offer much of an addition to her education. On May 15 Emily Fowler's father preached there upon the death of Jacob: "And when Jacob had made an end of commanding his sons, he gathered up his feet into the bed, and yielded up the ghost" (Genesis 49:33). To Emily Dickinson, this text— so pregnant with meaning for those who were wrestling for faith—may have seemed unusually portentous. The next day she wrote Abiah Root for the last time from Mount Holyoke:

I tremble when I think how soon the weeks and days of this term will all have been spent, and my fate will be sealed, perhaps. I have neglected the *one thing needful* when all were obtaining it, and I may never, never again pass through such a season as was granted us last winter. Abiah, you may be surprised to hear me speak as I do, knowing that I express no interest in the all-important subject, but I am not happy, and I regret that last term, when that golden opportunity was mine, that I did not give up and become a Christian. It is not now too late, so my friends tell me, so my offended conscience whispers, but it is hard for me to give up the world.[58]

As it happened, Emily Dickinson would have one last wrestle with the Lord before finally concluding that even Heaven was an insufficient barter for autonomy.

It was more than a year after Dickinson's return from Mount Holyoke when her final crisis occurred. The winter and spring of 1850 brought a great revival to Amherst. Indeed, it was a season for awakenings: Lavinia, who was attending the Ipswich Academy, wrote Austin and Emily in early March, "Oh! Austin, if the Spirit of God has awakened *you,* I entreat you not to grieve it away. Do become a Christian *now.* How beautiful, if *we three* could all believe in Christ. . . . Does Emilie think of these things at all? Oh! that she might!" In mid-March Emily Fowler, who had been confined with illness for a time, wrote Austin and Emily: "Just now God is reminding us of our duty and our happiness in a different way than usual. I feel sure that there will be nothing of bravado or sneer about you, or of affectation or indifference—You would be above such miserable pretence. No one can be utterly thoughtless, if they are a spark raised above the brute, and the higher and clearer and more powerful the mind, the more eagerly will they seize these wondrous truths—Christ died for sinners, and we are all sinners." [59]

At Amherst College, a great hush of grace fell over the students and faculty. On Sunday, March 17, Professor Smith preached a mighty sermon, "Almost persuaded to become a Christian," and the revival began in earnest. The next day President Hitchcock decided to increase the evening prayer meetings at his home from one to two each week, and during the last half of March thirty-one students were converted along with "several individuals in the families, worshipping in the Chapel." [60] On April 3 Emily Dickinson wrote Jane Humphrey:

How lonely this world is growing, something so desolate creeps over the spirit and we dont know it's name, and it wont go away, either Heaven is seeming greater, or Earth a great deal more small, or God is more "Our Father," and we feel our need increased. Christ is calling everyone here, all my companions have answered, even my darling Vinnie believes she loves, and trusts him, and I am standing alone in rebellion, and growing very careless. Abby, Mary, Jane, and farthest of all my Vinnie have been seeking, and they all believe they have found; I cant tell you *what* they have found, but *they* think it is something precious. I wonder if it *is?*[61]

The whirlwind of revival had been tightening ever closer to Emily Dickinson. At first, in the Awakening of 1845–46, the meetings had been at the College; when she was worried lest she "be deceived" and fearful that she could not "trust" herself, she was able to stay away and remain apart from the powers of persuasion. The following year, at Mount Holyoke, the pressure was unrelieved, to be sure; however, Mount Holyoke was not home, and Dickinson could escape by visiting her family in Amherst—eventually, could leave Mount Holyoke altogether. But now the Lord of the covenant had been admitted into her own house—"farthest of all"—and even Vinnie had begun to give way to His imperious courtship.

For the women especially, this Christ Who came to call for them so importunately—offering Himself as the "Bridegroom" of salvation and beseeching them to become "brides of Christ" by accepting faith—could be a compelling Suitor. Some young women seemed transfigured by the love of this wooing. Abby Wood "talks of herself quite freely," Dickinson told Abiah Root in mid-May, "seems to love Lord Christ most dearly, and to wonder, and be bewildered, at the life she has always led. It all looks black and distant, and God, and Heaven are near." Yet Dickinson still considered God's courtship entirely too imperious, and she continued to decline the invitation of the Lord.

[Abby can tell you] how the "still small voice" is calling, and how the people are listening, and believing, and truly obeying—how the place is very solemn, and sacred, and the bad ones slink away, and are sorrowful—not at their wicked lives—but at this strange time, great change. *I* am one of the lingering *bad* ones, and so *I* slink away, and pause, and ponder . . . and do work without knowing why—not surely for *this* brief world, and more sure it is not for Heaven—and I ask what this message *means* that they ask for so very eagerly . . . will you *try* to tell me about it?[62]

Although Dickinson still asked to know "what this message *means*," she had actually begun to find her *own* message.

As early as April she had hinted of it to Jane Humphrey: "I have dared to do strange things—bold things, and have asked no advice from any—I have builded beautiful temples, yet do not think I am wrong."[63] In the May letter to Abiah Root, the tenor of Dickinson's rebellion became stronger: "Where do you think I've strayed, and from what new errand returned? I have come from '*to* and *fro,* and walking up and down' the same place that Satan hailed from, when God asked him where he'd been, but not to illustrate further I tell you I have been dreaming, dreaming a *golden* dream, with eyes all the while wide open."[64] The Book of Job was repeatedly used by preachers to demonstrate the imperative need for faith, given the fact of a God whose act of Primal Creation passed rational, human understanding. Electing blasphemy here, Dickinson has turned the Biblical text against itself, choosing for herself the role not of an accepting Job, but rather of rebellious Satan, who had challenged God's ability to extract faith from creatures that must bear the afflictions of their terrible Creator.

The Great Revival of 1850 continued to sweep through the village like a raging conflagration. As summer came, the work of the Lord went on.

Including seven from the families of the Faculty, there were thirty-three persons who, together, presented themselves at the altar, almost filling the broad aisle, all in the bloom of youth, and who now, for the first time, dedicated themselves, by their own voluntary consecration, to the service of their Maker, Redeemer and Sanctifier. This was on the 23rd day of June, 1850—a day long to be remembered, not only by the persons themselves, and their youthful companions, not only by the numerous families whom they represented, and to whom it caused great joy, but doubtless to be remembered forever, as a day when there was joy in the presence of the angels of God, and of the redeemed in heaven.[65]

On August 11 Edward Dickinson came to conversion, stiff-necked and unbending until the ultimate moment: "His pastor said to him in his study—'You want to come to Christ as a *lawyer*—but you must come to him as a *poor sinner*—get down on your knees & let me pray for you, & then pray for yourself.'"[66] And Edward bowed in faith before the Lord. In November his daughter Lavinia also entered the church by a profession of faith.

Not yet twenty, Emily Dickinson elected the path of *Non Serviam*. At the close of the year she wrote to Abiah:

You are growing wiser than I am, and nipping in the bud fancies which I let blossom—perchance to bear no fruit, or if plucked, I may find it bitter. The shore is safer, Abiah, but I love to buffet the sea—I can count the bitter wrecks here in these pleasant waters, and hear the murmuring winds, but oh, I love the danger![67]

Thus was it ended. She had refused faith. Perhaps, however, she had begun to compose poetry.

IV ❧ *The 1850s: Apprenticeship and Vocation*

There is a difference between attempting poetry and being a poet, for the second demands commitment to a way of life: a poet has accepted a calling and embraced a vocation; she has resolved to define identity itself in terms of the art she will create. In 1850, Dickinson was still merely feeling her way with language, uncertain of her final course. No one can ascertain the precise moment when experimentation left off and dedication began; no single reason can be advanced to explain Dickinson's willingness to accept the renunciation that such a calling requires. Nor was it the case that a general air of solemnity dominated her existence: even during the devout revival year of 1850, for instance, the three young Dickinsons led an active social life. "Amherst is alive with fun this winter," Emily Dickinson wrote her young uncle, Joel Norcross, in January; and in the same month she gave a more circumstantial account to Jane Humphrey:

There is a good deal going on just now—the two last weeks of vacation were full to the brim of fun. Austin was reading Hume's History until then—and his getting it through was the signal for general uproar. Campaign opened by a sleigh ride on a very magnificent plan to which my dear Jane would have been joyfully added—had she been in town—a party of ten from here met a party of the same number from Greenfield—at South-Deerfield the evening next New Year's—and had a frolic, comprising charades—walking around *indefinitely*—music—conversation—and supper—set in most modern style; got home at two o'clock—and felt no worse for it the next morning—which we all thought was very remarkable. Tableaux at the President's followed next in the train—a Sliding party close upon it's heels—and several cozy sociables brought up the rear. To say nothing of a party *universale* at the house of Sydney Adams—and one *confidentiale* at Tempe Linnell's. How we miss *our friend* at all of these things! . . . Tolman [Albert Tolman, a tutor at Amherst College] I do not see—guess he is pining away—and cant say I blame him in view of the facts in the case. I shant tell you what ails him—for it is a *private* matter—and you ought not to know! How could you be so cruel Jane—it will certainly be the death of him— and t'will be laid at *your* door if it *is*. Write me soon darling![1]

Some of Dickinson's activities combined this fun with intellectual pursuits. "We had a Shakespeare Club," Emily Fowler later recalled,

—a rare thing in those days and one of the Tutors proposed to take all the copies of all the members and mark out the questionable passages. . . . Finally we told the men to do as they like, "we shall read everything." . . .

. . . [Emily Dickinson] once asked me, if it did not make me shiver to hear a great many people talk, they took ["]all the clothes off their souls"—and we discussed this matter. She mingled freely in all the companies and excursions of the moment and the evening frolics. . . . Emily was not beautiful yet she had great beauties. Her eyes were lovely auburn, soft and warm, and her hair lay in rings of the same color all over her head, and her skin and teeth were good. . . . When "we girls" named each other flowers, and called her sister, the *Pond Lily,* she answered quickly, ["]and I am the *Cow Lily*["] referring to the orange lights in her hair and eyes.[2]

Yet the most intimate account of the Dickinsons during this period comes not from one of the girls' acquaintances, but from Austin's friend Joseph Lyman.

Lyman had been Austin's classmate at the Williston Academy in 1844–45, and when Father decided to have Austin return home in early 1846, Joseph Lyman was invited to come with him and remain as a guest in the Dickinson home until he went down to New Haven for college. During the protracted visit, he developed warm friendships with both girls. Just turned fifteen, Emily already was more reflective than her pretty, vivacious sister, and ten years later Joseph would recollect the quiet evenings he had spent with "Emily Dickinson who used to read German plays with me and sat close beside me so as to look out words from the same Dictionary."[3] During his years at Yale (1846–50), Lyman continued his intimate relationship with the Dickinson children, and little by little he and Vinnie developed a special fondness for each other. While Mother and Father remained discreetly absent, the couple spent long hours together courting in the manner of the day. "I remember," Joseph Lyman wrote his fiancée, Laura Baker, six or seven years later

how [Vinnie] used to take her little red ottoman and with almost childish grace come and set it close by my chair on the left side of me and lay her arm across my lap and put the book she was reading up against me and look from its pages into my face & read to me—and then follow me out at the front door with Austin and say "Don't be gone very long Joseph" and meet me at the front door when I came back—remembering all these things, her beauty, her grace & gentleness, & how I read her Virgil lessons to her & walked with her to the [Amherst] Academy gate carrying her books, the simple unalloyed happiness of those sunny hours came over me. . . . I was very happy once in Vinnies arms—very happy. She sat in my lap and pulled the pins from her long soft chestnut hair and tied the long silken mass around my neck and kissed me again & again. She was always at my side clinging to my arm. . . . Her arms were fat & white and I was very, very happy with her.[4]

Vinnie was only seventeen when Joseph Lyman graduated from Yale in 1850, young enough to make immediate marriage an unlikely choice. Moreover, Joseph was uncertain about his feelings for her: he could not yet support a wife, and though he was a Massachusetts boy, had ambitious thoughts of traveling beyond the cloistered world of Amherst to make a fortune.

He remained in New England for almost a year after graduation, but in the spring of 1851 he went south (first to Tennessee and then to Louisiana, where he eventually settled). In late March 1851 he made a farewell visit to Amherst, having told Vinnie that he expected to return after a two-year trial period in the South. "A gay party of us went up from Amherst to Montague on a Sugar Excursion," he recollected later:

I was with the Dickinson family. I was about to leave for the South uncertain when if ever I might return. Vinnies Love was shed around me softer than the balmy air. We spent all the afternoon in the woods there rambling about, laughing, talking. I had been with Emily a good deal & with Jane Hitchcock and Mary Warner—towards the last of our being there, just before we went to our carriages I, thinking of all the past . . . thinking too *of all the future*—what I should become, when I should come again & about Vinnies Love, & what I could do with it during the years, I strolled away w[ith?] myself and sat down on a rock beside a spring. Then Vinnie came unto me & took my hand & said—"O Joseph I haven't seen much of you today. Howell has been with me all the afternoon but I would so much rather have been with you." I said "My dear Vinnie, I thought it best under the circumstances not to pay you very marked attention before all these people. I would avoid every thing like gossip." Vinnie loq. "I know Joseph, but I love you, and I am proud of you and of your love—I want people to know that you love me—come, Joseph, they are all going to the carriages. Let me take your arm and we will sit together in the carriage.—O Joseph *must* you go tomorrow!"[5]

Vinnie never fully relinquished her affection for him. On March 26 she wrote in her diary: "Walked with Joseph. Now he is gone! . . . Had maple Sugar. Joseph has gone, two years is a long time!"[6]

Joseph did not return to claim his Vinnie. She moped and attempted to console herself; and her diary suggests that she had plenty of company to cheer her up.

April 3. Parents gone to Monson, Jennie called, Sawyer spent the *morning* . . . the Misses Gilbert, Howland & Bowdoin spent the evening here. Funny times, these!

April 4. Gave Tutor Edward, flowers. Emilie Fowler spent the morning here. Bought a collar, made cake. Walked with Jennie, Parents returned. Received letter from H. *Billings.*

April 7. Father is gone to Boston—Walked with Aunt *Lavinia*. . . . Jane & Howland supped here. Sawyer, Howland, Misses Fowler & Gould spent evening. Had gay *times*.[7]

On August 15, 1851, Vinnie noted laconically that she had "Refused a heart"; on October 8 she wrote, "Received offer of *marriage*."[8] Affectionate and outgoing, Vinnie was not a great beauty, but she was very pretty and continued for many years to have a plentiful supply of suitors. For one thing, Mrs. Dickinson offered a tempting table. (As Joseph Lyman later recalled, "Vinnie's mother was a rare and delicate cook in such matters as crullers and custards and she taught the girls all those housewifely accomplishments.")[9] And even Father could be magisterially tolerant since many of the girls' friends were young men who had come to Amherst to read law with him.

Vinnie's suitors were charmed by her warmth and her pretty, girlish manner; however, the young men who paid court to Emily were those who had the habit of reflectiveness. Even Joseph Lyman, who was attracted to Vinnie's unquestioning affection, could perceive the rare felicity that characterized her sister's perceptions. "Emily Dickinson . . . used to say of me that I seemed ever to carry an arrow in my hand," he wrote Laura Baker, "so distinctly and persistently did my whole nature point to what was before me."[10] Not surprisingly, Emily was drawn to young men who could share her fastidious sensibility and take an interest in the poetry she had begun to write: Ben Newton, a law student with a literary turn of mind; George Gould, the editor of the Amherst College magazine, the *Indicator;* Henry Vaughan Emmons, who gave her a volume of Poe's poetry when he left Amherst in 1854. Almost certainly, however, she never met during these years a young man who was her intellectual equal, for her letters demonstrate the emergence of an intelligence that was increasingly rare in its power and audacious in its capacity for compressed, but brilliantly precise expression.

Although neither Austin nor Lavinia could touch Emily's genius, both were quick-witted; all three took a delight in language, and Vinnie had considerable comic talent. "Vinnie grows only *perter* and *more* pert day by day," Emily wrote Austin in 1851.[11] Vinnie shared her mother's reluctance to put pen to paper, "Though I've allways [*sic*] had a great aversion to writing, I hope, by constent [*sic*] practice, the dislike will wear away, in a degree, at least," she wrote Austin in the spring of 1850 from the Ipswich Academy, where she was a student. Promptly after inscribing this resolve, she spilled her ink: "Oh! dear, was ever any thing more unfortunate! two wretched blots have I made, & these, added to the other deformities of this sheet, render it quite unfit for inspection." By comparison with her brother and sister, Vinnie never did write much, but the few remaining letters capture her pungent turn of comedy: "The parlour carpets have been taken up & put down again &

none of us killed," she wrote Austin in 1851; two years later she observed, "Joel [Norcross] has made us a visit & I'm glad its over, for I have got tired of hearing about *Ego altogether*. He is never informed on any other subject."[12] Ebullient by nature, sociable and gossipy, Vinnie thrived on parties and flirtation, and it is much more remarkable that *she* never married than that her sister did not.

Vinnie bustled about—redecorating the house to make it prettier or busying herself with Emily's appearance, as adolescent sisters sometimes do: "Emilie's hair is cut off & shes very pretty," she informed Austin in June 1852.[13] Yet the dependency between these two continued beyond youth and remained unabated throughout their adulthood. More than a decade later, Emily wrote Joseph Lyman, "Vinnie is in the matter of raiment greatly necessary to me; and the tie is quite vital."[14] Often Vinnie and Emily played off against each other humorously, employing their brother as audience: "Austin wont you try to be careful?" Emily wrote during a season of flu. "I know *my* sake a'nt much, but Vinnie's is considerab[l]e—it weighs a good many pounds—when *skin and bones* may plead, I will become a *persuasion,* but you have *other* friends who are much more substantial."[15] The next day Vinnie wrote: "Emilie has fed you on air so long, that I think a little 'sound common sense' perhaps wouldnt come amiss *Plain english you know* such as Father likes." Four months later Vinnie took up the running jest once more: "I think Emilie is very much improved. She has really grown *fat,* if youll believe it. I am very strict with her & I shouldnt wonder if she should come out bright some time after all."[16]

Close in age (Austin, Emily, and Vinnie had been born within a span of fewer than four years), the three young Dickinsons had always relied heavily upon one another's company. As they grew older, the intense emotional tie grew even stronger: dissimilar in disposition and natural gifts, these sisters and their brother nevertheless seem to have regarded themselves almost as a single unit. Emily Dickinson's much-cited question "What makes a few of us so different from others?" is often understood as if it were a reference to the entire family, children *and* parents. In fact, the children had learned early to band together fiercely because Mother and Father were generally so unavailable to them.[17] Mrs. Dickinson had been inclined to withdrawal and depression even before her children were born, and motherhood did little to transform her fundamental nature. ("I called . . . on Mrs. E. Dickinson," a family friend Ann Shepard wrote her sister in 1843; "she was as usual full of plaintive talk."[18]) By the time her daughters had become young women, Mother tended increasingly to withdraw from the rest of the family with a series of illnesses, some identifiable and some vague and ephemeral. The children were thrown upon one another for solace, and each felt personally wounded when one of the others was absent. They varied in their tolerance for separation, the girls being more vulnerable than Austin in this respect.

Alone of the three, he spent two protracted periods away from Amherst, first teaching in Sunderland and Boston (1850–52), then attending Harvard Law School (1853–54); his absences caused both sisters genuine pain. "Mother has been sick for two days & Father 'is as he is', so that home has been rather a gloomy place, lately," Vinnie wrote Austin in 1852. "You are at home so little, that you see only the sunshine & none of the clouds, but clouds there are & very black ones sometimes, which threaten entirely to obscure the sun."[19]

Emily, the middle child, was most easily desolated by any separation from brother or sister. She acknowledged her susceptibilities, and puzzled over them. "I cant help wondering sometimes if you think of us as often as we all do of you, and want to see us *half* as much," she wrote Austin in 1853; "I think about this a great deal, and tho' I dont talk with Vinnie . . . about it, yet it often troubles me. I think we miss each other more every day that we grow older, for we're all unlike most everyone, and are therefore more dependent on each other for delight."[20] Perhaps it is not too much to say that Emily Dickinson could feel that she was securely *herself* only when Austin and Vinnie were there to listen and respond to her meditations or to share the complex sense of humor that never required explanation—fixed poles to steady her through the difficult hours. The effects of Mother's inability to convey affection and Father's many absences, those elements of early life that had made it difficult for Emily Dickinson to define her identity with confidence, could be repaired to some extent by the intimacy that she so perfectly shared with her brother and sister. For many years, then, this compensatory relationship with Vinnie and Austin was the basis for a viable solution. There had been interruptions when one or another of them was away: Austin's time at the Williston Academy during the spring and summer of 1842 and the school year 1844–45 (but not his college years, for these were spent at Amherst); Vinnie's time at the Ipswich Academy (1849–50); and Emily's own time at Mount Holyoke (1847–48). Yet these had been, by definition, limited variations in an established routine. "Normal" life during the years of childhood and adolescence was home-centered. One of the three might go away, but he or she always expected to return and re-establish the bond that was of singular importance to them all.

However, once they began to move toward maturity, the stability of this relationship was threatened, and Emily, especially, found the unbalancing effect almost intolerable. Thus her messages to Austin often betray a species of "homesickness":

To look at the empty nails, and the empty chairs in the kitchen almost obscures my sight, if I were used to tears. . . . I wish we were children now. I wish we were *always* children, how to grow up I dont know. . . . I feel very sure lately that the years we have had together are more than we shall have—I guess we shall journey separately, or reach the journey's end, some of us—but we don't know. . . . Oh for the pleasant years when we were young together, and this was *home—home!*[21]

Dickinson was writing these letters in an age when childhood had become idealized. The Sentimentalists and the Romantics construed "childhood" in many ways: it was a period of innocence, a time of freedom from responsibility, even an extended moment of privileged insight into transcendent reality. However, the wish Emily Dickinson expresses in these letters that she and her brother and sister might be "*always* children" reflected few of these current notions; instead, it had a quite explicit meaning that was rooted in the priorities of her life thus far. "Childhood" was that time when the three Dickinson children had all been together and Emily had experienced the deep, intuitive understanding that her nature craved; "adulthood" entailed the possibility of prolonged, perhaps permanent loneliness—and it was a threat not merely to her happiness, but to the integrity of her very self.

A voracious need to hold fast to the few whose company could console her can also be seen in the letters to close acquaintances. In some measure, the ardor of Dickinson's language in her letters to them must be seen as a reflection of the current conventions for correspondence between intimate friends.[22] In addition, the typological thinking of Amherst Trinitarians had led so stolid an imagination as Edward Dickinson's to assume that separation was a "type" of death.[23] Nonetheless, even when an adjustment is made for the fashionable effusiveness of girlish letter-writing and the studied pessimism of this Trinitarian way of "seeing" the world, Emily Dickinson's letters remain extravagant. To be sure, by the 1850s she was trying her hand at stylized writing. But her anxiety at having been left behind whenever she is separated from a close friend and the urgency with which she sought to mend the breach—anxiety and urgency that are often expressed in the language of "eye" and "face"—transcend every embellishment of style and become at their extremity an impassioned assertion of the need to protect herself from extinction. Emily Dickinson consistently construed separation as a kind of "death"—death of the beloved friend or disintegration of her own sense of coherent identity.

"It seemed so pleasant to have you—to know that I might see you—that I sank into a kind of stupor—and didn't know—or care—or think that I could not see you always," Dickinson wrote to Jane Humphrey in 1850.

The immortal Pickwick himself couldn't have been more amazed when he found himself soul—body and—spirit incarcerated in the pound than was I myself when they said *she* had gone—gone! Gone *how*—or *where*—or *why*—who saw her go—help— hold—bind—and keep her. . . .

Vinnie you know is away—and that I'm very lonely is too plain for me to tell you—I am *alone*. . . . When I knew Vinnie must go I clung to you as the dearer than ever friend—but when the grave opened and swallowed you both . . . Oh ugly time—and space—and boarding-school contemptible that tries to keep us apart—laugh now if you will—but you shall howl hereafter! Eight weeks with their bony fingers still poking me away—how I *hate* them.[24]

Two years later, in early 1852, a letter to Abiah Root expresses the same sentiments and contains the same series of associations:

I shall not break or reproach by speaking of the links which bind us to each other, and make the very thought of you, and time when I last saw you, a sacred thing to me. . . .

Amherst and Philadelphia, separate indeed, and yet how near, bridged by a thousand trusts. . . . Very likely, Abiah, you fancy me at home in my own little chamber, writing you a letter, but you are greatly mistaken. I am on the blue Susquehanna paddling down to you; I am not much of a sailor, so I get along rather slowly, and I am not much of a mermaid, though I verily think I shall be, if the tide overtakes me at my present jog. Hard-hearted girl! I don't believe you care, if you did you would come quickly and help me out of this sea; but if I drown, Abiah, and go down to dwell in the seaweed forever and forever, I will not forget your name, nor all the wrong you did me![25]

There is a studied style in this prose, a heightening of tone that approaches the Gothic, and this hyperbole was surely intentional. More important, however, is a pattern that is probably un-self-conscious and that runs throughout the letters of this period.

In mid-nineteenth-century New England information about absent loved ones was so difficult to obtain that it was only natural to worry about the health of a friend or relation when direct access to them was impossible. Not surprisingly, the letter writer did not worry about his or her *own* well-being (for that was not a matter of doubt); instead, the correspondent asked anxiously for reassurance that the absent person was still alive and well. In striking contrast, Emily Dickinson's letters express concern not so much for the condition of the one who has left as for her own safety. As a consequence of the separation, Dickinson construed herself as menaced by nothing less than annihilation itself—the bony fingers reaching out after her in the letter to Jane Humphrey and, most striking of all, the gradual dissolution of identity in the second letter, as the metaphor of writer-as-sailor is transformed into woman-as-mermaid, and finally into live-person-as-dead-body dwelling in "the seaweed forever and forever." Separation is construed as a wound to the one who has been *left behind,* and each of the letters reproaches the recipient in some measure for having inflicted such a blow (even though the second letter explicitly denies reproach). Finally, although conversation must have played some essential role in her pleasure at having the person in her presence, it is the inability to *see* them that Dickinson explicitly mourns in these letters to them.

God's Heaven was the only remedy Amherst society had postulated for such dilemmas, a place where separation would nevermore occur. However, even the hope of Heaven was an insufficient stay against these fears, for the winning of a happy afterlife entailed not one but two unacceptable submissions: the giving up of self to conversion and the obliteration of self by death. Autonomy was still better than Heaven. "The path of duty looks very ugly . . . and the place where *I* want to go more amiable. . . . I dont wonder that good angels weep—and bad ones sing songs."[26]

Although the resident population of Amherst was astonishingly constant during Emily Dickinson's lifetime, young men were always passing through. Boys came to Amherst College for their education; sometimes they stayed on as tutors or as Father's students reading law. Eventually, however, virtually all of them left. If one of them married an Amherst girl, she would have to leave with her husband to set up house elsewhere, often far from family and girlhood friends. "I know I cant have you always," Dickinson wrote to Emily Fowler; "some day a 'brave dragoon' will be stealing you away and I will have farther to go to discover you *at all*."[27] Of course Dickinson was correct: Emily Fowler married Gordon Ford in 1853 and went to live in Brooklyn. So it was with other confidantes as well: Abiah Root married the Reverend Samuel Strong in 1845 and settled in Westfield; Jane Humphrey married William Wilkinson in 1858 and moved to Southwick. One by one, most of Dickinson's valued friends slipped out of sight, and her feelings about this quite normal process are nowhere more movingly and candidly articulated than in the letters to Susan Gilbert, the young woman who was to become Austin's wife.

Susan Gilbert and her sister Martha had been born in Greenfield, just north of Amherst. Susan, the youngest of the large family, was only nine days younger than Emily Dickinson; Mattie was a year older.[28] The family was not a distinguished one, for the girls' father had kept a tavern and a livery stable in Amherst. Both parents died young—the mother in 1837 and the father in 1841—and their minor children were sent to live with relatives. Mattie and Susan divided their time between an aunt in Geneva, New York, and a married sister in Amherst, Harriet Gilbert Cutler. Susan Gilbert may have met one or more of the Dickinson children in 1847, when she was a student at the Amherst Academy; by 1850 both Mattie and Sue were in Amherst.

Mattie and Susan looked alike, and although their dispositions were dissimilar—"always Martha seems the gentle and submissive one, with Susan more forthright and self-possessed"[29]—people called them "twins." Emily Dickinson could not have been more delighted at their acquaintance. Susan especially was very gifted, quick enough to offer Emily Dickinson appreciative companionship. By the fall of 1851, when Susan, unwilling to continue as a financial burden to her brother-in-law, went to Baltimore to teach school, Emily Dickinson had already come to think of her as a valued friend. Yet Emily was not displeased when Austin seemed at first to favor Mattie, for she would willingly have welcomed either as a sister-in-law. "Susie and Mattie come often," she wrote Austin in June 1851. "Sue was here on Friday, for all afternoon yesterday—I gave the *manslaughter* extract to the infinite fun of Martha! They miss you very much—they send their 'united love.' "[30] By the time six more months had passed, Emily seems to have accepted both of the Gilberts as "sisters." Yet such affection was scarcely free from anxiety, for insofar as Mattie and Sue *were* responsive, they began to become as important to Dickinson's sense of well-being as even Austin and Vinnie.

In January 1852 Mattie contracted a severe case of flu and spent several weeks in bed. Emily wrote what seems to have been intended as a reassuring letter to Sue, who was still in Baltimore. "Dont feel anxious, dear Susie," she urged; "Mattie is only sick *a little* and Dr Smith and I, are going to cure her right away in a day." However, she had scarcely gone beyond this reassurance when the configuration of her own anxiety began to shape the letter. "I told Mattie this morning, that I felt all taken away, without her, or Susie, and indeed I have thought today of what would become of me when the 'bold Dragon' shall bear you both away, to live in his high mountain—and leave me here alone; and I could have wept bitterly over the only *fancy* of ever being so lone—and then Susie, I thought how these short adieus of our's might—Oh Sue, they *might* grow sadder and longer, and that bye and bye they would not be said any more, nor any more *forever,* for that of our precious band, some *one* should pass away." Now the "brave dragoon" of the letter to Emily Fowler has become transformed into a "bold Dragon" on a "high mountain," ready to consume unwary young women. In the end, marriage, too (as an event that would separate Dickinson from the friends whom she had come to need), began to seem a "type" of death. Indeed, the language of the letter even leaves it unclear who is to "pass away"—Sue, once she has married, or Emily Dickinson, who has been left behind, or both. Repeatedly, then, the letters of this period return to the variations that can be invented for the themes of separation and marriage—always construing them as mortal wounds that threaten death, disintegration, or even madness.[31]

These were the years of Emily Dickinson's own season for courtship: Ben Newton had left Amherst, but in 1851 George Gould was still calling at the Dickinson house to see Emily, and he continued his relationship with the family at least until 1852. Henry Vaughan Emmons attended Amherst College from 1850 to 1854, and during these years Emily Dickinson welcomed his companionship. Her handsome cousin John Graves frequented the house and was privileged, some years later, to receive a number of her most candid letters. When, in the spring of 1852, Austin's affections settled decisively

upon Sue, Emily Dickinson became, perhaps, overly involved in their relationship; however, in some measure she was testing the wind for herself.
What might marriage mean? It might even be that perfect form of intimacy
she had yearned after for so many years. "Those unions," she wrote to Sue
in June 1852, "by which two lives are one, this sweet and strange adoption
wherein we can but look, and are not yet admitted, how it can fill the heart,
and make it gang wildly beating, how it will take *us* one day, and make us all
it's own, and we shall not run from it, but lie still and be happy!" Paradoxically, however, the very possibility of passionate fulfillment engaged her deepest anxieties: any love strong enough to satisfy her craving would offer the
certain danger of an unacceptable loss. Marriage might bring a bliss too blest
to endure.

You and I have been strangely silent upon this subject, Susie, we have often touched
upon it, and as quickly fled away, as children shut their eyes when the sun is too
bright for them. . . . How dull our lives must seem to the bride, and the plighted
maiden, whose days are fed with gold, and who gathers pearls every evening; but to
the *wife*, Susie, sometimes the *wife forgotten,* our lives perhaps seem dearer than all
others in the world; you have seen flowers at morning, *satisfied* with the dew, and
those same sweet flowers at noon with their heads bowed in anguish before the
mighty sun; think you these thirsty blossoms will *now* need naught but—*dew?* No,
they will cry for sunlight, and pine for the burning noon, tho' it scorches them, scathes
them; they have got through with peace—they know that the man of noon, is *mightier* than the morning and their life is henceforth to him.

Even love, then, was potentially wounding—"scorching" and "scathing"—
and this wound, like all the others, threatened a blow to identity, perhaps
even a relinquishment of the self altogether: it entailed a "giving up" that
was not unlike the sacrifice of autonomy that had been required by a conversion to faith (indeed, there are echoes of conversion language here—"gold"
and "pearls"). "Oh, Susie, it is dangerous, and it is all too dear, these simple
trusting spirits and the spirits mightier, which we cannot resist! It does so
rend me, Susie, the thought of it when it comes, that I tremble lest at sometime I, too, am yielded up."[32] In the end, her fears about marriage for herself
were complex. The voracious intensity of the relationship might swallow up
her independence and autonomy; reliance on another left her vulnerable to
exquisite pain should she lose him; and marriage to almost any young man
of her acquaintance would require her to leave Amherst and her family.

By the spring of 1853, Mattie Gilbert had moved away (she married in
1857 and settled in Geneva, New York). Emily Dickinson tolerated the loss
of Mattie surprisingly well, for Austin and Susan had begun to take the first
steps toward a permanent commitment. Although each stage of their courtship had been deeply troubled, they were engaged by Thanksgiving of 1853.[33]

Now Emily had reason to suppose that she would never again have to fear the absence of this friend, so like a second sister. Yet, as she soon discovered, one last, terrible trial remained.

Susan Gilbert was a practical young woman and an astute observer of the Dickinson family. Austin was certainly considered a prime catch for any girl in town—an attractive red-headed man with the expectation of a sizable inheritance. Nonetheless, the situation in Amherst had serious drawbacks. Emily's affection was valuable, but often too possessive. More important, if Susan and Austin remained there after the wedding, Austin would certainly become subordinated to his father. Susan had assiduously cultivated Edward Dickinson's good opinion, but she could have had few illusions about his willingness to give Austin a free hand. Dwight and Frank Gilbert, Susan's two older brothers, had both made a lot of money in Michigan, and they were eager to have the couple move to the Midwest after marrying. Susan, farsighted enough to see that men of ambition ought to follow the wildfire of American urban expansion, convinced Austin at least to take a look at the situation before settling on a final course. Thus in early August 1854, Sue went to her aunt's home in Geneva, New York, and sometime in the fall, probably in October, she and Austin went to Michigan.

Even these tentative investigations of a move away from Amherst threw Emily's relationship with Sue into a crisis, and there is a quality of rage and reproach in several of the letters from this period that cannot be found anywhere else in Dickinson's correspondence.

[late August 1854] . . . Thro' Austin, I've known you, and nobody in this world except Vinnie and Austin, know that in all the while, I have not heard from you. . . . Never think of it, Susie—never mention it. . . . I do not miss you Susie—of course I do not miss you—I only sit and stare at nothing from my window, and know that all is gone—Dont *feel* it—no—any more than the stone feels, that it is very cold, or the block, that it is silent, where once 'twas warm and green, and birds danced in it's branches.

I rise, because the sun shines, and sleep has done with me, and I brush my hair, and dress me, and wonder what I am and who has made me so. . . . And prithee, what is Life? . . .

. . . It's of no use to write to you—Far better bring dew in my thimble to quench the endless fire—My love for those I love—not many—not very many, but dont I love them so?

[about 1854] . . . You need not fear to leave me lest I should be alone, for I often part with things I fancy I have loved,—sometimes to the grave, and sometimes to an oblivion rather bitterer than death. . . .

Sue—I have lived by this. It is the lingering emblem of the Heaven I once dreamed. . . .

Few have been given me, and if I love them so, that for *idolatry* they are removed from me—I simply murmur *gone,* and the billow dies away into the boundless blue, and no one knows but me, that one went down today. We have walked very pleasantly—Perhaps this is the point at which our paths diverge—then pass on singing Sue, and up the distant hill I journey on.[34]

The language here is a distillation of the verbal patterns that characterize so much of the correspondence after the mid-1840s. Ardent affection is construed as necessarily entailing separation ("no use to write . . . better bring dew in my thimble to quench the endless fire"); loneliness is depicted as a disruption of vision ("I only sit and stare at nothing"); separation is a mortal wound, both for the departed and for Dickinson herself—a death that kills the integrity of self—and the sea is a formless force that both absorbs self ("the billow dies away") and presents an impassable, infinite divide ("boundless blue"). What is the remedy for such dangers as these? The permanence of poetry: "then pass on singing Sue, and up the distant hill I journey on." The second of these letters concludes with a poem that begins, "*I have a Bird in spring / Which for myself doth sing,*" and ends, "*Then will I not repine, / Knowing that Bird of mine / Though flown / Shall in a distant tree / Bright melody for me / Return.*"[35]

It has been an easy matter for some of Dickinson's critics to take the letters to Sue from this period as the "symptom" of some grave mental derangement, for the tone is strikingly heightened. There is no gainsaying Emily Dickinson's excessive anxiety and anger at the prospect of losing not merely Susan but what was much more important, her brother Austin. However, our judgment must be tempered by the fact that she was giving voice to more than her own personal emotions: the entire family was shocked to discover that Austin and Sue might be seriously considering such a move, and there is good reason to suppose that all expostulated strenuously with him. In March 1855 Austin was still deliberating about his future. However, by mid-May Edward Dickinson had seized the opportunity to purchase the Brick House on Main Street. Appalled by the possibility of his only son's removal, he offered to build Austin and Sue a grand house on the lot adjoining the western border of the property if they would only take up permanent residence in Amherst.[36] Altogether, the barter he offered seemed too good to refuse; by late spring, the couple had decided to give up all notions of leaving. "Austin's plans are now definite as he is writing to you—tho' they have resulted very differently from our previously formed expectations," Sue wrote her brothers in Michigan; "we are both happy in them, and hope they may strike you as pleasantly—Austin's Father has over-ruled all objections to our remaining here and tho' it has been something of a sacrifice for Austin's spirit and rather of a struggle with his pre-conceived ideas, I feel satisfied that in the end it will be best and he will be fully rewarded for his filial regard—He goes into partnership on even terms with his Father the first of June."[37] Thus was Father's long-term preference for his only son at last given permanent, tangible expression. One of Emily Dickinson's dilemmas was resolved by Father's action: she would not be forced to endure separation from Austin and Sue. Yet the same stroke merely intensified another problem, her keen sense of rivalry with her brother.

It can never have been easy for Emily Dickinson to be the daughter of Edward Dickinson, especially since the precocious girl had grown into a woman of such intellectual power. Vinnie had elected one option: despite her native wit, despite even the strength of character she could sometimes demonstrate, she played the role of pretty, coquettish gossip. She was willing not to be taken seriously, and she seems to have found the duties of a traditionally defined feminine, domestic role entirely congenial, as her early willingness to "regulate" household affairs indicates. Moreover, as Mother's illness made her less and less active, Vinnie was not averse to taking over the management of Father's home instead of marrying and establishing a home of her own. For a long while, the tradition of the New England spinster suited her quite well.[38]

Emily was different. Many years later, after the poet's death, Vinnie tried to describe the diverse roles that had been pre-empted by various family members: "Father was the only one to say 'damn.' Someone in every family ought to say damn of course. As for Emily, she was not withdrawn or exclusive really. She was always watching for the rewarding person to come, but she was a very busy person herself. She had to think—she was the only one of us who had that to do. Father believed; and mother loved; and Austin had Amherst; and I had the family to keep track of."[39] By the time of this remark the many skirmishes had been fought, and the major battles were long past: every combatant save Vinnie herself had passed away. In the early 1850s, however, it was not yet an accepted fact that the older daughter's job was "to think"; Emily Dickinson was still struggling to define a unique course for herself, one that would give her talent and ambition full rein. None was readily offered by her environment. Amherst during the mid-1850s did not take a particularly enlightened attitude toward women's activities; and although there is little evidence that Father interfered with any of the young men who came to court his daughters, there is every reason to suppose that he had no sympathy for Emily's literary activities. Throughout his life, his hostility toward intellectual women remained unchanged.

In 1874, during his final term in the Massachusetts legislature, Edward Dickinson wrote a testy letter home to Austin:

This forenoon, I went into the Hall of the Ho. of Reps. to hear the Women's Suffrage People argue pro & con,—heard some women speakers, on both sides—some sentimental, some belligerent, some fist shakers—some scolds—and was disgusted with the class of females which gathered there. I hope we shall soon have a chance at the subject, & begin to clear off the scum—they don't expect to get what they ask, this year, as most of them say, but threaten to agitate till they find a legislature weak enough to report in their favor.[40]

Such remarks might be dismissed as the crotchets of an elderly man (Edward was by then seventy-one years old) if there were not such cogent evidence that he had always taken this attitude toward uppity women.

He had chosen to marry a woman who shrank from direct assertiveness and who achieved her ends, when she did, by more passive forms of aggression. And during 1826 and 1827, in the midst of his engagement (when he was perhaps more than usually inclined to imagine what an ideal woman might be), he had published a series of five articles on "Female Education" under the pseudonym "Coelebs" in the *New England Inquire,* a short-lived Amherst newspaper; these amount to a kind of manifesto of his attitude toward females and their role in life, and his antagonism toward intellectual women is so pronounced that his sister Mary, who was teaching school at the time, wrote to chastise him for it.[41]

He begins with a premise that anticipates the general course of the articles quite well: Women's "sphere is different from that of men. They have their appropriate duties to perform; and the object of these [essays] will be to show how they can be the best prepared for their performance, and how the happiness of society, with which females are so closely and inseparably connected, can be the best promoted." In the second essay, Edward deflects one possible line of criticism with an interesting assertion: "It is immaterial to me whether the *natural abilities of the sexes are equal,* or unequal: whether they would make equal improvement with the same means of education, or not. It is best, for all practical purposes that each should think that they are not *inferior* to the other, but *exactly equal.* And taking that for granted will not affect the argument. The best way to determine what kind of education is the most proper, is to inquire what will promote, in the highest degree, the happiness of society."[42] It is not surprising that he asserted such a view, or that he at least felt it prudent to make this pronouncement in an Amherst newspaper; after all, the premise on which the Amherst Academy had been founded was that boys and girls would be given the same training. However, a problem inheres even in this seemingly mild beginning.

If it is "best" to assume that the "natural abilities" of women *are* "exactly equal" to men, why ought their "sphere" be "different from that of men"? Or, to restate the problem from Emily Dickinson's personal perspective, if Father really assumed that she was intellectually "equal" to Austin (probably she was a good deal *more* gifted, of course) and if she was equally well educated, why did the world of Amherst (in which Father played such an active part) provide no adult roles for her that would allow her to make use of this intelligence and education? Why, like some Cinderella from the world of nightmare, must she suddenly discover that science and literature and questions of theology or philosophy will all vanish from her sphere when she quits school? For such was precisely her experience when she returned to Father's house from Mount Holyoke. "The Sewing Society has commenced again," she wrote to Jane Humphrey in January 1850, "and held its first meeting last week—now all the poor will be helped—the cold warmed—the warm cooled—the hungry fed—the thirsty attended to—the ragged clothed—and this suffering—tumbled down world will be helped to it's feet again—which will be quite pleasant to all. I dont attend—notwithstanding my high approbation—which must puzzle the public exceedingly. I am already set down as one of those brands almost consumed—and my hardheartedness gets me many prayers."[43]

Not even Edward Dickinson could have changed the public mores single-handedly; however, he might have given his daughter private support, as some fathers did. Or at least he might have paid minimal, courteous attention to her serious discourse. However, everything about the subsequent routine in his house confirms the tone of scornful dismissiveness that he takes in these early essays toward any woman with ambition or serious intellectual aspirations.

What duties were females designed to perform? Were they intended for Rulers, or Legislators, or Soldiers? Were they intended for the learned professions;—to engage in those branches of business, which require the exertion of great strength, or the exercise of great skill? . . .

Do you wish to be instructed in matters of state—to have every position you advance denied—every remark criticised? Should you like to dispute daily upon politics and religion, in your family—and above all, to be edified, at every interval of leisure, when you retire from the bustle of business to spend an hour in your family . . . to relax from severe employment with an interesting disquisition upon some abstruse point in metaphysics, by all means make sure of a *literary* wife. This is all you have to do. Open your house and sit down. Literature will support you. It will fill and warm and clothe you—T'will make your beds and sweep your rooms—wash and mend and cook for you.—You have merely to fold your arms, and be quiet.—Give the reins to your wife, and she will drive you to pleasure & honor and happiness. . . .

She will introduce your guest to the contents of the last "Quarterly," or the last production of the "Great Unknown."—She will tell them of the beauty of one passage, or the defects of another;—she knows what sentiments are correct, and what are absurd. . . . She will tell you of language "*superlatively elegant,*" & of figures the most "*barbarous;*" of scenes the most "*exquisite fine,*" and of plots developed with "*infinite ingenuity:*" . . .

Modesty and sweetness of disposition, and patience and forbearance and fortitude, are the cardinal virtues of the female sex. . . . These will atone for the want of brilliant talents, or great attainments.[44]

Even in the Amherst of 1826–27 the content of these essays was inflammatory, and after the third of them had been published, several letters of complaint found their way into print. Thus the last two essays, capturing Edward Dickinson in an attitude of modified retreat, are largely given over to listing the many fields of study that women might study with profit. English grammar, geography, history, rhetoric, logic, chemistry, botany, natural theology—virtually the entire curriculum that would later be available to Emily Dickinson found its way into the list. However, the fundamental premise was not altered in the slightest: whatever native intelligence a woman might have, however well educated she might become, her "proper" sphere would always be limited to the domestic realm, and the *only* appropriate application of her learning would be the comforting of her husband and the elementary instruction of her children.

The problem that these essays illuminate is not merely one of a man who would be hostile to "intellectual" women, especially if they presumed to be members of his immediate family. That would have been disagreeable, especially so for a daughter with Emily Dickinson's talents and proclivities, but it would at least have been simple and straightforward. Instead, Edward espoused two mutually contradictory attitudes—that women should be excellently educated (and encouraged to take their studies seriously enough to do well in schoolwork), but that upon completing school, they should forget their education and entirely commit themselves to providing domestic comfort. The contradiction that is articulated so clearly in these early essays was put into practice in the household he eventually headed. In some respects, a girl was to be treated as if she were exactly equal to a boy: thus until she was eighteen, Emily Dickinson was given an education that was virtually identical to that of her brother. When she reached maturity, however, and it was time to take her place in society, Father expected her to put aside all of the energies and talents that had been awakened and nourished by her schooling and to become domesticated. This renunciation of many years' intellectual training was not expected of Austin, of course, so it is not surprising to find that shortly after she returned home from Mount Holyoke, Emily Dickinson's letters began to voice her resentment at having no more significant status than that of an insignificant little sister.

In October 1850 Austin was teaching at Sunderland and living away from home; it was his first full-time job, and he often neglected to write the family. His sister Emily undertook to chide him, and although the humor of her letters was surely intended primarily to amuse, the sharp bite of her jealousy and anger soon emerged.

An affection of *nin*[e]teen years for the most ungrateful of brothers jogs now and then at my elbow, and calls for paper and pen. Permit me to tie your shoe, to run like a dog behind you. I can bark, see here! Bow wow! Now if that is'nt fine I don't know! Permit me to be a stick, to show how I will not beat you, a stone, how I will not fling, musquito, I will not sting. Permit me to be a fowl, which Bettie shall dress for dinner, a bantam, a fine, fat hen. . . . Herein I "deign to condescend to stoop so low," what a high hill between me, and thee, a *hill,* upon my word, it is a *mountain,* I dare not climb. Let's call it "Alp," or "*Ande,*" or yet the "Ascension Mount." I have it!—you shall be "Jove" a sitting on great "Olympus," a whittling the lightnings out, and hurling at your relations. Oh, "Jupiter"! fie! for shame! *Kings* sometimes have fathers and mothers.[45]

What was perhaps worst for Emily Dickinson was the fact that the father who had inveighed so movingly against the horrors of a "*literary* wife" was evidently delighted at the prospect of a literary *son.* When Austin did write the family, Emily could see that Edward Dickinson treated his son's words like pearls of wisdom. Thus she wrote to Austin with some asperity:

Father perused the [your] letter and verily for joy the poor man could hardly contain himself—he read and read again, and each time seemed to relish the story more than at first. Fearing the consequences on a mind so formed as his, I seized the exciting sheet, and bore it away to my folio to amuse nations to come.

"If it had only come" in the language of your Father, "a single day before," in the twinkling of an eye "it had been transferred to the *Paper*" to tell this foolish world that one man living in it dares to say what he *thinks.* . . . So soon as he was calm he began to proclaim your opinion—the effect cannot be described—encomium followed encomium—applause deafened applause—the whole town reeled and staggered as *it* were a drunken man—rocks rent—graves opened—the sun went down in clouds—the moon rose in glory—Alpha Delta, All Hail![46]

A theme runs through both of these letters that is reiterated again and again in the letters to Austin from this period. Placed in hyperbolic juxtaposition to the little sister is a mythic, even a Godlike figure of a brother; the accord he receives is not a response evoked by some splendid feat or even by some incomparable talent. Instead, the glory, the attention and the praise are all a birthright. Emily Dickinson understood this fact with unblinking clearsightedness, so whenever Austin returned home to visit, she took a hand in getting the "old plantation" up for an inspection by the heir. "The carriage stands in state all covered in the chaise-house—we have one *foundling-hen* into whose mind I seek to instill the fact that 'Massa is a comin!' "[47]

Against achievement, perhaps even against talent, there might be some avenue of retaliation. Against a *birthright,* no other claim, however compelling, can prevail. "Father takes great delight in your remarks to him," Emily

Dickinson wrote to Austin while he was in Boston at law school, "puts on his spectacles and reads them o'er and o'er as if it was a blessing to have an only son. He reads all the letters you write as soon as he gets [them] at the post office, no matter to whom addressed. . . . then he makes me read them aloud at the supper table again, and when he gets home in the evening, he cracks a few walnuts, puts his spectacles on, and with your last in his hand, sits down to enjoy the evening. . . . I believe at this moment, Austin, that there's no body living for whom father has such respect as for you."[48]

Part of Austin's inheritance was the freedom to go out in the great world beyond Amherst—to see, smell, hear the busy life of the mid-nineteenth-century American city. Amherst was a backwater, staid and unchanging. Parochial and old-fashioned as Emily Dickinson's own routine was, she knew there was a different kind of existence elsewhere, one to which she had little or no access. "I had forgotten *Pussy*," Dickinson wrote her brother in 1853:

if she knew it was "Master Austin" [I was writing to,] I guess she would send some word. . . . I've half a mind to tell her how you have gone to Cambridge, and are studying the law, but I dont believe she'd understand me.

You cant think how delighted father was, with the account you gave of northerners and southerners, and the electioneering—he seemed to feel so happy to have you interested in what was going on at Cambridge—he said he "knew all about it—he'd been thro' the whole, it was only a little specimen of what you'd meet in life, if you lived to enter it." I couldn't hardly help but telling him that I thought his idea of life rather a boisterous one, but I kept perfectly still.[49]

Dickinson did not leave evidence of any desire to side with the women of Seneca Falls. She certainly had mutiny on her mind by this time, but her target was of a different order from the ship of state. Nonetheless, the unbroken front of male faces that constituted any political gathering understandably aroused her rage. In 1852, when Father attended the Whig convention in Baltimore, he delivered a letter from Emily to Susan Gilbert, who was teaching in the area. The postscript reads: "Why cant *I* be a Delegate to the great Whig Convention?—dont I know all about Daniel Webster, and the Tariff, and the Law? Then, Susie I could see you, during a pause in the session—but I dont like this country at all, and I shant stay here any longer!" The letter concludes with an adaption of Cato's immortal battle cry against Carthage: "'Delenda est' America, Massachusetts and all!" And above the signature it reads, "open me carefully."[50] Emily Dickinson's rage was a veritable time bomb!

Although Dickinson's conception of herself and of the role she would play had begun to undergo a significant transformation, the outward events of the early 1850s gave few indications of it. To a large extent, the life of the entire family was an extension of the lives of Father and Brother: if Austin was the heir apparent, Edward was the undisputed sovereign. He was at the height of his public success now, and most of the significant episodes in the family's social life were a consequence of his commitments. Railroads were the passionate interest of Edward Dickinson's adult life, and for a number of years he had been eager to bring a spur to Amherst; finally, in May 1851, the General Court granted a charter to the Amherst & Belchertown Rail Road, and on February 6, 1852, the Amherst *Express* reported a gala celebration, with Edward Dickinson officiating as the director of the company.

Hon. Edward Dickinson made a few remarks. He recounted the first meeting for agitating railroad matters in this vicinity, held in Sunderland, nearly eight years ago, and faces gathered there . . . had grown familiar to him from seeing them at meetings held for a similar purpose, since that time. . . .

A salute of ten guns fired in this town on Thursday afternoon, in honor of the completion of the Railroad subscriptions and the contracting for its construction. We'll have another bout when the road is built![51]

In December of that same year, Edward Dickinson was elected to the United States Congress; he served one term in the House of Representatives, from 1853 to 1855.

By June 1853 the railroad to Amherst was completed, and the first cars had come up from New London. There was a great celebration in town. Of course Father was at the center, "Chief Field Marshal of the day," while his womenfolk were relegated to the satellite role of providing refreshments for his many guests, among them the Hollands, whom Emily Dickinson met now for the first time. Mother was exhausted by the strenuous domestic duties that followed upon Father's success, and during the summer of 1853 her daughters were obliged to do even more cooking and straightening and cheerful greeting than usual. Dickinson was a dutiful daughter, but as she explained to Austin, she had no liking for the role of mess sergeant and hostess: "Our house is crowded daily with the members of this world, the high and the low, the bond and the free, the 'poor in this world's goods,' and the 'almighty dollar,['] and 'what in the world are they after' continues to be unknown—But I hope they will pass away, as insects on vegetation, and let us reap together in golden harvest time—that is, you and Susie and me and our dear sister Vinnie must have a pleasant time to be unmolested together, when your school days end."[52]

Emily was strongly disinclined to join in these general celebrations of Edward Dickinson's triumph. Indeed, there are intimations that as she matured she was not unreservedly approving of Father's way of dispatching the ghost of the Dickinson past, and although she was inevitably implicated in his choices so long as she remained under his roof, she could not suspend her intelligence or her analytic capacity. She cherished moments when Father's behavior betrayed a vein of spirit or imagination: Father mimicking the minister—"he said he ran out of the meeting for fear somebody would ask him what he tho't of the preaching. He says if anyone asks him, he shall put his hand to his mouth, and his mouth in the dust, and cry, Unclean—Unclean!!"[53]—or Father ringing the church bells so that all of Amherst would turn out for a display of northern lights. But most of the time Father was dry and literal-minded; his life was not punctuated with moments of greatness. Emily Dickinson's propensity to characterize Father in heroic terms was an act of love, not a striving for accuracy; it tells much more about *her* capacity for passion and aspiration than it does about Edward Dickinson's behavior. Not surprisingly, the most movingly effective descriptions are those that suggest what Father "might have been," for these render something of the pathos in his limitations.

During his period in the United States Congress, the pre–Civil War frenzy had reached its height, but Edward Dickinson was not in the fray. He was on the floor to hear the Kansas-Nebraska bill debated, but no righteousness kindled his powers of public persuasion. He remained committed to the moribund Whig Party, the political affiliation of his own father; and when he ran for a second term as representative, he lost—partly because of his old-fashioned Whig sentiments and partly because he had repeatedly cut short his time in Washington to return home and attend to private business.[54] Personally ambitious as he seems to have been, he was cautious in money matters. He watched American urban expansion primarily with an eye for the ready dollar; he understood that fortunes could be made by bold ventures, but the father who had shackled his son to Amherst was scarcely prepared to pursue the wild fire of expansion himself. Instead, he stayed in Massachusetts and made a tidy sum buying and selling real estate long-distance. Ultimately, his vision extended little further than three blocks from the intersection of Pleasant and Main streets. The very concept of the "House of Dickinson" was reduced by Edward's willingness to construe it in the limiting, literal terms of brick and mortar: by 1855 he had become well-to-do by Amherst standards, and he used his hard cash to buy back the Homestead his father had built. In the fullness of his maturity, he was known widely for his financial responsibility and his attention to duty—but never for generosity or geniality or boldness of enterprise.

Even his commitment to God was hedged. He had always read the Bible aloud and conducted prayer service every day when he was home, and he educated all three of his children in the rigorous religion of their forebears, although he himself was not yet a believer. He delayed conversion until well into middle age, and after his eventual submission he still displayed no change, no mark of singular devotion; he always defined his vocation in terms of business and was not inclined to explore the mysteries of the Divinity. Nonetheless, later—years later—he wrote, "I am even now while I write, melted to tears at the remembrance of what we saw and felt at the working of God's spirit among us in 1850"; and in 1874, when he died in his room at the Tremont House in Boston, they found a card upon his person with these words penned in his own hand: "I hereby give myself to God. Edward Dickinson, May 1, 1873."[55] In public he remained proud to the end, driving hard bargains and living ostentatiously; in private he worshipped a God whom, perhaps, he feared more than he loved.

Emily Dickinson's plans for her own future were on a different plane—subtler, quieter, and infinitely further-reaching. There are hints of it throughout the letters of this period. Writing to Austin in 1851, she captured the delicacy of her relationship with Father: "We dont *have* many jokes tho' *now,* it is pretty much all sobriety, and we do not have much poetry, father having made up his mind that its pretty much all *real life.* Father's real life and *mine* sometimes come into collision, but as yet, escape unhurt!"[56] The biggest "joke" is only implicit in her note. Father, whose family ghost had originally instilled the imperative quest for honor and glory, was an essentially prosaic human being. It was his *daughter* (not even his son) who possessed the imagination and grace for greatness—"poetry," as she calls it here.

The early 1850s marked a crucial juncture in Emily Dickinson's life: the friends of her girlhood had begun to marry and move away; correspondence with them dwindled and then ceased, and they were replaced by the friends she would keep until her death—Fanny and Loo Norcross, Elizabeth Holland, and (once the Michigan threat was over) Susan Gilbert, who married Austin. There was no grand renunciation of marriage on Emily Dickinson's part. However, it gradually became clear that she would not choose the readiest way for a woman to define an empowered adult identity, would not leave Father's house to become mistress of her own; and this fact presented her with a series of related quandaries.

Some were the concomitants of those persistent adversaries, lingering illness and death. Millicent Todd Bingham refers to this period as a time of "funerals and fears," and she lists the names of thirty-three young people from the area who died between February 1851 and November 1854—all acquaintances of Emily Dickinson.[57] Natural theologians and ministers might enjoin their students and congregations to look upon the world with the new eyes of faith and "see" man's life replete with signs that promised a new life to come; in fact, what Dickinson all too often *saw* was the visible evidence of active decay. Among those to die now was Emily Lavinia Norcross, who finally succumbed in July 1852. After the girls roomed together at Mount Holyoke, she had often visited Emily Dickinson in Amherst to continue the friendship that had first begun in 1833. For almost twenty years Emily Lavinia had defied death. Yet death triumphed at last. The end was swift and fearfully disfiguring: there "was a large funeral & *many* mourners aside from her relatives—her face could not be seen so changed & so soon."

Nor could Dickinson evade a confrontation with death's ravages by leaving Amherst. In 1855, during Father's final year in the House of Representatives, she and Vinnie made a trip of several weeks down to Washington, Baltimore, and Philadelphia; in Philadelphia they stayed with Eliza Coleman, a distant cousin on the Norcross side of the family. Eliza's older sister, Olivia, had already been carried off, but Eliza remained just beyond death's grasp for more than three decades. An acquaintance observed in 1854, "Miss Coleman is a beautiful and accomplished girl but is I fear destined to an early death. Her only sister died at twenty of consumption and their remarkable beauty seems only a symptom of decay."[58]

Even Austin, who did not submit to a conversion until 1856, was moved to question the authority of a Divinity Who claimed to be both omnipotent and kind, and yet Who permitted such suffering and extinction: "I ask myself, Is it possible that God, all powerful, all wise, all benevolent, as I must believe him, *could* have created all these millions upon millions of human souls, only to destroy them? That he *could* have revealed himself & his ways to a chosen few, and left the rest to grovel on in utter darkness? I *cannot* believe it. I can only bow & pray, Teach me O God, what thou wilt have me do, & obedience shall be my highest pleasure."[59] Before life was done, Austin would become a man of many sorrows, and the loss of loved ones to death would be among them. But as Vinnie was to observe, Austin had Amherst; that is to say, he had conspicuous opportunities in the social world to win public acclaim as a balance against the private agonies of disease and death. Perhaps public success, even greatness, can never be a sufficient compensation for intimate despair, but it is at least a palliative; no such easement was available to Emily Dickinson. Most women married and became mothers, and this role was perhaps the most effective opposition to time and death, a new birth against the force of annihilation. However, when she rejected woman's traditional resort, Dickinson thereby created the need to discover some other role to play—some sufficient "self" to counter the dark menaces of oblivion.[60]

Other quandaries had more directly to do with Father's attitudes. He had clearly construed the matter of "Dickinson Honor" or the "House of Dickinson" in terms of male lineage—Samuel Fowler, Edward, Austin—and his female children were casually consigned to the peripheries of importance. How, then, could Emily Dickinson assert an empowered, autonomous "self" while continuing to live in Father's house? Indeed, how could she sustain the love she felt for him without repudiating her righteous anger? How could she permanently dispatch the ignominy of being no more than a "little sister" to the favored brother? And, most difficult of all, how could she gain the greatness that her deepest nature increasingly craved with such passion?

Although the goad of ambition prodded her with implacable insistence, there were few options readily available to the women of Emily Dickinson's world, and few of those that *were* available offered anything resembling greatness. For all of these dilemmas, she had to invent her own answers— new and unique resorts to satisfy her needs. Thus it came to pass that she confided her faith not to God unseen, but to the power of her own "Word."

The letters demonstrate that Dickinson had begun to write systematically by the mid-1850s. Often she made preliminary drafts of her correspondence, which she evidently kept to refer to when shaping the style of subsequent letters. Thus a poignant sentiment in one of the reproachful letters to Sue during the Michigan visit—"not one word comes back to me from that silent West. If it is finished, tell me, and I will raise the lid to my box of Phantoms, and lay one more love in"—is reiterated later in a much more subdued letter to John Graves—"Ah John—*Gone?* Then I lift the lid to my box of Phantoms, and lay another in."[61] Correspondence was still primarily a vehicle for communication with those whom she could not see in person; however, it had become something else as well, a self-conscious, disciplined exercise in the artful use of language. Indeed, there is even reason to suspect that some of the major poems had their inception during this period, for snatches of language in these letters—some of them even as long as a short paragraph— appear to be prose variants of language that can be found in the mature verse.[62]

Gradually, this command over words gave her the means to craft a uniquely powerful adult identity. Having forfeited society's cooperation in defining self when she rejected the roles usually available to women, she discovered that *this* "I," the "poet," was in some ways better than the roles offered by Amherst to anyone (man or woman), a secret, privileged inner self that could observe life to analyze and criticize with complete safety. One early way of invoking this identity was by citing that wily fellow of fabled cunning: "I am *something* of a fox," she wrote to Austin in 1853, "but you are more of a hound!" Later she expanded and slightly altered the image in a letter to Sue: "I asked Austin if he had any messages—he replied he—had not! That good for nothing fellow! I presume he will fill a fools Cap with protestations to you, as soon as I leave the room! Bats think Foxes have no eyes—Ha Ha!!"[63] In the poetry, the fox who can see and yet remain unseen would become a way of defining that complex game of hide-and-seek that a poet may play with her reader.

> *Good to hide, and hear 'em hunt!*
> *Better, to be found,*
> *If one care to, that is,*
> *The Fox fits the Hound—*
>
> *Good to know, and not tell,*
> *Best, to know and tell,*

> *Can one find the rare Ear*
> *Not too dull—*[64]

The silent language of eye and face having failed, Emily Dickinson would find in poetry the way to create a superior language and a uniquely privileged self.

Poetry lent itself to Dickinson's particular need as no other verbal formulation could. Indeed, her trope of fox and hound for poet and reader anticipates by a century the insights of twentieth-century psychologists and psychiatrists. D. W. Winnicott gives an account of several young patients who might be the pallid, less gifted descendants of Emily Dickinson. One, an adolescent girl, had a book

in which she collected poems and sayings, and she wrote in it "My private book." On the front page she wrote: "What a man thinketh in his heart, so is he." . . .

Here is a picture of a child establishing a private self that is not communicating, and at the same time wanting to communicate and to be found. It is a sophisticated game of hide-and-seek in which *it is a joy to be hidden but a disaster not to be found.*

Winnicott explains the origin of this way of defining the self: "In the early phases of emotional development in the human being, silent communicating concerns the subjective aspect of objects"—that is, in the primitive state of eye / face communication, the infant initially believes herself to possess the entire world, for everything that is "seen" seems to be a part of the self. Later, this feeling of empowered possession can be retained in artistic creativity, as the account of a conversation between Winnicott and another of his patients suggests.

X. then went on to talk about the glorious irresponsibility of childhood. She said: "You see a cat and you are with it; it's a subject, not an object."

I said: "It's as if you were living in a world of subjective objects."

And she said: "That's a good way of putting it. That's why I write poetry. That's the sort of thing that's the foundation of poetry."

She added: "Of course it's only an idle theory of mine, but that's how it seems and this explains why it's men who write poetry more than girls. With girls so much gets caught up in looking after children or having babies and then the imaginative life goes over [to] the children. . . ."

She said: "Now I only write down things that I feel in poems; in poetry something crystallizes out." . . .

When she needs to form a bridge with childhood imagination it has to be crystallized out in a poem.

In Dickinson's case, the decision not to marry left her with quandaries, to be sure. However, this same decision probably contributed to her art: she relinquished a socially sanctioned mode of defining adult femininity for the supremely subtle definition of identity that she achieved through her poetry. Nor is such behavior the sign of disease. "I suggest," Winnicott concludes, "that in health there is a core to the personality that . . . never communicates with the world of perceived objects. . . . Although healthy persons communicate and enjoy communicating, the other fact is equally true, that *each individual is an isolate, permanently non-communicating, permanently unknown, in fact unfound.*"[65]

Dickinson's poetry apotheosizes this central human paradox: the poignant, inevitable isolation of each human being—the loneliness and the yearning to be seen, acknowledged, and known—on the one hand; on the other, the gleeful satisfaction in keeping one part of the self sequestered, sacred, uniquely powerful, and utterly inviolate—the incomparable safety in retaining a secret part of the "self" that is available to no one save self.

Not surprisingly, poetry and the use of words in general became an issue in Dickinson's relationship with Austin. She wanted him as an audience: her artful letters could be an apprenticeship to poetry only if they found a suitable recipient; in fact, one reason she ceased writing to such girlhood friends as Abiah Root (while she continued to write to Sue even after Sue had come to live next door) may have been that Abiah and the others like her did not develop sufficient subtlety of intellect to understand the complex and compressed form of discourse that Dickinson was perfecting. For a while, then, Austin was her principal "public." Of course, *Father* was inclined to rhapsodize over *Austin's* literary style, reading his son's letters aloud to anyone who would listen and praising every line of them without reservation. Emily Dickinson understood that her brother was the unassailable heir to all the material prizes and public offices that constituted the "House of Dickinson." However, she also understood that her writing was a profound act of rebellion against Father and an unbeatable form of competition with Austin: in the matter of authorship, *she* intended to win unquestioned ascendancy.

Occasionally, Austin offered resistance. In June 1851, at the beginning of the period of most intensive correspondence between brother and sister, there was a skirmish for dominance. Emily Dickinson began with disarming affection: "At my old stand again Dear Austin, and happy as a queen to know that while I speak those whom I love are listening." Yet, once into the body of the letter, she marshaled an unmistakable attack to establish and protect her territory. She enjoyed his last letter:

I like it grandly. . . . I feel quite like retiring, in presence of one so grand, and casting my small lot among small birds, and fishes—you say you dont comprehend me, you want a simpler style. *Gratitude* indeed for all my fine philosophy! I strove to be exalted thinking I might reach *you* and while I pant and struggle and climb the nearest cloud, you walk out very leisurely in your slippers from Empyrean, and without the *slightest* notice request me to get down! As *simple* as you please, the *simplest* sort of simple—I'll be a little ninny—a little pussy catty, a little Red Riding Hood, I'll wear a Bee in my Bonnet, and a Rose bud in my hair, and what remains to do you shall be told hereafter.

And, having ridiculed his objections so that she might take possession of the Empyrean heights herself, she issues a dictum or two:

Your letters are richest treats, send them always just such warm days. . . . A little more of earnest, and a little less of jest until we are out of August, and then you may joke as freely as the Father of Rogues himself.[66]

The camouflage of humor does not obscure her majestic air: a "queen" in her position of writing, she will not brook criticism or competition.

In 1853 Austin took a short turn at writing verses himself, and she warned him off in no uncertain terms.

And Austin is a Poet, Austin writes a psalm. Out of the way, Pegasus, Olympus enough "to him," and just to those "nine muses" that we have done with them!

Raised a living muse ourselves, worth the whole nine of them. Up, off, tramp!

Now Brother Pegasus, I'll tell you what it is—I've been in the habit *myself* of writing some few things, and it rather appears to me that you're getting away my patent, so you'd better be somewhat careful, or I'll call the police![67]

She did not have to issue the warning again. Austin was welcome to his inheritance of "Dickinson"—a respectable legal career in this little New England town. His sister had begun to invent a new and more lofty destiny for herself.

Many years later Dickinson admonished her sister-in-law: "Cherish Power—dear—Remember that stands in the Bible between the Kingdom and the Glory, because it is wilder than either of them."[68] The sentiment thus stated sounds cryptic; however, an 1864 letter to Susan had explained that for Emily Dickinson, Poetry was Power: "I knew it was 'November,' but then there is a June when Corn is cut, whose option is within. That is why I prefer the Power—for Power is Glory, when it likes, and Dominion, too."[69] This statement codifies a conviction that had already become fixed during the decade of the 1850s: "It's a great thing to be 'great,'" Dickinson wrote her cousin Loo Norcross, "and you and I might tug for a life, and never accomplish it, but no one can stop our looking on, and you know some cannot sing, but the orchard is full of birds, and we all can listen. What if we learn, ourselves, some day! Who indeed knows?"[70]

For Emily Dickinson, to "sing" by writing poetry was an act of grandeur. Her language in discussing verse is quite uniform in this regard. Upon receiving a book of Poe's poetry from Henry Vaughan Emmons, she wrote, "I thank you for them all—the pearl, and then the onyx, and then the emerald stone. My crown, indeed! I do not fear the king, attired in this grandeur." Little by little, she was able to envision her *own* future in this mighty kingdom of immortal verse: "Longfellow's 'golden Legend' has come to town," she wrote to Susan,

and may be seen *in state* on Mr. Adams' bookshelves. It always makes me think of "Pegasus in the pound"—when I find a gracious author sitting side by side with "Murray" and "Wells" and "Walker" in that renowned store—and like *him* I half expect to hear that they have *"flown"* some morning and in their native ether revel all the day; but for our sakes dear Susie, who please ourselves with the fancy that we are the only poets, and everyone else is *prose,* let us hope they will yet be willing to share our humble world and feed upon such aliment as *we* consent to do![71]

The antecedents for this way of thinking—Poetry as Kingdom, Power, and Glory or as an estate of opulent golden and jeweled splendor—can be traced not to some other poet but, rather, to the language that had described the estate laid up for the "believer," the reward that awaited those who were willing to yield self to God and become newly born in Christ—the "wall of jasper," the "city of gold," and the "crown" of salvation.

Even when Dickinson first hinted at the beginnings of her poetic ambition in letters to Jane Humphrey and Abiah Root, she had already begun to preempt God's regal language of princely reward and to apply it to her own work: "I have been dreaming, dreaming a *golden* dream," she told Abiah. And to Jane Humphrey she said, "I have builded beautiful temples, yet do not think I am wrong." As she became increasingly committed to her vocation, she determined that gold would become her *independent* estate. Others might grapple with the Angel of the Covenant to win salvation, but she would engage her energies to win a different reward. "Life has had an aim," she wrote Jane Humphrey, "and the world has been too precious for your poor—and striving sister! . . . What do you weave from all these threads, for I know you hav'nt been idle the while I've been speaking to you, bring it nearer the window, and I will see, it's all wrong unless it has one gold thread in it, a long, big shining fibre which hides the others."[72] Emily Dickinson had determined to win a "crown" not through *relinquishment* of the self, but through the *assertion* of self in golden lines of verse.

In 1855 the drama of the Dickinson Fathers came full circle. This was Edward's final year in the House of Representatives. Then, on April 20, 1855, a notice appeared in the Amherst *Express:*

SALE OF REAL ESTATE.—The elegant place where the late venerable Dea. Mack resided for upwards of twenty years, has been recently sold by his son, Samuel E. Mack, of Cincinnati, to the Hon. Edward Dickinson, whose father, Samuel F. Dickinson, formerly owned the place. Thus has the worthy son of an honored sire the pleasure of possessing the "Old Homestead."[73]

By May Edward had begun to hire workmen to do the extensive renovations he had planned—adding a cupola and two chimneys, and providing other ostentatious evidences of success. It was also in this month that Susan wrote the letter to her brothers informing them that Austin had decided after all to remain in Amherst and go into partnership with Father.

The days of Samuel Fowler Dickinson were not removed by a great span of years from the events of 1855–56. Grandfather had built his Brick House in 1813, and he had mortgaged his material wealth to the evangelical vision of Amherst College in 1821—not long ago as history is measured. And yet, for Edward and Austin, the heroism of those heady days belonged to an ancient and irrecoverable past. Edward had embraced principally the material side of the Dickinson legacy, and he calculated the accomplishments of his life in prudent, hard-eyed, bookkeeping terms. "As he looked about," Bingham writes, "Edward Dickinson could feel justified in indulging a sense of satisfaction. He had retrieved the family fortunes. In the community his place was secure, not to say honored. . . . His wife and daughters were settled in the homestead, built by his father . . . and Austin was established next door. There was a feeling of permanence in his status, not to say an expectation of perpetuity, for by Austin's marriage the succession was assured."[74] The continued perpetuation of the *name* "Dickinson": this was the entire focus of Edward's interest in his son and heir. Austin soon grew docile to the notion of following his father's lead. He was more likable than Edward; his nature was gentler and more generous, and he had an aesthetic sensibility, collecting paintings and investing his desultory energies in beautifying Amherst. Nonetheless, Edward and Austin were more like each other than either was like Grandfather. Samuel Fowler Dickinson's glorious dream had looked beyond the superficial, material world toward a compelling, transcendent reality; and if in the end his ardor was compromised by his sense of betrayal and failure when the profits of his earthly success had been spent, he had understood what it meant to be seized by grandeur. He had known passion. Perhaps, for one brief moment, he had even heard the voice of Divinity calling him from the still, calm center of the whirlwind. By comparison, the life his son and grandson had chosen was a diminished thing.

Edward's public triumph was more than matched by the family's private woe in 1855. When, after six months for renovations, the family took possession of the Homestead in mid-November, Mother fell into some nameless, disabling apathy, apparently as a direct result of her return to the Brick

House. "I cannot tell you how we moved," Emily Dickinson wrote Mrs. Holland:

I had rather not remember. I believe my "effects" were brought in a bandbox, and the "deathless me," on foot. . . .

. . . It is a kind of *gone-to-Kansas* feeling, and if I sat in a long wagon, with my family tied behind, I should suppose without doubt I was a party of emigrants!

But, my dear Mrs. Holland, I have another story, and lay my laughter all away, so that I can sigh. Mother has been an invalid since we came *home,* and Vinnie and I "regulated," and Vinnie and I "got settled," . . . and mother lies upon the lounge, or sits in her easy chair. I don't know what her sickness is.[75]

Nor was Mother's illness of short duration. Austin and Sue were married the following July; the ceremony took place not in Amherst, but in Geneva, New York, where Sue's aunt lived, a deviation from the norm that was almost certainly owing to Mother's intractable affliction. Two years passed, and Mother still spent her days in a state of despondency. Whatever sorrows the Brick House held for her—the memory of that desperate time two decades earlier during Samuel Fowler's last days and months in Amherst, perhaps, or the recollection of the years spent weeping while Edward went as represent-ative to Boston—the sickness that left her body so weak was not merely physical in origin. Her infirmity was a deep despair: its seeds had been pres-ent from even the earliest days of the marriage, and now it had taken root and immobilized her. Throughout the length of her acute sickness, which did not abate until the early 1860s, Vinnie and Emily took up the burden of the housekeeping and, what was even more exhausting, the "watching." Some-one had to be available to Mother most of the time; usually it was Emily.[76]

If Father (and perhaps Austin, too) was able to focus his attention on the brick-and-mortar world of everyday reality, Emily Dickinson had begun to look with increasing consistency toward the transcendent reality that Grand-father had glimpsed. "We shall be in our new house soon," she had written Jane Humphrey before returning to the Homestead, "and—Jennie, we have *other* home—'house not made with hands.' "[77] Edward's vision of the world was defined by possibilities for advancement and success—meetings, busi-ness deals, contracts, court appearances, elections, and applause. His daugh-ter Emily sought the other half of the patrilineal inheritance, the realm of heroism: when *she* looked upon the world, she sought to discover the linea-ments of ultimate Power.

She had been given years of instruction in the correct way to adjust her vision of the Being Who had created man and Who continued to spell man's fate: teachers had directed her to see signs that would sustain hope in this concealed Divinity; ministers had commanded her to recognize the evidences of a new birth in Christ scattered throughout the natural world. Yet she had refused faith and the promises held out by conversion. Instead, she had clung to independence and the inviolate integrity of an isolated self. When Emily Dickinson looked into the void just behind life's veil, she apprehended a terrible Force of desertion, destruction, and death. It had been thus from the beginning of her life: as an infant, she had encountered death walking the corridors of the Norcross farm; later she had looked upon death in the face of Sophia Holland; eventually, she had seen death's triumph in the contagion that had ravaged the face of her cousin Emily Lavinia Norcross. Even now she could see death lurking in Eliza Coleman's febrile beauty, and Mother's persistent, nameless infirmity merely confirmed this vision of life as a condition always haunted by the presence of death. By November 1858 Emily Dickinson's sight had become saturated with evidence of the tireless activities of extinction. "Good-night!" she wrote the Hollands:

I can't stay any longer in a world of death. Austin is ill of fever. I buried my garden last week—our man, Dick, lost a little girl through the scarlet fever. I thought perhaps that *you* were dead, and not knowing the sexton's address, interrogate the daisies. Ah! dainty—dainty Death! Ah! democratic Death! Grasping the proudest zinnia from my purple garden,—then deep to his bosom calling the serf's child.

Say, is he everywhere? Where shall I hide my things? Who is alive? The woods are dead. Is Mrs. H. alive? Annie and Katie—are they below, or received to nowhere?

I shall not tell how short time is, for I was told by lips which sealed as soon as it was said, and the open revere the shut. You were not here in summer. *Summer?* My memory flutters—had I—was there a summer? You should have seen the fields go—gay little entomology! Swift little ornithology! Dancer, and floor, and cadence quite gathered away, and I a phantom, to you a phantom, rehearse the story![78]

Who could give comfort in the face of such a Force? She had been instructed to call it "Father."

By 1858 she had begun to sew the fascicles together, but as early as 1856 the poet had been born out of the labors of apprenticeship: visionary authority had entered Emily Dickinson's discourse.

[To John Graves, late April 1856] . . . I'll tell you what I see today, and what I would that you saw—

[To Mrs. J. G. Holland, early August 1856] . . . If God had been here this summer, and seen the things that *I* have seen—I guess that He would think His Paradise superfluous.

[To (Uncle) Joseph Sweetser, early summer 1858] . . . Strange blooms arise on many stalks, and trees receive their tenants. I would you saw what I can see, and imbibed this music.[79]

The infant who had fallen into words because the silent language of eye and face had failed; the girl who had preserved autonomy by refusing the pledge of faith to a God unseen; the brilliant young woman whose father could see talents and virtues only in a son—all of these lonely, angry, defiant, ambitious "selves" came together in a "new birth"—that of the heroic poet-seer.

Uniquely transformed, Emily Dickinson proposed to enter into an epic struggle in behalf of all humanity. Living in Amherst she had nonetheless been nourished by an exotic atmosphere: the village was secluded, even quaint, and far from the metropolitan centers of burgeoning America; at the same time, however, the crosscurrents of intellectual thought swept through this New England hamlet, the ancient inheritance of our Puritan fathers confronting new sciences that would eventually transform not merely the nation but the world. Edward Dickinson had been born the scion of a great house, the inheritor of an American tradition that had begun with Winthrop's call to build a New Jerusalem; yet he had turned from every opportunity for glory to become no more than a man of property. Perhaps it was a fitting irony, then, that his daughter—excluded from the world of money and politics and material gain—should fashion this destiny of heroic conquest for herself: Emily Dickinson would engage in an Armageddon of her own making against the God of death. Kingdom, Glory, and above all Power—these were to be the wagers. The archetypal hero and the informing poetics of her vocation would both be fetched from the struggle that was the core of every revival she had scorned: the moment when God and man had met face to face for the final time—Jacob's wrestle with the Lord.

Part Two ◆ *Interlude: Context and Subject*

GENESIS. 32:24   *And Jacob was left alone; and there wrestled a man*
with him until the breaking of the day.

25   *And when he saw that he prevailed not against him,*
he touched the hollow of his thigh;
and the hollow of Jacob's thigh was out of joint,
as he wrestled with him.

26   *And he said, Let me go, for the day breaketh.*
And he said, I will not let thee go,
except thou bless me.

27   *And he said unto him, What is thy name?*
And he said, Jacob.

28   *And he said, Thy name shall be called no more Jacob,*
but Israel: for as a prince hast thou power with God
and with men, and hast prevailed.

29   *. . . And he blessed him there.*

30   *And Jacob called the name of the place Peniel:*
for I have seen God face to face,
and my life is preserved. . . .

35:11   *And God said unto him . . . be fruitful and multiply;*
a nation and a company of nations shall be of thee,
and kings shall come out of thy loins. . . .

13   *And God went up from him in the place*
where he talked with him.

Two swimmers wrestled on the spar—
Until the morning sun—
When One—turned smiling to the land—
Oh God! the Other One!

The stray ships—passing—
Spied a face—
Upon the waters borne—
With eyes in death—still begging raised—
And hands—beseeching—thrown!

(#201)

This has proved a puzzling piece of verse. Several critics have argued that it depicts some internal struggle, "as if two parts of a divided self were fighting for survival."[1] The patterns of language in Dickinson's letters offer a few clues: the spare but explicit rendering of the second swimmer in the poem, no longer alive and no longer really whole (just a meager concatenation of "face," "eyes," and "hands—beseeching—thrown!"), echoes those eye / face locutions that run throughout the correspondence. There, Dickinson customarily used such language to render her desolation at the pain of separation from loved ones, for separation not only made the ideal, silent discourse of "interview" impossible, but seems to have threatened the integrity of her own sense of identity as well. What is more, there is precedent in the correspondence for a depiction of "two parts of a divided self," as Dickinson-the-writer created an image of Dickinson-the-afflicted; in one letter to Abiah Root, the affliction was even construed as a death by water—to "drown . . . and go down to dwell in the seaweed forever and forever." Yet even when the letters are artfully crafted to heighten the tone, even when they invoke powerful Biblical language—the "face-to-face" of mankind's ultimate encounter with God, for example—there is still nothing essentially cryptic about them. The primary, manifest meaning is rooted in the events of Dickinson's life: thus the nature of the separation and loss is explicit and clear, and Dickinson's fears are discoverable. A reader might wonder why Dickinson regarded separation with such apprehension or why she chose to use this habitual mode of expression to give voice to her anxiety, but a reader would not usually be confused about the immediate occasion for the apprehension expressed in any given letter.

By contrast, even if a reader is willing to accept the notion that this piece of verse represents some struggle between the members of a "divided self," its primary subject, its fundamental meaning, still remains puzzling, for unlike a letter, the poem seems entirely to lack context. The habitual verbal patterns of Dickinson's correspondence—patterns that are carried into her poetry as well—suggest that the struggle and anguish of this brief lyric may be related in some way to separation and a threat to coherent identity. However, more precise understanding is still elusive. The poem remains only an outline of agony, a veiled after-image of desolation. Nor is the dilemma limited to this one poem, or to a mere handful like it; much of Dickinson's strongest poetry is inaccessible—that is, it is difficult to determine precisely what such poetry is "about." Thus problems of context and subject are at the very center of any serious investigation of Dickinson's work.

Because the poems are both powerful and enigmatic, many readers have sought to understand her writing as an extension of the events in her life; the subject, they have assumed, was Dickinson's unique, personal feelings, and the context was the series of particular circumstances that combined to form her private existence. Of course, the most cogent reason to consider the influence of life upon work was the hope that the cryptic poetry might thereby be deciphered. As luck would have it, however, this tactic has not been successful. Few of the details of Dickinson's adult life have been recorded; as a result, there are long periods of time—weeks, months, and on one occasion an entire year—for which not even the simplest quotidian activity of her routine can be ascertained. Whom she saw, whether she was sick or well, whether she was happy or sad—such information is generally not available. Moreover, the information that does remain suggests only that she pursued a relatively quiet course. There is no concrete evidence for an event or series of specific events that would "explain" her remarkable poetry.

Confronted with this vexing lack of information but nonetheless irrevocably committed to the proposition that "personal life" is the correct context in which to understand the poetry, some readers have turned the usual relationship between life and work upside down: instead of discovering the events of the life in order to understand the poetry, they have supposed that the poetry might be used to infer the events of the poet's life. So, for example, if there are poems about madness, these must constitute "proof" that the poet experienced an emotional breakdown. And once this insidious process is begun, it is difficult to know where to cease. The actual records give so little explicit factual information that the gaps in it are susceptible to many different interpolations; many different "lives" can be postulated, many different "contexts" proposed for the poetry, and what began as an attempt to solve a puzzle produces instead a problem of even vaster proportions. As an ultimate reversal, the poetry is construed not as literature but as a series of "clues."

Perhaps it is a supreme irony, then, that Emily Dickinson, who was reticent to the point of silence when pressed for an explanation of any given poem, went out of her way to speak with deliberate precision about the *context* in which her art was to be judged. The fullest statement was given in her fourth letter to Thomas Wentworth Higginson, July 1862.

In 1862 Emily Dickinson was no longer a girl but a mature woman in her early thirties; there is evidence that she had been writing poetry seriously for some years, four years certainly and probably much longer, perhaps ten or twelve years. Thus the statement about her work in this letter was not a promise or an avowal of intention about hypothetical poetry that might be forthcoming; instead, it was the assertion of a self-conscious poet who had by now a sizable accumulation of finished work. Although she lived in a small, religiously conservative New England town, Dickinson numbered two important literary men among her friends—Samuel Bowles, editor of the Springfield *Daily Republican,* one of the most influential newspapers in the country, and Josiah Holland, who worked with Bowles on the *Republican* until 1870, when he left to take over *Scribner's Monthly.* Conscious of current literary values, then, she "placed" her own poetry quite explicitly by quoting from Emerson: "When I state myself, as the Representative of the Verse—it does not mean—me—but a supposed person."[2]

In Dickinson's poetry, the Emersonian allusions are usually light, even mocking; she did not construe her *poetry* as imitative of Emerson's. However, like Whitman, she did accept at least part of Emerson's description of "The Poet." Confident that Higginson would be familiar with this celebrated definition, she invoked it to establish her own position: "The poet," Emerson claimed,

is representative. *He* stands among partial *men* for the complete *man,* and apprises us not of *his* wealth, but of the common wealth. . . . *He* is isolated among *his* contemporaries by truth and by *his* art, but with this consolation in *his* pursuits, that they will draw all *men* sooner or later. For all *men* live by truth and stand in need of expression. In love, in art, in avarice, in politics, in labor, in games, we study to utter our painful secret. The *man* is only half *himself,* the other half is *his* expression.

. . . I know not how it is that we need an interpreter, but the great majority of *men* seem to be minors, who have not yet come into possession of their own, or mutes, who cannot report the conversation they have had with nature. . . . The poet is the person in whom these powers are in balance, the *man* without impediment, who sees and handles that which others dream of, traverses the whole scale of experience, and is representative of *man,* in virtue of being the largest power to receive and to impart.

It is difficult now, more than a century later, to appreciate the audacity of Emily Dickinson's quiet assertion. In this excerpt from Emerson, a reader must substitute some form of feminine pronoun or some collective noun for each of the words I have italicized to understand the scope and boldness of her claim. The Poet: "She stands among partial human beings for the complete person, and apprises us not of her wealth, but of the common wealth"—this daughter of Edward Dickinson, lawyer and sometime politician, this sister of the heir apparent to the legacy of the "Dickinson name." Most important of all is the context Dickinson demands for her work. The poetry is not offered as a record of individual introspection, however intelligent and sensitive that might be: Dickinson does not intend to speak for herself, uniquely fashioned; she intends to speak of the general condition and for all men and women.

To be sure, the decision to dedicate herself to this life work satisfied many intensely personal needs. Moreover, the "Representative Voice" that Emily Dickinson devised necessarily reflected the unique experiences of her own life; indeed, that Voice changed over the years, even as Dickinson herself changed and gained riper knowledge. Nonetheless, the fundamental, informing premise remained always the same: the correct context for her poetry was not narrow, but all-embracing; not personal, not "the particular series of events that made up the life of Emily Dickinson," but panoramic: "America—mid-nineteenth century," perhaps, or "Everywhere—All Times."

She confronted any number of practical problems. She understood very well that the greater part of America was moving away from the kind of world Amherst still preserved. Increasingly, America would be a nation of cities: Walt Whitman (whom she knew at least by reputation), a Long Island boy who grew up in Brooklyn, appeared ideally situated to speak to this new and burgeoning America. Emily Dickinson would appear to have been doubly handicapped, then, not merely by her sex, but also by the isolation of her experience. Perhaps that is why it is so difficult fully to credit her stated determination to become America's "Representative Voice." Yet her poetry only confirms the uncompromising assertion she made to Higginson. "*This is my letter to the World / That never wrote to Me— / The simple News that Nature told—With tender Majesty / Her Message is committed / To Hands I cannot see— / For love of Her—Sweet—countrymen— / Judge tenderly—of Me*" (#441). It is as if she were speaking here and now, to you or to me, magically alive and ardent (perhaps as her grandfather had been) with the spirit of vocation.

Although she did not have access to the crossroads of America, to the ports and cities and highways, she did have New England in her blood and bones. "*The Buttercup's, my Whim for Bloom— / Because, we're Orchard sprung— / . . . Without the Snow's Tableau / Winter, were lie—to me— / Be-*

cause I see—New Englandly—" (#285). To be "Orchard sprung" in New England at that time was to know Eden after the Fall: Eve's apple not only tasted, but accepted as a staple food. Mankind's accommodation to the freedom and peril that were the dual consequences of the Fall lay at the heart of one dominant strain in the American experience; and New England culture as Dickinson knew it, the last great re-animation of American Puritanism, was a final distillate of that strain. At this moment in America, a new kind of heroism was being invented in teeming New York, in the sprouting, sprawling, boasting Midwestern cities, and on the far plains where fortunes beckoned and money vied with piety for place in men's minds. Here in Amherst, however, a more ancient heroism was still waiting to be won.

Dickinson's rejection of faith in 1850 was not, as a modern reader might suppose, a renunciation of the belief that God exists: in some manner, she retained a deeply rooted conviction in the *existence* of God until the day she died; the terms of her belief fluctuated, but the flame of it was never quenched. What she rejected in 1850 was the *conventional definition of God's nature.* Hitchcock and the others urged hope upon their flock—enjoined them to believe that God was loving and benevolent, that despite the evidence of disease and death, God would lead the chosen into a joyous Eternal Life, that those beloved who had been separated by death would be united forever in the Hereafter. And it was this optimistic interpretation of God's character, this utter acceptance of the promises of Christ, to which Dickinson would not assent. When Emily Dickinson wrote Jane Humphrey in April 1850 that she was "standing alone in rebellion," her statement addressed a transcendent isolation. To be sure, friends and family and clergy all urged her to submit, but their insistence was not severe; she was in no manner shunned because of her independence. Rather, she was "alone" in the presence of Him Who wields ultimate Power. Without companion, without even a confidence in the promises of Christ to sustain her, Emily Dickinson determined to hunt out that immortal Divinity Who dwells silent and unchanging just beyond the world of appearances. And even a woman in the nineteenth century might undertake this epic challenge, might commit herself to heroism without ever leaving home: standing in Amherst, Emily Dickinson could look into the heart of Eternity.

Thus it was that she might speak as "Representative"—not merely for herself or for her time, but for all men and women and for all time. If the poet can stand bold in the face of truth, sooner or later all will seek her here, in Amherst. It avails not, time nor place—distance avails not. Are we not *all*, children of Eve, in some manner "Orchard sprung"? So Dickinson would claim. *"The Queen, discerns like me— / Provincially"* (#285).

In the province of God called Amherst, He made Himself known through the Bible and the practices of the Congregational Church.[3] He called men and women to Him in revivals, and His servants enjoined the congregation to emulate Jacob the wrestler. The Protestant tradition had for many centuries looked upon Jacob as a kind of Everyman figure:

The Lord when hee appeareth most familiarly to *Jacob,* hee exercises him with a wearisome wrestling. . . . Hee tosses and shakes him too and fro, and exercises him with fighting and struggling [*sic*] all the night long! . . . And in this is shadowed unto us, the manner of that victory, which the children of God obtain in their wrestlings, to wit, that it was such a victory as is not without a wound. . . . As it was with Jacob, so it is with all the true Israelites of God; wrestling abides them, and in wrestling they must be exercised.[4]

By Emily Dickinson's time, the model of Jacob had acquired new emphasis. The Bible tells us that Jacob obtained his inheritance not by right of birth, but by cunning; similarly, he acquired a covenant from God not through passive obedience to the Lord, but by means of active combat with Him. Moreover, Jacob was the first Biblical patriarch to win inheritance and covenant in such a way. Amherst Trinitarians held that each individual could play an essential and active role in his or her own salvation; therefore, they urged all hopeful Christians to exert a supreme spiritual effort to win faith and the chance for salvation; and they construed *Jacob's* wrestle with God as the archetypal model for every man and woman who sincerely strove for belief. So it was, then, that Jacob was everywhere in Dickinson's experience. In childhood she had heard his name invoked when the adults enjoined one another to embrace God's will; as a girl at Mount Holyoke, she herself had been instructed to wrestle as Jacob and thus to enjoy the coveted goal of confident faith. Even after her renunciation during the revival of 1850, she could scarcely forget him, so much were Jacob's name and legend woven into the process of conversion.

In the hours when she was not writing or working, his shadow might flicker across her imagination. For instance, she marked the passage in Vaughan's "Early Rising and Prayer" that recounts Jacob's struggle with the Lord:

> Serve God before the world, let him not go
> Until thou hast a blessing; then resign
> The whole unto him, and remember who
> Prevail'd by wrestling ere the sun did shine;
> Pour oil upon the stones and weep for thy sin,
> Then journey on, and have an eye to heaven.[5]

Idly, perhaps, one day while composing, Dickinson transcribed the angel's demand of triumphant Jacob on the back of one of the work sheets for her own verse: "Let me go for the Day breaketh."[6] Six of her poems are explicit recastings of the moment when Jacob struggled with the Lord—and many, many more touch lightly upon that unique moment by their use of the words "wrestle," "grapple," and "strive," each one of which, in Dickinson's world, carried the association of "a struggle with faith" or "a struggle with the Lord."[7]

The enigmatic verse "Two swimmers wrestled on the spar—" becomes a good deal more accessible when it is put into such a context. The notion that the two swimmers really are "two parts of a divided self," a reading that seemed intuitively sound, can now be grounded in the context of the artist's larger poetic mission. In Dickinson's day, the ceremonial moment when self was expected to "wrestle" against self was that moment in the revival (or even in an isolated conversion) when Jacob's wrestle with the Lord was ritually re-enacted. Traditional religion held that a Christian might *win* in this encounter only by submitting self to Christ in conversion. But Dickinson thought otherwise. "Self" was too high a price to pay, even for the hope of Eternal Life: thus in 1850, when she had turned away from God, she wrote to Jane Humphrey, "the world has been too precious for your poor—and striving sister." And it is Dickinson's contrary, *rebellious* interpretation of mankind's wrestle with belief and trust in God that this verse recounts: the swimmer who has chosen the world and turns to "land" is "smiling"; the swimmer who has turned his hope to God has become no more than an empty face with blinded eyes. The elements of separation and the threat to coherent identity that Dickinson's eye / face language so often conveys are indeed central to this poem. In the letters, the dangers had been construed at the individual level, potential dangers for Emily-Dickinson-the-woman. Now they have become universalized. To be sure, both the moral decision that is rendered by the course of the poem and the habitual modes of verbal expression that can be discovered in it are inextricably linked to the history of Dickinson's own experiences. Nonetheless, once she had achieved the beginnings of mastery in her art, she was able to move beyond the merely personal. Separation and isolation—random, cosmic threats to identity—these are the conditions that confront *all* human beings after the Fall. We are all cast away from God and mocked by the paradox that we must lose the autonomous self (through "beseeching" faith) if we are to gain even a chance for salvation. But most of all, we are wounded—wounded by the tribulations permitted by a Deity Who is indifferent to human suffering, and wounded finally and inevitably by death.[8]

Now, at a distance of so many years, it is no easy thing to recover the emotional force and complexity of this legend or its sense of immediacy and timeliness more than a century ago. Like many fabled events, Jacob's encounter with God was susceptible to many interpretations. Although it was primarily construed as that moment when man first strove with God to obtain the blessing of a covenant, the same text was also used to cite the danger of taking issue with received interpretations of the Bible—a practice called "wrestling Scripture."[9] Dickinson's creative imagination was not the only one to be captivated by the power and subtlety of Jacob's story: Melville realized that this archetypal struggle between man and God was pregnant with possible meanings, and so the restive hero from Genesis appears over and over again in Melville's work—in the poetry as the Master Singer, in *Moby Dick* as the unmasted, epic overreacher, and in *Israel Potter* as both wanderer and model for the confidence man.

One distinguished critic has even declared that Jacob is the prototype of the American poet. In an essay entitled "Religious Poetry in the United States," R. P. Blackmur makes a provocative assertion:

I would say . . . that it is the great wrestling tradition which has inhabited the great majority of religious poets since the Council of Trent, . . . a wrestling with God, with the self, with the conscience, and above all in our latter day with our behavior. . . . It is astonishing that we do not have poems called "The Place Peniel" and "The Sinew that Shrank"; for there is in this adventure of Jacob half the subject-matter of modern poetry. . . . What seem to be the beginnings of American religious poetry—Anne Bradstreet and Edward Taylor—illustrate the theme in its simple form as the versification of typical experiences and enthusiasms, of doctrine and behavior, where versification is a kind of rehearsal for an act or a role yet to be undertaken.[10]

Blackmur does not seem to know that the encounter between Jacob and the Lord served as archetypal model for New England Protestant conversions (at least in the middle years of the nineteenth century); nor does he attempt any correlation between the story of Jacob and the poetry of Emily Dickinson. However, if he had done so, he might have posited that in Dickinson's work the "rehearsal" of Bradstreet and Taylor was boldly taken forward, and that in Dickinson's hand, *poetry itself* had become the medium of epic encounter.

The world her gaze fell upon was replete with the consequences of divine power. If she had submitted to conversion, her vision of that world would have been "adjusted," and she would have discerned evidences of Christ's promises throughout the universe. Yet she had not submitted. She concurred in the belief that the created world retained signs of the nature of its Creator; having subjected God's handiwork to ruthless appraisal, however, she saw in it not hopeful promises, but shabby deceptions. Such was the "nature" that her poetry necessarily addressed.

Because Dickinson did not assent, even reluctantly, to God's dominion, she set herself apart from the great tradition of religious lyric. The ambition of her verse transcends the ambition of conventional Christian verse. Traditionally, the religious poet saw himself as inevitably subordinate to God. He might discover cunning new devices for singing God's grandeur, or he might

Emily, Austin, and Lavinia Dickinson
by O. A. Bullard
1840

Edward Dickinson
by O. A. Bullard
1840

Emily Norcross Dickinson
by O. A. Bullard
1840

View of Amherst, Massachusetts

Amherst Academy, Amity Street

Emily Elizabeth Dickinson
1847 or 1848

Austin Dickinson

Lavinia Dickinson
1852

The Edward Dickinson / Orris Bigelow House
North Pleasant Street, Amherst

dare to chant of God's darker and more frightening aspect, or he might even complain, resisting and resenting the rigors of God's discipline. Yet in all of these attitudes, the essential assumption remains unchanged: God is a divine Being; His essence lies beyond mankind's reach. Thus religious poetry may approximate praise or complaint, but it cannot hurl mortal beings into God's realm. The poet is unable to *compel* God to engage in discourse; he can "capture" God only insofar as God chooses to reveal Himself or to make the poet *His* instrument. Dickinson was content with none of these premises for poetry.

Her refusal of faith had not sprung from indifference. She accepted Jacob's wrestle with the Lord as a moment of unparalleled importance. In surprising and uncanny ways, this archetype even echoed elements central to her own personal experience. It was as if history had deliberately waited for this moment, the intersection of this unique life with this particular time and place in Christianity, so intimately was Jacob's legend fitted for Dickinson's telling.

To understand its unique aptness—even more, to understand the vision of the universe that impelled her to the vocation of poet—we must understand Jacob's wrestle as Emily Dickinson understood it. Genesis. 32:24–30 and 35:11, 13, "And Jacob was left alone. . . ."

The text is a tale of irreparable loss. In the early days of creation, God had walked the earth and mingled with man even as a Father might. Jacob's grandfather Abraham had strolled the heights with Him and received the gift of covenant in person: "God talked with him, saying, As for me, behold, my covenant is with thee, and thou shalt be a father of many nations" (Genesis 17:3–4). In those days women, too, could seek out the Lord if they wished to put a question to Him. Thus when Jacob's mother, Rebekah, felt the struggle of her twin boys, Jacob and Esau, even in the womb, "she went to inquire of the Lord," who told her of the fateful wrestlings to come (Genesis 25:22 ff). Although the Almighty Creator possessed fearsome power, He could be seen face to face; He would listen to our troubles and sorrows and complaints, and give us answers to our question. Now at this fateful moment, just as the sun rose over the Peniel Hills, Jacob confronted God the Father face to face; and it was the last time any human being would thus behold Him so long as men shall live and the earth survive. When the wrestle had been concluded, "God went up from Him." Our Heavenly Father never again returned.

In Emily Dickinson's judgment, this primal scene was the turning point for all subsequent history, and she reckoned all human life as scarred by the God Who had withdrawn from us to prowl behind the veil of the visible world. Her belief could extend to the fact of His existence, but search as she might, she could never know His nature save by indirection—and all the ills of human life pointed to some inscrutable force of destruction and annihilation. What are we to make of the Creature's insistence that we address Him as "Our Father"; what are we to do when (like some cruel parody of a Master Poet) He hides Himself so pitilessly only to command that mankind find Him out and affirm that He is benevolent? "*I know that He exists. / Some-where—in Silence— / He has hid his rare life / From our gross eyes. / 'Tis an in-stant's play. / 'Tis a fond Ambush— / Just to make Bliss / Earn her own surprise! / But—should the play / Prove piercing earnest— / Should the glee—glaze— / In Death's—stiff—stare— / Would not the fun / Look too expensive! / Would not the jest— / Have crawled too far!*" (#338)

After 1856, when Austin submitted to conversion, all the other members of Emily Dickinson's family had professed their confidence in the promises of Christ and the new birth to come. For the poet, however, the fact that she could never glimpse the Face behind the veil made even the process of assigning a name to God problematic. How does one *name* an absence—and what credence can one give to that "promised" resurrection when the Author of this unlikely pledge remains unseen? "*My faith that Dark adores—,*" Dickinson wrote with bitter irony, "*Which from it's solemn abbeys / Such resurrection pours*" (#7). Sometimes Dickinson resorted to that only thing in nature which is a darkness visible, understanding full well the malignity such an epithet might imply. All her family was religious, "except me—," she explained to Higginson, "and address an Eclipse, every morning—whom they call their 'Father.' " [11] This dilemma of naming such a God provided the impetus for a new and separate vocabulary, and certain words accrued special import from Dickinson's way of construing this disappearance of the Lord: "eclipse" and "veil" intimated concealment and exclusiveness, a refusal to engage face-to-face communication—for God, a hostile withdrawal; for Dickinson the poet, a retaliatory interposition of her verse between self and God's annihilating power (because the Voice immortalized in the verse was exempt from God's agent, death).

Nor was the Incarnation of Jesus Christ construed as a remedy for our plight: the promise of Christ seemed as distant from her as the epoch so many thousands of years earlier when God the Father had walked among us. Christ's Resurrection was not assurance that mankind or some portion of it would be joyfully united with God in Heaven; rather, Christ's rising from the dead was a searing reiteration of Jacob's loss in Genesis, and the implication of this second desertion was more desolating still. It spelled the loss even of hope. "*If He dissolve—then—there is nothing—more— / Eclipse—at Mid-night— / It was dark—before— / Sunset—at Easter— / Blindness—on the Dawn— / Faint Star of Bethlehem— / Gone Down!*" (#236)

The determination to confront the full barrenness of human fate was one of the principal sources of Dickinson's poetry—not a personal grievance, but a universal tragedy. "*Parting is all we know of heaven,*" she wrote bleakly, "*And all we need of hell*" (#1732). In one sense, there was an element of terrible fulfillment in her vision. The language of "eye" and "face" had spoken of loss and anguish since the earliest letters of her girlhood; now, at last, she had discovered a cosmic event commensurate with her furious passion, God's desertion of mankind. It was, withal, an horrific discovery. If God's moral order is but sham, what confidence can any of us repose in His natural order—or in any of the orders of life upon which our fragile existence depends? *"Sunset at Night—is natural—* / *But Sunset on the Dawn* / *Reverses Nature—Master—* / *So Midnight's—due—at Noon.* / *Eclipses be—predicted—* / *And Science bows them in—* / *But do one face us suddenly—* / *Jehovah's Watch— is wrong."* (#415). When the "face" of God shows naught but "Eclipse" and the disorder of Jehovah's "Watch" is not merely a derangement of hours, but a lapse in that divine watchfulness standing between humanity and oblivion, then not even the integrity of personal identity is safe from annihilation.

Indeed, Jacob's wrestle with the Lord demonstrates that God is primarily a Destroyer and not a Preserver, for when the combat shifts against Him, He uses the force of the Godhead to wound: "And when he saw that he prevailed not against him, he touched the hollow of his thigh; and the hollow of Jacob's thigh was out of joint, as he wrestled with him." God's touch is not vitalizing, but injuring, a dislocating thrust to the groin—a castrating motion to maim and unman. Melville's Ahab, crazed in his attempt to "dismember the dismemberer," is an American Jacob, "touched" by divine violence and determined to seek out and challenge again and again until mortal combat be done: "To the last I grapple with thee"—the final speech he flings upon the wind. And Ahab bears the scar of his first wrestle, the mark of mutilation: "It resembled that perpendicular seam sometimes made in the straight, lofty trunk of a great tree, when the upper lightning tearingly darts down it, and without wrenching a single twig, peels and grooves out the bark from top to bottom, ere running off into the soil, leaving the tree still greenly alive, but branded." It is not the reassuring lesson of Emerson's *Nature*, then, that informs Dickinson's poetry, but Ahab's lesson—the lesson of Jacob. *"Nature— sometimes sears a Sapling—* / *Sometimes—scalps a Tree—* / *Her Green People recollect it* / *When they do not die—"* (#314). Heaven itself cannot be won without the mark of God's malice. *"How many <u>Bullets</u> bearest?* / *Hast Thou the Royal scar?* / *Angels! Write 'Promoted'* / *On this Soldier's brow!"* (#73)

Jacob's encounter with God signals a conclusion, an end to the era when God walked among men. Yet it marks a beginning as well: Jacob's victory has won him a new identity and a new name: "Thy name shall be called no more Jacob, but Israel": subjugator and progenitor, Jacob becomes a prototype for heroism; "Israel" means "he who strives with God."

In the telling of this legend, the framers of the Old Testament perpetuated ancient myths concerning the power of a name: one's name was a talisman of the role he was expected to play, so Jacob's new name signified a fundamental change of identity—a new "self" empowered to exercise the authority he had won. This attitude toward names pervades the Bible; however, in the case of Jacob, an additional complexity enriches the text. In the original Hebrew, the term used in these passages for "wrestle" is "abhaq," and this is the only place in the Scriptures that the word "abhaq" is used. Now the *word* "abhaq" is a play upon the *word* "Jacob"—a pun, almost an anagram for it: to be a Jacob is to seek martial engagement (through wrestling); and the quintessential attribute of this hero is cunningly compressed into the name itself. The clergymen of Amherst could understand the importance of naming. They could appreciate as well the complex compression of language that characterized the interplay between Jacob's name and his deeply rooted inclination to strive for authority and seek out disputation. A familiarity with Hebrew was one of the most important marks of learning among these men of God (and it was, after all, the desire to establish a professorship of *languages* at the Amherst Academy that began the endeavor out of which Amherst College was born). Yet it was not necessary to be a clergyman in order to know about such plays upon the word: sermons and serious Biblical instruction illuminated the intricate web of meanings that a short passage like this one might contain. Melville's epic overreacher, Ahab, carries the imprint of his complex destiny in *his* name: Ahab was the name of a wicked king of the Hebrew nation; however, "Ahab" is also an anagram of "abhaq," and Melville's epic challenger is, paradoxically, a "Jacob" figure as well.[12]

Emerson called the poet a "namer," and Dickinson's understanding of such power was almost certainly reinforced by this assertion in his widely read essay "The Poet." However, Emerson's influence came late. The foundation for Dickinson's work, her most enduring conviction about the uses to which language might be put, derived from her own earliest personal experience—experience that was reinforced by the Trinitarian culture of the town of Amherst during her formative years, by instruction from teachers who understood the complexity of Biblical compression, and by the regular use of a Lexicon that insisted upon the moral force of the word.

The outcome of Jacob's wrestle is a prize: God awards it to him just before He retires into Heaven, nevermore to confront humanity in person. In some measure, perhaps, the nature of the award speaks directly to the loss of God's presence. "Be fruitful and multiply; a nation and a company of nations shall be of thee, and kings shall come out of thy loins." There will be new life to replace the lost Deity; what is more, the new life will carry an entitlement to vast royal wealth. For Jacob many eons ago, the spiritual component of this encounter with God was balanced by material rewards. He sired twelve sons; they matured to rule over the twelve powerful tribes of Israel; and at the height of their glory, the Hebrews built the shining city of Jerusalem. Revivals of Emily Dickinson's day repeatedly invoked this image of golden triumph—looking backward to resurrect Jerusalem the golden from the Old

Testament, looking forward to anticipate the glorious gem-graced kingdom of God to come in Revelation.

Dickinson, too, would claim that there was a great estate and golden glory to be won; however, in *her* formulations, this prize went not to patriarchs, but to poets.

Even her youthful discussions of poets and poetry—the remarks about Poe and Longfellow—postulated a royal station for the one who could demonstrate mastery over the word. Once she had accepted the vocation of poetry herself, she laid claim not only to golden glory, but to the second of Jacob's rewards as well: the possibility of generating life. With the "Breath" of her verse she would vie with the God of Genesis Who had breathed life into dust and made man. "*For this—accepted Breath— / Through it—compete with Death— / The fellow cannot touch this Crown— / By it—my title take—*" (#195). Indeed, Dickinson exercised the power of Jacob's inheritance to its uttermost. She claimed these rights, and she endeavored to force God to acknowledge His loss—even as Jacob had coerced a blessing. The Old King must yield to this parvenue, and the majestic word will no longer be God's, but the poet's. "*Ah, what a royal sake / To my necessity—stooped down! / . . . Get Gabriel—to tell—the royal syllable— / Get Saints—with new— unsteady tongue— / To say what trance below / Most like their glory show— / Fittest the Crown!*" (#195)

Here in Jacob's legend there is a beginning, then, not only for such as would *act* heroically, but also for those who pursue the heroic quest by wrestling with the word and creating even as God had created, by sowing Logos. Jacob the wrestler was a model for the poet-pugilist; Jacob's struggle was a starting point for Dickinson as artist. Sometime in 1859 she transcribed these words:

> *A little East of Jordan,*
> *Evangelists record,*
> *A Gymnast and an Angel*
> *Did wrestle long and hard—*
>
> *Till morning touching mountain—*
> *And Jacob, waxing strong,*
> *The Angel begged permission*
> *To Breakfast—to return—*
>
> *Not so, said cunning Jacob!*
> *"I will not let thee go*
> *Except thou bless me," —Stranger!*
> *The which acceded to—*

> *Light swung the silver fleeces*
> *"Peniel" Hills beyond,*
> *And the bewildered Gymnast*
> *Found he had worsted God!*

(#59)

This poem subjects the Biblical event to the reordering vision of Dickinson's own language. The tone that dominates most of the poem is deceptively moderate; only at the conclusion does the magnitude of this transaction become evident. But, then, *God's* method has been most often to offer palliatives in the face of horror. So at first the dawning "fleeces" recall us to God's promise that we shall be washed in the blood of the lamb. Yet, as the poem implies, these fleeces of Peniel are in reality no precious prize, no golden fleeces for which Jason journeyed far. They are, correctly seen, the mark of a falling away: our golden age, the age when God moved among men, has concluded, and a lesser age of silver has begun.

The fleeces also remind us of Jacob's saving resourcefulness. Jacob "fleeced" his brother Esau by pulling the wool over their father's eyes. Jacob had followed his twin Esau into the world, and thus it seemed impossible for him to obtain the blessing of the firstborn. But Jacob was unwilling to accept his fate passively: he purchased his brother's birthright for a mess of potage and deceived his blind father by throwing a goat's hide over his own smooth skin; thus did he master an apparently irrevocable loss. The implications of this maneuver had a personal meaning for Emily Dickinson, who had been excluded from the family's quest for honor while her older brother was accepted as "natural" heir to the task of perpetuating the Dickinson family's reputation. Yet the fact that Jacob was an artful strategist is most significant because it can be applied even to our universal plight. Once the wrestle had been concluded, God became forever afterward a camouflaged antagonist. Jacob's wrestle, conducted as it was face to face, could not show subsequent nations how to fight a divine Antagonist who has removed Himself from sight. Yet the "fleeces" in Dickinson's poem recall Jacob's earlier resourcefulness and cunning. And all human beings can turn to such talents as these to counter the new dangers of a Divinity Who has hidden Himself.

It is impossible to emphasize too strongly the importance of the transition that took place at Peniel: God concealed His face and gave us a *word* in its place—humankind's first tragic fall into language. And Dickinson's poem recalls the immediate effects of this transaction, too.

Moses, who followed close upon the time of Jacob, chafed under the prohibition against seeing God's face, and he was wooed by the insinuating promises of a disembodied voice. "I am the LORD," God declared, while hiding His face, "And I appeared unto Abraham, unto Isaac, and unto Jacob, by the name of God Almighty, but by my name JEHOVAH was I not known to them" (Exodus 6:2–3). God has disappeared, but He has left words in His wake and *signs* as well (so Dickinson's poem clearly suggests). Jacob's "bewildered" condition reminds us of God's annihilating power: for God decreed that Moses and the chosen people should wander forty years in the wilderness before entering the Promised Land; and ever thereafter when He discovered a backsliding among the Jews, He threatened to scorch the earth—"I will make thee a wilderness, and cities which are not inhabited" (Jeremiah 22:6). Yet the "silver fleeces" that swing (perhaps "lightly") seem a sign that prefigures God's guidance in the wilderness; for although He consigned them to wander, God placed a pillar of cloud by day and a pillar of fire by night to lead them in their long flight from Egypt. Destroyer and Preserver—God's ambiguous nature seems delicately poised at the conclusion of the poem. Yet even in this apparent balance, there is nonetheless a reiteration of wounding. For the "Light" itself, construed as a force—to swing the clouds, to lead mankind throughout our entire earthly captivity— is both an evidence that the Father exists and a reassertion of the finality with which He has withdrawn from us forever.

Having removed His person, God leaves only fitful glimmerings of His power. "Thou canst not see my face," God told Moses, "for there shall no man see me, and live" (Exodus 33:20). He was a God of consuming brightness, and when He ceased to walk the earth, the most usual sign of his presence was light. Yet even this talisman of God was wounding: Jacob's wrestle with God on the road to Seir was reiterated many centuries later by Paul's encounter with the Lord on the road to Damascus. Both men unexpectedly confront God; both are wounded; but because God departed from the earth long before the age of the Apostles, Paul is wounded not by God's *person*, but by His illumination.

The Bible tells us that Paul, who had not yet been converted to the teachings of Christ, was confounded by a great "light from Heaven." Astonished and blinded, Paul fell to the ground; and even as he fell, he heard an angry voice crying out of the Heavens, "why persecutest thou me?" (Acts 9:4) Trembling with weakness and fear, Paul was three days without sight, regaining it only after he had submitted himself entirely to the Lord's direction. Thus what remains to mankind, even after the Redeemer has come and gone, is still a God Who wounds—a grand, random ambuscade, a "*Truth*" that must "*dazzle gradually / Or every man be blind—*" (#1129). The gift of enlightenment is *blinding*, then; and in some measure it was precisely this, the *blinding* truth of God, that Dickinson was urged to accept almost two thousand years after the Redeemer had come and gone. Whenever an individual had been converted, her *sight* would be "adjusted" so that she could "*see*" the evidences of God's promises throughout creation. After Saint Paul's sight had been restored, God asserted, Paul "is a chosen vessel unto me, to bear my name before the Gentiles, and kings, and the children of Israel: for I will show him how great things he must suffer for my name's sake" (Acts 9:15–16). Paul regained his "sight," but he had lost his "I" to faith. Ravished by God, Paul was no longer his own man, but now merely a "vessel" of the Lord. And such was the state urged upon Emily Dickinson's generation as well.

The gift of "enlightenment" will be blinding: so it was for Saint Paul; so it was still in 1850 for God's people in Amherst. What is more, they risked not merely mutilation; they risked the autonomy of the self entire, that eye/I which is both vision and identity.

God's sun burns steady, day upon day—the emblem of authority and the visible power of generation. The hero-poet must scan it. To look full upon the face of God's powers is to risk mutilation; yet only by such risk may a challenge take place—autonomy and integrity be saved. Mad Ahab understood the significance of the "'diver sun—slow dived from noon. . . . I'd strike the sun if it insulted me,'" he vows. Eschewing rant, Dickinson's poetry often issues from the dread security of accepted agony, that "*Quartz contentment*" (#341) of relinquished hopes and existential isolation, "*Contented as the Eye / Upon the Forehead of a Bust— / That knows—it cannot see*" (#305).

The silver fleeces that cast their glow upon Jacob's Peniel Hills herald the breaking of day, the demonstration of an "eastering" impulse. That, too, is a sign, or so we have been led to suppose—the promise of a reunion that will heal the schism between God and man, of a time when the Word will again become flesh, when man and God once again look upon each other face to face. The sun rises; if Jesus, Son of our Heavenly Father, truly rose into Heaven, then perhaps we, too, will rise. Yet when Dickinson looked for confirmation of such a promise, she found only the leavings of some terrible, transcendent butchery.

One Sunday in April 1856, Emily Dickinson wrote to her cousin and intimate friend, John Graves. The rest of the family had gone to church, but she had remained behind to look for God.

You remember the crumbling wall that divides us from Mr. Sweetser—and the crumbling elms and evergreens—and *other* crumbling things—that spring, and fade, and cast their bloom within a simple twelvemonth. . . . Much that is gay—have I to show, if you were with me, John, upon this April grass—then there are *sadder* features—here and there, *wings* half gone to dust, that fluttered so, last year—a mouldering plume, an empty house, in which a bird resided. Where last year's flies, their errand ran, and last year's *crickets fell!* We, too, are flying—fading, John—and the song "here lies," soon upon lips that love us now—will have hummed and ended.

To live, and die, and mount again in triumphant body, and *next* time to try the upper air—is no schoolboy's theme!

It is a jolly thought to think that we can be Eternal—when air and earth are *full* of lives that are gone—and done—and a conceited thing indeed, this promised Resurrection![13]

"Conceited"—perhaps Dickinson meant merely to suggest that mankind inflated its own importance in supposing that it alone among all of God's creation should be raised from the "crumbling things—that spring, and fade, and cast their bloom within a simple twelvemonth." Perhaps (it is a blasphemous thought) God Himself manifests His own unwholesome pride through this magician's trick of striking down only to demonstrate that He can triumphantly raise from the dead. Or perhaps Dickinson meant to imply both meanings, with the necessary admonition that God's *disclosure* of these meanings has proceeded by way of signs and metaphors all compressed into the "conceits" of God's communication.

If God's absence is compensated by words and signs, these are forms of compensation that merely extend His propensity for wounding; they work not by bruising our bodies, but by insinuating falsehoods into our beliefs—revising our "sight" so that we can accept His mutilations without complaint. God urges us to seek Him, but when "enlightenment" comes, it is knifelike and cold—"*a certain Slant of light, / Winter Afternoons*—" (#258). Its song is but the "oppression" of a funeral dirge. Nor does it really clarify our understanding: God still refuses to loosen the Seal of Revelation; instead, He inflicts the "Seal Despair"—the injury that leaves no physical traces, "*But internal difference, / Where the Meanings, are*—" (#258). And this, too, invades the coherence of the self: the light may shine, quick and sharp; we close our eyes, but the after-image lingers on the retina. God's prevarications and false promises call beckoningly to us: they offer consolation and order; we try to turn away from these false allures, and still the mind has been violated and sullied—even if only by the desire for hope.

The auctioneer of parting "brings his Hammer down"; the "*Faint* Star of Bethlehem" has "*Gone Down*" from the firmament even as the children of Israel went down into Egypt-land and captivity. And we remain—captive, unransomed, and still bereft even unto the present day.

Emily Dickinson determined to devote herself to the vocation of poetry. Yet every form of usual religious poetry celebrated a God Whose ways she had come to condemn. Milton offered the mode of grand epic response to the struggle between God and His rebel-angels, a model that presumes that the poet will "justifie the wayes of God to men." The Psalmist urges the prototypical Christian lyric upon the artist, a jubilation over the Lord's creation and a submission to His rule: "Make a joyful noise unto God, all ye lands: Sing forth the honor of his name: make his praise glorious" (Psalms 66:1–2). And Keats recasts the Psalmist's exclamation into secular terms by transforming the act of rejoicing into the ceaseless rapture of an "immortal Bird"; the art of singing, then, becomes a spontaneous effusion—"pouring forth thy soul abroad / In such an ecstasy!" Yet Dickinson could not temper her insight to accept these traditional modes: how can we "make a joyful noise unto God" when God's creatures "crumble" and "moulder" and "fade" and "fall" on a sunny April Sunday? How can we "justifie the wayes of God to men" or sing forth the "honor" of God's name when His signs are deceits and His promises are belied by unending spectacles of death? God's wounding extends throughout creation—affecting even the music His singers may make. He invalidates joyful noise or Keatsian rapture; His every motion denies the justification for Miltonic Christian epic. If He could, God would rob us of song altogether.

Sometime in 1866 Emily Dickinson transcribed these lines; they function to refute the informing poetics of Milton, of Keats, and of the Psalmist; and they were written, with ironic fittingness, on part of a tradesman's bill:

> His Bill is clasped—his Eye forsook—
> His Feathers wilted low—
> The Claws that clung, like lifeless Gloves
> Indifferent hanging now—
> The Joy that in his happy Throat
> Was waiting to be poured
> Gored through and through with Death, to be
> Assassin of a Bird
> Resembles to my outraged mind
> The firing in Heaven,
> On Angels—squandering for you
> Their Miracles of Tune—
>
> (#1102)

What lesson, then, does such a universe imply, and to what use must we put our appalling knowledge? Melville saw the world as Job had seen it—as the work of a Creator whose voice echoes with thunder and whose hand has fashioned the behemoth and the grinning leviathan. Dickinson saw the same vision domestically rendered: young women with death etched into their pale, tubercular beauty; the crisis of pneumonia—fever, labored breathing, and then silence; the baby who dies without having been named; scarlet fever, typhoid, dysentery—the watches of the women alone at night. Death was always the same, by sea or by land: sometimes easier at sea, when the body could be slipped quietly into the water—certainly easier than midsummer putrefaction, buried in haste for fear of the stench.

The customary lesson of such spectacles was submission. In *Moby Dick*, Father Mapple extracted a Jobean lesson from the tale of Jonah: " 'If we obey God, we must disobey ourselves; and it is in this disobeying ourselves, wherein the hardness of obeying God consists.' " In Amherst, did not Susan

Gilbert submit to conversion in August 1850, directly after her sister's death in childbirth? And in the earliest ages of mankind, the original model for this lesson was Abraham, grandfather of Jacob and founder of the original covenant.

God had made His covenant not with Abraham alone, but also with the sons of Abraham's wife, and with all the generations to follow them. Abraham had no child by Sarah, his wife—only the handmaiden's son, Ishmael—and Sarah was beyond the age of childbearing. But God promised a miracle to Abraham: "Sarah thy wife shall bear thee a son indeed; and thou shalt call his name Isaac: and I will establish my covenant with him for an everlasting covenant, and with his seed after him" (Genesis 17:19). In time, it came to pass as God had said, and Abraham walked in God's way and praised His name. Nonetheless, God devised an experiment to test Abraham's obedience, asking from him the only thing that would make the covenantal promise void and meaningless—the life of Isaac, who was to inherit the covenant and sire sons to inherit from him in their turn. Abraham had been a doubting and defiant man before, had reared his own will up against the Lord's. Now God demanded absolute submission. And in this extremity, Abraham disobeyed his own will and prepared to submit to the will of the Lord. Then God did "tempt Abraham, and said unto him . . . Take now thy son, thine only son Isaac, whom thou lovest, . . . and offer him . . . for a burnt offering" (Genesis 22:1–2). Dickinson underlines the lesson of this event with bitter hymnal cadence. "*Not a hesitation— / Abraham complied— / Flattered by Obeisance / Tyranny demurred— / Isaac—to his children / Lived to tell the tale— / Moral— with a Mastiff / Manners may prevail*" (#1317). So Isaac lived to beget Jacob, who heard the tale of God's experiment with Abraham and Isaac. And in his own time Jacob grew to manhood and wrestled with the same savage Divinity. However, Jacob did not yield, but "prevailed." And only Jacob's story stands against all these other lessons.

The hero who would retain autonomy and integral identity and the poet who construes the task of singing in heroic terms—such as these must return to the legend of Jacob to discover a model.

The wrestler can bring forth new life. Dickinson saw that it was so. In a letter to Elizabeth Holland in 1859, just after the birth of Mrs. Holland's son, Dickinson wrote, "I pray for the tenants of that holy chamber, the wrestler, and the wrestled for. I pray for the distant father's heart, swollen, happy heart."[14] Mr. Holland's heart may have been "swollen," as Dickinson states; however, it was swollen not with progeny to be issued forth, but only with happiness over the fecundity of his wife. The poet takes this capacity of women one step further: the poet is that mortal by whom both the Flesh and the World are made Word—thus "reborn" into a life beyond time's effacement.

Yet if the poet wants to do more even than to create a permanent Voice beyond the reach of fleshly decay—if the poet wants to wound *God*, even as humanity has been wounded by this abandoning "Father"—she must find some way to reach beyond material reality. The world we know stands already finished and complete, its Author having vanished to prowl behind its veil. We see Him not, but encounter only His mask. Ahab refused to accept the finality of God's retreat and required some direct, physical match. " 'All visible objects . . . are but as pasteboard masks,' " he rants. " 'If man will strike through the mask! How can the prisoner reach outside except by thrusting through the wall!' " And Ahab was crucified upon the back of the broad leviathan—grim mockery of his profane ignorance. No human being can penetrate the mask. Still, Ahab's fury captures every man's rage at the absence of the Divinity, and in shaping his rebel, Melville surely hoped to create a Representative spokesman for this central human anguish.

Dickinson's hero-poet confronted two dilemmas: to seek out the hidden God so that an attack might be mounted; and to find some weapon adequate to pitch against the mighty force of the Godhead. As solution to both of these, Dickinson returned to the power of the Word.

We can never reach God directly: Ahab's lesson teaches us this much; but so, too, does the lesson of Moses, of Paul, and of every man who has followed in the wake of the fateful sunrise that shone upon Jacob's Peniel Hills. It is an inescapable truth: the Creator has vanished behind the mask of His world. But He is also lodged *in* that mask. The material world is only dust reshaped; the meaningful world of spiritual truth lies in the significance we attribute to the components of the material world. And here is where the fusion of Maker and mask occurs. God exercises dominion over us while we are in the world only insofar as we accept *His* definition of the meaning of it—adjust our vision to "see" the evidences of Christ's promises and use language correctly to "name" these promises and to affirm our faith in and submission to the God we cannot apprehend directly. To this end God gave us a world of types and emblems and signs; and the words and phrases that name these constitute a language of immense power, for it extends beyond the immanent world to touch the Divine. Thus even if mankind cannot wrestle with God directly, face to face, there is still this one area from which God dare not retreat lest He lose dominion over us altogether. Dickinson grasped this vulnerability of the Lord, the exposure He must risk because of His desire to retain humanity in His thrall. She saw, too, that because of this weakness in God's relationship to us, mankind is enabled to seek Him out for combat.

Some of God's weapons can never be turned against Him. Yet insofar as words can be used as the force to bind us to God, they have as well the contrary capacity to sunder those bonds. If we are empowered by a religiously inflected language to identify not only material objects but spiritual truths, then the poet can wreak vengeance upon the Deity by exposing His frauds and renaming the transcendent meaning of the world so as to reveal the true relationship between the Lord and His subjects. By this prodigious act of usurpation, the poet will challenge God's claim to sovereignty; eventually, through the act of *re-creation,* the poet may even wrest dominion from the Deity altogether. The metaphor that informs this daring adventure—that fusion of parturition and epic challenge—is arrogant; perhaps (like the language that informs God's activities) it is necessarily "conceited." But if it is, it sweeps even nature before it—mimetic of the hero-poet's bold enterprise. "*Musicians wrestle everywhere—* / *All day—among the crowded air* / *I hear the silver strife—* / *And—waking—long before the morn—* / *Such transport breaks upon the town* / *I think it that 'New Life'!*" (#157)

The poet begins in a world corrupted by the deceitful *mythos* of a fraudulent Divinity. The poet turns the force of God's myth-laden language *against itself,* so that the Creator may be wounded just as He sought to wound mankind. In this colossal wrestle with the Lord, the poet purges God's language, even as Jesus purged the merchants from the Temple, and the poet sings Truth. And in all of these deeds, the poet works in isolation—self-creating and self-sustaining. Other craftsmen, other artisans of the word, may look toward God, our Father, for comfort and support and enlightenment. They may seek to "justifie" the ways of God to man, or they may plead with God to "batter" the heart. Yet such postures reveal that these artisans are only children after all, seeking a parent's blessing. The poet must stand alone, and the poet's word shall be *itself* a blessing.

Emily Dickinson died in May 1886. Sometime during this her last, lingering spring, she wrote to Higginson, pre-empting at the conclusion of her life even the power of God to bless: "Audacity of Bliss, said Jacob to the Angel 'I will not let thee go except *I* bless *thee*'—Pugilist and Poet, Jacob was correct."[15]

Part Three ◆ *Pugilist and Poet*

My God, my God, . . . thou art a figurative, a metaphorical God . . . a God in whose words there is such a height of figures, such voyages, such peregrinations to fetch remote and precious metaphors, such extensions, such spreadings, such curtains of allegories, such third heavens of hyperboles, so harmonious elocutions, so retired and so reserved expressions, so commanding persuasions, so persuading commandments, such sinews even in thy milk, and such things in thy words, as all profane authors seem of the seed of the serpent that creeps, thou art the Cove that flies. . . . Neither art thou thus a figurative, a metaphorical God in thy word only, but thy works, too. The style of thy works, the phrase of thine actions, is metaphorical. . . . Neither didst thou speak and work in this language only in the time of thy prophets; but since thou spokest in thy Son it is so too. How often, how much more often, doth thy Son call himself a way, and a light, and a gate, and a vine, and bread, than the Son of God, or of man? How much oftener doth he exhibit a metaphorical Christ, than a real, a literal?

—*John Donne,* <u>*Devotions,*</u> *#xix*

In placid hours well-pleased we dream
Of many a brave unbodied scheme,
But form to lend, pulsed life create,
What unlike things must meet and mate:
A flame to melt—a wind to freeze;
Sad patience—joyous energies;
Humility—yet pride and scorn;
Instinct and study; love and hate;
Audacity—reverence. These must mate,
And fuse with Jacob's mystic heart,
To wrestle with the angel—Art.

—*Herman Melville*

I ◆ The Voice

Only one photograph of Emily Dickinson exists, and it is a poor one. A daguerreotype taken when she was about seventeen, it shows an awkward, skinny girl holding her body stiffly. In repose, the face is plain, and it reveals little hint of the animation and wit that the family members all attested to, little of Dickinson's intelligence and power of mind, little of her mischievous, irreverent humor. Probably Emily Dickinson herself felt that the picture failed to capture any essential element of self, for when Higginson explicitly requested a photograph of her, she sidled into prevarication and told him that none had ever been taken. She wanted him to know her through her writing—the poetry and letters—and in the end he was forced to accept her on her own terms. The path prescribed for Higginson has become the paradigm for subsequent generations. Emily Dickinson led such an unremarkable, quiet life that few details of her day-to-day existence survive. Principally, she must be known through her written remains. The extant photograph has the quality of a memento; it satisfies a certain curiosity for many readers; however, few feel it has captured the real Emily Dickinson. The *real* Emily Dickinson resides in the poetry. Life has been supplanted by art.

Indeed, given the degree to which life has been supplanted by art in Emily Dickinson's case, it is astonishing how many of her audience feel that somehow they know her personally. This disarming intimacy is, perhaps, the central paradox of Dickinson's achievement. Hundreds of thousands of readers have responded not merely to her superb verbal artistry, but to a felt presence, her "self." How can this be?

Poets are often the best guides to Dickinson's work, and poets are uniquely qualified to comprehend the extraordinary vitality that invests her mere words-upon-the-page with personality and life. Archibald MacLeish addresses this puzzle by describing the "Voice" of the verse. No one can read Emily Dickinson's work, MacLeish remarks, "without perceiving that he is not so much reading as being spoken to."

There is a curious energy in the words and a tone like no other most of us have ever heard. . . .

Breath is drawn and there are words that will not leave you time to watch her coming toward you. Poem after poem—more than a hundred and fifty of them—begins with the word "I," the talker's word. . . .

And ... the voice ... not only speaks but speaks to *you*. We are accustomed in our time—unhappily accustomed, I think—to the poetry of the overheard soliloquy, the poetry written by the poet to himself or a little group of the like-minded who can be counted on in advance to "understand." ...

But [Dickinson's] poems ... were never written to herself. The voice is never a voice over-heard. It is a voice that speaks to us almost a hundred years later with such an urgency, such an immediacy, that most of us are half in love with this girl. ...

There is nothing more paradoxical in the whole history of poetry, to my way of thinking, than Emily Dickinson's commitment of that live voice to a private box full of pages and snippets tied together with little loops of thread.[1]

The "problem of publication" is a necessary consideration for all who study Dickinson's work. Why did she not publish; did she *want* to publish and fail; is her inability to get poetry into print the sign of an unreceptive society, or is it some symptom of a neurotic nature? Such questions must be entertained, but they are not really exhaustive. Moreover, the problem of publication is largely extrinsic to the poetry. What demands our full analytic attention is the Voice of the verse, as MacLeish so rightly suggests—the energy and vitality of it, the reader's sense of being in touch, not with an artful set of words, but with another human being, insistent and intense. It is the creation of this Voice that is the great wonder. And the implications of Dickinson's failure to publish during her lifetime are magnified and rendered significant by the conversational imperative of her poetry. (What if her work had never been found—had even been destroyed?) The consigning of "that *live voice* to a private box full of pages and snippets" is what engages readers' sympathies and anxieties. It is like a burial alive.

How are we to understand the process by which that remarkable, importunate Voice came into being?

Examining the events that constituted the poet's adult life simply compounds the dilemma: there is no "tragedy" sufficient to account for the force of the verse, and her daily existence was so simple that even the usual rages and passions of ordinary life seem to have been largely excluded from it. Only two known crises punctuated her adult life—eye trouble that became acute between 1861 and 1865, after which time it seems to have abated, and the death of her father in June 1874. Both were bruising not merely because they were traumatic in and of themselves, but because they reawakened the fears, failures, and unhappy memories of her childhood. The first of these, her eye disorder, occurred while she was at the height of her creative powers.

All three Dickinson children suffered from recurrent eye disease (as did their mother); Austin's eyesight seems to have been worse than Vinnie's, and Emily suffered the most serious episodes of failed vision.[2] Austin and Vinnie do not seem to have been emotionally distressed by the weakness of their eyes and the need to rest them from time to time; however, Emily panicked when recourse to the written word was denied her. In her second letter to Higginson, written in April 1862, she speaks of "a terror—since September—I could tell to none—and so I sing, as the Boy does by the Burying Ground—because I am afraid."[3] For a long time critics supposed that this "terror" was some disappointment in love. Common sense in some measure argued against such an inference: she scarcely knew Higginson at the time of this letter, and it would be astonishing to find her alluding to such an intimate matter in so early a note. Moreover, "terror" is a curious word to use about a broken love affair: "loss" or "disappointment" would surely be more apt. When the letters she wrote to Joseph Lyman were discovered, they put such romantic speculations to rest: her fear had nothing to do with blighted affections; she had begun to experience periods of severely impaired vision. "Some years ago I had a woe," Dickinson wrote,

the only one that ever made me tremble. It was a shutting of all the dearest ones of time, the strongest friends of the soul—BOOKS[.] The medical man said avaunt ye books tormentors, he also said "down, thought, & plunge into her soul." He might as well have said, "Eyes be blind", "heart be still" [sic]. So I had eight weary months of Siberia.

Well do I remember the music of the welcome home. . . . Going home I flew to the shelves and devoured the luscious passages. I thought I should tear the leaves out as I turned them. Then I settled down to a willingness for all the rest to go but William Shakespear [sic]. Why need we Joseph read anything else but him.[4]

It is impossible to know exactly when the illness began. Probably the most severe symptoms first appeared in the fall of 1861 (though milder trouble with her vision may have begun even before this time). Some degree of impaired vision evidently persisted for several years.

Thus the extraordinary number of poems "in the handwriting of 1862" most probably has a simple, if horrifying, explanation: Emily Dickinson feared (with cogent reason) that she was beginning to go blind. Under such circumstances, any poet with an accumulation of ten or twelve years' work would set about putting her papers in order—making fair copies of the verses she intended to save and discarding earlier versions of them lest they be taken as final. And under such circumstances, any serious artist would husband her energies and time.

Before the problem with her eyes became acute, Emily Dickinson maintained a modest but entirely unremarkable social life. In the early years of their marriage, Austin and Sue began to entertain in the gracious manner that would characterize evenings at the Evergreens throughout most of their years there. During this period, Emily Dickinson often shared in the hospitality next door. Never fond of travel, she nonetheless made short trips from home—visiting her cousin Eliza Coleman Dudley in Middletown, Connecticut, and making the jaunt to Springfield to visit the Hollands. After the early 1860s, however, she kept increasingly to Amherst; little by little, she even became reluctant to join in the festivities next door. In 1864 and again in 1865, she was obliged to spend long months in Cambridge undergoing medical treatment. She was not allowed to read during this term, and much of the time she was even prohibited from writing; bright light evidently hurt her eyes. Her few letters home capture the mood of desperate vulnerability.

[To Lavinia, July 1864] . . . It is a very sober thing not to have any Vinnie, and to keep my Summer in strange Towns . . . but I have found friends in the Wilderness.

You know "Elijah" did, and to see the "Ravens" mending my stockings, would break a Heart long hard—Fanny and Loo [Norcross] are solid Gold, . . . and the Doctor enthusiastic about my getting well—I feel no gayness yet. I suppose I had been discouraged so long. . . .

Emily wants to be well and with Vinnie—If any one alive wants to get well more, I would let Him first.

[To Susan, September 1864] . . . [I am] At Centre of the Sea—. . .

It would be best to see you—it would be good to see the Grass, and hear the Wind blow the wide way in the Orchard.

[To Lavinia, November 1864] . . . *Does* Vinnie think of Sister? Sweet news. Thank Vinnie.

Emily may not be able as she was, but all she can, she will. . . .

I have been sick so long I do not know the Sun.[5]

Clearly her Norcross cousins were kind and attentive; however, despite their ministrations, the "terror" she had felt intermittently in 1861–62 seems to have dominated her life throughout this trying period. While she was away from Amherst, she focused all her attention on the recovery that would allow her to return home, and once she returned home for the second time, in October 1865, she became fixed in her determination never again to leave for any length of time.

The practice of finding excuses to avoid the daily round of social activities had begun as early as Emily Dickinson's return from the Mount Holyoke Female Seminary in 1848. This trouble with her eyes, not in and of itself a cause of her choice to lead a retired life, immensely reinforced the inclination to withdraw. Once she had begun the pattern, it was easy as the years passed to fall increasingly into the habit of pursuing a secluded existence. Eventually, other events further reinforced her decision. One year after Edward Dickinson's death in June 1874, his wife suffered an incapacitating stroke. According to Vinnie, one of her daughters must be constantly at home; Emily chose this part and, finding the life with her books and nature so congenial, continued to live it, always seeing her chosen friends and doing her part for the happiness of the home.[6]

By the last years of her life, Emily Dickinson had become altogether home-bound, probably phobically so. Yet there was nothing abrupt: Vinnie always claimed that her sister's retirement was "only a happen"—a slow process, the result not of one dramatic tragedy, but rather of many separate, small decisions.

Although it is important to dispel the melodramatic aura that has attended so many accounts of Emily Dickinson's life, this matter-of-fact explanation for the cloistered quality of her existence runs the risk of oversimplification. It paints the picture of a shy woman, awkward in her dealings with others and most comfortable in the familiar surroundings of her home—a woman who managed her anxieties by systematically eliminating every cause for anxiety from her life. There is truth in such an account, but only a partial truth. Other, equally important factors played a role in shaping the course of Emily Dickinson's existence: her decision to lead a life devoid of significant event may well have been the necessary condition for her art.

For most people—ordinary, normal people—a full life entails some combination of real-world relationships and rewards: marriage, children, an ongoing sense of membership in the larger community, a job or profession that allows one to exert one's talent in a productive way, a willingness to explore the diversity of society. It is by some such standard that people generally measure "success" or "emotional fulfillment," and according to this standard Emily Dickinson's life was sorely straitened. Yet by the simplest measure of all, Emily Dickinson was not "normal." She was preternaturally gifted—sensitive and immensely intelligent. The world is not organized to meet the demands and capacities of a few such extraordinary people, and it is scarcely surprising that highly creative men and women often do not lead lives that are "successful" when measured by normal standards.

Emily Dickinson confronted an additional obstacle. She was a woman, and mid-nineteenth-century America offered women few opportunities to reap the full rewards of a "successful" life. They might have marriage and children. However, membership in the larger community was severely limited. They could not vote; under many circumstances, they could not even hold property in their own right. The arena allowed to a woman for the exercise of her talents was mostly defined by the domestic sphere (and it is perhaps a supreme irony that, more than a century later, people conclude that Emily Dickinson must have been peculiar precisely because she thus constricted herself). A few women did manage to explore some of society's diversity, but the public code of dress for females—floor-length skirts and

inflexible corsets—is probably a telling index of the freedom and encouragement they were given to do so. It is true that Dickinson's life must be described as a deviation from the norm; yet it is equally true that her strategy
in fashioning such a mode of being had a decidedly positive dimension.

Once Emily Dickinson had accepted the vocation of poet, the expected
relationship between life and work was inverted. And here, the insights of
the poet Adrienne Rich can help to explain the origin of that compelling
Voice of the poetry. "I have a notion," Rich writes,

that genius knows itself; that Dickinson chose her seclusion, knowing she was exceptional and knowing what she needed. It was, moreover, no hermetic retreat, but a
seclusion which included a wide range of people, of reading and correspondence. . . .
She carefully selected her society and controlled the disposal of her time. . . . Given
her vocation, she was neither eccentric nor quaint; she was determined to survive, to
use her power, to practice necessary economies.

Suppose Jonathan Edwards had been born a woman; suppose William James, for
that matter, had been born a woman? . . . Even from men, New England took its
psychic toll; many of its geniuses seemed peculiar in one way or another, particularly
along the lines of social intercourse. . . . Emily Dickinson—viewed by her bemused
contemporary Thomas Higginson as "partially cracked," by the twentieth century as
fey or pathological—has increasingly struck me as a practical woman, exercising her
gift as she had to, making choices. I have come to imagine her as somehow too strong
for her environment, a figure of powerful will, not at all frail or breathless. . . .

The terms she had been handed by society—Calvinist Protestantism, Romanticism, the nineteenth-century corseting of women's bodies, choices, and sexuality—
could spell insanity to a woman genius. What this one had to do was retranslate her
own unorthodox, subversive, sometimes volcanic propensities into a dialect called
metaphor: her native language.[7]

Rich's assessment is acute: Dickinson's "life" served her poetry precisely in
its simplicity, in the *absence of significant event*. The act of "retranslating" her
insights and passion into "metaphor"—poetry—was for Dickinson the central activity of her existence. "Self" and "life" were syphoned out of the time-
bound parochial world of Amherst and poured into her work. In a literal and
quite self-conscious way, Emily Dickinson elected to expend her vital force
in creating and sustaining that Voice of the poetry.

To be sure, in fashioning a biography of "Emily Dickinson," one must
begin with the child and the young woman, with the family and environment
and culture that shaped her thought and defined the options available to her.
However, little by little, as the woman becomes Poet, biography must shift
its principal focus from the person to that Voice of the verse, for it was in her
poetry and not in the world that Emily Dickinson deliberately decided to
"live." Strict chronology, the primary concern with events that follow one

another in orderly file—these must yield to the panoramic prospect of a larger view. Dickinson dealt with a series of dilemmas in her work: some dominated the earlier stages of her writing; some occurred later. However, because the Voice of Dickinson's poetry was not constructed as a mechanical entity that followed rigid rules of development, the reassuring confinements of temporal order must be loosened. The mind that gave life to that Voice was complex—restless, questioning, always turning back upon itself to re-view and re-examine old answers and old assumptions. It is this *process* that the biographer of Emily Dickinson must try to capture, subtle and elusive as it may be. Still, there are immense rewards. Emily Dickinson the woman existed in time, and today she is dead and gone: the Voice of the poetry, importunate and quick with energy, is as vital today as it was when it was breathed into being more than a century ago.

I ❖ The Poet's Problem with a "Woman's Place"

Possibly all major artists repose some element of self in the enduring master-works that survive them; however, in Dickinson's case the transposition was virtually complete. The members of her family gradually understood the terms of this existence and accepted the autonomy it conferred upon her. "Her love of being alone up in her room was associated with her feeling for a key, which signified freedom from interruption and the social prevention that beset her downstairs," her niece recalled.

She would stand looking down, one hand raised, thumb and forefinger closed on an imaginary key, and say, with a quick turn of her wrist, "It's just a turn—and freedom, Matty!" ... Her loneliness has been much deplored; but where and with whom would she not have been lonely? Her kind of loneliness was the gift whose riches she herself pronounced beyond the power of "mortal numeral to divulge." And what society of her contemporaries would have made up to her for the loss of the precious guest of her solitude she named "Finite Infinity"?[8]

Those outside the family circle understood her desire for seclusion less well, perhaps because they were unable to comprehend that her art originated in a metaphysical imperative—not in mere lachrymose sensibility. To be a great artist in any age requires an exceptional self-consciousness about the terms of one's existence; thus in mid-nineteenth-century New England, any woman who wished to be a major poet was forced to think with brutal honesty about the implications of her gender.

Rich cites a poem, "I would not paint—a picture—," which, she asserts, "struck me at the age of sixteen and which still, thirty years later, arrests my imagination. . . . This poem is about choosing an orthodox 'feminine' role," Rich's gloss reads in part. "The receptive rather than the creative; viewer rather than painter, listener rather than musician; acted-upon rather than active . . . The strange paradox of this poem—its exquisite irony—is that it is about choosing not to be a poet, a poem which is gainsaid by no fewer than one thousand seven hundred and seventy-five poems made during the writer's life, including itself."[9] This dilemma, whether to *create* beauty or to *be* beautiful, seems to have hounded almost every significant woman writer; and Dickinson was no exception.

Emily Dickinson confronted a painful double bind when she fixed upon her vocation: on the one hand, she could become a strong poet only if she was assertive and used language forcefully; on the other hand, in the mid-nineteenth century, the mores of Amherst—indeed, of America in general—did not condone assertiveness or outspokenness in women. Moreover, these social prejudices had been strongly reinforced in the Dickinson household. Father had praised his *son's* letters to the skies, proclaiming them "altogether before Shakespeare" and vowing to "have them published to put in our library"; at the same time, however, Father had never taken the least notice of his *daughter's* precocity or literary genius. Father had a public life and was a notable orator; Mother was so self-effacing and silent that her taciturnity had become almost a family joke. If anything, Emily Dickinson's domestic existence had exaggerated society's dictum that women be silent and passive.

There are family legends that suggest just how unwilling Emily Dickinson was to conform to such injunctions or to emulate her mother's habit of resignation.

Edward Dickinson was quick to notice any lapse of attention on the part of his womenfolks. In his code there was no room for carelessness. . . . The well-known anecdote of the plate illustrates the point. One day, sitting down at the dinner table, he inquired whether a certain nicked plate must always be placed before him. Emily took the hint. She carried the plate to the garden and pulverized it on a stone, "just to remind" her, she said, not to give it to her father again.[10]

Language, of course, was a far subtler weapon than a hammer. Dickinson's verbal maneuvers would increasingly reveal immense skill in avoiding a frontal attack; she preferred the silent knife of irony to the strident battering of loud complaint. She had never suffered fools gladly. The little girl who had written of a dull classmate, "He is the sillyest creature that ever lived I think," grew into a woman who could deliver wrath and contempt with excruciating economy and cunning. Scarcely submissive, she had acquired the cool calculation of an assassin.

There are many evidences of her mature mastery over the expression of rage and derision and rejection. Some can be found in her letters, especially those she wrote to Higginson. Even more can be found in the poetry, of course, and the poem Adrienne Rich singled out for praise is a good place to begin. It is a superbly controlled, subtly complex examination of the plight of woman-as-poet.

> *I would not paint—a picture—*
> *I'd rather be the One*
> *It's bright impossibility*
> *To dwell—delicious—on—*
> *And wonder how the fingers feel*
> *Whose rare—celestial—stir—*
> *Evokes so sweet a Torment—*
> *Such sumptuous—Despair—*
>
> *I would not talk, like Cornets—*
> *I'd rather be the One*
> *Raised softly to the Ceilings—*
> *And out, and easy on—*
> *Through Villages of Ether—*
> *Myself endued Balloon*
> *By but a lip of Metal—*
> *The pier to my Pontoon—*
>
> *Nor would I be a Poet—*
> *It's finer—own the Ear—*
> *Enamored—impotent—content—*
> *The License to revere,*
> *A privilege so awful*
> *What would the Dower be,*
> *Had I the Art to stun myself*
> *With Bolts of Melody!*

(#505)

It is true, as Rich has observed, that the speaker makes an apparent renunciation of her vocation as poet and that the renunciation is ironically refuted by the mere *existence* of the poem. However, the most telling evidence of Dickinson's comfort in violating the social restrictions that prohibited women from asserting themselves is not the poem's existence, but its high comedic tone. This verse exhibits a superb legerdemain in the management of its major themes, and it takes a rare stance for Dickinson: a tongue-in-cheek assertion of the necessarily "androgynous" nature of the Poet.

The poem is one of Dickinson's most complex, and the reader is forced to confront its difficulties at the very beginning. There is resistance to the notion that artistic creativity can be an uncomplicated process. This attitude is reinforced by a series of paralleled opposites: verbs of being juxtaposed to verbs of doing, and a puzzling procedure in which opposite elements conspire to nullify each other, "Despair" canceling "delicious" in stanza one (this in addition to the oxymoron of "sumptuous Despair"). In stanza two, there is the compressed contradictions of "Cornets," a word that signifies several quite different things: it is "an instrument of music," a horn; it is also, however, "an officer of cavalry"—thus are song and warfare concisely combined. Moreover, while "horn" recalls the male sexual organ, to one who speaks "New Englandly" the "cornet" is also that horn of plenty, the cornucopia of the Thanksgiving feast—full-fruited harvest pouring from a container fashioned in a patently sexual configuration, the female organs in the process of birthing.

In sharp contrast to the fecundity of the cornucopia, there is the disturbing evidence of dismemberment here—the introduction of mere disembodied "fingers" at first, then a single lip, and finally an ear. This odd assortment of body parts recalls God's assault upon the coherent "I" that begins with a demand for faith and submission to conversion, and that culminates in an extinction of self which is death. Dickinson returned repeatedly to the spectacle of God's slaughterhouse; yet in *this* poem about song, God is not the culprit, for the wrenching, mutilating divisions have been decreed by the dictates of social propriety.

The Lord is a Creature of covenants, and Dickinson here toys with the irony that man exceeds even God in the establishment of ill-drawn or self-contradictory "laws." "License" is a "permission; authority or liberty given to do or forbear any act"; it is also, however, "excess of liberty . . . freedom abused, or used in contempt of law or decorum." "Privilege" is "a particular and peculiar benefit . . . beyond the common advantages of other citizens"—that is, a right that exceeds or ignores the law. "Dower" seems the most inconsistent of all; it is also the only term here that applies explicitly to the relationship between men and women. A "dower" is "the property which a woman brings to her husband in marriage"; however, it is also "the gift of a husband for a wife."*

---

* With all of these legal terms, there is good historical reason for the different definitions, which ultimately seem to contradict each other—none more than "dower." Anyone who had read the novels of Samuel Richardson (a readership that probably included virtually every educated American in the early nineteenth century) knew that the money a wife brought as "dower" into the marriage generally determined how much "pin money" her husband allowed her and how much of a widow's "dower" she was left after his death. Dickinson knew this, too—she was,

Dickinson affirms the *physical* differences between the sexes. To "wonder how the fingers feel / Whose rare—celestial—stir— / Evokes so sweet a Torment—" is, perhaps, to be a woman aroused, pleased with erotic stimulation and simultaneously curious about the feelings of her partner. Similarly, a woman satisfied in the enactment of love *must* be "Enamored—impotent—content," for she does not have the physical equipment to be *potent* in her active pleasure. It is not such differences that trouble Dickinson (indeed, the tone suggests quite otherwise). Yet, when society attempts to legislate permissible activities according to differences in anatomy, impose social restrictions according to gender, the result can only be deforming. Thus the legal language is contradictory, most blatantly so when it seeks to make distinctions between the different rights or duties of men and women. And the most intolerable example of such "legislation" occurs when society construes "potency" in figurative ways that then *deny women access to various forms of power* (including the power to be an artist). Thus the string of images becomes increasingly grotesque with each stanza, and culminates in the absurdity of the last two lines. Such prescriptive attitudes are vicious and mutilating of women's "selves" (and probably of men's as well), and it is this form of wounding that the theme of dismemberment running throughout the poem is meant to capture. In usurping God's power to create, let us not, Dickinson implores, emulate His penchant for destructiveness as well.

The linguistic pacing of the poem is superb; and the compression of sexuality, legal rights, and the power of art is both suitably unsettling and insightful. However, one must not take so sober an attitude toward the verse that the joke of it gets lost. This is a cartoon of a poem, bombastically satirical and very funny. The speaker is not angry at the *reader;* instead, she invites the reader to join with her in laughing (somewhat bitterly) at the follies of mankind.

A number of Dickinson's critics have been at pains to suggest that she suffered neurotic or psychotic disorders of a primarily sexual nature. It is worth noting, then, the ease with which she deploys the phallic image of the fondling fingers, the physical fact (not tragedy) of women's *literally* "impotent" condition. Moreover, these physical images of male sexuality are paralleled by the cornucopia image of female sexuality—with this difference: women are usually construed as "naturally" constructed for the process of reproduction. The *poet* must combine power (or "potency") with productivity (or "fecundity"). At this point a final meaning of "cornet" becomes significant: phallic symbol of aggression, feminine symbol of birthing—the cornet is, in addition, a "crown." With this complex insight as preamble, the

---

after all, a lawyer's daughter. Yet the *law* as an institution was under particular attack (from such novelists as Dickens) during the mid-nineteenth century. Emily Dickinson reveals in her poetry a doubting attitude toward the efficacy of laws (especially God's), and she certainly intended the internal contradictions here as ironic.

climax of the poem (which is a sexual climax as well as an artistic one) can be seen as pointedly and comically paradoxical: to "stun" oneself "With Bolts of Melody!" is, given the highly charged sexual context, either to be masturbating or to be coupling with oneself (as hermaphrodite?). The first is sterile, the second impossible; and taken together, they describe a form of artistic creativity that is essentially barren.

There is ample evidence throughout the letters and poetry that Emily Dickinson was able to express a wide assortment of strong feelings; furthermore, there are such dazzling displays of ingenuity in the rendering of these emotions that one cannot conclude that she was in any serious way crippled by a fear of being inappropriately "active" or "assertive." Yet there was another, inviolable constraint for women artists in America of the mid-nineteenth century, and this proved much less susceptible to ingenious evasion.

At the time Emily Dickinson began her career, American poets could command considerable respect as thinkers because poetry, even the poetry of a waning Romantic age, was held to serve a significant intellectual function. The citizens of this still-new nation were willing to believe that the men who wrote serious verse might be able to teach them how to think. Nor was serious poetry relegated to a small audience of literati. In 1858, Longfellow's narrative poem *The Courtship of Miles Standish* sold more than fifteen thousand copies on its first day in print in England and America, and for nearly twenty years Longfellow taught at Harvard and served as an arbiter of taste and thought among educated Americans. Emerson rejected the church and for many years the academy as well, yet he lectured everywhere, and his writings were so widely read that he managed to fuse the roles of poet and intellectual leader without the security and sanction of a professorship at Harvard. Walt Whitman's career demonstrated that even a radical poet might become a shaper of American ideas: a steel engraving of the author, nonchalantly dressed in workman's clothes—hand on hip, collar unbuttoned—appeared as the daringly iconoclastic frontispiece of *Leaves of Grass* in 1855. This was part of a larger effort, conducted principally through the medium of his poetry, by which Whitman insisted upon identifying the poet as an ordinary man who could exert his influence at the personal level, as brother or friend rather than as formal teacher. If he was thought disgraceful at first, by the mid-1860s he had already begun to be called the "Good Gray Poet," and gradually his work was exalted as the testimony of a Christlike man of untiring compassion. By the time of his death in 1892, Whitman, too, had been acknowledged as an artist who had provided his countrymen with new categories to help formulate Americans' most important thoughts.

In the case of men, then, it was assumed that the craft of writing might have a significant intellectual component. Such was not the case with women.

Certainly women lectured in public, on issues like abolition, temperance, or female suffrage; but this endeavor was all too often dismissed as the merely political expression of an essentially exhibitionistic or sentimental need and not taken seriously as an intellectual activity. Certainly women might write and publish. As early as 1820, one-third of all American novels were being written by women, and the proportion increased as the century moved on. Women published poetry, too: Emily Dickinson would have had to look no further than the Springfield *Republican* to discover strain after strain of "feminine" melancholy or saccharine sensibility. By mid-century, women had grown so prolific that "serious" male writers like Hawthorne expressed anxiety and outrage about the competition they offered and the standards they were beginning to set for America's reading public. Nonetheless, women continued to write and publish. There were only these tacit stipulations: women's work must be relentlessly domestic and emotional; a female author must make *no claim for herself as a serious intellectual;* women might write and publish only so long as they did not also presume to *think.* Not surprisingly, women authors were relegated to what has been termed the "status of sublime amateur. . . . Theirs was an unconscious and compulsive art, untouched by intellectualism or artifice."[11] They were expected to exercise their emotions, but not their intelligence; they might write as a way of relieving the strain of strong feelings, but not as a systematic, strong-minded endeavor. Margaret Fuller made surely the most powerful attack upon this attitude toward the female intellectual, and her fate was not so much to succeed in altering people's opinions as merely to make the male intellectuals around her uncomfortable. In *Ernest Linwood* (1856), the popular Southern novelist Caroline Lee Hentz describes the creative process of women who write in an appropriately "feminine" way: "'Book! Am I writing a book? No indeed! This is only a record of my heart's life, written at random and carelessly thrown aside, sheet after sheet, sibylline leaves from the great book of fate.'"[12] Even when Dickinson's poetry was about to see print in book form for the first time (in posthumous publication), it was her fate to be judged by just such standards. In 1890, two months before the publication of *Poems by Emily Dickinson,* Thomas Wentworth Higginson wrote these introductory remarks in an essay discussing her work:

Emerson said, many years since in the *Dial,* that the most interesting department of poetry would hereafter be found in what might be called "The Poetry of the Portfolio"; the work, that is, of persons who wrote for the relief of their own minds, and without thought of publication. Such poetry, when accumulated for years, will have at least the merit of perfect freedom; accompanied, of course, by whatever drawback from the habitual absence of criticism. Thought will have its full strength and uplifting, but without the proper control and chastening of literary expression; there will be wonderful strokes and felicities, and yet an incomplete and unsatisfactory whole.[13]

Even today, some readers still unselfconsciously employ these nineteenth-century categories in assessing Dickinson's poetry.

Vinnie's assessment of the different roles pre-empted by the various members of the immediate family takes on a new significance when it is seen in this context: " 'Father was the only one to say "damn." . . . As for Emily, she was not withdrawn or exclusive really. . . . She had to *think*—she was the only one of us who had that to do.' " Emily Dickinson's enduring regard and respect for Austin's wife, Sue, is also more understandable when the prevalent attitude toward intellectual women is taken into account. Over the years, the poet had many differences with her sister-in-law, some of major proportions. Sue could be argumentative; she appears to have taken offense easily; and during the later years of the poet's life, Austin's marriage to Sue was sorely strained. Nonetheless, the tie between the two women remained strong. In 1882 (only four years before her death) Dickinson sent this short note across to the Evergreens: "Dear Sue—With the exception of Shakespeare, you have told me of more knowledge than any one living—To say that sincerely is strange praise." [14] Susan Dickinson was Emily's most consistent audience. Two hundred and seventy-six poems were sent to her, almost three times as many as were sent to Higginson. Like Emily Dickinson, Susan was a woman determined to "think." In her case, intellectual activity took the form of inviting the most interesting minds she could find to come to Amherst and enjoy her hospitality: she entertained Emerson, Henry Ward Beecher, Harriet Beecher Stowe, Frederick Law Olmsted, and many, many others.

There were but few friends outside of Amherst with whom Dickinson was willing to be candid about the scope of her vision, and of these by far the most significant were Fanny and Loo Norcross, Aunt Lavinia's daughters. The correspondence with them surely constitutes the most straightforward, confiding group among Dickinson's letters. As early as 1859 Dickinson wrote to Loo:

I have known little of you, since the October morning when our families went out driving, and you and I in the dining-room decided to be distinguished. It's a great thing to be "great," Loo, and you and I might tug for a life, and never accomplish it, but no one can stop our looking on, and you know some cannot sing, but the orchard is full of birds, and we all can listen. What if we learn, ourselves, some day! Who indeed knows? [15]

Almost certainly it was a considerable relief to be able to write to someone in this unguarded and ingenuous way about her work. In late 1861, for example, she sent the Norcross cousins a mordant comment upon the discrepancy between the passive, maidenly comportment women are taught as girls and the "potency" they can possess if they become major writers. "That Mrs. Browning fainted, we need not read *Aurora Leigh* to know, when she lived with her English aunt; and George Sand 'must make no noise in her grandmother's bedroom.' Poor children! Women, now, queens, now! And one in the Eden of God. I guess they both forget that now."[16]

Given the objective social prohibitions Emily Dickinson confronted—given especially her own father's view that daughters were unimportant creatures while sons were valuable, worthy of praise and attention—it would have been an easy thing for the poetry to become contaminated with resentment. One of Dickinson's greatest personal victories is that she did not allow this contamination to take place. She was astute enough to realize how urgently the quality of her art depended upon her success in reaching her readers. Thus when she wrote poetry, she never fell into an adversarial relationship with her audience. She was not self-indulgent, not unreflective, not undisciplined. She could not afford laxity. She was willing to transfer all of the energy of living into the creation of poetry—willing to exchange a transient but nonetheless palpable "self" for a disembodied Voice that exists intact and unchanged now, more than a century later to breathe "words that will not leave you time to watch her coming toward you"—a vibrant, often commanding Voice that "not only speaks but speaks to *you*." The exchange was not effortless, however. That Voice was carefully, meticulously considered. Emily Dickinson wrote scores of poems that deal directly or indirectly with the problem of establishing "Voice," dozens more about the nature and function of poetry. She was a woman, and although she did not necessarily want to exploit that fact, neither did she intend systematically to deny it. With this precondition, she did not want the Voice of the verse to be incongruous or susceptible of dismissal; above all, she wanted to speak as a "Representative Voice," not querulously—not with the keening voice of the "overheard soliloquy." She sought to *engage* her readers, male and female, to talk to each personally.

In sum, she wanted to make the terms of existence that were meaningful to the Voice of her poetry relevant to the terms of existence by which her readers defined their own lives—whoever those readers might be, in no matter what time or place. And the miracle is, she succeeded.

In the end, there were many "Voices." This fact has sometimes puzzled Dickinson's readers. One poem may be delivered in a child's Voice; another in the Voice of a young woman scrutinizing nature and the society in which she makes her place. Sometimes the Voice is that of a woman self-confidently addressing her lover in a language of passion and sexual desire. At still other times, the Voice of the verse seems so precariously balanced at the edge of hysteria that even its calmest observations grate like the shriek of dementia. There is the Voice of the housewife and the Voice that has recourse to the occasionally agonizing, occasionally regal language of the conversion experience of latter-day New England Puritanism. In some poems the Voice is distinctive principally because it speaks in the aftermath of wounding and can comprehend extremities of pain. Moreover, these Voices are not always entirely distinct from one another: the child's Voice that opens a poem may yield to the Voice of a young woman speaking the idiom of ardent love; in a different poem, the speaker may fall into a mood of almost religious contemplation in an attempt to analyze or define such abstract entities as loneliness or madness or eternity; the diction of the housewife may be conflated with the sovereign language of the New Jerusalem, and taken together, they may render some aspect of the wordsmith's labor. No manageable set of discrete categories suffices to capture the diversity of discourse, and any attempt to simplify Dickinson's methods does violence to the verse.

Yet there is a paradox here. This is, by no stretch of the imagination, a body of poetry that might be construed as a series of lyrics spoken by many different people. Disparate as these many Voices are, somehow they all appear to issue from the same "self." (Hence MacLeish speaks of "words that will not leave you time to watch her coming toward you"—"*her*," a single person, not a delegation.) It is the enigmatic "Emily Dickinson" readers suppose themselves to have found in this poetry, even in the extreme case when Dickinson's supposed speaker is male. One explanation for this sense of intrinsic unity in the midst of diversity is the persistence with which Dickinson addresses the same set of problems, using a remarkably durable repertoire of linguistic modes. Evocations of injury and wounding—threats to the coherence of the self—appear in the earliest poems and continue until the end; ways of rendering face-to-face encounters change, but this preoccupation with "interview" is sustained by metaphors of "confrontation" that weave throughout. The summoning of one or another Voice in a given poem, then, is not an unselfconscious emotive reflection of Emily Dickinson's mood at the moment of creation. Rather, each different Voice is a calculated tactic, an attempt to touch her readers and engage them intimately with the poetry. Each Voice had its unique advantages; each its limitations. A poet self-conscious in her craft, she calculated this element as carefully as every other.

2 ❖ *The Voice of the Child*

The Voice of the child contributed to some of Emily Dickinson's strongest poems; paradoxically, it also figured in her most embarrassingly coy and sentimental verse.

By the middle of the nineteenth century, poetry about children and lyrics spoken by a child had become a standard part of American culture. To a society that prohibited women from entering the realm of "serious" intellectual pursuits, this art of the nursery world seemed entirely appropriate to the feminine sensibility. The Voice of the child was permitted to female poets and was thus available to Dickinson. However, insofar as Dickinson had a *literary* source for the rendering of children in her poetry, it came primarily from her novel reading and not from the work of other poets. Dickens was the family favorite, and Emily Dickinson was so steeped in his work that tag phrases from his novels and the names of his characters are found throughout her own correspondence as a kind of playful private code to be used with close friends.

Like many nineteenth-century novelists, Dickens often had a significant practical purpose in mind when he created his fictions: if he could cause his readers to feel pity and sympathy for the fictional children whose lives had been ruined by pervasive social evils—the horrors of the orphanage or the workhouse, for example—then the power of this moral sentiment might serve to initiate reforms. Pity was not usually construed as an end in itself: instead, it was intended to be a force that motivated onlookers, adults within the fictional world or the audience of readers living in the real world, who could *act* forcefully to redress the specific social evils that had been portrayed. The victims, often children, seldom pitied themselves: sometimes they expressed innocent bewilderment or pain, sometimes courage and endurance. When they did lapse into self-pity, their capacity to engage the sympathy of others quickly vanished.

There were many problems inherent in this model, but two gave Dickinson particular difficulty. In Dickens's novels, the children who were objects of pity seldom had a strong, distinctive Voice. Dickens and others did develop a language of sentimental sympathy, but it was spoken by adult narrators or observers, not by the suffering child. When Emily Dickinson attempted to have the child speak directly, all too often the result was bathetic complaint or coy entreaty. Few modern readers can admire the prayer that begins, "*Papa above! / Regard a Mouse*" (#61); and even direct allusions to Dickens's fictional children could not save the situation. Dickens had published *A Christmas Carol* in 1843, shortly after his first American tour. In 1860 the figure of the patient cripple, Tiny Tim, needed no gloss. "*We dont cry—Tim and I, / . . . Tim—reads a little Hymn— / And we both pray— / Please, Sir, I and Tim— / Always lost the way! / We must die—by and by— / Clergymen say— / Tim— shall—if I—do— / I—too—if he— / How shall we arrange it— / Tim— was—so—shy? / Take us simultaneous—Lord— / I—'Tim'—and—Me!*" (#196). Alas, the Tiny Tim of this poem does not touch a reader's heart, and the cloying supplications of the child-speaker sink into such plaintiveness that the verse hovers at the edge of inadvertent caricature. Sometimes a poem of this stamp will begin vigorously enough, only to betray itself. "'*Houses*'—

so the Wise Men tell me— / 'Mansions'! Mansions must be warm!" (#127): such a tone renders the promises of Christ's Father in an idiom of almost Biblical simplicity. Yet as the poem moves forward and the language strives more and more overtly to coerce sympathy (*"Mansions cannot let the tears in, / Mansions must exclude the storm! / . . . Could the Children find the way there— / Some, would even trudge tonight!"*), the sinewy strength of the opening grows flaccid, and the verse cannot sustain the reader's emotional commitment.

The second problem with the sentimental model was even more serious. Pity is earthbound. Sympathy can move human beings to change the social arrangements that inflict pain; however, no power of sympathy can do away with transcendent ills. Death cannot be corrected. Oblivion cannot be furnished with comforting amenities. Thus transcendent pain demands some stronger reaction than pity. The strategy of the following poem addresses precisely this demand as it makes the effort to move beyond mere pity. It begins:

> On such a night, or such a night,
> Would anybody care
> If such a little figure
> Slipped quiet from it's chair—

Initially, the poem appears to be no more than an attempt to extract sympathy for the infant that has passed silently away. Yet the situation is not quite that simple, for the poem concludes:

> There was a little figure plump
> For every little knoll—
> Busy needles, and spools of thread—
> And trudging feet from school—
>
> Playmates, and holidays, and nuts—
> And visions vast and small—
> Strange that the feet so precious charged
> Should reach so small a goal!

> (#146)

The cemetery is filled with the dead, and under "every little knoll" there lies someone who was once a child, plying its tasks and pursuing its dreams; yet all are now equally dead, equally far from life's pleasures. *"As in sleep— All Hue forgotten— / Tenets—put behind— / Death's large—Democratic fingers / Rub away the Brand—"* (#970). Confronted with the absolute annihilation of death, can anyone make distinctions? Children die "too soon," some might say. Dickinson would answer: the injury is not *too soon,* the injury is *death itself*—death of the small and young, death of the aged and great. There is never a "right time to die." We may think ourselves clever and strong when we elude death for a while, and we even forget his long shadow falling across our paths. But in the end, the Angel of Death dispatches us all. Even Abraham's son, once miraculously spared from death by God's reprieve, was eventually constrained to accept our universal fate. "Isaac pleads again," Dickinson wrote during the last days of her own life, " 'but where is the Lamb for the Sacrifice?' The clock's sweet voice makes no reply."[17] When a child dies, its early death merely emphasizes the fate we all must accept in the end: the *correct* reaction, then, is not pity, but rage or terror.

Yet if Dickinson wished to express strong feelings like rage or terror, she would have to overcome the several difficulties of finding a language that was deemed appropriate for her. In Amherst, language was fettered by a religiously encoded vision of the world. For any woman who wanted to write poetry, there was the further impediment of a language smothered by the ornate embellishment of emotionalism. And for all American poets who wished to treat subjects of intellectual importance, there was the customary Latinate formality of "serious verse."

Male poets did not confront the same constellation of difficulties. Walt Whitman, writing poetry during the same period, also found the received conventions for American poetry too limited for his intentions: like Dickinson, he intended to speak as "Representative Voice," and he took upon himself the task of fashioning a new kind of poetic line and a novel notion of poetic diction. In the preface to the first edition of *Leaves of Grass* (1855) he articulated his views of American poetry and poets. "The genius of the United States," he claimed, is "always most in the common people. Their manners speech dress friendships—the freshness and candor of their physiognomy—the picturesque looseness of their carriage." According to Whitman, an American poet was not required to burden his native tongue with "proprieties" of Latinate speech. "The English language befriends the grand American expression. . . . It is brawny enough and limber and full enough. . . . It is the dialect of common sense." He set many pages of type in this first edition himself, for his long cadences did not easily lend themselves to the usual poetic arrangements of "feet" and "lines." He included the frontispiece of himself in laborer's clothes, and in the text he introduced himself with every appearance of intimacy and informality in a plausible rendering of "common" language. Without a doubt he was direct.

I loafe and invite my soul,
I lean and loafe at my ease observing a spear of summer grass.

My tongue, every atom of my blood, form'd from this soil, this air,

Born here of parents born here from parents the same, and their parents the same,
I, now thirty-seven years old in perfect health begin,
Hoping to cease not till death.

(from "Song of Myself")

None of this was usual. Much of it was shocking. Some of it was even judged obscene (though none of the material quoted here earned that censure).

Although there was a great deal of invention in Whitman's revolutionary work, he built upon a foundation that was already clear, direct, available, and acceptable: the ordinary language of the "common man," the workingman and laborer—the man of the street. Whitman transformed the language with which he began, but he had something to begin with.

Dickinson would have found Whitman's call for a "common" language in poetry entirely congenial—even, perhaps, compelling—for he gave formal utterance to many attitudes that lie behind her work; however, she faced a serious challenge in attempting to implement such a proposal. "Direct" language in a woman was always "domestic" language: there were no women of the street (save for prostitutes), no workingwomen or women laborers. Even female domestic servants were something of an oddity until the mass immigrations began in 1848. What could be the foundation for Dickinson's experiment—a language that was clear, direct, available, acceptable in a female, and replete with power? The answer was the language of the child. The child could serve as an Everyman because every adult had once been a child. Moreover, in childhood the prescribed roles for "appropriate" male and female behavior were not yet fully enforced. Indeed, in mid-nineteenth-century America, little boys and little girls even looked very much the same: girls' hair was often cut very short, and boys regularly wore dresses until the age of six or seven, when they went to school. The child-as-Everyman was no ideal answer, but it was better than none.

One of Dickinson's accomplishments, then, was a transformation of the language of children—of the home, the school, and the playground. In poems that adopt this strategy, Dickinson did not take fictional children for her model; certainly she did not adapt the cloying postures of the child in sentimental poetry. Rather, she attuned her ear to the often strident, often impassioned tones of actual boys and girls: she fashioned a poetic Voice from the components of the brash, not-yet-"civilized" *real* child.

The setting is, perhaps, a Sunday-school class; the lesson, a verse from the New Testament, Matthew 16:28. "Verily I say unto you, There be some standing here, which shall not taste of death, till they see the Son of man coming in his kingdom." Some restless little girl with an active imagination has let her attention wander from the theological lesson, and she raises her voice above the teacher's to introject a question:

> *Do People moulder equally,*
> *They bury, in the Grave?*

Dickinson has deployed this interrupting Voice with its specific and faintly indelicate question to achieve that sense of direct address that Whitman also craved. Without any warning, the reader is accosted and plunged into the midst of a transcendent puzzle: how can mortals not "taste of death"? The poem continues:

> *I do believe a Species*
> *As positively live*
>
> *As I, who testify it*
> *Deny that I—am dead—*
> *And fill my Lungs, for Witness—*
> *From Tanks—above my Head—*
>
> *I say to you, said Jesus—*
> *That there be standing here—*
> *A Sort, that shall not taste of Death—*
> *If Jesus was sincere—*
>
> *I need no further Argue—*
> *The statement of the Lord*
> *Is not a controvertible—*
> *He told me, Death was dead—*

(#432)

Begun with the insistent child, the poem has quickly become the property of a poet-speaker, one familiar with biology and chemistry (from the Amherst Academy, perhaps) and given to irreverent flights of high humor. The Voice is conversational and perpetually present ("*As I, who testify it / Deny that I—am dead—*"), employing a strategy not unlike Whitman's eternally suspended "now" ("I, now thirty-seven years old"). The very *vitality* of this Voice is proof of the argument the Voice intends to make, such telling proof, indeed, that at the conclusion of the poem we are returned politely to Sunday school. "So when this corruptible shall have put on incorruption, and this mortal shall have put on immortality, then shall be brought to pass the saying that is written, Death is swallowed up in victory" (I Corinthians 15:54). In the Bible it is God's victory; in the verse it is the poet's.

Emily Dickinson has taken the word of the prophet Isaiah, 11:6—"and a little child shall lead them"—and turned it entirely to her own purposes.

The world of the child is a realm of absolutes: feelings have not yet been moderated by the demands of propriety. "Growing up" and learning how not to seem "crazy" both require a relinquishment of these absolutes. They require as well that social interactions follow the local rules of law and decorum: one must not initiate a conversation at will with a stranger; one must not ask impertinent questions; one must not simply react to life spontaneously without first considering the effect of that reaction upon others; when asked a question, one must not tell the truth straightforwardly if it is shocking; and one must not make observations about the facts of life and death aloud that offend or frighten other people. One is permitted to do none of these things—unless one is a child. Thus when the Voice of Dickinson's poetry availed itself of the privileges of childhood, it gained precisely these options of speaking intensely, frankly, and familiarly. It is the freshness and apparent spontaneity of her work that so often catches adult readers off guard, and it is the readers' intuitive recognition of the figure of the child behind the verse that has led so many to take as literally true such statements as "*I was the slightest in the House—*" (#486). Only the conspiratorial invitation of youth could so consistently beguile readers into answering "yes" to the question "*I'm Nobody! Who are you? / Are you—Nobody—too?*" (#288) Only the Everyman figure of the child could convince each single reader that he or she was in league with this Voice against the rest of the world—them, the "public," grown-ups.

Yet Dickinson's Voice of "the child" was, of course, an amalgam: the artist availed herself of any number of speech patterns, inflections, tones, attitudes, and freedoms that were associated with the verbal habits of children—sorting them, making choices among them, and structuring them with her own adult intelligence. In any given poem, the selection varies, and so does the degree to which the adult consciousness can be seen to intrude. When the speaker has been explicitly *defined* as a child, the directness and apparent simplicity of the verse can be charming; in this case, it is the intrusion of sentimental ornamentation, the vestige of society, that can vitiate the poem. Of course, the artist's skill has contrived even this sense of direct address, but the adult intellect is almost entirely obscured by the illusion of unreflective candor. Poems like "*I would not paint—a picture—*" are more complex and more discomfiting. In this poem there is a childlike air of license and unconstraint, a relaxed playfulness and humor that admit fairy-tale, cartoon-sized fantasies, each more absurd than the last. Yet at the same time there is an inescapably mature mind carefully modulating the images and formulating the sophisticated compressions—a mind that is most powerfully present, perhaps, in the informing notion that serves as a premise for the entire poem: society has decreed that men may make art while women may play the part only of audience.

There are poems that deploy the child's insights and assertions with such puzzling force that many readers may not know quite how to react.

> *Volcanoes be in Sicily*
> *And South America*
> *I judge from my Geography*
> *Volcanoes nearer here*
> *A Lava step at any time*
> *Am I inclined to climb*
> *A Crater I may contemplate*
> *Vesuvius at Home*
>
> (*#1705*)

The vision is that of a child—old enough to go to school, but young enough still to say aloud the truth that adults push from consciousness, that violence is not found exclusively "someplace else." The Voice is that of a student—measured and bookish, preoccupied with newly acquired geography and geology. However, still lingering in this student's memory is the recollection of an earlier time of life when absolute rage and voracious passion found forthright expression. Such emotions can never be eliminated; instead, they are covered over with layers of moral injunction and social propriety. Yet, being volcanic, they sometimes still erupt through the many strata of these prohibitions, unexpectedly hissing violence in their path. Domestic brutality is the most ancient of crimes, and the playground is the last remnant of our unsocialized selves.

If the Voice of the child can be resurrected with its full range and amplitude, then cadences of insolent candor, rage, rebelliousness, grief, and unadulterated terror can be readied for the poet's art, an arsenal of incalculable force to use in her rebellion against the Divinity.

In His role of Creator, God had fashioned a world shaped by time and death. The Voice of Dickinson's verse could confound death and transcend time by springing to life anew for every reader. Her poetry, then, stands as rival creation to God's. "*A Word that breathes distinctly,*" Dickinson wrote of her own work, "*Has not the power to die / Cohesive as the Spirit / It may expire if He—*" (*#1651*). Within the context of this *alternative* "Creation," Dickinson undertook to defy the Deity in a second way, by subverting the power of God's various forms of art, His "language." It came to her in several forms: there were the legends of the King James Bible; there were the many names of God's "signs" in the natural world; and there were the meters of the hymns used by Amherst Congregationalists. Dickinson rebelled against all of these. Her defiance of the first two can be discerned in the content of her poems— Biblical tales retold for the purpose of exposing God's perfidy and weakness, and the "signs" of the world reinterpreted to reveal His hypocritical dealings with mankind. Her rebellion against the rhythms of religious song, however, was asserted through the *form* of her poetry, a reworking and disrupting of the patterns of English hymnody.

It has long been recognized that the underlying metrical structure of Dickinson's work is the pattern of English hymnody. Hymnal measures were a "metric form familiar to her from childhood as the measures in which Watt's hymns were composed. Copies of Watt's *Christian Psalmody* or his collection of *The Psalms, Hymns, and Spiritual Songs* were fixtures in every New England household. Both were owned by Edward Dickinson."[18] The rhythmic configuration of hymns is not obscure; the same configuration or a similar one can be found even in common nursery rhymes, alternating lines of eight syllables and six syllables—"eights and sixes," as they were called. It is surprising, then, that Dickinson's resort to them was not immediately apparent to her first readers. But it was not. If anything, for many years she was treated as a poet who worked entirely without metrical rule, and her poetry was much admired by those who worked with *vers libre*. One reason for this misunderstanding was the flood of corrupted and "corrected" texts of Dickinson's poetry, the only copies available until the Johnson edition of 1955. Another reason, however, is that, although Dickinson did rely upon these metrical forms for the basis of her poetry, she often used them as a model to strain against and violate. The same can be said for her patterns of rhyme. "True rhyme" is the ideal lurking behind Dickinson's verse; however, she employed many deviations from it—half-rhyme, consonant rhyme, eye-rhyme, and the like. Sometimes she scarcely rhymed at all. And although there was precedent for this practice in Emerson's work, the music of her verse was new enough to seem revolutionary, discordant (and to many unacceptable). Grounding her work in the commonest denominators, she pulled against them so vigorously that for many years she was thought to have employed no system at all.

Modern critics have devised a number of subtle ways to describe the poet who wrestles with the work of some prior artist. Dickinson herself, self-conscious as always, put the matter in simple terms: Disobedience, mankind's first sin and the quintessential transgression of youth—a crime that can be committed *only* when there is a "parent" in charge.

> *So I pull my Stockings off*
> *Wading in the Water*
> *For the Disobedience' Sake*
> *Boy that lived for "or'ter"*
>
> *Went to Heaven perhaps at Death*
> *And perhaps he did'nt*
> *Moses was'nt fairly used—*
> *Ananias was'nt—*
>
> (#1201; var. "or'ter")

Another child. She has been taking Bible lessons and is still young enough to raise impertinent questions. Ananias followed the Apostles after Christ's death; he was supposed to give all his possessions away to the Christian community, but in a moment of dishonesty he kept some back. God's wrath was instantly upon him, and He struck him dead. Moses's case was even harder. The great prophet had served God faithfully for forty years, with but a single minor transgression. He led a stiff-necked and querulous people through the wilderness toward the Promised Land, and at journey's end God's "reward" was so ungenerous that it assumed in Dickinson's eyes the character of a cruel and taunting punishment. God conducted the aged patriarch to the top of Mount Nebo: "This is the land which I sware unto Abraham, unto Isaac, and unto Jacob, saying, I will give it unto thy seed: I have caused thee to see it with thine eyes, but thou shalt not go over thither. So Moses the servant of the LORD died there in the land of Moab" (Deuteronomy 34:4–5). God is almighty and eternal: man is poor, weak, and mortal. God's wrath is implacable: even trivial offenses against Him receive a mighty reprisal, for God is also jealous and unforgiving. Does such a God deserve obedience? Will He honor it if He receives it? The child in the poem concludes that the record speaks against God, and so this child chooses Disobedience *for its own sake:* "Wading in the Water."

The joke is buried deep in the poem, but it is there. A matter of "feet," ten human toes, perhaps, released from the tight sock of decorous dress; or perhaps a line of *metrical* rebellion, "feet" that are allowed freedom from the conventions of rhyming "eights and sixes."

Over and over again, Dickinson plays with the pun on feet and on the proper functions of feet—walking, running, dancing. It is a commonplace of Dickinson study that the real subject of the poem "*I cannot dance upon my Toes— / No Man instructed me—*" (#326) is the poet's refusal to accept the awkward, deforming poetic feet of conventional poetry. However, it is generally not noticed that the exhilaration of creativity that is the subject of "I taste a liquor never brewed—" is captured in the swaying, effervescent country dance, the reel: "*Inebriate of Air—am I— / And Debauchee of Dew— / Reeling—thro endless summer days— / From inns of Molten Blue—*" (#214).

The pun sometimes found its way into her letters, though always in connection with the poetry. In 1861 Dickinson sent a number of successive versions of "*Safe in their Alabaster Chambers*" (#216) across the hedge to her sister-in-law, Susan Dickinson, and the two discussed the merits of several alternative second stanzas. When the decision had been made and the poem had earned Sue's approval, Dickinson wrote, "Your praise is good—to me— ... Could I make you and Austin—proud—sometime—a great way off— 'twould give me taller feet—"[19]

Sue, an intimate, could probably understand the ambition expressed in this pun with no difficulty. Others were not so adept at following the quick kaleidoscope of Emily Dickinson's discourse. The third letter to Higginson, like the short note to Sue written a year earlier, also dealt with the poet's ambitions for her work. Higginson had been reserved in his judgment of the verse she had sent him: the unfamiliar and (to his ear) unruly meters and rhymes seemed not ready to be issued to the public. Dickinson responded:

I smile when you suggest that I delay "to publish"—that being foreign to my thought, as Firmament to Fin—

 If fame belonged to me, I could not escape her—if she did not, the longest day would pass me on the chase—and the approbation of my Dog, would forsake me—then—My Barefoot-Rank is better—

 You think my gait "spasmodic"—I am in danger—Sir—

 You think me "uncontrolled"—I have no Tribunal.[20]

Austin remarked that she liked to adopt theatrical postures in the Higginson letters. She was at least ambivalent about publication (as the note to Sue affirms), but she had too much integrity and pride to petition for it—or perhaps her image of "fame" was too colossal to be framed in less than Biblical terms. In any case, the "Barefoot-Rank" signifies not rustic modesty, but incorrigible impudence: the "gait" he deemed "spasmodic" seems not clumsy to her, but "better." This letter was written in June 1862; two months later she sent him the virtuosic verse "*I cannot dance upon my Toes*," a dazzling display of varied footwork, to articulate the same impertinent, unyielding position. She wanted to demonstrate her capacity to write the rhythmically regular verse he demanded; and she wanted him to realize that the issue of metrical feet had been the subject of her most scrupulous thought. The rhythmic patterns that had appeared merely "uncontrolled" to him had actually been deployed as part of her self-conscious strategy of artistic rebellion.

 Many of the advantages inherent in pre-empting the license and language of childhood can be summed up in the word "no." There is a time in infancy when the child prefers this word above all others—gives it as response to every query, request, and command—a time when the child's attitude toward all accrued wisdom, conventional religion, and accepted propriety is entirely concentrated in this single response: the flailing, shouting roar, "NO"; the tight monosyllabic shake of the head, "no." In the course of human life, this epoch of "no" is a time of momentous transition; it marks the beginning of autonomy and effective action in the world and the relinquishment of the illusion of absolute power. In the beginning, the world is brought to the infant—the baby's demands and needs are satisfied by others when they discern his or her desires—and as the baby begins to grow increasingly conscious of the relationship between "self" and "others," it seems at first that the others are under the control of self. Thus in the natural course of things, we all begin life supposing we have magical power over all that we survey. Somewhat later in childhood we come to accept the fact that our power as individuals is very limited; this limitation of our sense of power is in some measure compensated by the pleasure we can take in negotiating the world with increasing skill and effectiveness. Thus is the fantasy of absolute autonomy relinquished for the actuality of real but limited power. Between these two periods of life lies the epoch of "no," when the child realizes his or her power without yet accepting the fact that this power is circumscribed.[21]

During that epoch, when everything is rejected equally and "no" is the answer to every question, the child's negativity is not resistance to some *particular* thing; it is, instead, a refusal to accept the fact that choices must be made and that the significant categories of the world have already been defined by others. Relinquishing the imperious "no" is a painful capitulation. Adults tolerate this season of "insanity," knowing that in time, as the child matures, it will pass; yet the child's impervious resistance to reasonableness and placation is very difficult to live with, and occasionally parents fall in with the momentary lunacy by matching absurdity to absurdity. "Would you like a cookie?" "No." "Would you like to play?" "No." "Would you like to *go outside?*" "No." "Would you like to *stay inside?*" "No." The pattern of this more or less playful exchange demonstrates the parent's intuitive understanding of the meaning of the child's "no": the assertion of equal indifference to everything is tantamount to claiming an infinite remove from the world of finite possibilities; it is disdain for all values that have been set by others; it is the child's last opportunity to pretend at being God.

Certainly Dickinson could capture the insouciance and pertness of the poet-as-two-year-old: *"The Missing All, prevented Me / From missing minor Things. / If nothing larger than a World's / Departure from a Hinge / Or Sun's extinction, be observed / 'Twas not so large that I / Could lift my Forehead from my work / For Curiosity"* (#985). However, the very flippancy that makes a poem like this one appealing also robs it of authority. Moreover, although readers may be willing to accept an image of the artist as someone odd or "half-cracked," that image renders a socially sanctioned form of disrespect and dismissiveness for the poet and her work. Thus if Dickinson was to use this idiom of "no" as a Voice of *power,* she was obliged to disentangle it from the merely infantile and from the nearly mad.

There is, of course, one further category of people in whom society sanctions an attitude of disdain and indifference to all the things of this world: the Saint. The tradition of "dying to the world"—a tradition that is ceremonially enacted when an adult enters a sectarian order, relinquishes his or her "given" name and selects a new one, severs the bonds of family ties, discards the dress of the street for the religious habit, and submits to a life-long discipline of indifference to physical comforts—has long commanded society's respect. Dickinson understood the implications of such a life, and in some ways seems to have admired it: *"To put this World down, like a Bundle—*

/ And walk steady, away, / Requires Energy—possibly Agony— / 'Tis the Scarlet way" (#527). Yet there was an insurmountable obstacle to her employing the Voice of the Saint without essential alterations: customarily, the Saint has authority in this world precisely insofar as he or she has relinquished "I" to "God."

It is not personal authority at all that is communicated by the Saint's rejection of worldly categories, then: it is merely God's judgment and will exercised through the medium of an earthly agent. Unlike the child, the Saint cannot assert *autonomy* through the idiom of "no"; rather, the Saint has exchanged the world's categories (which will at least allow an individual to make a series of choices) for God's categories (which allow for very little choice at all). So Dickinson wrote of the prototypical Saint's vocation:

> *Renunciation—is a piercing Virtue—*
> *The letting go*
> *A Presence—for an Expectation—*
> *Not now—*
> *The putting out of Eyes—*
> *Just Sunrise—*
> *Lest Day—*
> *Day's Great Progenitor—*
> *Outvie*
>
> (#745)

The God Who has withdrawn His face is rendered here not as "Eclipse," but as "Expectation": Saints have relinquished the "Presence" of the visual world to fix their attention upon absence and hope. Again there is wounding; but now it is self-mutilation—"The putting out of Eyes"—the abnegation of a child's right to confront a Father and grapple for power, and the yielding of identity to a void. The pacing of the poem's "footwork" describes the process, as the span of the speaking Voice is methodically contracted, mimicking the mathematical process by which a number approaches zero.

Poems of renunciation can be found throughout Dickinson's work. When the subject is construed in its traditional context, as a renunciation of the world for God, the self is often perceived as both compromised and diminished. Yet this same transaction *redefined* provides the basis for one of her most powerful poetic Voices. Nowhere is such renunciation better exemplified than in a poem of the classroom and parlor where "dying to the world" gives "birth" to the Voice of a poet.

> *A Clock stopped—*
> *Not the Mantel's—*

Geneva's farthest skill
Cant put the puppet bowing—
That just now dangled still—

An awe came on the Trinket!
The Figures hunched, with pain—
Then quivered out of Decimals—
Into Degreeless Noon—

It will not stir for Doctor's—
This Pendulum of snow—
The Shopman importunes it—
While cool—concernless No—

Nods from the Gilded pointers—
Nods from the Seconds slim—
Decades of Arrogance between
The Dial life—
And Him—

(#287)

We begin with the schoolgirl's text, Paley and the argument by "Design" for the existence of God: "Suppose I had found a *watch* upon the ground." Just as the existence of a watch indicates the existence of a watchmaker, so all the ordered processes around us indicate the informing presence of a Master Craftsman. Nature—the orderly panorama of the seasons, the rules of Newtonian physics, even the miniature "Clock" that is our own body ticking its way toward death—all of these operate according to laws whose existence both proves the necessary existence of a Supreme Being and confirms His authority.

Yet these scientific laws prove more than the mere existence of the Divinity; they articulate the poverty of our power in relation to God's. A law "implies a power," Paley asserts, "for it is the order according to which that power acts."[22] So long as we live on earth, we are in thrall to God's power as it is exerted through unvarying natural laws. Thus because we cannot change them, we bow to the tyranny of time and to a cosmos whose significant categories and regulations have already been defined by the Deity. To escape the reach of His power, we must somehow escape His "Design." "Death's large—Democratic fingers" offer one release, for they put all at an infinite remove from both mankind's values and God's natural laws. Yet such release is scant comfort, for we are transported either to oblivion or to an uncertain eternity where we must confront the Avenger unmasked. If we could "die" alive—if we could find a way to step out of time without stepping into the wilderness of hereafter, if we could reject "Design" while preserving the "I"

intact and strong—then perhaps we might command the power and authority to counter the assaults of the Divinity.

Such paradox as this was Dickinson's achievement: a fusion of infinity
and nothingness. To create a Voice of power for her own use, Emily Dickinson conflated the freedom, autonomy, isolated arrogance, and absolute egoism of the child with the solemnity and high purpose of the Saint. She
invented a new vernacular of "No."

In many ways a quintessential classroom exercise, "A Clock stopped—"
is a virtuoso demonstration of Dickinson's ability to manipulate mathematics
and science and to insinuate them into her work, a deliberate appropriation
of one essential element in God's great "Design." The informing metaphors
of this verse pivot upon the notion of "degree," just as its linear construction
rests upon the fulcrum of "Noon"—a word that occurs precisely in the
middle of the poem, as it does in seven others.[23] Noon is a "Degreeless" hour
because when both minute and hour hand point to twelve, they are superimposed: there is no angle between them; they are separated by *zero* degrees.
Moreover, the word "Noon" as an object in itself has properties that render
it expressly useful for Dickinson's purposes. It has zero at the center—twice
zero, in fact, which as Lear's Fool has informed us, is still zero. Construed
somewhat differently, however, it may be seen to have infinity at the core (∞);
thus are boundlessness and nothingness fused in this single syllable. In addition, it is a one-word trope for eternity, a palindrome of a word with no
beginning and no end, the same word whether read backward or forward.
And, perhaps uniquely important to Dickinson, it is the word "no" placed
"face-to-face." The word "Noon" is so consistently associated with the same
themes of life and death, eternity and oblivion—so often carefully centered
in a poem—that it begins to serve the function of a "sign" created not by
God, but by the poet. "Noon" is *both* a zero hour and eternity. And neither
zero nor eternity can be computed in "degrees."

"Degree" is not merely a scientific term; its more general usage has to do
with power and station, "a step . . . in elevation, quality, dignity, or rank; as
a man of great *degree*." What the verse chronicles is a titanic but quiet
struggle for supremacy. Like "Two swimmers wrestled on the spar—," this
poem deals not with an individual crisis, not even with literal death (although
most critics have read it as a rendering of the moment when the body yields
its spirit up); instead, it offers the outline of a general case, an individual
struggling against God's powers and persuasions for utter independence and
autonomy. And if, as the poem seems to suggest, this paradoxical triumph of
a "death" that produces a "new birth" has special relevance to the vocation
of Poet—a victory that is a matter of tone and structure and Voice—nonetheless, Dickinson offers a strategy that can be translated back into every
human life.

In the thirty-seven words that precede "Noon—," the "Clock" is presented in ambiguous, sometimes diminishing terms. Rendered disparagingly as a mechanism that is intrinsically dependent upon external agency, it is a "puppet" or a "Trinket," and its usual behavior is obeisance—the obsequious perpetual motion of "bowing," acknowledging subservience to a Master of superior degree. Nor does this action even indicate an individual decision; as the puppet is manipulated by a showman's strings, so are we all compelled to our knees by the fear of God's laws, the implacable agents of His power—time, death, decay. Yet even in this first half, there is an undercurrent of stubborn resistance. Although the initial sentence does not reveal who stopped the "Clock," subsequent statements suggest that somehow, in defiance of all usual laws and expectations, the mechanism has stopped itself. The practitioner from Geneva who is the first to attempt re-animation of the ticking, bobbing sycophant is both an ambassador from the capital of clocks and a missionary from Calvin's Geneva Convention—the foundation upon which New England Protestantism was built. His efforts fail, and the second stanza concludes with an agony of "awe" as the "Clock" moves definitively beyond the reach of time.

In the thirty-seven words that follow "Noon—," the power relationship has been reversed. A "Doctor" and a "Shopman" come to complete the trinity of those ministering to the obstinate machine, and all three are but different guises of the Master Craftsman, God Himself. Yet even He Who has bestowed life cannot force life upon this rebel, and now it is the "importuning" Deity Who is forced into an attitude of supplication. If the "Clock" had died in the literal sense, it would have moved into some beyond—eternity or void—where God holds sway. However, it has not. It is still *in* the world, but no longer *of* it, poised in an enigmatic equilibrium that is captured by the impossible image, "This Pendulum of snow—." Dickinson often used "snow" as a synonym for her own poetry, the veil she interposed between self and the savage God. However, this poem offers a lesson that goes beyond Dickinson's personal case. The essence of human existence can be altered by the kind of transaction that has taken place here. The ticking heart is not merely hardened to God's entreaties (this would be the standard Trinitarian formulation), but it has become suffused with disdain and is thus entirely unavailable to Him. The integrity of such a position is captured by "cool—concernless No—," a dismissiveness of utter indifference. In her role as poet, Dickinson could create artful formulations of verse, "snow," that serve to reiterate the negative that is at the heart of "snow"—"no."

Ironically, in the concluding sections of the poem it is God Who is still trapped within the rigid regularity of time; for insofar as He requires its bowing obsequiousness to confirm His own supremacy, *"Nods from the Gilded pointers— / Nods from the Seconds slim—,"* to that extent is He dislodged from the eternal and the infinite. The fraudulence of such authority is rendered by "Gilded," a superficial appearance that merely simulates the "golden" promises of conversion. And in the brief second or two that allows God to reckon His might, the newly liberated "Clock" has already conquered "Decades."

Dickinson was fascinated with mathematics and sometimes measured the significance of an object or event in terms of ratios. Very often the intrinsic worth of an object was a function of its distance from the observer: the farther away it was, the more valuable it was. The ratio of *infinity* to any number, however large, is infinite: Heaven is of inestimable value precisely because of its incalculable distance from us, and a being trapped in the web of the world's limits can never summon a great enough force to confront an infinite Deity on equal terms. Yet *"A Clock stopped—"* suggests a tantalizing strategy to overcome the infirmity of human limitation: the ratio of any number to *zero* is also infinite; thus infinity and zero are *equally distant* from the world of finite objects, measurable time, and bounded distances. To the extent that Dickinson's poetic Voice can assume a posture of radical diminishment, ideally one that can be identified as "zero," it has thereby established a relationship to the finite world that is the mirror image of God's infinite remove—and equivalent to it in value. Such is the logic by which infinity and zero can be conflated in this poem.

Throughout much of the poetry, then, there is a transvaluation of values according to which assertions of self-abasement and apparent humility become affirmations of power and worth. *"Size circumscribes—,"* mocks the Voice of a prodigious child, impatient with a world managed by slow-witted adults and a universe ruled by a clumsy colossus; *"it has no room / For petty furniture— / The Giant tolerates no Gnat / For Ease of Gianture— / Repudiates it, all the more—"* (#641). The derision of the rhyme, furniture / Gianture needs no gloss. Nor should a reader be startled when the initially meek Voice of *"I'm Nobody!"* executes an about-face into contempt (and again the rhyme captures the scorn of dismissal): *"How dreary—to be—Somebody! / How public—like a Frog— / To tell your name—the livelong June— / To an admiring Bog!"* (#288) The daughter of the politician had seen many pompous would-be solons proclaiming their virtues in public. Similarly, the student at the Amherst Academy and the Mount Holyoke Seminary had heard many self-important ministers enjoining their congregations to listen for the "still small voice" that had called to the prophet Elijah during Ahab's reign in Israel (I Kings 19:12); and the student-become-poet knew that "small," too, could be transformed into a declaration of power. *"All I may, if small, / Do it not display / Larger for the Totalness— / 'Tis Economy / To bestow a World / And withold a Star— / Utmost, is Munificence— / Less, tho larger, poor"* (#819). Just as "noon" contains both zero and infinity and "snow" contains "no," so "small" contains "all."

Dickinson's cryptic utterance to Higginson at the beginning of their correspondence, "My Business is Circumference," has fascinated and puzzled her readers. Charles Anderson rightly cites the *Religio Medici* of Sir Thomas Browne as the principal source for her interest in this figure: "In his effort to define [circumference] as a sense of boundlessness radiating out from a center, opposite to the normal sense of a limiting circle, [Browne] cited the formulation of Hermes: The sphere of which the center is everywhere, the circumference nowhere. . . . [Dickinson] expanded it into a symbol for all that is outside. Her center is the inquiring mind whose business is circumference, intent upon exploring the whole infinity of the universe that lies before her." Sensing Dickinson's ambition and the audacity of her enterprise, Anderson concludes: "The most startling use of the term occurs in a late letter: 'The Bible dealt with the Centre, not with the Circumference.' This pronouncement is not so much baffling as unexpectedly bold. Set beside her own boast, 'My Business is Circumference,' it seems little short of blasphemous. Her poems are to accomplish something the Bible does not? . . . The immediate leap into God is impossible, the poet cannot be like the aurora. He must go back to the earth, the human experience of pain and suffering, and work out from there toward the divine reality."[24] Dickinson would answer that the poet *can* leap into God's realm. So long as God cares to demand our obedience and worship, He is ensnared in the very "Design" that seems to separate the finite world from His realm of infinity and eternity. And insofar as she can locate the crucial areas where God's majesty requires mankind's cooperation, the poet can accomplish something the Bible does not: she can repossess language, using it to expose God's tyranny. As Representative for us all, she can develop a Voice—a posture, a set of values, a tone of address—that will counter God's attempts to dominate us.

The Voice of "no" is more than merely an aesthetic achievement, then; it can articulate one form of release. If we are not frightened of death or suffering, if we can tolerate loss and retain personal integrity, if we are utterly unmoved by the promise of some Heaven to come—then God has no hold upon us. By the same token, if the world's rewards cannot tempt us—if we disdain the celebrity of public office and the wealth of kings—then we can have the power to be sufficient entirely in ourselves. And *this* is freedom. Perhaps it is the only "salvation" available to us.

The Voice of "no" has yet another mode: the profession of supreme importance merely by defiance or self-assertion. "*Me, change! Me, alter! / Then I will, when on the Everlasting Hill / A Smaller Purple grows—*" (#268). Politicians are confirmed by election; God maintains authority by tempting us with a different kind of Election. Dickinson engrosses both into her poetry, re-animating and confirming self each time a reader's eye scans the page. "*My Reward for Being, was This. / My premium—My Bliss— / An Admirality, less— / A Sceptre—penniless— / And Realms—just Dross— / When Thrones accost my Hands— / With 'Me, Miss, Me' / I'll unroll Thee— / Dominions dowerless— beside this Grace— / Election—Vote— / The Ballots of Eternity, will show just that*" (*#343*). These were serious matters to Dickinson. Nonetheless, she could approach even considerations of eternity and oblivion with whimsy or riddle or anagram; she was ready to employ all the aspects of language that are summoned by parlor games like charades or by acrostics and other puzzles of the pen. Even the shape of a poem could play a role in its meaning. Thus in the preceding poem the circumference that is sometimes zero and sometimes infinity is embedded in the form, which is circular: strictly speaking, the most appropriate logical sequitur of its *last* line is its *first* (i.e., "*The Ballots of Eternity, will show just that* / *My Reward for Being, was This [poetry]*").

The affirmation of self, too, was subject to witty forms of poetic invention. "I" could be asserted merely by sound; death by shifting from long "i" to short "i"—closing the "eye / I" (so after death, a person's body is generally referred to as "it"). Even before she was fifteen, the letters show her experimenting with this device. In an early note to Abiah Root, six closed "eye / I"s anticipate the chill stroke of extinction: "I have heard some sweet *little birds sing,* but I fear we shall have more cold weather and their *little bills will* be frozen up before their songs are finished."[25] Perhaps she was already making private copies of her own correspondence, or perhaps her memory for sound was as phenomenal as her capacity for verbal compression. In any case, the very same manipulation, in a more trenchant examination of the same subject, can be found in the first line of a poem written out twenty-one years later: "*His Bill is clasped—his Eye forsook—*" (*#1102*), the second half of the line iterating the fact that is conveyed phonetically by three closed "eye / I"s in the first three words. The self-consciousness of the device is patent in the vowel transformations of some of the lesser work: "*If I should'nt be alive* / *When the Robins come,* / *Give the one in Red Cravat,* / *A Memorial crumb.* / *If I could'nt thank you,* / *Being fast asleep,* / *You will know I'm trying* / *With my Granite lip!*" (*#182*). Yet at other times the tactic is so startling and iconoclastic that its power obscures the artifice; the strength of the Voice makes the poem seem almost emotive, and the reader may have the illusion of being directly in touch with the author herself in a mood that borders on mania.

Probably no "I" poem has elicited so much critical consternation as this one:

> *Mine—by the Right of the White Election!*
> *Mine—by the Royal Seal!*
> *Mine—by the Sign in the Scarlet prison—*
> *Bars—cannot conceal!*
>
> *Mine—here—in Vision—and in Veto!*
> *Mine—by the Grave's Repeal—*

Titled— Confirmed—
Delirious Charter!
Mine— long as Ages steal!

(#528)

What belongs to this speaker? Everything, it would seem. Little wonder, then, that so many readers have dismissed the Voice as merely Emily-Dickinson-in-the-throes-of-personal-crisis. This kind of response is a defensive tactic that establishes a safe distance between the reader and the violence latent in the verse. Such an approach may not get at the meaning of the poem, but it stands as unselfconscious witness to the extravagant vitality and power of this Voice.

Although the mode of address is strangely extra-social, the speaker is clearly an adult, capable of using the language of legal authority, titles, and contracts—familiar with Christ's promise of Election and with the religious myth that is consummated in the visionary Book of Revelation. Thus a few critics have rightly seen that the proper context for this unorthodox poem approximates the religious: the speaker has actively chosen the vocation of poetry, and by virtue of this "Election" she has gained some "Royal" reward that transcends time. Inexplicably, however, the insistent Voice of the poem is not fulfilled and at rest, but is still pitted against some undesignated antagonist. With the first line of the poem, the reader is flung into the middle of a territorial dispute: ownership has been challenged, and the more useful question is not *what* the speaker wants, but *who* the other member of the ongoing controversy might be.

Perhaps the most interesting strategy of this poem is the mixture of unlike elements. The adult intelligence of this Voice combines with the use of religious terminology to suggest some characteristics of the Christian saint; however, there is also a menacingly uncivilized quality in its posture, for "I" is the overwhelming and unmitigated claim throughout. "Mine . . . Mine . . . Mine" is a childlike chant familiar to those who have passed time in the company of two-year-olds. It is tolerable (barely) when the refusal to acknowledge social categories or limitations of any sort issues from someone too immature to enforce his or her will. But when, as in this poem, the imperious voice clearly belongs to an adult, the result is of stunning force. Perhaps nowhere else in Dickinson's work are the Voices of child and Saint so explosively fused: freedom, autonomy, isolated arrogance, and absolute egoism are merged here with a sense of solemnity and high purpose. Sometimes, as in "A Clock stopped—," the product of this coalescence is the artfully restrained Voice of the tight, quiet, but decisive "no." In this poem, however, it is the roar of "NO" transformed into a vaunting, sovereign assertion of self, unlimited and unqualified: the Voice of "I." The only worthy opponent of such a Voice is God Himself.

This Voice—the "I" in "mine" that permeates the poem in echoing assonance—stands outside the limitations of ordinary grammar: just as there is no specific referent for the pronoun, so there is no limited, finite verb and no circumscribed object. Syntactically, then, this "I" exists beyond God's temporal "Design" even as it dominates the tonal design of the poem. Ironically, God *is* subject to the limitations of time and space implicit in usual syntactic constructions: the "Bars" of the "Scarlet prison" in which He has pent every human soul "cannot conceal" the speaker's triumph; even inexorable time, slipping slowly along, cannot "steal" so much as a scintilla from the force of this Voice. And these failures, in contrast to the speaker's victories, are recounted according to the delimiting grammatical laws of subjects, finite verbs, and predicates. In fact, if goods have been stolen and laws broken, it is the poet who is culprit, for she has turned God's mystical language of the Covenant, the Apocalypse, and Salvation—"White," "Election," "Royal Seal," "Vision," "Titled," and "Charter"—to the aggrandizement of that "eye / I" whose poetic vision and impassioned veto of God's proffered contract confer a superior state. A traditional Christian lyric would celebrate God's supremacy; this heretical hymn glorifies the individual's ability to remain intact despite cosmic threats and bribes. Perhaps it intends to engross even God into the domain of self, no more than one additional prize of the sweeping despotism asserted by "Mine."

This potent poem is not unique among Dickinson's works: several other verses are hauntingly similar, though few others achieve the high pitch of hypnotic intensity. #431, for example, is a lesser instance. "*Me—come! My dazzled face / In such a shining place! / Me—hear! My foreign Ear / The sounds of Welcome—there! / The Saints forget / Our bashful feet— / My Holiday, shall be / That They—remember me— / My Paradise—the fame / That They—pronounce my name—*" This may seem at first to be a poem about the entrance into Heaven; however, the allusion to "feet," which in this poem are anything but "bashful," signals that the subject is in reality the kind of "Election" conferred upon poets (as in #343, "*When Thrones accost my Hands— / With 'Me, Miss, Me'*"). But most of all, the cadences of the verse have become no more than a naked trumpeting of self—"Me, Me, Me" and "My, My, My." Similarly, #174 ("*At last, to be identified! / At last, the lamps upon thy side / The rest of Life to see!*") is a hymn to eye / I—as is the more complex poem beginning "*Title divine—is mine! / The Wife—without the Sign!*" (#1072) The salient feature of such poems is the speaker's self-achieving, self-supporting isolation.

Sometimes the posture of opposition or renunciation may have a "saner," more civilized tone. A speaker may reject both the world and God; nonetheless, they are of value in the poem because they provide a context for the speaker's act. The following example, often anthologized and justly praised, rehearses the complexity of this stance with model economy.

> *The Soul selects her own Society—*
> *Then—shuts the Door—*
> *To her divine Majority—*
> *Present no more—*
>
> *Unmoved—she notes the Chariots—pausing—*
> *At her low Gate—*
> *Unmoved—an Emperor be kneeling*
> *Upon her Mat—*
>
> *I've known her—from an ample nation—*
> *Choose One—*
> *Then—close the lids—of her attention—*
> *Like Stone—*
>
> $\qquad\qquad$ (#303; var. "lids—")

Here is hubris nicely delineated. "Society" can move in two directions away from the speaker. One supplicant is God (the "divine Majority," where "Majority" literally indicates one of higher degree or rank), and His suit is rendered by alterations in the language of revivals. The "Soul *selects*" instead of waiting for Election; the strait gate of conventional conversion has become the narrowed and barred pathway to the Soul; instead of beseeching faith, the Soul rejects the presence of the Deity, even though *He* may humble Himself before her. Equal indifference is accorded the riches and titles of worldly renown, a "Society" of emperors or kings. The address of both the "divine Majority" and the "Emperor" has an explicitly sexual connotation (as both advance in an attempt to pass through "the door" and the "low Gate"); however, the feminine Soul has rebelled against the passivity that is mandated for women by the conventions of classic courtship. Instead, *she* chooses "One" from an "ample nation," and then closes her "eye / I" altogether. And as in "Renunciation—is a piercing Virtue—," the conclusion of the final stanza renders the speaker's withdrawal by a radical reduction toward zero, both in line length and in vowel sound—although here, because the speaker has included "One" other with herself, the final line is a two-word spondee.

The resultant Voice is recognizably human and patently sane. It is, therefore, not threatening, but available to the reader; and its fine, discriminating judgment is in some measure susceptible of imitation. The difference between this poem and the ones discussed immediately preceding it which trumpet "I" nakedly and voraciously is the sculptured delineation of the speaker: the God of transcendence and the representatives of the immanent world provide significant "others" to interact with the "self" of the speaker and thus to define it. The situation is universal, and the decision is entirely without particularizing detail; however, the *means* of establishing identity in this poem are those employed in every human life: an interaction between "self" and "other." We are dealing with a socialized speaker—an adult Voice that understands and accepts the *fact* that the world has evolved categories to define and limit human behavior, even though it may *reject* the world (and the world's God) altogether once it has fully assessed their worth. It is a prideful Voice, but it is mannerly, elegant, even aristocratic.

By contrast, the Voice of the other poems is primitive, atavistic, sometimes inchoate. *"Mine—by the Right of the White Election!" "Title divine—is mine!"* The Voice of such utterances might issue from a cloud or from the white heat of flame: it is unfathomable, Godlike. It is a self in the process of creating and sustaining self by an act of naked, relentless incantation. It is vastly more powerful than the more socialized Voices of renunciation and exclusiveness; at the same time, perhaps inevitably, it is cryptic and not fully humanized. In striving for a Voice of power, Dickinson may not have sufficiently disentangled this thundering rhetoric of "I" from the merely childish, the nearly mad, and the purely visionary.

Thus for some readers, *this* Voice cannot stand as "Representative." For these, Dickinson was obliged to invent other Voices, which could speak the language of daily life as it really was in mid-nineteenth-century America, what Charles Anderson called "the human experience of pain and suffering."

3 ◆ The "Wife's" Voice

Unwed in fact and destitute of child, Emily Dickinson could nonetheless appropriate the *Voice* of the "Wife" for her verse, a Voice of maturity—and intimate with pain.

For all that she was talented and intellectually prodigious, Emily Dickinson was in many ways like other girls and young women. She loved to play with variations of her own name and signature. As a little girl, she signed her letters simply "Emily," occasionally expanding it to "Emily E. Dickinson"; however, soon after she turned seventeen, she began to alter the spelling of her first name to a more romantic form, "Emilie." On and off for a number of years, she signed herself variously: "Emilie," "Emily," "Emily E. Dickinson," "Emilie E. Dickinson," "Emilie E.," and sometimes merely "E." or "E.E.D." In 1860, the year she turned thirty, Emily Dickinson relinquished the girlish "Emilie" forever; however, the name change that had already come to most of her friends, giving up the maiden name for the name of a husband's family, had not come to Emily Dickinson. It never did. Nonetheless, she did not abandon her propensity for changing the name she went by;

as late as 1878, the poet still idled time away by practicing her signature in the worksheets of her poetry. Emily Dickinson, who never took a husband, chose to define her status through her art; and she attached this ritual of name change to the act of writing poetry.

The adult letters give evidence of a remarkable series of innovations. For instance, in the eighty-one letters that remain from Dickinson to Higginson, she did not sign herself "Emily" or "Emily Dickinson" a single time. The very first letter is not signed at all: the body of the letter is on a sheet of stationery with no name attached; in a small envelope accompanying the letter is a card on which Emily Dickinson wrote her name. In subsequent letters to Higginson, she sometimes signed herself "E. Dickinson" (which might have been either her father's or her mother's signature as well). Frequently, she signed herself merely "Dickinson," as a man might. Other letters are concluded not with a name, but with an epithet, usually "Your Scholar," but occasionally such others as "Your Gnome" and "Barabbas" [*sic*]. And finally, after many years of correspondence, she fell into the habit of not signing some of her letters to him at all, repeating the format of the very first letter but not bothering to include the accompanying card—confident that her handwriting and distinctive style were by now a sufficient identification.

The entire Dickinson family was obsessed with the importance of "name." Edward hovered over his only son anxiously—eager that he marry, settle in Amherst, and produce a son of his own. This was not affection, but a strain of entrenched fanaticism concerning the "House of Dickinson." He expended no similar concern about his daughters' future: one or the other might marry and produce children, but if she did, these would carry their own father's name; the daughters might retain the Dickinson name and remain at home, but then they would be childless and thereby unable to perpetuate "Dickinson." Everybody in the family understand Father's scenario, and so did the rest of Amherst. Mabel Loomis Todd's daughter writes, "Whether the girls ever married was beside the point. It was not family *traits* [italics mine] which must be perpetuated so much as the Dickinson name."[26] Susan Gilbert was well aware of her father-in-law's eccentricity, and the mandate for grandchildren caused tension in her marriage to Austin from the beginning. Finally, on June 19, 1861, five years after their marriage, Austin and Sue had their first child, a son. As was the custom, the baby, who was sickly, remained unnamed for a number of months; the family called him "Jackey," patriotically nicknamed for the Union Jack. Finally, in December, he was given a proper name. Possibly the name of Austin's first son had been settled tacitly even before the marriage: "Jackey" was named not for his own father, but for his paternal grandfather.

BEFORE DECEMBER 6. *Edward Dickinson receives a request from his new grandson (via Susan):* I have been in this great world ever so many days, and have'nt got any name yet but Jackey—My Mother says you have a very nice name, and I may ask you if I can't have one just like it—If you are willing such a little bit of a man should have such a big name like yours, please tell me—

DECEMBER 6. *Edward Dickinson replies:* I have rec^d your letter, asking me if I am willing that you should have a name like mine—And I say, in this reply, which you can *read*, as well as you could *write* the other, that if you will be a good boy, ride in your carriage & not cry, and always mind your father and mother, I will consent to your being called Edward Dickinson; and promise you a Silver Cup to drink from, as soon as you are big enough to hold it in your hands. Your affectionate Grandfather . . .[27]

Thus would "Dickinson" be perpetuated by the little boy, who was thereafter called "Ned"—or so the old man thought. However, Edward's daughter Emily did not write off her *own* claim to the "Dickinson" heritage so readily. Thus when Ned was nearly five years old, she wrote Mrs. Holland, "Ned tells that the Clock purrs and the Kitten ticks. He inherits his Uncle Emily's ardor for the lie."[28]

Although Emily Dickinson watched the performance in December 1861 without any direct comment that has been preserved, there is an indirect clue to her reaction. Four months later (in April 1862) she wrote her first letter to Higginson, and by 1866, when he had received enough of her poetry to comprehend her sense of vocation, she had begun signing herself simply "Dickinson." After her father's death in 1874, more often than not she signed all letters "E. Dickinson." And in 1885, when Emily Dickinson knew that she lay dying, she concluded a letter to Mabel Loomis Todd, who was in Europe, with this sentence: "The Savior's only signature to the Letter he wrote to all mankind, was a Stranger and ye took me in." She signed herself with pristine simplicity: "America."[29]

In a way that her husband was not, a wife was accountable for every aspect of the lives of those in her house.[30] She tended their sicknesses; she supervised their meals and clothing; she gave her children their earliest lessons in letters and numbers and religion. It is true that a mother might stir the cozy custards of the nursery; but when death visited the home, killing the resident grandparents or brothers and sisters with equal indifference, it was Mother who had to explain the universal impassivity of death and disease to her children. Women were assigned the responsibility for imposing day-to-day order on life's chaos—for sustaining a regulated life and emotional continuity.

Thus when Emily Dickinson appropriated the Voice of the "Wife" for her poetry, it was a Voice of maturity and responsibility, wounded and sobered by pain, but nonetheless seeking to retain coherence and to assert the sanity of everyday domestic routine. It acknowledged the responsibility to care for others. And when anguish extended beyond even the range of comforting, the Voice of the "Wife" summoned the courage to meet reality face to face, however diminished from human hope reality had become, and to seek out truth. Paradoxically, this Voice, too, could speak as Everyman, even though not everyone had been a "Wife" (not even every woman), for its province encompassed the personal recesses of every life. Not all can enter the perpetually shifting shadow-masque of markets and money, politics and wars; but everyone enacts some essential role in the short, intimate drama that is begun in birth and ended in death—and it is private drama that falls within the "Wife's" domain as Dickinson construes it.

> I'm "wife" — I've finished that —
> That other state —
> I'm Czar — I'm "Woman" now —
> It's safer so —
>
> How odd the Girl's life looks
> Behind this soft Eclipse —
> I think that Earth feels so
> To folks in Heaven — now —
>
> This being comfort — then
> That other kind — was pain —
> But why compare?
> I'm "Wife!" Stop there!
>
> (#199)

The "footwork" and tone of the poem are a masterful demonstration of the sentiment it states—a self-confident claim to adulthood. Yet paired with this tone of assurance is a deliberate tentativeness in locution. What name, the speaker asks, can I assign to this new state? Like "*Two swimmers wrestled on the spar*—," the fair copy of which was inscribed on the verso of the sheet bearing this text, it is a lean poem, so spare with language that both problem and resolution must be inferred from method as much as from verbal content.

If the speaker's endeavor is to discover a designation for her newly gained status, the movement of the poem makes it clear that a title will be adequate only if it is entirely independent—absolute and not comparative. The irony of the twelve-line poem is this paradox: the quest is concluded in the very first two words with a term that seems by definition to be *both* dependent and comparative. The speaker must go through the process of testing that makes up the text of the poem in order to discover that a Poet can transform " 'wife' " into " 'Wife!' " The first is merely a social term, one that makes a woman's status entirely contingent upon her relationship to a man—a "'wife'" is the legal consort of the man whose family name she bears; the second, "'Wife!,'" is self-defined and self-conferred, and it designates a poetic Voice of experience and authority.

Initially, the distinction seems one of gradation: the highest eminence and majesty ("Czar") or simply the achievement of greater age ("'Woman'"). One pertains primarily to power (and is by stipulation masculine), the other to maturity (and is by stipulation feminine), but both are measures of a maximum degree; thus both need some inferior alternative ("That other state—") to make the title meaningful. The second stanza essays a different kind of comparison. It inverts traditional expectations so that the speaker's condition becomes the measure of those in Heaven, and it concocts the immeasurable ratio between the finite pleasures of earth and the infinite bliss of Heaven— a ratio that must itself always be infinite and thus "Degreeless." By this juncture the reader may have begun to understand that this "'wife,' . . . Czar, . . . 'Woman'" station cannot be designated by readily available criteria. It remains vexingly ill-defined—provocatively so. In fact, the most usual associations are systematically denied. The poem begins with a statement of fact ("I'm 'wife'—"), yet everything that follows this initial assertion pulls immediately and dramatically away from customary inferences. There is no man in the poem at all—no husband to serve as the primary figure according to whom the wife's necessarily subordinate status has meaning—no male term at all save "Czar," which the speaker has appropriated for herself. Eventually, the omission itself becomes a form of assertion. *This* state of "'Wife!'" must somehow be contingent upon no one else. It is a gaining of the "wife's" role without the simultaneous gaining of a husband; it is a fulfillment of feminine potential that permits a woman to keep an independent status, not predicating "self" upon her relationship to a man. The initial line of the third stanza confirms as much: "This being comfort—then" is an absolute construction, a verbal form that exists outside finite, temporal boundaries, always in the suspended state of "now." A final comparison is begun, then impatiently cast aside: comparison is a dependent form of definition. "Wife!" must be absolute.

Like the shift in a lantern show when two dimensions suddenly become three, the ontological status of the language is abruptly transformed. Poetic discourse is converted into the imperative mode, present tense, and the speaker springs to sudden life. "I'm 'Wife!' Stop there!" An *acceptable* "other" has been found to complete the definition, the "reader"—any reader at any time. Thus does the poet escape the tyranny of "Design."

Essential elements of this Voice—of its nature, status, and attitude—resemble those of the "child / Saint": it is contrived to exist outside of time; it is exalted, "Degreeless"—here, neither by the transvaluation of values that wrings "all" from "small," nor by superlative boasts, but merely by its confidence, self-sufficiency, and maturity. "Snow," with its rejection of both heavenly and earthly values, had been an apt name for the poetry of "no." With this new Voice, Dickinson continues the assumption that God's withdrawal from mankind must be matched by a poetic veil, yet disdain no longer dominates the tone. The "soft Eclipse" of verse stands as demarcation between "Girl's life" and " 'Wife,' " and it functions as a kind of screen to throw the earlier period into shadow—a transition that is made not contemptuously, but with wonder. "Soft Eclipse" reiterates God's withdrawal from mankind, with but one exception: God went up to Heaven and hid behind the veil of the material world, leaving words in His wake to replace the lost Presence; the poet, too, replaces person with Voice or Word. However, what had been cowardice in God's case is ingenuity, even triumph, in the case of the artist.

Even more important than these evidences of continuity and consistency, however, are new elements that find their way only tentatively into this poem: "safer . . . comfort . . . pain," a hint of sorrow and the acknowledgment that damage and loss are inescapable components of human existence. These notions lay at the heart of the relatively weak poetry that addressed the child sentimentally, but the puissant Voice of the "child / Saint" rejected this vulnerable side of life—the child by the overpowering roar of "Me, My, Mine," and the Saint by a chill indifference that rendered loss impotent to threaten "self." However, the most significant difference is the new notion that poetry might bring balm to the wounds of mortal creatures—to the poet herself and to the reader as well. Thus the Voice of the "Wife" is capable of recognizing the pain in other lives, and it often seeks to tender assistance, either by example or by direct address. God was primarily "Father" to the rebellious, disdainful Voice of child and Saint; for the "Wife," the example of the Christ takes precedence.

God made the prize of Heaven unattainable to those whose "eye / I" had not been wounded. Even Jesus paid the toll. Did not Jesus die? Did not even Jesus say in *His* extremity, "not as I will, but as thou wilt" (Matthew 26:39)? In a similar manner, the "eye / I" of the "Wife" gains credence through its unblinking recognition of the perils in ordinary existence. "*A Wounded Deer—leaps highest— / I've heard the Hunter tell— / 'Tis but the Extasy of death— / And then the Brake is still!*" (#*165*) Dickinson's acquaintance with Shakespeare may first have introduced her to that Elizabethan commonplace, the trope of Hunter and Deer for courtship; almost certainly it was Shakespeare who made her familiar with the Elizabethan pun for sexual climax— "death." However, she needed no Shakespeare at all to see that in mid-nineteenth-century Amherst, the "hunt" of courtship and the "death" of active feminine sexuality all too often brought the wife a finality that was not in the least figurative—death to the newborn, death in the throes of labor. There were signs of visible decay embedded even in feminine beauty: "*A Cheek is always redder / Just where the Hectic stings!*" (#*165*) And "Hectic," the "habitual fever" of consumption, still haunted the Norcross family when the poet was at the height of her powers.

Unnoticed, generally uncomplaining and self-effacing, the "Wife" instantiated a humble form of heroism in her daily round of work and love, and she was perpetuated not by legends of a single great act, but by the modest duties and small kindnesses of countless, anonymous women—worn and faded—who have been willing to accept the burden of caring.

> How many times these low feet staggered—
> Only the soldered mouth can tell—
> Try—can you stir the awful rivet—
> Try—can you lift the hasps of steel!
>
> Stroke the cool forehead—hot so often—
> Lift—if you care—the listless hair—
> Handle the adamantine fingers
> Never a thimble—more—shall wear—
>
> Buzz the dull flies—on the chamber window—
> Brave—shines the sun through the freckled pane—
> Fearless—the cobweb swings from the ceiling—
> Indolent Housewife—in Daisies—lain!
>
> (#187)

The slow, heavy dactyls and trochees render a different attitude toward poetic rhythms—not the rebellious, impatient foot of the child who feels at liberty to disobey, but the tired tread of the woman at work in her home. These "low feet" spell the slow metric of unending domestic obligation.

The identification with Jesus is present, but muted: the burden of the cross intimated by "staggered"; the nails of the Crucifixion recalled by "rivet." Overwhelming these, however, is the evocation of the coffin and death—death, which converts a living body and compassionate spirit into something not human, an immobile mask, gelid as metal. The incipient Gothic mood is so compelling that the poem might well have been developed by expanding this tone; however, Dickinson chooses to focus not on extinction, but on the ever-shifting tension between the forces of death and the minute triumphs of everyday vitality. As in "I'm 'wife'—," the speaker employs the imperative mode to reach some sentient "other" ("Try—. . . Try—"), for we can better tolerate the assaults of oblivion when we minister not only to our own needs, but to the needs of others as well. Thus as soon as the daily duties of the wife are recalled in stanza two, the dead body becomes recognizably human; it has been dissected by death (existing only in fragments of "forehead . . . hair . . . fingers"), but it is no longer a monstrosity.

Nonetheless, as the poem draws to its conclusion, the busy wilderness has already begun to assert its claim: the carrion fly (who becomes a major actor in one of Dickinson's most famous poems) batters the window; spiders spread their webs. Their adversary, the "Indolent Housewife," has passed beyond combat. There is bitter irony in the double meaning of "Indolent": "Habitually idle or indisposed to labor . . . Free from pain." Those who have never had the duty of keeping a home and attending to the helpless of all ages might suppose that women had no labor of *real* consequence. However, the women who engage with death every day on the domestic battleground can understand that *this* "Housewife" at least was finally "free from pain."

Although the catalogue of housewifely rituals is brief and stylized here—adapted to the larger issue of the poem—Dickinson could turn a great many seemingly trivial routines of the home into signs of the simple dignity with which housewives mediate between the family and the hostilities of God's natural forces. Women in nineteenth-century Amherst were in charge of both light and heat. "A wood box in the kitchen was filled by men, but the women kept the fires burning. In a climate as harsh as that of New England, just to keep warm in winter took a good deal of time. As there was neither gas nor electricity, lamps must be cleaned and filled with whale oil, a daily task for which a shelf in the back pantry was reserved. Tallow candles, often made at home, lighted the family to bed."[31] God gave us a sun; it can smile fruitfully on our endeavors. Yet He demands a return for this "gift"—we must fuel *His* lamp with our bowing obeisance. The women of the house provided Dickinson with an alternative model—generosity that is undemanding and uncomplaining. Thus the poet who employs the Voice of the "Wife" can leave a surer beacon than God's. "*The Poets light but Lamps— / Themselves—go out— / The Wicks they stimulate— / If vital Light / Inhere as do the Suns— / Each Age a Lens / Disseminating their / Circumference—*" (#883).

Dickinson did not enjoy sewing: poetry was her handwork, and she preferred the pen to the needle as her instrument. Yet she understood that needlework could also be a form of art. In samplers and other fancy stitchery, it was a visual art; in the endless yards of seams and hems, it became the art of affection.

> Don't put up my Thread & Needle—
> I'll begin to Sow
> When the Birds begin to whistle—
> Better Stitches—so—
>
> These were bent—my sight got crooked—
> When my mind—is plain
> I'll do seams—a Queen's endeavor
> Would not blush to own—

Hems—too fine for Lady's tracing
To the sightless Knot—
Tucks—of dainty interspersion—
Like a dotted Dot—

Leave my Needle in the furrow—
Where I put it down—
I can make the zigzag stitches
Straight—when I am strong—

Till then—dreaming I am sowing
Fetch the seam I missed—
Closer—so I—at my sleeping—
Still surmise I stitch—

(#617)

In his three-volume edition of her work, Thomas Johnson appended a comment to this poem: "The spelling of 'Sow' and 'sowing' (lines 2 and 17) is undoubtedly a mistake for 'sewing.'" Spelling was not Dickinson's principal talent; however, we must assume an intentional pun to make sense of line 13. In fact, Dickinson may well have had Emerson's essay "The Poet" explicitly in mind here.

Already famous and influential by the time Dickinson wrote this poem, Emerson's essay is relentlessly masculine in its orientation, and it presented Dickinson with a statement of the ostensible limitation of her right to be "Representative." Thus, when Emerson asks, "Who loves nature? . . . Is it only poets, and men of leisure and cultivation . . . ? No; but also hunters, farmers, grooms and butchers, though they express their affection in their choice of life and not in their choice of words," there is the implicit premise that only men will be poets. Emily Dickinson realized that if the "Wife" could sew / sow, she enacted the farmer's "poetic" mission, with this difference: hunters and farmers "love nature" by leaving home to do a job; the "Wife" expresses this same affection privately and personally in her unobtrusive domestic chores.

The explicitly poetic element here is the line that is repeatedly appealed to, though never named, as the measure of straight seams; these are an accomplishment of eye as well as of hand and have a royal stamp in this poem. Moreover, "seams" are lines that unite rather than divide, and just as stitches join pieces together into a garment, so the wife's ministrations knit the family into a coherent, viable unit and the poet's lines serve to make a connection between speaker and reader. The wife's species of heroism is invisible, seldom celebrated or proclaimed aloud; thus when Dickinson has recourse in this poem to the strategy of rendering a reduction toward zero, its meaning is altered. In geometry, the line is a figure that has length, but not breadth, and it is one-dimensional; the "dot" or point is a figure that has *no* dimensions. A "dotted Dot" is twice nothing, then, like the double zero of "Noon." However, here the trope does not render the speaker's withdrawal from the world as it had in "*A Clock stopped—*"; instead, it captures a form of Christlike charity that is so self-effacing that it becomes invisible—and this implication is anticipated by the "sightless Knot" of line 10.

Dickinson did not suppose that a life of heroic charity was limited exclusively to women or to feminine speakers. For example, although she customarily referred to her poetry as a "veil" or "flowers" or "snow," there were exceptions to this nomenclature. "*The Products of my Farm are these,*" one poet-speaker says of the following words: "*Sufficient for my Own / And here and there a Benefit / Unto a Neighbor's Bin. / With Us, 'tis Harvest all the Year / For when the Frosts begin / We just reverse the Zodiac / And fetch the Acres in*" (#*1025*). Although the Voice here might be a woman's, this farmer is more likely to be a man; it might even belong to that husband-man of Emerson's essay, but with this proviso—the definition of his achievement must follow the priorities Dickinson has set for her "Wife" speaker. Thus his aim is a form of charity that nullifies the rigidly punitive rules of God's "Zodiac" of seasons.

Still, more often than not these postulations of the heroism that inheres in simple acts of charity do recall women rather than men, for they are so frequently grounded in domestic routine. More than 10 percent of Dickinson's poems utilize images of food and drink, the primitive comfort that is the nucleus of the home. Yet these images have none of the sensuous detail that would render the palpable reality of actual food: we learn nothing of its savory aroma or exquisite taste, nothing of its appearance. It is not food *per se* that so captures the poet's attention (although in her own adult life, elegant cooking was the one household chore she took upon herself with happy creativity), but what food and drink could be made to represent.[32]

Perhaps the primary implication is the rendering of a rudimentary emotional hunger that only God can satisfy. "*We thirst at first—'tis Nature's Act— / And later—when we die— / A little Water supplicate— / Of fingers going by— / It intimates the finer want— / Whose adequate supply / Is that Great Water in the West— / Termed Immortality*" (#*726*). However, primordial anguish alone is seldom sufficient to support a strong poem. Dickinson often construed hunger and thirst as the necessary prerequisites for comprehending the worth of food and drink: deprivation becomes the rule by which we measure satisfaction. "*Who never lost, are unprepared / A Coronet to find! / Who never thirsted / Flagons, and Cooling Tamarind!*" (#*73*) This formulation eschews the merely petulant: primitive need yields to the more complex notion that loss can be a postponement of gain or satisfaction. Yet this informing notion is apt to produce verse that hovers at the level of maxim or aphorism, and more powerful poetry issued from a speaker's rejection of satisfaction or comfort. "*Who never wanted—maddest Joy / Remains to him unknown— / The Banquet of Abstemiousness / Defaces that of Wine— / Within it's reach, though yet ungrasped / Desire's perfect Goal— / No nearer—lest it's penury— / Should disenthrall thy soul—*" (#1430; var. "*it's penury*"). The paradox of a "Banquet of Abstemiousness" draws upon some of the same elements that had informed the poetry of renunciation, yet it differs from these by rendering relinquishment *itself* as a sensual delight. In this respect it seems to border on the perverse; and while responding to its resonances and unstated nuances, a reader may at the same time shy away from its deliberately tortured assessment of human satisfactions. What is the meaning of this "Banquet of Abstemiousness," then, and why do we find it nonetheless captivating our reluctant attention?

The answer to the puzzles presented by the food imagery in Dickinson's poetry lies not in some unique peculiarity of the poet's own emotional configuration, but in her adaptation of a complex scheme of ancient emblems that can still speak poignantly to a modern audience. Although the poems revert again and again to oral modalities, the range of food and drink named is astonishingly small: no meat or vegetables, occasionally fruit, but generally such Biblical fruit as the Tamarind of the Holy Land or the Edenic apple; and for the rest—water, wine, and bread—the essential elements of the Lord's Supper. At the literal level, the "Wife's" sphere of influence encompasses the kitchen: she gives immediate comfort by providing food and drink. Yet the "Wife's" ministrations also address more comprehensive human woes, and it is precisely in this way that she can become Christlike. In order to render the scope of the "Wife's" charity, Dickinson moves the food-and-drink imagery of her poetry beyond the merely mundane to invoke a series of transcendent transactions. Throughout the Bible, God's pledges are rendered by candid appeals to our most primitive hunger: His help and promises are "food." In the Old Testament, the earthly kingdom that would come to the Israelites was figured as "a table . . . in the presence of mine enemies" (Psalms 23:5). In the New Testament of Grace, at the Last Supper, Christ replaced a limited, earthly reward with an eternal one by promising that the faithful would be reunited with Him forever in a Heavenly Kingdom.

Almost invariably, then, when food-and-drink imagery appears in Dickinson's work, it is meant to invoke not primarily the creature comforts that can be found in this world, but the more sweeping promises of reward and happiness that have been described in the Bible and especially in the New Testament. Furthermore, the specific constellation of water, wine, and bread (or some one or two of them) that appears in the poetry with such consistency is no accidental conjunction: for Emily Dickinson, as for all Amherst Congregationalists of the mid-nineteenth century, these represented the most important ceremony of the church, the Lord's Supper.

In Dickinson's day the mystery and piety of this hallowed rite still occu-

pied a privileged place in the collective imagination: the momentous significance of this sacrament for each Christian's life had altered little if at all, and
the attitudes of Dickinson's friends and neighbors in Amherst toward the
Lord's Supper resembled the reverence and seriousness of their seventeenth-
century Puritan forebears more than the falling away of their secularized
inheritors. In each of the three poems just cited, there is some hint of this
Biblical implication—sometimes a good deal more than a hint. No reader
can understand Dickinson's work, therefore, without some appreciation of
the meaning of the rite that is so often invoked by these images. No reader
can fathom the sweeping power of the Voice of the "Wife" without appre-
hending the full implication of her "Christlike" behavior.

Christ's Last Supper—the prototype for all re-enactments of the Lord's
Supper or the sacrament of Holy Communion—had been crucially important
to his followers for several reasons. First, Christ announced the New Covenant of Grace on this occasion. No longer would mankind be held to the
strict Old Testament measure of inflexible justice and revenge; instead, embraced by the loving sacrifice of Christ's death on the cross, mankind would
be granted mercy and the hope of a Heaven to come (and it was the "signs"
of *this* promise that a Christian was expected to "see" throughout nature
after experiencing a conversion to faith). Second, Christ announced that He
would be leaving His Apostles. Third, He promised that they would be reunited with Him in His Father's House after death. Fourth, He instituted the
ritual of the Lord's Supper as He presided over the bread and water mixed
with wine—and He commanded His followers to repeat this ritual as a way
of recollecting the promised reunion—saying, "Do this in remembrance of
me" (Luke 22:19).

And as they were eating, Jesus took bread, and blessed it, and brake it, and gave it to
the disciples, and said, Take, eat; this is my body. And he took the cup, and gave
thanks, and gave it to them, saying, Drink ye all of it; For this is my blood of the new
testament, which is shed for many for the remission of sins. But I say unto you, I will
not drink henceforth of this fruit of the vine, until that day when I drink it new with
you in my Father's kingdom. [Matthew 26:26–29]

For all Congregationalists this was the foundation of the New Law of faith.
However, it presented a knotty problem of interpretation.

The Catholic Church had had no difficulty interpreting the significance of
the Last Supper: Holy Communion was a sacrament; during the saying of
the Mass, bread and water mixed with wine were miraculously transformed
into the body and blood of Christ, retaining their own appearance or "acci-
dents," but informed with the essence of God—a miracle called "transub-
stantiation." Thus Catholics could be comforted by the belief that every time
a Mass was celebrated, Christ actually came into the presence of His people.

For all Puritans, however, this episode of the New Testament (reported in essentially the same words by three of the four Gospels) presented a considerable dilemma. Puritans had rejected the "magical" properties of sacraments, viewing them as just another manifestation of decadence in the Church of Rome. In the case of every sacrament except Holy Communion or the Lord's Supper, this "purification" could be justified without tendentious argumentation because there was no Biblical text imputing miraculous transformations to them. However, for the Lord's Supper there was. Jesus Himself had said, "Take, eat; this is my body. . . . Drink ye all of it; For this is my blood of the new testament." What kind of accommodation could be formulated to evade the implications of this text?

Calvin wrestled with the problem presented by these accounts of the Last Supper, and his conclusion was that Christ had been speaking not literally, but figuratively—even poetically. Thus when He said, "This is my body," Christ had been employing the trope of metonymy, the substitution of something associated with a person to name the person himself. Those who suppose that bread can *become* the body of Christ "have recourse to a gloss which is forced and violently wrested," Calvin claimed:

> . . . I say that the expression which is uniformly used in Scripture, when the sacred mysteries are treated of, is metonymical. . . . Although the sign differs essentially from the thing signified, the latter being spiritual and heavenly, the former corporeal and visible, . . . why should not its name be justly applied to the thing? . . .
> . . . Let our opponents, therefore, cease to indulge their mirth in calling us Tropists.[33]

According to this reading, Christ did not leave us with a sacrament that would reunite us with the absent Redeemer; He left an ordinance that exhibited *signs* of His promise—mere metaphors for his body and blood. Indeed, like His Father before Him, He gave us words and emblems to replace the lost Presence.

In Dickinson's estimation, the loss obliterated the promise. This was a *second* tragic fall into language: first the Father at Peniel, now the Son at the Last Supper. Thus the sacramental vernacular of water, wine, and bread, which gave hope to so many other Christians, spelled anguish to Emily Dickinson, misery and betrayal. As poet, she would deploy precisely this vernacular, then—this limited, Biblical evocation of food and drink—in order to explore the comprehensive desolation of all human beings—spinning through empty space and irretrievably isolated from their mysterious, metaphorical God.

Christ played a strangely mixed role in this universal drama of pain and desertion. Insofar as He had been a man—had suffered physical agony and cosmic betrayal, had come with affection and mercy to minister to the afflictions that He shared with us, had even died—to this extent He was worthy of our love and admiration. However, insofar as He had been God—winning our loyalty only to desert us and retreat into Heaven, leaving only words in His wake—to that extent He had proved no more than the traitorous agent of the Father. Dickinson yearned for the trust in the promise of succor that bread, water, and wine were said to signify; sometimes her poetry touches Christ's promise with tones of tentative faith. More often, however, confidence eluded her, and the Voice of the verse turns away from Christ's overtures.

"Abstemiousness," then, is preferable to the Supper of Our Lord ("that of Wine"): it "defaces" God's "penury" by rejecting the empty promise of a face-to-face reunion with Christ, and it enables the abstainer to savor the rich independence that is the only sustenance we can assuredly obtain. Thus the compelling oxymoron, "Banquet of Abstemiousness," is not perverse: it is a scathing denunciation of the emptiness of sacramental signs. The phrase tugs persistently, even at a modern sensibility. Although most of us do not scrutinize the language of the New Testament, "Banquet" and "Wine" echo in the ear when they are joined, waking dormant hope and reviving, if only for a moment, ancient anticipations of some eternal realm of moral grandeur.

Having renounced Christ's promises, then, Dickinson took the love and mercy that sometimes seemed essential to His mission and incorporated them into the accents of the "Wife," whose sacrament is the poem itself, reaching across time to proffer understanding and comfort to each reader anew.

> *I bring an unaccustomed wine*
> *To lips long parching*
> *Next to mine,*
> *And summon them to drink;*
>
> *Crackling with fever, they Essay,*
> *I turn my brimming eyes away,*
> *And come next hour to look.*
>
> *The hands still hug the tardy glass—*
> *The lips I w'd have cooled, alas—*
> *Are so superfluous Cold—*
>
> *I w'd as soon attempt to warm*
> *The bosoms where the frost has lain*
> *Ages beneath the mould—*
>
> *Some other thirsty there may be*
> *To whom this w'd have pointed me*
> *Had it remained to speak—*

And so I always bear the cup
If, haply, mine may be the drop
Some pilgrim thirst to slake—

If, haply, any say to me
"Unto the little, unto me,"
When I at last awake.

(#132)

Not blessed by the "custom" of the church or tradition, this "wine" ministers not by promising eternal reunion and transcendent glory, but by the eloquent offer of simple charity and the shared hope—not the guarantee—of eternity.

Maturity is essential to the attitude and tone of this Voice; "little" and "small" become attributes not of the "*I*," but of the "*other*"—the reader, the sufferer, all who need understanding and consolation. Barefoot defiance is, perhaps, an important part of the past, but power in these poems derives principally from fortitude. *The Prelude*, Wordsworth's great autobiographical poem, traces the development of his own creative powers; like much Romantic work, it focuses on a particularized self. Dickinson, who wrote so many poems about poetry and the role of the poet, also examined this process of "becoming" as it pertained to the artisan of words; typically, her thoughts are compressed into brief, lyrical form, and her verse addresses not her own particular case, but one that is Representative.

I can wade Grief—
Whole Pools of it—
I'm used to that—
But the least push of Joy
Breaks up my feet—
And I tip—drunken—
Let no Pebble—smile—
'Twas the New Liquor—
That was all!

Power is only Pain—
Stranded, thro' Discipline,
Till Weights—will hang—
Give Balm—to Giants—
And they'll wilt, like Men—
Give Himmaleh—
They'll Carry—Him!

(#252)

This remarkable utterance begins with a jubilant reverberation of the tone that suffuses such poems as "So I pull my Stockings off"; however, with the unexpected introduction of "Grief," the mood shifts. The mien of the child is put aside, and maturity begins.

"Pools" has two Biblical precedents—the primordial vitality in the sea of Genesis and the annihilation of Noah's Flood, life pulled from briny fathoms and death by water. Throughout the letters, Dickinson invoked both implications: immortality was "the Flood subject"; death was "the deep Stranger"; and passionate love was an "exultation" that "floods" the self.[34] The "Grief" that has introduced sober maturity into the child's defiant gesture seems at first to herald the kind of experience that can bring only unhappiness. Yet the strategy of this poem is to hold destructive and creative forces in tension, demonstrating that good can come of apparent ill—not indirectly, through the miracle of Christ's Crucifixion, but immediately and personally.

The "story" of this verse is elliptical, and its message may seem as perplexing as the taste for a "Banquet of Abstemiousness." The speaker begins by embracing "Grief," preferring it even to "Joy": initially, the reason for this choice is not clear, but it seems to have something to do with "New Liquor." The second stanza explains the speaker's rationale. In order to win "Power," an individual must accept "Pain." Indeed, the danger that one might sink irretrievably into a flood of anguish can be averted only through an exercise of the kind of "Discipline" whereby one can be "Stranded"—according to Dickinson's "Webster's," "driven on shore . . . as, a ship *stranded* at high water." The image echoes Noah's fate, but it teaches a different lesson: Noah had been saved by his unquestioning obedience and his faith in things unseen; this speaker demonstrates that each human being can save him- or herself. Indeed, the salvation proffered in *this* model confers such strength that the one who was so recently in peril of drowning can now support weights without difficulty. It is always thus, so the final four lines assert: attempts to blunt the force of feeling are diminishing; they can make even strong men impotent. By contrast, new and ever-increased challenges of pain elicit the strength of an Atlas.

The poem addresses human response to adversity and suffering, and it offers the Poet as model. "Joy" must be banished: the least hint of it will falsify the faltering metrical movement, for the "feet" of this verse are appropriately staggering, like the gait of the careworn "housewife," and they stand in explicit contradiction to the kind of dancing, carefree rhythms of the "Reel" that capers skyward in "I taste a liquor never brewed." The "Liquor" here celebrates a new testament of pain, and at every moment in the poem, the speaker's experience is measured against a shadow-play of Christ's suffering.

Thus although the "New Liquor" recalls the Last Supper—conflating the new Covenant pronounced there with the wine that was ever after a sign of

Christ's promise—it recalls even more explicitly Jesus's description of His intention to replace the rigid laws of the Old Testament with a new lesson of love and generosity. His parable took the form of a story about wine. "Neither do men put new wine into old bottles: else the bottles break, and the wine runneth out, and the bottles perish: but they put new wine into new bottles, and both are preserved" (Matthew 9:17). Implicit in Christ's mission was the offer to alleviate our unhappiness. The Redeemer would take our sins upon Himself and sacrifice Himself in our behalf, giving us balm to numb our human anguish. Here Dickinson explicitly argues against accepting any surrogate: permit no one to suffer in your behalf, the poem entreats, for when you seek to evade sorrow, you only relinquish the means to strength. Even God's *mercy* can be castrating. Thus Dickinson rejects Christ's errand of love, flouting the gift that the Lord's Supper signifies. Similarly, the meters of the poem are unruly, bursting the confinements of hymnody—indeed, of all conventional metrical schemes, the "old bottles" that cannot contain the heady "new wine" of Dickinson's powerful verse.

Poetry itself can be a manifestation of strong feeling mastered by the ordering imperatives of art. Repeatedly, Dickinson construed her vocation in this way. "*Bound—a trouble— / And lives can bear it!*" (#269): such is the lesson of one poem whose lines are regulated by complex patterns of echoing consonants. Another, more traditional formulation can be found in a verse about the religious lyric. "*The Martyr Poets—did not tell— / But wrought their Pang in syllable— / . . . The Martyr Painters—never spoke— / Bequeathing— rather—to their Work— / That when their conscious fingers cease— / Some seek in Art—the Art of Peace—*" (#544). These poems of suffering celebrate another of the poet's gifts: the activity of writing as "Representative." Each life provides its own unique array of torments and its own means of endurance and discipline. The Poet selects one form of regulation when she transforms raw emotion into the cadenced images of verse, speaking to others out of the isolation of her own life. Yet all can find some appropriate way to "discipline" the suffering of life, and thus all can acquire the "Power" that includes both "Kingdom" and "Glory."

Virtually every one of these poems touches upon the model offered in Christ's Passion and death; at the same time, a great many suggest that this model of the creative potential in commonplace pain is essentially domestic. "*This was a Poet—It is That / Distills amazing sense / From ordinary Meanings— / And Attar so immense / From the familiar species / That perished by the Door— / We wonder it was not Ourselves / Arrested it—before—*" (#448). A nineteenth-century Congregationalist reader would immediately have recognized "amazing sense" as a rejection of John Newton's hymn, "Amazing Grace," a song of thanks for the gift of Christ's promised redemption.[35] What is more, all would have known that the homely task of compounding potpourri and distilling "Attar" was a housewife's art. "*Essential Oils—are wrung— / The Attar from the Rose / Be not expressed by Suns—alone— / It is the gift of Screws—"* (#675), an art of Christlike pain and love.

Wars may be concluded; kings may die and presidents be elected: heroism in the public world often assumes a shape, and concludes with pleasing finality. Although Christ's gift was a personal offer of affection and mercy, His heroism took this public form—terminating with the triumphal entry into Jerusalem, the public trial, the Crucifixion, and the miraculous Resurrection. The lesser trials of ordinary lives do not have such artful climaxes. Housewives know that there are always feelings to be mended, sicknesses to ease, sorrows to be comforted back to happiness: success in such heroic endeavors as these is never complete, never fully finished. The most difficult lesson to be taught by the Voice of the "Wife," then, is that "Power," even when won by disciplining the most primitive emotions, cannot be absolute. To be sure, there can be an air of triumph in this Voice, a regal tone (acknowledged by "Czar" in "I'm 'wife' "). But it is not the deaf, arbitrary despotism of "Mine . . . Mine . . . Mine"; the speaker has earned her authority by acknowledging the needs of others and by wringing strength from the travail in her own life. She has won a spiritual ascendancy that explicitly surpasses the glorious crown that was claimed by those who had experienced a conversion to faith.

Repeatedly, the "Wife" seeks to bring order into a world of chaos; often, there are moments of bliss and rejoicing. However, no victory is final, no triumph complete: one who accepts the burden of pain must accept as well the fact that just as good can come of apparent ill, so a reign of order will periodically fall before the encroachments of destruction.

It would never be Common—more—I said—
Difference—had begun—
Many a bitterness—had been—
But that old sort—was done—

Of—if it sometimes—showed—as 'twill—
Upon the Downiest—Morn—
Such bliss—had I—for all the years—
'Twould give an Easier—pain—

I'd so much joy—I told it—Red—
Upon my simple Cheek—
I felt it publish—in my Eye—
'Twas needless—any speak—

I walked—as wings—my body bore—
The feet—I former used—
Unnecessary—now to me—
As boots—would be—to Birds—

I put my pleasure all abroad—
I dealt a word of Gold
To every Creature—that I met—
And Dowered—all the World—

When—suddenly—my Riches shrank—
A Goblin—drank my Dew—
My Palaces—dropped tenantless—
Myself—was beggared—too—

I clutched at sounds—
I groped at shapes—
I touched the tops of Films—
I felt the Wilderness roll back
Along my Golden lines—

The Sackcloth—hangs upon the nail—
The Frock I used to wear—
But where my moment of Brocade—
My—drop—of India?

(#430)

Many of the familiar elements are here: the royal state that is conferred by poetry; the peace and "Easier—pain—" that inhere in artistic discipline. The "Cheek" that in the other poem was redder from the "Hectic's" sting now blushes with pride, "Red" from "so much joy." After the transformation that is recorded in the fourth stanza, where "feet" become the winged poetic feet of the artist, the speaker becomes both wifely and Godly, "Dowering" the world with her bounty. Unlike God, Who left a silver age behind Him at Peniel, the poet returns us to a golden Adamic era: meanness and sin seem not yet existent as the speaker puts her "pleasure all abroad." Perhaps the "word of Gold" that is dealt to "every Creature" is merely munificent good will; perhaps it is the naming of a world miraculously made anew. In either case, *this* "Gold" repudiates the pinched and fallen world from which God has fled not once, but twice.

Yet even India ink cannot permanently dispel the forces of disintegration. Just as the spider and the fly assailed the small circle of domestic peace as soon as the "Indolent Housewife" had been laid to rest, so the busy wilderness waits to intrude upon even the order of art. The ever-shifting balance of power between the creative forces and the forces of destruction swings against the poet, and the effort to impose order must begin once again.

Unlike the audacious, imperious child / saint, the "Wife" acknowledges that the flesh harbors ineluctable death. Words can endure. Accents of comfort can span the silent decades to address generations as yet unborn; but the author herself must perish, and each reader, too, must confront some last frontier of eternity. "*All but Death, can be Adjusted*— / *Dynasties repaired*— / *Systems*—*settled in their Sockets*— / *Citadels*—*dissolved*— / *Wastes of Lives*—*resown with Colors* / *By Succeeding Springs*— / *Death*—*unto itself*— *Exception*— / *Is exempt from Change*—" (#749). In the midst of these metaphors of creation and destruction, of accounts come due and final payments, there is the delicate undertone of a last, futile wish to mend and make anew. But the woman who seeks to sew / sow affection understands that the range of her talent is cruelly curtailed. The sorrows of life can be "Adjusted" and tailored to fit more comfortably; rents in the fabric of happiness can be gaily resewn just as spring renews the year with her bounty. But death is an ultimate barrier to solace.

Christ claimed that He had triumphed over death for everyone: His Resurrection was only the beginning; all men and women would be delivered from the grave. The flesh would be reconstituted, transfigured, and made eternal. "It is sown in corruption; it is raised in incorruption: . . . it is sown in weakness; it is raised in power: It is sown a natural body; it is raised a spiritual body. . . . Death is swallowed up in victory. O death, where is thy sting? O grave, where is thy victory?" (I Corinthians 15:42–44, 54–55). "All but Death, can be Adjusted—" explicitly denies this passage in the New Testament—indeed, denies it by employing the same metaphors that Saint Paul had used to affirm it: Christ's promise of a life after death cannot be trusted. The "Wife" could take upon herself many of the tasks Christ had pursued; however, she could not destroy death, and thus her ability to repair the Divinity's deficiencies stops abruptly when life is ended.

4 ❧ *The Proleptic Voice*

Although all of the many variations of "Voice" in Dickinson's poetry are designed to circumvent time, none could alter the reality of death that each reader would eventually confront. Still, because the poet did not want to ignore this lonely terror, she was obliged to discover an attitude and a mode of discourse—a tone, diction, and syntax—that could speak to the fear that rests in the quiet, cold center of every human consciousness.

Dickinson's poetry is often very difficult to read aloud: without the regularized punctuation that has become standard in the twentieth century (but was not for *anyone* in Dickinson's family), often elliptical at its most critical moments, pivoting upon puns and compressions—double and triple meanings, sometimes more—it forces the reader to render syntax, diction, and their ambivalences in subtle shadings of the voice and to supply the missing elements with just the correct length and "tone" of pause. Yet, skillfully read aloud, much of the poetry is astonishingly conversational.

In August 1862 Dickinson responded to a note from Higginson that had evidently taken her to task for not mixing more actively in society. "Of 'shunning Men and Women'—they talk of Hallowed things, aloud—and embarrass my Dog—He and I dont object to them, if they'll exist their side."[36] In Dickinson's time and place, it was difficult to talk aloud for any length of time without touching upon "Hallowed things."

A letter from Emily to Austin during his courting season, in the fall of 1851, illustrates the unselfconscious intermingling of life and death in the epistolary style of all the Dickinsons.

Martha is very long talking of you and Susie, she seems unreconciled to letting you go away. She is down here most every day—she brings Sue's letters and reads them. . . . Vinnie tells me *she* has detailed the *news*—she reserved the *deaths* for me, thinking I might fall short of my usual letter somewhere. In accordance with her wishes, I acquaint you with the decease of your aged friend—Dea Kingsbury. He had no disease that we know of, but gradually went out. Martha Kingman has been very sick, and is not yet out of danger. Jane Grout is slowly improving, tho' very feeble yet. . . .

Emeline and Henry are just learning to say "*we*," I think they do very well for such "new beginners."[37]

Sickness, death, marriage, birth: these moments in the cycle of life were artlessly integrated into the usual course of social exchange. However, it would have been rare indeed for an individual to drop a rehearsal of his or her own ultimate demise into a letter or conversation. Everyone thought about it, worried about it, feared it; but as a rule, one seldom discussed it with others.

The process of dying is not convivial: we must perish each alone, and once we have crossed into whatever lies beyond life, none can return to tell the tale of passage. The Voice of the "Wife" captures accents that can be heard in the home; the Voice of the child / Saint usually does not issue from adults in the real world, but any adult who has listened to the chatter and railing of children has heard such tones. These Voices and all the modulations, combinations, and variations that grew out of them have their familiar counterparts in the lives of every reader. Thus none was entirely appropriate for poems that treat the process of dying, for in Dickinson's estimation the most enigmatic part of death was the gradual isolation of an increasingly helpless self moving toward the horror of the utterly unknown: " *'Tis not the Dying hurts us so—* / *'Tis Living—hurts us more—* / *But Dying—is a different way—* / *A Kind behind the Door—*" (#335). The submerged image of "Eclipse" is applied even to this process—here, the interposition of the "Door" of death, that separates the moribund from all human contact. The attempt to conjure the consciousness as it passes out of life must always be a bravura feat of the imagination, and the Voice created for this purpose—proleptic, Gothic, suffused with transcendent knowledge—is essentially and deliberately literary. It speaks aloud, often indifferent to the listener. It does not trouble to aggrandize the self: no one but death is competing for pre-eminence. Insofar as it seeks power, it has but one end: discovering a strategy to hold identity together as the bland force of extinction systematically dissolves it.

In approaching this subject, Dickinson had to contend with a peculiarly convoluted attitude toward the woman-as-poet. The unrivaled master of American Gothic poetry was Poe. His theoretical pronouncements did not receive the widespread respect that had been accorded the New England transcendentalists (a fact that galled him until the day he died); nonetheless, the influence of his work could be observed in the poetry and fiction that were published throughout New England during Dickinson's life, in such exalted literary journals as *The Atlantic Monthly* and in countless now-forgotten small-town newspapers. In his essay "The Philosophy of Composition," Poe took a craftsmanlike attitude toward the writing of poetry that may have recommended itself to Dickinson even though the sing-song rhymes and rhythms of his verse did not compel her imitation. "Beauty is the sole legitimate province of the Poem," he began. "Melancholy is . . . the most legitimate of all the poetical tones," he continued.

Now, never losing sight of the object *supremeness,* or perfection, at all points, I asked myself—"Of all melancholy topics, what, according to the *universal* understanding of mankind, is the *most* melancholy?" Death—was the obvious reply. "And when," I said, "is this most melancholy of topics most poetical?" From what I have already explained at some length, the answer, here also, is obvious—"When it most closely allies itself to *Beauty:* the death, then, of a beautiful woman is, unquestionably, the most poetical topic in the world—and equally is it beyond doubt that the lips best suited for such topic are those of a bereaved lover."

To a woman seeking to be a Representative Voice, this claim (based, according to Poe, on a *universal* understanding of mankind) posed a special problem. Even more categorically than Emerson's definitions of the "Poet," it assumed that the active role, *creator of beauty,* would belong to a man, while the passive role, *beautiful object,* would fall to the woman. To fulfill Poe's prescription, Emily Dickinson would have to die before she could be considered "poetical," and then some bereft suitor would have to pen a verse or two about her demise. It is a comical notion, but perhaps it is equally ludicrous to suppose that the *real* horror of death could be rendered by a mourning, lovesick (but perfectly healthy) swain. Dickinson had observed the "beauty" of lascivious death—in her cousin Emily Lavinia Norcross and, even more strikingly, in the Coleman sisters. Women who sat the "watches" did not fancy that the final loss of a beautiful woman was, in Poe's sense, "poetical."

Not surprisingly, Dickinson did not accept Poe's initial premise, that "Beauty" (to the exclusion of Truth) was the "sole province" of poetry; for many reasons, Poe's pronouncements about the "Poet" were less relevant to Dickinson's endeavor than Emerson's were. Yet they could not be entirely dismissed. Popular periodicals inundated her with evidence that accounts of women's deaths touched some universal nerve of pain. Thus when Dickinson sought a "Voice" to deal with death—not the unhappiness suffered by those still living, but the panic of slow dissolution as consciousness disintegrates— she performed radical surgery on Poe's pronouncement. The death of a woman (though not necessarily a beautiful woman) would be the subject, but the Voice reporting the event would be that of the woman herself.

Several variations of tone resulted from this audacious experiment. One tone is distinctly Gothic, derived in some measure from Poe, from the school of Ann Radcliffe, from Byron, and from every other practitioner of the ghostly art. At other times the tone is a shimmering adaptation of the prophetic, dreamlike cadences of the Book of Revelation. Sometimes, a poem has the domestic accents of the "Wife"—accustomed to the humble routines of cleaning and sewing and feeding her family, and attempting unsuccessfully to tailor quotidian language to an hallucinatory turmoil of failing perception. All of these Voices have one thing in common: they are not essentially of this world; to a reader who does not understand Dickinson's motives and strategies, they may seem little more than an evidence of unloosed hysteria.

One bold justification for the proleptic or Gothic Voice is an extension of the "Wife's" willingness to renew the mission of Christ through her own affection. The "Wife" could not destroy death, and neither can this Voice; yet in fashioning the latter, Dickinson was inventing another kind of "Representative" speaker. In effect, she proposed to her readers that a surrogate might "die" for them—men and women, aged and infant. Christ had claimed to do as much; however, Christ's sacrifice had told us nothing about the experience of crossing over into the uncharted world beyond. Instead, He had offered promises, but not proofs, that whatever horrors might be entailed in the passage, after the "abomination of desolation," all human creatures would be raised from the dead. This vague, impalpable assurance of some place in "My Father's House" balanced inadequately against the visible suffering of those dying and the frightful uncertainty that haunted all when they attempted to prepare for the moment when "self" would be relinquished. What Dickinson could do through the poetry, then, was to create variations on the process of dying, arming her readers with vivid and specific anticipations of the climactic moment itself.

If we could know death as intimately as we know other forms of danger and pain, if we could anticipate the worst of its ravages and prepare ourselves to endure them, then one might *truly* exclaim, "Death is swallowed up in victory. O death, where is thy sting? O grave, where is thy victory?" What extraordinary power such an experiment could confer!

> 'Tis so appalling — it exhilirates —
> So over Horror, it half Captivates —
> The Soul stares after it, secure —
> To know the worst, leaves no dread more —
>
> To scan a Ghost, is faint —
> But grappling, conquers it —
> How easy, Torment, now —
> Suspense kept sawing so —
>
> The Truth, is Bald, and Cold —
> But that will hold —
> If any are not sure —
> We show them — prayer —
> But we, who know,
> Stop hoping, now —
>
> Looking at Death, is Dying —
> Just let go the Breath —
> And not the pillow at your Cheek
> So Slumbereth —
>
> Others, Can wrestle —
> Your's, is done —
> And so of Wo, bleak dreaded — come,
> It sets the Fright at liberty —
> And Terror's free —
> Gay, Ghastly, Holiday!
>
> (#281)

Many things in this poem toy with blasphemy, but the most clearly irreverent is Dickinson's mocking usurpation of the language of revivals: to read a work of this nature is to "grapple" — not with God or faith, but with death — and in the course of *this* encounter, a Christian "conquers" the inclination to accept faith on any terms. Nor is this sacrilegious use of "grapple" casual or unsuited to the subject. The conversion experience and death were the two moments in every Christian's life when God required total relinquishment of the "eye / I." Thus at the conclusion of the poem, those who still strive for faith are, ironically, "lost" because of their eternal and unceasing bondage: "Others, Can wrestle—"; but for the one who has summoned the courage to confront *death* "face to face," the wrestle is done. He or she has preserved the "eye / I" and gained liberation from the fear of God's threats.

Other elements in the poem develop a strategy for living from this encounter with death. Each of the four stanzas that anticipate the climactic fifth (which recounts not "Death," but the banishment of struggle and fear) makes paradoxical use of the power of vision. We cannot be entirely certain what the "Soul stares after"; some vision of the moment of death, perhaps, or some afterthought of the life that was. But death has no body, and thought no substance. The second, third, and fourth stanzas continue the tactic, admitting that these attempts to "envision" something defy ordinary visual powers: "To scan a Ghost, is faint. . . . If any are not sure— / We show them—prayer. . . . Looking at Death, is Dying—." This progression of actions whereby we are encouraged to "look" at things that cannot be seen compels a reader to understand that for Dickinson, eyesight or vision is more than the capacity to look at the objects in this world; it is that power by which individuals impose order on human experience and thereby assert authority over it. Thus is it a principal means by which we can assert independence and autonomy.

The imperative force of this conviction originated in Dickinson's earliest experiences with her family, and it was reinforced by Trinitarian demands for a reordered vision. However, at the adult stage of her life, it was surely fueled by current cultural trends as well, the loose Emersonian notions that had permeated New England thought by the later 1850s and early 1860s. Emerson's classic statement in chapter 1 of *Nature* asserts that man's power of sight is in harmony with the transcendent force of creation.

When we speak of nature [here], we have a distinct but most poetical sense in the mind. We mean the integrity of impression made by manifold natural objects. It is this which distinguishes the stick of timber of the wood-cutter from the tree of the poet. The charming landscape which I saw this morning is indubitably made up of some twenty or thirty farms. Miller owns this field, Locke that. . . . But none of them owns the landscape. There is a property in the horizon which no man has but he whose eye can integrate all the parts, that is, the poet. . . .

. . . Standing on the bare ground,—my head bathed by the blithe air and uplifted into infinite space,—all mean egotism vanishes. I become a transparent eyeball; I am nothing; I see all; the currents of the Universal Being circulate through me. I am part or parcel of God.

In Dickinson's poetry, "landscape" always echoes Emerson's usage here: not the natural world as material entity, but an individual's integrated, coherent understanding of the *meaning* of the "seen" world and of one's experiences in it. Yet, far from allowing this "vision" of the landscape to uplift her "into infinite space" where "all . . . egotism vanishes," Dickinson clung to "egotism" and posited *her* vision against God's attempts to force meaning upon us. Far from being "nothing . . . part or parcel of God," Dickinson wrestled in her work to individuate self from God and to counter His power to blind humankind.[38]

The most famous of the proleptic poems maintains a tension between the capacity of vision and the meaning of its extinguishment, between that which is willed and that which must be accepted passively. And it offers yet another application of "Eclipse."

> *I heard a Fly buzz—when I died—*
> *The Stillness in the Room*
> *Was like the Stillness in the Air—*
> *Between the Heaves of Storm—*
>
> *The Eyes around—had wrung them dry—*
> *And Breaths were gathering firm*
> *For that last Onset—when the King*
> *Be witnessed—in the Room—*
>
> *I willed my Keepsakes—Signed away*
> *What portion of me be*
> *Assignable—and then it was*
> *There interposed a Fly—*
>
> *With Blue—uncertain stumbling Buzz—*
> *Between the light—and me—*
> *And then the Windows failed—and then*
> *I could not see to see—*

(#465)

What compels our attention is the quiet of the Voice, the simple fortitude that will serve as guide through the suburbs of the Wilderness. A reader who can recollect "How many times these low feet staggered—" knows that shortly "dull flies" will thump triumphantly upon "the chamber window" and a "Fearless" spider will swing his skein from the ceiling. Chaos will resume its swift work. But for the moment of this poem, we are poised fastidiously between the order and coherence of life and the disintegration of death.

Death is a "*Bisecting / Messenger*" from eternity (#1411), a caller with a "*bisected Coach*" (#1445) who will divide body from soul. Thus two different kinds of creature wait in the bedroom to divide the spoils: the "King," God or some regal ambassador, is ready to take possession of the spirit; and the carrion fly rumbles its impatient anticipation of the feast of flesh. Both are present; neither is yet empowered. Nonetheless, a quasi-legal transaction has already begun to take place, the fulfillment of that dread phrase, "Thy will be done"; and the presence of onlookers assures that this "will" may be duly "witnessed." One more mortal going to the grave; dust to dust without exception.

Throughout, the "eye / I" of the speaker struggles to retain power. Ironically, although the final, haunting sentence has to do with sight, "I could not see to see—," at no time in the course of the poem can the speaker maintain an ordered visual grasp of the world. "The Ear is the last Face," Dickinson wrote to Higginson. "We hear after we see."[39] Thus is it in this work. We begin this poem about seeing—with sound.

In the first stanza, the "I" can still assert straightforward utterances of fact in a comprehensive manner; however, the faculty of sight has already begun to slip away. In the following stanza, "Eyes" belong only to others— ghostly, anonymous presences gathered to attest to God's action. The speaker no longer retains either an autonomous "I" or the physical power of eyesight. A volitional self is recollected in stanza three, but the memory is one of relinquishment, the execution of the *speaker's* last "will" and testament. Indeed, one element of the poem's bitter contrast is concentrated in the juxtaposition of the ruthless will of the Deity, Who determines fate, and the speaker's "will"—reduced by now to the legal document that has been designed to restore order in the aftermath of dissolution. And at this moment of double "execution," when tacit acknowledgment of God's ineluctable force is rendered, identity begins to fritter away. The speaker formulates thought in increasingly strained synecdochic and metonymical tropes. The possessions of the dying Voice are designated as the "portions of me [that] be / Assignable—," not as discrete objects that belong to someone and are separate from her, but as blurred extensions of a fraying self that can no longer define the limits of identity. The "uncertain" quality that inheres in the speaker's eyesight is assigned to the "stumbling Buzz" of the fly; it is the speaker's faculties that have "failed," but in the verse, the speaker attributes failure to the "Windows." The confusions inherent in this rhetorical finale of the poem aptly render the atomizing self as the stately centrifugal force of dissolution begins to scatter being and consciousness.

Like many other proleptic poems, "*I heard a Fly buzz*—" serves several functions. It does provide a means of "Looking at Death"; in addition, however, it strives to define both death and life in unaccustomed ways. Thus it is centrally concerned to posit "seeing" as a form of power: "to see" is to assert authority and autonomy—the authority to define life in ways that will be meaningful not only to oneself, perhaps, but to others as well, and the autonomy to reject the criteria and limits God would force upon us, even if such an act will inevitably elicit God's wrath. Death robs us of all bodily sensations; more important, however, it wrests this autonomous authority from us, the final and most devastating wound, "I could not see *to see*—." Ironically, the strategy of the poem mimics God's method, for a reader is enabled to comprehend the value of "sight" here principally by experiencing the horror of its loss. Moreover, the poem even suggests that some ways of engaging with the world during "life" may be no more than forms of animated death. Eating, sleeping, exercising the physical faculties—these alone do not describe "life"; and many pass through existence with a form of "blindness" that fatally compromises the integrity of self. Thus the poem offers a counsel to the living by strongly implying the crucial importance of daring "to see" while life still lasts, and one way in which the poet can be Representative is by offering a model of active insight that is susceptible of emulation.

Most of Dickinson's work presupposes a model of identity in which the "self" can be described according to the way it organizes its perceptions of the world, formulates its goals, and arrives at judgments. God can impose any situation or bodily configuration upon us that suits His whim: the "self" nonetheless supersedes all apparent limitations inherent in God's action. "*The Outer—from the Inner / Derives it's Magnitude— / 'Tis Duke, or Dwarf, according / As is the Central Mood—*" (#451). Thus a woman can be a poet; thus either man or woman can be Representative. Indeed, we derive the essential force of our being from the fact that this internal structure is coherently integrated and inviolate. God can threaten us, inflict pain upon us, cajole us, implore us; but so long as we remain alive and volitional, He cannot force the faith that would be expressed by assenting to *His* characterization of our plight. "*To be alive—is Power— / Existence—in itself— / Without a further function— / Omnipotence—Enough— / To be alive—and Will! / 'Tis able as a God— / The Maker—of Ourselves—be what— / Such being Finitude!*" (#677) However, insofar as death obliterates self, it robs us of this power.

At the end of "*I heard a Fly buzz—*" the speaker has been winnowed by death, and the integral self is scattered outward and destroyed by dispersal; that poem concludes when vision has failed. Another of the proleptic poems begins after the power of seeing has been lost altogether.

> *I felt a Funeral, in my Brain,*
> *And Mourners to and fro*
> *Kept treading—treading—till it seemed*
> *That Sense was breaking through—*
>
> *And when they all were seated,*
> *A Service, like a Drum—*

Kept beating—beating—till I thought
My Mind was going numb—

And then I heard them lift a Box
And creak across my Soul
With those same Boots of Lead, again,
Then Space—began to toll,

As all the Heavens were a Bell,
And Being, but an Ear,
And I, and Silence, some strange Race
Wrecked, solitary, here—

And then a Plank in Reason, broke,
And I dropped down, and down—
And hit a World, at every plunge
And Finished knowing—then—

(#*280*)

Here the process of annihilation is inverted: the fragile membrane that sepa-rates "self" from "outer world" has been ruptured, and the surroundings flood into consciousness with a force like that of sexual violation. There are no distinct "others" (not even the anonymous "Eyes" that had indicated mourners to witness death in "*I heard a Fly buzz—*"), nothing but a lone speaker whose mind has been filled with a jumble of sensations, as if it were no more than an empty vessel. Throughout, the speaker seems to strain after coherence, and the poem's compelling attraction derives in large measure from its ability to lure the reader into joining the speaker in this pursuit. It even seems apparent that Dickinson intends this prolonged and unresolved tension: at the beginning we are given to hope that "Sense was breaking through," and this expectation is not undercut until the end, when "a Plank in Reason, broke." The poem taunts with its invitations and frustrations, and ultimately forces us to ask what we know, how we know—whether "life" and "death" are susceptible to understanding.

The poem is taut in its movement, for there are at least three forces at work to set the verse in motion and structure its course. The one that is clearest and most available to the reader is the step-by-step scenario of "Fu-neral," a familiar ritual whose configuration has been decreed by society. All Congregationalist funerals followed very much the same outline, and few readers will have difficulty in recognizing it: the mourners who pay their respects, the church service, the removal to graveyard and burial, the tolling of the bell as friends and family leave to resume the pursuits of the living. What makes this poem startling, of course, is that the ritual observed in real life by the mourners is reported here by the deceased itself.

Although it is an impossible feat, seeing one's own funeral and reading one's own obituary are among the most common fantasies of our culture, and they have become stock components of our literature as well. Congregationalist ministers enjoined the members of their congregations to reflect upon the moment of death as a spiritual exercise, to imagine how family and friends would feel (would they be confident of meeting the deceased in Heaven, or would they fear an eternity of separation because the life of the deceased had given no signs of saving Grace?). Mark Twain played humorously with the remnants of this religious notion in *The Adventures of Tom Sawyer;* and in the twentieth century Thornton Wilder's *Our Town* dramatized the pathos in life by using a proleptic narrator who sees, among other things, her own funeral. The premise behind all of these is the same: from the absolute vantage of death, we will be able to ascertain what is really important in life—what events were significant, what values are enduring. At last, perhaps, we can know what people really thought of us or how God will ultimately judge us: seeing our funeral might allow us finally to understand our "self." This poem is grotesque, and deliberately so, principally because Dickinson's rendition of the convention turns all the usual advantages of these literary devices against themselves. No information about life or self can be gathered from *this* funeral. The mourners are silent, muffled figures whose movement, though constant, "treading—treading," leads only "to and fro"; the funeral service has no sound but the relentless "beating—beating" of the unmusical, toneless "Drum." One horror, then, is the hollow abstraction of this retrospective view. Instead of confirming the importance of certain particular events and values, instead of revealing the true feelings of people for a specific soul now deceased, it suggests that nothing and no one can have enduring value. The only lasting value is the unvarying ritual itself *as ritual,* and both the reader and the proleptic Voice cling to the formal, abstract structure of the ceremony that alone seems capable of imposing order upon death.

In ironic juxtaposition to the regularized, conventional progress of the funeral rites is the second force in the poem, the disruptive capacity of death—a jumbling together of all categories that apply to the speaker and serve to define identity. The funeral is "felt"; the "Mind" becomes "numb"; the coffin is lifted "across" the soul; being is reduced to "an Ear," as speaker and "Silence" become members of the same "strange Race" of creatures. The speaker's plight in the penultimate stanza of the poem recollects Dickinson's assertion that Immortality is "the Flood subject," for even the possibility of consciousness after death becomes confused and terrifying when both speaker and "Silence" find themselves "Wrecked, solitary, here." The "Plank" of reason in the last stanza may seem cryptic to a modern reader; however, a contemporary reader might well have recognized Dickinson's allusion to the iconography of conservative, mid-nineteenth-century religious culture. In Holmes and Barber's *Religious Allegories* (1848), there is an emblem called "WALKING BY FAITH" (modeled on the passage from II Corinthians 5:7, "For we walk by faith, not by sight"). It depicts a man "just starting from what appears to be solid ground, to walk upon a narrow plank [with the word 'FAITH' imprinted on it], stretched across a deep "gulph" and which ends nobody knows whither."[40] On one side is life, and on the other is Heaven; only the plank of "FAITH" can provide transport—so this emblem asserts. Yet having renounced faith, Dickinson substitutes a "Plank in Reason," which breaks because no rational explanation can be adequate to bridge the abyss between earth and Heaven. The poem concludes with a fall that is an apotheosis of confusion. Perhaps it recapitulates that first fall into Hell (the poem's recourse to the emblem tradition supports this inference); perhaps it is the horror of a residual self, dropping endlessly through infinite, interstellar space ("And hit a World, at every plunge," seems to confirm this reading)—no Heaven or Hell, just unbounded and eternal loneliness; perhaps it is a surrealistic fall into some dark, endless, undefined interior of being (the initial placing of the funeral "in my Brain" encourages this inference). And of all these possibilities, the first is perhaps the most comforting because the resort to a familiar mythic world makes it at least partially comprehensible.

This is an extraordinarily self-conscious piece of verse, with Dickinson making both artifice and the relationship between art and life explicit concerns of the poem. Thus two forces, the familiar order of ritual and the expanding disjunction of categories that are used to define the speaker's existence, function to balance each other in some measure. Without the systematic, articulated ceremony of the funeral rites, a reader might have no idea what the speaker was describing, and the poem would lack coherence and unity; without the steady distortion of the terms by which self is defined, the reader could not apprehend the full experiential anguish of the process. Yet they work together in one respect: each in its own way tacitly argues that human beings must *create* their own order, for we live in a universe that has an imperative only for annihilation.

The ultimate horror is this: that the inescapable activity of destruction derives much of its fearsomeness from being tied to the laws of unvarying and intractable movement—time, the third major force at work in the poem. And whereas the sequential order of the funeral and the violating disorder of disrupted categories are conveyed through diction, time's indifferent ruthlessness is rendered less directly—through absences and through syntactic and rhythmic structures. Thus the reader *feels* the force of time in the poem more keenly than he or she apprehends it intellectually.

We feel it first because of the oddities in the account of the funeral. In the latter-day Puritan culture of Emily Dickinson's Amherst, funeral services were forms of proto-narrative: since the ceremony was stylized, different por-

Holmes and Barber offer many visual renditions of the Christian poised at the edge of some bottomless gulf; however, this plate seems most directly relevant to Dickinson's poem.

In the conventional model, the shining city of Heaven awaits—a reward for blind faith. Hence the Christian in this emblem looks not forward, but down at the Bible in his hand. The plank is labeled "FAITH" so that the reader will make no mistake about the force that can carry all across the dangerous chasm. In Dickinson's poem, of course, the plank is in "Reason."

tions of it were not of equal importance, even though they might take equal amounts of time to enact. The "narrative structure" of the funeral rite was dominated by the sermon, which summed up the life of the deceased and served as the centerpiece of the ritual: everything that preceded it was merely anticipatory; everything that followed was anticlimactic. A funeral told the tale of transition from earth to afterlife, and its sermon was the dead person's final "earthly appearance." Drawing upon a tradition of many centuries, the minister would begin with a suitable text from the Bible; he would then select the most significant events in the dead person's life in order to reveal his or her essential Christian nature; finally, he would draw a conclusion concerning the spiritual state of the newly deceased—sometimes even estimating the chances for salvation. Although soul had been severed from body at death, society's *formal recognition* of this event did not occur until this moment, when the body lying in the casket was explicitly distinguished from both the mortal being who had lived on earth and its soul, now departed. The invariable chant at the graveside—"ashes to ashes, dust to dust"—gives articulation to this recognition. Pivoting upon the sermon, then, the funeral service balanced hope against apparent loss: all that was essential to the nature of the departed had moved to an afterlife, saved (it was hoped) by the merciful sacrifice of Christ; the mortal remains were thus no occasion for grief, for the "fall" into the grave could be canceled by the "rise" into Heaven. Funeral sermons were so important as exemplary renditions of Christian character and explicit instances of God's mercy that they were very often printed and published, to be read devotionally. Many of Heman Humphrey's and a number of Edward Hitchcock's still survive in this form.[41]

Any accurate recapitulation of the funeral "narrative," then, would be shaped to mirror this structure, and such a recapitulation would of course reflect the crucial significance of the sermon as final exegesis of identity. A merely sequential movement of the verse would have to be modulated to highlight the central importance of this moment. However, such is not the case in Dickinson's version here. *There is no narrative center to this poem.* Quite the opposite: there is a curiously detached, even clinical tone, an apparent determination to tell only "what happened" in orderly, impartial, and merely temporal sequence, a fading out at the end into terrible uncertainty. Thus, although Dickinson employs the successive stages in the funeral ritual to establish a recognizable sequence in the poem, she does not "shape" this temporal arrangement to make the sermon take precedence: the "Service" is but one event among many, each of apparently equal consequence. This is a brutal violation, this flattening of the narrative so that temporal sequence provides the only order; and it accomplishes one part of its effect merely through a felt absence. There *is* no sermon in this service. The proleptic speaker's individual character does not dominate even her own funeral.

The second way a reader feels time's force in this poem, however, is probably its prominent feature: immutable clock-time conveyed grammatically through the driving, implacable forward movement of parataxis. Events occurring without pause, without yielding insight, without any logical relationship to one another, without any ordering of importance: life is swept remorselessly along in the swift current of time, swept over the edge, perhaps to come to rest in some unfathomed end, perhaps merely to fall forever. There is virtually no syntactic subordination in this poem; the few instances are either hypothetical ("As [if]") or, more commonly, temporal ("till . . . when . . . till . . . then . . . then . . . then"). The insistent beat of "when" and "then" merely reinforces the drumming tattoo of ticking time, which becomes more insistent with each stanza and climaxes with the paratactic thumping of

"And" that is concentrated in the fifth stanza ("And . . . And . . . And . . . And") as the Voice recounts its final, undefined descent beyond understanding. It is thus that the reader is propelled forward by the driving force of time: urgent, impatient, uncaring. Here, the metrical dominance of "eights and sixes," hymnal cadence, serves as bitter irony—the hope offered by Christ utterly forsworn by the bleak vision of the verse; and probably Dickinson intended a trope for metrical foot in the image of "those same Boots of Lead, again"—death busy about his usual work of blight and annihilation.

The somber implication of paratactic movement is by no means confined to this one poem: it is rendered unmistakably (though unobtrusively) in "*A Clock stopped—*" by "*Nods from the Gilded pointers— / Nods from the Seconds slim—*"; and the irony in that poem is that God is as completely entrapped by the inflexible nature of His invention as mankind is. Indeed, throughout Dickinson's work, the use of parataxis almost always signals the inexorable drive toward death.

Everything in Emily Dickinson's education had taught that all historical narratives had a "shape" over and above simple sequence, a shape that had been imposed by God. The Bible offered a panoramic chronicle that showed the compassionate outlines of God's plan for humanity; histories of both ancient and modern life were another, more immediately social embodiment of God's providential design. The narrative design of the funeral service, then, was intended to mimic the shapeliness that had been imparted to time by God, a shapeliness that told the unvarying story of divine love. The leveling parataxis of "*I felt a Funeral, in my Brain*" is an explicit refutation of the claim that time has been shaped by God's merciful actions; and in here, the reader can *feel* the ominous, undifferentiated forward movement toward inescapable death.

Other poems also serve to refute this standard notion of time as shaped by God, but they do so at a more explicitly intellectual level:

> *Crumbling is not an instant's Act*
> *A fundamental pause*
> *Delapidation's processes*
> *Are organized Decays.*
>
> *'Tis first a Cobweb on the Soul*
> *A Cuticle of Dust*
> *A Borer in the Axis*
> *An Elemental Rust—*
>
> *Ruin is formal—Devil's work*
> *Consecutive and slow—*

Fail in an instant, no man did
Slipping — is Crashe's law.

(#997)

The definition comprised by this verse states that time is linear and undifferentiated. Here, however, the device that mimics this linear process is not
parataxis, but the slow, incremental accumulation of examples that follows
the definition in the first stanza. These quite nicely illustrate the notion of
"Consecutive and slow—," and become another way of suggesting movement through time that is undifferentiated and unshaped by God's mercy,
every moment like every other, and each inching all of us irresistibly toward
death. Sometimes Dickinson conjured eternity, at least, in nonlinear terms;
however, sometimes God's Domain was itself presumed to be no more than
an extension of the doggedly linear quality of the life He created for earth
and its creatures.

Forever — is composed of Nows —
'Tis not a different time —
Except for Infiniteness —
And Latitude of Home —

From this — experienced Here —
Remove the Dates — to These —
Let Months dissolve in further Months —
And Years — exhale in Years —

Without Debate — or Pause —
Or Celebrated Days —
No different Our Years would be
From Anno Dominies

(#624)

Insofar as time has gradations, Dickinson asserts here, these are structures
that have been imposed upon it by mankind, "Dates ... Months ... Years
... Celebrated Days"; without them, there would be only the dissolving,
exhaling incoherence of "Anno Dominies," time as arranged by God.

"I felt a Funeral, in my Brain" is narrated in the past tense despite the
fact that the possibility of such a narrative vantage is explicitly denied in the
concluding stanza. The Voice arrests us with an exotic timbre; it is an acknowledged artifact, like some marvelous automaton, and it exists for the
sole purpose of this single performance, the uttering of the poem—trailing
no past, presuming no future save extinction. Yet there is an inherent paradox

to this plan: parataxis is the grammatical representation of the passage of time, and it demands the existence of some temporal continuum. However, the temporal continuum that we know on earth precludes any realistic possibility of a dead person's speaking; and a Voice that can use the past tense to narrate events that end with a fall into nothingness is difficult even to imagine. Moreover, the difficulty offered by this poem is not unique to it: others like *"Twas just this time, last year, I died"* (#445), *"I died for Beauty—"* (#449), and *"Because I could not stop for Death—"* (#712) present variations of the same dilemma. When we read them, we must presume (perhaps unconsciously) that although they give accounts of action that takes place over the course of "time," the temporal continuum of each poem exists independently of the clock time in which both author and reader exist. Nor do these poems take place in the same "region" or the same temporal continuum: they are not related to one another. Each presents a single, isolated nightmare.

All of these poems in some measure lack a logical center or fail to move toward a clear resolution; all posit the relationship of events exclusively in terms of temporal sequence. However, the distinct, self-contained temporal integrity of each short verse itself offers a compensating unity. Each poem in its entirety is a small, distinct system—an artifact that has been concocted for the reader's inspection and analysis. It is true that an absolute barrier exists between the reader and the Voice of such verse; and the distance such a barrier imposes coerces the reader's attention precisely because it so severely strains our powers of understanding and defies our deepest intuitive notions. This is perhaps the greatest strength of such work. At the same time, however, such a barrier discourages sympathetic identification. Probably it is not surprising that critics who have read Dickinson's poetry as a relatively unselfconscious outpouring of personal emotion often assert that these poems offer the strongest "proof" of her madness.

In fact, Dickinson employs this deliberately unrealistic Voice precisely in order to force each reader to re-examine the premises about life and death that he or she has taken for granted. We can tolerate the inevitability of our demise, Dickinson would argue, largely because there is the myth of some possible new life in the Heaven of an afterworld, a myth that rests on the spurious notion of a continuum of "time" from life to death. Thus the speaker of " *'Twas just this time, last year, I died"* (#445) concludes her narrative of the process of death with an expression of wishful expectation for just such a temporal continuum between life and eternity: *"But this sort, grieved myself, / And so, I thought the other way, / How just this time, some perfect year— / Themself, should come to me—."* The poet thus compels us to wonder whether the reassuring focus of the Christian myth derives its power primarily from our desperate need for hope and continuity. In this capacity

the poet is not so much namer as shaper. She asks us to examine the implication of the *forms* by which we give structure to the many narratives that
recount our lives.

The Voice of the "Wife" accepts the suffering and the mission of mercy
that is usually associated with Christ. The proleptic Voice itself bears no
closer relationship to Christ than it does to any earthly speaker; however, in
creating such a Voice, Dickinson appropriated one element of Christ's role
for the poet—that of a messenger who travels between time and eternity.
Many critics have remarked upon Dickinson's skill in capturing the essence
of a single short stretch of experience. Nowhere is this talent more clearly
demonstrated than in proleptic poems and in those poems that address the
process by which one becomes poet of the proleptic.

> *Just lost, when I was saved!*
> *Just felt the world go by!*
> *Just girt me for the onset with Eternity,*
> *When breath blew back,*
> *And on the other side*
> *I heard recede the disappointed tide!*
>
> *Therefore, as One returned, I feel,*
> *Odd secrets of the line to tell!*
> *Some Sailor, skirting foreign shores—*
> *Some pale Reporter, from the awful doors*
> *Before the Seal!*
>
> *Next time, to stay!*
> *Next time, the things to see*
> *By Ear unheard,*
> *Unscrutinized by Eye—*
>
> *Next time, to tarry,*
> *While the Ages steal—*
> *Slow tramp the Centuries,*
> *And the Cycles wheel!*

(#*160*)

The Flood subject, immortality, hungers menacingly at the outskirts of this
poem. The speaker, like Melville's Ishmael, has looked upon the face of death
and lived to tell the tale; and although the mortal struggle is not quite a
wrestling match, it has surely been some kind of heroic encounter. There is
an air of victory in the verse, a tone of entitlement and privileged insight. In
the final analysis, perhaps the poem recounts a kind of "death" and "rebirth"—the transformation of woman into poet.

The belief that all historical narratives have a shape carries an implicit notion of time: thus, if we believe that God has embedded a myth in the Bible to elaborate the benign plan of His dealings with mankind, we will also believe that time is "anisotropic"—that there have been privileged moments, like God's sparing Isaac or Christ's gift of the Crucifixion, that are more important than other moments in revealing God's benevolence. The structure or shape of time, then, consists in the pattern of such moments, their relationship to one another. If, on the other hand, we believe that time has *no* intrinsic form, that it is "isotropic," we will presume that every moment is of equal importance with every other moment insofar as each impels us equally toward death: time, like a string of beads, moves forward in a rapid succession of "nows," second following second in an incessant and uniform way— having no aim, embodying no intrinsic order, contributing to no grand plan save God's plan of annihilation. (And if time *is* shaped, it is fashioned to tell only this tale of systematic brutality.) This notion of "isotropic" time is implicit in such poems as "*I felt a Funeral, in my Brain.*" "*Forever—is composed of Nows—*" takes the notion of isotropic time one step further by arguing that human society and its customs impart the saving remnant of order to an otherwise unstructured field of time and space. Such order is better than none—it is better than being trapped in the ever-fleeing "now" that marks the changing moment between past and future—however, it has no *focus*, no goal, no implicit point of view. The poet, Dickinson suggests, can supply that focus: because God has not imparted privileged moments of truthful narrative to the passage of time, the poet must repair God's deficiency by recounting the privileged insights from her moments of heightened perception. The poet can be guide, and the poet's willingness to confront even death can qualify her to understand both life and eternity, and to explicate the very process of annihilation. It is this ability that is asserted in "*Just lost, when I was saved!*"

The first stanza begins in the past tense, almost as if it were the beginning of one of the proleptic poems, and the initial parataxis ("Just lost . . . Just felt . . . Just girt") provides the syntactic expression of a time that leads only to death. Yet here there is a counterforce to death and time; this Voice hovers at the edge of existence, but has not yet moved beyond it. The expanse between time and eternity has been reduced to a "line," a term that has two primary meanings in this poem: it is the boundary that separates life and death, and it is a unit of poetry. Thus the counterforce to predatory eternity is "breath," the poet's creative, ordering capacity. At the conclusion of the first stanza, the forces of annihilation have been bested by "breath," and they are contained by the past tense that has dominated that stanza. The second stanza's first line introduces a remarkable and unique present tense, "I feel." "*To feel*" is here an intransitive verb that Dickinson's dictionary defined in the following way: "To have the sensibility of the passions moved or excited.

The good man *feels* for the woes of others." The reward for this willingness to confront eternity, then, is the capacity to "feel" the truths of time and eternity and to "tell" them to others.

The notion of "line" soon dilates with implication. It is the equator, a measure of "circumference," the place where the two hemispheres meet, and the only way around the earth that is a perfect circle; seamen who had "sailed the line" told frightening tales of instruments that went awry on the equator when the tools for calibrating became suddenly unreliable. The equator is also the only figure of earthly measurement that is both line and circle. The "line" may be a plumb line as well, exploring the recesses of human possibility with John of Patmos in the Book of Revelation at "the awful doors / Before the Seal!" The rapid proliferation of implications that follows this pivotal line (which contains the only present-tense verb in the poem, "Therefore, as One returned, I feel") is matched by an explosion of time. Having passed through the past and lingered for but a single moment in the present, the speaker moves permanently into the infinitive mode: "to tell . . . to stay . . . to see . . . to tarry." The beating repetition that had spelled the imprisoning "Now" has been transformed into a pattern of possibilities and promises, time that can be ordered through the poet's permanent and unchanging vision.

5 ❖ *The Possibilities for Publication*

Many of Dickinson's critics are rightly hesitant to posit a path of growth or development in the poetry copied out in 1862–63 or earlier—that is, all poems with a Johnson number of 807 or lower; the dating of probable composition for all of these must be so tentative that no clear path of artistic or personal change can be clearly spelled out. Reservations must also be offered concerning the preceding discussion of Voice. Unlike such poets as Tennyson and Browning, Emily Dickinson never wrote dramatic monologues; her poems are not renditions of a series of individualized speakers, each different from the others. Rather, there is a continuous speaker, and this speaker adopts a variety of tones and postures: different Voices. Occasionally these are relatively unmixed: "*We dont cry—Tim and I*" is a poem in which the speaker adopts the posture of an actual child; "*Dont put up my Thread and Needle—*" is dominated by accents of the "Wife," though this case is somewhat more complex, for the conflation of seamstress and poet is implicit throughout. "Voice," then, identifies not a person, but an attitude—a way of looking at the world, a set of categories in terms of which the relationship between speaker and reader can be defined, a system of priorities that determine what is of value and what is not, a vocabulary and syntax for rendering the speaker's sentiments. These different Voices do not always agree with one another: the child's outspoken disobedience and the child / Saint's arrogant indifference cannot be made compatible with the "Wife's" self-effacing inclination to comfort others, or with her appreciation of the value of pain. Both child / Saint and proleptic Voice are at considerable remove from the world, whereas the "Wife" pursues her calling within a context that is defined domestically.

Nevertheless, the various Voices have many things in common: all are fundamentally preoccupied with the relationship between "self" and "other," and all perceive the "self" as in constant peril of violation or disintegration; all look upon life as a process of pain, threatened with cosmic wounding and limited by the absolute blow of physical demise; all address the force of time and seek, somehow, to confound it. Most important, all originate in a need to compensate for the indifference, inadequacies, or hostilities of an absent God.

These Voices are not fixed, unchanging entities. The proleptic Voice is always distinctive: readers know when they are being addressed from beyond the grave. Yet the Gothic resonance of this Voice finds its way into other kinds of poetry, and in her later years Dickinson found further strategies to deal directly with death. The impudent, taunting tones of the playground characterize a number of poems throughout her work in a Voice that is recognizably childlike; however, in suitably modulated form these tones are also found in a caustic, ironic, satiric adult Voice that has graduated from laboratory and classroom to rebuke a derelict God or renounce a commercialized society. Sometimes it is no more than the capacity for examination, analysis, and report that recollects this school-aged Voice. The mature, caring tones of the "Wife's" Voice are subjected to the most strenuous transformation. Many of Dickinson's poems, especially the late poems, seem to issue from a speaker whose gender and station in life are indifferent. This Voice comprehends the vantage of Ecclesiastes: "One generation passeth away, and another generation cometh: but the earth abideth for ever. . . . The thing that hath been, it is that which shall be; and that which is done is that which shall be done: and there is no new thing under the sun" (1:4, 9). An ageless, timeless Voice, familiar with pain and great loss—honest, compassionate, wise, and content to relinquish warfare.

Although we cannot know by what process Dickinson perfected the poetry before 1862–63, it is clear that by that time she had already laid the firm foundation of her work. She had an astonishing versatility at her command; the verse was dense with compression and smooth in the management of its tonalities and themes. The full range of the Voice was not yet complete, and the consequences of her various poetic attitudes were yet to be fully discovered; nonetheless, the major strategies of the Voice had been established, and her apprenticeship—whatever form that had taken—was clearly over. Although she never wished for publication so ardently that she was willing to have the verse see print at no matter what cost, it seems clear that she was at least willing to consider publication, perhaps more than willing. During the years 1858–63 she tested the waters.

There were several avenues open. The most handy was no farther than a block or two away. In 1860 Amherst boasted at least two printers, Henry A. Marsh and The Express Job Printing; in the decade between 1860 and 1870, six more firms entered the market (some also left it after a very short life in the trade). In some respects, the business of getting manuscript copy into print then had much less the air of "art" about it than a modern audience is apt to realize. In this era before quick copying, even before the time when typewriters and carbon paper made it relatively easy to produce more than a single copy of a document, any written work that was meant to be read by more than a very small selection of people had to be set in type and run off in print. Every town of any size had its printers, and Emily Dickinson's society was a culture not merely of the written word, but of the *printed* word. Thus in 1851, when Father had declared that Austin's letters to his family were "altogether before Shakespeare" and had postulated the possibility of having "them published to put in [the family] library," he had been making tacit allusion to the busy industry of job printing. Any private occasion might naturally lend itself to printed record and limited distribution: the *Reunion of the Dickinson Family at Amherst, Massachusetts, August 8th and 9th, 1883* was published under such circumstances, as was Austin's modest essay of 1889, "Representative Men of the Parish."[42]

Paradoxically, private printing may have been both too lofty and too limited for Emily Dickinson's use. Usually, Amherst printers ran off sermons, broadsides, town publications, manuals for use at Amherst College or at the Agricultural College, society minutes, catalogues, and scientific publications (often Edward Hitchcock's). It would not have been impossible or outrageous to use the printers for a private edition of poetry, but it would have been somewhat outdated. Earlier, in the 1840s, a more varied list had issued from Amherst printing shops: *Letters to a Son in the Ministry* by Heman Humphrey; *Sketches* by Mme. Sigourney; *A Wreath for the Tomb* by Edward Hitchcock. However, by 1860 Amherst publishers had become organs of a public world—the College and the township; as a rule, local printers published "official" documents, and they distributed them on a very limited basis.

In 1855 Walt Whitman availed himself of the services of a printer, had his own iconoclastic verse set in type, paid for the job privately, and sent copies of the finished *Leaves of Grass* to influential literary men who could help him further his career. Ralph Waldo Emerson was one such selected reader, and in August 1856 Emerson wrote a now famous encomium to the brash new poet: "I greet you at the beginning of a great career." In the retelling, it seems a thrilling success story; in fact, Walt Whitman had no "great career" until many years had passed and he had expended a significant portion of his energies actively promoting it. The day of the private press as a vehicle for literature was fast disappearing, and Whitman's poetry would probably never have found its vast audience if Whitman himself had not been an insider of the publishing trade—working the rounds of Manhattan and Brooklyn newspapers and knowing the right people. Emily Dickinson did not publish her poems privately: that is the only fact we know. Possibly she realized that without expert knowledge and the kind of contacts in the literary world that she did not have, she could never have promoted her poetry into prominence (as Whitman had). She was caught in an epoch of transition in both the status of literature and the process of publication.

In earlier times, American literature had addressed serious, genteel readers. By Dickinson's time, things had changed. "Until the early nineteenth century, authorship had not been a profession in the modern sense of the word: it had been a matter of finding a paying patron rather than of pleasing a reading public. In 1820, the books sold in the United States netted half a million dollars; in 1860, this figure had risen to twelve and a half million." Even by the mid-1850s, literature had become a business. It had rapidly centralized: 92 percent of all fiction was published in Boston, Philadelphia, or New York; and literature was not just business, but *big* business. "In 1826, Cooper's *The Last of the Mohicans,* a popular book of the time, sold 5,750 copies; in 1853, Fanny Fern's *Fern Leaves from Fanny's Portfolio* sold 80,000 copies and was read literally from coast to coast. . . . The Harper's motto was cheap prices and large circulation; they capitalized on religious family series and educational libraries. Like their competitors, the brothers encouraged writers to suit the supply to the demand."[43] Whitman did not supply what people were demanding any more than Dickinson did; but New York was a publishing center, and Amherst was not. Moreover, Whitman was willing to market both his poetry and his personality, while Dickinson was not.

After the middle of the century, many popular authors had begun to be not so much artists as celebrities: some could be both (Whitman and Twain are cases in point); but the era of the widely read *serious* author was drawing to a close. There is no doubt that a great many writers were compelled to sell themselves to the "people" when they sold their work. They traveled to promote sales; they gave public readings; sometimes they even allowed the style of their personal lives to become part and parcel of the sales package. This was, perhaps, especially so with popular women writers, whose names became synonymous with whatever sentiments their work evoked. Begun in the 1850s, this trend escalated at a dizzying rate after the conclusion of the Civil

War. Thus Dickinson had a serious consideration to ponder: to what extent would she be willing to submit to some ransack of her privacy for the sake of publication? And this quite objective problem doubtless fueled the ambivalences she might already have had about submitting her work to the judgment of a possibly harsh and ill-informed audience.

Even if Dickinson *had* unambivalently sought publication, she confronted obstacles. How could a writer so isolated from commercial centers—a poet who nonetheless thought of herself as America's "Representative" Voice— reach the kind of readership that would confirm her all encompassing ambition? It was difficult for an unknown author simply to walk into a major publishing firm unannounced; however, there was an intermediary step, publication in magazines or prominent newspapers (which, unlike today's newspapers, printed fiction and poetry as well as news). And here Emily Dickinson had a contact: Sam Bowles, who had succeeded his father in 1851 as editor of the Springfield *Daily Republican* and transformed it into one of America's most influential journals.

Bowles was an extraordinary man, Byronically handsome, with deep, intelligent eyes. He was neither literary nor bookish; indeed, very much a man of his times, Sam Bowles was like an updated, successful, commercial variant of Samuel Fowler Dickinson. A zealot, not for religion, but for politics and business.

Bowles was everywhere, doing everything, poor at delegating responsibility and exacting maximum results from himself and from everyone who worked for him. He expanded far beyond his own community. . . . His journalistic efforts took him deep into local, state, and national politics. As a matter of principle, he never ran for office himself, but he was close to many who did, from the lowest to the highest. He enjoyed the political world and became an important influence in it. . . . He was a child of the young democracy, socially as well as politically. . . . Dr. Josiah Holland, his colleague on the *Republican* for years [and husband of one of Emily Dickinson's closest friends], must have thought him . . . "irreverent, not to say heathenish." "I think," said Holland, "that his strongest passion was the love of power"—the power, that is, of manipulating men and influencing decisions.[44]

It is not difficult to understand why Emily Dickinson felt a kinship with this man, in so many ways different from her. His energy, quick wit, and irrepressible humor made him stimulating company, and she valued his friendship until the day of his death. Yet their attitudes toward literature could not have been more different.

In Boston, the premier publishing house was Ticknor and Fields: they published the work of Emerson, Longfellow, Hawthorne, Thoreau, and many other New England luminaries; in addition, the firm published two distinguished magazines—*The Atlantic Monthly* (first issued in 1857) and *The*

North American Review (1854–64). James Fields, owner of the Old Corner Bookstore, was the more literary of the two partners; he served as editor of *The Atlantic Monthly* from 1861 to 1871, and wrote several volumes of poetry and essays. His wife, Annie Adams Fields (1834–1915), was famous in her own right; a minor poet and biographer of her husband, Annie Fields had a sharp-eyed understanding of the vagaries of temperament that characterized the members and near-members of the literary establishment. For many years she conducted a distinguished *salon* in her home (possibly the model for Susan Dickinson's intellectual gatherings at the Evergreens); her acquaintance was much sought after, and she met virtually everyone of importance in the American world of arts and letters. She was not charmed by good-looking Samuel Bowles. A diary entry for January 30, 1867, reads in part:

Mr. Bowles is quite handsome and would be altogether so if he had elegance of manner to correspond with what nature has done for him in giving him fine eyes, but he is an ambitious man, ambitious to be known as a literary man, but apparently mistaking popularity for fame[] he has learned to know almost everybody of literary celebrity, to be on the top word continually, to keep open house, to be a general good fellow, which combined with real ability has made him widely liked & given him a brilliant restless way, which marks so many Americans. His book "Across the Continent" which appeared last summer was intensely interesting & valuable but inelegant and of momentary value comparatively speaking, from the careless writing and careless thinking which distinguished it. He is very able as an editor & J.T. F[ields] says more to be dreaded were he to start an opposing magazine than any other man in New England.[45]

Bowles had energy and an immensely quick mind, but little capacity for trenchant discrimination. He was too fast-moving and impatient to enter seriously or deeply into intellectual pursuits, and these characteristics were reflected in his choice of literature for the Springfield *Republican.* "His taste in poetry was completely conventional. . . . The columns of the *Republican,* for instance, were famous for their hospitality to lady poets, like young Colette Loomis, Lizzie Lincoln of Hinsdale, N.H., Luella Clarke, Ellen P. Champion, and 'Fanny Fern' (Sarah Willis Parton)."[46] "Fanny Fern" was read from coast to coast; after the golden spike had been driven, they named a Pullman car after her.

Thus confronted with genius, Sam Bowles failed to notice it—failed much more grievously than Higginson, who thought that Dickinson's poetry was difficult and strange, but also that her mind was worthy of his time and attention. Bowles had a sure ear for the coming fad, for sensation, for pathos. He was a man of public power first, a businessman second—and last, far down the line, a man of letters. Women writers of a certain type were enjoying quite a vogue in popular literature; Bowles made sure to publish their work.

Bowles was not alone in determining editorial policy in the *Republican:* he was assisted by Josiah Holland until 1870, when Holland moved to New York to become the first editor of *Scribner's Monthly,* a post he held until his death in 1881. Not surprisingly, he and Bowles held much the same opinion of women intellectuals and women artists—a complicated mixture of benevolent tolerance, implicit condescension, and the desire to capitalize on their popularity. In fact, Bowles and Holland printed essays in the *Republican* outlining their views about such women. The first, "Employment for Women: A Few Words to Those who 'Write for the Papers,'" appeared on December 6, 1865. It reads in part:

There is already, says [the *Phrenological Journal*], a surplus of teachers, and the prospects in that line are discouraging. The next resort is usually authorship. Others have won gold and laurels, says the eager aspirant, why should not I? Ask the editor, whose waste basket groans under rolls of flowery manuscript, improbable tales and verbose sketches, where rhetoric and euphony are up in arms against each other, and inane reminiscences of successful school compositions struggle with milk-and-watery imitations of Thackeray and Miss Mulock! . . .

Most of the trash which finds its grave in the editorial waste basket comes, we venture to say, from others than those who write or work in any way for a living. . . . The writings of one upon whom the terrible realities of suffering and destitution have begun to bear, will possess much earnestness and force, whatever other graces they may lack. They will be far more likely to compel attention than the work of the novice who writes to while away a leisure hour . . .

Again, a large class of young people, especially women, write to console themselves under sorrows either real or imaginary. To some temperaments the need of sympathy is imperative. . . . Now and then there is a true pathos in the complaint which makes the world listen to it . . .

But toward the "unappreciated" young women of the present day—of whom, alas! there are many—we have no such tenderness. What you need is to be set to work at some useful occupation, the homelier the better till such meditations as you now indulge are driven out of you. . . . You feel hurt if you are asked to mend a coat or wash the dishes, do it poorly and sulkily, and then go and write some stuff that you call poetry, about your "Unanswered Longings," or "Beautiful Visions," or what not! You ought to be put on short allowance of ink and paper till you have learned to be thoroughly ashamed of yourselves.

The second appeared in the *Republican* almost two years later, on November 20, 1867. Entitled "Women as Artists," it begins benignly, "Genius has no sex, according to its manifestations," and goes on to praise the Cooper Institute for giving its female students good instruction in the art of painting. Soon, however, this essay, too, adopts a scolding posture:

The only thing to be feared is that too many susceptible women will at once think they were born artists, and only need development, and will perhaps put themselves outside the pale of domestic life and the society which they naturally require, to nourish their mistaken endeavors. But the sensible women of taste will outnumber the foolish ones, and it will be no more terrible to have the country flooded with mistaken women-artists, so called, than with mistaken women-poets, who are so numerous lately.

Perhaps the final irony is that these sentiments appeared in a newspaper that habitually printed the work of popular "women-poets."

The attitude manifested by Bowles and Holland set up a situation in which there was no way for Dickinson to win. Insofar as she wrote carefully crafted, intellectually serious verse, she did not fit the salable stereotype: she would not please their readers, and they would not be tempted to publish her. Insofar as she might write appropriately "feminine" poetry, they might publish her, but they could not treat her as a serious intellectual presence.

Of the 1,775 poems Emily Dickinson wrote, eleven were published during her lifetime; of these, six appeared in the Springfield *Republican*. The first, assigned the title "A Valentine," " '*Sic transit gloria mundi* '" (#*3*), was a product of her earliest days as a writer, a witty but dismissable poem; the second, entitled "*Nobody knows this little Rose*" (#*35*) and printed in August 1858, was originally a *private* message to Mary Bowles; neither ought to be put into the same category as her other published work. All of the others she published in the *Republican* are significant: "*I taste a liquor never brewed*—" (#*214*), entitled "The May-Wine" and appearing May 4, 1861; "*Safe in their Alabaster Chambers*—" (#*216*), entitled "The Sleeping" and appearing March 1, 1862; "*Blazing in Gold and quenching in Purple*" (#*228*), entitled "Sunset" and appearing March 30, 1864; and "*A narrow Fellow in the Grass*" (#*986*), entitled "The Snake" and appearing February 14, 1866. All of these poems are immensely better than the general lot of poetry in the *Republican* during this time, and some are even among the superior run of Dickinson's work. However, all are, if not conventional, at least accessible, and all take subjects that appear to be within the prescribed limits for "lady poets." There is evidence that Emily Dickinson attempted to draw Sam Bowles into the kind of serious contemplation of life that her strongest poetry addressed, but her efforts were unsuccessful. Perhaps, given his ebullient, hard-driving, practical nature, no one could have thus engaged him. He was a go-getter in an age of go-getters; Emily Dickinson was the last lingering remnant of an earlier age.

No one knows exactly when Emily Dickinson first met Sam Bowles and his wife, Mary, probably sometime in 1858 when he began to form an intimate friendship with Austin and the couple was entertained by Sue and Austin at the Evergreens. This was a difficult time for Sam and Mary Bowles. Although Mary eventually bore seven healthy children, three sons and four daughters, in the late 1850s she had three stillborn babies. After the second stillbirth, in May 1858, Sam Bowles wrote to Austin, "We claim your sympathy in our sorrow. Our expected babe was born to another world. Mrs. Bowles has been sick all day—suffering greatly as is her wont,—& to-night at 8 she was relieved of a dead boy; the repetitions of a disappointment of her last confinement."[47] Emily Dickinson wrote her own short note to the bereaved mother:

Since I have no sweet flower to send you, I enclose my heart; a little one, sunburnt, half broken sometimes, yet close as the spaniel, to it's friends. Your flowers came from Heaven, to which if I should ever go, I will pluck you palms.

My words are far away when I attempt to thank you, so take the silver tear instead, from my full eye. . . .[48]

It was a season of sickness and death for the Dickinson household as well. Bad times had begun with the move back to the Homestead in late 1855 and Mother's subsequent collapse. In 1858, with Mother still an invalid and Austin sick, Emily Dickinson wrote the Hollands a despairing letter—"Ah! dainty—dainty Death! Ah! democratic Death! Grasping the proudest zinnia from my purple garden,—then deep to his bosom calling the serf's child!" Shortly thereafter, in February 1859, Lavinia left Amherst to go to Boston and nurse Aunt Lavinia Norcross. Death, the deep stranger, and immortality, the "Flood subject," suffuse Emily Dickinson's correspondence at this time. After Mary Bowles bore her third stillborn child in 1859, Emily Dickinson wrote her with great compassion and perhaps even empathy.

Don't cry, dear Mary. Let us do that for you, because you are too tired now. We don't know how dark it is, but if you are at sea, perhaps when we say that we are there, you won't be as afraid.

The waves are very big, but every one that covers you, covers us, too.

Dear Mary, you can't see us, but we are close at your side. May we comfort you?[49]

By September 1859 Aunt Lavinia's condition had worsened, and Emily Dickinson wrote the Hollands in distress.

Indeed, this world is short, and I wish, until I tremble, to touch the ones I love before the hills are red—are gray—are white—are "born again"! If we knew how deep the crocus lay, we never should let her go. . . .

Mother's favorite sister is sick, and mother will have to bid her good-night. It brings mists to us all;—the aunt whom Vinnie visits, with whom she spent, I fear, her last inland Christmas. Does God take care of those at sea? My aunt is such a timid woman![50]

In April 1860 the dear aunt "at sea" finally encountered the deep stranger; Aunt Lavinia Norcross died. Never had the issue of faith in Christ's promised rebirth seemed so near and importunate; never had the meaning of nature's "signs" appeared more puzzling. "Will she look down?" Emily Dickinson wrote her sister, who was still in Boston. "So many broken-hearted people have got to hear the birds sing, and see all the little flowers grow, just the same as if the sun hadn't stopped shining forever!"[51]

During this tumultuous period of anxiety and grief, Emily Dickinson wrote Sam Bowles two very short letters: they are unlike any that immediately precede them or follow them, and they contain the first poems she is known to have sent him. In them, Dickinson attempts to communicate both the central subject of her poetic enterprise and the particular anxieties about faith and the hereafter that she felt most keenly now (anxieties that he and his wife might be expected to share, given their recent losses).

The first letter evidently follows a particular conversation that had ended inconclusively; it places the traditional wrestle for faith that occurred during the conversion experience almost surrealistically—in the midst of the "sea" that had dominated so many of Dickinson's letters during the recent harrowing of pain and loss. Even "at sea," she suggests, one might choose autonomy and the inviolable self over an easy, optimistic, complaisant acceptance of the promises of Christ. In its entirety, the letter reads:

I cant explain it, Mr. Bowles.

> *Two swimmers wrestled on the spar*
> *Until the morning sun,*
> *When one turned, smiling, to the land*
> *Oh God! the other One!*
> *The stray ships—passing, spied a face*
> *Upon the waters borne,*
> *With eyes, in death, still begging, raised,*
> *And hands—beseeching—thrown!*

The other letter (although both were written at about the same time, no clear sequence can be established) treats the same themes more literally and without resort to archetypal imagery. In its entirety it reads:

Dear Mr. Bowles.

Thank you.

> "Faith" is a fine invention
> When Gentlemen can _see_—
> But _Microscopes_ are prudent
> In an Emergency.

You spoke of the "East." I have thought about it this winter. Dont you think you and I should be shrewder, to take the _Mountain Road?_

The _Bareheaded life_—under the grass—worries one like a Wasp.

The Rose is for Mary.

Emily.[52]

Not all of the allusions in this letter can be clear, for like the other, it clearly follows and continues a specific conversation; however, the same themes of death and faith dominate this missive. Among the Trinitarians, "East" or "Eastering" were common coinage for a resurrection after death—in short, going to Heaven. (Thus, when Austin married, even though his new home was just beyond the Homestead's _Western_ boundary, Emily said he had "gone East"—that is, to Paradise.) The _Mountain Road_ was the arduous pathway to God's realm, "the steep and rocky way to the towers of the Heavenly City, up which only a few faithful pilgrims struggle, in order to reach at last the shining gate of paradise."[53] Emblems depicting this pathway could be found in such works as Holmes and Barber's _Emblems and Allegories_ or even in the work of painters like Thomas Cole. That "_Bareheaded life_—under the grass" needs no explanation: it is what every reflective man and woman fears, and inevitably submits to.

Neither of these letters elicited Bowles's responsive interest, and subsequent correspondence is entirely different in tone. Although further notes contained other poems—thirty-seven in all—none touched again upon this brutal confrontation between man and Maker. There would have been no point in dispatching poems with an essentially religious structure to Sam Bowles: he would not have responded to their complex resonances, for he was an intrinsically secular man. Thus despite the important role he would play in Emily Dickinson's life, Sam Bowles could not help her gain an audience for that Representative Voice.

George S. Merriam, Bowles's biographer, asserts with the tone of pride that might be expected when old-fashioned religion has been replaced by a rational, enlightened code of ethics: "The generation to which 'Sam Bowles' belonged . . . was the generation in which New England broke through the sheath of Puritanism, and flowered into broader and more various life." Bowles was a Unitarian; his minister, William B. O. Peabody, "was a man of piety, refinement, and intellectual cultivation." Everything in Bowles's environment dismissed the culture that still nourished Emily Dickinson's art.

Moreover, he was a man; and increasingly during the latter portions of the nineteenth century, when men's work took them away from home for long periods, the terrors of sickness and dying (in the case of Mary Bowles, of difficult labor and stillborn babies) were entirely the province of women. "Mrs. Bowles is perhaps less comfortable than is common," Sam Bowles wrote a friend after his wife's first stillbirth, "but with good fortune she will mend rapidly. She feels her loss terribly. Though a disappointment, it is a small matter to me, only as it affects her."[54] Such language may sound cruelly hardhearted, but it was not unique to Bowles. The specter of death was becoming entirely divorced from the major occupations of a man's life; business had to go on, and it would not go on efficiently if men paused to ponder issues of faith, death, and a rebirth in Christ. So Emily Dickinson had to search elsewhere for a receptive reader who might issue her letter to the world.

Almost two years passed before she found another literary man to help her gain entrée into the world of commercial publishing: Thomas Wentworth Higginson. No one could have been more different from Sam Bowles than Higginson. Although both were generally thought to be handsome, the similarity ended there. Higginson was an earnestly moral man, trained at the Harvard Divinity School and ordained as a Unitarian minister. He was politically liberal, in striking contrast to Bowles's staunch conservatism; indeed, although there is no way of knowing exactly how much acquaintance Dickinson had with Higginson's wide reputation before she wrote to him in 1862, Sam Bowles knew the man's reputation very well, and the *Republican*'s editorial policies were consistently at odds with Higginson's reforming activities. Higginson attempted to organize groups for women's rights in the 1850s, and the *Republican* reported this fact with scorn; Higginson was sympathetic to spiritualism, and the *Republican* sneered at him for it; when Higginson lectured in Springfield, the *Republican* gave the event the slightest possible notice consistent with accurate reporting. Most important of all, Higginson was a vigorous activist during the decade preceding the Civil War; the *Republican* vehemently opposed any form of civil disobedience, and Higginson's valiant activity in behalf of Southern blacks was scarcely noted in that paper—though it was widely reported elsewhere.[55]

Edward Dickinson was, if anything, more conservative than Sam Bowles; and Emily Dickinson's decision to write to Higginson had somewhat the character of "domestic" disobedience. No one would have attempted to stop her; evidently, no one even offered a reproof. However, it would have been clear to everyone that she was going far afield in this correspondence. That fact alone suggests that by 1862 she had some concern lest her poetry never see print. "I found a bird, this morning, down—down—on a little bush at the foot of the garden," she wrote to the Hollands in the summer of 1862;

"and wherefore sing, I said, since nobody *hears?* One sob in the throat, one flutter of bosom—'*My* business is to *sing*'—and away she rose!"[56] Perhaps Dickinson, too, could continue to sustain the belief that her "business" was to "*sing*," but by 1862 it may have become increasingly difficult to do so without an audience.

Emily Dickinson once claimed that she had read everything Thomas Wentworth Higginson had written. By April 1862, twenty-two of his essays had appeared in *The Atlantic Monthly*. The Edward Dickinsons had been charter subscribers to the new journal, and Emily Dickinson must have read a substantial number of these before her first letter. They reveal Higginson as fundamentally different from two other most significant men in her immediate environment, Edward Dickinson and Sam Bowles.

The Alpha and Omega of Father's views about the place of women could be defined by his early essays on the education of women and his ready anger at suffragettes during his last term in the Massachusetts legislature: his views changed little if at all throughout his adult life. Women's place was in the home; women ought not to vote; women ought not to pursue a vocation. Sam Bowles was a much more complex case. He seems to have craved affectionate attention from everyone whose friendship he enjoyed. Merriam observes that a "charming address came to be his spontaneous habit whenever he was free from the absorption of work and the depression of suffering nerves. He conquered hearts like a charming woman, and with a feminine sense of power and pleasure in his conquests. Nor did he lightly abandon them." This "power" was exercised most with women. Merriam attempts to reconstruct these relationships along lines of chivalry and purity: "He honored good women, he learned of them, and he used to say that the best wisdom and inspiration of his life had come through them. His attitude toward them in personal intercourse was manly and delicate. In the homage he paid, there was nothing of perilous sentiment, no philandering or flirtation."[57] However, Sam Bowles's relationship with the Austin Dickinsons and their friends belies Merriam's account. His open flirtation with Susan drew his own wife's outspoken resentment, and only six months after Mrs. Bowles's third stillbirth, he was plotting strategies to slip away and spend time with Susan's widowed friend, Kate Turner. "I would that I might see your wife's beautiful friend," he wrote to Austin in January 1859, "but *how* can I? Mrs. Bowles is very liberal in her government: would it be fair to take advantage of it to go 40 miles over railroads to see beauty & grace & wit in that most enticing of mortal packages, which the elder Weller has so immortally warned all susceptible Samuels against?"[58] Samuel Bowles liked the ladies and enjoyed publishing their poetry and pretty fictions, but unlike Higginson, he seldom wrote about them as if they were his intellectual equals.

Much has been made of Higginson's essay "Letter to a Young Contributor," which was the immediate occasion for Emily Dickinson's initial letter to him. Without doubt the content of that essay bears scrutiny. But perhaps a better introduction to Thomas Wentworth Higginson and his views about women can be provided by an earlier essay published in the February 1859 issue of the *Atlantic,* "Ought Women to Learn the Alphabet?"

The piece is so elegantly written, and so persuasive in its muted passion in behalf of women's rights, that the temptation is to cite virtually all of it as a representation of the man with whom Dickinson corresponded for twenty-four years. A few excerpts must suffice, but even these make it inescapably clear that the foundation of Higginson's beliefs was simple and unwavering: women are the equals of men, and they ought to be treated as such.

The point of departure for the essay is a satirical plan drawn up by Sylvain Maréchal during the reign of Napoleon—a "Plan for a Law prohibiting the Alphabet to Women."

Maréchal exhausts the range of history to show the frightful results which have followed this taste of the fruit of the tree of knowledge; quotes the Encyclopédie, to prove that the woman who knows the alphabet has already lost a portion of her innocence. . . .

We take it, that the brilliant Frenchman has touched the root of the matter. Ought women to learn the alphabet? There the whole question lies. Concede this little fulcrum, and Archimedea will move the world before she has done with it; it becomes merely a question of time. Resistance must be made here or nowhere. . . . Women must be a subject or an equal; there is no middle ground.

. . . Lawyers admit that the fundamental theory of English and Oriental law is the same on this point: Man and wife are one, and that one is the husband.

Yet behind these unchanging institutions, a pressure has been for centuries becoming concentrated, which, now that it has begun to act, is threatening to overthrow them all. It has not yet operated very visibly in the Old World. . . . But in this country, the vast changes of the last twelve years are already a matter of history. No trumpet has been sounded, no earthquake felt, while State after State has ushered into legal existence one half of the population within its borders. Every Free State in the American Union . . . has conceded to married women, in some form, the separate control of property. . . .

[It had long been argued that women are "inferior."]

Now this impression of feminine inferiority may be right or wrong, but it obviously does a good deal towards explaining the facts it takes for granted. If contempt does not originally cause failure, it perpetuates it. Systematically discourage any individual or class, from birth to death, and they learn, in nine cases out of ten, to acquiesce in their degradation, if not to claim it as a crown of glory. . . . All generations of women having been bred under the shadow of intellectual contempt, they have of course done much to justify it. They have often used only for frivolous purposes even the poor opportunities allowed them. . . .

All this might perhaps be overcome, if the social prejudice which discourages woman would only reward proportionately those who surmount the discouragement. The more obstacles the more glory, if society would only pay in proportion to the labor; but it does not. Women, being denied not merely the antecedent training which prepares for great deeds, but the subsequent praise and compensation which follows them, have been weakened in both directions. The career of eminent men ordinarily begins with colleges and the memories of Miltiades, and ends with fortune and fame; woman begins under discouragement, and ends beneath the same. . . .

. . . Training and wages and social approbation are very elastic spring-boards, and the whole course of history has seen these offered bounteously to one sex and as sedulously withheld from the other. Let woman consent to be a doll, and there was no finery so gorgeous, no baby-house so costly, but she might aspire to share its lavish delight;—let her ask simply for an equal chance to learn, to labor, and to live, and it was as if that same doll should open its lips, and propound Euclid's forty-seventh proposition. . . .

Now all this bears directly upon the alphabet. What sort of philosophy is that which says, "John is a fool; Jane is a genius; nevertheless, John, being a man, shall learn, lead, make laws, make money; Jane, being a woman, shall be ignorant, dependent, disenfranchised, underpaid." Of course, the time is past when one would state this so frankly, . . . but this formula really lies at the bottom of the reasoning one hears every day. The answer is: Soul before sex. Give an equal chance, and let genius and industry do the rest. . . .

. . . As matters now stand among us, there is no aristocracy but of sex: all men are born patrician, all women are legally plebeian; all men are equal in having political power, and all women in having none. This is a paradox so evident, and such an anomaly in human progress, that it cannot last forever. . . .

. . . Who believed that a poetess could ever be more than an Annot Lyle of the harp, to soothe with sweet melodies the leisure of her lord, until in Elizabeth Barrett's hands the thing became a trumpet? Where are gone the sneers with which army surgeons and parliamentary orators opposed Mr. Sidney Herbert's first proposition to send Florence Nightingale to the Crimea? . . . First give woman, if you dare, the alphabet, then summon her to her career; and though men, ignorant and prejudiced, may oppose its beginnings, there is no danger but they will at last fling around her conquering footsteps more lavish praises than ever greeted the opera's idol,—more perfumed flowers than ever wooed, with intoxicating fragrance, the fairest butterfly of the ball-room.[59]

Here was a voice of strength and encouragement. Although the ultimate goal of this essay is more political than literary, Higginson echoes many of the sentiments Dickinson herself had expressed during those years in the early 1850s when Austin was being groomed for a career and a future consonant with the glorification of the Dickinson name while his sisters were being enlisted in little more than the daily round of household routine. Higginson even offers a confident assertion that the rights and achievements he pleads for are not "unfeminine"; that women can in fact win love as men do—by the exercise of their intellect, character, and talents.

This 1859 essay invited no letters from its readers—indeed, gave little opening for such a response. However, it did establish Higginson as a man who could respect a woman's intellect as he might a man's. He adopted no airs of condescension or contempt, an element in his nature that would have eliminated at least one of the obstacles that had made Bowles impossible as Dickinson's "John the Baptist." Other obstacles appeared, however, and many were of Emily Dickinson's own making.

By April 1862, when Higginson's essay "Letter to a Young Contributor" was printed in *The Atlantic Monthly,* Emily Dickinson was in a very low state. She had probably been writing seriously for more than a decade, and as yet she had had very little success in reaching a reading public. What is more, Sam Bowles, whose companionship she valued, despite the fact that he failed to appreciate her vocation, was himself in ill health; early in 1862 he left America for a six-month rest cure in Europe. Worst of all, the "terror since September," failing eyesight that might spell a finality of blindness, made her desperately anxious. Thus when she read Higginson's essay and undertook to write him a letter about her own work, she was not at her best, and she made grievous mistakes. For one, she misunderstood his posture toward *all* writers.

Although Higginson began his essay by deliberately addressing both sexes as potential authors (and such an approach surely recommended itself to Dickinson), this piece is not a plea in behalf of women for equal rights with men in the publishing world. Unlike the 1859 essay, it is not even primarily directed at women. Most of the essay is devoted to practical suggestions about the presentation of a manuscript to a commercial publisher. It is encouraging to the as-yet-unpublished author, but unblinkingly matter-of-fact.

[There is not] the slightest foundation for the supposed editorial prejudice against new or obscure contributors. On the contrary, every editor is always hungering and thirsting after novelties. To take the lead in bringing forward a new genius is [a] fascinating . . . privilege. . . .

Do not despise any honest propitiation, however small, in dealing with your editor. Look to the physical aspect of your manuscript, and prepare your page so neatly that it shall allure instead of repelling. Use good pens, black ink, nice white paper and plenty of it. . . .

On the same principle, send your composition in such a shape that it shall not need the slightest literary revision before printing. . . .

The first demand made by the public upon every composition is, of course, that it should be attractive. . . . Charge your style with life, and the public will not ask for conundrums. . . . If, therefore, in writing, you find it your mission to be abstruse, fight to render your statement clear and attractive, as if your life depended on it: your literary life does depend on it, and, if you fail, relapses into a dead language. . . .

Strive always to remember—though it does not seem intended that we should quite bring it home to ourselves—that "To-Day is a king in disguise," and that this American literature of ours will be just as classic a thing, if we do our part, as any which the past has treasured.[60]

Many years later Dickinson told Higginson that he had saved her life in 1862. Surely his friendship and interest in her work came at one of her lowest ebbs. However, nothing in this essay was supportive of the poetic vocation as she had defined it. Indeed, in order to wrest substance and support from it, she seems to have misread it seriously. Higginson's essay was "actually very hard-bitten. Stripped of its pieties, the point of his Letter was that the literary marketplace was a tough and competitive arena, in which only disciplined professionals could survive. He spoke of the 'interests' of author and editor with only a thin veiling of gentility. He talked of literary 'productions' whose 'value' had to be measured. He talked of the value of an editor's time and attention. He spoke of verbal felicities as being 'coined' and 'exchanged.' In fact, his Letter is almost a model of the ways that a half-century of experience had taught the realities of the market and the pieties of transcendentalism not only to lie easily together, but curiously to exemplify each other."[61] Such "realities" were anathema to Dickinson: if true, they spelled the impossibility of having the poetic vocation, as she had defined it, take a public form. This difference in attitude toward poetry presented one barrier between Dickinson and Higginson; another—perhaps more easily surmountable— was presented by the highly particularized religious context of the poet's work.

Bowles and Higginson were both Unitarians; however, the genteel course of ethical instruction that Bowles had been given as "religion" was vastly different from Higginson's systematic training in the ministry. Higginson did not believe what Trinitarians believed, but as a consequence of his schooling, he at least *knew* what they believed, and he might have been expected to recognize Biblical allusions, and allusions to the iconography of the Christian emblem tradition. However, it would have been neither instinctive nor natural for him to read poetry with the tradition of New England Trinitarianism in mind. Thus if he was to read Dickinson's poetry with *understanding*, he needed help from the author. It was of essential importance that she be explicit and direct in her mode of address to him, that she give him the clues and information he needed to place her work. Instead—perhaps because she was hesitant about the bold step she was taking in writing to him, perhaps because she had by now become defensive about her work—Dickinson was arch, coy, gnomic, and reticent. She offered mystery, not illumination. And Higginson, a practical man despite all his political daring, was not capable of penetrating such mystery as Emily Dickinson could concoct—nor of effectively countering the undertone of anger that tinged her prose.

Even if these problems in dealing with Higginson could have been overcome, one final, insuperable obstacle remained to discourage publication. Like Melville, Dickinson was an anachronism. Writing rebelliously, but writing nonetheless within the great tradition of latter-day Puritanism, Emily Dickinson was a time traveler from an earlier epoch. She was determined to construe writing as an heroic undertaking, literature as the vehicle for epic activity; if such were not the case, poetry would not be worth pursuing. Higginson had explicitly denied the practical possibility of this way of construing poetry: "If, therefore, duty and opportunity call," he admonished, "count it a privilege to obtain your share in the new career; throw yourself into it as resolutely and joyously as if it were a summer-campaign in the Adirondack, but *never fancy for a moment that you have discovered any grander or manlier life than you would be leading every day at home.*" [62] However, it was grandeur, only grandeur—and Power—that Dickinson wanted. She wanted to be America's Representative Voice, and she wanted that Voice to challenge God Himself and wrestle for dominion. Yet even Emerson, in his greeting to Whitman, had welcomed the younger poet to a "great *career.*" By the mid-nineteenth century, poets had to content themselves with precisely this kind of success—circumscribed and limited to this world. What would it have meant to Emily Dickinson to be merely a published poet, perhaps even a *minor* published poet? With the vision of transcendent heroism that she had formulated, how could Emily Dickinson settle for a "career"?

From the beginning, then, she vitiated her letters to Higginson with mixed clues about her aims and intentions. The first letter, unsigned and containing a calling card with her name on it, signaled not a professional inquiry, but a social one. Decades earlier in America, when authors sought patrons instead of publishers, such an overture might have been appropriate. But in 1862 it was not. The note itself was anything but a business letter.

Mr. Higginson,   15 April, 1862

Are you too deeply occupied to say if my Verse is alive?

The Mind is so near itself—it cannot see, distinctly—and I have none to ask—

Should you think it breathed—and had you the leisure to tell me, I should feel quick gratitude—

If I make the mistake—that you dared to tell me—would give me sincerer honor—toward you—

I enclose my name—asking you, if you please—Sir—to tell me what is true?

That you will not betray me—it is needless to ask—since Honor is it's own pawn—[63]

The author of this letter appears to want a sponsor, a supporter, a teacher, even a pastor, perhaps. There is little to indicate the explicit desire for publication. Indeed, in the wake of Higginson's hardheaded essay, Emily Dickinson's letter seems rather pointedly to renounce such a desire. Although no twentieth-century reader can disentangle the many nuances of her feelings, clearly no one can fault Higginson for not pressing publication upon her after he had read this note.

This first letter to Higginson reveals the complexity of her ambivalence toward a "career"; her fourth letter to him suggests her ambivalence and anger at the plight of the woman poet's ambiguous relationship to aesthetic evaluations. Not surprisingly, it is filled with the idiosyncratic preoccupations of the poet in question. Thomas Wentworth Higginson had asked her for a picture of herself, and she opens by responding to his request. "Could you believe me—without?" Austin might have been able to tell Higginson that Emily Dickinson was engaged in her favorite game here—hide-and-seek. Read the *words*, she is saying, for that is the only "self" I wish you to know. And there is a jest as well as an admonition in this apparently simple beginning. He is a *Thomas*; she wants to know whether he is a *doubting Thomas*, whether he can "believe" without seeing. Finally, the query puts her concisely into Christ's role, while placing Higginson unambiguously in the role of a disciple. (To a twentieth-century reader, the remark is yet another piece of evidence to document her preoccupation with eye / face communication: she retains power as God does, by withholding her face.)

The many-layered meaning of so apparently innocuous a beginning might have warned Higginson of the compression that was to follow when she began to talk about his judgment of her work.

Will you tell me my fault, frankly as to yourself, . . . I shall bring you—Obedience— the Blossom from my Garden, and every gratitude I know. Perhaps you smile at me. I could not stop for that—My Business is Circumference—An ignorance, not of Customs, but if caught with the Dawn—or the Sunset see me—Myself the only Kangaroo among the Beauty, Sir, if you please, it afflicts me, and I thought that instruction would take it away.[64]

It is impossible to know what Higginson made of this extraordinary utterance: even modern readers who are prepared to accept the fact of Dickinson's prodigious talent have found her stance puzzling. Indeed, the passage becomes comprehensible only if it is read as a complex and ultimately unsuccessful attempt on the poet's part to present herself as a serious artist. There is genius at work; however, it is a form of genius that is unwilling to make the least concession.

At the outset Dickinson asks for colleagueship (treat my verse with the scrutiny you would give your own work). Then, as if suddenly conscious of the limitations "propriety" has imposed upon women, she adopts a submissive attitude. However, both falsify her fundamental goal and set her aim far too low: Dickinson's "Business is Circumference," the matters with which generally only God concerns Himself. It is not that she is ignorant of the customary rules for poetry; rather, she intends to transcend them. How could a woman convey such intense arrogance and importunate requirement to this well-intentioned but relatively limited man? Of course, nineteenth-century America did encourage women to invest enormous emotion in their own personal appearance. Thus Dickinson the active creator decided to adapt for her own needs the language of anxiety and intensity that was deemed appropriate to discussions of *passive* feminine beauty: she construed poetry as an extension of self. An impartial observer, Higginson is in a position to make an aesthetic judgment of the "self" that is the poetry. So she implores him to tell her whether there are disfiguring flaws, whether *her way* of representing nature, "the Dawn—or the Sunset," has succeeded; for if she has missed the mark badly, she will feel personally grotesque, "Myself the only Kangaroo among the Beauty." And this is a "womanly" feeling that he might be expected to understand and wish to alleviate.

No one can fault Dickinson's resourcefulness in conveying the complexity of her needs. Moreover, this is a dazzling display of verbal dexterity (possibly contrived as such for the purpose of impressing Higginson). Yet the letter does seem to have failed to communicate adequately with its recipient, and in this respect it is like many others of equal brilliance. The problem lies in part with the quick shifts of imagery and in part with the relationship between the tone of the letter and the message it ostensibly carries.

A poet entirely unknown to Higginson, Emily Dickinson appears to claim that she is a neophyte, unsure of her abilities. There is no reason for Higginson to doubt such a disclaimer, especially after the naïveté of her first letter to him. Dickinson was virtually unpublished, living in rural isolation far beyond the intellectual aura of Boston; there was no reason to suspect that she was other than the fledgling she proclaimed herself to be. Yet the sophistication and intricacy of her prose entirely undercuts this assertion: indeed, if Higginson is to grasp the deft shifts of the highly condensed language in this letter, he must ignore her explicit statements about her own naïveté and begin his reading with the premise that he is dealing with a mind of rare literary gifts and an artist of polished proficiency. Not surprisingly, he failed to see through Dickinson's demurs into the heart of her genius. Yet he *could* see that this was no ordinary missive, that it did not fall into any one of the usual styles adopted by aspiring writers. Thus he seems to have concluded that Dickinson was strange, perhaps not altogether normal.

Those who enjoyed intimacy with her—not from intellectual equality, but from sustained emotional contact—her family and especially Austin, could apprehend her rare quality. Sometimes they understood the play among many levels of meanings (probably Sue was best at this), and sometimes they understood only that she was having fun in her own way. Mabel Loomis Todd claimed that the correspondence with Higginson was never "of a private nature, and as to the 'innocent and confiding' nature . . . Austin smiles. He says Emily definitely posed in those letters, he knows her thoroughly, through and through, as no one else ever did." [65] Higginson did not have Austin's advantage of constant proximity, and lacking that, he was not up to Dickinson's brand of wit.

Moreover, it would be a mistake to view Dickinson's behavior as merely reactive: woman-as-victim. Although there is a potent subtext of pain in the correspondence with Higginson, there is active malice, too, and Vesuvial rage—not at him personally, but at the frustrations of her situation. It is not merely that she "posed" in her letters; she indulged in a certain vindictiveness. Once she found that this literary man had no extraordinary creative gifts or capacities for insight, once she understood that his mind could not keep pace with hers, she did not alter her high pitch of verbal play one iota. She utterly refused to "write down" for an audience of lesser gifts than her own. Thus she talked over his head; she spoke gnomically; she answered direct questions obliquely (when she answered them at all). And when he finally did pay a visit to Amherst in 1870, she continued this act in person, pattering in and whispering like a child-woman.

Such behavior is revealing. It demonstrates a reluctance to enter into cooperative exchange, for all *cooperative* conversation will require both parties to adjust their modes of discourse to suit the other. This is, perhaps, the inevitable result of the "fall into language" that Dickinson had experienced in her earliest days. Her attitude toward Higginson suggests, too, an enormous pride: her reader must rise to *her* requirement (something that is true of the poetry as well). Finally and most important, these strategies give powerful evidence that although she was aware of society's expectations that women be passive, she was not in the least prepared to follow them.

The components of this ambivalence did produce an effect: Emily Dickinson's behavior probably reduced the possibility of publication. It is difficult to suppose that this result was deliberate or even conscious; however, it may accurately reflect her ultimate preference. No one can know now whether in 1862 America would have recognized Dickinson's genius under even the best of conditions. The fact is that Dickinson's behavior did not give her the best of conditions. Years later, as she lay dying, she meditated with prophetic confidence upon her eventual fame, and perhaps posthumous renown was the only reward she could have received with unmixed emotions. Hers would become a Voice crying to the wilderness: it is better to have been a seer than to have had a career.

Emily Dickinson continued her correspondence with Thomas Wentworth Higginson until the conclusion of her life. Not her last letter, but her next-to-last was written to him. Intransigent to the end, she invoked Jacob in a farewell note, even though she knew that Higginson would not understand the deep echoes and (by that time) complex ironies of her last messages.

The saga of the publication of her poetry did not end with the exchange of 1862. In 1864 five of her verses found their way into print in the New York metropolitan area. Several old friends and acquaintances were connected with journals there: Gordon Ford and his wife, Emily Fowler Ford (Noah Webster's granddaughter); Charles Sweetser (a relation on the Dickinson side of the family); and the Reverend Richard Salter Storrs (a prominent alumnus of Amherst College) all seem to have been instrumental in the publication. Perhaps they put poems that they had received in letters into print without asking permission; more likely, Dickinson knew that the poems were to be published and gave her tacit consent and / or assistance; we cannot know which was the case.[66] But this short flurry came to naught.

No enthusiastic following would cheer her along the way; no readers would respond with questions and praise. Writing would always be for her a solitary pursuit. It may be that Emily Dickinson had suspected, even before she was well under way, that such would be the case: wrestling the Lord is an intimate undertaking, not a public entertainment. She had courage. She had faith—not in the Divinity her forebears had followed, but in her own intelligence and fortitude. She continued to pursue the Mastiff behind the mask. And ultimately, she went her way alone, scrupulously fashioning a Voice to address a future that she could see only in her superb imagination.

II ◆ The Wrestle for Dominion: God's "Supernatural" Redefined

In his essay "The Protestant Mystics," W. H. Auden has observed that the Crucifixion and the Resurrection offer different problems of faith to different ages of Christianity. In the earliest days of the church, the Resurrection was nothing extraordinary to believe, for Christ was God, and God could surely rise from the dead and ascend into Heaven; however, the Crucifixion, the death of God in agony upon the cross, beggared the imagination and cried out for explanation. In the modern age, the reverse is true: the fact of Christ's death gains easy acceptance; it is His Resurrection that confounds faith. To some degree, Auden's observation can be applied usefully to distinguish between the early days of American Puritanism and that point in the late nineteenth or early twentieth century when a disenchanted land began to repose its faith in the power of the dynamo and to employ secular notions of "progress" and "success" when defining the course of human existence.[1]

There was a prolonged period of transition between these two eras of New England culture—a time during the middle decades of the nineteenth century when the fury of religious fervor had generally passed away and the despair (or complaisance) of a world without informing belief had not yet fallen upon the land. For many, possibly for most, this in-between period combined the most comforting elements of past and future. Especially in the cities, where Unitarianism had rapidly begun to supplant the more rigorous creed of traditional Congregationalism, there was a sentimental attitude toward the Deity: religion had lost its primitive aspect, and the harsh discipline of the past had softened into a creed of passive, unselective, universal love. The thundering threats of Old Testament prophets and the horror and brutality of Christ impaled upon the cross were more or less ignored as ministers and congregations focused their attention instead upon the joyful promises of the Resurrection. Belief in God's existence and faith in His promises could be sustained largely because God's nature had been radically simplified: society no longer bothered to wonder why an omnipotent, benevolent God permitted suffering and death to afflict His creatures. This newly sentimentalized creed forgot God's role as Avenger and Destroyer; instead, He became a Creature of caring, even motherly generosity. Death was seen as no more than a brief transition from earth to the certain bliss of Heaven.

New rituals and new literature were created to sustain this domesticated religion: "Changing funerary practices were intended to rob death of its proverbial sting; hymnology facilitated the process by ignoring hell and high-lighting heaven; and readers were eagerly devouring a new literature of death, 'consolation literature' that portrayed the deceased in a comfortable heaven waiting to be reunited with friends and loved ones forever."[2] Trinitar-ian garrisons like Amherst, Hanover, and Williamstown held to the old ways until the Civil War; nonetheless, the literature of religious sentimentalism insinuated its way even into such strongholds as these. As early as the 1840s, an Amherst printing house was issuing the work of Madame Sigourney, the premier author of saccharine elegies for children and verses about infants who awaited their parents in a Heaven that seemed little different from Mother's realm, the ideal home. Nor was Emily Dickinson isolated from the new religious sentimentalism. How could she be, when it appeared in such immediate sources of daily reading as the Springfield *Republican* or Ik Mar-vel's romantic fantasies?[3]

She read it. In the case of Ik Marvel she seems even to have been attracted by it. However, though her weak poetry sometimes lapses into its cloying cadences, her strong work pulls violently against it. Often consolation liter-ature spoke from beyond the grave with a Voice that was proleptically reas-suring, and poems like "*I felt a Funeral, in my Brain*" are pitched with biting satire against this current vogue for posthumous comfort. Much of Dickin-son's poetry was timely, then, offering a corrective for this "liberalized" reli-gion; indeed, the poet was entirely self-conscious about the relationship between her beliefs and those put abroad by the popular preachers of insipid sensibility. In December 1872 she enclosed this scornful poem in a letter to Higginson:

> He preached upon "Breadth" till it argued him narrow —
> The Broad are too broad to define
> And of "Truth" until it proclaimed him a Liar —
> The Truth never flaunted a Sign —
>
> Simplicity fled from his counterfeit presence
> As Gold the Pyrites would shun —
> What confusion would cover the innocent Jesus
> To meet so enabled a Man!
>
> (#1207)

Thus had the gold coinage of revival language been debased.

Like the Christians of that primitive age, Emily Dickinson did not doubt God's reality. A simple declarative sentence begins the poem that describes God's game of cosmic hide-and-seek (#338): "*I know that He exists.*" How-ever, unlike those early Christians, unlike the earliest American Puritans— unlike even the devout, conservative proclaimers of faith in her own generation—she could not believe in the promises of the Resurrection. Tens of centuries ago, Christ came; subsequently He left: these were certitudes. Yet the *meaning* of it all could not be gleaned at this distance of time. A Redeemer? "*My eyes just turned to see, / When it was smuggled by my sight / Into Eternity*" (#263). Out of "sight," God is out of sound as well: "*I have a King, who does not speak*—" (#103). Jesus had promised a loving response to prayer: "Ask, and it shall be given you; seek, and ye shall find . . . for every one that asketh receiveth; and he that seeketh findeth . . . Whatsoever ye shall ask in my name, that will I do, that the Father may be glorified in the Son. If you shall ask any thing in my name, I will do it" (Matthew 7:7–8; John 14:13–14). Had she followed Jesus's injunction to pray?

> *Of Course—I prayed—*
> *And did God Care?*
> *He cared as much as on the Air*
> *A Bird—had stamped her foot—*
> *And cried "Give Me"—*
> *My Reason—Life—*
> *I had not had—but for Yourself—*
> *'Twere better Charity*
> *To leave me in the Atom's Tomb—*
> *Merry, and Nought, and gay, and numb—*
> *Than this smart Misery.*
>
> (#376)

Perhaps early life had made trust too difficult; perhaps rigorous, intellectually stimulating scientific training at school had been too persuasive. For whatever reason, Dickinson dismissed prayer as an act of desperation: we resort to it only because face-to-face communication is impossible. "*Prayer is the little implement / Through which Men reach / Where Presence—is denied them. / They fling their Speech / By means of it—in God's Ear—*" (#437). On the whole, she was inclined to believe in the evidence of *things seen,* and the realities she confronted were uniformly disillusioning. Jesus had assured us of personal care from a loving God, but life offers a parade of unassuaged sorrows. Jesus had promised, "Ask, and it shall be given you"; but even modest requests, prayerfully framed, bring nothing except empty silence. The only reason that we have to believe in a Resurrection that will vanquish death is the promise of the Man who called Himself the "Christ." Yet if all of these other promises have proven false, is there not compelling reason to suppose that the anticipation of rising in triumphant body is no more than a fool's hope? "*I'm glad I dont believe it / For it w'd stop my breath— / And I'd like to look a little more / At such a curious Earth!*" (#79).

It is too little to say that faith eluded Emily Dickinson. Her poetry, the

"Breath" that could compete with death, was founded on the conviction that a genuinely religious poet would have to grapple earnestly with faith by matching Christ's fable and the promises in it against the evidence offered by the visible world. The fruit of her struggle would be an independent song of truth, even when the truth was terrible to hear.

She began with death, the only certainty in life. The Gospels tell us that even Jesus died, and whatever else can be said about the New Testament, this fact at least is certainly true. The modern era accepts this truth without astonishment, virtually without remark, yet for Dickinson it was central—and horrific. Ironically, had she believed less ardently in the existence of God, the Crucifixion would have been a matter of less importance: the sentimental religionists did not worry themselves with the paradox of a God-man in the throes of death. Their belief in God had become too attenuated, too secularized and domesticated and comforting, for them to recognize the savage implications of this element in the myth that informed their faith.

The rich irony of Emily Dickinson's position was that although she could not relinquish reason and accept the reassurance of some "birth" after death, neither could she shake her tenacious belief in the existence of the God Who had become man only to die on the cross. The strength of this belief impelled her to confront the dark implications of that execution in the ancient past.

And when they were come unto a place called Golgotha, that is to say, a place of a skull, . . . they crucified him, and parted his garments. . . .

And there were also two other, malefactors, led with him to be put to death . . . one on the right hand, and the other on the left. . . . And the people stood beholding. And the rulers also with them derided him, saying, He saved others; let him save himself, if he be Christ, the chosen of God. . . .

And one of the malefactors which were hanged railed on him, saying, If thou be Christ, save thyself and us. But the other answering rebuked him, saying, Dost not thou fear God, seeing thou art in the same condemnation? And we indeed justly; for we receive the due reward of our deeds: but this man hath done nothing amiss. And he said unto Jesus, Lord, remember me when thou comest into thy kingdom. And Jesus said unto him, Verily I say unto thee, To day shalt thou be with me in paradise. . . .

Now from the sixth hour there was darkness over all the land unto the ninth hour. And about the ninth hour Jesus cried with a loud voice, saying, Eli, Eli, lama sabachthani? that is to say, My God, my God, why hast thou forsaken me? . . . Jesus, when he had cried again with a loud voice, yielded up the ghost.

[Matthew 27:33–35; Luke 23:32–43; Matthew 27:45–50]

Jesus's death is framed by ill omens. It is introduced by the universal symbol of terror—the faceless face, the mask without eyes, Golgotha, the place of the skull. It is concluded with that most primitive terror—separation, aban-donment, the convulsive despair of the God-man's cry, "Sabachthani . . . why hast thou forsaken me?" Was Jesus "willing to die," then? Or at the end, did even Jesus fail in faith? Dickinson's meditations upon such mysteries reached backward in time to the sacrifice upon the cross only to soar forward again and lodge in the unfolding tapestry of her poetry.

Importunate moments in the New Testament returned again and again to give shape to her puzzlement, rage, and horror. More than once she referred to the thief's request. Sometimes the allusion may seem casual: "Tell Mrs. Holland she is mine," a letter of 1858 concludes. "Ask her if *vice versa?* Mine is but just the thief's request—'Remember me today.' Such are the bright chirographies of the 'Lamb's Book.'" Yet the letter that is concluded with this sentiment is the one containing that desolate account of universal death: "Dainty—dainty Death! Ah! democratic Death! . . . Say, is he everywhere? Where shall I hide my things? Who is alive? The woods are dead. . . . I shall not tell how short time is, for I was told by lips which sealed as soon as it was said. . . . Dancer, and floor, and cadence quite gathered away, and I a phantom, to you a phantom, rehearse the story!"[4] The "bright chirographies of the 'Lamb's Book'" tell a brutal tale that culminates in the blood sacrifice at Calvary; the thief's request may have seemed, then, the only suitable way to end a letter that catalogued unrelieved devastation.

In November 1862 Thomas Wentworth Higginson went to South Caro-lina, commanding a Negro regiment for the Union cause during those early days of the Civil War. "Perhaps Death—gave me awe for friends—striking sharp and early," Dickinson wrote in her first letter to him at war, "for I held them since—in a brittle love—of more alarm, than peace. I trust you may pass the limit of War, and though not reared to prayer—when service is had in Church, for Our Arms, I include yourself. . . . I was thinking, today, . . . that the 'Supernatural,' was only the Natural, disclosed—. . . Should you, before this reaches you, experience immortality, who will inform me of the Exchange? Could you, with honor, avoid Death, I entreat you—Sir—It would bereave."[5] She ended her second letter to him in battle with the Biblical phrase—"Mine is but just the Thief's Request—Please, Sir, Hear"—and with the last stanza of a poem, the complete text of which had been copied out two years earlier:[6]

> That after Horror—that 'twas <u>us</u>—
> That passed the mouldering Pier—
> Just as the Granite Crumb let go—
> Our Savior, by a Hair—
>
> A second more, had dropped too deep
> For Fisherman to plumb—

> *The very profile of the Thought*
> *Puts Recollection numb—*
>
> *The possibility—to pass*
> *Without a Moment's Bell—*
> *Into Conjecture's presence—*
> *Is like a Face of Steel—*
> *That suddenly looks into our's*
> *With a metallic grin—*
> *The Cordiality of Death—*
> *Who drills his Welcome in—*

(#286)

The letters and this poem cluster around some of the most troubling elements of the New Testament. The thief was the first man to be saved under the New Covenant of Grace. By what judgment was *this* scoundrel assured a precious place in Paradise? And by what measure or whimsy will the eternal fate of all other men and women be decided? Why did a God of "love" require the sacrifice of His only Son as appeasement for the trivial disobedience of man's having sampled the forbidden apple? Why did the Father withhold reassurance and love in Jesus's hour of extremity? And with this example, what hope can any merely mortal creature have when death approaches? Indeed, what confidence can we repose in any of the promises given so many centuries ago by a Son of God who failed to save even Himself?

In traditional Christianity, mankind's first sin provides the defining category for the human condition. We are a "fallen" race, a "postlapsarian" breed. Yet Emily Dickinson had other criteria to assess our state. We have been abandoned by the Father: this is primary, fundamental to our misery. And in this vulnerable, bereft condition, we have been exposed to a "Horror," the bestial blood-lust of a God Who required the execution of His own blameless Son. We have witnessed the unspeakable appetite of God the Father; we have witnessed the excruciating death of God the Son. We are that "*after Horror.*"

The poem has an hypnotic, surrealistic tone that derives in part from the fact that its structure is defined by the embrace of smug and smiling death. The reader is enabled to stare through time as if looking down the long shaft of a fathomless grave. At the farthest distance is the era of the New Testament with its condemned Redeemer; nearest is present death—invisible, patient, waiting to lay hold of each of us without warning. Contrary to the reassurance of Scriptural promises, Christ's death in the distant past has not disarmed present death; the decomposing elements of that ancient era offer a lesson of decay and corruption, not of victory and resurrection. The image that rivets the first two stanzas to the third is that of the gravestone whose granite essence is introduced in line 3 and whose death's-head finally makes an appearance in line 12. No vital Voice of life counters death in this poem: the speaker is ageless, sexless, and without any individual distinctions; it speaks not as "I" (which might affirm self), but collectively—"*us* . . . Our . . . our's." With the audacity of the child / Saint, it lays hold of Biblical and religious notions and combines them with the language of nineteenth-century science or industrial efficiency to make a reader feel the immediacy of the dilemma with agonizing urgency. Finally, the premise of the poem is that after Christ's death, *all* human "life" must be viewed as if from the grave.

In their review of the promises of Christ, the first two stanzas employ the same kind of imagery that can be found in "I felt a Funeral, in my Brain" (#*280*); in #*286*, however, the images are grotesquely conflated with the traditional story of Christ's death. The image of the "mouldering Pier—" derives from the emblematic representation of "faith" as a bridge. Repeatedly Dickinson's poetry returns to this visual image of faith: sometimes she renders it as a "*Pierless Bridge*" (#*915*); sometimes as a bridge with "*brittle . . . Piers*" (#*1433*). Here the emblematic bridge of faith is transformed by the horror of that moment in the proleptic poem (#*280*) when consciousness begins to fail, "*And I dropped down, and down— / And hit a World, at every plunge, / And Finished knowing—then—*" The result is a bizarre and uniquely powerful notion: Christ must walk the bridge of faith Himself—walk it not merely once in His own behalf, but over and over again in perpetuity. Indeed, the action has been repeated so long that the bridge has finally begun to collapse: *faith itself* has begun to crumble and wear away. Thus speaker and reader observe the endless, ancient ritual, and they pass "*the mouldering Pier— / Just as the Granite Crumb let go— / Our Savior, by a Hair—*"; it is no mere human falling now, but Christ the Saviour Who experiences the horror of this drop into unknowable depths. The Apostles were called "fishers of men," sending their nets into the water and bringing up followers for Christ; after his death, it was they who kept his legend alive. Yet even their capacity to renew our faith through the Gospels has been weakened by the length of time that has passed between their era and ours; indeed, the speaker fears that, had even one more second passed, Christ would have "*dropped too deep / For Fisherman to plumb—*." The poem, then, records the final moments of Christ's hold over our collective imagination, the twilight of the Christian era when strong, confident faith is disjointedly falling apart.

This savage, mysterious poem conveys several horrors. One is the span of time that has elapsed without any direct communication from the invisible Deity; however, another has less to do with time than with degree. Perhaps the "miracles" of Crucifixion and Resurrection overtax our capacity for belief; perhaps the fable of a God Who died and was compelled to test the bridge of faith Himself—a God Who *failed* in faith and cried, "Sabachthani"—is so intrinsically terrifying that no "Fisherman" / gospeler's line

It is difficult to improve upon the stark eloquence of the image itself: Death staring with uncompromising directness from the headstone of the grave.

The image could be found in graveyards throughout New England, and it took many highly stylized forms (see below); yet all retain the same primitive, dehumanized, masklike quality. They seem monstrous, hungry, and predatory.

could be strong enough to "plumb" the depths and fetch up the Redeemer Who has not risen, but fallen. The mystery is "too deep" for human minds to fathom, and even the effort to comprehend its scantest outlines "Puts Recollection numb—."

The first two stanzas are an unrelieved catalogue of despair: the death of God, the horror of a "drop" that seems to have no end. Is there nothing but anguish? a reader might demand. Christ told His disciples at the Last Supper that He would leave them, but He also pledged a reunion. Is there no remnant of the Promise? The poem yields a bleak response: the "Granite Crumb." Nothing left but a petrified scrap.

In the final stanza, this conundrum from the past fades swiftly before the pressing dilemma of every living moment: imminent death that strikes without mercy and without warning. The sustained trope of these last eight lines is a series of variations upon the "face-to-face" encounter with the Godhead that we have been promised. At first, we are offered "Conjecture's presence." Yet any residuum of hope that may have lingered in the notion of "Conjecture" is swiftly swept away by the thrusting apparition of *"a Face of Steel— / That suddenly looks into our's / With a metallic grin—."* This may be the helmeted presence of the bloodthirsty Divinity; it may be a ghastly mirror image, one's own face congealed into a caricature that destroys all traces of the sentient self, features pulled and distorted by the *rictus sardonicus;* or it may be some modern engine of efficient destruction that "drills his Welcome in—." In truth, the "choice" among such an array makes little difference. All of these "faces"—neither human nor beatific—are really the same face, variations of the traditional death's-head that was carved on so many New England gravestones. All are manifestations of the skull. And thus this poem ends where the Crucifixion began, with Golgotha, the place of the skull.

Dickinson toyed with one variant for this poem: for "drills his Welcome in—" she posited, "nails his Welcome in," a wording that would have specifically recalled the Crucifixion. This interchangeability of "drills" and "nails" is a fitting irony with which to conclude. The death of mere mortals in the up-to-date, efficient mid-nineteenth century is no different from the death of a God in the age of the New Testament.

Emily Dickinson is not an accessible poet, yet this verse is cryptic even by the standards generally invoked for the study of her work. Why does she so torture meaning here? Why does she engage in compressions that so mystify a reader's understanding? One answer might take this form. Some of the terms of each human demise are clear: uncertainty as to time, but certainty of execution; possible pain; then, an impassable barrier between the living and the dead. However, our notions of what comes after death must be based not upon direct information or clear evidence, but upon promises and uncertain inferences. In Dickinson's estimation, such "information" about the afterlife was cryptic indeed. Any poem that undertakes a serious examination of the meaning of Christ's sojourn among us—that attempts to extract the meaning of that most mysterious of all events, Christ's mortal agony upon the cross—must reflect God's own mystifying methods. By what *easy* or *simple* terms could any mortal explain the implications of God's death?

Thus it was the blood rite of the Crucifixion and not the glory of the Resurrection that cast its decisive shadow over Dickinson's poetry. Sometimes the poet seems to have derived a modicum of hope from Jesus's death: *"Jesus! thy Crucifix / Enable thee to guess / The smaller size! / Jesus! thy second face / Mind thee in Paradise / Of our's!"* (#225). Yet more often, the desire to accept faith was confounded by the imponderable mystery of God's demise.

This World is not Conclusion.
A Sequel stands beyond —
Invisible, as Music —
But positive, as Sound —
It beckons, and it baffles —
Philosophy — dont know —
And through a Riddle, at the last —
Sagacity, must go —
To prove it, puzzles scholars —
To gain it, Men have borne
Contempt of Generations
And Crucifixion, shown —
Faith slips — and laughs, and rallies —
Blushes, if any see —
Plucks at a twig of Evidence —
And asks a Vane, the way —
Much Gesture, from the Pulpit —
Strong Hallelujahs roll —
Narcotics cannot still the Tooth
That nibbles at the soul —

(*#501;*
var. *"Sequel" and "prove it"*)

Although the effect of this poem upon the reader cannot compare with the palpable menace in #286, it nonetheless warrants attention because of the systematic way it examines the leakage and finally the loss of faith.

It begins with an assertion that seems clear. "This World is not Conclusion." The next three lines reinforce a reader's inclination to understand "Conclusion" as "end, close, . . . last part." Yet as the poem moves forward, another meaning of the term increasingly begins to dominate: "the close of an argument, debate or reasoning." The deft play upon this pun carries the verse to its first major turning point: although reasoned inferences from the Design of the world have led human beings to postulate a Deity Who created man for something more than death, whenever "Philosophy" presses the matter, it can give no "Conclusion" because it cannot derive a formal proof of the hypothesis. "And through a Riddle, at the last — / Sagacity, must go —," the riddle of death. The next major division of the verse begins not with confident assertion, but with consternation: "To prove it, puzzles scholars —." A second resort, then, is to turn not to reasoning, but to the study of martyrology, "Contempt of Generations." Yet this move leads to an even more mysterious horror—not merely human death, but the death of God. So, when "Crucifixion" is announced, "Faith" (now rendered as a timid, stumbling bird) adopts a series of embarrassed and self-conscious postures, finally preferring the fickle directions of a weather vane to the promises of Christ.

The concluding coda of four lines summarizes the plight of Dickinson's generation with poignant honesty. Many preachers of her time affirmed God's love with satisfied self-confidence. The "Narcotics" of this sentimentalized religion could dull our awareness of the constant peril in life; however, it could never cure the condition of being "That after Horror." There is even a timely flourish of the macabre in the last image. Americans of the nineteenth century had a homely nickname for tuberculosis: it was "the mouse in the breast," gnawing away at breath and finally at life. Here Dickinson stipulates that the flamboyant attitudes and impassioned rhetoric of ministers who preached consolation are no more than a surface allure, like the dreadful beauty of consumption, an illusion of health that only conceals the putrefaction "That nibbles at the soul."

Nature, the essence of the conversion experience, the events of the Old Testament, even the promises of Christ—all bear the subtle imprint of deceit, corruption, and annihilation. Even the abstract pattern of all human life spells a message of divine sadism. If the " 'Supernatural' " is truly "only the Natural, disclosed," then death and that archetypal horror of the Crucifixion inform its essence. An enigmatic universe, tyrannized by brutality and destruction, provided the subject for Emily Dickinson's probing eye.[7]

1 ❖ *The Ravishment of Faith*

The fable of mankind's first fall and the subsequent drama of sin and guilt did not lay hold of Emily Dickinson's imagination; a concern with sin or human evil scarcely touches her poetry, and the word "fall" is seldom employed. Yet a similar word, "drop," resounds with implication: "drop" differs from "fall" because it shifts the responsibility for our cosmic isolation from ancient human errors to continuing divine neglect or malice. A people that are "fallen" have brought the plight upon themselves by error or foolhardiness or misadventure; if we have been "dropped," we are the victims of *God's* actions. Deaf to our prayers and silent in the face of our loneliness, He has dropped us into time to tarry for but a life's short span; when death comes, He lets us drop once again, now into some fathomless chasm of nightmarish space, perhaps never to stop. The notion of a fall into sin that may lead to a further fall into Hell, while frightening, has at least the advantage of limitation: we know who we will be and where we will be. By contrast, a drop that never ends—just "I dropped down, and down"—robs us of any referent of person or place or time according to which we might locate and define the self.

If the terms of our existence thus conspire to affront our coherent sense of self, so do the terms of salvation: God courts us with the promise of a splendid afterlife, yet the winning of this prize requires a yielding of identity. Such are the terms by which "faith" and "conversion" have been defined. In seeking to dramatize the plight of one caught between the allure and the danger of this dilemma, Dickinson employed a different use of the word "drop."

> The Drop, that wrestles in the Sea—
> Forgets her own locality—
> As I—toward Thee—
>
> She knows herself an incense small—
> Yet <u>small</u>—she sighs—if <u>All</u>—is <u>All</u>—
> How <u>larger</u>—be?
>
> The Ocean—smiles—at her Conceit—
> But <u>she</u>, forgetting Amphitrite—
> Pleads—"Me"?
>
> (#284)

At first glance, this conversion poem seems to bear a striking resemblance to "Two swimmers wrestled on the spar—"; however, in the other poem, when the conflict was between two parts of a divided self, the sea was a location, a barren wilderness outside the reaches of human civilization. Here Dickinson renders the tantalizing but dangerous elements of conversion with an entirely different tone. The "I" and "Thee" are mortal woman and possessive God; the "Drop" is a Christian who has already won faith, and the "Sea" is the primordial power of the Divinity. There are, perhaps, echoes of the great waters of Genesis and of Noah's Flood in this evocation; however, for the brief period of this poem, the creative and destructive impulses of the Godhead are held in check as "Drop" and "Sea" take part in mannerly conflict. Explicitly characterized as a wrestling match, the engagement has such an appearance of chivalric restraint that even insightful critics have read this as a love poem.

The notion of the "Drop" is useful here primarily because its identity is unstable, dilating and finally dissolving when it touches a larger body of water; and the complex terms of the conflict are predicated upon this notion. Because the "Drop" is "in" the Sea, it has no independent form or identity;

it has altogether merged with the water in which it is immersed. Forgetting its "locality," it strives for freedom. At one level, the argument is played out with words: this would-be rebel, like the Voice of the audacious child, knows that the word "*small*" can contain "*All*," but that the word "*All*," however great in implication, cannot contain "*small*." Yet the word play mirrors a more complicated mathematical argument: "*Unto the Whole—how add? / Has 'All' a further Realm— / Or Utmost an Ulterior? / Oh, Subsidy of Balm!*" (*#1341*). *All*, like infinity, is an absolute term: it cannot be augmented. If God is truly infinite, then He needs no "Drop," for infinity plus any increment, however large, is still infinity unchanged. Divinity cannot be glorified or altered in any way by the acquisition of one small soul. Such is the burden of the second stanza: "if <u>All</u>—is <u>All</u>— / How <u>larger</u>—be?" It follows from this premise that an infinite God ought not to mind the loss of the "Drop" that wants to be free, for infinity *minus* any increment, however large, is also still infinity, unchanged. And such a "Conceit" or flight of mathematical fancy leads the Drop to plead her case— " 'Me'?"

Given the sophisticated, learned terms of the argument thus framed, the "Drop" would appear to have won the debate. She gets the last word, and it is an assertion of self, albeit courteously framed as a request. The courtly tone of the poem seems only to reinforce her case. Though she reasons with the casuistry of a Jesuit, she "sighs" like the maid of a romance; and although the relationship is defined as a combat, she twice relaxes into forgetfulness. For his part, the silent Ocean "smiles," as if prepared to be indulgent. Still, the brutality that is latent in "wrestle" does not disappear: if the Drop is capable of "forgetting Amphitrite," the Ocean may smile precisely because he remembers. Amphitrite became the wife of Poseidon under the most unpropitious circumstances. One day this ruler of the waves saw her dancing innocently upon the shores of Naxos; he commissioned his emissary the dolphin to go steal her from her father's home, and when she was brought to him, he raped her. Confirmed as the consort of this jealous and vicious ruler, she was condemned to dwell forever in the dark, undulant depths of an unfamiliar world of water. Entitled to wear a crown as "queen," she could never again be inviolate or free—an apt rendering of the woman "blessed" with the "crown" of conversion as Dickinson construed it.

When Jesus came to save us, He presented Himself as the bridegroom claiming his beloved: "Can the children of the bridechamber mourn," he asked, "as long as the bridegroom is with them?" (Matthew 9:15.) The glorious reunion in Revelation, when all shall see God face to face, is the pledged fulfillment of Jesus's ardent courtship: "The holy city, new Jerusalem, [came] down from God out of heaven, prepared as a bride adorned for her husband. . . . A great voice out of heaven [said], Behold, the tabernacle of God is with men, and he will dwell with them, and they shall be his people, and God himself shall be with them. . . . And God shall wipe away all tears from their eyes; and there shall be no more death." (Revelation 21:2–4.) Dickinson was thoroughly conversant with this notion of God's relationship to His people; sometimes she captured its exotic nuances in a tone of elegant urbanity: "*God is a distant—stately Lover— / Woos, as He states us—by His Son— / Verily, a Vicarious Courtship— / 'Miles', and 'Priscilla', were such an One— / But, lest the Soul—like fair 'Priscilla' / Choose the Envoy—and spurn the Groom— / Vouches, with hyperbolic archness— / 'Miles', and 'John Alden' were Synonyme—*" (#357). There is no doubt that Dickinson could feel an affection for gentle Jesus that she could not feel for the God Who stayed in Heaven; yet the terms of the Crucifixion had made it clear that even though Jesus was not one with the Creator, His mission of love on earth was fatally compromised by the same ferocity that mars the Father. "*At least—to pray— is left—is left— / Oh Jesus—in the Air— / I know not which thy chamber is— / I'm knocking—everywhere— / Thou settest Earthquake in the South— / And Maelstrom, in the Sea— / Say, Jesus Christ of Nazareth— / Hast thou no Arm for Me?*" (#502)

It is a barbaric courtship. The bridegroom promised a Heaven and a place for the bride in this kingdom to come. Yet, to win the bride's place in the hereafter, we must relinquish autonomy and reason, the core of identity in the world that we know, to faith. And *all* must pay the price of death, even though Jesus Himself had acknowledged that not all would gain Heaven.

> *What would I give to see his face?*
> *I'd give—I'd give my life—of course—*
> *But that is not enough!*
> *Stop just a minute—let me think!*
> *I'd give my biggest Bobolink!*
> *That makes two—Him—and Life! . . .*
>
> *Now—have I bought it—*
> *"Shylock"? Say!*
> *Sign me the Bond!*
> *"I vow to pay*
> *To Her—who pledges this—*
> *One hour—of her Sovreign's face"!*
> *Extatic Contract!*
> *Niggard Grace!*
> *My Kingdom's worth of Bliss!*

(#247)

Who is this courting God? A ruthless Shylock demanding his pound of flesh, without exception and without compassion. His contract is literally "*Extatic,*" for its terms demand that the soul be wrenched from the body. Yet even when the bloody bond has been accomplished, payment is still uncertain—and parsimonious if made: "*Niggard* Grace!"[8]

There is something perverse about God's insistence that He must woo us through death. The Elizabethan pun, death as synonym for sexual climax, acquires an eerie, necrophiliac tonality when our "marriage" to the Redeemer can be consummated solely by some literal loss of life. Nor can we ever elude our lithe, persistent lover. "*Death is the supple Suitor / That wins at last— / It is a stealthy Wooing / Conducted first / By pallid innuendoes / And dim approach / But brave at last with Bugles / And a bisected Coach*" (#1445). God is patient; God is willing to wait. If we cannot come conveniently, He will courteously send His own carriage to fetch us.

The poem that may be Dickinson's best known and most discussed addresses just this specter of genteel carnality.

> *Because I could not stop for Death —*
> *He kindly stopped for me —*
> *The Carriage held but just Ourselves —*
> *And Immortality.*
>
> *We slowly drove — He knew no haste*
> *And I had put away*
> *My labor and my leisure too,*
> *For His Civility —*
>
> *We passed the School, where Children strove*
> *At Recess — in the Ring —*
> *We passed the Fields of Gazing Grain —*
> *We passed the Setting Sun —*
>
> *Or rather — He passed Us —*
> *The Dews drew quivering and chill —*
> *For only Gossamer, my Gown —*
> *My Tippet — only Tulle —*
>
> *We paused before a House that seemed*
> *A Swelling of the Ground —*
> *The Roof was scarcely visible —*
> *The Cornice — in the Ground —*
>
> *Since then — 'tis Centuries — and yet*
> *Feels shorter than the Day*
> *I first surmised the Horses Heads*
> *Were toward Eternity —*

(#712)

"I felt a Funeral, in my Brain" is a useful touchstone for this poem; more expressly even than that earlier work, "Because I could not stop for Death—" turns its attention to the structure of narrative as an ordering force. Whereas the other poem had pitched itself against the proto-narrative form of the traditional Congregational funeral, this poem might best be read against a purely literary model, the novel of seduction.

The seduction novel was perhaps the first fictional form to find its way into the American tradition. Following the example of Samuel Richardson's *Clarissa Harlowe*, published in England in 1747–48 and widely read in American until at least the mid-nineteenth century, American novels of seduction like *Charlotte Temple* (1791) or *The Coquette* (1797) were strenuous, Puritanical moral tracts. The plot is begun when a young woman is persuaded rashly to leave home and run away with her lover; the crucial difficulty is introduced when she responds to his sexual advances without being legally married to him; the most strenuous tension inheres in the heroine's moral anxiety, her realization that she has lost her virginity to a man she cannot in conscience wed; and it is resolved when she undergoes a heartrending repentance and consigns herself to the service of the Lord. American seduction novels employed this model with great consistency (echoes of it can be found even in *The Scarlet Letter*). Indeed, the reader's primary satisfaction in reading the formulaic versions was in having the anticipated resolution re-enacted.

When the bride-of-Christ tradition is fused with the narrative of seduction as it is here—God's emissary, "Death," becoming the suitor to carry the runaway heroine to some undefined lovers' rendezvous—the perverse elements of the Christian tradition are laid bare: the prurience of God's role as the bridegroom awaiting His bride; the macabre unnaturalness of any courtship that must be conducted by means of the grave; the sadism of an omnipotent Being Who claims to woo us as a lover, but Who nonetheless sends "Death" to carry us away whether we are willing to come or not. Strangest of all, such a fusion *seems* to allow the narrative of seduction to have a "happy ending." The maiden need not repent her elopement; instead, she can submit to the ghostly lover's advances with pleasure, anticipating the glorious ascension into Heaven where God in His magnificence is ready to receive her. In fact, of course, a "happy ending" of this sort is abhorrent: the frankly passionate sexuality that infuses the novel of seduction with power is entirely inappropriate to any relationship between God and mortal woman; and the notion of embracing "Death" with pleasure can be little more than a Gothic horror.

Thus the stroke of fusing two narrative forms is the first step toward displaying the inherent ghoulishness of God's styling Himself as a bridegroom. The conclusive steps are taken by Dickinson's pacing of the poem's narrative so that ultimate victory goes not to God, but to the poet; and this triumph is achieved by a masterful refusal to bring the poem to any climax at all.

The poem opens with the echoing cadences of "I could not stop" and "He kindly stopped." Although the difference in meaning is clear—I could not be troubled to stop what I was doing, so he kindly stopped his carriage to accommodate me—the mirror-image diction establishes a tone of balance. This suspension of dominant will or force is sustained by the following stanzas. Thus the parataxis that might drive percussively toward death ("We passed . . . We passed . . . We passed") is neutralized by Dickinson's use of several methods to shift movement away from both speaker and death before any conclusion can be reached. As early as the third stanza, activity is imputed to others (the "Children strove"), and this shift prepares the reader for the shift in the locus of movement that takes place at mid-poem: "Or rather—He passed Us—." After this point, no further motion is reported. The cessation is not equated with death or with any other momentous turning point; rather, it seems a shift of attention as much as anything. Perhaps the speaker is still traveling; "We paused" in stanza five implies as much. The reader cannot know.

In "*I heard a Fly buzz—when I died—*" (#465) metonymy and synecdoche were used to exemplify the palpable disintegration of consciousness; here, however, metonymy is introduced so unobtrusively that its potential for rendering such disruption is explicitly foresworn. It must have been the speaker who was "Gazing," although this action is imputed to the "Grain"; one might even say that the speaker's life is "Setting," although this declivity is quite plausibly assigned to the "Sun." Still, by the time the capacity to "pass" has been transferred to the *Sun,* and "The *Dews* drew quivering and chill—," readers may have grown so accustomed to a diffusion of agency that they draw no inference at all. Does the exchange of activity express the speaker's bodily death? It is impossible to tell—impossible, perhaps, because the real subject of the poem is not "Death," but "Immortality."

What holds the poem so remarkably taut is the steady, unruffled tone in which the speaker issues her astonishing narrative. When, in the last stanza, she shifts into the present tense, she does not thereby brandish victory and trumpet the change with a clarion claim. If anything, the unobtrusive alteration establishes a closer intimacy between reader and speaker, both now regarding an event that happened "Centuries" ago. Still, the aesthetic bravura of this easy finale in the present *is* a victory, the poet's victory over time and mortality. By this point a ruminative reader must realize that "He kindly stopped for me—" has a meaning that may not have been altogether apparent upon first reading. Although "Death" has carried the speaker away, he has won no victory, for "Death" has been arrested by the artist: the ticking of God's Design has been stilled. At the conclusion of the poem, movement has altogether stopped. Yet *nothing is ended.* The Voice of the verse is suspended in the perpetual present, forever exempt from change; and "Death's" attempted ravishment is defeated. Any narrative form that depends upon a Heaven ruled by God for its completion—be it the American seduction novel or the New Testament tradition of the bride of Christ—offers nothing but a sham. This sham can be rejected if the denouement of the narrative form is refused. "Immortality," the most mysterious passenger in the carriage, will accompany not the converted Christian, but only the Voice of the poet.

Dickinson sometimes calls our attention to the monstrosity of the bride-of-Christ myth by casting the sexual elements of divine wooing into explicitly perverse terms. For example, Christ may be exposed as a voyeur: *"Just so— Jesus—raps— / He—does'nt weary— / Last—at the Knocker— / And first— at the Bell. / Then—on divinest tiptoe—standing— / Might He but spy the lady's soul—"* (#317). Sometimes, violation takes the form of coercion that would force the new vision of redemption upon an unready or unwilling recipient.

> *She lay as if at play*
> *Her life had leaped away—*
> *Intending to return—*
> *But not so soon—...*
>
> *Her dancing Eyes—ajar—*
> *As if their Owner were*
> *Still sparkling through*
> *For fun—at you—*
>
> *Her Morning at the door—*
> *Devising, I am sure—*
> *To force her sleep—*
> *So light—so deep—*
>
> (#369)

This poem returns to the notion that *"Dying—is a different way— / A Kind behind the Door"* (#335) and plays upon the specifically sexual connotations of that image—it is something done secretly, in the intimacy of one's chamber. Thus, in the second stanza of #369, when the dead girl seems to be hiding behind a door, teasing the observer to enter it, the sexual innuendo becomes patent. And in the last stanza when "Her Morning at the door—" impatiently schemes "To force her sleep—," sexuality becomes violent: prying these eyelids open so that they *must* regard the new day of Heaven is but ravishment displaced.

In other poems, "Redemption" is rendered even more violently explicit in terms of phallic fury and brutality.

> If the stillness is Volcanic
> In the human face
> When upon a pain Titanic
> Features keep their place —
>
> If at length, the smouldering anguish
> Will not overcome —
> And the palpitating Vineyard
> In the dust, be thrown?
>
> If some loving Antiquary,
> On Resumption Morn,
> Will not cry with joy "Pompeii"!
> To the Hills return!
>
> (#175)

It is a nightmarish image, God's "Volcano" spewing molten death to entomb us so that we must await a Saviour Who will come later to unearth us. Indeed, even the wrestle of conversion itself can betray the phallic rage of the Divinity.

> He strained my faith —
> Did he find it supple?
> Shook my strong trust —
> Did it then — yield?
>
> Hurled my belief —
> But — did he shatter — it?
> Racked — with suspense —
> Not a nerve failed!
>
> Wrung me — with Anguish —
> But I never doubted him —
> 'Tho' for what wrong
> He did never say —
>
> Stabbed — while I sued
> His sweet forgiveness —
> Jesus — it's your little "John"!
> Dont you know — me?
>
> (#497)

Begun innocently enough as a tilt for faith and love, the encounter soon begins to go badly awry. Like some Creature who has tasted flesh, Christ seems unable to put a halt to His unloosed violence: what ought to be a bloodless engagement degenerates first into cruelty and then into deadly penetration.

Emily Dickinson was quite self-conscious in her refusal to accept the bride-of-Christ metaphor for salvation. God may pretend to woo us as if he were preparing for a marriage, but He cannot be trusted to keep the blood lust at bay. Too often, then, what takes place is not courtship, but rape. Part of Dickinson's contempt for sentimentalized religion was focused explicitly on its refusal to acknowledge the brutalities that are latent in even the prettiest conventions of Christianity. Women who wrote saccharine poems about God's universal benevolence held but "Dimity Convictions." Their tepid beliefs and infantile passivity left them ill-equipped for anything so strenuous as the kind of salvation God actually offers. "*One would as soon assault a Plush— / Or violate a Star— / . . . It's such a common—Glory— / A Fisherman's—Degree— / Redemption—Brittle Lady— / Be so—ashamed of Thee—*" (#401). This poem that scorns the "Dimity Convictions" of the stereotyped nineteenth-century American woman has become a favorite. It is refreshing for readers of Dickinson's work to realize that she was able to see through the falsities of her own time, was perhaps even able to take pleasure in the power of her own talent in a way that her contemporaries could not: she was different from other women, perhaps stronger. Such a response does not play the poem false. It does, however, somewhat miss the principal thrust of derision. Yes, the porcelain females are laughable; however, it is the God Whose "Redemption" can occur only if He "assaults" us and "violates" us Who is the real target of the poem's outraged contempt.

Although the New Testament is artfully constructed to show that Christ's mission is a fulfillment of Old Testament promises of hope and deliverance, Dickinson could see that it was chiefly the savagery of the Old Testament that Christ's mission brought to culmination. In some of the strongest bride-of-Christ poems, then, the Godhead is represented as an undifferentiated force of primordial brutality.

> *He fumbles at your Soul*
> *As Players at the Keys—*
> *Before they drop full Music on—*
> *He stuns you by Degrees—*
>
> *Prepares your brittle substance*
> *For the etherial Blow*
> *By fainter Hammers—further heard—*
> *Then nearer—then so—slow—*
>
> *Your Breath—has chance to straighten—*
> *Your Brain—to bubble Cool—*

> *Deals—One—imperial Thunderbolt—*
> *That scalps your naked Soul—*
>
> *When Winds hold Forests in their Paws—*
> *The Firmaments—are still—*

(#315,
packet copy; var. "scalps")

This fourteen-line poem is not a sonnet. Instead of regular iambic pentameter, it has a pantingly irregular series of lines cut to the shorter measure of three or four feet—3344, 3343, 3343. Instead of true rhyme throughout, there is rhyme only in alternate lines, and even this inconsistently—the true rhymes of "Key . . . Degree" and "Blow . . . slow" yielding first to slant rhyme and then to consonant rhyme in "Cool . . . Soul . . . still." Nonetheless, the faint form of the Shakespearean sonnet of courtship may linger just palpably enough for this verse to make an impression of artistic creativity that deliberately pulls away from order. The import of the final couplet, traditionally a sentencious summing up, underscores the horror of such a radical loosening of restrictions. In the presence of the Mastiff / God, the "Firmaments" are "still": they are "silent," with dread, and they exist still suffused with fear even today. The quality of continuing to endure is inextricably linked with the terror all creation feels, clasped forever in the "Paws" of the Cosmic Destroyer.

The images, too, shift with carefully measured adjustments toward ineluctable brute force. At first God may seem merely a clumsy musician who "stuns you" with a virtuoso performance. Yet many people think of the soul as lodging with the heart; and to a woman, this fumbling "at your Soul" suggests the attempt to open the bodice of a dress—thus is sexual molestation hinted, even at the beginning. By the second stanza, all possibilities for positive association have been eliminated; the hammers of the keyboard instrument have been transfigured into tools of the forge, and the rape of conversion is begun in earnest. If a soul will not come freely when God desires it, He beats it into compliance with the practiced authority of a blacksmith at his trade. "*Dare you see a Soul <u>at the White Heat</u>? / Then crouch within the door— / Red—is the Fire's common tint— / But when the vivid Ore / Has vanquished Flame's conditions, / It quivers from the Forge / Without a color, but the light / Of unannointed Blaze*" (#365). So it is in #315. The individual self is to be extinguished—color, cast, denomination all obliterated—not by "Blaze" but by the shattering force of an "etherial Blow."

In the third stanza, this progress toward extinction is brought to an inclusive finale: God rapes us one by one; however, He has violated us collectively, too, for His violence has vitiated the very culture in which we have been reared. America was settled by the Puritans who came here in order to establish the New Jerusalem, God's kingdom upon earth. When they encountered native red men who raped and scalped their women, they thought that the devil incarnate inhabited this wilderness, waiting to seize God's people and mutilate them. In this poem the acts of raping and scalping are rendered in precisely those savage terms; yet they are enacted not by Indians, but by the Lord Himself. It was not the *devil* who molested these journeying Puritans, so the verse avers, but rather the bloodthirsty Deity to Whom they had relinquished their destiny.

Certain words in this poem echo the language of other conversion / rape poems. God may "drop . . . Music" upon us, but His cacophonous harmonies will surely rend us; His melody celebrates only the art of brutality. The notion of an "etherial Blow" to devastate our "brittle" selves recalls all those poems that touch upon the grapple for faith—recalls a God Who has repeatedly "hurled" our beliefs. There is danger to everyone, then, and not merely to the "Brittle Ladies" of "Dimity Convictions." Surprisingly, perhaps, the Voice of the "Wife," an attitude and posture that on abstract grounds might seem suitable to this poetry of "courtship," virtually never appears: the disruptive forces are so powerful that a Voice without devices of self-protection, one open enough to have compassion for the suffering of others, could not survive. For behind the bride-of-Christ tradition, behind the rape that so quickly overtakes the conventions of wooing, there is indifferent barbarity. Conversion is a crime of violence.

No capitulation can be made with tyranny of this order. Our only recourse is to turn God's methods back upon Himself, matching rage to primitive rage.

> *I think just how my shape will rise—*
> *When I shall be "<u>forgiven</u>"—*
> *Till Hair—and Eyes—and timid Head—*
> *Are <u>out of sight</u>—in Heaven—*
>
> *I think just how my lips will weigh—*
> *With shapeless—quivering—prayer—*
> *That you—<u>so late</u>—"<u>Consider</u>" me—*
> *The "<u>Sparrow</u>" of your Care—*
>
> *I mind me that of Anguish—sent—*
> *<u>Some</u> drifts were moved away—*
> *Before my simple bosom—broke—*
> *And why not <u>this</u>—if <u>they</u>?*
>
> *And so I con that thing—"<u>forgiven</u>"—*
> *Until—delirious—borne—*

By my long bright—and longer—trust—
I drop my Heart—unshriven!

(#237)

The speaker weighs Christ's promises, the "prayer" that must be "shapeless" because it issues from a creature who has relinquished autonomy, the "Anguish" that God allows—this Father Who claimed to watch the very sparrows of the air. She measures the Lord's willingness to "'forgive,'" wondering how so "timid" a creature can have offended an infinite Divinity. And finally, not "*extatic*" as God would have her, soul severed from body and mortgaged to some Shylock of the skies, but rather "delirious" from attempting to resolve the equation of absolute agony balanced with niggardly grace, she can "drop" the "Heart" herself that Christ so covets as His prize—"*unshriven,*" unconverted, and beyond His power to ravish.

2 ❧ "Nature" Reviewed

Not surprisingly, much of the poet's wrestle with God was focused upon nature; strife for dominion became a dispute concerning the inherent meaning of the natural world and man's intrinsic relationship to it. There were several different reasons for this preoccupation. Although Dickinson was by no means a conventional Romantic writer, no serious poet could afford to ignore the transformation of poetry that had been wrought by the British Romantic poets and especially by Wordsworth, who in his most hopeful moods had postulated that man and nature might have a benign, reciprocal relationship. Dickinson was not an Emersonian transcendentalist, either; however, any American poet who wished to be "Representative" was constrained to address Emerson's optimistic assessment of the meaning a poet would discover in the landscape. In short, as an artist working in the aftermath of these attitudes, Emily Dickinson became a new kind of "nature poet," one who could articulate the ambiguity and latent violence that mankind must constantly confront in the course of ordinary existence. Finally—and surely most important—the Congregational faith of Dickinson's youth had consistently instructed conscientious Christians to scrutinize the Book of Nature in order to find the evidence of God's promises there. This religious inheritance offered the most highly structured interpretation of nature—a comprehensive set of signs and emblems that were believed to represent the Divinity's benevolent intentions. Yet in Dickinson's estimation, the semiology of latter-day American Puritanism was no more than a system of falsehoods. Thus insofar as all three of these traditions postulated that the poet might perceive some benevolent supernatural force working through nature, Dickinson stood in opposition to them. The disagreement assumed varying degrees of particularity.

Dickinson's most general objections were raised against the optimistic proclamations that characterized the initial phase of British Romanticism. In the widely read and immensely influential *Preface* to the second edition of *Lyrical Ballads* (1800), Wordsworth had described the poet and his relationship with nature in this way:

[The poet] is a man speaking to men—a man, it is true, endowed with more lively sensibility, more enthusiasm and tenderness, who has a greater knowledge of human nature, and a more comprehensive soul, than are supposed to be common among mankind; a man pleased with his own passions and volitions, and who rejoices more than other men in the spirit of life that is in him; delighting to contemplate similar volitions and passions as manifested in the goings-on of the universe. . . . He considers man and nature as essentially adapted to each other, and the mind of man as naturally the mirror of the fairest and most interesting properties of nature.

Wordsworth's statement assumes either that nature has an inherent volition or that some transcendent Will flows through nature—and that in either case this Will is accessible to the sentient observer. It also accepts as given that nature (or the power infusing it) is candid and has no intention of deceiving man, and that nature and the "volitions . . . of the universe" are either one and the same or are in harmonious accord with each other. Although Dickinson never explicitly mentions having read Wordsworth's *Preface,* there is every reason to suppose that she did. Certainly she knew the English Romantic credo: "I think of your little parlor as the poets once thought of Windermere," she wrote the Norcross cousins, "peace, sunshine, and books."[9] Typically, Dickinson locates Wordsworthian "peace" and "sunshine" inside the house, for in her estimation *nature* was seldom able to offer comfort or reflect happiness.

To be sure, Dickinson was not immune to the attractiveness of Wordsworthian optimism, and occasionally she does refer to nature as if it were an independent force with which humans might have a positive relationship. "*Nature—the Gentlest Mother is, / Impatient of no Child— / The feeblest—or the waywardest— / Her Admonition mild—*" (#790). Yet much poetry of this sort has an air of wishful thinking, for the Christian myth as Dickinson understood it could not sustain such an attitude. The Crucifixion had left its stamp upon the world, and like the Christ, nature must bow to the Father's pleasure and submit to His will. Thus, one of the strangest and most arresting of Dickinson's poems chooses as its speaker not some human creature, but "nature" itself.

> *The Winters are so short—*
> *I'm hardly justified*
> *In sending all the Birds away—*
> *And moving into Pod—*
>
> *Myself—for scarcely settled—*
> *The Phebes have begun—*
> *And then—it's time to strike my Tent—*
> *And open House—again—*
>
> *It's mostly, interruptions—*
> *My Summer—is despoiled—*
> *Because there was a Winter—once—*
> *And all the Cattle—starved—*
>
> *And so there was a Deluge—*
> *And swept the World away—*
> *But Ararat's a Legend—now—*
> *And no one credits Noah—*

> (#403)

The poem has an air of naïve puzzlement, even querulousness. Certain motions must be gone through, certain changes made; and like a housewife who is being forced to rearrange her parlor over and over again, nature complains at the continual disruptions. The habits of thought that dominate the first two and a half stanzas reveal no grasp of the cyclical order of the seasons, no ability even to understand underlying causation. "Winters" that seem "so short" and then the appearance of "Phebes" to demand an open house again: these are listed not as integral elements of some coherent plan, but as "interruptions" that merely irritate and mystify the speaker.

With "despoiled" at the end of line 10, however, the tone shifts. Nature begins to cast about for some explanation that can justify the necessities that govern her activities; and with a supremely quiet irony, Dickinson imputes to nature the same process of reasoning that Paley and Butler and Hitchcock had recommended to human beings, a rudimentary form of *inference by analogy*. Men and women had been told to look to nature for analogies that would illuminate the meaning of God's Design; however, *nature* must look somewhere else for instruction. Thus this speaker turns to the legends of an ancient Biblical past, and when she does, the telltale word "so" appears. The ravishment that characterizes God's transactions with His people afflicts His use of nature, too. "Summer—is despoiled—." Nature does not dispatch it, nor does it depart of its own accord; rather, it is "robbed" or "stripped" away. Hard upon this acknowledgment of ravishment, the poem moves into recollections of mythic devastation. The "once" that describes "Winter" has less the quality of naming a specific era than of invoking some expanse of past during which there was utter extinction—once upon a time. Unselfconsciously, perhaps, the speaker lapses into the familiar beat of determined death, "And . . . And . . . And," as the winter of starving ineluctably recalls that even more ancient moment of archetypal destruction by water: "And so there was a Deluge—/ And swept the World away—." No argument can counter the implacable power of the Divinity; no comfort can assuage the pain of His victims. Thus the poem ends abruptly, with a dismissal rather than a conclusion.

Like men and women, nature can even confront the necessity of engaging in a wrestle for "faith."

> I know a place where Summer strives
> With such a practised Frost—
> She—each year—leads her Daisies back—
> Recording briefly—"Lost"—
>
> But when the South Wind stirs the Pools
> And struggles in the lanes—
> Her Heart misgives Her, for Her Vow—
> And she pours soft Refrains
>
> Into the lap of Adamant—
> And spices—and the Dew—
> That stiffens quietly to Quartz—
> Upon her Amber Shoe—
>
> (#337)

The "struggle" here is for a belief in the possibility of renewed life despite "Adamant" adversity. Reasoned inferences from experience would counsel Summer not to exert her efforts against the force of extinction, here construed as "Frost." Yet the poem's poignant record captures Summer's persistent striving, even in the face of perennial loss. Oddly, then, nature *can* sometimes be a "mirror" of mankind, but when she assumes that relationship to human beings, it is principally their wrestle with God that she reflects. At other times, nature is simply impassive to our plight—neither rejoicing with our happiness nor sympathizing with our pain. "*The Morning after Wo—/ 'Tis frequently the Way—/ Surpasses all that rose before—/ For utter Jubilee—/ As Nature did not care—/ And piled her Blossoms on—/ And further to parade a Joy/ Her Victim stared upon—*" (#364).

Emily Dickinson began her poetic mission with the belief that the relationship among God, nature, and humanity takes several different forms. Occasionally, "nature" is the embodiment of some soothing or regenerative force like that given by "soft Refrains." Then its action is contrary to the principal thrust of the Divinity: "nature" and God are at odds, and God always triumphs in the end. At other times nature is neutral—evidently indifferent to both Deity and humanity. More often God lays hold of nature to do His bidding; at these times the forces of nature are annihilating: the "*Earthquake in the South— / And Maelstrom in the Sea—*" (#502). Finally, nature can be construed not as a force, but as a repository of evidence that will reveal God's true intentions.

A poem with a particularly American stamp offers the spare existential outline of God's handiwork:

> *The Angle of a Landscape—*
> *That every time I wake—*
> *Between my Curtain and the Wall*
> *Upon an ample Crack—*
>
> *Like a Venetian—waiting—*
> *Accosts my open eye—*
> *Is just a Bough of Apples—*
> *Held slanting, in the Sky—*
>
> *The Pattern of a Chimney—*
> *The Forehead of a Hill—*
> *Sometimes—a Vane's Forefinger—*
> *But that's—Occasional—*
>
> *The Seasons—shift—my Picture—*
> *Upon my Emerald Bough,*
> *I wake—to find no—Emeralds—*
> *Then—Diamonds—which the Snow*
>
> *From Polar Caskets—fetched me—*
> *The Chimney—and the Hill—*
> *And just the Steeple's finger—*
> *These—never stir at all—*
>
> (#375)

The poem's initial irony is a play upon the confident enthusiasm of Emerson's *Nature:* in chapter I of that widely read work, Emerson had defined "nature" as "the integrity of impression made by manifold natural objects," and he had asserted that "there is a property in the horizon which no man has but he whose eye can integrate all the parts, that is, the poet." Self-consciously, Dickinson echoes Emerson's usage of "landscape," a talismanic word in her time; just as shrewdly, she reiterates his notion of an "integrity of impression" in her word "pattern": the speaker of this verse is surely a poet by Emerson's definition, someone who can "see" the comprehensive plan of nature. Yet this landscape is little more than a Design of desolation. Behind the civilized locutions of the popular nineteenth-century essay still lurks a Divinity of Flood and Fire, the angry, jealous God of Jacob.

The Connecticut valley was a scenic place. Although American painters focused their vision on the Hudson River and, somewhat later, on the national parks of the Far West, the art of American lithography found suitable subjects in the rural and village scenes of western Massachusetts. The Ox-Bow of the Connecticut River at Northampton was a favorite pictorial prospect, as was the vista from Mount Tom in Holyoke; Edward Hitchcock included both a view of Amherst College and a panorama of the "Confluence of the Connecticut and Deerfield Rivers" in his *Religious Lectures*. Of course, Hitchcock drew theological inferences from the pictures he placed among his essays, but he shared one thing with the popular lithographers: a sense of openness and space in the scenes that were sketched, an implication that America offers rich "prospects" that are more than merely visual. These lithographs of the Connecticut River valley and its villages were so well known and widely circulated that all, and not merely Hitchcock's moralized offerings, were integral to Dickinson's culture. Thus the narrow, pinched spareness of the poet's "Landscape" in this poem must be measured against the habit of expansiveness in the standard lithograph if we are to appreciate the radical reduction of field in the verse.

The speaker is given no circumference to view, no more than an "Angle," and a narrow one at that—only what can be glimpsed by lifting the outer edge of a curtain and peering between it and the wall to look outside, a "Crack" as narrow as the space between the slats of a venetian blind. Nor does the speaker *choose* such an awkward way to observe the world. This poem still trails the accents of the verse of divine seduction and rape: the "landscape" pushes its way into the speaker's bedroom and "Accosts [her] open eye." "Ample" is surely intended as irony, for the range here is limited indeed; yet in one sense the space is as wide as a church door. It is enough to see the litter of the slaughterhouse.

The elemental structure upon which all else must build is scant: "*a Bough of Apples*—... *the Sky*—... *a Chimney*— / *The Forehead of a Hill*—... *a Vane's Forefinger*—." There are hints of face and hand, but they have been fused quixotically, first with nature and then with a trivial human artifact. The pattern of these fragments is little more than a concatenation, dismembered parts jumbled together without order or apparent function. No whole entity has issued from God's atelier, and no positive cosmic aim can be inferred from this collection of scraps. Time is the only force for change here. At first, time seems to sustain a positive Christian myth, beginning with the apples of Eden and concluding with Emily Dickinson's favorite part of the Bible, the "Gem Chapter," where God claims His bride and the New Jerusalem is brought forth resplendent. "And the building of the wall of it was of jasper: and the city was pure gold, like unto clear glass. And the foundations of the wall of the city were garnished with all manner of precious stones . . . jasper . . . sapphire . . . emerald . . . topaz. . . ." (Revelation 21:18–20.) Yet these emeralds vanish before the winds of winter, and the diamonds spell extinction, not bedazzling transfiguration. Thus the movement of time that had seemed to hint at glory concludes with a bleak finality of "Polar Caskets"—death in a cold climate.

In the end, all that remains is the immovable, elemental structure—an outline sketched with mutilated remnants. Hope and color have disappeared with Edenic apples: only "Chimney," "Hill," and "Steeple's finger" are left. "These—never stir at all—." They are a rudiment. They have not yielded to time. However, they are utterly devoid of life.

Most terrible of all, perhaps, the "Landscape" is still. Amherst revivals had fixed upon the hypnotic phrase that described the voice of God calling softly in a "still small voice" (I Kings 19:12), and New England ministers had bullied and cajoled the members of their congregations to listen attentively for that voice calling for submission to faith. When Emily Dickinson fashioned her own poetic Voice, she recollected the Biblical phrase she had heard so many times. The notion of "small," along with the complex inventions that could be performed upon the configuration of the word itself, became integral to her work. So did the notion of "still." Dickinson knew perfectly well that this intimate summons from God—the "still small voice"—had called to the prophet Elijah in order to demand a great bloodletting, the ruthless slaughter of all His enemies. Hence "still" can carry a deadly, multiple message in her work: quiet; enduring; and without movement or life. The wounding at Peniel is thus reiterated throughout the world, and the full irony of a universe that endures as dismembered fragments can be fully understood only when this "meaning" is measured against the munificent promises of a new birth from the grave.

> Some things that fly there be—
> Birds—Hours—the Bumblebee—
> Of these no Elegy.
>
> Some things that stay there be—
> Grief—Hills—Eternity—
> Nor this behooveth me.

> *There are that resting, rise.*
> *Can I expound the skies?*
> *How still the Riddle lies!*

> (#89)

Christ assured us that some of those now "resting" would "rise," but Christ has gone, and since none of us can "expound the skies," nature continues to embody the most urgent puzzle of all existence: "How still the Riddle lies!" Is the "Riddle" the all-too-real dead body, waiting to be magically resurrected from decay into that new life? How "still," how quietly and lifelessly, it lies in the ground! Is the "Riddle" the promise of Redemption? How "still," how persistently and enduringly, it "lies" and deludes us!

As a post-Romantic poet, Emily Dickinson accepted all of nature as her subject; however, the several signs that had conventionally been cited by the Trinitarians became the object of her particular concern: this religious inheritance, unlike the poetic one from Wordsworth and Emerson, concentrated upon the meaning of a relatively small collection of natural events. Although virtually all of these events, along with the signs that were supposed to spell God's generosity toward mankind, became part of the subject matter for Dickinson's work, some signs had a more sweeping implication than others.

God is no poet, but He has a "line"—the dawn / dusk line of sunrise and sunset. Both were claimed as traditional symbols of the promised Resurrection: sunrise was the talisman of God's New Day, the rebirth into eternity; sunset was the sign of going home to the Father. Insofar as these were the alpha and omega of hope, they became an appropriate place for the poet to initiate her questioning. "*Will there really be a 'Morning'? / Is there such a thing as 'Day'?*" one poem begins. The same poem concludes: "*Oh some Scholar! Oh some Sailor! / Oh some Wise Man from the skies! / Please to tell a little Pilgrim / Where the place called 'Morning' lies!*" (#101). Perhaps this New England "Pilgrim" seeks only directions to the place of eternal "Morning"; more probably, however, she seeks some explanation for the "lies" that have claimed each day's "Morning" as an *evidence* that God will rescue us from the grave.

Far from comforting us, then, the alluring promise of sunrise only arouses an unfulfilled hope that becomes its own form of injury.

> *As Watchers hang upon the East,*
> *As Beggars revel at a feast*
> *By savory Fancy spread—*
> *As brooks in deserts babble sweet*
> *On ear too far for the delight,*
> *Heaven beguiles the tired.*

> As that same watcher, when the East
> Opens the lid of Amethyst
> And lets the morning go —
> That Beggar, when an honored Guest,
> Those thirsty lips to flagons pressed,
> Heaven to us, if true.
>
> (#121)

The food imagery recalls the promise of the Last Supper: that we will rejoin the Lord Jesus in Heaven. Here, however, the symbol of food has been agonizingly elaborated by the imagination. We are faint with anguish, made vulnerable by our cherished expectation—hanging "upon the East" out of our desperate need to believe in God's day without end. And "Heaven beguiles the tired." Perhaps nothing displays the Deity's cunning so well as His ability to wound us with the force of our own desire for His presence, for even this glorious expectation is transformed into pain when it must remain uncertain so long as we live.

Thus the sky streaked with the crimson of dawn is rechristened by the poet: no longer the sign of resurrection to new life, it becomes instead the punctual reminder of God's phallic brutality. "*The Day came slow—till Five o'clock— / Then sprang before the Hills / Like Hindered Rubies—or the Light / A Sudden Musket—spills—*" (#304).[10]

If sunrise, properly limned, is the opening volley of God's assault upon mankind, Dickinson knew that, comprehensively understood, the story of sunset is an abomination.

> How the old Mountains drip with Sunset
> How the Hemlocks burn —
> How the Dun Brake is draped in Cinder
> By the Wizard Sun —
>
> How the old Steeples hand the Scarlet
> Till the Ball is full—
> Have I the lip of the Flamingo
> That I dare to tell?
>
> Then, how the Fire ebbs like Billows —
> Touching all the Grass
> With a departing — Sapphire — feature —
> As a Duchess passed —
>
> How a small Dusk crawls on the Village
> Till the Houses blot

> *And the odd Flambeau, no men carry*
> *Glimmer on the Street—*
>
> *How it is Night—in Nest and Kennel—*
> *And where was the Wood—*
> *Just a Dome of Abyss is Bowing*
> *Into Solitude—*
>
> *These are the Visions flitted Guido—*
> *Titian—never told—*
> *Domenichino dropped his pencil—*
> *Powerless to unfold—*
>
> (#291;
> *var. "Powerless to unfold"*)

The movement of day's end is characterized by the same kind of inexorable movement that drives an individual life to death. However, the import of this progress toward annihilation is more complicated when it encompasses all human life, for it presents unique problems to the artist.

The poem's termination is "Abyss" and "Solitude," alternative renderings of emptiness. "Abyss" was the state of the universe before the act of creation conferred structure and order. In Dickinson's dictionary it was defined as "A bottomless gulf; used also for a deep mass of waters [which] encompassed the earth before the flood . . . that in which any thing is lost." "Solitude" is an isolation from both humanity and God, a state that prohibits communication. The dire implication of these twin destinies of darkness at the conclusion of the poem may be obscured by the rich visual imagery with which the poem opens. However, even at the beginning, the progression of vivid moments creeps toward ineluctable loss: the scarlet blood and conflagration give way to the dead ashes of "Cinder"; the "Fire ebbs." If there is a touch of the gem-graced afterlife in "Sapphire," it fades so completely into the shadows of twilight that its grandeur quickly escapes us. Thus, by the midpoint of the poem, shadow has replaced the last flickering flame of day and has become an horrific, active force. "Dusk crawls"; even more improbably, "Houses blot"; and the entire universe acts in concert as a single, servile puppet— "Bowing" before the yawning void of the uncreating Word.

The great religious painters of the Italian Baroque, Guido Reni and Domenichino Zampieri, could paint madonnas and saints; Titian could render hair and rich brocades with an incomparable crimson depth. Yet who can limn a black inferno or this slipping into divine extinction?

When Dickinson wrestled with the problem of naming a hidden God in her letter to Higginson, she fixed upon "Eclipse" to spell the paradox of a darkness visible. As a poet dealing with nature, she confronted an even more intractable dilemma. Because the Design she discerned was a system of slow eradication, she was obliged to find language for a "creation" whose most salient feature was its implacable drive toward nothingness: she was obliged to invent ways of rendering the "Natural" world that would permit a reader to comprehend the "Supernatural" force of annihilation that lay behind it.

Still teasing the ambiguities of eastering and westering, Dickinson observes (#710), "The Sunrise runs for Both—": for some it is an eastering, the beginning of day; on the other side of the globe, however, it is a westering, the end. The poem continues: "Nor does the Night forget / A Lamp for Each—to set—." Where morning has begun, there is the sun; for night, "The North—Her blazing Sign / Erects in Iodine—," the northern lights to simulate the day. What can we make of these echoing elements—daylight and aurora borealis, or Janus-faced dawn and dusk? "Both lie—": the final line's brief, punning dismissal.

The terror of this "lie"—the paradox of God's "line" that deceives *both* as eastering and westering—becomes an ultimate model for the barrenness of a world filled with symbols of hope and promise, each one of which is false.

> Behind Me — dips Eternity —
> Before Me — Immortality —
> Myself — the Term between —
> Death but the Drift of Eastern Gray,
> Dissolving into Dawn away,
> Before the West begin —
>
> 'Tis Kingdoms — afterward — they say —
> In perfect — pauseless Monarchy —
> Whose Prince — is Son of None —
> Himself — His Dateless Dynasty —
> Himself — Himself diversify —
> In Duplicate divine —
>
> 'Tis Miracle before Me — then —
> 'Tis Miracle behind — between —
> A Crescent in the Sea —
> With Midnight to the North of Her —
> And Midnight to the South of Her —
> And Maelstrom — in the Sky —

(#721)

This superbly terrifying poem opens with what appears to be a precise set of distinctions that define the relationship between the immanent world and the transcendent. In the past, "Behind Me," there is "Eternity"; in the future,

"Before Me," there is "Immortality." The speaker is defined primarily by her location in the present: "Myself—the Term between—." When day comes to nature, it moves with the sun from east to west, and so long as we live, there is no way to escape this continuum. However, Christ promised that the supernatural realm that we can reach after dying stands outside of such a progression: at "Death," the redeemed will "Dissolve" into the "Dawn" of *God's* New Day. Entirely liberated from sublunary time, the Christian will discover a Kingdom where dawn can lead to a unique Day that is consummated "Before" the sun's movement "West" even begins. Thus the first stanza concludes with the traditional Christian formula for passing from this world into the timeless realm of Heaven.

Yet there are fundamental problems with this conventional formulation. "Eternity" and "Immortality" are similar insofar as each deals with an expanse that stands outside of time's passage. However, "Eternity" is a term that is coldly indifferent to the existence of both mankind and God; by contrast, "Immortality" refers explicitly to the infinite life of an integral consciousness, either human or divine. Without such a consciousness, immortality would be no different from eternity—"Behind Me" no different from "Before Me"—both blank nothingness. The "Me" on whom this crucial distinction may hinge is a weak force to begin with: the speaker identifies herself not as a person, but merely as a "Term," a period of time, perhaps, or one part of an equation or ratio (the finite portion as opposed to the two infinite portions). This "Term" is not distinct in and of itself; rather, its essential boundaries are set by "Eternity" and "Immortality," which lie on either side. Moreover, even these are unstable, for when Death arrives, the "Drift of Eastern Gray" dissolves one of the delimiting lines.

Fated to disintegrate into some other state, the speaker attempts to define the place that is the fabled prize awaiting those who possess faith. Yet her effort, begun in the second stanza, leads only to a wasteland. The "Kingdoms—afterward—" are perfectly static. No other selves exist in God's realm: only God exists, meditating endlessly upon Himself. Nor is God mindful of any other entity. All actions and definitions are entirely reflexive: "Himself—His Dateless Dynasty— / Himself—Himself diversify— / In Duplicate divine—." This spectacle is more than merely the mystery of the Trinity. It is the horrific proliferation of a house of mirrors: God existing everywhere, and everywhere impassively identical. Can *God's* consciousness give some shape to "Immortality" that will be meaningful to human beings, then, or does the reiteration of the Deity merely coil back upon itself like a series of concentric circles, endlessly expanding and yet always arrayed about the same minute center?

The speaker begins the third stanza still clinging to the hope encoded in the word "Miracle"; however, she issues a grim message. The syntactic pattern of her statement is essentially the same as that with which the poem opened; however, the altered diction indicates that an inference has been drawn. " 'Tis Miracle before Me—then— / 'Tis Miracle behind—." The difference between "before" and "behind" has been eliminated. No powerful pattern of consciousness has succeeded in converting "Eternity" into "Immortality." Heaven has no structure save the endless proliferation of an impassive Divinity.

And at this point of unbearable insight—inexplicably and without warning—the reader is made to *feel* mere anarchy unloosed upon the world, for the narrative center of the poem cannot hold: the first-person speaker utterly evaporates. The exact moment of its disappearance cannot be ascertained, but by the fourth line of the last stanza, "Me" and "Myself" have been replaced by "Her." This astonishing maneuver is entirely unexplained. It may be that horror at the prospect of the scene that she is conjuring causes the speaker to draw back from any implication in it: such things happen to others, she might think, but not to me—to *her* (some future self as the mind anticipates it). Or, more likely, the original speaker truly vanishes, sucked into the whirlpool even as she is about to tell us of it, and some entirely neutral and inhuman speaker intrudes to conclude the story. Only one thing is clear. In line 3 of the third stanza, chaos takes control. All of the ominous and potentially destructive elements that have been discussed or implied or hinted at suddenly break loose with full fury. The axis of the visual field is turned askew. The moon (or its reflection) can be seen only in the "Sea," and there not full, but fragmented as a "Crescent." Darkness descends from both poles. And in the sky an urgent turbulence of water, swirling up and up—absorbing human consciousness into oblivion.

It is useful to compare this poem with "Because I could not stop for Death—." There the speaker expressly declined to follow God's scenario for the conventional story of conversion-as-courtship; by refusing to bring her tale to a conventional conclusion, she retained control of the poem throughout; and at the end she was even speaking in the present tense, as comrade of the reader. By contrast, the speaker of this poem sets out with an acceptance of the symbolic meaning that God has assigned to sunset and sunrise, and she tells the traditional story of death-as-entry-into-God's-New-Day. Then the speaker who has accepted the plan of *God's* signs is erased without explanation.

This poetry that deals with the "Supernatural" is among the least accessible in the entire body of Dickinson's work. The obscurity is patently intentional, an artistic effort that compels the reader to confront the confusion and danger of our mortal condition. It seems incontrovertibly true that nature can instruct us about our ultimate fate; yet it is a tragic mistake to suppose, as Wordsworth did, that "the mind of man [is] naturally the mirror of the fairest and most interesting properties of nature." If the entire message of the Christ had been consoling, such an optimistic reading of nature might be possible: God magically rising from His own grave presents no horror, only reassurance. Yet God in the throes of death—impaled upon a cross and brought, at the terrible end, to despair—demands that each of us come to terms with the savagery of the Father's power. Often Dickinson captures the frustrations of our longing to believe in a Divinity Who works through nature to bless and comfort His children. Even more often, she depicts nature's intrinsic violence in order to expose God's duplicity and extract the *correct* emblematic significance. And in all of these endeavors, she is constrained to work at the very boundaries of human understanding.

3 ✧ A New Calendar of Signs

One of Dickinson's most familiar assertions about poetry constitutes the whole of a letter sent to Higginson, a single sentence written alone on a page: "Nature is a Haunted House—but Art—a House that tries to be haunted."[11] The Prime Mover hovers behind the natural world, seizing it to enact His will and scattering false emblems in it to deceive us about His purpose: thus is "Nature . . . a Haunted House." The poet's primary task is not merely to render the external reality, but what is much more difficult, to capture the Creator / Destroyer's essence as He exercises His power in this world. If the poet succeeds in rendering the pattern of this force and in reading the "signs" of nature correctly, then the "House" of her verse will be "Haunted."

In one respect Dickinson's nature poetry is entirely conventional: there are poems about the seasons; poems about flowers, about birds, about snow—about most of the subjects that an American "lady versifier" of the mid-nineteenth century might be expected to select. Some of her nature poetry is even quite ordinary by the standards of her day. Yet in her best work, Dickinson addressed these conventional subjects not to produce a superb example of the usual approach, but to pull strenuously against convention. Each of the seasons had its stipulated "signs" of the promised Resurrection; yet a trip through the calendar of Dickinson's work can become, instead, a systematic rebuttal of this Trinitarian symbol system. She had her own methods for construing the types and signs of nature. "There is a Dove in the Street," she wrote to Mrs. Holland one March, "and I own beautiful Mud—so I know Summer is coming. I was always attached to Mud, because of what it typifies—also, perhaps, a Child's tie to primeval Pies."[12] There is a down-to-earth, New England air in this invocation of typology: summer is coming for sure; the mud of spring is already here. And if Dickinson hints at a mythic world—"Mud," the elemental plaything of all children, serving as the raw substance from which God created the earth and its creatures, and the "Dove" that signaled the slow subsiding of Noah's Flood—she chooses prudently to look backward to a recollected or recorded past and not forward to a future that has only been promised.

When she undertook to summon the transcendent meaning of nature in her poetry, she revealed the same wry, practical turn of mind.

> A science—so the Savans say,
> "Comparative Anatomy"—
> By which a single bone—
> Is made a secret to unfold
> Of some rare tenant of the mold,
> Else perished in the stone—
>
> So to the eye prospective led,
> This meekest flower of the mead
> Upon a winter's day,
> Stands representative in gold
> Of Rose and Lily, manifold,
> And countless Butterfly!
>
> (#100)

Edward Hitchcock's scientific influence is inescapable here, for the speaker of this poem has surely learned her lessons in geology and fossil findings from him. As early as the 1840s, Emily Dickinson was taught the ways in which a paleontologist could reconstruct the entire skeleton of one of the region's prehistoric dinosaurs from just a handful of its bones. Reasoned intelligence (not faith) governed such investigations. The first stanza establishes the validity of this way of reading nature's meaning, and the second stanza then draws upon it. If a religious Christian were to interpret the flower found blooming in winter, he would say: Here is a sign that winter is not final and that spring will return; God created these natural emblems to show that Jesus's word will be fulfilled—that human death is not the end and that the faithful will be born again into incorruption. Yet the speaker of this poem rejects all such inferences. By parity of reasoning with stanza one, she constructs her own analogy: Here is the last remnant of a vanished past, a reminder that spring and summer have disappeared and that with them have gone all those supposed talismans of some human resurrection, "Rose and Lily, manifold, / And countless Butterfly!"

But the lily that emerges from a seemingly lifeless bulb, and the butterfly born from a chrysalis that has shown no evidences of vitality—surely these are clear enough signs of Christ's promise, the Amherst Trinitarians might argue. And against them Dickinson would reply:

> *So from the mould*
> *Scarlet and Gold*
> *Many a Bulb will rise—*
> *Hidden away, cunningly,*
> *From sagacious eyes.*
>
> *So from Cocoon*
> *Many a Worm*
> *Leap so Highland gay,*
> *Peasants like me,*
> *Peasants like Thee*
> *Gaze perplexedly!*

(#66)

True, nature offers instances of life emerging from apparent death. But what *conclusion* can we draw except "perplexity"? Do you want to discover God's ways by means of analogies in nature—do you want to fashion the rhetoric of your argument around a use of the word "so"?

> *So has a Daisy vanished*
> *From the fields today—*
> *So tiptoed many a slipper*
> *To Paradise away—*
>
> *Oozed so in crimson bubbles*
> *Day's departing tide—*
> *Blooming—tripping—flowing—*
> *Are ye then with God?*

(#28)

Sunset's unvarying bloodbath is the model: all life leads but to death.

In many of her better poems, Dickinson fused her insights with the direct, immediate experience of New England life.

> *New feet within my garden go—*
> *New fingers stir the sod—*
> *A Troubadour upon the Elm*
> *Betrays the solitude.*
>
> *New children play upon the green—*
> *New Weary sleep below—*

> And still the pensive Spring returns—
> And still the punctual snow!

> (#99)

There is a deceptive air of simplicity and unselfconsciousness about this poem. Although the soft, insistent beat of "New . . . New . . . New . . . New" moves the work forward, the verse contains all of the oldest and most common elements of a New England township. The "New feet" and "New fingers" recall familiar garden animals astir again among the tentative shoots of daffodils and lilies; and the poem's metric "feet" fall into the unbroken rhythms of Congregational hymnody—eights and sixes. Even the ghostly outlines of some small community linger in the invariable village "green" with its graceful "Elm" to give shade and lend a name, perhaps, to the principal street in town. Yet despite such traditionally hopeful material, the poem is surprisingly chill: not even the children's play can suffuse it with life and reassurance, for this poem rests upon an assumption that nature's continuity is provided not by renewal, but by loss.

Thus "solitude" and not song best suits this scene, and the bird's trilling "Betrays" or violates the mood. The same seasonal warmth that has lured boys and girls outside for recreation has also thawed the earth so that the winter's crop of dead may be buried—"New Weary sleep below—." The spring is "pensive," then, because it forces all to recollect that winter and death ever await us; indeed, they are so "punctual" that like the ancient Indians of this continent, we might count the passage of the years by their invariable arrival, as so many "snows" ago. The parataxis is unobtrusive, but it leads to death just the same; and the Voice of this poem about spring concludes with a finality of "snow," quiet and enduring, "still."

Behind the visible evidences of spring, Dickinson perceived a force whose power consistently vanquished growth and new life. Sometimes she construed it as busy Angels of Death, gathering young and old alike into eternity: "*Angels, in the early morning* / *May be seen the Dews among,* / *Stooping—plucking—smiling—flying—* / *Do the Buds to them belong?* / *Angels, when the sun is hottest* / *May be seen the sands among,* / *Stooping—plucking—sighing—flying—* / *Parched the flowers they bear along*" (#94). Perhaps the centuries-old battle between Christ and death is re-enacted by the activities of springtime; if so, far from vanquishing death, Christ saves us (insofar as He can) only by sly strategies of stealth.

> Dust is the only Secret—
> Death, the only One
> You cannot find out all about
> In his "native town."

Nobody knew "his Father" —
Never was a Boy —
Hadn't any playmates,
Or "Early history" —

Industrious! Laconic!
Punctual! Sedate!
Bold as a Brigand!
Stiller than a Fleet!

Builds, like a Bird, too!
Christ robs the Nest —
Robin after Robin
Smuggled to Rest!

(#153)

Again death is "Punctual." Again death is "Still." But now an admixture of Easter turned upside down makes death's activities even more ominous. Traditionally the risen Christ was figured as a bird whose soaring flight promised His followers a miraculous rebirth into life eternal. Here, however, it is death who "Builds, like a Bird"; those who are "Smuggled" to Heaven must be robbed from the cradle—before they have tried their wings or had any opportunity to sing.

Before the Civil War, Easter was the most important of all church holidays in Amherst. *Peterson's Magazine* for women included the lithographs of spring bonnets in its March and April issues so that they could be made up in time for Easter Sunday. Whereas Christmas did not merit an extended vacation from the Mount Holyoke Female Seminary and the exchange of Yuletide presents was very modest, Easter's mystery of life eternal was greeted with grateful displays. New England's long, gray sessions of snow were ending, and April was a month when keen winter remembrances were at last balanced by tentative summer anticipations. To Dickinson's eye, the Amherst town common could seem almost transparent during this season. Ladies in their fresh clothes and men driving buggies instead of sleighs—all this became an instantiation of that ultimate renewal that was chronicled in the Book of Revelation.

I cant tell you — but you feel it —
Nor can you tell me —
Saints, with ravished slate and pencil
Solve our April Day!

Sweeter than a vanished frolic
From a vanished green!

Swifter than the hoofs of Horsemen
Round a Ledge of dream!

Modest, let us walk among it
With our faces vailed—
As they say polite Archangels
Do in meeting God!

Not for me—to prate about it!
Not for you—to say
To some fashionable Lady
"Charming April Day"!

Rather—Heaven's "Peter Parley"!
By which Children slow
To sublimer Recitation
Are prepared to go!

(#65)

The poem rests upon the premise that "April" is a riddle. The function of the verse, then, is to "Solve" it—or if not to offer an answer, at least to indicate what problems exist and what kind of answers can be discovered.

April is a month of uncertain moods, sudden storms giving way to unexpected warmth. This poem mirrors April's cruel shifts in its structure, ensnaring an elusive present by moving quickly, often cryptically away from it, now backward to the past and now forward into the future—as present, past, and future all hover enticingly in the components of the visual scene. So children playing out of doors may be the stimulus that recalls a "vanished frolic" of some former day, while the gentle *plock* of trotters in the mud anticipates "the hoofs of Horsemen / Round a Ledge of dream!"—the four horsemen of the Apocalypse. "Sweeter" than those other times, perhaps by virtue of its immediacy, this April day is nonetheless "Swifter" than the "Ledge of dream" to come because it slips by us so rapidly and kaleidoscopically, now becoming then even as we pause to examine it. As if to demonstrate time fleeing before us, stanzas three and four move so elusively between present and future that we must tease the verse to discover where we are. The source for the informing train of images and associations in these two stanzas is the image of the "fashionable Lady," flirtatiously intriguing in her new spring bonnet: "*A Charm invests a face / Imperfectly beheld— / The Lady dare not lift her Vail / For fear it be dispelled— / But peers beyond her mesh— / And wishes—and denies— / Lest Interview—annul a want / That Image—satisfies—*" (#421). As it is with coy women, so is it with God. It was Isaiah who had seen the vision of "Archangels" with their faces covered (Isaiah 6:2). The prophet intended to convey a notion of God's grandeur in this vision; however, Dickinson thought otherwise. God hides Himself behind an April day because a hidden and unpredictable God seems more impressive than an accessible one. And with such a God it is both prudent and "Modest" to veil our own faces for protection.

The difficulty of holding on to the images that slip through the poem captures one part of the dilemma Dickinson intends to address. Not merely: What is the meaning of the ever-shifting "April" that we see about us? But even more troubling: How can anyone *speak coherently* of such mysteries? How can they be told?

Repeatedly, then, the poem returns explicitly to the problem of communication, especially communication through art. It begins with an apparent acknowledgment of failure: "I cant tell you—but you feel it— / Nor can you tell me—." Since the poem does not break off abruptly with this confession, we must conclude that Dickinson intends to solve the riddle of April in some way other than by merely *telling*. Certain forms of discourse are entirely dismissed. The "prate" of village gossip and polite, superficial chat that comprises the colloquy of those with "Dimity Convictions," for example: such a vernacular would be inadequate to render April's mystery. A better language is offered by "Heaven's 'Peter Parley'!" The "Peter Parley" books, published in America during the second quarter of the nineteenth century, were children's stories with a strongly moral cast; they were intended both as a supplement to Biblical instruction and as a guide to everyday life. However, "*Heaven's* 'Peter Parley'" is intended for grown-ups; for us the legends of the Bible and our relationship with the Deity while we are still in this world constitute a complex preparation for that "sublimer Recitation" in Heaven. If a poet wishes to "Solve" the riddle of "our April Day," it is to this lesson that she must turn.

Yet God's *answer* to the riddle God Himself has posed is "Saints, with ravished slate and pencil": brutality, silence, and anonymity. When Emily Dickinson studied mental philosophy in school, the texts she used offered a simple Lockean model of mental processes: individuals come into this world as *tabulae rasae*, blank slates; as they go through life, their experiences make impressions upon these slates, and the sum of the set of impressions on any given slate makes up an individual's "character." In this poem the rebirth that fulfills Easter's promise is tantamount to *losing* self—erasing the slate. As Christ the bridegroom "ravishes" us in conversion, so do we forfeit identity in the Heaven of God's New Day. Behind all of the restless, brooding moods of April, then, is this immutable fact of loss—God as pitiless Destroyer, stealing the very self He claims to save. Easter is indistinguishable from April Fool's Day. Thus is its "Riddle" derisively explained!

Dickinson understood that as artist of the "Supernatural," she would be obliged to vie with God for control over language and fable in order to tell the truth as *she* saw it. However, it was easier to do so in some cases than in others. When God has elaborated a myth concerning His relationship to the created world, the artist can refashion that myth to expose His dissimulation. When God treats us harshly while claiming to love us, the artist can give a circumstantial account of God's sadistic behavior, thus revealing His duplicity. Yet when God undertakes actively to obliterate and annihilate, the artist may find it difficult or impossible to give an aesthetic shape to this negative process without falsifying it. Thus when she rendered sunset as extinction, "*a Dome of Abyss . . . Bowing / Into Solitude—,*" Dickinson acknowledged that "*These are the Visions flitted Guido—*" (#291): the transcendent truth inherent in sunset—that the visible world's most salient feature is its slow disintegration into nothingness—is perhaps not accessible to an artist of gloriously resplendent oil paintings. How is it possible to *draw* extinction?

A similar problem vexes this poem. If the most intimate truth of April is God's propensity for tantalizing us with a promised afterlife and then hurling us into nothingness, will any combination of the Natural and Supernatural in a poem enable a reader to "feel" this insight? How can one write a poem about *nothingness* and *silence?* Insofar as a poem renders nature immediately and integrally, the undercurrent of dangerous transcendent meaning may elude us. (A poem like "*New feet within my garden go—*" skirts the edge of this dilemma.) Yet insofar as a poem focuses on the shifting deceptions of the Supernatural force that lies behind the visible world, a reader's felt experience of nature may be so thinly stretched that the poem becomes cryptic. To some extent, this is what one encounters in "*I cant tell you—.*"

The image of a "vanished frolic" may have been incited by children at play; the sound of horses in April mud may have initiated the train of thought that leads so rapidly to an evocation of the four horsemen of the Apocalypse. Yet in neither case is it easy for the reader to feel the sensuous manifold through which the Supernatural has become known. The entire second stanza is ephemeral, focusing on the transcendent world without a dense, mediating immanent world to give it concrete configuration. The same can be said of stanzas three and four, where Isaiah's prophetic vision obscures our sight of actual villagers coming and going or of any "fashionable Lady" parading her new spring hat. Some poets set out to write a verse of mystical visions; Dickinson did not. The real world is present in this poem, and the speaker asserts that we must "feel it" because this world is our necessary "Peter Parley" to the hereafter. Nonetheless, the voluptuous possibilities of the material universe do not engage our senses here. Thus although the work is hauntingly suggestive, it is not entirely successful.

Another description of the mystery of April's many moods solves the problems that plague "*I can't tell you—.*" One of Dickinson's finest poems, it achieves its effect by maintaining a superb balance between summoning the immanent world and invoking transcendence. Without apparent effort, the poem compresses several images together: there is the quixotic instability of

New England spring, sunny days yielding to the drench of sudden showers; there is the traveling circus, here today and tomorrow vanished without a trace; and there is the ancient myth of the Redeemer Who came only to depart and thus affirm our desolation.

> *I've known a Heaven, like a Tent—*
> *To wrap it's shining Yards—*
> *Pluck up it's stakes, and disappear—*
> *Without the sound of Boards*
> *Or Rip of Nail—Or Carpenter—*
> *But just the miles of Stare—*
> *That signalize a Show's Retreat—*
> *In North America—*
>
> *No Trace—no Figment of the Thing*
> *That dazzled, Yesterday,*
> *No Ring—no Marvel—*
> *Men, and Feats—*
> *Dissolved as utterly—*
> *As Bird's far Navigation*
> *Discloses just a Hue—*
> *A plash of Oars, a Gaiety—*
> *Then swallowed up, of View.*

(#243)

The first four lines anchor the verse firmly in the world of circuses and storms; the "shining Yards" of sunlight are swirled away as efficiently as the carnival's "Tent" is struck, its "stakes" and "Boards" vanishing like gypsies in the night. However, when the "Rip of Nail" and "Carpenter" introduce the notion of Jesus's Crucifixion, the tone of the verse shifts. The glory of nature's show, captured in the glittering image of the first two lines, is displaced by the void that is the paradoxical legacy of the divine Magician, the blank vision of "miles of Stare—." Now we must come to terms not with sunlit days a moment overcast, but with a Son Who has left us forever. The ultimate emptiness of the promised Resurrection is bitterest to a New England mind, for "North America" was to be the site of God's New Jerusalem, the city upon a hill. By Dickinson's day, little was left of that heroic legacy except "Retreat"; and this theme, announced at the conclusion of the first stanza, becomes the focus of the second.

Having opened so powerfully with the world of visible reality, the poem can convey a sense of felt loss through the systematic negation of that reality: "No Trace . . . no Figment . . . No Ring . . . no Marvel—." Like a series of lights going out, this vision is "Dissolved"; and the word conveys not a removal to another place, but something potentially more terrifying, some species of annihilation. Tentatively, the poem recalls spring in the final four lines with the introduction of the bird, yet this creature can provide no comfort. It is too distant and too ephemeral to return us to the apparent security of the visible world in which the poem began; and if it is truly an emblem of the risen God, its message is little more than stark warning. The bird soars aloft, delighting in its freedom and rowing the blue skies with insouciant "Gaiety—." And then it is gone, "swallowed up, of View." Not carried into a superior realm by the effort of its own flight, the bird has been consumed by a devouring power—"swallowed up." Has it entered an indiscernible Heaven? If so, the language of the poem asserts that the Creature Who awaits it is some unknown predator.

More than earlier times of the year, fall and winter cover the Connecticut valley with tumbling, huddling mementos of execution, and sometimes Dickinson strove to communicate this process through carefully limited, but vivid imagery. "*The name—of it—is 'Autumn'— / The hue—of it—is Blood— / An Artery—upon the Hill— / A Vein—along the Road— / Great Globules—in the Alleys— / And Oh, the Shower of Stain— / When Winds—upset the Basin— / And spill the Scarlet Rain— / It sprinkles Bonnets—far below— / It gathers ruddy Pools— / Then—eddies like a Rose—away— / And leaves me with the Hills*" (#656; var. "*And leaves me with the Hills*"). Yet the carmine artistry in such a pageant engages the visual imagination so fully that its aesthetic power counters the very destruction it renders, a permanent presence to serve as partial replacement for the wholesale destruction it paints. Loss and betrayal can be felt more keenly when they are held in tension with both the vibrancy of human experience and the magnanimity of divine promises.

Jesus selected Apostles because He needed help to reap the bounteous crop of those to be saved: "The harvest truly is plenteous, but the laborers are few; Pray ye therefore the Lord of the harvest, that he will send forth laborers into his harvest" (Matthew 9:37–38). This image had always been popular in American Puritan culture, and nineteenth-century Trinitarian revivalists spoke repeatedly of the preacher as a farmer gleaning the fields for Christ: "The husbandman is not always employed in gathering in his harvest. When one is over, he prepares his grounds for another. He sows for a new crop, though he may not expect it to take root and spring up at once. So the spiritual husbandman, who 'goeth forth and weepeth, bearing precious seed, shall doubtless come again with rejoicing, bringing his sheaves with him.' "[13] Amherst historians writing about the great revival years of the 1840s and 1850s consistently described the moments when Christians pledged themselves to the Lord as great "harvests of the souls," and the term had such currency during Dickinson's most creative years that the seasons of reaping could scarcely be mentioned without invoking images of Christ's promised salvation. Just as New England's protracted winters made the signs of spring especially attractive, so the harvests of summer and autumn, hay and apples and grains, were dearly prized because ineluctable cold lay just beyond Indian summer to bring another starving time. Christ had formulated his metaphor of this harvest of souls in the fertile crescent to the east of the Mediterranean—a land unfamiliar with snow. Thus it is not difficult to sympathize with the good men and women of Massachusetts who supposed that His way of representing the promise of eternal life was particularly suited to their experiences in the New Jerusalem of America.

In his *Religious Lectures* Edward Hitchcock perpetuated this New England habit of mind by pointing to the ways in which new spring growth is nurtured by the fallen leaves of the previous year, finding in this natural phenomenon a chemical "sign" of God's promised Resurrection. Emily Dickinson responded directly, with concise asperity, to his tutelage: "*Fainter Leaves—to Further Seasons— / Dumbly testify— / We—who have the Souls— / Die oftener—Not so vitally—*" (#314). Trees can tell us only about other trees. In human existence, death knows no seasons: when we die, our demise nurtures none; and if we are to be raised to new life, it must be by some extra-natural process. The time to live is very short, and nothing endures but dissolution.

Harvest time in New England is heavy with the aroma of apples, pears, and quinces. Pendulous, they stir with the wind, and the orchard's silence is so deep that no sound seems to break it except now and then the soft thump of an apple that drops into the grass. The promise of Heaven and a harvest of souls may seem never so immediate as in this orchard of ripe Edenic fruit—a potent sign of God's promise.

> A Solemn thing within the Soul
> To feel itself get ripe—
> And golden hang—while farther up—
> The Maker's Ladders stop—
> And in the Orchard far below—
> You hear a Being—drop—
>
> A Wonderful—to feel the Sun
> Still toiling at the Cheek
> You thought was finished—
> Cool of eye, and critical of Work—
> He shifts the stem—a little—
> To give your Core—a look—
>
> But solemnest—to know
> Your chance in Harvest moves

> A little nearer—Every Sun
> The Single—to some lives.

(#483)

Others felt the hope that was urged upon them by harvest, but Dickinson felt most of all the danger.

The first two and a half lines of the poem articulate the meaning of this scene in conventional emblematic language: the "golden" gift of faith ripens until the worthy Christian is ready to be gathered unto the Father. "The Maker's Ladders" are an explicit invocation of Jacob—not yet having wrestled with the Lord, and privileged to see into Heaven itself.

And Jacob went out from Beer-sheba, and went toward Haran. And he lighted upon a certain place, and tarried there all night, because the sun was set; and he took of the stones of that place, and put them for his pillows, and lay down in that place to sleep. And he dreamed, and behold a ladder set up on the earth, and the top of it reached to heaven: and behold the angels of God ascending and descending on it. And, behold, the LORD stood above it, and said, I am the LORD God of Abraham thy father, and the God of Isaac: the land whereon thou liest, to thee will I give it, and to thy seed. [Genesis 28:10–13.]

Yet just as it denies the efficacy of the promise, so this poem inverts the terms of the vision. Whereas Jacob's ladder was set upon the earth, the ladder of the verse begins in Heaven, reaching down to "stop" somewhere well above the speaker's place in the tree. Thus situated, the speaker is suspended between two alternatives: she might remain in the tree to be gathered in; or like other "Beings" in the orchard, she might not survive long enough. In that case, she would "drop"—not into a plash of grass but into some fathomless abyss. Her glimpse into Heaven, then, is not glorious but terrifying.

In the second stanza, any lingering grandeur of Jacob's celestial vision has vanished. Two images of the Lord are brought together: God as the brutal artist who "*fumbles at your Soul / As Players at the Keys*" (#315); and God as voyeur, "*on divinest tiptoe—standing— / Might He but spy the lady's soul—*" (#317). Here, however, these guises and practices of the Deity are displaced onto God's agent in nature, the "Sun." Thus although the stanza begins with the assertion that it is a "Wonderful" thing "to feel the Sun / Still toiling at the Cheek," the paradox of a sun that is "Cool of eye, and critical of Work" rather than generously and effusively generative instills a wonder of distaste, not of admiration. Nature's handling of the speaker is casual and familiar, even blatantly sexual—touching up the color of her cheek, turning her about and shifting "*the stem—a little— / To give [her] Core—a look—.*" By the final stanza, the speaker has begun to understand that this process of gathering in the souls is not a *promise* at all, but merely a *"chance* in Harvest," a risk that changes with every day and every shift of the fickle weather vane. If it holds out the hope of eternal life, it offers the more imminent danger of an unspeakable drop into nothingness. And for some, the fearful drop is no further than one day's sun away.

In three poems of varying degrees of mastery, Emily Dickinson addressed the period of transition between summer and winter. Though all are poems of autumn, the first two focus upon that peculiarly American season that our forebears named "Indian summer." All three address the problem of giving artistic and especially linguistic representation to loss. They are poems that fall with a dying cadence into silence.

> *These are the days when Birds come back—*
> *A very few—a Bird or two—*
> *To take a backward look.*
>
> *These are the days when skies resume*
> *The old—old sophistries of June—*
> *A blue and gold mistake.*
>
> *Oh fraud that cannot cheat the Bee—*
> *Almost thy plausibility*
> *Induces my belief.*
>
> *Till ranks of seeds their witness bear—*
> *And softly thro' the altered air*
> *Hurries a timid leaf.*
>
> *Oh Sacrament of summer days,*
> *Oh Last Communion in the Haze—*
> *Permit a child to join.*
>
> *Thy sacred emblems to partake—*
> *Thy consecrated bread to take*
> *And thine immortal wine!*
>
> (#130)

With contrariety, the poet rejects the usual emblematic tropes of the season: this is not a poem of harvest. Instead, Dickinson turns her attention to the profound promise of the Lord's Supper for an informing emblem of transcendence. Thus the crucial terms are "Sacrament," "Last Communion," "sacred emblems," "consecrated bread," and "immortal wine!" After their appointed duration has passed, lazy yellow days still linger over New England. Summer seems suspended in time, and the season appears to defy the possibility of winter's coming. What do such feasts of nature portend? Are they signs, and if so what do they signify? In this poem Dickinson examines the following possibilities. Perhaps they are a kind of nature's "Last Supper." As Christ had told His Apostles that He would leave them, so Indian summer delivers the message that summer will fade; yet as Christ had also promised a time when He would be reunited with His people, so these days of tropical surprise avow that, despite a bitter winter, summer will return. Is there more than earthly meaning here? If summer invariably follows winter, is this, then, a sign that the promised new birth will follow death? The poem glances at this possibility as well.

The overriding question of "These are the days" is the relationship between the first four stanzas and the last two. The evocative sensuousness of the opening is unusual for Dickinson, who is more often a poet of spare precision. In part the richness devolves from visual imagery; even more, however, it emanates from sonorous language. Although the rhyme pattern of the first four stanzas vacillates between true rhyme ("bear . . . air" and the somewhat attenuated "Bee . . . plausibility") and more discordant configurations ("back . . . look" and "resume . . . June"), assonance weaves throughout the lines like a haunting oboe, seeming to render a melody inherent in nature itself. Yet the logical import of the content cruelly undercuts this harmony. These beauties are "sophistries"—"reasoning [that is] sound in appearance only." Thus the "blue and gold" are a "mistake," attractive though they may be; the mellow season is a "fraud" to entice the "belief" that full summer may still be at hand. Only the speaker is fooled. The Bee is not deceived: despite appearances, the odors of ripeness have passed. Moreover, although nature's lovely false face may persuade a *poet* to convey the essence of this moment with intimations of weaving woodwinds, nature's own songsters, the birds, are silent. They return, but only to look, not to warble.

The fourth stanza turns away from this allure: here are the evidences of decay that "bear witness" to an oncoming season of cold: "ranks of seeds" and "a timid leaf," both dropping. The only suggestion of some possible rebirth in the poem is these "seeds," which, though a preparation for spring, cannot be understood to guarantee it, especially since nature has proven so meretricious. What, then, do the last two stanzas convey? They might be a conventional prayer—a supplication to be included in some cycle of rebirth or a yearning that this season be the sign of life after death. Yet nowhere in the first four stanzas is there evidence that Indian summer contains a promise for mankind; if there is any "meaning" here, it is more likely to be nature commenting only upon itself and its own motions of death and renewal.

However, there is another possibility. The yearning to partake of "consecrated bread" and "immortal wine" may pertain not to a promised rebirth through Christ, but rather to that never-ending life in art itself. What lingers forever in this poem, poignant and painful, is the tragic understanding that can be felt by means of the speaker's rehearsal. There is a season of lush, ripe nature; there is the yearning for a faith that summer will never leave; and then, there is the disillusionment—a recognition not just that winter is imminent, but that nature "cheats" us with "frauds" and "sophistries." The poem's poignant beauty demonstrates how ardently we *want* to believe in the reciprocity that Wordsworth had postulated between mankind and nature, and how cruelly nature allows us to deceive ourselves into precisely such expectations. In Dickinson's hands, the sonorous music of the verse is used to allure us so that we may be disabused of false hopes and beliefs. Thus the poem itself becomes Dickinson's own "Sacrament": each time it is read, poet and reader are magically brought together. Christ had offered Heaven; the poet offers truth.

Still, the poem as a whole is unbalanced. Though the first four stanzas are brilliantly effective, the prayer at the end is so loosely connected to the earlier portion that a reader may be justifiably confused about its relevance. In 1866, about seven years after the composition of "These are the days," Dickinson returned to the subject of Indian summer and the sacrament of the Lord's Supper to write one of her finest pieces of verse.

> *Further in Summer than the Birds*
> *Pathetic from the Grass*
> *A minor Nation celebrates*
> *It's unobtrusive Mass.*
>
> *No Ordinance be seen*
> *So gradual the Grace*
> *A pensive Custom it becomes*
> *Enlarging Loneliness.*
>
> *Antiquest felt at Noon*
> *When August burning low*
> *Arise this spectral Canticle*
> *Repose to typify*
>
> *Remit as yet no Grace*
> *No Furrow on the Glow*
> *Yet a Druidic Difference*
> *Enhances Nature now*
>
> (#1068)

When the poet sent a copy of this poem to the editor Thomas Niles, she alluded to it as "My Cricket"; however, Higginson's reaction may be more accurate, for he tentatively entitled it "Insect-Sounds."[14] The "minor Nation" is the inclusive world of chirping, buzzing, humming crickets, gnats, and flies. Unlike the birds in the earlier poem, the creatures here make sounds; yet theirs is an utterance either of monotony or of gentle cacophony, and it is "Pathetic" rather than joyous or sensuous. Nature does have an intrinsic noise; however, one would probably not call it song. There is nothing violent in the verse—ruminative, low-voiced, and solemn, it honors some magic moment when the present and the far-distant past seem in mystical communication. Nonetheless, this is a poem of ineluctable loss, and one way of defining the focus of the verse is to construe it as concerned with the problem of naming. How can a civilized, mid-nineteenth-century speaker describe the age-old process by which summer slips into the bleak death of winter? What words will suffice to capture the onset of silence? Dickinson's superb solution is the invocation of a succession of religious vocabularies.

With the first stanza, she begins in a familiar present with the ritual of the Mass. A Catholic custom, the sacrifice of the Mass differs in one way from its Protestant cousin, the ceremony of the Lord's Supper: since it is a symbolic re-enactment of the Crucifixion, every celebration of the Mass explicitly recalls God's death upon the cross. However, in a Mass, the horrifying elements of Christ's Passion are almost entirely absent, for what was an actual death two thousand years ago has been converted into a stately ceremony through the use of prayer, ritual, and symbol. Furthermore, the "Ordinance" of the Mass, the sacrament of Holy Communion, gives an unambiguously positive message: it confirms Christ's pledge of a rebirth from the grave. Thus the poem begins with hope. However, as soon as the speaker searches for this sacramental sign of reassurance, "No Ordinance be seen"; instead of a Holy Communion to make Indian summer a promise of the unending summer of Heaven to come, this "Custom" in nature merely enlarges "Loneliness," and the consoling expectations of the beginning must be forsworn.

Whatever is "felt" seems most foreign to the contemporary sensibility—"Antiquest"—"at Noon," when the sun is brightest; and in an attempt to capture the experience of the past's intrusion, the speaker relinquishes the language of Christianity and calls upon the language of the Old Testament. To a modern ear, "Canticle" may seem no more than a synonym for song; however, among Congregationalists of Dickinson's day the word had a very precise meaning. The Canticles were the Songs of Solomon, glorious celebrations of joy and affirmations of life. Yet here, the "Canticle" is not vibrant, but "spectral," and it typifies (or anticipates) not some new life to come, but "Repose"—the long sleep of inevitable winter and uninterrupted death. Finally, in the last stanza, what had begun primarily as a problem of naming becomes increasingly a serious dilemma of seeing as well, as if the light were fading even as we watch. Nothing visible has altered: the ceremony has neither given nor decreased "Grace"; the "Glow" upon the face of August does not yet reveal a "Furrow." Yet something has changed. The long, graceful drop of the poem—away from faith, away from even present safety—concludes in the last two lines: "Yet a Druidic Difference / Enhances Nature now." A pre-Celtic, pre-Christian sect of priests and magicians, the Druids celebrated successive transformations of an eternal matter: vitality flowed indiscriminately through humans, animals, fire, water, trees, and other parts of nature; life was unending, but there could be no "rebirth" from the grave, for any particular consciousness was violated by the endless transformations. Dickinson may or may not have been familiar with these Druidical theories of "immortality." However, she certainly knew one thing, because Caesar and many of the other Latin authors with whom she was familiar had commented upon it at length: the Druids were most remarkable for their pagan superstitions, their bloodthirstiness, and their cruelty; they routinely engaged in human sacrifice. Thus the verse that began with the *symbolic* sacrifice of the Mass concludes with a primitive religion where *any* human may be literally sacrificed to unappeased deities.

In such poems as "Further in Summer than the Birds," the sinew of the verse results from Dickinson's quiet, stark acknowledgment of the loss that is an elemental fact of life. There is no straining stridency, no consuming rage to distract the reader from the eloquent gravity of her insight. What is more, the poetic problem of rendering deprivation or nothingness without creating an aesthetic structure whose power vitiates the sense of privation is resolved here by vocabularies of ceremony and ritual that drop further and further away from the safety of a familiar, regulated, compassionate social system in the present. The movement of the verse describes the descent to an ancient, pre-Christian state, and there Dickinson discovers a correlative to the destruction that must follow the lull of Indian summer. Probably it is not surprising, then, that Dickinson issues her most explicit rebuttal to the Romantics and pre-Romantics in a poem that construes autumn as a season of subtraction: "*A few incisive Mornings— / A few Ascetic Eves— / Gone— Mr Bryant's 'Golden Rod'— / And Mr Thomson's 'sheaves.' / Still, is the bustle in the Brook— / Sealed are the spicy valves— / Mesmeric fingers softly touch / The Eyes of many Elves—.*" Nor is the prayer that concludes this poem of slow paralysis susceptible of misunderstanding: "*Grant me, Oh Lord, a sunny mind— / Thy windy will to bear!*" (#131)

In the final analysis, this season of harvest simply falls still.

> *The murmuring of Bees, has ceased*
> *But murmuring of some*
> *Posterior, prophetic,*
> *Has simultaneous come.*
> *The lower metres of the Year*
> *When Nature's laugh is done*
> *The Revelations of the Book*
> *Whose Genesis was June.*
> *Appropriate Creatures to her change*

> *The Typic Mother sends*
> *As Accent fades to interval*
> *With separating Friends*
> *Till what we speculate, has been*
> *And thoughts we will not show*
> *More intimate with us become*
> *Than Persons, that we know.*

> (#*1115*)

Here, nature's "Typic Mother" spreads the signs of the future delicately before us. This poem is another evocation of the low, buzzing hum that fails to become song; however, the declivity of metrical complexity in nature's tune, away from clearly accented feet into the "lower metres" of unstructured "murmuring," now clearly describes a movement away from any poetic possibility toward total inarticulateness. Summer's last reprieve is construed as its "Book" of "Revelations," yet this is a paradoxically negative indictment. In the Bible, the Book of Revelation recounts the fulfillment of Christ's promise in a glorious description of the New Jerusalem; by contrast, nature here has no grandeur, only loss, as summer fades quietly into solemn, gray cold. Soon, the possibilities for poetry, speech, sound of any kind are all gone as "Accent fades to interval." At the end, we are left alone with our own most frightening speculations. Silence. Winter is truly upon us.

Ironically, it is not in spring's promise, summer's lushness, or fall's harvest that the clear truth of God's divinity can be observed, but only in winter. The cool, white knife of winter's sun illuminates a frozen wasteland to bring our ultimate insight, the burden of despair. *"There's a certain Slant of light, / Winter Afternoons— / That oppresses, like the Heft / Of Cathedral Tunes— / ... When it comes, the Landscape listens— / Shadows—hold their breath— / When it goes, 'tis like the Distance / On the look of Death—"* (#*258*). Spare and dominated by destruction, winter's rigors fulfill the intimations of privation and mutilation that are postulated by "The Angle of a Landscape—." The legacy of Jacob is realized once again; but in winter, it is not the injunction to be fruitful and multiply, not even the wrestle, but only the castrating wound that remains.

> *As Frost is best conceived*
> *By force of it's Result—*
> *Affliction is inferred*
> *By subsequent effect—*
>
> *If when the sun reveal,*
> *The Landscape hold the Gash—*
> *If as the Days resume*
> *The Blackened countenance*

> *Cannot correct the crease*
> *Or counteract the stain—*
> *Presumption is Vitality*
> *Was somewhere put in twain.*
>
> (*#951;*
> *var. "Landscape hold"*
> *and "Blackened")*

Though it can only be inferred, the blow has left shockingly explicit evidence: the "Gash," the "Blackened countenance," the "crease," even the "stain" (to suggest menstruation)—all recall the external female sexual organs. It is tempting to suppose that this wound reveals Dickinson's envy of men because they possess a penis; yet her poetry is not preoccupied with phallic imagery, and "*I would not paint—a picture—*" (*#505*) deals humorously and matter-of-factly with women's "impotent" condition. Indeed, what Dickinson postulates in that poem is a correlative female power of physical fecundity to match the man's literal potency: the sexes are different, but equally valuable, vigorous, and strong. Something has been lost when "As Frost is best conceived" begins; however, it is not the male organ, but the capacity to bear fruit and multiply. The pun of "conceived" is particularly cruel, for physical conception can no longer take place; and just as a woman's monthly cycle of bleeding occurs only when she is not with child, so the "stain" of this garden is a sign that it contains nothing quick with life. Some negative force has been at work: although the poem begins and ends with the language of birthing, the ability to breed has been nullified. God has imposed His will upon the world, and He leaves only wilt and putrefaction to signify His passing.

Dickinson could adapt the notion of castration to render a feminine sensibility. It is equally true, however, that winter's wounding might be dealt by a deadly beau, prepared to ravish us into oblivion.

> *A Visitor in Marl—*
> *Who influences Flowers—*
> *Till they are orderly as Busts—*
> *And Elegant—as Glass—*
>
> *Who visits in the Night—*
> *And just before the Sun—*
> *Concludes his glistening interview—*
> *Caresses—and is gone—*
>
> *But whom his fingers touched—*
> *And where his feet have run—*

And whatsoever Mouth he kissed—
Is as it had not been—

(#391)

Here at last is the promised face-to-face "Interview" with the force of divinity, but instead of fulfilling existence, it erases it. There is an indecent familiarity, the fondling fingers that "touch" or "Caress"; there is violation, the deep kiss that does not linger on the lips, but plunges into the "Mouth"; and there is a kind of death—not the delicately suggestive Elizabethan pun for sexual ecstasy, not even the gelid finality of cessation, but an eradication so thorough that both being and all recollection of it are utterly nullified: "*And whatsoever Mouth he kissed— / Is as it had not been—.*"

The Book of Job had taught Dickinson that God resides in the North and rejoices in ruination: "Dead things are formed from under the waters, and the inhabitants thereof. Hell is naked before him, and destruction hath no covering. He stretcheth out the north over the empty place." (Job 26:5–7.) God's frigidity can even become perversely intermingled with the generative force that moves creation. "Out of whose womb came the ice? and the hoary frost of heaven, who hath gendered it? The waters are hid as with a stone, and the face of the deep is frozen." (Job 38:29–30). Divinity seems to applaud nothing so much as a devastation by cold, for "By the breath of God frost is given" (Job 37:10); and this lesson was re-enacted with invariable regularity in Emily Dickinson's own garden. "*Apparently with no surprise / To any happy Flower / The Frost beheads it at it's play— / In accidental power— / The blonde Assassin passes on— / The Sun proceeds unmoved / To measure off another Day / For an Approving God*" (#1624). Seek Him, then, and you must look to the North; beseech His mercy, and you must tolerate acres of frozen wilderness. "*God grows above—so those who pray / Horizons—must ascend— / And so I stepped upon the North / To see this Curious Friend—*" (#564). Melville's Ishmael had sailed an untamed ocean to find God, and if there were leviathans to harm him, there were countless forms of teeming life to sustain the human quest. Cooper's Pathfinder had paced the forest and finally the vast sea of grass in the plains; these, too, had hidden danger, but these, too, were vigorous and sustaining. A God of the North is utterly sterile: He inhabits "*Vast Prairies of Air / Unbroken by a Settler*" (#564). Nothing about His nature will support us in our pursuit of Him or reward our efforts—except, perhaps, the consummate privation that can inspire art.

The insidious force of winter's cold invades every other season. Tentative fingers of April cannot push the "punctual snow" far enough away to allow spring a secure sovereignty; summer must "strive" impotently against a "practised Frost"; and autumn inevitably dissolves into "interval"—a frigid expanse of silence. Some alien soldier from the forces of cold always lingers on the pale verges of civilization: "*The Flowers notice first / A Stranger hovering round / A Symptom of alarm / In Villages remotely set.*" Roused to action, we can muster only ineffectual resistance: "*But search effaces him / Till some retrieveless Night / Our Vigilance at waste / The Garden gets the only shot / That never could be traced.*" When the Angel of Death carries an up-to-date weapon and his shotgun invariably does its dreadful work, what are we to think? "*Unproved is much we know— / Unknown the worst we fear— / Of strangers is the Earth the Inn / Of Secrets is the Air— / To analyze perhaps / A Philip would prefer / But Labor vaster than myself / I find it to infer*" (#1202). Jesus so often spoke in parables and riddles that even the Apostle Philip requested undisguised information about the new birth and the "Father" that none had seen.

Let not your heart be troubled: ye believe in God, believe also in me. In my Father's house are many mansions [Jesus said]. . . . If ye had known me, ye should have known my Father also: and from henceforth ye know him, and have seen him.

Philip saith unto him, Lord, show us the Father, and it sufficeth us. Jesus saith unto him, Have I been so long time with you, and yet hast thou not known me, Philip? he that hath seen me hath seen the Father; and how sayest thou then, Show us the Father? [John 14:1–2, 7–9.]

Even further from the Father than the Apostle, Philip Dickinson had been instructed to discover His face in the workings of the natural world; but winter is God's perennial season, and anguish rather than faith and love was the lesson she learned.

None of this would matter so urgently if it were not for death, and during Emily Dickinson's lifetime, death was as close as the next room. Winter and cold compelled attention because death was the consummation of their power. " 'Twas warm—at first—like Us—," a poem begins, the Voice studious and probing—staring at the process of dissolution with patient curiosity, as if naming it and following its progress might prise the mystery that separates the warm living from the cold dead.

> 'Twas warm — at first — like Us —
> Until there crept upon
> A Chill — like frost upon a Glass —
> Till all the scene — be gone.
>
> The Forehead copied Stone —
> The Fingers grew too cold
> To ache — and like a Skater's Brook —
> The busy eyes — congealed —

> It straightened—that was all—
> It crowded Cold to Cold—
> It multiplied indifference—
> As Pride were all it could—
>
> And even when with Cords—
> 'Twas lowered, like a Weight—
> It made no Signal, nor demurred,
> But dropped like Adamant.

(#*519*)

The homely objects in a world of gaiety have been transformed. Winter's frosted window, cozy to those whose pleasure in their own warmth is enhanced by its tracery, is conflated with the mirror held against a dying mouth to test the residue of breath within—macabre mockery of God's promised "face to face." The shouting capers of the skating pond have been drawn into the fatal stillness of gelid eyes, "congealed" to see no more. To be sure, the frozen pane and the glassy brook had always held the potential of becoming such grisly emblems, but few can see their lurking implications until death forces recognition upon us. And just as all things contract in the cold, so death can pull an entire sentient world into the compass of a consciousness that will dwindle and dwindle until it has contracted into nothingness.

It is difficult to fix the moment when the observed subject is no longer "like us"; there are "eyes" in line 8, but in the next three lines, the "i" has been closed, and a human being has become "it." All of the changes are minutely incremental, proceeding in a simple sequence that accelerates only as the creeping cold gains sway. Science defines cold as an absence of energy; however, Dickinson perceived it as a quintessential weapon of the God Who was Himself "Eclipse," a darkness visible, and it is this force of cold that pulls us to the frozen edges of eternity. By the final stanza, identity has been vanquished without having given any "Signal": being is no more than "Weight"; its residual function, to "drop." Nothing has been learned. Or perhaps the only thing that can be learned is the process itself. Life: begun in warmth, concluded with a short, cold drop into the grave.

One of Dickinson's best-known poems and surely one of her finest converts the glorious promises of Christ into an honest vernacular of unchanging frozen death.

And seeing the multitudes, he went up into a mountain: and when he was set, his disciples came unto him: And he opened his mouth, and taught them, saying, Blessed are the poor in spirit: for theirs is the kingdom of heaven. Blessed are they that mourn: for they shall be comforted. Blessed are the meek: for they shall inherit the earth. [Matthew 5:1–5.]

The body that drops "like Adamant" offers a gloss upon the Beatitudes that explicates the meaning of Jesus's message with bitter cruelty: Yes, you shall inherit the earth, just acreage enough to be buried in.

> *Safe in their Alabaster Chambers—*
> *Untouched by Morning*
> *And untouched by Noon—*
> *Sleep the meek members of the Resurrection—*
> *Rafter of satin,*
> *And Roof of stone.*
>
> *Light laughs the breeze*
> *In her Castle above them—*
> *Babbles the Bee in a stolid Ear,*
> *Pipe the Sweet Birds in ignorant cadence—*
> *Ah, what sagacity perished here!*

> (#216)

This verse exists in two different finished versions, a rare occurrence in Dickinson's work. A fair copy of the first (above) was made in about 1859; one of the few poems published during the poet's lifetime, a slightly emended version of this 1859 poem was printed in the Springfield *Daily Republican* on Saturday, March 1, 1862, with the subscript, "Pelham Hill, June, 1861." Dickinson's friendship with Samuel Bowles makes it unlikely that he would have run it without her permission, especially with the accompanying attribution. Sufficiently satisfied with this form of the poem to give it a public airing, Dickinson had nonetheless reworked its second stanza during the summer of 1861 (perhaps in anticipation of publication), and she sent three variant forms of it across the hedge for Susan Dickinson's inspection. Somewhat less than a year later, in April 1862, when she initiated the correspondence with Higginson, she included "Safe in their Alabaster Chambers" with one of the *variant* second stanzas in her very first letter to him. At about the same time, she made a second fair copy of the poem for herself, using the original first stanza virtually unchanged and the Higginson second stanza; on the same page, she included fair copies of the two other variant second stanzas. No one can know with certainty which of the versions she ultimately preferred: probably she judged all to have some merit. The four variant second stanzas are in some respects quite different from one another, yet all employ the language of nature ironically to address the hollowness of Jesus's munificent promise.[15]

There is such a monied complaisance in the first word: "Safe." Dickinson was not deaf to the fact that although some of the Beatitudes promise an exclusively eternal recompense, some promise a no-nonsense earthly payoff.

The poet defined ultimate victory as a complete renunciation of God's market-place morality, whether He promises gold here or glory hereafter: "*A Triumph—when Temptation's Bribe/Be slowly handed back—/One eye upon the Heaven renounced—/And One—upon the Rack—*" (*#455*). It is a nice inversion of reward, then, to have these sleepers in sole possession of the only ground that no one cares to occupy. The hint of "Satin" covering the coffins echoes the tradition of the bride of Christ. Yet these "members of the Resurrection" are still innocent of divine molestation: "untouched" by the passage of time, they have been passed over by immortality as well. And so they remain—still—in austere isolation, each to his or her appointed plot.

There is double irony in the juxtaposition of the second stanza and the first. Initially, one feels the gaiety with which the world gambols on, insensitive to the once-human horror just below. The bitterness of the contrast is intensified by the fact that the specific season raging overhead is spring, with its many signs of the promised rebirth in Christ. The "cadence" of the "Birds" is "ignorant" in several respects: it is "unacquainted with" the dead in the ground; it is "unenlightened," having no transcendent significance as an emblem of resurrection; and, finally, it is unskillfully made, for its merry "Piping" cannot begin to render the complexity and tragedy of the comprehensive situation. What "sagacity" has "perished"? The ancient discipline of natural theology, which found evidence of God's goodness and love scattered throughout the natural world.

This version of the poem is subtle and understated. There is irreverence in the image of these "members of the *Resurrection*" whose inertia is so defiantly drawn. There is the scorn of dismissal in the second stanza's rendering of a thoroughly frivolous natural world. And the interment of the Christian emblem tradition in the final line is little less than blasphemy, casually and disarmingly phrased. The unifying insight of the poem is the falsity of Christ's promises and of the natural symbols that are said to portend them. Yet this insight is presented without rage or terror, and its sacrilege is conveyed with such delicacy of tone that it would not offend even the refined readership of Sam Bowles's *Republican*—a group whose literary sensibilities had been tutored by the sweetmeats of consolation literature. One guess, then, is that Dickinson returned to this poem because she found its second stanza too muted for the power of the first.

All three of the variant second stanzas are studies of cold, the two stanzas not sent to Higginson even more obviously so than the one selected for his examination.

[VARIANT I]

Springs—shake the sills—
But—the Echoes—stiffen—

Hoar — is the window —
And numb the door —
Tribes — of Eclipse — in Tents — of Marble —
Staples — of Ages — have buckled — there —

[VARIANT 2]

Springs — shake the Seals —
But the silence — stiffens —
Frosts unhook — in the Northern Zones —
Icicles — crawl from Polar Caverns —
Midnight in Marble — Refutes — the Suns —

In variant 1, some spring of the seasons or of Easter's promised redemption endeavors to open the tomb that has been closed by death, but the frost of extinction has so thoroughly shrouded the souls within that "Echoes — stiffen" like the corpses themselves, and the "door" is as "numb" as the bodies within. Instead of life's reanimating the sleepers, the active force of cold manages to chill even the returning warmth that has come to release them. I Corinthians 15:25–26 had promised a repeal of the grave's power: "For [Christ] must reign, till he hath put all enemies under his feet. The last enemy that shall be destroyed is death." In the poem this promise has been horrifically reversed: the cold of the grave freezes the power of spring and rebirth, and the Saviour's mission is defeated. With the hope of the New Testament lost, the poem retreats into an Old Testament past, recalling the tribes of Israel who wandered in the desert waste. The "Tribes" here, however, have not even the guidance of a pillar of fire or of cloud: they are the chosen people of a *hidden* God, an "Eclipse" that will never serve as guidance in the wilderness. "Staples" recalls Christ's mission and the nails of the Crucifixion; now they release none, but rather affix the "meek members of the Resurrection" forever in their tombs, "buckled" securely in the coffins that will cherish them for eternity.

Variant 1 is dominated by patterns of Judaeo-Christian mythology. Although Variant 2 retains this focus upon the legend of Father and Son, it is clearly the product of a modern sensibility—one tutored (by Edward Hitchcock, perhaps) in the mysteries of a glacial age with seas of ice, a silent, frozen wilderness slowly moving to engulf the world. Again the Bible is invoked, but now the reference is to the "Seals" in the Book of Revelation, which will be broken when the New Jerusalem is at hand. Yet just as the tomb rebuffed Easter's promise of release, so it "stiffens" against the fulfillment of Revelation. Instead of heavenly release, a new ice age begins. Dinosaurs had roamed the upper Connecticut valley eons before the coming of the Puritans; now, monstrous tentacles of cold from "Polar Caverns" rouse themselves to begin a leisurely descent. Worse than the most ferocious dinosaur, they move with the slow, insidious "crawl" of the snake. Perhaps these "Icicles" constitute an Antichrist triumphant at the end of time: a power of darkness, "Midnight," that "Refutes" the Sun / Son.

The first stanza holds the sensuous world in tight conjunction with the world of myth. "Meek members of the Resurrection—" clearly carries us back to the Beatitudes; both "Morning" and "Noon" invoke Heaven; and "satin" recalls Christ as the bridegroom. Yet the palpable images of "Alabaster Chambers" with the coffin's satin "Rafter" and the grave marker's "Roof of stone" lodge the mythic firmly in a world of everyday reality. The 1859 version of the second stanza tips the poem decisively in the direction of the quotidian—by the mere vividness of the day that "Babbles" above; even more, perhaps, by the patent disavowal of the possibility that this scene may provide signs of redemption. Variants 1 and 2 overbalance the second stanza in the opposite direction—summoning a world of myth and legend that encroaches upon ordinary sanity. Both variants are effective in creating terror, but neither sustains the careful balance of the first stanza.

Perhaps it was for this reason that Dickinson decided in the end to send Higginson a version of the poem that holds the relationship between the world of myth and the world of everyday affairs constant throughout.

> *Safe in their Alabaster Chambers—*
> *Untouched by Morning—*
> *And untouched by Noon—*
> *Sleep the meek members of the Resurrection,*
> *Rafter of Satin—and Roof of Stone—*
>
> *Grand go the Years,*
> *In the Crescent above them—*
> *Worlds scoop their Arcs—*
> *And Firmaments—row—*
> *Diadems—drop—*
> *And Doges—surrender—*
> *Soundless as Dots,*
> *On a Disc of Snow.*

The stately passage of the "Years," public time that is dominated by the "Diadems" of kings and "Doges," accents the merely earthly meaning of "Morning" and "Noon" in the first stanza. Similarly, the series of half-circles implied by "Crescent," "scoop," and "Arcs" contrasts the time frame of all human kingdoms with the perfect circle of God's eternity. This much is clear and can be tolerated. Horror begins with the fact that human volition concludes in the familiar "drop—," an undefined descent into uncertainty. Nor is it possible for the sleepers ever to reach the realm of God's impassive perfection, for His circle (recalling the last vestige of earth life, a snowflake) is a "Disc of Snow," a two-dimensional kingdom of absolute cold: even if we "surrender," a phantasmagoric reduction to zero is thrust upon us; if we enter the divine presence, we are utterly bereft of voice—"Soundless"—and entirely without dimension—"Dots." We become *nothingness* in the unending winter of God's nature.

"The Angle of a Landscape" is, it would seem, too generous a vantage to describe the chances God has given us. Existential possibilities are meager, and humanity is brutally assaulted and wounded: these truths can be observed in the remnant of Edenic "Apples" and the "Forehead of a Hill" that compose nature's scenery. But the ultimate truth of human destiny can be found only in the "Polar Caskets" of winter, for winter has but one face—a flat and featureless expanse of cold.

4 ❧ The Masks of Divinity and the Coordinates of Heaven

In his Gothic fable of the Inquisition, "The Pit and the Pendulum," Edgar Allan Poe posited a grotesque form of torture: a prisoner is cast into a dungeon; at its center is a pit inhabited by ravenous rats; from the ceiling far above, a razor-sharp pendulum swings back and forth, marking the remorseless passage of time, and as it swings, it descends lower and lower to threaten maiming at first and at last a hacking to death; and finally, as if these were not enough, the walls of the dungeon gradually begin to warm and then to glow with hellish heat, forcing the prisoner toward the center where the pit and the pendulum vie for his execution. Yet Poe's story concludes with a reprieve. Just at the moment when a drop into agony, mutilation, and annihilation seems unavoidable, the forces of the Spanish Inquisition are defeated by a conquering French army, and the prisoner is released. Since the author explicitly disavowed any intention of giving an outline of transcendent realities, the story is only a fantasy that offers a *frisson* of horror; the nightmare, limited and susceptible of termination, can thrill in the reading and then be dismissed: therein lies much of its strange charm.

Dickinson's examination of nature introduces a sobering fear: perhaps the kind of hallucinatory vision that is rendered in Poe's tale has more truth than fancy; perhaps this God of absolute cold has concocted a cosmos that functions primarily as an experiment in human anguish.

A Pit — but Heaven over it —
And Heaven beside, and Heaven abroad;
And yet a Pit —
With Heaven over it.

To stir would be to slip —
To look would be to drop —
To dream — to sap the Prop
That holds my chances up.
Ah! Pit! With Heaven over it!

The depth is all my thought —
I dare not ask my feet —
'Twould start us where we sit
So straight you'd scarce suspect
It was a Pit — with fathoms under it
Its Circuit just the same
Seed — summer — tomb —
Whose Doom to whom?

(#1712)[16]

Interestingly, the first stanza offers two different versions of the spatial relations that define the moral universe. The first line, along with lines 3 and 4, presents a variation of the traditional view: below, the "Pit" of damnation; above, the salvation of "Heaven"; between, the Christian poised in uncertainty. If this were the only spatial array offered, the dilemma sketched in the poem might follow the usual outlines of Puritan moral tales or of the emblems and visual allegories drawn by artists like Quarles or Holmes and Barber. Each human must walk the precarious path of life: if he or she falls into sin, that fall will be consummated after death by descent into the unending punishment of Hell; if he or she pursues the strait and narrow pathway of God's righteousness, then a reward of eternal happiness in Heaven above awaits. Yet line 2 complicates this vision: "Heaven" is not merely above, but "beside" and "abroad." However, its proximity offers no solace; instead, "Heaven" seems to swirl around us like the empty ether of interstellar space, a barren configuration that is incapable of sustaining life. These several "Heavens" recall that other freakish vision of "Kingdoms — afterward": "*Whose Prince — is Son of None — / Himself — His Dateless Dynasty — / Himself — Himself diversify — / In Duplicate divine —*" (#721), the deranged house of mirrors created by a sterile God.

This terror in the first stanza — a tension between the hope for Heaven as reward and the fear of Heaven as nightmare — is sustained by the pervasive anxiety of the succeeding stanzas. One is not able to walk even the path of righteousness in safety, for "To stir would be to slip"; nor can one easily investigate the terms of this existential dilemma, for "To look would be to drop." Indeed, should attention to holding "straight" wander for so much as an instant, the lapse might prove fatal to "the Prop / That holds my chances up." Life must be contracted, then, to mere static concentration upon our plight. A state of existence that is thus defined cannot breed poetry, for one dare not start the "feet." In fact, without any chance for investigation, question, debate, complaint, or even worship, all human possibility is reduced to the merely vegetative: "Seed—summer—tomb—." Fate is homogenized, and separate, integral identity becomes irrelevant: "Whose Doom to whom?" In "*Behind Me—dips Eternity—*" (#721), the narrative center could not hold, and the visual plane aligning earth and sky slipped askew. "A Pit—but Heaven over it" takes this distortion one step further by suggesting that the intrinsic construction of the cosmos is itself so radically destabilizing that we are in constant menace of a disintegration that would pitch self into plumbless "fathoms" of oblivion.

The lessons of nature could never be entirely abandoned. Nonetheless, a system of natural signs and emblems was insufficient to convey the complexity of Emily Dickinson's vision. She was not content to limit herself to limning God's force as it could be perceived in nature; like the great Christian epic poets, she aspired to map the essential elements of the larger spiritual universe. Interestingly, she had little interest in the underworld: the "Pit" was not important enough to warrant her intention. She was concerned, however, to examine the notion of Heaven with rigor and to achieve some comprehensive understanding of the Almighty Being Who waits to receive us after death. It was an ambitious enterprise with roots in the Bible, in Dante, and in Milton's epic vision. Christ Himself had offered the original model for such an inquiry. God was His "Father"; and "In my Father's house are many mansions" (John 14:2).

Occasionally Dickinson toyed with the simple and seemingly accessible notions that the Scriptures had offered—the palace of God as a well-appointed Victorian home with "*parlors, shut by day*" (#103), for example. Yet the earthly resting place of those whom God had already called to His bosom left so powerful a vision of the grave, a "place" that was all too easily defined, that death and the cemetery obscured the comforting image of Heaven-as-home. "*What Inn is this / Where for the night / Peculiar Traveller comes? / Who is the Landlord? / Where the maids? / Behold, what curious rooms! / No ruddy fires on the hearth— / No brimming Tankards flow— / Necromancer! Landlord! / Who are these below?*" (#115) The Bible also suggests that Heaven can be described as a shining city: "the holy Jerusalem, descending out of heaven from God, Having the glory of God: and . . . a wall great and high, and . . . twelve gates" (Revelation 21:10–12). Would the golden city in the sky be as familiar as the township of Amherst, then? "*What is— 'Paradise'— / Who live there— / Are they 'Farmers'— / Do they 'hoe'— / Do they know that this is 'Amherst'— / And that I—am coming—too— / . . . I shant walk the 'Jasper'—barefoot— / Ransomed folks—wont laugh at me— / Maybe—'Eden' a'nt so lonesome / As New England used to be!"* (#215) Yet if Heaven is essentially the same as earth, why must there be the fearful interruption of death? Why would a benevolent God subject His creatures to such uncertainty and pain? Is it not a cruel practice to force us to lose the earth we know and love, only to transport us to a Heaven that is no more than earth's extension? Under these conditions, Dickinson was more than willing to trade the Heaven to come for the vivid life she already knew. *"Of Heaven above the firmest proof / We fundamental know / Except for it's marauding Hand / It had been Heaven below"* (#1205). Repeatedly, both in the letters and in the poetry, she affirmed that life—with its admixture of pain, which accentuates pleasure—offers everything we need of Heaven.

At one level, such meditations in verse might seem merely deft manipulations of familiar Biblical passages and common religious notions—the clever inventions of a precocious student of theology. Yet serious considerations lie behind these poems about Heaven as a house or a town. When any individual life is ended, the body remains, and we can see that a rapid process of decay occurs. Eventually, every distinguishing physical component of identity is erased. Thus if some integral "I" remains after death, it must exist in a form we do not know on earth. "Without any body, I keep thinking," Dickinson wrote many months following her father's death. "What kind can that be?" Nor was this concern about the terms of an "afterlife" unique to Emily Dickinson. Many ruminative Christians of her time and place pondered its puzzle: "Austin and I were talking the other Night about the Extension of Consciousness, after Death and Mother told Vinnie, afterwards, she thought it was 'very improper'" Emily Dickinson wrote Mrs. Holland. "I dont know what she would think if she knew that Austin told me confidentially 'there was no such person as Elijah.'" In the New Testament, Jesus said that after "the resurrection [those who have been saved] neither marry, nor are given in marriage, but are as the angels of God in heaven" (Matthew 22:30); in a letter to Otis Lord, Dickinson mused playfully upon the dilemma posed to earthly love by this bodiless, transcendent state. "In Heaven they neither woo nor are given in wooing—what an imperfect place!" Yet identity as we define it during life is essentially dependent upon our interactions with others; if those in Heaven "neither marry, nor are given in marriage," the absence of the emotional tie is a wounding of that identity. Jesus did not discourse upon the relationships between parents and children or sisters and brothers in Heaven; however, Emily Dickinson, along with family and friends, worried about the possibility of that deprivation, too. "Are you certain there is another life?" Emily Dickinson wrote to Charles Clark shortly after his brother's death: "Your bond to your brother reminds me of mine to my sister— early, earnest, indissoluble. Without her life were fear, and Paradise a cowardice, except for her inciting voice."[17] How can we *"be"* in Heaven if the very relationships that have sustained us here cannot be continued there?

In truth, it is not an easy task to translate the notion of Heaven as a house or a town. Houses, cities, kingdoms—all of these images used throughout the Bible to describe God's Heaven—are actually arrangements on earth to accommodate the needs of the body and to structure and facilitate relationships among people. Houses have kitchens because our bodies need food, bedrooms because the flesh must sleep; cities have neighborhoods where friends can congregate and different members of the same family can live near one another. There are markets to sell clothes, printing houses for newspapers and books, firehouses, jails, schools. All such businesses and institutions, along with the government that imposes order, are what constitute a "city," and without these the notion of a "city" of Heaven cannot assume any coherent, reassuring, familiar form. In his *Religious Lectures,* Edward Hitchcock returned many times to the puzzle of individual identity and human relationships in God's Heavenly "city," realizing how painfully the members of his audience worried about the problem.

Who of us have not sometimes been afflicted in the removal of those whose forms and features have been ever since remembered with the deepest interest. . . . And how deep was our anguish, when we last looked upon them . . . as we saw the grave closing over their remains. . . . If they were the true disciples of Christ, they shall be restored to us in the resurrection morning, and we shall recognize them amid the millions, who then awake from the grave. . . . There shall be a characteristic something in their spiritual bodies, that will lead us at once . . . to fly to their embrace.[18]

In support of this assertion, Hitchcock offered not proof but analogies from nature—and Dickinson was not persuaded by such theodicy.

In her view, Heaven offered not village or home, but a new kind of wilderness; even the belief that Heaven exists and that the "true disciples of Christ" may await us there could not ease her apprehension.

> *Their Hight in Heaven comforts not—*
> *Their Glory—nought to me—*
> *'Twas best imperfect—as it was—*
> *I'm finite—I cant see—*
>
> *The House of Supposition—*
> *The Glimmering Frontier that skirts the Acres of Perhaps—*
> *To Me—shows insecure—*
>
> *The Wealth I had—contented me—*
> *If 'twas a meaner size—*

Then I had counted it until
It pleased my narrow Eyes—

Better than larger values—
That show however true—
This timid life of Evidence
Keeps pleading— "I dont know."

(#696)[19]

This is a particularly American interpretation of the panoramic, unknown afterlife—God's "House of Supposition." The long, billowing exhalation of line 6 mimics the uncompassed vistas of the New World's own Western wilderness, not yet fully explored or completely mapped in the late 1860s. Instead of cities, vast regions of untilled land spread as far as the eye could see—expanses of prairies or immense, particolored deserts. Yet the prairies were richly fertile, and the deserts glowed with warmth and an intimation of gold, whereas Heaven's "Glimmering Frontier" hints only at white light reflected from unending tracts of ice, the essence of God's frigid, annihilating power. Life on earth has schooled this speaker to trust only in "Evidence"; when confronted with a promised Heaven of hypothetical happiness, she must plead, " 'I dont know.' " What she can see is best, even if its rewards are finite; and the incoherence, even danger of an unseeable, unexplored Paradise is rendered here by the substitution of abstract nouns, "Supposition" and "Perhaps," for the concrete nouns that would complete such locutions if they referred to that earthly frontier, the burgeoning American West.

We have been encouraged to think of Heaven as a place; yet the very notion of "place" presupposes the coordinate notion of a body. Dickinson's dictionary defined "place" as "a particular portion of space of indefinite extent, occupied or intended to be occupied by any person or thing, and considered as the space where a person or thing does or may rest or has rested, as distinct from space in general." Given this definition, she could see the fallacious logic inherent in traditional notions of Heaven as a "place" for entities without material form of any sort.

We pray—to Heaven—
We prate—of Heaven—
Relate—when Neighbors die—
At what o'clock to Heaven—they fled—
Who saw them—Wherefore fly?

Is Heaven a Place—a Sky—a Tree?
Location's narrow way is for Ourselves—
Unto the Dead
There's no Geography—

> *But State—Endowal—Focus—*
> *Where—Omnipresence—fly?*

> (#489)

We, the living, gossip about "Heaven" as if it were Hadley or Northampton—a township one can visit for the day on a jaunt with scheduled times for leaving (but not for returning). This "narrow way" of alluding to Heaven as if it were a "Location" serves the interest only of those on earth. If Heaven does exist, it must be some different condition for the dead, some "State—Endowal—Focus—." Presumably, to be in Heaven is to be with God. And yet here is the paradox: God is *everywhere*, "Omnipresence." Where is He *not*? Where is He *more*? Can we be *with* Him? Can we be *without* Him? Where does He "fly?"

Dickinson's determination to undertake the tasks of conceptualizing "Heaven" and "God" presented complex problems, then. The consolation literature of her day was all too ready to take a simplistic attitude, never analyzing the concepts it employed and construing both God and His realm as nothing more complicated than a superior sort of domestic arrangement. Thus this component of the poet's work was a timely corrective to the easy optimism of the popular press. Dickinson was not alone in this endeavor: although Melville did not attempt to map the topography of Paradise, he did scan the world to find the masks of the Divinity. Like Dickinson, he discovered the Creator / Avenger in nature. Yet Melville found God's likeness in certain human forms, too. Melville set his novel *The Confidence Man* on a riverboat because he claimed to have discovered God's earthly counterpart there in the person of a swindler who wears a series of disguises in order to bilk the passengers of their money and to coerce unwarranted affection from them; in Melville's estimation, the "Heaven" to come was devalued by the expectation that nothing but further deceptions could follow the kind of life we are forced to lead on earth. Almost certainly, Emily Dickinson was unfamiliar with this last novel issued during Melville's lifetime (it was published, fittingly, on the first of April 1857—April Fool's Day). Yet she, too, sauntered through the world searching out the masks of the hidden God. She did not go to sea, was not familiar with the seamy riverboat traffic up and down the Mississippi; but she found the devious Divinity behind many worldly masks, nonetheless.

One of Dickinson's maneuvers was similar to Melville's characterization of God as a riverboat crook. As always, however, Dickinson's vision has the distinctive tonality of New England about it. Although there was no theater in the Amherst of Emily Dickinson's youth, traveling shows, carnivals, and circuses regularly put up their tents in town, and once the family had returned to live in the Brick House, Emily Dickinson could watch from her bedroom window and see an outlandish parade as the crews trooped from Pelham into Amherst along Main Street. The juxtaposition of carnival and the hallowed ground of her forebears arrested her imagination. One spring day she wrote, "Again the Procession from Algiers will pass the Chamber-Window." And another time: "There is circus here, and Farmer's Commencement, and Boys and Girls from Tripoli, and Governors and swords, parade the Summer Street. They lean upon the Fence that guards the quiet Church Ground, and jar the Grass, now warm and soft as a Tropic Nest."[20] Jugglers and tumblers, flea-bitten animals in cages and magicians: all of this menagerie provided one possible mask for the Divinity. Perhaps God is only the harmless Master of our entertainment. *"Like Mighty Foot Lights— burned the Red / At Bases of the Trees— / The far Theatricals of Day / Exhibiting—to These— / 'Twas Universe—that did applaud— / While Chiefest—of the Crowd— / Enabled by his Royal Dress— / Myself distinguished God—"* (#595).

However, even this strategy of disarming transcendence by construing God as the Master of Ceremonies to some splendid circus of the skies could not efface the doubts and fears that pervaded Dickinson's explorations of the Supernatural. Whenever the tents were thrown up in town, prudent New Englanders were inclined to hide their silver lest it be pilfered, and every carnival had its con man. Nature's entertainments can cheat us, too—by encouraging us to suppose that the magnificence of their outer display is the entire truth. *"Dew—is the Freshet in the Grass— / 'Tis many a tiny Mill / Turns unperceived beneath our feet / And Artisan lies still—."* Perhaps the use of "lies" here implies "rests"; however, the other meaning, "exhibits a false representation," seems the overriding implication—a deceit of nature that may be carried into poetic "feet" by writers who fail to realize that nature's beauties can cover a multitude of snares. *"We spy the Forests and the Hills / The Tents to Nature's Show / Mistake the Outside for the in / And mention what we saw. / Could Commentators on the Sign / Of Nature's Caravan / Obtain 'Admission' as a Child / Some Wednesday Afternoon"* (#1097). One key to nature's riddle, then, is Heaven, the *inside* of nature's "Tents." Perhaps it is the only key worth having, for the panoramic promise of Heaven holds the answer to death's mystery as well.

Like God, Heaven is hidden; like death, Heaven can never be experienced during life. Nonetheless, each of us is constrained to try to imagine what Heaven is like, for it offers the only hope of existence after our time on earth has passed.

> It knew no Medicine—
> It was not Sickness—then—
> Nor any need of Surgery—
> And therefore—'twas not Pain—

It moved away the Cheeks —
A Dimple at a time —
And left the Profile — plainer —
And in the place of Bloom

It left the little Tint
That never had a Name —
You've seen it on a Cast's face —
Was Paradise — to blame —

If momently ajar —
Temerity — drew near —
And sickened — ever afterward
For Somewhat that it saw?

(#559)

Dying being (in #335) "a different way — / A Kind behind the Door," this poem attempts to infer what has been glimpsed on the other side, when the portal to "Paradise" has been left "momently ajar." The unthinkable possibility offered, more terrifying in its way than Poe's elaborately calculated machine of torture, is that there is some essential part of God's afterlife that, could we but see it, would leave us "sickened — ever afterward." Can it be that Heaven is really no more than another version of the "Pit"?

Ultimately, even the notion of Paradise as some transcendent entertainment can become horrific. Perhaps after our life on earth, we will enter into a state of static isolation, as if the silence of the hidden God infected everything about Him with exile.

Departed — to the Judgment —
A Mighty Afternoon —
Great Clouds — like Ushers — leaning —
Creation — looking on —

The Flesh — surrendered — Cancelled —
The Bodiless — begun —
Two Worlds — like Audiences — disperse —
And leave the Soul — alone —

(#524)

In its invocation of "Ushers" and "Audiences," this poem summons the image of God as the Master of Ceremonies. Yet the ritual that is begun here is a mockery of any acceptable notion of entertainment. Although the poem encompasses both an ending and a new beginning, only in the ending is there so much as an echo of other sentient beings: "Departed" carries an after-image of life—the train station at Pelham, perhaps, or the coach stop in the middle of Amherst, or even mourners at the grave; and "Judgment" implies the presence of both culprit and magistrate. Yet as soon as the first line has concluded, all familiar signs of vitality and social interchange vanish entirely, replaced by metaphors of abstractions. Nor does the speaker reach the destination she expects, for despite the assertion of the first line, there *is* no "Judgment" in the poem.

Biblical descriptions of the Judgment Day picture a crowded affair. The Disciples taught that "we must all appear before the judgment seat of Christ; that every one may receive the things done in his body, according to that he hath done, whether it be good or bad" (II Corinthians 5:10). The image they conjured was clearly an ordeal passed in the company of others, and the prophecies in Revelation confirm this vision, giving explicit reference for the "Pit" in Dickinson's lean existential equation.

Lo, a Lamb stood on the mount Zion, and with him a hundred forty and four thousand, having his Father's name written in their foreheads. And I heard a voice from heaven, as the . . . voice of harpers harping with their harps: And they sung as it were a new song before the throne, . . . and no man could learn that song but the hundred and forty and four thousand, which were redeemed from the earth. . . . And I saw an angel come down from heaven, having the key of the bottomless pit and a great chain in his hand. . . . And I saw the dead, small and great, stand before God. . . . And I saw a new heaven and a new earth. [Revelation 14:1–3; 20:1, 12; 21:1.]

In the Bible and in every conventional account of the Judgment and a life after death, all anxiety is focused upon the possibility of an unending punishment of pain in Hell, the "Pit"; Heaven is viewed as a desirable and delightful reward. Yet paradoxically, it is Heaven Emily Dickinson seems to have feared. Thus, in "Departed—to the Judgment—," desolation derives not from punishment, but from solitude.

If it were not for the word "Judgment," a reader might even have difficulty in defining the spectral ceremony that is enacted. In every place where people or God would be expected, there is instead an abstraction or some element of the universe that lacks consciousness. Thus it is "Great Clouds" that play the role of "Ushers"; the "Audience" is "Creation," later more explicitly defined as "Two Worlds"; and the speaker even limns self not as an integral person, but first as "Flesh" and then as "Soul." This is clearly God's realm, but Dickinson employs poetic devices that the great Christian poets had conventionally used to depict Hell. For example, in *Paradise Lost* Milton used abstract nouns where the concrete would be expected in an attempt to render the incoherence of the underworld: "Regions of sorrow . . . The seat of desolation" (book I, lines 65, 181). In *"Their Hight in Heaven comforts not—,"* in *"Departed—to the Judgment,"* and in other poems about Paradise,

Dickinson appropriates this strategy to capture the fearsome essence of Heaven, defiantly juxtaposing her alternative transcendent vision to that of the poet who sought to "*justifie* the wayes of God to men." The presence of "Ushers" hints at the possibility of a wedding (or at the bride-of-Christ tradition), and this hint is sustained in "The Flesh—surrendered—"; but with the introduction of "Cancelled," every positive possibility drops away. Indeed, the train of movement set in motion by "Cancelled" plays out a kind of antiwedding, a severing rather than a joining together and the beginning of a "Bodiless" state in which sexual union and fruitfulness are impossible. The wound of bisection that strikes "Flesh" out of existence reverberates with cosmic import, and another kind of bisection occurs: "Two Worlds . . . disperse," leaving the mutilated speaker "alone" in an empty universe. Not dead, but without any medium for defining self or confirming vitality. And such horror as this is the conclusion to the Master Showman's "entertainment."

There were other masks of the Divinity that could be invoked to make God's nature manifest; and to find them Emily Dickinson was not obliged to venture any farther than her own father's law offices, two blocks away, in the center of Amherst. The daughter of Hampshire County's most successful lawyer, Dickinson was inordinately conscious of the legalistic language in which our destiny has been cast, a diction dominated by covenants and judgment; she also perceived that *God's* legal preoccupations have more to do with business transactions than with dispensing even-handed justice. "*You're right—'the way is narrow'— / And 'difficult the Gate'— / And 'few there be'—Correct again— / That 'enter in—thereat'— / 'Tis Costly—So are purples! / 'Tis just the price of Breath— / With but the 'Discount' of the Grave— / Termed by the Brokers—'Death'!*" Thus far, divine practices are at least in accord with hard-driven deals in Amherst. Yet when God's final verdict must be described, His Judgment is so arbitrary that the whimsy can be rendered only by a violation of the formal pattern in the verse:

> And after *that*—there's Heaven—
> The *Good* Man's— "*Dividend*"—
> And *Bad* Men— "go to Jail"—
> I guess—

> (#234)

Under these circumstances, it is not surprising to discover that the vaunted prize of Heaven is not very different from a prison.

> Doom is the House without the Door—
> 'Tis entered from the Sun—

> *And then the Ladder's thrown away,*
> *Because Escape—is done—*
>
> *'Tis varied by the Dream*
> *Of what they do outside—*
> *Where Squirrels play—and Berries die—*
> *And Hemlocks—bow—to God—*

(#475)

If it were not for the words "Doom" and "Escape," the first stanza might offer a relatively conventional depiction of Paradise: it arches above us, entered by the "Sun"—a hatchway to Heaven, perhaps, or an entrance opened by the Son of God, Who came to be our Redeemer. The ladder of Jacob's legend has evidently permitted access to the distant skies, and when a human has finally arrived, it can be "thrown away." Yet the reality of Heaven *is* "Doom," and once the ladder is gone, "Escape" has been forfeited. The second stanza reveals wherein the "Doom" of Heaven lies; it is static, a prison of ennui. Too late, earth is recognized as preferable to Heaven. Homesick for variety, the inmates amuse themselves with the "Dream" of "what they do outside—" the residence of this Northern Deity: the play of "Squirrels," the death of "Berries," the obeisance of "Hemlocks" who "bow—to God—."

Yet, if God was to be found in downtown Amherst, his most usual guise would be as buyer and seller of goods on Merchant's Row. God proffers Paradise; in exchange, He demands nothing less than self. Often Jesus spoke in parables that revealed the rates of exchange. The Kingdom of Heaven is a "pearl of great price"; and when we discover its existence, we should emulate the prudent "merchant man . . . Who, when he had found one pearl of great price, went and sold all that he had, and bought it" (Matthew 13:45–46). Perhaps Christ's parable of the rich young ruler gives the clearest and most extensive description of God's demands.

And, behold, one came and said unto him, Good Master, what good thing shall I do, that I may have eternal life? And [Jesus] said unto him, . . . If thou wilt enter into life, keep the commandments. . . . The young man saith unto him, All these things have I kept from my youth up: what lack I yet? Jesus said unto him, If thou wilt be perfect, go and sell that thou hast, and give to the poor, and thou shalt have treasure in heaven: and come and follow me. But when the young man heard that saying, he went away sorrowful: for he had great possessions.

Then said Jesus unto his disciples, Verily I say unto you, That a rich man shall hardly enter into the kingdom of heaven. And again I say unto you, It is easier for a camel to go through the eye of a needle, than for a rich man to enter into the kingdom of God. [Matthew 19:16–24.]

It was not the young man's wealth that Jesus wanted; it was the renunciation that would have been entailed in giving up that wealth—the abject surrendering of self to follow God without question. This lesson of yielding the individual will to God was everywhere reiterated in Dickinson's culture, and what often captivated her imagination was that often the barter was so baldly represented in the hard-cash terms of a deal or a bargain to be struck with the Lord, an "*Extatic* Contract!" (#247)

The question of what a person would be when he or she had sold the self entirely to God was left unasked, and the poet sometimes considered this quandary. Can anyone who has relinquished will and autonomy be left in a condition to appreciate Paradise or God's presence in it? The focus of *this* query is not so much upon Heaven—its status as a place, its spatial configuration, its temporal condition—as upon the personal integrity of a human being who has surrendered autonomy to purchase celestial life.

> *He put the Belt around my life—*
> *I heard the Buckle snap—*
> *And turned away, imperial,*
> *My Lifetime folding up—*
> *Deliberate, as a Duke would do*
> *A Kingdom's Title Deed—*
> *Henceforth, a Dedicated sort—*
> *A Member of the Cloud.*
>
> *Yet not too far to come at call—*
> *And do the little Toils*
> *That make the Circuit of the Rest—*
> *And deal occasional smiles*
> *To lives that stoop to notice mine—*
> *And kindly ask it in—*
> *Whose invitation, know you not*
> *For Whom I must decline?*

(#273)

God evidently uses a satchel to carry the deeds of "Dedicated" lives; and when a transaction has been completed, he gathers His papers, puts them inside, pulls the "Belt" around his old-fashioned briefcase, and closes the "Buckle" so that none will be lost. The lawyerly image of the Deity remains strong in this poem, and there is an aura of the regal as well. Of course, it is the speaker and others like her who have made Him "imperial" by giving what the rich young ruler of the parable was unwilling to yield, the entire "Kingdom" at her disposal. Ironically, although the speaker contributes to God's grandeur, she is able to gain no eminence for herself: on her side, everything about this transaction spells loss. She has not established an intimate relationship to the Lord, nor has she even retained the unique entitlement to life that she had possessed before; instead, she is "A Member of the Cloud." Identity has been atomized and mingled indiscriminately with all those other surrendered lives that have been scattered throughout Heaven.

Inevitably, this poem recalls "The Drop, that wrestles in the Sea—": there is the same dissolution of self, the same innuendo of a courtship and marriage whose subtly elegant terms conceal callous brutality and absolute possessiveness. In fact, if a woman poet wished to write the kind of defiant, almost parodic version of the parable of the rich young ruler that is found in this poem, she had few alternatives but to turn to some tradition like that of the bride of Christ. In mid-nineteenth-century America, most women had little to offer except themselves, for the property rights of daughters and wives were so ill-protected by the law that, as often as not, the "Title Deed" to all a woman's wealth would have been synonymous to a "Deed" for "Self." With the rarest exception, women did not become rulers with vast riches to relinquish, royal booty to sell, or a throne to abdicate; thus the parable of the rich young ruler as it was formulated in the Gospel could but seldom apply to women. The *female* response to the injunction, "Come and follow me," might be to accept the stereotyped role of the submissive wife; and it is this response that Dickinson renders in the second stanza of "He put the Belt around my life." What this speaker will "be" in Heaven, then, is the one who responds automatically to everyone else's beckoning. All the strength and compassion that the "Wife's" Voice can communicate elsewhere in Dickinson's poetry is missing here. A grotesque caricature of the *empowered* "Wife," this speaker is little more than a servant; her ministering to others springs not from vitality and generosity but from abject submission, and it is not surprising that the reader sees no evidence that she is able to confront pain or nourish hunger. By the poem's conclusion, her sphere has dwindled from giving at least small comforts to occupying herself with the trivial round of making calls and receiving visitors, always willing to "decline" should her master so decree.

A Christian's meditations upon Heaven can go through several stages. Initially, the prospect may seem almost too good to be true. " *'Tis so much joy! 'Tis so much joy! / If I should fail, what poverty! / And yet, as poor as I, / Have ventured all upon a throw! / Have gained! Yes! Hesitated so— / This side the Victory!"* What an opportunity Heaven appears to be. There is a gamble: one must be willing to chance everything for an unknown reward; perhaps the uncertainty even causes one to "Hesitate." And what a pity, this hesitation, should one be on the verge of "Victory." Surely it is better to take the gamble and face the risk. *"Life is but Life! And Death, but Death! / Bliss is but Bliss, and Breath but Breath! / And if indeed I fail, / At least, to know the worst, is sweet! / Defeat means nothing <u>but</u> Defeat, / No drearier, can befall!"* Even if one embraces faith and there is no Heavenly reward, then, life is still life, the bliss of earth still bliss, and "Death, but Death"—not made worse by an unfulfilled hope of Paradise. *"And if I gain! Oh Gun at Sea! / Oh Bells, that in the Steeples be!"* What a triumphant decision this confidence in Heaven would turn out to have been. Or would it?

> *At first, repeat it slow!*
> *For Heaven is a different thing,*
> *Conjectured, and waked sudden in—*
> *And might extinguish me!*
>
> (#172)

Ironically, the ultimate danger is not that Heaven might *fail* to exist, but that it might *prove* to exist.

So long as Heaven is potential, we can know it only internally, as a concoction of our own imagination: Jesus's promises, preachers' wheedlings, the descriptions in Revelation—all of these may attempt to present us with a notion of Heaven, but each individual's conception of it has shape internally, informed perhaps by the preachments of others, yet essentially his or her own. So long as we live, then, Heaven is our possession, and we can make of it what we want—the triumph of a "Gun at Sea" or "Bells" pealing for joy. Once dead, however, we might discover that "Heaven is a different thing"— something that will "extinguish" self.

Repeatedly Dickinson returned to this possibility. Sometimes she feared the "self" would be entirely engrossed into some larger, amorphous entity, God or the cloud of saved souls. *"This Dust, and it's Feature— / Accredited— Today— / Will in a second Future— / Cease to identify— / This Mind, and it's measure— / A too minute Area / For it's enlarged inspection's / Comparison— appear— / This World, and it's species / A too concluded show / For it's <u>absorbed</u> Attention's / Remotest scrutiny—"* (#936, *my emphasis*). The pun twists the knife: on earth, our attention may be "absorbed" by the expectation of Heaven, each of us preoccupied with his or her own daydreams of Paradise; after death, our separate identities will be "absorbed" into a collective silence.

The ultimate mask of God, then, is that of some transcendent travel agent, transporting us not to our stipulated destinations but to parts unknown; and He commands exorbitant fees. *"I asked no other thing— / No other—was denied— / I offered Being—for it— / The Mighty Merchant sneered— / Brazil? He twirled a Button— / Without a glance my way— / 'But— Madam—is there nothing else— / That We can show—Today?'"* (#621) The poems about this transaction, both the journey to Heaven and the arrival there, are among the most strenuous and unsettling in all of Dickinson's work. They turn upon the intrinsic connection between the ability to *locate* the self with regard to other beings or things and the ability to *define* the self with coherence and precision.

All human beings think of the self as a consciousness that is situated in some specific place; thus the capacity to identify "me" is contingent upon the ability to designate some surrounding space that is "not me." Moreover, we define where we "are" in large measure by where we "have been" and where we "are about to go." And as soon as these fundamental spatial and temporal notions begin to fritter away, nightmare descends.

> *Our journey had advanced—*
> *Our feet were almost come*
> *To that odd Fork in Being's Road—*
> *Eternity—by Term—*
>
> *Our pace took sudden awe—*
> *Our feet—reluctant—led—*
> *Before—were Cities—but Between—*
> *The Forest of the Dead—*
>
> *Retreat—was out of Hope—*
> *Behind—a Sealed Route—*
> *Eternity's White Flag—Before—*
> *And God—at every Gate—*
>
> (#615)

At first, the situation described in the poem appears clear; yet as soon as the reader attempts to formulate a coherent image of the event that is being described, the obstinate paradox of virtually every significant mapping element in the verse frustrates the most persistent effort. What begins with apparent clarity concludes with hallucinatory confusion.

The poem opens with an entirely conventional notion: life is a journey toward death; after death there are the two alternative afterworlds, Heaven and Hell; eternal bliss is to be found by the saved in Heaven, eternal pain by the damned in Hell. Yet in the poem this usual notion of a "journey" is vitiated at once, for Hell seems not even to exist as a possibility; there is no "Pit" to concern us here, merely the "Heaven over it." A reader might expect the verse to render a glorious and reassuring vision, then. Instead, it offers an ingenious form of anguish in the baffling maze of options that follow. A "Fork" generally implies *two* courses (and the use of the word again recalls the religious alternatives, Heaven and happiness or Hell and misery); yet this is an "odd Fork"—one that cannot have an even number of possibilities. Finally, the first stanza concludes by intimating that there was never a "Fork" at all, for in the end only one option is given—"Eternity." Thus the visual array has shifted, and the initial image of a "Fork" in the road has given way to the vision of a single road with no choice at all. In the distance there are "Cities," perhaps some welcome destination like the Heavenly Jerusalem. Yet an obstacle lies between, "The Forest of the Dead." This verbal formulation summons the primitive fear of children's fairy tales—"The Babes in the Wood," perhaps, or some other story of little lost ones. Yet the poem's image adds one further horror: it is the "Forest of the *Dead—*." Can such a "Forest" be of trees? Perhaps it is a barren moonscape of sterile rock, immense, phantasmagoric gravestones clustered like a wood, so dense one can find no pathway, so vast that it strikes "awe." Almost certainly it is intended to recall the spectral woods in canto XXXI of Dante's *Inferno*—"strange trees" that imprison the shades of the damned in the seventh circle of the second ring of Hell. By the end of the second stanza, then, the meaningful image that has been invited by the notion of the Christian's "journey" toward Heaven has dissolved into nightmare.

The third stanza dispels even the possibility of a coherent visual construct. As in "Their Hight in Heaven comforts not—," an abstract noun is used where reason begs for the concrete: thus "Retreat" is "out of Hope—." Moreover, the Biblical *conclusion* of the Christian journey that leads to an opening of the "Seals" of Revelation has here been put *"Behind"* in the "Sealed Route," and the reader must suppose that such a "Seal" as this can never be broken. Finally, the "Cities" that had seemed to offer hope in stanza two now merely complete the terrifying series of reversals. Like Cerberus, the three-headed dog who had guarded the gates to the underworld of the ancient Romans, "God" is "at every Gate" of the twelve-gated city ahead, the menace of His presence an inescapable finality. The surrealistic geography of this poem concisely renders the impossibility of Heaven as a "place." Moreover, the reader's efforts merely to follow the course of the verse and extract a plausible vision of the "journey" to it produce inevitable frustration. And the feelings of helplessness and anxiety that the poem thus engenders are precisely mimetic of our feelings when we attempt to clarify the notion of Heaven that God has offered to us.

One part of Heaven's anarchy inheres in the paradox of spatial and temporal relations that it presents. However, another part of its fearful chaos has to do with disruptions of the usual relationships between people, and this subject, too, is touched upon here.

The speaker of this poem addresses us from beyond the grave; yet, remarkably, she speaks not merely for self but for at least one other as well—possibly many others—"*Our* journey." However we have no idea as to the identity of the others who may be involved in the speaker's ordeal, nor can we know what relationship the speaker bears to her companions. In fact, although Dickinson has improbably designated *one* Voice to speak for *many* from beyond the grave, it seems that the presence of these others has made no difference to the speaker's ordeal—all have experienced the same nightmare, paradoxically isolated while they move in undifferentiated unison ("Our journey . . . Our feet . . . Our pace . . . Our feet"). They have provided no company for one another, offered no comfort or reassurance to one another, neither rejoiced with others nor sorrowed for others. Each might as well have been alone. Hitchcock's assurance that we will recognize a "characteristic something" in others after death that will allow us to "fly to their embrace" is explicitly denied by the mute anonymity of this ghostly group that moves toward doom in dumb accord, like a row of puppets. Insofar as "feet" represent poetic activity, they are understandably "reluctant" to be "led" toward the paralyzing end point; for if there is no communication and no articulation of the distinct self, there can be no poetry.

Finally, there is a "Term" attached to "Eternity" in this poem. It cannot pertain to time, for a "Term" is "any limited time," and "Eternity" can know no boundaries. But the word "Term" has a legal connotation as well: in a covenant, terms are "propositions stated or promises made, which when assented to or accepted by another, settle the contract and bind the parties." The precise nature of Eternity's "Term" is stipulated only at the poem's conclusion—"Eternity's White Flag," the talisman of surrender. The city is not prepared to surrender to those advancing toward it: God's face "at every Gate" is armament enough. Rather, each human being is required to surrender before entering. It is a surrender that reiterates the loss of self first experienced in the act of conversion when a Christian accepts the terms of God's covenant of faith; and its effects have begun to be seen in the hollow sameness of the creatures whose fateful "journey" is traced in this poem, for an appalling erosion of human identity is already well under way.

Horrifically, this erosion is accomplished neither by some death that is a drop into nothingness, nor by consignment to the eternal suffering of the "Pit"—but by salvation. One of Dickinson's most complicated poems treats this perverse truth as a kind of Biblical riddle. A reader can best understand the following verse, then, if the terms of the puzzle are made clear. Question: what is the unstated antecedent of "It" in the first line? Answer: the resurrection from the grave into Heaven.

> *It was not Death, for I stood up,*
> *And all the Dead, lie down—*
> *It was not Night, for all the Bells*
> *Put out their Tongues, for Noon.*
>
> *It was not Frost, for on my Flesh*
> *I felt Siroccos—crawl—*
> *Nor Fire—for just my Marble feet*
> *Could keep a Chancel, cool—*

And yet, it tasted, like them all,
The Figures I have seen
Set orderly, for Burial,
Reminded me, of mine —

As if my life were shaven,
And fitted to a frame,
And could not breathe without a key,
And 'twas like Midnight, some —

When everything that ticked — has stopped —
And Space stares all around —
Or Grisly frosts — first Autumn morns,
Repeal the Beating Ground —

But, most, like Chaos — Stopless — cool —
Without a Chance, or Spar —
Or even a Report of Land —
To justify — Despair.

(#*510*)

The clues proceed by negation: "not Death . . . not Night . . . not Frost . . . Nor Fire." Thus although "It" is stipulated as opposite to these, the power of the carefully consecutive signs of death and damnation drive us in the direction of nightmare. Ironically, it is the supposed opposite of nightmare that is being identified, the resurrection from the tomb into Paradise.

Dickinson begins the poem by making the solution of the riddle quite patent, in terms both of the standard religious conventions of her day and of her own well-established linguistic patterns. In the New Testament, "to stand" always has two implications. While alive, Christians are enjoined to stand unshaken in faith—"Watch ye, stand fast in the faith, . . . be strong" (I Corinthians 16:13); after death, it is precisely this steadfast faith that will enable each of the saved "to stand up" in the grave, miraculously renewed. Paul wrote, "Not for that [Christ's Disciples] have dominion over your faith, but are helpers of your joy: for by faith ye stand" (II Corinthians 1:24); thus when the time for Judgment had arrived, all true Christians would rise to their feet and receive everlasting life—"For the great day of his wrath is come; and who shall be able to stand?" (Revelation 6:17.) The Biblically encoded meaning of "stand" in Dickinson's culture was so strongly felt, the joyful message of standing up in the grave to receive Christ had been incorporated into so many popular hymns, that the meaning of "I stood up"— especially when it was juxtaposed to "It was not Death"—would have been inescapable: deliverance from death and salvation, and entry into God's New Day. After beginning with the Lord's language of redemption, Dickinson continues the clues with her own consistent talisman of Heaven, the magic moment of "Noon," when eternity and nothingness are briefly conflated. "Noon" named the poet's state of unchanging permanence ("cool—concernless No—" in #287); at the same time, the word "Noon" stood for God's realm of absolute, perpetual power.

Yet having pinned the speaker unmistakably to Paradise both with God's semiotics and with her own, Dickinson deflates every conventional expectation, and none of the anticipated glory of such a moment leaks into the verse. Instead, the poem progresses through a series of explicit contradictions of happiness and grandeur: the obscene image of Noon's bells with their tongues wagging in derision, the snakelike familiarity of "Siroccos"—the steady winds of southeastern Italy, "said to resemble the steam from the mouth of an oven"—a demonic force now wantonly fondling the speaker's body. "Marble feet" suggests that poetry has become immobile, impossible, petrified. Yet a tradition of New England folk emblems makes this image, too, overdetermined to stress sacrilege.

New England graves had headstones, sometimes called "bedbacks," and it was on these "bedbacks" that the Angel of Death was so often emblazoned; since many graves had a footstone as well, the configuration of headstone and footstone in the cemetery could be seen to resemble a bed, thus becoming a visual trope: the death of the righteous is but a brief sleep from which they will awaken when the final trump is sounded. In this poem, the graveyard's visual trope for death has been surrealistically conflated with the "Chancel," that portion of the church just next to the altar or communion table where the Lord's Supper is celebrated. This grotesque fusion, then— cemetery casting its pallid "cool" upon the site of the Lord's Supper—is a metaphorical nullification of Christ's promised reunion. Indeed, this last and most daring poetic figure, "Marble feet" superimposed upon the "Chancel," explicitly reverses the familiar Biblical passage to which Dickinson so often returned. Christ "must reign, till he hath put all enemies under his feet. The last enemy that shall be destroyed is death. For he hath put all things under his feet. . . . O death, where is thy sting? O grave, where is thy victory?" (I Corinthians 15:25–27, 55). In Dickinson's poem, Christ's promise is put under *death*'s feet, and the *grave* is victorious.

Thus the anguish of the speaker's existential dilemma is captured by the wrenching conflict between the fact that is stated at the outset, "It was not Death," and the impressions captured by this complex imagery—all the loathsomeness that we have been taught to associate with dissolution and damnation.

Involuntarily, perhaps, the speaker reveals the extremity of her plight by the very terms she employs to state her perplexity: "And yet, it *tasted*, like them all." Jesus sometimes verbalized His promises in striking ways: "Verily I say unto you, There be some standing here, which shall not taste of death"

(Matthew 16:28). The pledged reunion was also formalized by a ceremonial act of eating, the sacrament of water, wine, and bread. Yet here it is the atavistic and potentially nauseating element of these words that dominates. The speaker recollects Christ's bizarre phrase and attempts to render what is happening to her by using the verbal formula of His promise; the result is ghoulish and grotesque. Taste is the most primitive sense, food the most fundamental gratification, and the notion of *tasting* all these grisly pieces of evidence as a way of discovering their meaning suggests that other, more usual and effective means of discernment have been lost and that the speaker has dropped back to the basest human level.

Little by little, she confesses the loss even of her own sense of personal identification: thus she searches for external things that can "Remind" her of the last self that she knew, her body "Set orderly, for Burial." Stanza four seeks even more anxiously for an answer to the questions "Who am I?" or "What have I become?" and the speaker proceeds by similes that recall the penultimate image of conversion in "He fumbles at your Soul": "Deals— One—imperial—Thunderbolt— / That *scalps* your naked Soul—." (italics mine). Now, the speaker's "life," named as such in the middle of line 13, is synecdochally reduced by the end of that line to a *scalp* that has been "shaven / And fitted to a frame"; the speaker posits herself as part of some ghostly musical instrument—the bellows of a church organ, perhaps—that cannot "breathe" song without a "key," and this spectral vestige of music, a parody of the "new song before the throne," is the only remnant of vitality. The bizarre image is delivered in a quick tattoo of parataxis ("And fitted . . . And could . . . And 'twas"), the syntax Dickinson so often employs to represent the drive toward death or dissolution. However, even such clear conclusions as death have been forfeited here, and the rapid parallel structures lead only to a halt that is no halt at all: "When everything that ticked—has stopped— / And Space stares all around—."

Time has ceased. The visible world has evaporated. Yet nothing has come to take their place, and we find ourselves in some stark winter of the soul. God's essence extends throughout the universe, but now it is revealed in its simplest, elemental form—the force of "frosts" that silence the "Beating" of earth life altogether—a purely retrograde power. And what follows is not a glorious Golden City, but "Chaos," the abyss that existed before Genesis. However, now that the epoch of existence in the world has been completed, "Chaos" is a condition from which none can be rescued; it is a new deluge state, different from Noah's because reprieve is now impossible. "Stopless— cool— / Without a Chance, or Spar—." The brief term of Creation has been concluded. Nightmarishly—Consciousness remains, but it is isolated in an eternal, tumbling, empty, unstructured void.

Nowhere else does Dickinson's arrogant, revisionary image of Heaven come so close to Milton's depiction of Hell—"Without dimension, where length, breadth, and highth, / And time and place are lost" (*Paradise Lost,* book II, 893–94); yet Hell as Milton described it was full of fire, and Satan had at least the companionship of other fallen angels in his misery. Here, Dickinson renders the Heaven of a silent, hidden God, and the speaker is entirely alone. There are no other beings—not souls or God or angels or devils. There is no temporal or spatial structure whatsoever, merely an unmeasurable, unending state of flux and confusion. In such a situation, it is not possible to have coherent emotions, for there can be no standards for assessing one's own reactions, no alternative situations against which to measure one's own plight, no God of perfect goodness to allow a calibration of loss. Thus if one is not apprised of *any* options, it is possible "To justify" neither hope nor "Despair." The speaker may continue to exist—forever, perhaps. But now, eternal life has been revealed as a state of amorphous isolation that never changes and never, never ceases. *This* state has not even the desperate hope that might be offered by a death that leads to oblivion.

A spatial and temporal impossibility, a loss of integral identity—our only certainties are that Heaven cannot be the simple bliss Christ promised, and that God is more monster than affectionate parent. "*Far from Love the Heavenly Father / Leads the Chosen Child, / Oftener through Realm of Briar / Than the Meadow mild. / Oftener by the Claw of Dragon / Than the Hand of Friend / Guides the Little One Predestined / To the Native land*" (#1021).

Perhaps the Bible postulates a Heaven less to console us than to assert the arbitrary will and ineffable grandeur of the Creator. Or perhaps (paradoxically) nothing more aptly predicts what we will discover in Heaven than the notions we can formulate here on earth about Hell. An eternity of chaos, or an unspeakable, inescapable assignation with the vagaries of Ultimate Power.

Behold, he cometh with clouds; and every eye shall see him, . . . and all kindreds of the earth shall wail because of him. Even so, Amen. I am Alpha and Omega, the beginning and the ending, saith the Lord, which is, and which was, and which is to come, the Almighty. [Revelation 1:7–8.]

5 ❖ Experiment

Emily Dickinson's schooling differed markedly from that of the average young woman of her day: she was given more instruction in current mathe-

matics and science than the average American school*boy* is given now. To be
sure, there was a great deal less science known and less to learn then; but
because Amherst Trinitarians thought that there were intrinsic connections
between science and religion, virtually everything that was available elsewhere in mid-nineteenth-century America was available and taught in Amherst. Hitchcock's influence was felt throughout every educational institution
that Emily Dickinson attended. Even the building program at Amherst College was affected by his devotion to the cause of modern science: although
systematic expansion of the library did not begin until 1850, two substantial
science buildings, the Woods Cabinet and the Lawrence Observatory, were
already completed by 1848. In the opinion of the evangelical ministers who
made up the faculty of Amherst College, taught at the Amherst Academy,
and lectured and preached at Mount Holyoke, God was a Master Craftsman
by way of being the Supreme Scientist of the universe.

According to this view, God created the magnificent systems of mathematics and natural laws so that we might discover His face therein. Hitchcock enunciated the typical attitude:

The eminent saints of ancient times were watchful observers of the objects and operations of nature. In every event they saw the agency of God; and therefore they took
delight in its examination. For they could not but receive pleasure from witnessing
the manifestations of His wisdom and beneficence, whom they adored and loved. . . .
The ablest philosophers of modern times . . . maintain, that a natural law is nothing
more than the uniform mode in which God acts; and that after all, it is not the
efficiency of the law, but God's own energy, that keeps all nature in motion: that he
operates immediately and directly, not remotely and indirectly, in bringing about
every event: and that every natural change is as really the work of God, as if the eye
of sense could see his hand turning round the wheels of nature.[21]

Biblical phenomena and the manifestations of natural science are not essentially different, then: both the wondrous events of the Bible—God's relatively
direct communication with the earliest prophets in the Old Testament and
Jesus's miraculous manifestations of His Godhead in the New Testament—
and the most recently discovered phenomena of science are expressions of
the same direct relationship between God and His people. Look to the Bible,
look to the immense laboratory of the world; the force and nature of God
will be found equally in both places.

Emily Dickinson was willing to grant this premise; perhaps natural theologians were even correct to think that it was in *this* mask, the guise of the
inventor or the scientist, that God's nature was revealed most starkly. Yet
Dickinson differed from her teachers in one respect: whereas they found evidence of benevolence and harmony in both the Bible and the workings of the

world, the poet discovered principally malice, capriciousness, and the terrifying drive toward extinction.

> It's easy to invent a Life —
> God does it — every Day —
> Creation — but the Gambol
> Of His Authority —
>
> It's easy to efface it —
> The thrifty Deity
> Could scarce afford Eternity
> To Spontaneity —
>
> The Perished Patterns murmur —
> But His Perturbless Plan
> Proceed — inserting Here — a Sun —
> There — leaving out a Man —
>
> (#724)

This is quintessentially a nineteenth-century poem, perhaps quintessentially an American poem as well. Franklin and Jefferson, giants of the Revolution and architects of the Constitution, had been inveterate tinkerers and inventors. When Fulton sailed his steamboat, the *Clermont,* up to Albany in 1807, he inaugurated an epoch in which scientists and inventors would capture a large measure of the public's heroic imagination. During the nineteenth century, America would celebrate new machines of all sorts and eventually (after Dickinson's death) the dynamo that struck Henry Adams with awe and dread.

Yet in the 1850s and 1860s, Emily Dickinson still looked to the eternal workings of God's machine, the cosmos, in search of truth and hope; what she found was the unchanging element of annihilation. The Divinity uses His capacity for calling creatures into being as a kind of boyish frolic: the only thing that is essential to creation is the raw, untempered assertion of God's power. His right to rule us, exact obedience, and demand love are all fundamentally rooted in the fact that just as He made us, so He can extinguish us. Thus in this poem there is appalling whimsy in the image of God-the-amateur-empiricist—puttering in His workshop, trying now this and now that new creation, playfully romping with His capacity to call absolutely anything into being (be it beautiful or deformed, good or nasty) and then as quickly nullify it if it does not amuse His fancy. "Efface it," extinguish its identity entirely. The progress of His work is not subject to appeal: if He has a "Plan," it is "Perturbless." And the structure of the universe He has concocted does not reveal an ordered, loving intelligence at work, but the ruthless and impervious exertion of random energy "inserting Here—a Sun— / There—leaving out a Man—."

The Lord is a sloppy worker, yet this is a very tidy piece of poetry. The balanced structures of the verse ("It's easy to invent . . . It's easy to efface . . . Here—a Sun—. . . There . . . a Man—") are deployed as a mocking parody of God's anarchic methods. Indeed, their prim irony recalls the skills of Dryden or Pope. Nor is this echo surprising. Students at the Amherst Academy learned to write gracefully by studying the great English stylists of the eighteenth century—Addison and Steele, Dryden and Pope—and Dickinson continued this study of style at Mount Holyoke.

The greatest of the English Augustans, Alexander Pope (1688–1744) lived in an age of new science himself, not the machinery and electricity that captivated the nineteenth-century imagination, but the elegant order of Newtonian physics, a set of relatively simple laws that could be applied to all physical processes. Many Christians of Pope's time and place felt that Newton had posed a serious threat to conventional theology by asserting that the universe moved not at the direct and immediate commands of God, but rather as a system that was governed by invariable rules of motion; in his lengthy poem *An Essay on Man,* Pope undertook to demonstrate that Newtonian physics offered no contradiction to traditional notions of God. On the contrary, they served to demonstrate the order and harmony of God's nature and thus to reassure us that the Lord works in a consistent and benevolent manner. Like Milton, Pope sought to justify God's ways. "Expatiate free o'er all this scene of Man; / A mighty maze! but not without a plan / . . . Together let us beat this ample field, / Try what the open, what the covert yield; / The latent tracts, the giddy heights explore / Of all who blindly creep, or sightless soar; / Eye Nature's walks, shoot Folly as it flies, / And catch the Manners living as they rise; / Laugh where we must, be candid where we can; / But vindicate the ways of God to Man." (*An Essay on Man,* epistle 1, lines 1–16.) Like many of his contemporaries, Pope postulated the existence of a "Great Chain of Being." This was an orderly system that proceeded step by step (never omitting a step), starting with the lowest and most elementary created thing and progressing with stately regularity through higher and higher levels of being—up to mankind, beyond man to the angels, beyond even the angels up to God Himself. Pope embedded the order of Newtonian physics in this vast map of creation—embedded in it even as much of Newtonian dynamics as he could understand—thereby hoping to persuade the reader that, far from contradicting traditional notions of the Divinity, the "new science" of the eighteenth century affirmed God's benevolent nature. The existence of this Great Chain of Being was the best proof one could have of a reliable, compassionate Deity, Pope urged.

Emily Dickinson did not read Pope's poetry with very much pleasure (though she clearly learned semantic skills from it). The lofty philosophy preached by its Great Chain of Being left her thoroughly unmoved: in November 1847 she wrote Abiah Root from Mount Holyoke, "At .11. I recite a lesson in 'Pope's Essay on Man' which is merely transposition."[22] Still, she tucked Pope's *Essay* into her memory as an excellent example of the poet dealing with God-as-scientist; and in "It's easy to invent a Life—" she returns to the Augustan master, not to imitate him but to explode the plausibility of his vision of an ordered world supervised by a God Who is wise and kind.

The passage she has in mind comes from the first epistle of that poem—a long, tendentious section designed to persuade mankind to *"Submit"* to God's will, despite the objections our limited capacity for reason might raise.

> Heav'n from all creatures hides the book of Fate,
> All but the page prescrib'd, their present state; . . .
> Oh blindness to the future! kindly giv'n,
> That each may fill the circle mark'd by Heav'n;
> Who sees with equal eye, as God of all,
> A hero perish, or a sparrow fall,
> Atoms or systems into ruin hurl'd,
> And now a bubble burst, and now a world.

(An Essay on Man,
epistle 1, lines 77–78, 85–90)

Possibly this passage offered an especially appealing target for Dickinson because Pope's defense of God's ways here is based upon modalities of seeing: mankind occupies its own place in the Great Chain of Being, Pope observes, and can see only its own state, know only its own needs; God can extend His vision throughout creation, knowing the past, present, and future of each and every step in the Great Chain. Thus only God, Who "sees with equal eye . . . / A hero perish, or a sparrow fall, / Atoms or systems into ruin hurl'd, / And now a bubble burst, and now a world," is able to understand the integral relationship between these apparently disparate events and then to act for the good of all. What may appear to be whim or even malice is really benevolence, systematically applied. Dickinson pitches the cadences of her verse against Pope's in order explicitly to refute such a claim; and she uses balanced Augustan diction to assert not approval, but derision. God acts without any intent, "inserting Here—a Sun— / There—leaving out a Man—." What appears to be whim and malice is just that—whim and malice, the "Gambol of His Authority."

Although *An Essay on Man* commanded a great deal of respect when it was published (1732–34), even then some readers were not prepared to accept an argument that limitations and miseries in this world all served some larger plan for good. Immediate pain was more telling than the merely hypothetical benefits that only God could see. By Emily Dickinson's day, the very notion of a Great Chain of Being had become difficult to sustain. Geologists had discovered the existence of great glacial ages in the ancient past, which had swept away entire categories of created life. Eons earlier, enormous dinosaurs had dominated the Connecticut valley, but such mighty animals as these had become entirely extinct. Even creatures whose characteristics seemed too human for comfort had flourished long ago and been extinguished. By the midpoint of the nineteenth century, then, it had become clear that God does not create out of expansive joy, filling in each minute step in a Chain of Being so that the cosmos will be blessed with unity and harmony. Indeed, at just the time when Dickinson was writing, the venerable tradition of the Great Chain of Being was coming to an end. The new discoveries in geology and comparative anatomy suggested that many links in such a Chain have been destroyed. Not effusive, God is more like a "thrifty" amateur or dilettante: He may call entities into existence as a way of amusing Himself, but when He doesn't like them or they fail to function in quite the way He had hoped, He "effaces" entire classes, unwilling to squander space in Heaven on His mistakes. Although these "Perished Patterns" may protest, the ruthless forces of creation and destruction proceed "Perturbless."

Dickinson's poetic method here, discovering a major author who has acted as apologist for a vision of the world she wishes to refute and then appropriating some central element of that writer's work for her own uses, is consistent with her practices elsewhere, for there is a powerful intertextual component in Emily Dickinson's poetry. The Bible was the text she most consistently sought to undermine—God's only published work. Yet she also refuted the usual notions of conversion by attacking the tradition of the bride of Christ and deflecting her poetry off the literature of courtship and the novel of seduction. She rejected Wordsworth's claim that the mind of man was the "mirror" of what was most beautiful in nature. She set herself in opposition to Emerson's optimistic view of nature by appropriating the word "Landscape" (a word Thoreau also used); and then she redefined "Landscape" in the narrowest, most mutilated terms. She averred that an accurate map of the relationship between the immanent world and the transcendent realm would look more like Poe's Gothic scenery than the epic models proposed by Dante and Milton; indeed, she even went so far as to claim that the epic model is true only by inversion—Heaven is really like the place Dante and Milton had described as Hell. Enormously self-conscious as a literary craftsman, Dickinson composed her work in the context both of a long religious tradition and of an Anglo-American literary tradition. The *line* of her poetry wrestles principally against the meters of hymnody, and its dissonances strain against a reader's expectation for true rhyme. Yet in the case of the specific works and authors to which her verse responds, it is not the *line* that she wishes to refashion but the *vision* and the *valenced language* in which that vision is rendered. Above all other things, Emily Dickinson desired to confirm her own assessment of the world. Her poetry could serve that end only insofar as she could maintain precise control over the word itself and permit no spurious mythic implications to soften the brutal truth of her existential vision.

Her concern for raw honesty was nowhere more urgent than in this examination of God's empiricism, perhaps because the "scientific" religion of mid-nineteenth-century "natural theology" dominated the milieu in which she lived. Emerson and Milton could at least be put to rest unopened on the bookshelf; however, she mingled daily with dictatorial Trinitarians. Thus her uniquely personal concerns were directly assailed by this tradition, its world view, and its assumptions about language. It is perhaps ironic, then—Amherst, Massachusetts, being such a small New England town—that her private anxieties coincided so exactly with the inexorable movement of intellectual concerns elsewhere in America and Europe. Having been reared in the antique beliefs of latter-day Puritanism, Emily Dickinson anticipated many of the puzzles that were to bedevil the modern world.

The most recent experiment in God's vast laboratory is mankind. Will He tire of us, too? Shatter us as a bored child breaks his toys, cast us into an extinction so deep that creation can go on as if we had never existed? Not Heaven; not Hell; not even palpable chaos; but utter obliteration of the very fact that once there were such things as human beings.

Dickinson looked to the Bible as well as to nature in her search to understand the terms of God's experiments with mankind. Jacob's wrestle revealed a cowardly God Who retreated from us forever rather than risk combat again; the arbitrary demand that Abraham make a blood sacrifice of his only son (never mind that the command was canceled at the final moment) showed the Divinity baring Its fangs like a Mastiff, bloodthirsty and unpredictable. Even the great prophet Moses had been subjected to a series of cruel experiments, and the poet could draw conclusions about the Deity from these, too.

It always felt to me—a wrong
To that Old Moses—done—
To let him see—the Canaan—
Without the entering—

And tho' in soberer moments—
No Moses there can be
I'm satisfied—the Romance
In point of injury—

Surpasses sharper stated—
Of Stephen—or of Paul—
For these—were only put to death—
While God's adroiter will

> *On Moses—seemed to fasten*
> *With tantalizing Play*
> *As Boy—should deal with lesser Boy—*
> *To prove ability.*
>
> *The fault—was doubtless Israel's—*
> *Myself—had banned the Tribes—*
> *And ushered Grand Old Moses*
> *In Pentateuchal Robes*
>
> *Upon the Broad Possession*
> *But titled Him—to see—*
> *Old Man on Nebo! Late as this—*
> *My justice bleeds—for Thee!*
>
> (#597;
> var. "But titled Him—to see—")

Here is the same streak of childish malice that is revealed in "It's easy to invent a Life—." Dickinson had been taught that before the era of Christ, God acted as a force for justice, swift and ruthless, eye for eye and tooth for tooth. Yet banishing the faithful prophet Moses while allowing the quarrelsome, complaining tribes of Israel to enter the Promised Land demonstrates no more than the "tantalizing Play" of unrestrained willfulness. Since there is no acceptable explanation for such behavior in a just God, He must be unjust—mean, perhaps, and petty and sadistic. What is more, He is insecure in His authority. It does not suffice the Lord to know that He is almighty. He needed to create us so that He would have some means for affirming His sense of His own importance: over and over He must "prove ability" by taunting humanity with its helplessness before His power. In the case of Moses, God heightened the enjoyment of His pleasure by forcing the old man to look upon the Land of Canaan he could never enter: "Thou shalt see the land before thee," He said as He commanded Moses to climb Mount Nebo and survey the horizon; "but thou shalt not go thither unto the land which I give the children of Israel" (Deuteronomy 32:52). The same God Who eludes the force of our eye / I by hiding His face from us played upon Moses's visionary power with perverse skill: the old man gazed out obediently over the forbidden kingdom, and only then was he allowed to die.

The story of Moses is significant because his anguish is a type for future human experience. God always takes pleasure in teaching us what is good by taunting us with satisfactions that we have been denied. *"Water, is taught by thirst. / Land—by the Oceans passed. / Transport—by throe— / Peace—by it's battles told— / Love, by Memorial Mold— / Birds, by the Snow"* (#135). The poet's willingness to address pain is a way of responding to God's practice: *"I like a look of Agony,"* Dickinson wrote, *"Because I know it's true— / Men do not sham Convulsion, / Nor simulate, a Throe— / The Eyes glaze once—and that is Death— / Impossible to feign / The Beads upon the Forehead / By homely Anguish strung"* (#241).

The notion of some desirable Heaven is essential, then, to this part of God's experiment with mankind: He uses it not to instruct us or to deliver us, but merely to raise hope so that He can snatch hope away. *"The nearest Dream recedes—unrealized— / The Heaven we chase, / Like the June Bee—before the School Boy, / Invites the Race— / Stoops—to an easy Clover— / Dips— evades—teases—deploys— / Then—to the Royal Clouds / Lifts his light Pinnace— / Heedless of the Boy— / Staring—bewildered—at the mocking sky—"* (#319). Heaven is never *"now."* Its authentic sign can be found only in those delights of nature that dip and sway always just beyond our reach. The Lord hid His own face from "bewildered" Jacob; in the same way, the quest for this unattainable Heaven leaves us all "Staring—bewildered—at the mocking sky," God's derisive joke, endlessly re-enacted in the natural world.

Insofar as Heaven can mean "happiness," like God, it will always exist in a state of eclipse.

> *"Heaven"—is what I cannot reach!*
> *The Apple on the Tree—*
> *Provided it do hopeless—hang—*
> *That— "Heaven" is—to Me!*
>
> *The Color, on the Cruising Cloud—*
> *The interdicted Land—*
> *Behind the Hill—the House behind—*
> *There—Paradise—is found!*
>
> *Her teazing Purples—Afternoons—*
> *The credulous—decoy—*
> *Enamored—of the Conjuror—*
> *That spurned us—Yesterday!*
>
> (#239)

This poem is a compendium of the Judaeo-Christian experience. Its consummate woe is that of all the alluring delights it mentions, only the Edenic apple actually hung near enough for man and woman to grasp it and be lost: with this ancient irony the poem is begun. The "Cruising Cloud" recollects God's sign leading Moses through the wilderness—by day a pillar of cloud and by night a pillar of fire. Yet "the interdicted Land—" affirms God's inexplicable cruelty in forbidding the prophet's entry into Canaan. "Behind the Hill—the House behind—" echoes Jesus's repeated references to His Father's many mansions, the only "House" that can never be seen by human eye. Heaven's "teazing Purples" recalls Christ's stipulated ransom of our souls. Yet "Purples" can perplex our expectations, the color of mourning and the color of majesty: when Jesus was condemned to die, "they put on him a purple robe, And said, Hail, King of the Jews!" (John 19:2–3.) The ultimate "Conjuror," Jesus demonstrated His imperial power by rising magically from the dead; once risen, Christ "spurned us" by retreating to Heaven as His Father had done before Him. Are we to praise Him, then, or to sorrow in His having come only to depart?

This is not a catalogue of unrelieved pain. It is something worse—the chronicle of a cycle of torture that will last until the end of time. God restrains His cruelty just long enough to give us optimism and ensnare our trust; once we relax our vigilance, He strikes us and wounds again. Yet as soon as we recoil and turn away, God woos us with the blandishments of eternal life and happiness. Like a cat with a mouse, He prefers torture to instant execution.

Beneath all other patterns of divine "providence" is this elemental structure—this pattern of taunting uncertainty that is laid out before us in the Bible and reaffirmed by the experience of every human life; and the signs of it can be found throughout the created world. Here, then, is the ultimate target of all Dickinson's investigations of narrative form and structuring orders; and taken together, the poems that expose God's invariable experiment constitute a biting, scathing, bitterly satirical refutation of the Biblical claim that humans can always discern a pattern of benevolent providential history in the workings of the world.

Pagan peoples of the northern climate often held ritual celebrations on the shortest winter's day and made offerings to the gods to implore the sun's return from exile. However, by Dickinson's time sophisticated scientists had observed the periodicity of the planets through their telescopes, and they inferred that spring will always come: this fear of unending cold was but a naïve, primitive fantasy, they affirmed. Yet the poet recalled God's frigid, punitive nature and His promises in the Bible, and she was not lulled into complaisance by the "certainties" of modern science; although Christ had affirmed the Father's loving watchfulness, He had also assured us that the stars will fall and the world will end. In such a pitiless laboratory as this world, it would be insanity to count on spring's return.

> *A little Madness in the Spring*
> *Is wholesome even for the King,*
> *But God be with the Clown—*
> *Who ponders this tremendous scene—*
> *This whole Experiment of Green—*
> *As if it were his own!*
>
> (#1333)

The conjunction of "Madness," "King," and "Clown" recalls Shakespeare's *King Lear*, summoning up the faint memory of that drama's tumultuous world, a raging scenery of storms and devastation. The nihilistic vision of Shakespeare's play affirmed that tragedy is not personal but universal—that it inheres in nature's impassive violence, death inflicted upon all in some merely random order. Interestingly, Dickinson left evidence on a surviving work sheet of her care in choosing the phrase "Experiment of Green." She posited about a dozen alternatives; however, the one she pointedly favored as her second choice was "Apocalypse of Green." Perhaps "Spring" would not always be the beginning of life. Perhaps, one day, it would be the end.

If every spring tempts us with the "Madness" of believing we can master our fate and find life eternal, every dawn heralds another day in which God can test His inventions. And both are emblems not of hope, but of horror.

> *"Morning"—means "Milking"—to the Farmer—*
> *Dawn—to the Teneriffe—*
> *Dice—to the Maid—*
> *Morning means just Risk—to the Lover—*
> *Just revelation—to the Beloved—*
>
> *Epicures—date a Breakfast—by it—*
> *Brides—an Apocalypse—*
> *Worlds—a Flood—*
> *Faint-going Lives—Their lapse from Sighing—*
> *Faith—The Experiment of Our Lord—*
>
> (#300)

Emily Dickinson wrote a great many poems of definition, especially in the later years of her life, and virtually all of these have the same formulaic beginning, "X is," as in *"Bliss is the plaything of the child—"* (#1553) and *"Fame is the one that does not stay—"* (#1475). *"'Heaven'—is what I cannot reach!"* might fall into this general category: "Heaven" is the focus of attention, and the poem opens by attempting to ascertain its nature. However, *"'Morning'—means 'Milking'"* is not such a poem. The principal object of investigation here is not "Morning"; "Morning" is no more than a medium of communication between those on earth and the transcendent force that lies behind the material world. God communicates with us through such "signs" as this, and it is the *meaning* of God's message that the poem tracks.

Initially, the otherworldly focus of the verse is blurred. The first stanza is devoted to quotidian meanings of sunrise. For the "Farmer," time to get up and milk the cows; for the unchanging mountains, no more than "Dawn," the beginning of another day. Curiously, however, in the last three lines of this stanza, the poet introduces terminology that she employs elsewhere in a religious context. "Dice" is the game of chance that we play for salvation: "*Soul, Wilt thou toss again? / By just such a hazard / Hundreds have lost indeed— / But tens have won an all—*" (#*139*). "Revelation" is what we gain if we win this game—a reward described in the Biblical book that bears that name. Yet here, these terms seem to turn explicitly away from God's realm: the "Maid," the "Lover," and the "Beloved" are all engaged in the game of courtship. The sexual tonality, though clearly present, is tantalizingly ambiguous. Does the "Maid" gamble her affection or her chastity? Why is morning a "Risk" for the "Lover"? Is he stealing away from an illicit assignation? And what is the meaning of "revelation" to the "Beloved"? Is it merely the discovery of her admirer's identity, or is it that unique face-to-face encounter by which she is initiated into sexual pleasure? These ambiguities are made even more vexing by the poet's use of religious terms. Does our relationship with God hold such uncertainty as this—such a perverse mixture of orgastic delight and fatal loss?

The first line of the second stanza momentarily relieves the tension: perhaps we need not attempt to disentangle this mélange of powerful implications, after all. Yet this temporary relief merely mimics the pattern of all of God's dealings with us—a cycle of torture and reprieve—so after the brief respite, the poem delves back deeply into anguish.

For "Brides" the "Apocalypse" surely means new knowledge, hitherto forbidden; for the bride of Christ, an acquaintance with the New Jerusalem. Yet before the reward can come, there must be a destruction of all the earth, "the abomination of desolation. . . . For then shall be great tribulation, such as was not since the beginning of the world to this time, no, nor ever shall be. . . . The stars shall fall from heaven, and the powers of the heavens shall be shaken: And then shall appear the sign of the Son of man in heaven: and then shall all the tribes of the earth mourn" (Matthew 24:15, 21, 29–30). Death by Fire. In this poem the intimation of Christ as the bridegroom waiting would surely tip the balance of dual implication in "Apocalypse" away from destruction and toward glory if the following line did not hearken back to God's experiment with Noah. Death by Water. What "Morning" means to "Worlds" is another chance for annihilation, "a Flood—." Certainly this is the deep memory that haunts nature's musings upon the periodic devastation of winter: "*And so there was a Deluge— / And swept the World away—*" (#*403*). By this point, the poem pushes so strongly in both of the two opposite directions, destruction and rescue, that the penultimate line defies certain understanding. Does "Morning" mean death to "Faint-going Lives"; does it mean relief from the pain of a difficult night and new strength to greet the next day, "Their lapse from Sighing"; or does it mean salvation, the dawning of *God's* New Day, when all things are confirmed in everlasting life?

In a sense, the entire complex movement of the poem is directed at its final line, for here the vexed ambiguities come to culmination. "Faith" sees each new " 'Morning' " as a renewal of "The *Experiment* of Our Lord." This phrase so clearly echoes the formulation by which we affix dates, "the Year of our Lord," that "Experiment" summons recollections of the God-Man, unique among the Deity's inventions. Perhaps it pleased the Master Scientist to create this unique entity, the Self-as-Man—a daring invention indeed—a Son to bear the burden of all sin. Yet in Dickinson's time as in our own, when a scientific experiment was conducted upon an animal and the animal was badly maimed, it was killed at the experiment's conclusion. Then the scientist wrote at the end of his report, *"The animal was sacrificed,"* an invariable formulation. So it was with the God-man — sacrificed—the "Perished Pattern" of a species that lived and died with but one exemplar, Jesus Christ. Although this murder of the Deity is a horror from which we cringe, these darker implications of "Experiment" cannot be dispelled from the verse, for they are essential to an understanding of the poem's last line. Without Christ's sacrifice upon the cross, "Faith" in the new birth after death could quite literally not have come into existence.

And as it was for Christ, so shall it be for every human being: before possible resurrection, certain death. Every day we must contemplate death's immanence; every day, then, is an "Experiment" worked upon our peace of mind. God worries us, strains our beliefs with tribulations, taunts us with death, offers a brief reprieve only to taunt us with death again. In the great bell jar of earth and hovering atmosphere, no invention provides the Master Scientist with so much diversion as this game of cat-and-mouse He plays with humankind to test our "Faith." Will "Morning" mean oblivion or eternal life? *"Do we die— / Or is this Death's Experiment— / Reversed—in Victory?"* (#550).

Sometimes Dickinson sought to capture the perverse regularity and precision in the pattern of God's manipulation of the creatures He has invented. All of us are subjected to the same anguished equation: perhaps God despises us, or perhaps He thinks humans so trivial that His abuse needs no vindication. For whatever reason, the same alternation of pain and relief can be cited to describe all human existence. The following poem might be a riddle asking the identity of "it" in the first line ("[I]t was like . . .") if the course of the poem did not make the answer so agonizingly clear: "It" is the underlying pattern of life—God's "Experiment" with mankind.

> 'Twas like a Maelstrom, with a notch,
> That nearer, every Day,
> Kept narrowing it's boiling Wheel
> Until the Agony
>
> Toyed coolly with the final inch
> Of your delirious Hem—

And you dropt, lost,
When something broke—
And let you from a Dream—

As if a Goblin with a Guage—
Kept measuring the Hours—
Until you felt your Second
Weigh, helpless, in his Paws—

And not a Sinew—stirred—could help,
And sense was setting numb—
When God—remembered—and the Fiend
Let go, then, Overcome—

As if your Sentence stood—pronounced—
And you were frozen led
From Dungeon's luxury of Doubt
To Gibbets, and the Dead—

And when the Film had stitched your eyes
A Creature gasped "Reprieve"!
Which Anguish was the utterest—then—
To perish, or to live?

(#414)

The essence of these three experiments is mankind's inescapable progress toward death: death comes near, threatens the worst; inexplicably, death retreats. Over and over the ritual is enacted. The subject of the experiment cannot escape, nor can she affect the outcome (eventually, everyone dies). Thus sooner or later the experiment will be brought to a conclusion. Instead of retreating, death will continue its lurid advance until the unknown obliterates everything else: "The animal was sacrificed." The array of forces at work within the poem is relatively simple; the antagonists are time and mortality, God's ubiquitous instruments, and the protagonist is the speaker, one who has experienced the drama enacted within the poem and can describe its structure. In a sense, the heroine can never win: the conflict has already been defined as one in which eventually she must lose self to God in death. The central issue, then, is whether the speaker can find a way to convert the situation into a process whereby the subjects of God's experiment can become more than merely passive victims. Thus the function of this narrative is to demonstrate that the speaker can at least hold an integral self together until the inevitable end and that she can wrest meaning from her own travails and convey that meaning to others.

The speaker explicitly addresses the reader, "you," and without assuming the least hint of a didactic tone, the poem undertakes a clearly didactic as-signment. Moreover, although the Voice is not proleptic, the poem functions in many of the same ways as the proleptic poetry, for the speaker communi-cates in the aftermath of some severe trial. Nowhere is Dickinson's desire to speak as "Representative" more clearly demonstrated: everyone must endure the process that the verse describes; most do not understand the ordeal that they are going through; many attempt ineffectually to alleviate pain with hope and faith. This speaker has cast such remedies aside. She has accepted the full force of the Lord's assaults; she has not submitted to despair or sunk to pleading; instead, she has plunged into confusion, anxiety, and danger. By the conclusion, she has discovered the full scope and shape of our misery. Through her courage, the speaker has won the only kind of freedom that is available on earth, and it is this freedom that the speaker offers to the reader. Thus the aesthetic structures of the poem serve a crucial moral function: they reiterate the progress of the travail in an orderly sequence that allows a reader to experience it safely—vicariously and coherently—without the full force of anxiety and chaos that the speaker was constrained to endure; and they give the clearest evidence of victory in their superbly controlled modu-lation away from despair toward power. Every segment of the verse succeeds in conveying one or another aspect of the entire lesson, yet each succeeds in a distinct way. This is how it would have been for "you," the speaker says, if you had looked, as I have, upon the cold, systematic torment of God's ways with mankind. So the poem begins.

The first episode (contained in the first two stanzas) accomplishes two things: it enables us to feel the enormity of dread and danger that are con-cealed in the patterns that govern everyday existence, and it demonstrates the potentially disintegrating effect of this nightmare reality upon individual con-sciousness. As she has done elsewhere, Dickinson communicates terror by radical compression of imagery and by techniques of spatial disorientation. At the outset, the speaker's location is deliberately obscure: she seems sur-realistically suspended over a whirlpool, held aloft, perhaps, only by the force of her determination not to drop into the perilous unknown. A reader of Dickinson's poetry will have encountered the "Maelstrom" elsewhere—"*in the Sea*" (#502) or even "*in the Sky*" (#721). It is the swirling, sucking force of God's intention to absorb us and annihilate each distinct individual ego. Yet the "Maelstrom" of this poem is unique, for it has a "notch"; it is not merely a "boiling Wheel" of water or air, but a cog in some strange cosmic machine. The technical term for a wheel with a notch is a "ratchet wheel," and Dickinson's own dictionary defined the word "ratchet" in terms of its function within a timepiece: "In a *watch,* a small tooth at the bottom of the fusee or barrel, which stops it in winding up." In short, Dickinson has con-flated the deadly funnel of the "Maelstrom" with the barrel of a watch stem, thereby locating us at the dark heart of God's "Design," *inside the Watch* that stands as proof of His existence while it simultaneously ticks our lives toward death. There is a terrible, ineluctable truth, then, in the surrealistic image with which the poem opens: the resistless force of time sucking us into oblivion. This is the essential meaning of "Design," the only verity that can be discovered through this journey to the dark heart of creation. God is a savage Scientist Whose natural laws are so obscene that their implications can be appreciated only with the excruciating difficulty and anxiety that the verse engenders.

As she has done so often before, Dickinson introduces the notion of a reduction to zero. The "narrowing Wheel" gets smaller and smaller as it approaches the moment of the drop, and the menace of this inexorable, slow constriction threatens to overwhelm coherence. The moment of unparalleled hazard—the speaker hovering uncertainly over a void, forced to recognize that God stalks her, taunts her, sets traps to ensnare her—delivers an insight too devastating to be absorbed with impunity. Sanity itself falters at the realization, and the integrity of the ego begins to disintegrate. Thus the speaker feels her own emotions not as part of a coherent self, but as if they were elements of the outside world. "Agony" is projected onto the whirlpool that circles below; and although only a human being can feel "delirious," here that state is attributed to the "Hem" of the speaker's dress. Such a scattering of identity recalls the slow winnowing process of death: were it to proceed unchecked, the self would be atomized into extinction—whether by death or madness is irrelevant. Thus at no point in the poem is individual coherence more desperately in peril than here, at the outset, when the systematic ritual of laceration strains our power of comprehension to the limit.

Still, even at the beginning we can understand certain crucial things. The predatory implement can be defined as a "Maelstrom, with a notch"—a combination of the natural and the mechanical. Such a way of naming it asserts that the very distinction between the two categories is specious and that nature can sometimes act as a machine to perform God's experiments with mankind. What is more, we are able to understand that "every Day" catastrophe draws nearer. This is an experiment conducted in part by the passage of time, which is why the heart of darkness is the inside of a deadly watch. Initially, it would appear that time can be a force acting only against the interests of humanity, every dawn a new beginning only insofar as it announces yet another enactment of God's investigations. Indeed, the movement of the poem mimics repetitive movement through time. The second episode reiterates the action of the first, the third follows the pattern of the second—just as over and over God torments us with the same, unchanging specter of death. One challenge, then, is to wrest the power of time away from God and to put it to our own advantage.

Success in responding to this challenge begins to occur in the second episode (recorded in stanzas three and four). Like the first, this transaction has its surrealistic element, the bizarre linking of the "Goblin" from fantasy land with the almost industrial precision implied by the "Guage." It is the same experiment as before, and again it is ghoulish and sadistic. God's methods have not altered, and it is clear that for Him, the passage of time has made no difference. Even so, changes have occurred in the terms of the poem. The very fact of having withstood the shocking insight of the first two stanzas has given the speaker strength: there is understanding and a certain capacity for analytic thinking here that were not present during the first episode, and these gains are reflected in the structure of the verse. Although metrical irregularities remain (line 12 is short by one foot), the stanzas have become uniform, and the gasping quality of the second stanza is no longer present; moreover, the narrative content is clearer—on the most literal level, it is easier to understand what is taking place. Thus in this second scenario it becomes apparent, as it was not in the first, that these are not extraordinary occasions, but merely part of the grotesque back-and-forth movement toward death that all must follow. Probably there was no actual "Maelstrom" (" 'Twas *like* a Maelstrom"); yet the stunning force of condensed insight at the opening of the poem obscured that fact. Here, however, it is entirely clear that there was no actual "Goblin": rather, the events were so contrary to our usual understanding of life that it was "*as if* a Goblin with a Guage— / Kept measuring the Hours—." Finally, we can even begin to appreciate the extent to which God Himself was implicated in the outrage—if only by His failure to intervene more quickly and halt the torture.

When we reach the last two stanzas, we can recognize that the principal function of the poem as a series of verbal structures has been to reconstruct the implications of the fact that the entire universe stands under perpetual "Sentence" of death. Fittingly, the first twenty-three lines follow only the loosest syntactic structure: true, taken together they make one very long sentence; yet the subordinate clauses are jumbled and unfocused—as if the grammatical structures we have invented to discuss ordinary happenings cannot quite encompass this vision of life. However, the drive toward coherence and mastery begins to accelerate when we reach the last two stanzas: the verse is still tinged with Gothicism, but the narrative line becomes entirely comprehensible; and the clearly articulated question at the conclusion— "Which Anguish was the utterest—then— / To perish, or to live?"—stands in bold contrast to the syntactic disjointedness of the preceding lines. By this time, the speaker has become an integrated self with the courage and vision to grasp the nettle of despair. Life, the world, all of creation: these are no more than different rooms of the same prison. Once we have accepted the horror of this insight, we can even extract power from it.

So long as we anticipate release, hope for freedom or happiness or deliverance, our ordeal will be prolonged. So long as we experience life primarily as something snatched from the greedy claws of predatory death, life can never be more than the sustained "Anguish" of waiting for another mortal crisis to occur. So long as we entertain false hope, time will always be our enemy because time merely prolongs our misery while inexorably drawing us closer to the moment we fear. We can use time to our advantage only when we relinquish all of these forms of passivity and turn our energies instead to an analysis of God and His methods. No matter how many reprieves we are granted, we can never alter the fundamental terms of God's experiment; however, we can answer the question that is posed at the conclusion of the poem. "To live" *in peril and on God's terms* is as much an "Anguish" as "To perish." There is nothing to choose between them. Thus the only sensible course is to ignore the experiment entirely, thereby making ourselves immune to its torments. We cannot escape death, but we can escape the *fear* of death.

Implicitly, the poem offers much the same counsel as "A Clock stopped—," the tactic of "cool—concernless No—." Recognizing the twisted sadism of God's nature, recognizing His promises as no more than empty bribes that intensify our pain, we can turn away from His blandishments with justified pride and self-esteem. He will always retain the power to kill us, but He can torture us with fears and unfulfilled yearnings only to the extent that we allow Him to do so.

In the case of the poet, the same kind of experiment is conducted along somewhat different lines.

> The Soul has Bandaged moments—
> When too appalled to stir—
> She feels some ghastly Fright come up
> And stop to look at her—
>
> Salute her—with long fingers—
> Caress her freezing hair—
> Sip, Goblin, from the very lips
> The Lover—hovered—o'er—
> Unworthy, that a thought so mean
> Accost a Theme—so—fair—
>
> The soul has moments of Escape—
> When bursting all the doors—
> She dances like a Bomb, abroad,
> And swings upon the Hours,
>
> As do the Bee—delirious borne—
> Long Dungeoned from his Rose—
> Touch Liberty—then know no more,
> But Noon, and Paradise—

> The Soul's retaken moments—
> When, Felon led along,
> With shackles on the plumed feet,
> And staples, in the Song,
>
> The Horror welcomes her, again,
> These are not brayed of Tongue—
>
> (#512)

Again compression is used to convey a surrealistic ordeal; yet the forces at work here are more directly violent that those of "'Twas like a Maelstrom." In that poem, liberty could be achieved when any individual's own fear of death had been conquered: since the limitation was internal, anyone might win his or her own freedom. Here, however, God acts more directly and constrictively.

The image of "Bandaged moments—" captures the several principal issues of the verse. The displacement of the bandage from the "Soul" herself to the temporal term of imprisonment, "moments," suggest a force sufficiently brutal to fracture the integrity of consciousness. Yet such a blow to coherence is not of central importance here. The overriding issues are those of direct injury and literal constraint. If God cannot coerce us by threats, He can always retreat to His residual source of mastery: He is more powerful than we are; He can weaken us with sickness; if all else fails, He can execute us. Thus it is God's power to injure that this poem addresses, a power that can act quite literally as a prison.

Perhaps it is the power of vision—the poet's eye / I—that God most explicitly attacks. When the eyes are "Bandaged," one cannot see; and this speaker only "feels" the actions of the first stanzas, whereas the "Fright" is able "to *look* at her—." Yet "Bandaged" suggests some more general and inclusive wounding, the reiteration of God's attack upon Jacob that may come in any number of specific afflictions, sicknesses, or losses. Blinded and wounded, the "Soul" is probably also bound with shackles of some sort. Although it is true that she is "too appalled to stir—," the third and fourth stanzas make it clear that this alone does not detain her. Perhaps she is "Bandaged" with an anticipatory winding cloth—prepared for burial before the final stroke has fallen, forced to endure the familiarity and blatantly sexual fondling of some icy freak, a bridegroom divested of any allure or a deadly beau preparing to abduct her to "Polar Caskets" of absolute cold. And to all of these the "Soul" makes no response—clearly, the poem implies, because she has no opportunity to do so.

Unlike "'Twas like a Maelstrom," this verse does not grope for terrifying imagery to capture the horror that is latent in everyday existence; thus the Gothic elements here are not verbalized as similes. Rather, this poem depicts actual crises whose terrible nature cannot easily be rendered through ordinary diction and everyday imagery.

During the "moments of Escape—" when she manages to elude her warden, the "Soul" demonstrates the nature of the power that has been manacled and imprisoned; she is like a "Bomb," capable of "bursting . . . doors" and dancing abroad. Again there is an intertextual element at work here; however, this poem refers itself not to the verse of some other poet but to Dickinson's own earlier poem "*I taste a liquor never brewed—*" (#214). It poignantly recalls times that were filled with the innocent joys of exuberant, unfettered creativity; and these "moments of Escape" re-enact that flight of the "Inebriate of Air," drunk with the power of composition, "*Reeling—thro endless summer days— / From inns of Molten Blue— / When 'Landlords' turn the drunken Bee / Out of the Foxglove's door— / When Butterflies—renounce their 'drams'— / I shall but drink the more! / Till Seraphs swing their snowy Hats— / And Saints—to windows run— / To see the little Tippler / Leaning against the—Sun—*" (var. "*Leaning against the—Sun—*"). Evidently this reeling, carefree flight, gaining the upper air by the sheer force of poetic invention, grasping "Noon, and Paradise—" or "Leaning against the—Sun—," haunts God's peace of mind.

Because He cannot tolerate the poet who is at liberty to soar and sing, God stalks the "Soul" until she is "retaken" and "plumed feet" are chained. Every time God's withering force lays hold of the "Soul," her song is mutilated: the second stanza was painfully attenuated while the perverse courtship was conducted; now that the "Soul" is imprisoned again and can sing no more, the poem breaks abruptly off with but two lines of a stanza that will never see completion and a "Tongue" that can do no more than "bray." God's antipathy to song is puzzling. To be sure, the Divinity will respond when Its authority is attacked—when the poet explodes Christ's false promises and renames the signs of nature. Yet God's action here is not characterized as some response to the poet's explicit threat or challenge. Perhaps it is the poet's power to *raise self* from earthly limitations that God cannot tolerate. In this poem, for example, there is an eerie reversal of Christ's mission: the "Soul" is in prison as Christ was entombed; she gains freedom and "Noon" just as He awoke from the dead in Resurrection and rose into Heaven. Yet the "Soul" is "retaken." It is as if Christ could be pried out of Paradise and crucified once again—"staples" in His body, pinning Him to yet another cross—for after the exhilaration of the Soul's flight, her "retaken moments" have just this quality of outrage and violation.

God may be many things—the Master Craftsman of the world, a Merchant bartering for souls, a Travel Agent, a Lawyer, a Judge, a Scientist toiling in His laboratory, "*Burglar! Banker—Father!*" (#49)—but there is little to suggest that He might also be the Master Singer. When God's musical abilities are invoked, the result is cacophony and discord: He "fumbles . . .

at the Keys" (#*315*). In the poet God discovers a creature of His own making who can sing and dance as He cannot. How can it be that He Who called a universe into being is unable to do what the least of His creatures can do with effervescent ease? The mystery taunts and goads. And Dickinson's best-known poem about the Lord's vindictiveness toward poets opens with a line that formulates a derisive and ironic response to this question.

Gigantic and powerful, yet slow of wit, God shakes a diminutive bird, turning it around and around perplexedly. Then, like a child with a wonderful toy or a magical animal, He breaks it open in greedy irritation: where does the music come from?

> *Split the Lark—and you'll find the Music—*
> *Bulb after Bulb, in Silver rolled—*
> *Scantily dealt to the Summer Morning*
> *Saved for your Ear when Lutes be old.*
>
> *Loose the Flood—you shall find it patent—*
> *Gush after Gush, reserved for you—*
> *Scarlet Experiment! Sceptic Thomas!*
> *Now, do you doubt that your Bird was true?*
>
> (#*861*)

At its lowest level, this is a violent nursery tale: like the doltish farm boy who owned a goose that could lay golden eggs, God has a creature whose talents He cannot comprehend. Partly out of impatience (for the farm boy did not want to wait and receive only one egg every day; he wanted all his gold at once) and partly out of a primitive curiosity about the inner workings of the wonderful singer, God bisects the bird in the service of some clumsy scientific errand. And like the farm boy, God discovers no secrets—neither gold nor music, only gore and a "Lark" that can never give its magic gift again. If the rest of the poem left any doubt, the last line confirms that the speaker addresses herself to God: He has possessed Himself of the wondrous bird by the only means available to Him; He has killed it. Thus only at the gruesome conclusion does the now silent songster become "*your* Bird."

God's compulsion to maim and destroy is delivered here with vivid irony. The bird is a traditional emblem of spring, a sign of the promised rebirth after death. When God undertakes to "Split the Lark—," He discovers "Bulb after Bulb, in Silver rolled," as if He had cut open the root of a lily or a daffodil. And these vernal flowers, springing as they do from bulbs that have every appearance of death about them, are also traditional signs of Christ's promised eternal life. Yet when you slice a bulb in half, what you discover at its center is the tiny, delicate embryo of a flower: not the secret of the lily or the daffodil itself, only the promise of a bloom that now can never be. In dissecting these creatures of Eastertime, God cancels the very spirit of renewal and eternal life. Strangely enough, this God, "Father" and Creator, seems to know very little about the process of birth: His enterprises are tinged with the morbid curiosity of a scientist investigating the mysteries of pregnancy by dissecting the mother-to-be.

God's earlier experiments with mankind are recollected—the "Flood" that washed away the world in Noah's time and the God-man Who died in pain upon the cross—for the "Lark," split in two and spread-wing before the Deity is a grotesque re-enactment of the Crucifixion (Christ crying in bewilderment, "Eli, Eli, lama sabachthani? . . . My God, my God, why hast thou forsaken me?"). Yet if Christ did rise from the dead into Heaven, this "Lark" can never imitate His flight again.

But most of all, the poet / bird is a "Representative" victim of God's ignorance and dark violence. The Lord demands faith from each of us before we can enter into His kingdom, a faith in that which is *unseen*. After the Resurrection, one of the Apostles, Thomas, was told that Jesus had returned from the dead; but doubting Thomas refused to accept this information merely on faith. "Except I shall see in his hands the print of the nails, and put my finger into the print of the nails, and thrust my hand into his side, I will not believe." After eight days had passed, Christ appeared before Thomas and said, "Thomas, because thou hast seen me, thou hast believed: blessed are they that have not seen, and yet have believed" (John 20:25, 29). Nonetheless, for reasons Emily Dickinson could not begin to comprehend, God thinks it necessary to kill each and every one of us before He can determine whether we do, in fact, possess the requisite faith. Here He proceeds in a manner that seems a mockery of Christian custom. In ancient Rome, priests who were termed "augurs" foretold the future by observing the flights of birds or by interpreting the entrails of sacrificial animals. Now the Father of Christ Himself can be discovered following the practices of these pagans; and given His choice between observing a bird in flight or pawing through its bowels, He chooses blood. His "Scarlet Experiment" is invariable. He worries us, injures us, maims us, and concludes each life with death: "The animal was sacrificed."

What can He hope to find? Faith, like melody, is invisible—as "unseen" as the God Who left us long ago. The lingering, tragic irony is that like mankind, God, too, will remain "bewildered"—eternally dissatisfied in His pursuit of certitude—for He will never be able to *see* our golden faith. Thus God discovers only the "silver" that signifies a loss: the gold was there, but it lodged in the bird's song, not in her entrails. Still, God never stops the slaughter of those who might solace Him. And in the end, who could have proved devotion more ardently than the bird who longed after His company and made so much music to explicate her wrestle with the Lord?

When time has run out and the great epoch of creation is over, the brief equation that articulates God's dealings with mankind can best be formulated as a function of His way with songsters.

> At Half past Three, a single Bird
> Unto a silent Sky
> Propounded but a single term
> Of cautious melody.

> At Half past Four, Experiment
> Had subjugated test
> And lo, Her silver Principle
> Supplanted all the rest.

> At Half past Seven, Element
> Nor Implement, be seen —
> And Place was where the Presence was
> Circumference between.

(#1084)

The accuracy with which the bird's note is assigned an hour may have been suggested by Thomas Wentworth Higginson's essay "Water-Lilies": "Precisely at half past three, a song-sparrow above our heads gave one liquid trill."[23] Yet the abstract nouns throughout this poem compel the reader to infer that Dickinson is dealing here not with the material world, but with mythic time and archetypal events.

Christ died on the cross at three in the afternoon. The Resurrection did not occur until two days later, but by "Half past Three," the requisite offering to the Father had been made. Thus the warbler is emboldened to begin. Once before a "single Bird" had appeared in the aftermath of annihilation, but that earlier bird had pursued a silent mission: after the Flood, Noah sent out a dove to see whether the waters had subsided and death was done; when the bird left and returned bearing an olive branch, Noah knew that the oceans had begun to return to their shores, and when the bird left and returned not again, Noah knew that God's fury was spent and the time of Flood was over. Now that the God-man has come and gone, His barbaric sacrifice offered to the Father, *this* bird gathers courage to attempt to elicit some response, if only a tacit one, from the Being Who lives in a "silent Sky" above us. She has but one request, one stipulation, to make, and she offers it for His consideration with eloquent economy, as a "single term / Of cautious melody." Allow us to create, she pleads. Allow us to dance with quick feet; allow us to sing, even if You must remain silent Yourself; allow us to wrestle with all our might; allow us even to grasp "Noon, and Paradise" if we are able. Allow us to love you in our own way.

By "Half past Four," one hour of mythic time has passed. There is no way of computing how long a period that may be as we measure days and years on earth. All we can know with certainty is that it has been long enough for God's plan to have executed one more sequence of its mission. The "Experiment" has acquired a momentum of its own, and it seems to exist as an abstract force that is independent even of God. Like nature, "Experiment" is referred to as "she" or "her"; yet far from being a gentle mother, "Experiment" is an unloosed force of obliteration. Uncaring and unfeeling, it has an inexorable forward movement of creation and annihilation that offers no room for the individual plea, no opportunity for the kind of "melody" the bird has proposed. The golden song that might have been is rejected by the "silver Principle" according to which the "Experiment" runs its course; and as always in these encounters between transcendent force and the force of mankind, there is a falling away from grandeur. Yet the bird has spoken not merely for self, but as "Representative"; thus in having denied her request, God's plan has denied all poets and all mankind—"Supplanted all the rest"—rejected every tentative stirring that might be termed music.

By "Half past Seven," a terrible simplification of the universe has occurred: neither the bird ("Element") nor the melody ("Implement") remains. True, the force of the bird's simple song has been enough to establish a "Place" where its "Presence" used to be. But the "Place" is empty. And between this "Place" and the "single Bird" who has been so definitively swept away, there stands the prohibitive essence of God—"Circumference"—vacuous and empty, nothingness, zero. Although the Lord has refused song, He has nothing to put in its stead. *His* one creation is a term of existence that leads only to death and ultimate extinction.

By the conclusion of this poem, the sun has surely gone down: the era of God's Experiment with mankind has been completed. *The animal was sacrificed.* This is the way the world ends. Birds can make music no more.

III ◆ Love and the Love Poetry

There is a true covenant of faith, a New Testament of unstinting love and trust; however, Emily Dickinson found it not in the sacred traditions of Christianity, but in what has conventionally been termed "profane love"— the passion between a man and a woman: *"The Sweetest Heresy received / That Man and Woman know— / Each other's Convert— / Though the Faith accommodate but Two—"* (#387). God loves us by worrying our lives, testing faith, and concluding His experiment with an invariable sacrifice. Passionate love is a glorious repudiation of God's will to wound and annihilate. Constant and generous, it seeks to comfort, to shield from pain, to mend and make anew. *"Love is like Life—merely longer / Love is like Death, during the Grave / Love is the Fellow of the Resurrection / Scooping up the Dust and chanting 'Live'!"* (#491)

Not surprisingly, Jacob's wrestle finds its way into Dickinson's love poetry, too; here, however, it becomes not a striving for supremacy, but the consummation of love recorded in a subtle adaption of the *aubade*.

> *He was weak, and I was strong—then—*
> *So He let me lead him in—*
> *I was weak, and He was strong then—*
> *So I let him lead me—Home.*
>
> *'Twas'nt far—the door was near—*
> *'Twas'nt dark—for He went—too—*
> *'Twas'nt loud, for he said nought—*
> *That was all I cared to know.*
>
> *Day knocked—and we must part—*
> *Neither—was strongest—now—*
> *He strove—and I strove—too—*
> *We did'nt do it—tho'!*

(#190)

Not as uniformly strong as Dickinson's best love poetry, this verse nonetheless exhibits a number of themes and strategies that are repeated elsewhere in more effective form. For example, the balanced, reciprocal constructions

("He was weak . . . I was weak," "I was strong . . . He was strong," and "So He let me lead him in—. . . So I let him lead me—Home") give a syntactic representation for the underlying premise of most of her romantic poetry: whatever the superficial differences of size or age or worldly power, the lovers are essentially equal; neither wants to dominate, and their relationship is characterized by mutual magnanimity. "Home" may carry the primary meeting of domicile, but to one in love, the beloved's embrace is the ultimate resting place. God's destructive impulse culminates in a separation, the barrier of death: "*Dying—is a different way—/A Kind behind the Door*" (#335). By contrast, the lovers seek union; thus passion reverses God's destructive impulse, opens the "door," and even crosses the threshold, an image that conveys both emotional intimacy and delicately explicit sexuality. Indeed, passion vivid upon the beloved's countenance becomes its own radiance, a new sun to drive away the "dark," love thereby liberating the couple from the ordinary rules that attend the cycle of night and day. When Jacob wrestled at Peniel, the coming of the day signaled a necessary conclusion to the match; in the conventional *aubade,* dawn's rosy fingers demand an end to the tryst. In this poem, although the lovers both "strove" to submit to the usual demand for parting (a striving that reiterates the night's passionate encounter), they "did'nt do it . . .!" And their refusal to part overturns both Biblical precedent and the rules for courtly love.

The notion of striving is thus transformed in the love poetry: it alludes to the underlying affirmation of sexual love that permeates Dickinson's passionate verse, and it addresses the need that is felt by all lovers to fashion their own conventions for affection, a new "Saints' Lives." "*Read—Sweet—how others—strove— / Till we—are stouter— / What they—renounced— / Till we—are less afraid— / How many times they—bore the faithful witness— / Till we—are helped— / As if a Kingdom—cared! / . . . Brave names of Men— / And Celestial Women— / Passed out—of Record / Into—Renown!*" (#260)

Love imposes unique linguistic problems upon the poet; to some extent they are mirror images of the problems encountered in the nature poetry. There the dilemma consisted in finding words to render processes of annihilation and dissolution, the difficulty of naming an absence or a de-creating force or an unstructured abyss—"*the Visions [that] flitted Guido / Titian— never told— / Domenichino dropped his pencil— / Powerless to unfold—*" (#291). Here the artist is confronted with the need to capture desire's fervent immediacy or love's vital affirmation of life, having principally a language of quotidian experience at hand. So a poet-speaker laments: "*I found the words to every thought / I ever had—but One— / And that—defies me— / As a Hand did try to chalk the Sun / To Races—nurtured in the Dark— / How would your own—begin? / Can Blaze be shown in Cochineal— / Or Noon—in Mazarin?*" (#581). One of Dickinson's solutions is an inversion of the techniques that are employed in the nature poetry. The summer's dying fall is rendered in

verse that moves from uncadenced sound to silence: "*The murmuring of Bees
. . . The lower metres of the Year . . . Accent fades to interval*" (#1115). Love
begins with sensuous ripples of sound and expands to fill a universe with
harmony.

> *Many a phrase has the English language—*
> *I have heard but one—*
> *Low as the laughter of the Cricket,*
> *Loud, as the Thunder's Tongue—*
>
> *Murmuring, like old Caspian Choirs,*
> *When the Tide's a' lull—*
> *Saying itself in new inflection—*
> *Like a Whippowil—*
>
> *Breaking in bright Orthography*
> *On my simple sleep—*
> *Thundering it's Prospective—*
> *Till I stir, and weep—*
>
> *Not for the Sorrow, done me—*
> *But the push of Joy—*
> *Say it again, Saxon!*
> *Hush—Only to me!*
>
> (#276)

At first nature itself supplies the grandeur in counterpoint that becomes
increasingly complex: "Cricket" yields to the resonant echo of "Thunder's
Tongue"; the shifting tides of the Caspian Sea provide the several voiced in-
tonations of "Choirs"; and finally song itself appears in the "Whippowil—."
Hard upon this introduction of melody in mid-poem, the "bright Orthography" of verse is born. Yet—and this is the dilemma that most strenuously
vexes the poem—there is something second-best and even unnatural about
poetry's interruption here. The speaker awakens in a fitful flurry of tears—
not of sorrow, but of exquisite recollection and renewed longing. Roused thus
from warm sleep, would any woman want *poetry,* a formal and public mode
of expression? Or is not passion's best idiom a simple Anglo-Saxon diction
whispered close in the intimate dark while lovers strain the limits of delight:
"the push of Joy—/ Say it again, Saxon! / Hush—Only to me!"

Where love is concerned, language can do two things. Haltingly, perhaps,
and low, it can give immediate, direct expression to desire and affection. By
no means an end in themselves in this case, words become only one part in
the complex dialogue of glance, gesture, and act by which men and women
play passion out. The relationship itself, not the means by which it is con-

ducted, is of central importance; and in this most common art, the art of love, the poet enjoys little advantage over a candid but untutored suitor. Poetry *can* address love, of course; however, in this second case, language is more often descriptive rather than dynamic. Just as the word conferred power on Dickinson precisely because it could create an unchanging Voice that stands beyond time's reach, so her poetry could immortalize love; even more, if Dickinson could discover a language of power for *passion*, then the quality of the lovers' relationship could be revealed as a rebuking alternative to God's brutally selfish possessiveness. Thus might the "fall into language" be turned to advantage in treating even love. However, "Many a phrase has the English language—" raises a fundamental query. Which is better, the "bright Orthography" of love poetry or the "Hush" of love enacted? Might not the presence of the beloved and the possibility of intimacy's sweet delight displace the value even of verse? The tenacious shadow of this dilemma hangs over much of Dickinson's most poignant love poetry. Yet before art can be measured against life, art must come into being.

I ◆ *The Language of Love*

In Dickinson's work, the generosity of the lovers' affection and their willingness to treat each other as equals set them in direct opposition to God. Indeed, the force of their mutual devotion can overcome even the limitations that are imposed by the natural laws of the Divinity's devising, for lovers enjoy a privileged relationship to time and space.

> *Forever at His side to walk—*
> *The smaller of the two!*
> *Brain of His Brain—*
> *Blood of His Blood—*
> *Two lives—One Being—now—*
>
> *Forever of His fate to taste—*
> *If grief—the largest part—*
> *If joy—to put my piece away*
> *For that beloved Heart—*
>
> *All life—to know each other—*
> *Whom we can never learn—*

> And bye and bye—a Change—
> Called Heaven—
> Rapt Neighborhoods of Men—
> Just finding out—what puzzled us—
> Without the lexicon!

(#246)

This New Testament of passion and devotion replaces the Bible as a model for human behavior and mortal hope, and it is lovers who truly merit the language that has traditionally been reserved for the Divinity. Dickinson discovered an idiom of power for profane love by usurping God's language of transcendence.

The poem opens Edenically, invoking that moment in the ancient past when love began—Eve and Adam in Paradise catching sight of each other for the very first time, rapt with wonder and eloquently innocent. Dickinson infuses this mythic element into her poem by positioning the narrative of stanza one against Milton's classic account. Before the Fall, Eve speaks ingenuously of her first meeting with Adam and of their initial discourse: "What could I doe, / But follow strait, invisibly thus led? / Till I espi'ed thee, fair indeed and tall, / . . . back I turnd, / Thou following cryd'st aloud, Return fair Eve, / Whom fli'st thou? whom thou fli'st, of him thou art, / His flesh, his bone; to give thee being I lent / Out of my side to thee, neerest my heart / Substantial Life, to have thee by my side / Henceforth an individual solace dear; / Part of my Soul I seek thee, and thee claim / My other half." (*Paradise Lost,* book IV, lines 475–88.) Man and woman began in loving equality; yet the Christian tradition claims that such parity led humanity into perdition, Eve tempting Adam to taste the forbidden fruit. Thus our first parents were exiled from Paradise, and forever after woman was commanded to subject herself to man: "Children thou shalt bring / In sorrow forth, and to thy Husbands will / Thine shall submit, he over thee shall rule" (*Paradise Lost,* book X, lines 194–96; see Genesis III:16).

Dickinson's poem is a repudiation of this conventional view. Edenic equality can persist forever, the poet claims; when passion is generous, true lovers can make their own Paradise. Thus although the first two lines of the poem acknowledge disparity, in the three lines that follow all discrepancies between the couple are dispelled by their perfect union, "Two lives—One Being—now—," the speaker's "Brain" and "Blood" perfectly matched to her mate's. Indeed, by the conclusion of the first stanza, the lovers are so fully in accord with each other that a reader might even suspect that there had been some violation of the integrity of distinct identity—a process similar to the relinquishment of self demanded by God from all who "love" Him. The second stanza dispels such suspicions by moving from the Old Testament to the

The Dickinson Homestead

Susan Gilbert Dickinson

Austin Dickinson
about 1890

The Evergreens

Samuel Bowles

*Thomas Wentworth
Higginson with his
daughter on
a bicycle*

Josiah Holland

*Reverend Charles
Wadsworth*

Helen Hunt Jackson

Judge Otis Phillips Lord

AMHERST, MASS.

1886.

*The Honorable Edward Dickinson
(dated variously 1853, 1860, 1874)*

*Lavinia Dickinson
1896*

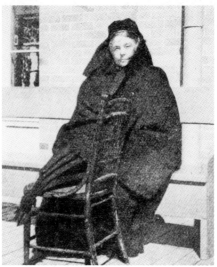

*Susan Dickinson
1897*

New, with the speaker accepting a Christlike role. "Smaller" at the opening of the poem and equal at the end of the first stanza, now the speaker is capable of accepting the "largest part" of her beloved's grief. The informing metaphor of this stanza, initiated by the striking phrase "Forever of His fate to *taste*—," is suggestive in several ways. It recalls Christ's assurance that there are those who "shall not *taste* of death," while affirming with the word "Forever" that it is the lovers who set the standard for such immortality. Perhaps the food imagery even recalls the Lord's Supper, the ritual reassurance of Christ's loving remembrance. But most of all, these simple transactions recall the loving Wife: if the husband is dispirited, she is willing to comfort him and take the burden of his pain upon herself; if there is "joy," she will put aside her portion for him like a dainty piece of pastry, an affectionate surprise saved for her "beloved Heart—."

By the third stanza, all considerations of size have become irrelevant, for the passionate mutuality of the lovers has made them infinite. Thus love is joyful discovery without end: "All life—to know each other—/ Whom we can never learn—." According to tradition, it is only God Whose endlessly complex nature can never be plumbed; according to tradition, it is precisely these intricate subtleties of the Divinity that impose coherence upon Heaven and give structure to eternity. Yet in much of Dickinson's poetry about Heaven, God fails to emanate order; thus everlasting life becomes no more than nightmare without end. Now the lovers succeed where God has failed. The third stanza of this poem is a new Book of Revelation: "Heaven" is a coherent place with "Neighborhoods of Men—," and its citizens spend their time catching up on the course of study that the lovers began on earth. Thus at first they are "puzzled" as the lovers were before they learned to know each other; however, with the "lexicon" of the couple's relationship patent before them, all those in Heaven can perfect their knowledge of love by studying the model of this man and woman.

In its way, "Forever at His side to walk—" provides an outline for the scope of love's errand: everywhere from Eden to eternity, man and woman can entirely displace God's authority (though even love cannot rob Him of His power to wound). For her part, the poet has leave to deploy the entire vocabulary of transcendence in her treatment of the subtleties of passion; and the several different Voices and stances that Dickinson draws upon in her wrestle with the Lord and her indictment of His ways can be adapted to this more agreeable task of displaying love's variety.

The attitude of the child—unsuited, one might suppose, to a love poem—gracefully lends itself to several purposes. Unlike God, the lovers express affection face to face in an exchange of candid, gazing eyes. Confirmed in passion's "Revelation," they discover that intimate understanding can carry them beyond all degrees of learning and into a state of inarticulate wonder. As if by magic, this new simplicity transforms them into children once again.

"We learned the Whole of Love— / The Alphabet—the Words— / A Chapter—
then the mighty Book— / Then—Revelation closed— / But in Each Other's
eyes / An Ignorance beheld— / Diviner than the Childhood's— / And each to
each, a Child— / Attempted to expound / What Neither—understood— / Alas,
that Wisdom is so large— / And Truth—so manifold!" (#568) Even the Voice
of the child, direct and unaffected by social constrictions, can be used to
convey the intimacy of lovers' diction. So the woman sportively invites the
man to make-believe passion's beginning. "Let Us play Yesterday— / I—the
Girl at school— / You—and Eternity—the / Untold Tale— / . . . Still at the Egg-
life— / Chafing the Shell— / When you troubled the Ellipse— / And the Bird
fell—" (#728).

Most of all, however, love is an awakening from childhood into maturity,
and the most elegant use of the child's Voice in Dickinson's love poetry can
be found in an intricately wrought "Anniversary" poem. The subject of the
verse is the speaker's emotional growth over the course of a year, and the
progress of her development is rendered in subtly modulated shifts of tone
and idiom: beginning with the strident accents of an impatient and imperious
child, the poem concludes with a woman's Voice, ripe with passion and with
pain.

> One Year ago—jots what?
> God—spell the word! I—cant—
> Was't Grace? Not that—
> Was't Glory? That—will do—
> Spell slower—Glory—
>
> Such Anniversary shall be—
> Sometimes—not often—in Eternity—
> When farther Parted, than the Common Wo—
> Look—feed upon each other's faces—so—
> In doubtful meal, if it be possible
> Their Banquet's real—
>
> I tasted—careless—then—
> I did not know the Wine
> Came once a World—Did you?
> Oh, had you told me so—
> This Thirst would blister—easier—now—
> You said it hurt you—most—
> Mine—was an Acorn's Breast—
> And could not know how fondness grew
> In Shaggier Vest—
> Perhaps—I could'nt—
> But, had you looked in—

A Giant—eye to eye with you, had been—
No Acorn—then—

So—Twelve months ago—
We breathed—
Then dropped the Air—
Which bore it best?
Was this—the patientest—
Because it was a Child, you know—
And could not value—Air?

If to be "Elder"—mean most pain—
I'm old enough, today, I'm certain—then—
As old as thee—how soon?
One—Birthday more—or Ten?
Let me—choose!
Ah, Sir, None!

(#296)

The poem is built upon a mathematical trope. At its beginning, the man is older than the woman; we do not know their exact ages, but we know there is a difference. By its conclusion, a reduction to zero has been accomplished: over the course of a twelve-month period, the lovers have defied all the laws of time and of natural processes; instead of merely growing one year older, they have become the same age (and in some respects, the same size). The differences between them have been eliminated. A linguistic jest mirrors the process: the first word of the poem is "One"; the last, "None!" Indeed, the strategy of the entire poem is predicted upon the assumption that to be able to *name* a thing fully and adequately demonstrates mastery over it. Thus when the verse recounts a sequence in which linguistic skills are accrued to render a complex emotional experience, it also demonstrates the process by which maturity is wrung from that experience.

Abruptly, the poem opens with the imperative mode. We find ourselves in a schoolroom or on a parlor floor with a little girl laboriously wielding a pencil and slate, doing sums and jotting down her computations, perhaps, or writing out a vocabulary lesson (for definition and numerical value are to some extent conflated in this poem). "One Year ago": how can she set down its incalculable meanings and implications? The child turns to "God," not with prayer, but in command: "spell the word! I—cant—." The difficulty in "spelling" here has little to do with finding the proper letters; some sort of magic has been worked, and an indefinable privilege lurks in the vexing term "One Year." Thus occult charm must be invoked to capture its sorcery. "Grace?" That is the "free unmerited love and favor of *God*"; intuitively, the child rejects the Divinity's suggestion. God tries again: "Glory?" Now there is a word that might do. The little girl picks up her slate: "Spell slower—Glory—."

The spell that has been cast by the lovers is intrinsically sacrilegious. Jesus had instructed us to pray to His Father: "For thine is the kingdom, and the power, and the glory, for ever." As poet, Emily Dickinson had pre-empted God's authority by seizing the "Power." Now we can see that lovers, too, have a claim upon that remarkable prayer, for theirs is the "Glory." And this poem even contrives to have God instruct the speaker to name it thus.

Having discovered the proper locution to name the meaning of "One Year," the speaker can begin to move toward maturity: a child at the beginning of the poem, she has acquired a woman's capacity for desire and desolation by the opening of the second stanza. If she is to express these, she must find still more ways of articulating emotion, and now she looks not to God, but only to her own resources. "Glory" has moved the relationship outside the temporal and into the transcendent realm; yet strictly construed, an "Anniversary" can occur only within time. Thus the speaker initiates a playful violation of temporal prohibition: "Such Anniversary" as this shall be "Sometimes," but "not often—in Eternity—." This fracturing of time's tyranny prepares us for the power of the temporal paradox contained in "When farther Parted, than the Common Wo—/Look—feed upon each other's faces—so—." At the most fundamental, syntactic level, the utterance is difficult to parse. The poem records the Anniversary of a parting that has not yet been mended. How, then, can the verbs "Look" and "feed" be in the present tense, haunting us with an action that seems forever suspended in time, unending and not subject to completion? We can postulate an expansion of the elliptical utterance that will handle this problem at its literal level: "Such Anniversary" will occur when two lovers are "Parted" who have been accustomed to "Look" and "feed upon each other's faces"; nor is it surprising that this tactic of reconstruction swings the lovers into unending time by using infinitive constructions to render their relationship. But expanding the expression to complete the ellipsis is clumsy and strained; moreover, it vitiates the force of "Look—feed." These verbs assault the reader with *now*, the lovers existing in some continuous present, their passion restructuring time to grant them an eternity.

Just as the expression "Look—feed" manipulates time's restrictions, so, too, does the lovers' "Banquet." As always in Dickinson's poetry, "Wine" recalls the Lord's Supper, yet here that ceremony is conflated with an earlier reflection of quite another order: the feast of love in the Song of Solomon. In that nuptial lyric, the bride mediates upon her beloved: "He brought me to the banqueting house, and his banner over me was love. . . . Let him kiss me with the kisses of his mouth: for thy love is better than wine" (Song of Solomon 2:4, 1:2). In Dickinson's poem, the speaker recollects her "careless" love with a poignant cry of awareness that has come too late: "I did not know the Wine / Came once a World." She had thought love's "Banquet" was the common way, and only abstinence has conferred the tragic realization that crucifies her now. Even Christ's "Thirst" upon the cross could be comforted with vinegar upon a sponge, but the speaker's rarer need can be slaked only by the beloved.

All of this work—groping for the word "Glory," discovering a way to speak the force of a passion that extends unaltered across time, even enduring the anguish of the recollected ecstasy—occupies the speaker until the mid-point of the poem. It recapitulates the grief and dawning knowledge that have filled the year since parting and gives a substantial account of the process by which she has achieved maturity. Brought by this recapitulation to the moment of her "Anniversary," the speaker adopts a different tone. Vexed syntax and a diction of agony drop away, and the accents of confident authority enter the poem. No longer engulfed in tribulation, she can achieve some distance from her ordeal—can even begin to see herself as the beloved has seen her. And it is not until this moment, perhaps, that she becomes his equal and is fully enabled to love.

Hers was an "Acorn's Breast." To the beloved, this fond expression spelled a poignant combination of sexual beauty and immaturity: firm, round breasts tapering to pointed nipples, yet a heart undeveloped in the knowledge of pain. The speaker can savor his compliment and appreciate his affectionate reservations, but now she knows one thing better than he; as the axiom avers, given time, the smallest acorn will grow into a tower of strength. Thus after one year's passage, she can return to him with a more accurate assessment: could you *now* but peer within, "A Giant—eye to eye with you, had been—." In God's Kingdom, the ultimate face-to-face encounter is possible only after death and the promised new birth in Christ; yet in the lovers' new mythic realm, this first "Anniversary" is "Birth"day enough.

In general, Emily Dickinson thought that love was for grown-ups—too complicated for the naïve to understand, too difficult a relationship for the child to take part in, too serious for any but the responsible adult to try. There are poems of initiation, to be sure, but these regard the girl's status as a mere beginning and not of intrinsic interest; it is the woman's or the "Wife's" state that is the goal. Thus one poem opens with an adolescent, almost gushing gait: "*He touched me, so I live to know / That such a day, permitted so, / I groped upon his breast—. . . .*" Yet it moves quickly to an assertion of change: "*And now, I'm different from before, / As if I breathed superior air— / Or brushed a Royal Gown—*" (#506). Sometimes the same emotional development is cast in specifically religious terms, but the value structure is the same. Real love is complex: its advent marks the conclusion to irresponsibility. "*I am ashamed—I hide— / What right have I—to be a Bride— / So late a Dowerless Girl— / Nowhere to hide my dazzled Face— / No one to teach me that new Grace— / Nor introduce—my Soul— / . . . Bring Me my best*

Pride— / No more ashamed— / No more to hide— / Meek—let it be—too proud—for Pride— / Baptized—this Day—A Bride—" (#473).

Love demands the capacity for many moods, many shifts of attitude and tone: impatience, longing, sorrow, passion, whimsy, humor—all the suns and storms and sleeting seasons that make up the full range of mature sexual love. Not even God in imperial power requires such a deft dance from the poet as the lover does. God is removed and refuses all mutual exchange, and our relationship with Him is founded upon the certainty that He will never come in answer to our longing. A mortal lover is more various—delightful and desolating in unpredictable ways.

> If you were coming in the Fall,
> I'd brush the Summer by
> With half a smile, and half a spurn,
> As Housewives do, a Fly.
>
> If I could see you in a year,
> I'd wind the months in balls—
> And put them each in separate Drawers,
> For fear the numbers fuse—
>
> If only Centuries, delayed,
> I'd count them on my Hand,
> Subtracting, till my fingers dropped
> Into Van Dieman's Land.
>
> If certain, when this life was out—
> That your's and mine, should be—
> I'd toss it yonder, like a Rind,
> And take Eternity—
>
> But, now, uncertain of the length
> Of this, that is between,
> It goads me, like the Goblin Bee—
> That will not state—it's sting.

(#511)

To some extent, this poem is a mirror image of "One Year ago—": it, too, is fashioned upon a mathematical trope, an expansion toward infinity instead of a reduction toward zero; and whereas the other poem concludes with the mature Voice, this poem opens with it. Interestingly, the beloved here is closely identified with a husband figure, and the ideal, away from which the poem moves with increasingly distressed strokes of imagery, is conjugal love. Given her choice, the speaker would elect a life in which marriage gives passion a permanent home. Any impediment will disrupt the speaker's capacity to continue normally in the Voice of a "Wife," and a significant obstacle will compel her to seek other strategies for self-expression.

At first the speaker's dilemma can be contained within the range of ordinary domestic experience. Because she knows the duration of the separation and has its conclusion within easy sight, she can discourse with smiling confidence. Nature's fulfillment, "Summer," and the intimations of death and carrion with which the "Fly" so often harasses the housewives of Dickinson's poetry are both dismissed with equanimous disdain. Yet as early as the second stanza the quotidian idiom of domestic chores is no longer adequate to convey the intensity of the speaker's painful desire, and she must resort to a radical compression of language to capture her bafflement and anxiety. The narrative account of a year's waiting is figured as a yarn (though the word itself never enters the poem), and this unspoken word is punned as the housewife winds the months into "balls" to be put away. Even this verbal legerdemain cannot quite contain the force of her yearning, however, and a surrealistic element enters: what had been "balls" of yarn becomes transformed into something else—balls of wax or of metal, or perhaps billiard balls with numbers on them, that must be stored in "separate Drawers," lest the heat of desire "fuse" them. Months, "a year"—these are lengths of time a woman might wait. "Centuries" introduces a different order of magnitude, and a new Voice must be tried, that of a child at play—now not for arrogance or imperiousness, but to offer a riddle, a game to distract the speaker from intractable anguish. The puzzle that is invoked was a popular, punning jest in Dickinson's day. The riddler would extend her hand, palm down, and one by one curl each finger under; the fingers were intended to represent people, and the riddler would demand to know where these disappearing folk had gone. The answer was "Van Dieman's Land"—i.e., "down under," the slang expression for Australia (Van Dieman's Land is Tasmania, an island off the coast of Australia).

But play is no more than play, and the child's game is but a brief respite from present pain. Thus the fourth and fifth stanzas leave the child and the "Wife" and the world of realizable passion behind; now the speaker adopts a Voice that looks not to this world, but to transcendence. To be sure, the poignant echo of the kitchen's domesticity remains in the "Rind"—all of life gladly discarded for an "Eternity" together. But even a "certain" meeting in some afterlife is denied. Tauntingly, like the "Goblin Bee—" that rumbles out of sight, always threatening yet never near enough to see, reunion hovers as a possibility whose accomplishment is never assured and never denied. Sexual congress, richly rewarding in so many other love poems, appears here as the painful thrust of the "sting." This "Goblin Bee" is an emissary from the same menacing realm as the "Goblin with a Guage," and its presence is a ghostly reminder that even lovers can be swept into the "Maelstrom" of time's tyranny, unwilling subjects in God's "Experiment" with mankind—that unpredictable alternation of torture and release that describes the universal journey to extinction.

The Voice of the "Wife" runs throughout Dickinson's love poetry. The state that fulfills her usual aspirations is the humblest and most common, just freedom from the uncertainty that besets the speaker in "If you were coming in the Fall," marriage or some other permanent arrangement for passion: "*No numb alarm—lest Difference come— / No Goblin—on the Bloom— / No start in Apprehension's Ear, / No Wilderness—no Doom— / But Certainties of Noon— / Midsummer—in the Mind— / A steadfast South—upon the Soul— / Her Polar time—behind—*" (*#646; var. "Wilderness" and "Noon"*). To be sure, the eloquence with which Dickinson could articulate love's nuances in her poetry set her apart from other women; yet the speakers of the verse are meant to be "Representative." Dickinson understood one exquisite paradox of affection: *all* couples suppose themselves unique in the consuming newness of their discovery and the compelling privacy of their feelings; hence, with a disarming intimacy, the poet tries to capture not what is rarest in passion, but what is delightfully and universally knowable. As one newly married speaker exclaims: "*Always Mine! / No more Vacation! / Term of Light this Day begun! / Failless as the fair rotation / Of the Seasons and the Sun. / Old the Grace, but new the Subjects— / Old, indeed, the East, / Yet upon His Purple Programme / Every Dawn, is first*" (*#839*).

The proleptic Voice does not readily lend itself to love poetry; however, Dickinson experimented with even this ghostly attitude in her exploration of the lyric possibilities for affection. Often the result is strained, the verse more macabre than ardent. "*I see thee better—in the Dark— / I do not need a Light— / The Love of Thee—a Prism be— / Excelling Violet*": these lines are laden with erotic potential, ardor concentrating the scattered infra-red beams in a darkened room like a powerful "Prism" to guide the lovers through their night. Yet when the shadows in the poem extend to include the casket, eroticism is vitiated by the grotesque: "*And in the Grave—I see Thee best— / Its little Panels be / Aglow—all ruddy—with the Light / I held so high, for Thee—*" (*#611*).

It is easy for the modern sensibility to dismiss such efforts as idiosyncratic or even deviant. But Dickinson aspired to be a poet of breadth, not narrowness; she lived in an age that admired the work of Poe and (what is worse) Poe's much less gifted imitators; and her approach to poetry was bold. Thus she tried the varieties that even proleptic love poetry offered. Sometimes it is easy to see how closely this mode of passionate poetry is tied to Dickinson's other verse. A Gothic poem that has sometimes been cited as an example of mere perversity becomes more comprehensible when its maneuvers are put into the context of the other poetry. The opening lines posit a request that allows the poet to employ the closed "eye / I" ("it" to demonstrate death's force): "*If I may have it, when it's dead, / I'll be contented—so—*" Neither Dickinson nor her speaker, we must suppose, actually wanted the lover's dead body; what *is* at stake is the ability to present a vision of the afterworld to him—some preparation for the ordeal he is destined to encounter. The exact nature of the ordeal becomes transparent when the language of this poem is placed against another's. The love poem begun above goes on to recount the message the speaker has for her beloved:

> *I'll tell Thee All—how Bald it grew—*
> *How Midnight felt, at first—to me—*
> *How all the Clocks stopped in the World—*
> *And Sunshine pinched me—'Twas so cold—*

> (#577)

And these lines are a variant of the speaker's nightmarish vision of the resurrection in "*It was not Death*" (#510): "*As if my life were shaven, / And fitted to a frame, / ... And 'twas like Midnight, some— / When everything that ticked—has stopped— / And Space stares all around— / ... But, most, like Chaos—Stopless—cool—.*" That is, the speaker in the love poem wants to prepare her beloved for the horrors of God's "Heaven."[1] Thus, although the verse does not succeed as a piece of love poetry, it is at least a comprehensible effort.

But perhaps the best such poetry eschews the first-person Voice that issues from beyond the grave and employs instead an omniscient Voice that can describe the singular events after death without distracting Gothic inflections.

> *'Twas a long Parting—but the time*
> *For Interview—had Come—*
> *Before the Judgment Seat of God—*
> *The last—and second time*
>
> *These Fleshless Lovers met—*
> *A Heaven in a Gaze—*
> *A Heaven of Heavens—the Privilege*
> *Of one another's Eyes—*
>
> *No Lifetime set—on Them—*
> *Appareled as the new*
> *Unborn—except They had beheld—*
> *Born infiniter—now—*
>
> *Was Bridal—e'er like This?*
> *A Paradise—the Host—*

And Cherubim—and Seraphim—
The unobtrusive Guest—

(#625)

Brazenly usurping the right of Christ to claim His bride, these lovers come together for the "last—and second time," and what ought by tradition to be the Judgment Day becomes instead a festive marriage ceremony. God takes up His role as the Master of Ceremonies or "Host," here entirely obscured by the glory of the "Fleshless Lovers"; and the relationship between the woman and man not only takes precedence over the Lord's activities, but also imposes structure upon eternity.

Every important element of the poem turns upon the use of the "eye / I." On earth, the lovers would have been "Unborn—except They had beheld" each other; after death, they are indeed Reborn "infiniter," not as convention would have it, by the power of Christ, but by "the Privilege / Of one another's Eyes." Such private law is postulated as the very definition of "Heaven," and it is not God but these lovers who impart meaning to Paradise. Indeed, Dickinson even dispatches the dilemma of passionate fulfillment in a place whose inhabitants "neither marry, nor are given in marriage" by translating the notion of intercourse into "Interview," the mingling of selves that can come with the lovers' eternally protracted "Gaze." Ironically, because God is excluded from their pre-emptory affection, He cannot participate in that ultimate "Heaven of Heavens" that is defined by their face-to-face reunion; thus are Deity, "Cherubim," and "Seraphim" all relegated to the same limited status as witnesses. But perhaps the cardinal virtue of this transcendent love is that it transforms salvation into an experience whereby self is neither forfeited nor atomized, but confirmed and sustained forever.

There was ample reason to write otherworldly, spiritual poetry. Even lovers must submit to death, and a meeting in Heaven necessarily becomes their final goal. Yet unlike some devoutly Christian poets, Dickinson never postulated a meeting in the hereafter as the ideal engagement for a man and woman in love. Earth provides the sumptuous opportunity to create a "*Heaven*" that will obscure God's Paradise entirely: "*Eternity—obtained—in Time— / Reversed Divinity—*" (#800). It was the immense and varied range of earthly relationships that Dickinson most often sought to capture, invoking a language of transcendence to show love's splendor, not its location.

Indeed, one of the most engaging attitudes to be found in Dickinson's love poetry is the humorous, candid, self-conscious impatience of a woman who has discovered that creating this Heaven-upon-earth is more easily said than done. The Voice issues vigorously from the page in an arrestingly forthright, conversational mode.

Doubt Me! My Dim Companion!
Why, God, would be content
With but a fraction of the Life—
Poured thee, without a stint—
The whole of me—forever—
What more the Woman can,
Say quick, that I may dower thee
With last Delight I own!

It cannot be my Spirit—
For that was thine, before—
I ceded all of Dust I knew—
What Opulence the more
Had I—a freckled Maiden,
Whose farthest of Degree,
Was—that she might—
Some distant Heaven,
Dwell timidly, with thee!

Sift her, from Brow to Barefoot!
Strain till your last Surmise—
Drop, like a Tapestry, away,
Before the Fire's Eyes—
Winnow her finest fondness—
But hallow just the snow
Intact, in Everlasting flake—
Oh, Caviler, for you!

(#275)

The general meaning of the poem is not difficult to understand. Its most striking characteristic is the speaker's command over a supple series of verbal attitudes in her wooing of the "Caviler" who has raised suspicions about her sincerity. The impatient hyperbole of the first stanza yields to an exaggeratedly religious tone in stanza two; however, stanza three carries this religious attitude in unexpected directions. Like many of the other love poems, this one merges Old and New Testament language. "Tapestry" and "snow" recollect the conclusion of the Book of Proverbs, the quintessential Old Testament description of a good wife, thereby providing the appropriately conclusive rebuke to the speaker's doubting consort: "Who can find a virtuous woman? for her price is far above rubies. The heart of her husband doth safely trust in her. . . . She is not afraid of the snow for her household. . . . She maketh herself coverings of tapestry" (Proverbs 31:10–11, 21–22). Yet here, the key words take on an explicitly sexual meaning as the verse plays upon the notions of "Heaven" (which is named in the poem) and Revelation (which is not) and moves into an attitude of frank invitation. The promised face-to-face encounter is transformed into that hushed moment when the "Tapestry" drops and the man first beholds her fair nakedness, when he first enjoys the secrets of her body, when he first tests the "flake" of her maidenhead, reserved for him alone.

There is playfulness in this poem, but no coyness; and the bold blasphemy in this notion of Revelation is used in other love poems with the same sure tone of wonder and ecstasy. A poem that begins, "A Wife—at Daybreak I shall be—," concludes with this remarkable meditation:

> *Midnight—Good Night! I hear them call,*
> *The Angels bustle in the Hall—*
> *Softly my Future climbs the Stair,*
> *I fumble at my Childhood's prayer*
> *So soon to be a Child no more—*
> *Eternity, I'm coming—Sir,*
> *Savior—I've seen the face—before!*
>
> (#461)

Elsewhere, Dickinson construes the disappearance first of the Creator and then of the Son as "*Eclipse—at Midnight—* /... *Faint* Star of Bethlehem— / *Gone down!*" (#236) Everything in the language of this marriage poem conspires to assert that the beloved can rectify that loss: although it is night, "Midnight" can be dismissed: the bridegroom / "Savior" *comes up* the "Stair" (almost as if he were climbing Jacob's ladder); "Childhood's prayer—" is left behind; and the "face" to be revealed is neither some fearsome, hitherto hidden God nor a phantom bridegroom coming for Jerusalem, but a familiar and welcome one that the speaker has seen "before!"

Like God, the lovers make the force of their presence felt in nature; the result is various, but never cold and never brutal or destructive. When the beloved is gone, the speaker's garden vividly reflects her sexual frustration: "*My Fuschzia's Coral Seams / Rip—while the Sower—dreams— /... My Cactus—splits her Beard / To show her throat—/... Globe Roses—break their satin flake—/ Upon my Garden floor—/ Yet—thou—not there—/ I had as lief they bore / No Crimson—more—*" (#339). "The Daisy follows soft the Sun—," another poem begins; yet this opening tone of hesitant reverence leads to a sumptuously sensual ending: "*Forgive us, if as days decline—/ We nearer steal to Thee! / Enamored of the parting West—/ The peace—the flight—the Amethyst—/ Night's possibility!*" (#106) And two of Dickinson's best-known and most widely anthologized poems define the lovers' relationship in language that explicitly reverses the usual Christian implications of nature.

> *Come slowly—Eden!*
> *Lips unused to Thee—*
> *Bashful—sip thy Jessamines—*
> *As the fainting Bee—*
>
> *Reaching late his flower,*
> *Round her chamber hums—*
> *Counts his nectars—*
> *Enters—and is lost in Balms.*

(#211)

Traditionally, "Eden" is notable first for innocence and then for the Fall. In his epic poem, Milton undertook to demonstrate that by virtue of God's mercy, it has proved a "fortunate Fall" because it allowed Christ to come to earth in loving sacrifice to save those who would otherwise have been "lost." These notions lurk behind the preceding poem along with one other: an unmarried woman who has engaged in sexual intercourse is a "fallen" woman.

Yet all such traditional notions are overturned here. "Eden" becomes a desirable state, not because it offers innocence, but because it allows another opportunity for the Fall; and the Fall is fortunate because it provides intense sexual pleasure. Indeed, this poem describes precisely the consummation that is denied in "If you were coming in the Fall," the Bee's penetration that is the intimate act of love—the man "lost," to be sure, but "lost in Balms." Perhaps even more striking than this audacious reversal of Christian salvation is the speaker's unhurried, deliberate tone. Neither hesitant nor flirtatious, she counsels a slow, self-conscious union where every element of the engagement can be savored.

After God's withdrawal at Peniel, He left a "bewildered Gymnast" behind—Jacob along with the rest of humanity dropped into a Wilderness without inherent order. The poet could dispel the Wilderness: "*I put my pleasure all abroad— / I dealt a word of Gold / To every Creature—that I met— / And Dowered—all the World.*" Yet God is enemy to the poet, and her sovereignty is subject to His attack: "*When—suddenly—my Riches shrank— / A Goblin—drank my Dew— / . . . I felt the Wilderness roll back / Along my Golden lines—*" (#430). Within the poetry, the Voice of the "Wife" most often seeks to bring coherence into a troubled Wilderness through the simple affection of the hearth and unprepossessing forms of domestic regulation. Yet the lovers can extend their spell into a Wilderness as well.

> *Wild Nights—Wild Nights!*
> *Were I with thee*
> *Wild Nights should be*
> *Our luxury!*

Futile — the Winds —
To a Heart in port —
Done with the Compass —
Done with the Chart!

Rowing in Eden —
Ah, the Sea!
Might I but moor — Tonight —
In Thee!

(#249)

If there were any doubt, the word "luxury" points explicitly to the lovers' pleasure: according to Dickinson's dictionary, it means "voluptuousness in the gratification of appetite . . . lust."

In a nice stroke of perversity, the speaker identifies the rolling, storm-tossed "Sea" with "Eden"; now the Fall that will cause expulsion brings the man and woman into the security of each other's arms—for like "Home" in "He was weak, and I was strong," "port" is, by clear implication, the safe harbor of sexual embrace. God's cosmic location is not forgotten: He is a Northern God, and the "Compass" needle would point to His abode. Thus "Compass" and "Chart" are dismissed along with everything else that would appeal to pre-existing arrangements or inherent limitations. Now the lovers' passion can ride the unleashed force of "Wilderness"—not subduing its power, but channeling it into their own relationship to intensify the delight that has become its own sufficient order.

The ultimate rebuke to God's brutality and possessiveness, this shimmering mass of love poetry ought to provide the culmination of Dickinson's artistic effort. In one respect it does, for nowhere is the tone surer or the use of language more exquisitely balanced. Yet Dickinson's love poetry is more than merely the conclusion to some abstract, transcendent dialectic; there is a powerful, idiosyncratic element, and the undercurrent of tragic loss that can be found in so much of the other poetry is here, too. Humanity lost its God: the Creator went up from the plain of Peniel and hid Himself; the Redeemer ascended into Heaven to reiterate that retreat. The love poetry records one more wounding, the loss of the beloved.

Over and over, in countless graceful ways, the same theme of loss is sung. And if, more often than not, the speaker's ambition is modest—not the sublime passion of "Wild Nights," but the ordinary Heaven of husband and home—it is also repeatedly denied. Thus the poetry that might have celebrated a Glory that is becomes a poignant requiem for the Glory that might have been. Indeed, a very great deal of Emily Dickinson's love poetry takes the form of "might have been"; the loving mutuality of passion, though authentic and potent, is consistently thwarted. And if the woman overtakes the poet in any respect, it is here, in a haunting conviction that runs like a crimson thread throughout this work. Separation: the besetting anxiety of Emily Dickinson's life is translated into the speaker's relationship with her beloved.

2 ❖ *Love in the Real World*

There is every good reason to suppose that Emily Dickinson fell in love. Most women do, and during her school years and those following, she displayed all of the ordinary flurries of excitement over young men that one would expect. The love poetry—not idealizing and incorporeal, but ardent and filled with sexual invitation—gives so much evidence of Dickinson's capacity for passion that for a while (now fortunately passed) critics generally supposed that the principal reason for her art lay in some unfulfilled affair of the heart. Two groups of love letters in draft give further fuel to this interest: three letters written in the late 1850s and early 1860s when Dickinson was at the height of her poetic powers are addressed to some unknown recipient; fifteen letters written in the late 1870s and early 1880s, long after the great love poetry was completed, are addressed to Judge Otis Phillips Lord, with whom Emily Dickinson is known to have had a late-blooming romance. Was Judge Lord Emily Dickinson's lifelong love? If he was not, was there some earlier, unhappy love affair during the years of her poetic outpouring? It is natural for Dickinson's readers to be curious. Unfortunately, such curiosity will probably never be satisfied. The evidence has been so extensively sifted that if some simple answer were there, it probably would have been discovered. On the face of it, this seems a great disappointment. But is it?

Everything about Emily Dickinson's poetic mission suggests that her work was part of an heroic quest whose scale far outran the outlines of any single life. The anguish and ecstasy of the *general* human condition is a fit subject for such a poet, and individual poems might seem so immediate and intimate that every reader could identify his or her dilemmas with the speaker's. However, poetry that was no more than a bill of particulars detailing the vicissitudes of Emily Dickinson's *personal* love life would not have served the artist's own aim. Although there is a significant tie between the life and the work where love is concerned, it has little to do with the identity of Emily Dickinson's beloved.

Dickinson viewed all of human existence as essentially wounded by the malignity of a disappearing God. Some people who held such a view would dismiss the transcendent realm altogether and turn their attention to the happiness that can be found in affectionate relationships on earth: God and Heaven may be unavailable, but husband or wife and children can provide a balm against the pain of this divine blow. Yet Emily Dickinson did not choose to seek fulfillment through quotidian happiness; instead, she embraced the vocation of poet and took up battle with the Lord. In doing so, she made a series of critical decisions: she chose *words* rather than people as her ultimate source of comfort, and she valued the creation of a permanent, unchanging Voice over the shifting, unpredictable relationships that make up a varied ordinary life. Instead of descendants, she would have readers—even a century after her death, she would be able to speak from the page with undiminished vitality. Such decisions grew out of uncountable personal choices. The preference for living under her father's roof; the desire to have Austin and Vinnie living always close at hand; the yearning for some vehicle to assert "self" in clear, uncompromising terms; the ambition to usurp the birthright and become, herself, the scion of the House of Dickinson; the lust for epic grandeur—these were a few. Most of the poetry is a natural outgrowth of her choices. If words provided the medium for engaging with the Divinity, they provided the link with generations to come as well. Even the Voice of the "Wife" could be given a meaningful role to play—reaching out with understanding and compassion to readers the poet herself could never see.

Love poetry need not have posed a particular problem. But it did. In some measure, love poetry focused many of the ambivalences that inhered in Emily Dickinson's initial decision.

Consistently, Dickinson's love poetry turns away from all of the usual strategies. She might have chosen to write about the fortunes of a typical courtship as the Elizabethan sonneteers did—the uncertainties and the rejections and the bliss of momentary understandings all providing a variety suitable for poetic inspection. She wrote a few such poems; however, by far the greatest part of the love poetry assumes that the difficulties that beset lovers come not from within, but without. Moreover, tacit in most of Dickinson's work is the notion that some arrangement like marriage that allows for sustained intimacy and the uninterrupted possibility for passion is the ideal toward which poetry best addresses itself. There is no intrinsic reason why Dickinson could not have written love poetry celebrating the dynamics of a happy marriage or even examining the difficulties of achieving that perfect union. Nonetheless, for the most part, she did not. Or her decision to turn away from worldly rewards might have led her to postulate unconsummated fidelity to a distant beloved as a glorious end in itself; the poetry of this pure adulation could become its own kind of prayer, an alternative, perhaps, to those directed toward God. Other poets have celebrated a spiritual love, but Emily Dickinson did not choose to do so. Finally, she might easily have elected not to write love poetry at all. However, she declined this path as well.

Instead, her poetry about love follows a peculiar, frustrating pattern. The same poetry that postulates marriage as the ideal also accepts as a given that this "marriage" can never take place. It is not that the lovers are joined only to discover that they are unhappy together; rather, two lovers, perfectly matched and deeply in love, are not permitted to remain together. Over and over again this pattern is repeated. And it is this persistent pattern that may be partially illuminated by an examination of her real-world relationships.

Of young men her own age, the group about whom the most is known is defined by the names she mentions in her letters: Ben Newton, Henry Vaughan Emmons, George Gould, cousin John Graves—even Jacob Holt, a young Amherst dentist of literary inclinations who was about eight years her senior and who died before she had turned eighteen. Probably she had girlish crushes on several of these boys (and on others, whose names have not been preserved). It seems incontrovertible that she had a brief flirtation with Henry Vaughan Emmons, with whom she went walking in the summer of 1852, but her feelings did not run deep. She accepted his attentions to another young woman in the autumn of 1853 with entire equanimity, and she greeted his fiancée as a new "friend" late in the summer of 1854.

Only the case of Ben Newton merits some attention. Nine years older than Emily Dickinson, Ben Newton was Edward Dickinson's law student until August 1849; after Newton left to begin practice in Worcester, he sent Emily Dickinson a copy of Emerson's *Poems*. When he married, in June 1851, Dickinson noted the fact at the end of a long letter to Austin without perturbation: "Emily Fowler inquires for you—also M[artha] and Susie—Give my love to my friends, and write me as soon as you can—the folks all send their love. *B F N. is married*." However, when he died in March 1853, Dickinson reported it to Austin with some anxiety: "Love from us all. Monday noon. Oh, Austin, Newton is dead. The first of my own friends. Pace." Dickinson had refused conversion herself only two and a half years earlier, and she had just begun the poetic wrestling with faith that would occupy her life. Questions about immortality were much on her mind. Thus, after some months' deliberation, she wrote Ben Newton's pastor, the distinguished Unitarian writer and minister Edward Everett Hale, to ask a question about Newton that was entirely conventional among the pious citizens of Amherst: was he willing to die?

I think, Sir, you were the Pastor of Mr B. F. Newton, who died sometime since in Worcester, and I often have hoped to know if his last hours were cheerful, and if he was willing to die. . . . You may think my desire strange, Sir, but the Dead was dear to me, and I would love to know that he sleeps peacefully.

... Mr Newton became to me a gentle, yet grave Preceptor, teaching me what to read, what authors to admire, what was most grand or beautiful in nature, and that sublimer lesson, a faith in things unseen, and in a life again, nobler, and much more blessed—

Of all these things he spoke—he taught me of them all, earnestly, tenderly, and when he went from us, it was as an elder brother, loved indeed very much, and mourned, and remembered. During his life in Worcester, he often wrote to me, and I replied to his letters—I always asked for his health, and he answered so cheerfully, that while I knew he was ill, his death indeed surprised me. He often talked of God, but I do not know certainly if he was his Father in Heaven—Please Sir, to tell me if he was willing to die, and if you think him at Home, I should love so much to know certainly, that he was today in Heaven.

Of all the young men in Dickinson's girlhood, Ben Newton is the only one she mentions in later years. He was her literary and spiritual "Tutor," an epithet she often included next to his name, instructing her about poetry and immortality. "My dying Tutor told me that he would like to live till I have been a poet," she writes in her third letter to Higginson, "but Death was much of Mob as I could master—then—."[2]

Probably in some respects Higginson replaced Ben Newton in Emily Dickinson's array of friends and confidants: they would have been about the same age (actually, Higginson was two years younger than Newton); and although Higginson could not teach Dickinson very much about "Death" or "his Father in Heaven—," he might well be expected to suggest "what to read" or "what authors to admire." Thus she concludes her third letter to him with a request that echoes the language about Ben Newton in the letter to Edward Everett Hale: "But, will you be my Preceptor, Mr. Higginson?" The poet signs this letter as she had signed the one before, "Your friend E Dickinson—"; however, she signs her next letter to him, "Your Scholar,"[3] and such was the epithet she most often used in lieu of signature in all sub-sequent letters. Ostensibly seeking guidance in her exploration of literature, she must have hoped that Higginson would give her one thing more that Ben Newton had offered freely, supportive encouragement. In the end, Higginson gave little of this. In her turn, Dickinson displayed little inclination to accept his advice. Yet they did discuss literature after a fashion, and the correspondence clearly answered her need to have contact with the world of letters.

For spiritual guidance, she turned to her Philadelphia correspondent, the Reverend Charles Wadsworth. Dickinson probably met Wadsworth during her trip to Philadelphia in 1855; one of the leading pulpit orators of his day (and often compared to that other eloquent man of God, Henry Ward Beecher), Wadsworth was pastor of the Arch Street Presbyterian Church, and he was probably friendly with the Colemans, with whom Dickinson stayed in 1855. All of the Wadsworth family records and letters reveal him as a busy, happily married man, deeply in love with his wife and much occupied with his professional activities: his emotional energies were fully engaged, and he could not have had much free time. It is highly likely that Dickinson heard him preach; it is even possible that she met him. In any case, Emily and Lavinia remained in Philadelphia for only two weeks, and Emily could not have come to know him well. Nonetheless, at some time after 1855, Emily Dickinson did initiate a correspondence with him that continued until his death in 1882. None of her letters to him survives. Only one of his to her remains, a very early letter, possibly even the first, given that he misspells her name.

My Dear Miss Dickenson

I am distressed beyond measure at your note, received this moment,—I can only imagine the affliction which has befallen, or is now befalling you.

Believe me, be what it may, you have all my sympathy, and my constant, earnest prayers.

I am very, very anxious to learn more definitely of your trial—and though I have no right to intrude upon your sorrow yet I beg you to write me, though it be but a word.

> In great haste
> Sincerely and most
> Affectionately *Yours*—[4]

The letter has no date, and there is no way of ascertaining what anxiety moved Dickinson to initiate the correspondence (perhaps Mother's protracted illness after the move to the Brick House in 1856). However, it is of a piece with her behavior at other times.

Personally shy in the company of strangers, Emily Dickinson had few if any reservations about writing to famous men. In every case she had a plausible reason for writing: concern over the circumstances of Ben Newton's death was sufficient to move her to write Edward Everett Hale because no one else could answer her needs; her desire to have some literary mentor and confidant, combined with her knowledge that Higginson was sympathetic to women writers, led her to write to him; Wadsworth's reputation as a preacher and his evident capacity for compassion encouraged her to suppose that he would be an adequate spiritual adviser. Yet taken together, these correspondences begin to reveal an interesting pattern. Although Emily Dickinson did not live in a metropolis, Amherst was an unusual country town—the seat of two colleges (in 1856 the Massachusetts Agricultural College took the first steps toward incorporation), it was filled with men of learning, a great many of them ministers. It is true that Emily Dickinson must have been more intelligent than virtually all of the men and women she met; it is also true that for pressing reasons, she may have valued confidentiality in both literary and spiritual matters. Nonetheless, it is very difficult to believe that her actual isolation was so great that she could find no better alternative than these correspondences to address her need for companionship and counsel. It is almost as if absence itself were the enabling virtue of the relationships. Thus although Higginson pressed Emily Dickinson for a picture, asked her to give a description of herself, invited her to Boston so that they might meet, she does not express any commensurate desire to get to know him better than their intermittent letters would allow. Emily Dickinson seems to have *preferred* distance.

Secrecy *per se* does not seem to have mattered: just as the family knew she wrote to Higginson, so they knew of her letters to Wadsworth. Still, Dickinson wanted to retain her privacy, and it was impossible to mail anything at all from the little post office in Amherst without having the entire town know the names of one's correspondents. Thus she employed various strategies to get her letters out of town anonymously: some (probably many to Wadsworth) were enclosed in letters to Bowles or to the Hollands, to be mailed from Springfield; in Dickinson's later life, her cousin George Montague addressed notes and packages for her. Yet her concern was aimed at the village gossips, not at the members of her family. Wadsworth called upon Emily Dickinson in Amherst twice, once in 1860 and again in 1880, both times as part of a more general visit to the area. These calls came entirely by surprise, for with Wadsworth as with Higginson, Dickinson seems neither to have urged nor to have expected face-to-face encounters.

Charles Wadsworth was friendly with James and Charles Clark of Northampton, and sometime in the 1860s Emily Dickinson was introduced to James Clark, who knew her father. Thus after Wadsworth's death James Clark sent several of his sermons to Dickinson, and the note she sent in thanks gives some idea of the peculiar mixture of affection and distance that characterized her friendship with the Philadelphia minister.

To James D. Clark . . .

Please excuse the trespass of gratitude. My sister thinks you will accept a few words in recognition of your great kindness.

In a [*sic*] intimacy of many years with the beloved Clergyman, I have never before spoken with one . . . who knew him, and his Life was so shy and his tastes so unknown, that grief for him seems almost unshared.

He was my Shepherd from "Little Girl"hood and I cannot conjecture a world without him, so noble was he always—so fathomless—so gentle.

I saw him two years since for the last time, though how unsuspected!

He rang one summer evening to my glad surprise. . . . He spoke on a previous visit of calling upon you, or perhaps remaining a brief time at your Home in Northampton.

I hope you may tell me all you feel able of that last interview, for he spoke with warmth of you as his friend. . . .[5]

Dickinson uses the word "intimacy" to refer to this relationship with her "Shepherd"; perhaps these two visits along with the letters—no friends in common, little or no knowledge of his ongoing life or of his own dreams and hopes and desires, no expectation of regular conversation—were as much of an intimacy as she could tolerate.

The more proximate friendship with Sam Bowles manifests this same un-usual combination of affection and distance—although because Bowles lived in nearby Springfield and was a frequent visitor at the Evergreens next door, Dickinson's strategies for achieving a balance were somewhat different. Moreover, her relationship with him was but one element (and a small one) in his complicated, busy life. In order to put Dickinson's feelings for him into context, it is necessary to take a brief glance at his relationship with his wife and the other women he admired.

There is no doubt that Emily Dickinson was deeply attached to the hand-some, ebullient editor of the Springfield *Republican*. His intelligence was quick, if not powerful, and his conversation was full of energy and wit. What must have been even more important, he was willing to pursue intellectual exchanges with women as well as with men, a rare quality in Emily Dickin-son's immediate experience. Yet his interests were more congenial to Susan Dickinson's than to those of her sister-in-law, Emily. Sue was well read and up-to-date, and she invited the most interesting men and women of the day to visit the Evergreens. Though she was no dilettante, she looked to the pres-ent and the future, whereas Emily Dickinson looked to the past and eternity. Early in their acquaintance, Dickinson had attempted to engage Sam Bowles in those questions about faith and the afterlife that most disturbed her own thoughts. Yet Bowles's responses made it clear that these subjects did not concern him. Steeped, perhaps, in the consolation literature that the Spring-field *Republican* so often published, Bowles turned his attention to the things of this world, confident in the belief that a generous and benevolent Deity was already taking care of any problems one might encounter in the next.

Sam Bowles liked the company of lively, witty, attractive women. His own wife more than fulfilled her marital duties, carrying ten babies to term. Yet she was not strong; her frequent pregnancies weakened her further; and the three stillbirths during the 1850s demoralized her terribly. After she had been married for several years, Mary Bowles developed symptoms of this frailty: asthma and the tendency to be jealous of her husband's relationships with other women. A strong bond of friendship existed between Sam Bowles and Austin Dickinson; however, Bowles had equally strong ties with Susan Dick-inson, perhaps even stronger than with Austin. Years later, in 1881, when Mabel Loomis Todd and her husband came to Amherst, Mrs. Todd reported the stories that had circulated concerning Mrs. Austin Dickinson's relations with Sam Bowles. Any flirtation between the two would have taken place years earlier, but village gossip dies hard. If there were only gossip, it would be easy to dismiss such stories. However, some estrangement is recorded in the family papers as well.

As early as January 1859, Bowles was urging Austin: "If *you* can't spend a whole week yourself [in Springfield], send your wife & one of the girls from the paternal mansion, and then come after them yourself." Bowles was certainly attracted by the possibility of spending time with Susan's sprightly friend Kate Turner, but Sue herself seems to have been the chief object of flirtation at this time. Almost certainly there was nothing more strenuous than flirtation at stake, but little by little Mary Bowles grew impatient of her husband's attentions to Austin's wife. By 1861 relations between the families had become strained, and Sam Bowles wrote Austin to apologize for his wife's behavior:

I want you to understand & appreciate & love Mary—to do this, you must make some allowances for her peculiarities,—& judge her by what she means, rather always than by what she says. Her very timidity & want of self-reliance gives her a sharper utterance. . . . I think she was somewhat disappointed in her Amherst visit— it did not turn out so pleasantly, as she meant to have it. Of course the fault was mainly hers, but it was also partly mine. I did not manage her as she wanted to be managed. The mischief I shall endeavor to remedy here, & without annoying you any more. But I am sore-distressed & weary at heart. My nature revolts at a divided, contradictory loyalty.

Although the families continued to be friendly, the strain between them persisted, at times intensifying. In 1863 there was another flare-up. Bowles wrote to Austin:

I will come & spend to-morrow with you, by way of Northampton, in the morning, returning by evening train. It is all I can do now. Mary will not come, of course. It could hardly be expected, since Sue has not been to see her, even though she has been to Springfield two or three times.[6]

Evidently Austin understood the harmlessness of Sam Bowles's attentions to his wife, even if village tongues were inclined to wag. Though relations were always touchy, Mary's animosity dwindled after 1863; she had other, more immediate targets for her jealousy.

However much Sam Bowles favored the company of Susan Dickinson, darkly attractive and incisive in discussion, his deeper affections were engaged elsewhere. At precisely the time that Emily Dickinson was becoming a close friend of Sam Bowles, his own closest female companion was Maria Whitney, a learned, sensitive young woman who lived in Northampton.

More susceptible to illness than his robust manner would suggest, Sam Bowles contracted a chill and sciatic inflammation on a trip through the snow from Amherst to Springfield in March 1861. Somehow he could not shake the illnesses; even the summer did not dispel them, and finally he decided to take a cure at the Hydropathic Institute on Round Hill in Northampton. He went up in mid-October and did not leave until late November. During his first week there he met Maria Whitney, the daughter of a Northampton banker who was distantly related to Mary Bowles. Sam Bowles and Maria Whitney seem to have taken to each other immediately. "I have had two or three long rides . . . with Mr Bowles & Maggies accompanying in a buggy," Maria wrote her brother on October 28. "It is exceedingly pleasant having Mr Bowles at Dr Deniston's, though we *are* sorry to have him need the treatment. We see him almost every day." Mary Bowles was again pregnant, and in an attempt to prevent yet another stillborn infant, she and her husband decided to go to New York City for the birth because more sophisticated medical treatment was available there; when Sam Bowles left Northampton at the end of November, he went directly to New York to join his wife. The baby, a boy, was delivered alive and well on December 20, and at about the same time or shortly thereafter, Maria Whitney went down to New York to be with them; she stayed with friends, but saw Sam Bowles regularly. "Mr & Mrs Bowles are still at the Brevoort house. She has a hearty little boy, & they are both as happy over it as the most youthful papa & mama could be—Mr B. comes here often, & I find him a most agreeable & delightful companion."[7] Mary and Sam Bowles remained in New York through March. Sam had still not fully regained his health, and on April 9, 1862, he sailed for Europe alone, hoping that a protracted vacation would restore him. He remained, traveling the Continent, until November; and Maria Whitney went home to Northampton, there to begin an active friendship with Emily Dickinson that was to last until the poet's death.

It is difficult to estimate Maria Whitney's relationship to the Bowles family during the early 1860s. She was their frequent visitor; she often traveled with them; she seems to have been on amiable terms with Mary Bowles; and she became virtually indispensable in helping to manage the Bowles children (whose number continued to increase). Finally, in July 1867, she took up residence in their Springfield home to help out, for Mary Bowles was pregnant yet again and doing poorly. There is no doubt that her presence was sorely needed. "Mrs Bowles is expecting to be confined in the fall, and it will probably be a long time before she will be able to take the direction of affairs in the house," Maria Whitney wrote home:

Sallie has [had charge of the house] ever since I was here last winter, & it has kept her out of school & is too confining & wearing for so young a girl—So unless I stay she must be sent away to school & a housekeeper substituted—I have promised to remain a year . . . and then at the end of that time I shall decide upon the question of a more permanent establishment here.

Yet by March 1868 Mary Bowles was already complaining about her husband's attentions to their guest / housekeeper. Maria got wind of Mrs. Bowles's complaints indirectly, from her family in Northampton, and she wrote home in indignation. "The friendship is as precious to me as to him, & he has not attempted at any time to persuade me to any thing that my judgment & inclinations did not sanction. I have staid here voluntarily."[8] Despite these protestations, Maria left the Bowles household under a cloud of bad feelings. Nonetheless, her close connection with Sam Bowles and his family continued. She accompanied two of his children when they went to school in Europe (1868 and 1871), and Bowles visited them during her stay there; indeed, he timed his vacations to coincide with her own, and she is frequently reported as having been a member of the "Bowles party" when traveling (though it is not clear whether Mary Bowles was also there). Though she held a post in modern languages at Smith College between 1875 and 1880, she was often in Europe during this time, attending to Sam Bowles and his offspring.

Sam Bowles died in 1878 at the age of fifty-two. All of the Dickinsons mourned him deeply. Emily Dickinson wrote two letters to Mary Bowles—a short note immediately upon receiving the news of his death, and a somewhat longer and more eloquent one when she had had the time to absorb the news. She also wrote at least four tender letters to Maria Whitney, who may have mourned Sam Bowles's death more profoundly than anyone else.

During the late autumn of 1861, when Bowles first met Maria Whitney and began to see her almost daily, he was also becoming more intimately acquainted with the Dickinson family; Northampton is but a short carriage ride from Amherst, and the long New England Indian summers make the open air inviting. Emily Dickinson was alert to the family's personal anxieties: she wrote Mary an affectionate note when the baby boy was born healthy and strong (urging, as she was to do several times, that he be named "Robert" after the poet Robert Browning, whose wife, Elizabeth Barrett Browning, had died in June of that year); and she wrote offering sympathy to Sam when his illness took a bad turn in early January ("When did the Dark happen?").[9] But most of all her letters focused on a subject that seems to have been central to their discussions while he was in Northampton, her commitment to the vocation of poetry.

Conversations leave no record, so it is impossible to know exactly what objections Sam Bowles had raised when Dickinson attempted to talk about her work with him; he did write in response to her letters, but because these notes were destroyed along with the rest of her correspondence after she died, his side of the dialogue must be inferred. One part of his puzzlement evidently had to do with her resolute willingness to renounce the world in order to write, especially when she was not publishing the bulk of her work. After all, the women whom he most admired employed their intelligence in quite different ways, and the few who wrote wanted to please the reading public and see the product of their imagination in print. To distinguish herself from these others, Dickinson spoke to him of her "snow," the name she employed for her poetry when she wished to convey its renunciation of both God and Mammon. The essence of "Snow" is "No!" In "A Clock stopped—," the timepiece acquires a "Pendulum of snow," indifferent to the Divinity's pleading; in "*Publication—is the Auction/Of the Mind of Man—*" (#709), the speaker expresses contempt for the possibility that she might "invest" her "Snow." Probably Dickinson had already introduced these notions into conversation with Bowles because she uses the word "Snow" in the clear expectation that he will understand its meaning here.

Dear friend   [early 1862]

If you doubted my Snow—for a moment—you never will—again—I know—Because I could not say it—I fixed it in the Verse—for you to read—when your thought wavers, for such a foot as mine—

> *Through the strait pass of suffering—*
> *The Martyrs—even—trod.*
> *Their feet—upon Temptation—*
> *Their faces—upon God—*
>
> *A stately—shriven—Company—*
> *Convulsion—playing round—*
> *Harmless—as streaks of Meteor—*
> *Upon a Planet's Bond—*
>
> *Their faith—the everlasting troth—*
> *Their Expectation—fair—*
> *The Needle—to the North Degree—*
> *Wades—so—thro' polar Air!*[10]

It is difficult to fathom whether Dickinson had discussed enough of her nature poetry with Bowles for him to understand that *these* "Martyrs" are enduring the trials that will lead them to a ruthless Destroyer-God in the North. However, she must have showed him more than a little of her verse, for the confident pun, "when your thought wavers, for such a foot as mine—," expects ready recognition.

Certainly it was not the best time for Dickinson to be attempting this rarefied discussion of her work. Bowles had Maria Whitney much on his mind; furthermore, both the Bowles family and the Austin Dickinsons were preoccupied with their roles as parents, for Sue was expecting her first child in June. Emily Dickinson was an anomaly in the midst of this flurry over wives and babies, and some of Sam Bowles's rather pointed comments about her commitment to poetry may well have taken the form of wondering why an intelligent, marriageable young woman would wish to shut herself away from domestic rewards and the protection of a husband. In any case, another letter is devoted to responding to questions like these. The note has no salutation and launches immediately into an exclamatory poem.

[early 1862]

Title divine—is mine!
The Wife—without the Sign!
Acute Degree—conferred on me—
Empress of Calvary!
Royal—all but the Crown!
Betrothed—without the swoon
God sends us Women—
When you—hold—Garnet to Garnet—
Gold—to Gold—
Born—Bridalled—Shrouded—
In a Day—
"My Husband"—women say—
Stroking the Melody—
Is this—the way?

Here's—what I had to "tell you"—
You will tell no other? Honor—is it's
own pawn—[11]

A variant of this poem was sent across the hedges to Susan Dickinson at about the same time it was sent to Bowles in New York, possibly because Sue had been part of the discussion that had prompted it. Scarcely a love poem, this might almost be called an "anti-love poem," so bitterly does it capture the smugness with which some women flaunt their married state—"Stroking the Melody," perhaps by intoning, "My *husband* says . . ."

Ironically, this poem does not employ the Voice of the "Wife"; instead, like "Through the strait pass of suffering," it trades upon the attitudes and tonalities of the saint, who is willing to renounce the rewards of this world. The chanting long "I" sound that dominates the first two lines recalls "Mine—by the Right of the White Election!"—the celebration of a self that is utterly independent and autonomous. A "Title divine" may be conferred by poetry, and a self may be created in verse that is unfettered by the dangers and limitations that confront those real-world wives who sometimes seem to be "Born—Bridalled—Shrouded— / In a Day—." Indeed, the poem adopts such an uncharacteristically negative attitude toward the wife's role that one wonders how explicitly it may allude to the current unhappiness of Mary Bowles and Susan Dickinson. Though Mary had at last given birth to a healthy child, the three stillborn babies were not lightly forgotten; moreover, always prepared to be jealous and often provided with ample cause, Mary may already have noticed Sam's blossoming relationship with Maria Whitney, who was at this very time in New York. In Amherst, Sue's confinement was producing its own worries because of Sue's phobic terrors concerning pregnancy and delivery. And in early 1862 Emily Dickinson was witness to all of this marital anxiety and misery.

Dickinson revered the wife's role; however, she realized that there were enough dangers and disappointments in marriage to discourage any woman from abandoning a true vocation in order to marry just for the sake of being married. Such is the burden of this letter to Sam Bowles. It was not an argument that Bowles was prepared to hear or respond to favorably. Two years later, in a letter to Austin, Bowles asked to be remembered to the family: "To the girls & all hearty thought—Vinnie ditto,—& to the Queen Recluse my especial sympathy—that she has 'overcome the world.'—Is it really true that they ring 'Old Hundred' & 'Aleluia' [sic] perpetually, in heaven—ask her; and are dandelions, asphodels, & Maiden's [vows?] the standard flowers of the ethereal?"[12]

Like the brief exchange of letters in 1860 over the matter of faith, this discussion of women and poetry was curtailed after a few notes had been sent back and forth. Neither party seems to have wanted to pursue the matter: each was too firmly entrenched to be persuaded by the other. Even if she could not make him understand her vocation, Dickinson could still admire Bowles for his wit and engaging manner. She missed him badly when he embarked on the long European sojourn in April 1862, and his leaving gave her one additional reason to initiate her correspondence with Higginson at that time. Indeed, all three Dickinson women were reluctant to see him go. Emily's farewell letter leavens genuine sadness with humor and more than a touch of anger, limning a literary set piece, the piteous picture of their desolation at his failure to pay a farewell visit.

You would come—today—but Sue and Vinnie, and I, keep the time, in tears—We dont *believe* it—*now*—"Mr Bowles—not coming"! . . .

. . . We cannot *count*—our tears—for this—because they drop so fast—and the Black eye—and the Blue eye—and a Brown—I know—hold their lashes full. . . .

Dear friend—we meant to make *you*—brave—but moaned—before we thought. . . . If we could only care—the less—it would be so much easier—Your letter, troubled my throat. It gave that little scalding, we could not know the reason for, till we grow far up.

I must do my Goodnight, in *crayon*—I *meant* to—in Red. Love for Mary.[13]

Their feelings for Bowles differed, but he was probably the closest male friend outside the family that any of the three Dickinson women would ever have.

Some of Dickinson's readers have speculated that Bowles may have been the object of her unrequited passion. There is no way to disprove such a theory, but it seems unlikely. It is easy to imagine Emily Dickinson's falling in love with a married man, especially if he returned her passion; it is easy to imagine her becoming resigned to never being able to marry him. But it is not easy to imagine her doing so when the married man in question was already engaged in flirtations of varying degrees of seriousness with her sister-in-law, one of her sister-in-law's friends, and a learned Northampton woman whose ardent feelings were reciprocated. Nothing in Emily Dickinson's character suggests that she would have been willing to become one of a *group* of admiring females. Furthermore, in this close and observant family where Sam Bowles occupied somewhat the status of community property, no one entertained the slightest notion that she was passionately in love with him. Perhaps the most telling evidence, however, is Bowles's inability to appreciate the power of her talent or the depth of her intelligence. What Dickinson consistently craved was a response to the subtlety and range of her own intellect, imagination, and sensitivity; the intractable loneliness that seems always to have beset her derived not primarily from her secluded life, but from the absence of genuine equals with whom she could be "herself." The love poetry speaks consistently of parity and mutuality, and whatever his other virtues may have been, Sam Bowles could probably not have offered these to any woman. It never seems to have occurred to him to offer them to Emily Dickinson. Dickinson sent him at least thirty-seven of her poems, but none was a love poem.

It is enough to know that Emily Dickinson had great affection for Sam Bowles because even with that level of involvement, her relationship with him is remarkable for the kind of emotional distance that she consistently maintained. In the case of Higginson and Wadsworth, separation was a given: the primary contact was by letter and not by direct discourse. However, in the case of Bowles, who came so frequently to call next door, separation had to be manufactured. To this end, her behavior with him was entirely contradictory. She often wrote urging a visit, and at the beginning of her friendship with the couple she wrote extravagantly. "I am sorry you came, because you went away. . . . I would like to have you dwell here. . . . You shall find us all at the gate, if you come in a hundred years, just as we stood that day." Yet when Sam Bowles did begin coming to Amherst with some regularity, she soon began to find reasons for not seeing him. As early as the fall of 1861 when Bowles was in Northampton, apologetic notes begin to appear.

Perhaps you thought I did'nt care—because I stayed out, yesterday, I *did* care, Mr Bowles. I pray for your sweet health—to "Alla"—every morning—but something troubled me—and I knew you needed light—and air—so I did'nt come. Nor have I the conceit that you *noticed* me—but I could'nt bear that you, or Mary, so gentle to me—should think me forgetful—[14]

This is the period when Dickinson was beginning to experience severe eye trouble, and the note might be dismissed as a by-product of her illness if it were the only one of its kind. But it is not.

After his seven-month European trip in 1862 (during which Dickinson wrote him often and affectionately), Bowles came up to Amherst in late November. The family greeted him warmly—all but Emily, who sent down a note apologizing for her absence. "I cannot see you. You will not less believe me. That you return to us alive, is better than a Summer. And to hear your voice below, than News of any Bird." After he had returned to Springfield, she wrote again—not explaining, but elaborating her apology. "Because I did not see you, Vinnie and Austin, upbraided me—They did not know I gave my part that they might have the more. . . . Did I not want to see you? Do not the Phebes want to come? Oh They of little faith! . . . Few absences could seem so wide as your's has done, to us—. . . . We hope often to see you—." For each of these instances in 1861 and 1862 one might postulate a perfectly reasonable explanation to account for Dickinson's behavior. However, they seem not to have been unusual instances but parts of a regular pattern. Emily Dickinson often saw Sam Bowles when he visited Amherst, yet just as often she chose not to do so. One incident in 1877 became the occasion for an amusing family anecdote. Bowles was downstairs borrowing a book. He asked for Emily, and she sent down word that she could not see him. Exasperated by this whimsy, Bowles shouted upstairs in annoyance: " 'Emily, you [damned] wretch! No more of this nonsense! I've traveled all the way from Springfield to see you. Come down at once.' She is said to have complied and never have been more witty." She included a loving poem in her next letter to him and signed herself, "Your 'Rascal,' " appending the footnote, "I washed the Adjective."[15]

For his part, Sam Bowles found Emily Dickinson " 'Near, but remote.' "[16] Dickinson surely made herself distinct and uniquely valued by this strategy of selective visitation. This was no small victory when dealing with a man like Bowles—busy, voluble, self-important, and all too inclined to take advantage of his attractiveness to women. Yet Bowles was only one of the many friends and loved ones with whom Dickinson deployed such tactics of distancing and selective separation. The most striking pattern occurs in her relationship with the one man whom she is known to have loved with passion, the man who returned her feelings in kind, Judge Otis Phillips Lord.

An 1832 graduate of Amherst College, Lord studied law and was admitted to the bar in 1835; in 1843 he married Elizabeth Farley, and the couple soon moved to Salem, where they lived for the rest of their lives. They had no children. Lord was a man of great intelligence. In his maturity, he was considered by many to be the most brilliant lawyer in the state. Like Edward Dickinson, he was active in Whig politics, and it was principally a loyalty to this dying party that prevented his enjoying much wider political success. He was a formidable orator, trenchant and possessed of a surprisingly playful sense of humor. Beginning in the 1850s and continuing until his death in 1884, he held a number of important state offices. As early as 1853, he was the "acknowledged leader of the [Massachusetts] House, in all its polemics," and he traveled the state as an articulate campaigner. An "eloquent and persuasive speaker," he appeared at a rally in Northampton on November 3 of that year; in December 1853 he became speaker of the Massachusetts House "by apparently universal whig consent."[17]

It is difficult to know precisely when "Phil" Lord first met the Dickinson family. As one of the leaders of the Whig Party, he must have met Edward Dickinson by 1853—probably long before then. Both attended the great Whig convention in 1855, and in 1857 they sat together on a Northampton commission. Yet Lord may have been introduced to the rest of the family even before the 1850s, because he regularly attended Class Day at the Amherst College commencement ceremonies. His trips to western Massachusetts became more regular and protracted when he was appointed to the Superior Court in 1859, for he was then obliged to preside in Northampton sessions twice a year—in April and October. In any case, there is an entry in Mrs. Lord's diary for June 9, 1860, indicating that both of the Lords had dined at the Homestead, and from that time forward they became regular visitors and close friends of the entire Dickinson family. Somewhat more than a year after Edward Dickinson died intestate, wills were drawn up for his wife and daughters (probably by Lord himself), and Elizabeth Farley Lord was one of the three who signed as witnesses for Emily Dickinson's will.

If Emily Dickinson met Lord in 1857, while he was serving on the Northampton committee, she would have been twenty-six, and he forty-five. There is nothing to prove that her relationship to him was particularly close. She may have felt more kindred spirit with the articulate, worldly man than with his wife; nonetheless, there is only the slimmest evidence that she manifested such a preference publicly (although after the couple's visit in October 1875 when she made her will, Emily Dickinson did write to Higginson as if Lord had been there alone: "You ask me if I see any one—Judge Lord was with me a week in October"[18]). Mrs. Lord died in December 1877, and very shortly thereafter (in a matter of months), Emily Dickinson's relationship with Phil Lord became overtly passionate: extant drafts of her love letters to him appear to have been written as soon as early 1878.

The speed with which Emily Dickinson and Phillips Lord declared their love for each other is remarkable, especially so because by the latter half of the nineteenth century the process of mourning had become a fixture of sentimental culture, according to which the newly dead were ritually sanctified and idealized. Thus one wonders whether the relationship had some longer basis. "My lovely Salem smiles at me. I seek his Face so often—but I have done with guises," a letter written in the hand of 1878 begins. It continues:

I confess that I love him—I rejoice that I love him—. . . the exultation floods me. I cannot find my channel—the Creek turns Sea—at thought of thee—. . .

Incarcerate me in yourself—rosy penalty—threading with you this lovely maze, which is not Life or Death—though it has the intangibleness of one, and the flush of the other—waking for your sake on Day made magical with you before I went. . . .

. . . my Darling come oh *be* a patriot now—Love is a patriot now Gave her life for its . . . country Has it meaning now—Oh nation of the soul thou hast thy freedom now[19]

"I have done with guises" suggests that she may have loved him and been constrained to conceal her passion; and such an inference is sustained by the glad exclamation, "Oh nation of the soul thou hast thy freedom now." The feelings between them may even have begun as early as the late 1850s. Unfortunately, there is no proof one way or the other.

All of her finished letters to him were destroyed—as were all of his letters to her; nothing of their correspondence remains except rough drafts of fifteen letters she wrote to him in the years 1878 to 1882, and these were strenuously edited by Austin and Lavinia before being turned over to Mabel Loomis Todd, whose daughter eventually published them in 1954. This is a vexingly small sample: Emily Dickinson and Phil Lord wrote weekly letters to each other during this period, sometimes more often. Yet even the little that remains is revealing. There is the persistent intimation that the passion that became open in 1878 had its origins much earlier. "Our Life together was long forgiveness on your part toward me. The trespass of my rustic Love upon your Realms of Ermine, only a Sovereign could forgive—I never knelt to other—." Sometimes the tone of her address seems exaggeratedly childlike to a modern ear; this was the fashion in late-Victorian America, but Dickinson so often violated the fashion that the nuance is unsettling here. Most often, however, her confident delight in having at last discovered an intelligence and a capacity for passion that could match her own is the dominant strain.

Ned and I were talking about God and Ned said "Aunt Emily—does Judge Lord belong to the Church"?

"I think not, Ned, technically."

"Why, I thought he was one of those Boston Fellers who thought it the respectable thing to do." "I think he does nothing ostensible—Ned." "Well—my Father says if there were another Judge in the Commonwealth like him, the practice of Law would amount to something." I told him I thought it probable—though recalling that I had never tried any case in your presence but my own, and that, with your sweet assistance—I was murmurless.

I wanted to fondle the Boy for the fervent words—but made the distinction. Dont you know you have taken my will away. . . .[20]

This conversation took place in 1878 when Ned was seventeen; its casual tone, taken together with the fact that Dickinson expresses no surprise at Ned's question, suggests that the entire family knew of her relationship with Lord.

But the most striking thing in these letter drafts is the unmistakable element of sexual passion. In this most intimate relationship, Emily Dickinson was very much like other women: Lord evidently pressed for sexual union; she held back, despite the potency of her own desire.

[about 1878] Dont you know you are happiest while I withhold and not confer—dont you know that No is the wildest word we consign to Language?

You do, for you know all things. . . . To lie so near your longing—to touch it as I passed, for I am but a restive sleeper and often should journey from your Arms through the happy night, but you will lift me back, wont you, for only there I ask to be. . . .

. . . I will not let you cross—but it is all your's, and when it is right I will lift the Bars, and lay you in the Moss—You showed me the word.

I hope it has no different guise when my fingers make it. It is Anguish I long conceal from you to let you leave me, hungry, but you ask the divine Crust and that would doom the Bread.

[about 1880] It is strange that I miss you at night so much when I was never with you—but the punctual love invokes you soon as my eyes are shut—and I wake warm with the want sleep had almost filled—I dreamed last week that you had died—and one had carved a statue of you and I was asked to unvail it—and I said what I had not done in Life I would not in death when your loved eyes could not forgive—. . . How could I long to give who never saw your natures Face—.

[April 30, 1882] . . . I do—do want you tenderly. The air is soft as Italy, but when it touches me, I spurn it with a Sigh, because it is not you.[21]

Otis Lord wanted to marry Emily Dickinson and bring her to live with him in Salem. After all the years of loneliness, Emily Dickinson might have grasped this happiness with eager hands, but she did not. She wavered. She was tempted. But she never left the Homestead to wed him.

There were objective obstacles, opposition on both sides to a marriage. Austin and Lavinia were pleased with Emily's new happiness; however, Sue seems to have been shocked at this late-blooming ardor. When Mabel Loomis Todd first questioned Sue about the sisters who lived next door, she was severely warned away from them. "You will not allow your husband to go there, I hope!" Sue sputtered. "They have not, either of them, any idea of morality. . . . I went in there one day, and in the drawing room I found Emily reclining in the arms of a man. What can you say to that?"[22] The objections in Salem had their origins not so much in false modesties as in considerations of hard cash. After Mrs. Lord's death, her sister and her niece kept house for the judge. The niece, Abbie Farley, was the chief beneficiary of Judge Lord's will, and since he was a man of considerable wealth, she stood to inherit a good deal so long as he did not marry. An intimate friend of Susan Dickinson's, Abbie Farley actively opposed the match; indeed, her hostility toward Emily Dickinson was so great that she destroyed everything the poet had written to Lord, letters and whatever poetry they may have contained. More important than such opposition, however, were the immediate claims upon Dickinson's loyalty and attention. In June 1875, almost a year to the day after Edward Dickinson's death, his widow suffered the stroke that would leave her incapacitated for the rest of her life. Fretful, sometimes mildly hallucinatory and easily agitated, she was unable to perform the simplest physical actions unaided. Emily and Vinnie cooperated in her care; if Emily had left, some other arrangement would have been required.

In November 1882 the elder Mrs. Dickinson quietly passed away. Dickinson's letters to Lord soon toy deliciously with the thought of marriage.

[November 1882?] The celestial Vacation of writing you after an interminable Term of *four Days,* I can scarcely express. . . . Emily "Jumbo"! [He has been teasing her about having gained a little weight.] Sweetest name, but I know a sweeter—Emily Jumbo Lord. Have I your approval?

[December 3, 1882] What if you are writing! Oh, for the power to look, yet were I there, I would not, except you invited me—reverence for each other being the sweet aim. . . . While others go to Church, I go to mine, for are you not my Church, and have we not a Hymn that no one knows but us?

. . . You said with loved timidity in asking me to your dear Home, you would "try not to make it unpleasant." So delicate a diffidence, how beautiful to see! I do not think a Girl extant has so divine a modesty.

You even call me to your Breast with apology! Of what must my poor Heart be made?

Yet time continued to pass, and for whatever reason, Emily Dickinson remained in Amherst. Lord had been critically ill in May 1882 but recovered; on March 11, 1884, he suffered a stroke, and two days later he died. "Dear Mr Lord has left us—," Dickinson wrote Mrs. Holland. "After a brief unconsciousness, a Sleep that ended with a smile, so his Nieces tell us, he hastened away, 'seen,' we trust, 'of Angels'—'Who knows that secret deep'—'Alas, not I—.' "[23] Even though she had never consented to marry him, Emily Dickinson carried her devotion to the grave. As she lay in her coffin, Vinnie put two heliotropes in her hand, " 'to take to Judge Lord.' "[24]

Even here, in this last love, Dickinson's earliest concerns creep into her language: "Oh, for the power to look," Dickinson writes—a face-to-face interview synonymous with the most profoundly intimate communication. Yet it was precisely such closeness that she rejected. After her father had died, after her mother, too, had passed away, she still elected a relationship mediated by the written word over one that permitted sustained, direct interaction.

In every separate case, a good reason can be adduced for Dickinson's decision to interpose a distance between herself and the men she most cared for: Wadsworth's friendship and spiritual counsel were valuable because he was outside of the closely knit group of ministers who conducted affairs in the township of Amherst and at the college; Bowles was probably all the more attentive to her for being kept in uncertainty about her willingness to see him; Lord's love was reciprocated, but it came at a time when duty to her failing mother prevailed. However, when they are evaluated as a group, these relationships combine to suggest a lethal conviction at the core of Dickinson's nature: deep affection for anyone outside the immediate family and passionate love both *necessarily entail separation.*

Such a paradigm reveals profound ambivalence, and Dickinson's behavior with all of her intimate friends conveys the same conflict: loneliness and a hunger for genuine companionship balanced against primitive, unutterable fear whenever she was engaged in a relationship of emotional intimacy. She seems to have had little or no flexibility, no capacity to enjoy personal exchange and closeness and then to let go, secure in the conviction that the valued friend or beloved would return to renew the bonds of familiarity. Thus the same woman who had required her sister, brother, and sister-in-law all to live in the same close compound—never to submit to definitive separation until death—also chose Mrs. Holland as her closest female friend, a woman who lived first in Springfield and then in New York and thus could be seen only at infrequent intervals. Outside the family, only those relationships that could be conducted largely through the written word were comfortable.

Dickinson had the courage to *write* to many people she had never met, some of them famous people: Edward Everett Hale, Thomas Wentworth Higginson, Charles Wadsworth, Charles and James Clark, Washington Gladden (a well-known Springfield minister whom she wrote after Lord's 1882 illness). Yet she chose to *see* very few. Nor was she always comfortable when she had the opportunity to meet with one of these correspondents in person (as the two interviews with Higginson suggest).

Interestingly, Vinnie seems to have manifested a variant of the same condition. Vinnie got out and around, was comfortable leaving the Homestead for lengthy visits; yet when a passionate relationship with a man was concerned, she, too, loved best out-of-sight. Joseph Lyman left Amherst in March 1851, just after Vinnie had turned eighteen; she was a pretty, popular girl who received at least one other proposal of marriage. Still, she fixed her heart upon this friend of Austin's who had taken up permanent residence in the Deep South. When he became engaged in December 1856, she wrote him a letter that employs many of the modalities of speech that characterize Emily Dickinson's letters:

My Dear Joseph—I remember & love you still. . . . I wonder if I shall ever see your face again. . . . I'm glad you have found a life-companion who pleases you. I wish I could see you *once more* before you are married. . . . Joseph Lyman, how would you & I appear were we to meet suddenly? . . . I wish we were all children again & lifes battle not begun.

Joseph Lyman wrote his fiancée, Laura Baker, a good deal about the Dickinson family. With the cruel insightfulness of the young and carefree, he analyzed Vinnie's attractions and her behavior toward him. In one letter, he composed an imaginative sketch of the kind of life he might have had if he had married the younger Dickinson daughter. The little make-believe drama opens with Vinnie speaking:

. . . O Joseph its so warm today! Dont go down after dinner, I've been so lonely all day I had a long letter from Amherst too—Joseph, cant we go out in June. The courts adjourn in July—it wont make much difference. I am afraid I shall get sick Joseph. [Joseph imagines his response.] Vinnie, I've sworn a great oath to stay & there's no use talking. Besides I think some of taking the stump this canvass—my friends are urging me & I dont know as I will go to Massachusetts at all. You can go with Mr so & So & wife, they're going directly to Boston.[25]

All her life, Vinnie languished for the absent Joseph Lyman. Yet he perceived *her* as primarily committed to Amherst, unable to endure a separation from home and family. It is interesting that in her 1856 letter to him she articulates the wish that they "were all children again"—echoing, albeit unselfconsciously, Emily Dickinson's letters to Austin in 1853, during his season of courtship. For both young women, the phrase clearly gropes for some way to prevent time from imposing separation. None of the Dickinson children managed separation well; both girls rejected marriage when it was offered, preferring to remain at the familiar Homestead and have an absent lover whose "companionship" could be summoned at will out of the imagination.

Emily Dickinson's fifteen letters to Otis Phillips Lord remain as evidence of a love affair late in her life; however, rough drafts of three earlier letters—according to the evidence of the handwriting, composed in about 1858, 1861, and 1862—offer testimony of an earlier passion.[26] Since they were written when Dickinson was at the height of her creative powers, there has been a great deal of speculation about their intended recipient, yet they remain shrouded in mystery. It is not even necessarily the case that finished copies of the letters were ever sent: Dickinson may have worked on them and then decided not to dispatch them. Nonetheless, these must be more than mere epistolary exercises, for certain details are quite specific: in one she mentions the recipient's recent bout of sickness; in another she reminds him of something he said to her when they last met and of their "awful parting" on this occasion. Yet no detail is precise enough to identify any man in particular. Wadsworth and Bowles have both been conjectured, but these are unlikely choices. Dickinson may well have been addressing herself to Judge Lord at a time when the love between them could not be socially sanctioned. Or she may have become emotionally involved with some other man whose identity is not known. By the late 1850s, a great many distinguished speakers came regularly to Amherst; what is more, the college had a collection of successful alumni who returned for commencement exercises, Class Day celebrations, or merely a visit. Men of the stature of Henry Ward Beecher came frequently to Amherst. At this distance of time, it would be difficult even to name all the men Emily Dickinson might have come to know during these years. However, the identity of the intended recipient is less important than the pattern of language and thought that is revealed in these "Master" letters.

The first is the shortest of the three notes, and also the one whose tone most closely approaches Dickinson's usual epistolary style.

Dear Master

I am ill, but grieving more that you are ill, I make my stronger hand work long eno' to tell you. . . .

. . . I wish that I were great, like Mr. Michael Angelo, and could paint for you. You ask me what my flowers said—then they were disobedient—I gave them messages. They said what the lips in the West, say, when the sun goes down, and so says the Dawn. . . .

Each Sabbath on the Sea, makes me count the Sabbaths, till we meet on shore—. . . . I cannot talk any more . . . tonight . . . for this pain denies me.

How strong when weak to recollect, and easy, quite, to love. Will you tell me, please to tell me, soon as you are well.

Perhaps the most interesting thing in this letter is the reference to her having sent him several pieces of poetry, the "flowers" he has evidently puzzled over. And if her mode of salutation adopts a modest mien, the estimation of her own work is as self-confident here as it is in her later letters responding to Higginson's criticism. She does not apologize for his puzzlement, and she states the aspiration to Michelangelo's greatness without the least qualification or excuse. If anything, when speaking about her poetry, she slips into attitudes of justifiable pride and mastery; thus the riddling response to his query ("They say what the lips in the West, say") gently takes *him* to task for the failure to understand. Confident in her craft and confident as well that they will meet again, she finds it "easy, quite, to love."

The second letter, written about three years later, is the longest of these missives. Something (we cannot know what) has gone awry in the relationship between them, and confidence has been replaced by anguish.

Master.

If you saw a bullet hit a Bird—and he told you he was'nt shot—you might weep at his courtesy, but you would certainly doubt his word.

One drop more from the gash that stains your Daisy's bosom—then would you *believe?* Thomas' faith in Anatomy, was stronger than his faith in faith. . . . I heard of a thing called "Redemption"—which rested men and women. You remember I asked you for it—you gave me something else. . . . I am older—tonight, Master—but the love is the same—so are the moon and the crescent. If it had been God's will that I might breathe where you breathed and find the place—myself—at night—if I . . . never forget that I am not with you—and that sorrow and frost are nearer than I—if I wish with a might I cannot repress—that mine were the Queen's place—the love of the Plantagenet is my only apology—. . .

These things are . . . holy, sir, I touch them . . . hallowed, but persons who pray—dare remark . . . "Father"! You say I do not tell you all—Daisy confessed—and denied not.

Vesuvius dont talk—Etna—dont—. . . One of them—said a syllable—a thousand years ago, and Pompeii heard it, and hid forever—She could'nt look the world in the face, afterward—I suppose—Bashful Pompeii! "Tell you of the want"—you know what a leech is, dont you—and you have felt the horizon hav'nt you—and did the sea—never come so close as to make you dance?

. . . I used to think when I died—I could see you—so I died as fast as I could. . . . Say I may wait for you—say I need go with no stranger to the . . . untried . . . fold—. . . What would you do with me if I came "in white?" Have you the little chest to put the Alive—in?

I want to see you more—Sir—than all I wish for in this world—and the wish—altered a little—will be my only one—for the skies.

... just to look in your face, while you looked in mine—then I could play in the woods till Dark—till you take me where Sundown cannot find us—...

I did'nt think to tell you, you did'nt come to me "in white," nor ever told me why,

> No Rose, yet felt myself a'bloom,
> No Bird—yet rode in Ether.

Although the first letter had offered information and sought information in return, the purpose of this letter is principally emotive: it attempts to convey her passion, her longing, and her sorrow; insofar as it argues, it does so by the poignant exhibition of pain. Although the letter nowhere mentions Dickinson's poetic ambitions, her vocation as poet is taken as a "given" throughout. Most striking, however, is the fact that when Dickinson seeks to give urgent form to her feelings, the language and categories of the poetry flood into the prose and overtake ordinary epistolary style.

Consequently, the microcosm of the lovers assumes the same tragic configuration as the macrocosm that is ruled by God: it is a world desolated by wounding and by the loss of face-to-face communication. What this letter records is yet another fall into language—here necessitated not by God's absence, but by the lover's.

The letter begins by playing upon the notion of what must be *told in writing* as opposed to what can be seen or heard. Strangely enough, given Dickinson's obsession with the importance of face-to-face communication, the second and third "Master" letters both suggest that there has been some grievous failure of speech (here, "You say I do not tell you all—"). Ironically, then, the assumptions that inform these letters reverse those behind so much of the poetry—that seeing and hearing are better than reading or writing. The image of bird and bullet with which the letter opens is so general that it leaves the exact nature of the blow to the poet / woman uncertain. Nonetheless, the letter clearly implies that although the beloved ought to have been able to infer her pain (even though she disavowed it when they were together), the written words of this letter must play a role in making the invisible wound apparent.

The notion of wounding is one element from the poetry that suffuses this letter with intensity; the ancient tale of Vesuvius and Pompeii is another—the unmitigated force of the volcanic eruption and the subsequent interment of Pompeii (here figured as feminine), the city that was constrained to await resurrection; horizons, too, are imported from the language of the poetry; and the ravenous sea is akin to that mythic force from the verse. In each of these tropes, the lover is loosely identified with the part that is given to God in the poetry; thus Dickinson construes herself as awaiting "Redemption." The "apology" that is offered to justify her wish for "the Queen's place" echoes the royal language of salvation, "the love of the Plantagenet." The reward she covets above all others is the Biblical one—Revelation—"just to look in your face, while you looked in mine."

Since the letter is a very rough first draft—with words scratched out and alternative phrases penned in—however high-pitched and involuntary the tone of emotional distress may seem, its register has been artfully calculated. The mode of address here differs markedly from the later love letters to Lord: no less carefully wrought, those notes deliberately put aside the mantle of poet so that Dickinson could write intimately, as woman. It differs, too, from the letters to Bowles, where the young woman encloses a poem and then comments on it in a voice approximating her own ("Here's—what I had to 'tell you'—"). In this "Master" letter, the person is almost entirely obliterated by the poet; and the note begins not with a woman in pain, but with a wounded "Bird." The vulnerability of the speaker, then, is carefully balanced against her power when manipulating the written word. The challenge "What would you do with me if I came 'in white?' Have you the little chest to put the Alive—in?" cuts two ways. At one level, "white" surely signifies here (as it sometimes does in the poetry) the virginal state, preserved for the one truly beloved; to put such a one in "the little chest" would be a species of burial alive—an outrage too terrible for contemplation. Yet "white" is the color of renunciation in the poetry: "Mine—by the Right of the White Election!" is the "Saint's" declaration of utter independence and autonomy. And *this* implication of "white" asserts not receptivity, but mastery and the will for self-determination. To come "in white" would be to come as poet in supreme confidence; the recipient would have no choice but to put the vibrant Voice of the page into "the little chest" where letters are kept—unchangingly "Alive," though entirely unapproachable as a real woman. The "Master" has evidently turned his hand to writing verse, some of which he has promised to show her. The reproach "you did'nt come to me 'in white,' nor ever told me why" closes the letter by putting him at a distinct disadvantage. What man in his right mind would compete with Emily Dickinson for pre-eminence in writing poetry?

In one respect this letter shows nothing so clearly as Emily Dickinson's all-too-human discomfort in suffering love's insecurity. Any woman might be expected to assert her strength in the face of such uncertainty or even rejection. Some might flaunt the presence of another suitor; Emily Dickinson gives a deft demonstration of her poetic powers. Yet there is a crucial difference between choosing between two suitors and choosing between poetry and a human lover. In the first case, a woman has already made the decision to find her reward in real-world relationships; her uncertainty is limited to discovering an appropriate consort. In Dickinson's case, the choice is between two different kinds of happiness—a precarious and changeable relationship with another human being, or an unchanging "life" through the Voice of the poetry (for in her own life, Emily Dickinson consistently construed the Word not as a supplement to ordinary human relationships, but as an alternative to them). The force with which the Voice of the poet dominates this letter suggests that at some level Dickinson had already made her choice—preferring the safety of mediating language.

There is no reason to doubt the eloquent testimony of Emily Dickinson's letters: surely she ached for Phil Lord's caress at the very time that she was refusing his invitation to marry. By the same token, she longed for Sam Bowles's congenial company even at moments when she denied him an interview. The anguish of these "Master" letters is certainly authentic; yet even her testament of pain cannot eliminate the intense ambivalence that runs throughout them. Like all the other emotionally charged relationships outside of the close circle of sister, brother, and sister-in-law, this relationship confirmed Emily Dickinson's deepest conviction: the world is blighted with the curse of loss, and all true affection bears some mark of its wound.

The third letter has no salutation; it is the least finished of the three and the least likely to have been sent.*

Oh, did I offend it—[Did'nt it want me to tell it the truth] Daisy—Daisy—offend it—who bends her smaller life to his (its) meeker (lower) every day—who only asks—a task—[who] something to do for love of it—some little way she cannot guess to make that master glad—

A love so big it scares her, rushing among her small heart—pushing aside the blood and leaving her faint . . .

Daisy—who never flinched thro' that awful parting, but held her life so tight he should not see the wound—. . .

Wonder stings me more than the Bee—who did never sting me—but made gay music with his might wherever I [may] [should] did go—Wonder wastes my pound, you said I had no size to spare—. . .

I've got a cough as big as a thimble—but I dont care for that—I've got a Tomahawk in my side but that dont hurt me much. [if you] Her Master stabs her more—

Wont he come to her—or will he let her seek him, never minding [whatever] so long wandering [out] if to him at last . . .

. . . I will be [glad] [as the] your best little girl—nobody else will see me, but

---

*This letter is a very rough draft; Dickinson's alternative suggested changes are in parentheses; words crossed out are in brackets.

you—but that is enough—I shall not want any more—and all that Heaven only will disappoint me—will be because it's not so dear

The letter may seem at first a gasping plea from this woman of thirty-one. However, anyone familiar with the habits of Dickinson's poetry can penetrate the appearances to perceive the complexity of her tone. The mien of humility and the grotesque girlish postures barely conceal the inrush of rage. Thus at its very beginning, the letter dismisses the recipient to the ranks of the dead: he is "it"; the "eye / I" has been *closed*. Moreover, the wound is now construed so explicitly as a painful sexual violation—the bee sting, the stab, and the Tomahawk—that any blissful, passionate resolution has clearly been forsworn. Language brimming over from the poetry inundates the missive with images of savagery; the man who might have delivered "Redemption" seems to have brought only a bitter confirmation of God's ravaging ways.

It is tempting to conclude that Emily Dickinson was the architect of her own unhappiness and that her expectation became its own tragic, self-confirming prophecy. There are elements in this letter to support such a view; despite the tone of distress, for example, the speaker gives every indication that it was she who precipitated the parting ("Did'nt it want me to tell it the truth"). Perhaps any fulfillment of passionate love was too threatening to Dickinson's sense of personal integrity to be endured—identity itself put in peril by the danger of being engulfed. The letter hints at this possibility: "A love so big it scares her, rushing among her small heart." However, no one can speak with authority about cause and effect now, so long afterward and with such meager evidence. It is sufficient to take note of the pattern.

After Emily Dickinson's death, her brother dismissed out of hand all the talk of blighted romance. True, she had gradually fallen into the habit of leading a cloistered life; however, her withdrawal had nothing to do with reversals of love. "Austin . . . was quite definite," Bingham reports.

He said that at different times Emily had been devoted to several men. He even went so far as to maintain that she had been several times in love, in her own way. But he denied that because of her devotion to any one man she forsook all others. Such an idea was mere "nonsense." Her gradual withdrawal, Austin insisted, was perfectly natural. . . . Little by little she withdrew from village life, seeing fewer and fewer acquaintances as time went on until, after her father's death in 1874, she became the recluse of the legend.[27]

For whatever reason, one after another the major friendships and passionate relationships of Emily Dickinson's life all confirmed her deepest conviction: where passion is concerned, there must be separation.

3 ❖ *At the Conclusion Was the Word*

Although separation was the constant in these many real-life relationships, the causes for the separation seem various. In the case of Dickinson's love affair with Lord, she was the decisive agent—not so much rejecting his proposals of marriage as lingering in indecision until his death made marriage impossible. The situation with Bowles was more mixed: the many demands of his own life allowed only a limited number of trips to Amherst, and thus Dickinson was often in a position of urging him to visit her; yet when he did, she frequently refused to see him. Higginson and Wadsworth lived at a sufficient distance to make separation the general condition of the friendship. The "Master" letters are inconclusive: neither the nature of the separation nor its cause can be discerned.

In the love poetry, however, the cause of separation is virtually always the same: it is a transcendent necessity; *God* decrees the distance. Nor is His action entirely without cause. The speaker in many of these poems claims to need neither the Divinity nor His Heaven: the lovers can make their own Paradise because the beloved is, himself, a sufficient redeemer.

> *There came a Day at Summer's full,*
> *Entirely for me—*
> *I thought that such were for the Saints,*
> *Where Resurrections—be—*
>
> *The Sun, as common, went abroad,*
> *The flowers, accustomed, blew,*
> *As if no soul the solstice passed*
> *That maketh all things new—*
>
> *The time was scarce profaned, by speech—*
> *The symbol of a word*
> *Was needless, as at Sacrament,*
> *The Wardrobe—of our Lord—*
>
> *Each was to each The Sealed Church,*
> *Permitted to commune this—time—*
> *Lest we too awkward show*
> *At Supper of the Lamb.*
>
> *The Hours slid fast—as Hours will,*
> *Clutched tight, by greedy hands—*

So faces on two Decks, look back,
Bound to opposing lands—

And so when all the time had leaked,
Without external sound
Each bound the Other's Crucifix—
We gave no other Bond—

Sufficient troth, that we shall rise—
Deposed—at length, the Grave—
To that new Marriage,
Justified—through Calvaries of Love—

(#322)

Although the word "Noon" does not occur in this poem, the scientific language makes it clear that this union is defined by some witchery of brilliant light—midday "at Summer's full." The "solstice" of the speaker's transforming love is literally a moment outside of time: "the point . . . at which the sun stops or ceases to recede from the equator." It is Heaven, then, "Where Resurrections—be—"; it is Revelation as well, "The Sealed Church." It surpasses speech; it surpasses even poetry—"The symbol of a word / Was needless." Could it but be sustained, it would be perfection. Yet the lovers have disrupted the mythic order in having experienced the Redemption before the Crucifixion. And unlike the poet, they cannot stop the Clock: "The Hours slid fast," driving them apart. They may look toward a "Marriage," but not on earth. Ironically, theirs is a too-perfect union for sublunary creatures; only Heaven can contain them, and they must earn that Paradise "through Calvaries of Love."

Sometimes, this anguish can be converted into a seeming virtue, and a rhetorical advantage can be wrung from the impediment to happiness. Thus the speaker of one poem assumes a Godlike role, waiting for the parade on Judgment Day to validate her choice of the beloved. "*Of all the Souls that stand create— / I have elected—One— / When Sense from Spirit—files away— / And Subterfuge—is done— / When that which is—and that which was— / Apart—intrinsic—stand— / And this brief Tragedy of Flesh— / Is shifted—like a Sand— / When Figures show their royal Front— / And Mists—are carved away, / Behold the Atom—I preferred— / To all the lists of Clay!*" (#664) The exquisite pacing of time's movement toward eternity and the slowly building import of the choice combine to invest the last two lines with such an exquisite air of triumph that centuries of separation seem almost inconsequential ("this brief Tragedy of Flesh"). Yet more often the love poetry returns to the heartbreaking fact of pain. Together the lovers are able to create what God had claimed the exclusive right to endow. Although he cannot deprive them of their capacity for Glory, He can intrude into the relationship and impose the wound of parting. "*I should have been too saved—I see—,*" the speaker in another poem muses, "*Too rescued—Fear too dim to me / That I could spell the Prayer / I knew so perfect—yesterday— / That Scalding One—Sabacthini— / Recited fluent—here—*" (#313). God had required even His own Son to experience the blow of abandonment and to recite the plea "Why has thou forsaken me?" Could He demand less of other human beings? And if the beloved's presence can repair the ancient loss of the Divinity by offering a union so perfect that it becomes wordless, then the beloved must be taken away so that the speaker is compelled to reiterate Christ's cry of loss: "Sabacthini."

What happens in many of these love poems is a subtle shift of attention from a primary focus upon the lovers' relationship with each other (or upon the speaker's passionate yearning for her beloved) to a predominate concern with the lovers' challenge to God. In effect, Dickinson's way of defining love's excellence—as an authentic New Testament of unstinting affection—leaves the poetry poised between two possible conclusions. On the one hand, the couple might adapt the perfection of their devotion to the humble routine of quotidian life, love infusing marriage with surpassing strength and delight; in this case, the Voice of the verse might be primarily that of the "Wife," immeasurably strengthened by her right to wield the terms of transcendent glory. Poems like "Forever at His side to walk," "One Year ago—jots what?," or "Doubt Me! My Dim Companion!" capture just such an attitude: the rapture partakes of Paradise, and it can be extended without change from earth into eternity; yet the flood of feeling engendered by the poem is primarily attached to the earthly enactment of love. On the other hand, the couple's relationship might become incorporated into the poet's larger concern, her ongoing wrestle with the Lord. However muted the militance may be, a line like "Each was to each The Sealed Church" flaunts God's supremacy, and instead of looking toward earthly life for fulfillment and focusing her attention exclusively upon the beloved, the speaker becomes preoccupied with the lovers' power to displace the Deity. Poems like "I should have been too saved—I see—" hover at the verge of this impulse, courting divine reprisal against lovers who have encroached into the eternal realm; the "Wife's" Voice is displaced by accents of the Saint, and renunciation rather than fulfillment is the necessary outcome.

It is the threat of this power to usurp the rights of the Divinity that brings the reprisal of separation. Thus when Dickinson's speakers seek to explain the Crucifixion of parting that is so often their lot, they are constrained to look toward the mythic realm for reasons: separation does not result from an incompatibility between the lovers; rather, it is the punishment exacted by a God Who is jealous of His Divine prerogatives.

> *They put Us far apart—*
> *As separate as Sea*

And Her unsown Peninsula—
We signified "These see"—

They took away our Eyes—
They thwarted Us with Guns—
"I see Thee" each responded straight
Through Telegraphic Signs—

With Dungeons—They devised—
But through their thickest skill—
And their opaquest Adamant—
Our Souls saw—just as well—

They summoned Us to die—
With sweet alacrity
We stood upon our stapled feet—
Condemned—but just—to see—

Permission to recant—
Permission to forget—
We turned our backs upon the Sun
For perjury of that—

Not Either—noticed Death—
Of Paradise—aware—
Each other's Face—was all the Disc
Each other's setting—saw—

(#474)

This is not one of Dickinson's better love poems, but its strategies can inform a reader's understanding of the better work.

It begins with the premise of separation, and the poem progresses through series of ever more strenuous efforts to break the lovers' bond; yet the triumph of the speaker lies in the fact that, as the means of prohibition become more punitive, the love only becomes commensurately more exalted. At the end, even "Death" and "Paradise" are eclipsed by the "Disc" of "Each other's Face." Strangely enough, however, although the force of mutual love is postulated as matching any force that can be mustered against it, the reader can in fact derive no sense of the beloved at all—indeed, no sense that he is even important to the speaker as a separate individual. Instead, what is important is the lovers' *power,* especially when it is measured against first earthly armies and then divine might. This power derives not from action, certainly not from the domestic round of activities that might combine to create a home, but rather, from a unique, wordless form of intimate communication: " 'These see'—. . . 'I see Thee.' "

The oldest and most primitive form of human communication, the face-to-face language of eyes, is here conflated with the most exalted form of enlightenment, the Biblical fulfillment in Revelation when men shall see God face to face, and both are imputed to the lovers. The Alpha and Omega of all human understanding can be contained in the mutual gaze of this man and woman. For lovers freely "to see" each other, then, is a form of extraordinary intimacy and worship, and together the man and woman can enact a unique form of idolatry that God will not allow. Thus the imperative to separate them derives from the essential nature of this love, a force that too nearly succeeds in displacing the Creator Himself.

Withal, there is a peculiar hollowness in the poem's conclusion. Through every trial the lovers hold fast to the gaze that spells their glory; thus "Death" and "Paradise" become not God's triumph, but their own—the ultimate justification of their fidelity to each other. Yet what do they gain save this victory over the Lord? These lovers, who are stipulated as sharing everything in general, seem to share nothing in particular: there is no record of small kindnesses; no gentle memories of hardships made easier by an affectionate understanding; no lingering traces of humor or delight; no passion; no winsome regret. In short, there is no real-world component to this love at all. Its nature is defined entirely by the transcendent, and ironically, its "triumph" cannot be felt by the reader as anything more than a sleight of hand with words.

Some of Dickinson's best love poetry is rooted in a simple conviction: love is a way of *being,* not a way of *speaking.* It is not surprising, therefore, that many of the most often repeated lines from this portion of her work—"*Come slowly—Eden!*" or "*Wild Nights—Wild Nights! / Were I with thee / Wild Nights should be / Our luxury!*"—are either anticipatory or hypothetical. When love can be actual and not merely potential, even a poet will prefer silence or whispered fragments of sound to the artful cadences of verse: "*Say it again, Saxon! / Hush—Only to me!*" Yet this simple conviction is tragically tied to another, which comes out of Dickinson's more general belief concerning transcendent reality: when they are together, the lovers are capable of *being* like God. It is this combination of convictions that compels Dickinson so often to conclude that the lovers of her poetry can never enact their passion on earth.

Ironically, then, just as it was humanity's wounding loss at Peniel that became the impetus for Emily Dickinson's poetic career, it is this wound of separation that makes the love poetry possible. If the lovers could be together, there would no need for poetry: they would possess the unrestrained, wordless capacity "to see." Because they are parted, words become necessary, and the need for poetry is born. In addition, the nature of this genesis decrees that more often than not, it will be a poetry of unconsummated love. Perhaps nowhere is the legacy of Emily Dickinson's earliest "fall into language" more painfully evident than in this imperative for love poetry: gaining power over the Word in order to create a verse of passionate affection is all too often accompanied by a loss of that loving intimacy whose face-to-face communion surpasses verbal formulation. Thus although her love poetry could be humorous and playful, it is seldom a jubilant celebration of love's fulfillment or love's inexhaustible variety. Instead, it takes other forms: it is anticipatory; it is hypothetical; it speaks with anguished recollection; it tells a tale of what might have been. Sometimes it sings the saddest of all songs—a lament for love's impossibility.

There is one final fact about the love poetry that to some degree sets it apart from Dickinson's other work. The struggle between the human and the divine that was external at Peniel is here internalized in a potent form of linguistic wrestle: a striving between the terms of this world and those of the next, an effort to find some domestic, real-world accommodation for Paradise, an attempt of the "Wife's" Voice to encompass and contain the Saint's. When she succeeds, Dickinson's achievement would seem intrinsically impossible; she allows her earthbound reader to feel something that approaches divine ecstasy or infinite sorrow. No poem captures these eloquent paradoxes more powerfully than Dickinson's most often repeated litany of loss.

> *I cannot live with You—*
> *It would be Life—*
> *And Life is over there—*
> *Behind the Shelf*
>
> *The Sexton keeps the Key to—*
> *Putting up*
> *Our Life—His Porcelain—*
> *Like a Cup—*
>
> *Discarded of the Housewife—*
> *Quaint—or Broke—*
> *A newer Sevres pleases—*
> *Old Ones crack—*
>
> *I could not die—with You—*
> *For One must wait*
> *To shut the Other's Gaze down—*
> *You—could not—*
>
> *And I—Could I stand by*
> *And see You—freeze—*
> *Without my Right of Frost—*
> *Death's privilege?*

Nor could I rise — with You —
Because Your Face
Would put out Jesus' —
That New Grace

Glow plain — and foreign
On my homesick Eye —
Except that You than He
Shone closer by —

They'd judge Us — How —
For You — served Heaven — You know,
Or sought to —
I could not —

Because You saturated Sight —
And I had no more Eyes
For sordid excellence
As Paradise

And were You lost, I would be —
Though My Name
Rang loudest
On the Heavenly fame —

And were You — saved —
And I — condemned to be
Where You were not —
That self — were Hell to Me —

So We must meet apart —
You there — I — here —
With just the Door ajar
That Oceans are — and Prayer —
And that White Sustenance —
Despair —

(#640)

The most famous of Dickinson's love poems, perhaps even the most familiar of all her works, this poem more than deserves the attention it has received. A masterful manipulation of emotional nuances, it elicits several different kinds of response simultaneously: by some measure, these ought to be contradictory; however, they are not. The most searing and definitive assertion of loss becomes at the same time the most stirring expression of passion as counterbalanced structures hold the poem in taut suspension, each pushing toward some resolution and each interacting with the others to prohibit any simple conclusion. There are at least four distinct patterns at work within the poem, leading variously to a culmination of exquisite ardor and terrible pain. The poem is about love, of course. Yet taken in the larger context of Dickinson's mission, it spells the fate of the poet as well. Perhaps in the end it tells us more about Emily Dickinson herself than any other single work.

The first pattern is suggested by one reading of the paradox in the opening lines: "I cannot live with You— / It would be Life—": a tension between "Life" as the term of earth's existence and "Life" eternal as that fulfillment in Heaven toward which we yearn. The classic Christian journey toward Heavenly Life, told in familiar allegorical works of art (*Pilgrim's Progress*, for example), has a denouement that is literally elating—both because it soars upward to Paradise and because a happy ending is assured to all the faithful. The skeletal outline of this story provides a kind of "plot," beginning in the first stanza and concluding in the punultimate. The terms of this plot are sketched by an inexorable verbal movement: to "live"; to "die"; to "rise"; to have God "judge"; to be "lost" or "saved." This push toward Paradise carries an intrinsic hope for unlimited delight, and Dickinson's use of this shadow-plan enables her to draw upon many readers' deepest longings. Yet Heaven exists only by virtue of God's authority and decree, and the triumph over death that allows for some eternal happy ending is a miracle whose efficacy we can trust only insofar as we can trust the Redeemer's power. The interdiction enunciated in the first two lines turns upon the fact that the very nature of the lovers' excellence is a force that might disable God if it were permitted to exist. Thus the magnet of "Heaven" that pulls the poem forward and tantalizes our expectations can exist only if the lovers' relationship is aborted. Their *unique* story becomes a desolating variation of this Christian allegory: "not live"; "not die"; not "rise"; stand outside God's capacity to "judge"; not be "lost"; however, not be "saved," either. In short, *not be*. Each stage in this anti-tale of salvation describes a greater loss. If this were the only movement in the poem, the story would recount unmitigated devastation, but such is not the case.

The second pattern at work within the poem grows out of a different interpretation of the puzzling contradiction in the first two lines: "Life" as God's realm of eternal bliss juxtaposed to the superior Paradise that would be created by the lovers' "Life" together—either on earth or in some after-world—a perfect union of eyes / I's. And this tension, unlike the first, is all-embracing, beginning in the opening stanza and concluding in the last. The first three stanzas linger in earthly existence; God's realm is remote, and the grandeur of His power is vastly attenuated. The "Life" offered by the Deity is defined not by the thing itself but only by the promise of Heaven that is embedded in the Lord's Supper—for it is the vessels of this ceremony of wine and bread that the Sexton keeps under lock and key. Yet just as God's exalted state is muted here, so is the lovers'; and the statement of acceptance, "I cannot live with You— / It would be Life—," has little initial force beyond the facile paradox. As the poem moves toward death, there is a modicum of amplification. "Die" carries the faint echo of sexual fulfillment, and intercourse is here construed as interview, a private code of law or "privilege" of eye / I. The first duty is "To shut the Other's Gaze down—," a modest act. However, there is a second, and in a line drenched with the sound of "I," its cry breaks into the poetry, "And I—Could I stand by." It is the "Right of Frost," death matching death even as life had matched life.

This behavior in life and death sets the lovers apart from all others; however, their full glory cannot be grasped until the poem enters the transcendent realm. The "New Grace" that had been promised by Jesus was *His* "New Testament of Love," the pledge that we shall "rise" from the grave into Heaven, born into a life where we will exist in the presence of God forever, once again able to see His face. Yet the lovers' "rise" would surpass even this miracle of Redemption "Because Your Face / Would put out Jesus'." The impact of the conversion experience can thus be entirely reversed: in submitting to faith, each Christian had allowed his or her eye to be put out; now the beloved can "put out" Jesus's face. Superior even to resurrection, the lovers stand beyond God's capacity to judge. The speaker's defiance even takes an epic turn: she cares naught for Heaven or Hell, immune to any "excellence" but the beloved's. Milton's Satan had claimed that his independence of God was a function of his own power: "The mind is its own place, and in itself / Can make a Heav'n of Hell, a Hell of Heav'n" (*Paradise Lost,* book I, lines 254–55). This speaker follows Satan in defiance; however, she knows that both "self" and "Heaven" are defined solely by the beloved's presence: "*And were You—saved— / And I—condemned to be / Where You were not— / That self—were Hell to me—.*" The duel of God's "Life" and the "Life" that could be created by the lovers becomes a complex dance as the Lord's effort is repeatedly matched and overmatched by the beloved. Still, the poem's premise does not change: the lovers can *possess* none of the would-be splendor that is rendered by this escalating series of comparisons, precisely *because* of their love's magnificence. Indeed, the wrenching irony of the progression that concludes this poem is that the measure of their love can be demonstrated only by articulating what they have lost. Paradoxically, then, the word of ultimate desolation—"Despair"—becomes the only way to give utterance to ultimate ardor.

The conclusion of the poem is so fraught with feeling—so perfectly poised between the extremes of love's intensity and the speaker's loneliness— that no single response can do justice to the complexity of the verse. Perhaps the sublime possibilities dominate at first, the wonder of a beloved who can best even the Godhead. Yet as the poem lingers in memory, other elements may begin to emerge with increasing clarity.

A third structuring pattern running throughout speaks in contradiction to this rhetoric of transcendence: a homely language of everyday conversation, a discourse of here and there, the "Wife's" vernacular. This mode of speech is strongest at the beginning, where it so fully dominates the tone that the sacramental invocation of the Lord's Supper may be all but lost. The forfeit "Life" is not far away, just "over there," as near as a neighbor, and the poem seems almost cluttered with the everyday: the "Sexton's" cares about the church and the various forms of common "Cup" that invoke the lovers' unnamed chalice of devotion. A reader may even grow impatient with the discourse here, especially upon a second or third reading when the sublime description of the lovers' Heaven can be anticipated. Still, the summoning of everyday ritual continues through the death: the closing of the corpse's eyes is stipulated; but the housewife's allotted task before the days of undertakers, washing the body and preparing it for burial, is only glancingly implied as the poem begins to ascend skyward. Perversely, it is only in Heaven that the power of this ordinary language begins to become apparent: "*Your Face / Would put out Jesus'— / That New Grace / Glow plain—and foreign / On my homesick Eye— / Except that You than He / Shone closer by—.*" The two stanzas that contain these lines constitute the middle of the poem, the hinge upon which the verse turns from earth into Paradise, and nowhere else in the verse is the language of glory more thoroughly commingled with the parlance of everyday speech—the speaker "homesick" for the "Life" that never could be, an ordinary, domestic life infused with the radiance of this love. True, the two kinds of language are united, at least in part, by way of reversal: it is God's "Grace" that is "plain." Still, the tonalities of everyday speech tug resolutely at emerging transcendence, mooring it to the things of this world—hoping, perhaps, for the impossible, a lovers' Heaven-on-earth.

Once the notion of Judgment enters the poem, this quotidian touchstone seems lost: the beloved is defined entirely by his superiority to God, and the speaker looks no longer to home, but to epic poetry when she seeks to amplify the meaning of her own feelings. However, the peculiar grace and effectiveness of the final stanza shows that this mode of speech was not lost, only suspended, for at the end, it reappears with unbearable poignancy. No longer commingled hopefully with the divine, everyday language now merely affirms the breach between the lovers by spinning out variations upon the theme "apart." There is a reiteration and expansion of the opening notion that perhaps "Life" is not too far away: "You there—I—here—." Yet now the possibility for proximity is repeatedly denied. The "Door ajar" recalls a home; yet "Oceans are" recalls a separation as profound as death itself. And "Prayer," an entity that might link the immanent and the transcendent, always spells despair in Dickinson's work; it thus merely completes the hopeless progression by taking it to infinity—to the silent God above, Whose face we can never see in this lifetime and Whose response will never come. Having opened with the most ordinary evocation of sacramental wine, the poem concludes with a commensurately lofty evocation of life's commonest staple, bread—"White Sustenance." Yet the "Sustenance" that prolongs the life of this love is "Despair—": a rehearsal of the existential impossibility of passion's fulfillment.

The linguistic back-and-forth between the terrestrial and the celestial is closely tied to the final structuring pattern of the work, a recursion to the Bible that allows Dickinson to treat some of the central problems of creativity. The large, architectural lines of the poem are an adaption of the account of the Last Supper as it is given in the four Gospels of the New Testament. Throughout most of this piece of verse, Dickinson alludes to the Bible through a series of reversals. Jesus began the Last Supper by asserting that one of the Apostles would betray Him to His enemies; with them at the time of the Supper, He further announced that He would soon leave them; afterward He blessed the food, first the bread and then the wine; during this blessing He enunciated a New Testament of Grace—the promise of a reunion in Heaven made possible by a resurrection of His followers from the grave; finally, He instituted the sacramental ceremony of the Lord's Supper by enjoining all Christians to commemorate His promised reunion with a celebration of bread and wine, hereafter to become the metaphorical embodiments of His lost presence. Here Dickinson juxtaposes the sustained fidelity of speaker and beloved to the assertion of betrayal with which the gospels begin; a leavetaking cannot be announced because the lovers are already separated; the order of sacramental food is inverted. But, most important, Dickinson also reverses the promise that suffuses the gospels with importance, the New Covenant whereby Jesus promised reunion; for the poem pivots upon the successive premises, "I cannot live with You . . . I could not die—with You . . . Nor could I rise—with You—."

However, there is one central element that this poem shares with the Lord's Supper: both are metaphorical embodiments of a presence that is absent, by virtue either of distance or of death. Just as it is Jesus's "presence" that infuses the sacrament with importance, so it is the magically vibrant Voice of the verse that creates something very close to "Life" out of mere paper and print. Indeed, there is one last way to understand the two lines that open the poem. "I cannot live with You— / It would be Life—": *Life*, not *Art*.

None of Emily Dickinson's readers has met the woman who lived and died in Amherst, Massachusetts, more than a century ago, but many feel that they know her, and all have heard a Voice that, though it surely is not hers, is so intimately defined by her habits of mind that it encourages friendship, familiarity, even affection. Nor was the poet Emily Dickinson unselfconscious about the enormously seductive, colloquial power of that Voice. "*I'm Nobody!*" the Voice asserts firmly, yet confidentially, "*Who are you?*" Or in a defiant mode, the Voice mocks the Christ: "*I do believe a Species / As positively live / As I, who testify it / Deny that I—am dead— / And fill my Lungs, for Witness— / From Tanks—above my Head—.*" These glorious verses expand with "Life" only because of the vitality that inheres in the Voice. After all, what sense can there be in the lines "*So We must meet apart— / You there—I— here—,*" unless "here" refers to the very page on which the poem is printed? Indeed, this short, two-line assertion might be taken as a true utterance about all of Dickinson's poetry: "We," reader and poet, do indeed "meet," but only "apart," through the mediating auspices of the Voice and the verse.

Although proximity is the necessary condition for making love, solitude is the necessary condition for writing love poetry. In fact, it is the condition of writing *all* poetry. If Jesus had stayed among us, we would not require the sacrament of the Lord's Supper; His absence is the facilitating virtue. Could Emily Dickinson have had both love and the love poetry? Could she have devoted her energies, her hopes, her passions to the Word if she had invested love and her relationship to other people with a consuming importance? Such questions cannot be answered. But this tragically beautiful love poem raises them with quiet insistence.

Part Four ◆ *The Razor's Edge:*
Some Specimen Poems

The Props assist the House
Until the House is built
And then the Props withdraw
And adequate, erect,
The House support itself
And cease to recollect
The Augur and the Carpenter—
Just such a retrospect
Hath the perfected Life—
A past of Plank and Nail
And slowness—then the Scaffolds drop
Affirming it a Soul.

(#1142)

Three hundred and sixty-six of Emily Dickinson's poems are in the handwriting of 1862; and whether she was making fair copies of more than a decade's work or whether she managed somehow to write about a poem a day, no one can doubt that Dickinson was at the height of her powers during this year.

America was raging with activity. The Civil War had begun the year before, and a government desperate for food to give the Union Army passed the Homestead Act in 1862. Under this legislation, any settler prepared to farm could purchase 160 acres of public land in Minnesota, Wisconsin, Kansas, or Nebraska for a nominal fee. Twenty-five million acres were sold on these terms during the Civil War. The allure of the Far West had already been established by the gold rush to Colorado in 1859, and in the decades following 1860 a great migration took place. Everywhere in the Northeast, rural population continued to move west or into the Eastern cities seeking better prospects than the farm could offer; at the same time, European immigrants poured into metropolitan areas all over America. The country was growing: the population in 1860 was 31,443,321; by 1870, despite the enormous casualties on both sides during the Civil War, it had increased to 38,818,449. Between 1870 and 1900 over eleven million additional immigrants entered the United States, and the nation was transformed.

In 1830 Emily Dickinson had been born into one of the last Puritan garrisons, a relic of America's great New England past; however, even as early as the mid-1850s, Amherst was no longer isolated from a culture that teetered on the edge of social revolution. By the time the Civil War was over, the town had lost most of its antique, God-fearing ways, and the changes that had been sweeping the rest of the country began to invade its boundaries. William A. Stearns, who became president of Amherst College when Edward Hitchcock resigned in 1854, had graduated from Harvard College in 1827, educated by the Unitarians. Although he took his degree in divinity at the Trinitarian Seminary at Andover, he did not have the evangelical fervor that had marked every earlier president of the College. During his tenure in office, the student body became largely secularized, and by 1871 three-quarters of the graduating class went into some profession other than the ministry. During the 1860s fraternities evolved from serious-minded literary organizations into mere social clubs; and in 1874 the graduating class decided to conclude its year with a public ball—this in a town that had not countenanced dancing even in private homes twenty years earlier. The impact of immigration was felt in Amherst, too: well-to-do citizens could find servants; and the monopoly on churches that had been held for so long by the Congregationalists gave way between 1860 and 1870 to an Episcopal church, a Methodist church, a Roman Catholic church, and a Zion chapel. Still a relatively secluded place, Amherst nonetheless lost its special spiritual kinship with America's Founding Fathers. By the end of the Civil War, the general custom of revivals had virtually been abandoned.

Literature was changing, too. In 1862 Henry David Thoreau died. Although Emerson lived until 1882, his later years were scarred by severely diminished capacities, and as early as 1866 he acknowledged that his writing career was in its decline. Nathaniel Hawthorne died in 1864. Melville lived until nearly the end of the century; however, he published no fiction after 1857, and the poetry that he wrote was issued in such small editions that it went largely unnoticed. The great days of American transcendentalism were waning, and the era of American realism was beginning. William Dean Howells, the "Dean" of American realism, began to work on the editorial staff of *The Atlantic Monthly* in 1866; in 1871 he became its editor-in-chief. Mark Twain published *The Celebrated Jumping Frog of Calaveras County, and Other Sketches* in 1867, and his reputation quickly soared: initially a local humorist and journalist in California, he soon became an author of national importance—a celebrity and an American spokesman. In general terms, what this change signaled was a difference in the appropriate subject matter for literature. Emerson, Thoreau, Hawthorne, and Melville all believed that there was a transcendent realm—a "higher reality." In their estimation, words had the power to name the higher reality that lay behind mere everyday objects, and it was the business of literature to reveal this transcendent realm and probe its meaning. By contrast, Howells, Twain, and others like them were preoccupied with the events of everyday experience. "Reality" in their work was an examination of worldly things: literature addressed the problems that men, women, and even children confronted in their daily interactions with one another, and language referred exclusively to the components of this everyday life. Words lost their power to name some transcendent reality: "dawn" was the beginning of another day, nothing more.

Emily Dickinson's work had always stood outside of the dominant transcendentalist movement: rooted in the convictions of latter-day Puritanism, she addressed not some impersonal "higher reality," but "God." Still, she was not untouched by the changes taking place in American literature, for she read voraciously. Even more important in her case, perhaps, was the fact that the demise of literary transcendentalism corresponded to a change that took place in her own community, the slow death of old-fashioned religious piety in the town of Amherst. For example, Susan Dickinson, who had so vehemently pressed conversion upon Emily in that momentous year of 1850—who had worried Austin on the subject of conversion until he, too, submitted to faith in January 1856, six months before his marriage—gradually turned her attentions away from religion and the spiritual realm. Sue never renounced the God of her youth or even came close to doing so; however, the early fervor of her faith dwindled into a comfortable acceptance of polite, Sunday-go-to-church religion. By the beginning of the Civil War, she was becoming a sophisticated matron, hostess to many distinguished guests:—celebrities from the literary world, distinguished politicians (including most of the governors of the Commonwealth of Massachusetts), and notable members of the cosmopolitan society that lay beyond the boundaries of Amherst. In 1861 Gertrude Lefferts Vanderbilt, a friend of Kate Turner's, was the guest of the Austin Dickinsons in Amherst; in 1863 Sue journeyed down to Flatbush, Long Island, to be the houseguest of the Vanderbilts. Thus the evaporation of Trinitarian intensity was demonstrated even so close to Emily Dickinson as next door.

Emily Dickinson's poetry reflects these many changes in Amherst, in America, and in the literature of the United States. Probably it would be incorrect to say that she was directly affected by the diminishment of Amherst's piety or by the surge of American realism: instead, her poetry ran a parallel course to these, and change had been inherent in its inception.

Dickinson was not the last great Puritan poet. If she had been, the religious significance of her work would have been apparent from the first moment it was read. She might not have been a popular poet, but at least her mission would have been clear because the language of her verse would have been consistently infused with the force of religious implication. Yet it is not: the otherworldly component of her poetic diction is often elusive and obscure, even in poems that deal with such commonplaces of religion as Heaven. Rather, Emily Dickinson was an artist of the age of transition. Her self-imposed labor was to question God's authority and to free language from the tyranny of His definitions; thus the diction of her poetry is in the process of revising transcendent implication and pulling away from it even as the speaker addresses herself to God.

It would be tidy (and convenient) if Emily Dickinson had begun her work using a language infused with transcendent meaning and gradually moved by regular steps to a language that was entirely freed from it. However, she did not: in the very last work there are a few poems that address her earliest concerns; and in the earliest work there are poems that use language as if it referred always and only to the things of this world. True, there are large outlines. The poetry written during or before 1862 or 1863 is much more explicitly imbued with defiant religious implication than that written later. However, the demarcation is far from distinct. Some poems hover enticingly. Sometimes the language of a given poem seems to draw upon the Christian myth for depth and complexity; yet on another reading the language of the same poem seems opaque—designed to name real-world phenomena and little else. Although it is not one of her best works, "The Props assist the House," the first draft of which was written in 1863, is an interesting example of this ambiguity.

The first term of the metaphor upon which the poem is built is clear at the simplest level: while a "House" is in the process of construction, it is surrounded with "Props" or "Scaffolds"; once finished, it can support itself, so these "drop" away as the workmen dismantle them. However, the second term is considerably less clear. What does it mean to say that a "Life" is "perfected"? Does the verse refer to adulthood, the maturity of a man or woman who needs no further parental direction? Does it allude to death and salvation, mortality discarded and the immortal self freed from its hindrances? Or does it point to that time when the human consciousness can confront eternity alone, unsupported by the "Props" of comforting religious myth? The differences among these ways of construing the poem emerge from different ways of understanding the key words: "Augur," "Carpenter," "perfected," "Life," "Plank and Nail," and "Scaffolds." All of these have the potential for religious implication; yet the thrust of mythic import here is neither strong enough nor coherent enough to allow an entirely unambiguous reading of the verse.

If the poem means to address salvation as the goal, it fails to present the standard Christian notion of a "perfected Life" clearly. "Augur" is a relic of the pagan past, naming a prophet among the Romans, while "the Carpenter" names the one true Saviour, Jesus Christ; in this poem, however, they are recollected equally. The "Soul" is surely affirmed in salvation by the Crucifixion; however, the locution "A past of Plank and Nail" utterly fails to capture the essential, propitiatory role that was played by this momentous event— the horror of God's death and its glory. In short, the epic force of this language is vastly attenuated, and a conventionally religious reading is either invalidated or at least seriously undermined.

Yet Dickinson's spelling of "Augur" (here punned with the word "auger," a carpenter's tool) makes it clear that she intends some reading that is other than exclusively literal. Thus perhaps the verse describes the process by which human beings gather the strength to confront life and death without the crutch of a promised afterlife. If it is a poem of dismissal, its casual equation of "Augur" and "Carpenter" becomes a rhetoric of freedom—both myths equally irrelevant. Similarly, the diction of "A past of Plank and Nail" captures just that nuance of indifference that attends a consciousness authentically emancipated from the shackles of the Christian tradition. What is more, this tone and attitude of indifference reinforce the implications of the word "adequate" and of the reflexive construction "support itself"—demonstrating the self-sufficiency that was merely asserted by those locutions.

Indeed, one might even elaborate this reading to infer that not only an individual self could be thus liberated, but the "House" of poetry as well.

The word "House" was fraught with significance for Emily Dickinson. The Homestead, which had been built by her grandfather, was usually named as "my father's House" in her letters, a phrase that echoes Jesus's reference to the Heaven of God the Father. For Edward Dickinson, the "House of Dickinson" (embodied in the Dickinson name and in the succession through the male lineage—himself, Austin, and Ned) was the informing commitment of his life; and he wished the reputation of this "House" to be cleansed of his own father's disgrace, once again honored by the citizens of Amherst. Both daughters had been excluded from their father's driving ambitions for the "House of Dickinson"; although Vinnie seems to have accepted this relegation to the rank of onlooker, Emily did not. She styled herself a usurper: through her poetry, she would lay claim to the "Kingdom, and the Power, and the Glory" of God's House; by the same means, she would redeem the name Dickinson, becoming its only true inheritor. Thus one way of defining the wordsmith was as a uniquely endowed builder of houses: "*Myself was formed—a Carpenter—/ An unpretending time,*" a poet-speaker asserts (#488). The notion of "House" brings together a number of Dickinson's concerns: her autonomy, her authority, her right to inherit the earth, her right to possess herself of God's heroic grandeur as well, and her right to create the poetry through which these ambitions could be realized. "The Props assist the House" might best be read as a description of the way Dickinson's work came into its own independence, then—"A past of Plank and Nail" all but forgotten as the Christian myth loses its hold over the creative imagination. "Adequate, erect," the "House" of poetry can be free now.

Ironically, however, the poem that expresses this remarkable notion is curiously bland. There is no sense of felt triumph, perhaps because the "House" itself does nothing but stand (its most assertive motion is to "support itself"). The "Carpenter" has built it; the "Props" have assisted it; and when liberation comes, "the Scaffolds drop." There is no interaction of opposed forces—no remnant of wrestle; and although individual words in this poem might resound with the echo of grandeur, the concatenation here entirely disarms them. Even the word "drop," which has such horrific force elsewhere, is entirely unremarkable. Although the poem claims to describe a process in which power is transferred, the poem itself is finally without power. And if the image of "Scaffolds drop" indicates liberation, it also carries the shadow image of an execution.

The poem does not fully succeed in any reading; still, its failures are interesting. This statement of independence is delivered in words that walk the razor's edge: perhaps they retain the lingering potency of language with the valence of the Christian myth; perhaps that valence—full of vigor, but unyieldingly rigid in its implication—has been so weakened that it can no longer be felt as a coherent force. The verse focuses upon a structure that can stand by itself, yet the poem fails because the subject is not articulated cogently enough to support it. A number of Dickinson's poems use language in a similarly ambiguous way—walking the razor's edge: on one reading they seem to retain the deep structures of the Judaeo-Christian myth and to draw upon them for subtlety and complexity; on another reading they seem to deal exclusively with the things of this world. It is by no means the case that all are failures; some are among her most brilliant successes. But all accept the challenge of immense risk; for as this poem demonstrates, the poet who has wrested liberty from the great Creator courts a new kind of danger, an execution of sorts—blandness, incoherence, or meaninglessness—verse that has been deprived of its ultimate resource of vitality.

Sometimes Emily Dickinson herself seems to have seen the danger.

> *Of Bronze — and Blaze —*
> *The North — Tonight —*
> *So adequate — it forms —*
> *So preconcerted with itself*
> *So distant — to alarms —*
> *An Unconcern so sovereign*
> *To Universe, or me —*
> *Infects my simple spirit*
> *With Taints of Majesty —*
> *Till I take vaster attitudes —*
> *And strut upon my stem —*
> *Disdaining Men, and Oxygen,*
> *For Arrogance of them —*
>
> *My Splendors, are Menagerie —*
> *But their Competeless Show*
> *Will entertain the Centuries*
> *When I, am long ago,*
> *An Island in dishonored Grass —*
> *Whom none but Daisies, know.*

> (#290)

This famous poem begins with an image that might recall the forge—not the golden promises of Revelation, but the metal of a fallen age subjected to fire and then hammered brutally into shape: "Bronze" and "Blaze." What is more, it locates this activity in the "North," where God generally keeps His Kingdom in Dickinson's work.

Indeed, this is only one poem of many to invoke an image of God toiling at the anvil; in other instances, however, God's action—though terrifying in its violence—is at least focused upon humanity. So in "He fumbles at your Soul" (#*315*), the speaker asserts that "*He stuns you by degrees*— / *Prepares your brittle Nature* / *For the Etherial Blow* / *By fainter Hammers*—*further heard*— / *Then nearer*—*Then so slow*": God gradually intrudes into our presence, and then He takes us by force. Violation, rape—these are the horrors of such a vision. But in "Of Bronze—and Blaze," the problem is opposite. If God does indeed exist, He is entirely secluded, indifferent, and "distant—to alarms—." The reason we do not experience Him as the Great Destroyer is that we do not experience Him in any conclusive way at all. The only thing we can know is the display, which may or may not portend a Presence behind it, and the speaker's use of language nicely captures this ambiguity: whereas her diction can be construed as implying an active agent, her syntax denies the possibility of any connection. With few exceptions, the verb "form" is transitive and must take an object to fulfill its meaning; here, there is no object to complete the implied transaction, and the verb hangs open-endedly. This interdiction of interaction is reinforced by the reflexive construction "preconcerted with itself." In short, the first seven lines describe a force of light that is essentially different from that which radiates from God's emblem, the sun. Embodiment of the Lord's generative power and grandeur, the sun directs its light earthward, and its relationship to mankind is double-edged: it can give heat and light, and at the same time it can put out the eye / I. The northern lights are different. Diffused throughout the atmosphere, they provide illumination of a sort; however, this is light without either force or life-giving energy. It will not harm us, but it is essentially sterile, a display that is capable of breeding nothing save, perhaps, admiration and vain emulation.

The implication is clear, if ominous: an artist who is liberated from the Divinity's power may be nothing more than an artist deprived of heroic possibility. Thus in "Of Bronze—and Blaze," when the poet-speaker attempts to imitate this species of beauty (for the relationship by its nature precludes the possibility of strife and usurpation), she is afflicted with a form of "infection" and falls into the ludicrous, contradictory effort to "strut" upon a "stem." True, the speaker can reap some success from her "disdaining" of "Men" and "Oxygen": she still speaks from the page, impertinent and possessed of a magical vitality. Paradoxically, however, she is still indivisibly tied to both "Men" and "Oxygen," for in order to "live," she must have some reader—a breathing, sentient, mortal being. The notion that her "Splendors" are "Menagerie" is one rather complex way of asserting this dependency. A "Menagerie" is a place where wild animals are kept: it might describe human beings in a wilderness—the men and women of a world without God's guiding, ruling power—in short, the future readers of this verse. Of course, it also glancingly alludes to a carnival's side show. Is this the ultimate fate of poetry? Are poets destined to be no more than circus animals? Although the speaker stops short of such a dismaying projection, disillusionment haunts the poem's conclusion. The "Competeless Show" of the North will endure forever. By way of attempted parity, the speaker swings into the present tense; elsewhere this is a bravura demonstration of power in Dickinson's verse, yet here the only thing that can exist in an eternal present is the undying assertion of inevitable annihilation. "I am long ago" (soon you, too, will be "long ago"), time fleeing from humanity while impassive nature continues unperturbed.

This image of nature as distant from human concerns and utterly independent both of God's force and of mankind's needs is sometimes invoked as an example of strength and endurance. "*Ah, Teneriffe! / Retreating Mountain! / Purple of Ages—pause for you— / Sunset—reviews her Sapphire Regiment— / Day—drops you her Red Adieu! / Still—Clad in your Mail of ices— / Thigh of Granite—and thew—of Steel— / Heedless—alike—of pomp—or parting / Ah, Teneriffe! / I'm kneeling—still—*" (#666). Yet the longing to personalize this eminence of ice and stone cannot be eliminated from the speaker's diction: the mountain is "Clad" in "Mail"; it has a "Thigh" that has never been wounded by some wrestle with the Lord. The impenetrable indifference of its endurance seems a kind of fortitude, worthy of admiration; and because the speaker knows no other way to manifest her respect, she concludes her meditation by "kneeling" in reverence—even though God's presence is never suggested and the inanimate mountain is not equipped to recognize obeisance. Often the urgency to discover some relevance or meaning, here submerged in anthropomorphic diction, breaks overtly into the verse. Thus a speaker who has been surveying nature's manifold glory concludes her observation with a question: "*Without Commander! Countless! Still! / The Regiments of Wood and Hill / In bright detachment stand! / Behold! Whose Multitudes are these? / The children of whose turbaned seas— / Or what Circassian Land?*" (#64) "Detachment" has a military implication to accord with the image of "Regiments"; however, the vision of nature standing "In bright detachment" conveys, as well, an unbridgeable chasm between the observed and the observer. And the fact that both the "Teneriffe" and these "Regiments" are "Still!" is a grim warning. Unmovable and unmoving, they are incapable of responding to mankind's supplication. When God refuses to acknowledge our prayers, it is a matter of His will; a reaction of anger is appropriate, and residual hope for some recognition can be sustained. Here, however, unresponsiveness is a matter of intrinsic incapacity, and both anger and hope seem absurd in the face of this inanimate impassivity.

Not surprisingly, many poems that walk the razor's edge—delicately balanced between a language that can summon the Divinity by describing the things of this world and a language that has been drained of transcendent implication—are meditations upon nature. The following poem was evidently of particular interest to Dickinson because she worked out two final versions of it. The first, printed below, is a variant dating from 1862.

It sifts from Leaden Sieves—
It powders all the Wood.
It fills with Alabaster Wool
The Wrinkles of the Road—

It makes an Even Face
Of Mountain, and of Plain—
Unbroken Forehead from the East
Unto the East again—

It reaches to the Fence—
It wraps it Rail by Rail
Till it is lost in Fleeces—
It deals Celestial Vail

To Stump, and Stack—and Stem—
A Summer's empty Room—
Acres of Joints, where Harvests were,
Recordless, but for them—

It Ruffles Wrists of Posts
As Ankles of a Queen—
Then stills it's Artisans—like Ghosts—
Denying they have been—

(#311)

"It" is never named, but no one needs such a stipulation to recognize this common winter scene in New England, gray clouds filling up the fields with snow.

The poem never moves beyond "It," never explicitly meditates upon the possibility of some force behind the display. Thus a reader might be justified in supposing that this poem addresses the scenic possibilities of nature and intends to focus upon no subject except the variety of images that can be conjured from the things of this world. Since the later version radically shortens the poem and alters it further in the direction of the merely scenic, such a reading might even seem mandated. Yet there are powerful elements in this poem that also seem to compel the reader to peruse this language for supernatural significance.

The first stanza seems merely quotidian, mingling images from the kitchen with images of a lady's dressing table: flouring the boards to bake and dusting powder over the tracery of wrinkles on a face. "Leaden" introduces the only ominous note: no cook would employ utensils of this heavy, soft, poisonous metal. If the poem progressed by elaborating other images from everyday life, the tincture of disharmony might pass unnoticed, but the verse rejects this option. Instead, its forward movement is possessed by some demonic energy, and the lines seem compelled to record an unrelenting process of annihilation. The sense of urgency is partly located in the chanting reiteration of the syntax—"It sifts . . . It powders . . . It fills . . . It makes . . . It reaches . . . It wraps . . . It Ruffles"—a resurgence of the parataxis that drives toward death. Indeed, the most definitive departure from the domestic world occurs in the break between the first and second stanzas: at the conclusion of line 4, the trope is still tame, still a benign extension of my lady's chamber; by line 5, the act of powdering has become a form of obliteration as the landscape is transformed into an "Even Face," distinguishing features entirely eliminated, "Unbroken Forehead from the East / Unto the East again—." The snakelike movement as the snow "reaches" and "wraps" is a cruel contrast to the images of "Fleeces" and "Celestial Vail"; indeed, the paradox "lost in Fleeces" becomes an agonizing denial of Christ's salvific power.

In the last two stanzas, the violence that had acted by stifling becomes associated with dismembering, and the farmland assumes the appearance of a barren battlefield or a frozen slaughterhouse. The barely tolerable images of "Stump, and Stack—and Stem—" yield to nightmare; "Acres of Joints, where Harvests were," the stubble of corn standing in mute testimony to the rich growth that has been mowed down like an army cut off at the ankles. Perhaps feet (and the possibility for poetry) still remain. If so, they have been covered with snow. The elegant "Ruffles" of the last stanza may obscure the Gothic implications—arms, hands, rising out of the ground in supplication, the rest swallowed up in sod and snow. Fittingly, the poem concludes with "Ghosts." All else having been rendered blanch and motionless, the "Artisans" themselves fall still as well.

The difference between a poem like "The Angle of a Landscape" and this one is difficult to define with absolute precision. The other poem has a speaker explicitly attempting to interpret what she can see; the word "Landscape" itself invokes Emerson's *Nature,* an essay asserting that there is an inherent meaning in nature; the progress of the seasons is paced along clearly Biblical lines; then the themes of barrenness and mutilation are explicitly played off against these invocations of transcendence. By contrast, "It sifts from Leaden Sieves—" is never explicitly pinned to the Christian myth— even though some of the diction clearly recalls it. Read once through, the poem might seem no more than a watercolor in words; read again, it might seem a bitter narrative of God's annihilation. It hovers between these, evocative, perplexing, teasing, ultimately unresolvable. Is it a still-vital remnant from a religious past, or are these mere echoes, no longer vigorous enough to dominate the verse?

If the differences between this poem and "The Angle of a Landscape" can be discerned only with difficulty, the differences between this poem and one like "*How the old Mountains drip with Sunset*" (#291) are even more elusive. sive. Truth to tell, a good deal of Dickinson's nature poetry comes close to the razor's edge, pulling away from the language of transcendence and an otherworldy focus even as it trades upon the force of them; one source of the power in such verse is precisely this tension. Yet "It sifts from Leaden Sieves" is uniquely well suited to demonstrate the incipient falling away because the second version of it definitively rejects any preoccupation with the supernatural. In 1864 Emily Dickinson undertook a major revision to produce this second version; and almost twenty years later, in 1883, the revision figured in her last, abortive flirtation with publication.

Years earlier, in Emily Dickinson's childhood, she had played with Helen Fiske, the daughter of an Amherst College professor. A lively girl, Helen Fiske had left Amherst during her early adolescence, and the two lost touch. Helen Fiske married a major in the army, Edward Hunt, and the couple met the entire Dickinson family in 1860, when they were entertained at the Homestead during an Amherst visit. Unexpectedly widowed in 1863, Helen Hunt turned to writing as a way of earning a living. Shortly after the Civil War she met Higginson and his wife when they were all living in Newport. Little by little Helen Hunt became one of America's most successful women writers, and at some point Higginson told her about the poetry that was being written by her girlhood friend. Thus in the early 1870s, Helen Hunt renewed her friendship with Emily Dickinson. After a while, Dickinson allowed her to read samples of the poetry—how much we cannot know—and in 1876 Helen Hunt Jackson (she had married again in 1875) requested Dickinson's permission to publish one of the poems anonymously in a forthcoming collection of verse. Dickinson gave approval of sorts—by withholding refusal— and "*Success is counted sweetest*" (#67) was subsequently printed in *A Masque of Poets,* published by Roberts Brothers of Boston.

Emily Dickinson received her complimentary copy of this volume from one of the editors, Thomas Niles, in 1878, and she began a desultory correspondence with him, sometimes writing to order books she wanted to read. In 1883 Niles raised the possibility of publishing a volume of her verse. She sent him a number of poems, including "It sifts from Leaden Sieves"; his response to them was such that discussion was politely suspended.

It is interesting that under these circumstances, when Dickinson presumably wanted to make a good impression, she sent Niles a redaction of the *revised* version of the poem. It reads:

S N O W

It sifts from Leaden Sieves—
It powders all the Wood—

> It fills with Alabaster Wool
> The Wrinkles of the Road—
>
> It scatters like the Birds—
> Condenses like a Flock—
> Like Juggler's Figures situates
> Upon a baseless Arc—
>
> It traverses yet halts—
> Disperses as it stays—
> Then curls itself in Capricorn,
> Denying that it was—[1]

Here there is a playfulness that is entirely absent from the earlier version, for the driving forward movement has been disrupted. "It scatters" serves precisely the end of unsettling momentum; if the snow is reconstituted when it "Condenses," its entire force is expended upon itself and cannot be deployed to affect the world through which it moves. The trope of the "Juggler's Figures" reaffirms the self-contained quality of movement and energy; in addition, it disarms the poem of any serious intent by emphasizing the value of mere entertainment. In the final stanza, the back-and-forth movement of the snow reaches a climax in "traverses . . . halts . . . Disperses . . . stays—," and culminates in the reflexive "curls itself." What had been the inexorable motion of devastation in the earlier version is here transmuted into complex, artful patterns of snow-swept air—nature's incomparable theatricals.

None can know what guided Dickinson's choice. She may have been moved by tact as much as anything else, for by 1883 the deep harmonic of religious implication that suffuses the earlier version would have seemed antique to the ear of a cosmopolitan publisher. Or perhaps she considered the later revision a better poem. If so she is at odds with most of her modern editors: the original is almost always reproduced when the poem is printed.

Dickinson assigned titles to only twenty-four of her poems, and the variant of this poem that she sent to Niles is one of them. It locates the subject unambiguously in the immanent world. "The Props assist the House" makes an unusual claim about the nature of the "perfected Life—": it has "cease[d] to recollect / The Augur and the Carpenter"; it has no consciousness of an accumulated past. Insofar as the "House" stands for poetry as well, one might say that the second version of "It sifts from Leaden Sieves—" fulfills the claim of that other piece of verse, for it is a poem without memory: it carries no encumbrance of myth. Its stipulated subject, "SNOW," is universal and ageless only to the extent that snowstorms come to many climates with the regularity of winter. Yet not everyone has seen snow; nor will everyone have the opportunity to see snow. And whether or not one does is an extrinsic, incidental, and perhaps trivial fact of existence. One can lead a full and fully examined life without ever coming to terms with the "SNOW" of the later variant; however, the earlier version may well render a force that none can evade and none can afford to ignore. Not explicitly addressed to the Christian myth, the diction of the 1862 variant of the poem carries at least the *memory* of that myth in the echoing cadences of language that hesitates at the edge of the modern era, but does not yet accept a thoroughly secular sensibility.

Part of the immense strength of Dickinson's poetry comes from the fact that she gives every evidence of being highly self-conscious about the problems that attended her mission and the consequences that flowed from it; sometimes the protean character of the language at her disposal became itself the subject of her scrutiny. Thus the following poem not only walks the razor's edge; unlike many other poems that contain the same sort of linguistic tension, it comments upon its own ambiguities.

> *You've seen Balloons set—Hav'nt You?*
> *So stately they ascend—*
> *It is as Swans—discarded You,*
> *For Duties Diamond—*
>
> *Their Liquid Feet go softly out*
> *Upon a Sea of Blonde—*
> *They spurn the Air, as 'twere too mean*
> *For Creatures so renowned—*
>
> *Their Ribbons just beyond the eye—*
> *They struggle—some—for Breath—*
> *And yet the Crowd applaud, below—*
> *They would not encore—Death—*
>
> *The Gilded Creature strains—and spins—*
> *Trips frantic in a Tree—*
> *Tears open her imperial Veins—*
> *And tumbles in the Sea—*
>
> *The Crowd—retire with an Oath—*
> *The Dust in Streets—go down—*
> *And Clerks in Counting Rooms*
> *Observe—"'Twas only a Balloon"—*

(#700)

This poem is a kind of Alpha and Omega, beginning and ending both compressed into the phrase "Balloons set." The initial announcement may seem puzzling, for lines 2–8 examine the opposite, a "stately" soaring toward

Heaven. Yet the verse fulfills its promise—in part by recording the fitful descent of the delicate creature, but even more by finishing with "The Crowd . . . The Dust in Streets . . . And Clerks in Counting Rooms." The poem opens with a diction that recalls the potency of the New England past, ardent Christian faith cast in a language of rising and setting; however, it concludes with an almost Howellsian realism, city streets and the bustle of business. What it records is a fall from the mythic into the flatly matter-of-fact.

The particolored hot-air Balloon that swings aloft in the opening stanzas trails the import of many legends. Primarily it recalls the Christ, a "Creature so renowned—," with torn "imperial Veins"; its intended destination is the gem-graced Kingdom of Heaven with "Duties Diamond—." Yet here the story of Christ's death and Resurrection has been turned upside down: the glorious rise comes first, and then, just before it has fully cleared the ground, the Balloon is overtaken by the throes of some "struggle," straining and spinning, eventually ripping open. Language that had echoed the Ascension now reverts to the Crucifixion; instead of disappearing above us, the Balloon falls, pell-mell, never again to rise. Faintly, this language even recalls the "struggle" for belief; and "strains — and spins — / Trips frantic in a Tree" echoes Dickinson's own earlier poem #*501*, in which "*Faith slips—and laughs, and rallies— / . . . Plucks at a twig of Evidence—*." However, both the allusion to Christ and the glance at the old-fashioned struggle for faith are lodged insecurely in this language, for the traditional Christian implications have been weakened to the point of losing dominance.

Thus, almost as if she felt the need to strengthen or reinforce this evocation of the supernatural, Dickinson mingles other mythic traditions with them. The shades of Daedalus, the master craftsman of the maze at Crete, and his son, Icarus, the overreacher who flew too close to the sun, are summoned when the Balloon "tumbles in the Sea—." Even more obvious is the invocation of all the lore associated with the death of the swan: this majestic bird, sometimes thought by the ancients to have prophetic powers, was best known for the poignant clarity of its death cry; not surprisingly, the swan, especially the dying swan, became eponymous for the poet. No simple story, then, this verse records a colossal decline as Christ, the overreacher, the poet, and the possibility for some transcendent meaning in our everyday world all subside together. Indeed, the poem delivers this message of loss even as it shrugs away from transcendent meaning altogether with "'Twas only a Balloon'—." The locution "Balloons set—" states a form of sunset: the shadows lengthen, and the heroic days of American literature draw to a close.

The swan's cry achieves its plaintive beauty only once, when the bird is dying; and Emily Dickinson herself seems to have understood that there was an inexorable tragic force infusing her verse with its rare grace, "Liquid Feet" that can no longer keep a bird aloft.

Indeed, it may well be that she could have written this shimmering collection of lyric poems at no other time and few other places in America; for mid-nineteenth-century Amherst contained an unusual combination of past and future, each to some degree empowered for a few scant decades until the past faded slowly away, without trumpets or the agony of defeat, but because of faint inanition. For Dickinson's poetry to retain its full initial strength and coherence, the momentary confluence of these two epochs would have had to be sustained: the language of transcendence would have had to remain current, and the forces of defiance and rebellion—indeed, of ultimate change—would have had to continue undefeated and unabated. Inevitably, such was not the case. Even when Emily Dickinson was at the height of her vocation, in the early 1860s, language was already beginning to be substantially drained of its otherworldly implications. Emblems, Biblical allusions, moments freighted with inherent spiritual significance—many of these components of her poetry might have been readily recognized by the men and women of an earlier generation (though they could have felt no sympathy for her heretical use of these elements). However, the members of her own generation in Amherst had begun to drift away from those soul-searing days of the Great Revival in 1850, and the readers of Dickinson's poetry in subsequent generations would surely have more in common with the secular indifference of "The Crowd" and the "Clerks in Counting Rooms" than with those final few who continued to wrestle with the angel of the Lord. And to these subsequent generations, Dickinson's poetry seems merely strange or idiosyncratic. As death inevitably follows the swan's song, so some lethal alteration in the relationship between reader and poem must follow the kind of verse Emily Dickinson wrote.

Probably the most destructive consequence is a failure of communication. Part of this failure follows from the extremity of Dickinson's insubordination. Had she couched her sentiments in lines that scanned and rhymed with regularity, the verse might be more accessible; had she been content with less radical compression of imagery or less violent ellipsis, her readers might tolerate the straining of traditional language more easily. Yet moderation did not figure in her plan. Perhaps she suffered from the same self-limiting pride that can be found in the Higginson correspondence. In any case, beginning with Higginson (or Bowles) and continuing until the present, people have been baffled by her poetry. They deem it to be great; at the same time, they find much of it essentially cryptic.

Thus a paradoxical situation may arise. One of Dickinson's poems may be regarded as strong and important, and a great deal of critical attention may be devoted to it. Nonetheless, commentators may disagree about it at the most rudimentary level, having come to no accord even about its principal subject. Perhaps the most famous such poem is the following riddle.

My Life had stood—a Loaded Gun—
In Corners—till a Day
The Owner passed—identified—
And carried me away—

And now We roam in Sovreign Woods—
And now We hunt the Doe—
And every time I speak for Him—
The Mountains straight reply—

And do I smile, such cordial light
Upon the Valley glow—
It is as a Vesuvian face
Had let it's pleasure through—

And when at Night—Our good Day done—
I guard My Master's Head—
'Tis better than the Eider-Duck's
Deep Pillow—to have shared—

To foe of His—I'm deadly foe—
None stir the second time—
On whom I lay a Yellow Eye—
Or an emphatic Thumb—

Though I than He—may longer live
He longer must—than I—
For I have but the power to kill,
Without—the power to die—

(#754)

The principal clue here is the paradox in the last stanza; indeed, these lines so patently announce a riddle that they might be extracted and posited alone, followed by the query "Who am I?" Most of the riddling aspects of Dickinson's poetry are intimately related to Biblical paradoxes and pertain to the enigmatic promise that we shall be delivered from death into the eternal life of Heaven. Not surprisingly, this poem fits that pattern.

In the early 1860s, the Trinitarians of Amherst still believed that the New Testament gives an account of Christ's coming that is specifically linked with certain Old Testament promises and prophecies. One such foretelling is in the Psalms: "Thou madest [man] to have dominion over the works of thy hands; thou hast put all things under his feet" (Psalms 8:6). Unexceptional to a modern sensibility, perhaps, this statement puzzled earlier readers of the Bible. If "all things" is taken literally, death must be included, and man must put even death "under his feet"; however, death has dominion over man, not the opposite. This paradox can be resolved by assuming that the assertion in Psalms has to do not with all men, but with a Saviour: the passage in question can then be interpreted as a prediction that some *unique* man would come and that He would vanquish death. When Christ, the God-man, was born, the first part of that promise was fulfilled; and when He died and arose from the dead, pledging that others would rise just as He had risen, the second part was fulfilled. In that famous passage from the Epistles, Saint Paul affirms just this consummation: "If Christ be not raised, your faith is vain; ye are yet in your sins. Then they also which are fallen asleep in Christ are perished. . . . But now is Christ risen from the dead. . . . For as in Adam all die, even so in Christ shall all be made alive. . . . *For [Christ] must reign, till he hath put all enemies under his feet. The last enemy that shall be destroyed is death.*" (I Corinthians 15:17–18, 20, 22, 25–26; italics mine.) Thus these two passages from Psalms and I Corinthians treat the same apparent impossibility: all men are subject to death, but a man Who has Himself died, the Christ, will triumph over death. Indeed, He *must,* so the epistle asserts; until death is put under Christ's feet, no Christian can be raised from the grave. This paradox—that death has power over *all* men, even Jesus Christ, and that death "must" nonetheless be destroyed by a *man*—was a key commonplace of Trinitarian culture, and it was still so current in Dickinson's day that it had the familiarity of a maxim—as did I Corinthians 15.

Put the isolated riddle again. "*Though I than He—may longer live / He longer must—than I— / For I have but the power to kill, / Without—the power to die—.*" Who am "I," and who is "He"? To an Amherst audience, even as late as Emily Dickinson's day, the answers would probably have been patent: death and Christ. Death "may" live longer than Christ, for Christ died on the cross; yet Christ "must" live longer than death, for the righteous cannot be raised from their graves unless Christ first vanquishes death.

For such an audience (and certainly for Dickinson herself), the remarkable feature of the poem would not be its riddling conclusion, the solution to which would have been apparent. The daring innovation that contradicts ordinary conventions is the colloquial bloodthirstiness of the first five stanzas. I Corinthians 15 exploits the paradox of a God-man who can be subjected to death and still destroy death. Dickinson's poem bitterly exploits the *opposite* paradox. Christ may be the God-man Who came to save us from death, but He is also one and the same as the Father, the Destroyer and Avenger Who employs death as His agent. Thus although Christ may triumph over death, death also acts as an instrument of Christ's will. And, most terrible of all, death *enjoys* his job.

In earlier days, death (personified) had traditionally been thought of as one who wielded a scythe or slung arrows; in this more up-to-date poem, the horrifyingly humanoid eminence of death carries a shotgun or a rifle. Nor is this personified figure of death dispatching us with a gun unique here. It occurs in one Dickinson poem where time fires the fatal "shot": "*The Second poised—debated—shot— / Another [second] had begun— / And simultaneously, a Soul / Escaped the House unseen—*" (*#948*). It occurs in another where the "Ordnance of Vitality," or the rules concerning life and death, is the subject: "*The Ordnance of Vitality / Is frugal of it's Ball. / It aims once— kills once—conquers once— / There is no second War*" (*#1188*). And in still a third, the figure of death holding a rifle emerges with fatal clarity: "*The event was directly behind Him / Yet He did not guess / Fitted itself to Himself like a Robe / Relished His ignorance / Motioned itself to drill / Loaded and Levelled / And let His Flesh / Centuries from His Soul*" (*#1686*).

Once a reader has accepted the premise that death is the speaker and God is the Master, certain other elements of the poem become clear. In the Bible, especially in the Old Testament, "death" was figured as an angel with a special assignment (see II Samuel, 24:15–17, for example); in America, this mythic creature took visible shape as the Angel of Death that appeared on so many New England headstones. Of course the angel in question had always existed and had always been capable of performing his eventual task; however, until God decided to use him, his singular role had not been "identified," and he had to wait like "a Loaded Gun / In Corners." Once chosen for his mission, he became the "Angel of Death" and could begin the relentless process of annihilation that all men and women must submit to. Thus as soon as the "Gun" has been "carried . . . away," Dickinson's usual syntactic pattern for the drive toward death is introduced into the poem: "And carried . . . And now . . . And now . . . And every time."

It is not difficult to understand that the activity described in stanzas two through five is the process of hunting and killing; therefore, the challenge of the poem rests in untangling its mingled tonalities and allusions. The "Sovereign Woods—" names a king's hunting preserve; in the case of God, of course, these comprise the entire world, a "Woods—" that suffers the force of His blood lust countless times each day. There is an unsettling sexual timbre in the poem that recalls the effete elegance of Elizabethan songs and madrigals where shooting the "Doe" was a synonym for seduction; the violence of this trope angrily captures the lascivious obscenity of a Christian tradition that accepts all the notions implicit in a bride-of-Christ fable. And although they look backward in time to the late sixteenth century, when English Puritanism began, these stanzas also communicate a pungent sense of nineteenth-century American culture. The hunt takes place in a "Valley" that "glows"; and "Mountains . . . reply" by echoing the gun's retort. Such a configuration mimics the geography of that Trinitarian bastion, Amherst itself, a town set among hills and mountains like a handful of pebbles at the bottom of a shallow bowl. Fittingly, the poem recalls an American song tradition, too, the rollicking, crudely bragging backwoods ballad, here evoked by the speaker's relish in his work and by his bald satisfaction in a good job of killing. All of these taken together suggest that the final inheritance of the great New England Puritan tradition is not a set of gentle pieties, but the persistent presence of a God motivated principally by phallic rage. Even the grave will not remove us from death's constant vigilance: just as the angel sat by his "Master's Head—" in the sepulcher (Mark 16:5–7), the Angel of Death is emblazoned on "bedback" tombstones throughout New England, an unmoving, unchanging, grotesque sentinel. And God's countenance, should we attain Heaven and glimpse it, will be a "Vesuvian face" that radiates deadly light like the blast of His agent's gun.

The poem's complex echo of these several traditions suggests that to some extent God and death have insinuated themselves permanently into our culture. Yet it was Dickinson's conviction that a poet could strike back. It may be true that the "tale" "Jehovah" told to "nature" was the "slumbering plan" of a "reticent volcano" (#*1748*), and that the world's ultimate destruction by fire will be "Volcanic"—the "smouldering anguish" inflicted by a wrathful Divinity (#*175*). Nonetheless, the hero-poet possesses her own immense retaliatory power as a counterbalance: "*On my volcano grows the Grass / A meditative spot— / ... How red the Fire rocks below / How insecure the sod / Did I disclose / Would populate with awe my solitude*" (#*1677*). The force of God's might is exerted through the tedious uniformity of death: by contrast, the force of the poet's power is demonstrated in the subtleties of satiric exposure and the glissando of derision that can be embedded in precisely such a work as this. Dickinson's confidence in her own force did not waver; almost twenty years after writing this poem, she sent a letter to the Norcross cousins that is relevant in its use of metaphor.

What is it that instructs a hand lightly created, to impel shapes to eyes at a distance, which for them have the whole area of life or of death? Yet not a pencil in the street but has this awful power, though nobody arrests it. An earnest letter is or should be life-warrant or death-warrant, for what is each instant by a gun, harmless because "unloaded," but that touched "goes off"?[2]

The diligence with which modern readers have sought to decode the meaning of this poem stands as ample justification for her confidence.

Nonetheless, one must question whether a poem that presents such difficulties can be considered fully successful. Virtually all readers acknowledge the vigor of this verse; many have been captivated by its mockingly enigmatic posture. If these qualities were accompanied by a greater measure of accessibility, the work would be a fully successful endeavor. Instead, despite its hypnotic power, it is to some extent a failure, seeming to many in Dickinson's audience essentially cryptic and possibly a little mad. The crucial "clue" of the final stanza is so particularly tied to the commonplaces of the poet's own world that once these elements of her Trinitarian culture had passed into desuetude, the central meaning of the verse was all but lost, and its subtle reversals and transformations could not be grapsed and savored. The poem as a whole strains too violently against the Christian myth: rather than walking the razor's edge, it drops into obscurity. Such a fate is incipient in poems like "*It was not Death*" (#510) or "*That after Horror—*" (#286); perhaps many readers consider these works to be fascinating failures, too.

By 1862 words were losing the transcendent valence of New England Puritanism. Or, as Dickinson sometimes saw it, nature was being drained of supernatural meaning.

> *A Light exists in Spring*
> *Not present on the Year*
> *At any other period—*
> *When March is scarcely here*
>
> *A Color stands abroad*
> *On solitary Fields*
> *That Science cannot overtake*
> *But Human Nature feels.*
>
> *It waits upon the Lawn,*
> *It shows the furthest Tree*
> *Upon the furthest Slope you know*
> *It almost speaks to you.*
>
> *Then as Horizons step*
> *Or Noons report away*
> *Without the Formula of sound*
> *It passes and we stay—*
>
> *A quality of loss*
> *Affecting our Content*
> *As Trade had suddenly encroached*
> *Upon a Sacrament.*
>
> (#812)

In many ways, this is a transparent poem. There is no ellipsis to create uncertainty or to allow for multiple meaning; few words seem dense with implication; the author's artistry does not much exercise itself in concocting tropes. What is more, the manifest meaning of the poem is perfectly clear. Does the verse have more than this manifest meaning: does it have any further subject than a silver sun's "Light" in "March"? Perhaps. But if it does, the ulterior meaning must be argued, for it is perfectly plausible to assume that this is a poem about the raw, clear, brightly uncompromising light of rural New England just before spring begins.

March is the beginning of hope in Massachusetts. Days grow perceptibly longer, and the belief in an eternal life is reaffirmed in Eastertide. "Light" ought to spell gain under these circumstances, but this is a poem of loss. Indeed, the wound is such that its damage cannot be coherently articulated. Does the "Light" lack some essential vitality? Or is light no more than a facilitator, enabling mankind to perceive a world bereft?

At first there seems a tremor of transcendence. "Science cannot overtake" the "Color" in the fields: it is ineffable; perhaps it is the remnant of some epoch when "Light" had not been comprehensively divided into a visible and an invisible spectrum. Yet in the poem this vestigial illumination is tauntingly elusive. It falls "On solitary Fields. . . . It waits upon the Lawn. . . . It shows the furthest Tree / Upon the furthest Slope you know." At hand and at length, it seems laden with the possibility of revelation. Hovering at the threshold of communication, "It *almost* speaks to you." Yet in the end it fails to make connection. "It passes and we stay—." Perhaps it even carries the world of empowered myth in its wake. When "Horizons" move along and "Noons report away / Without the Formula of sound," this alteration might indicate no more than the progression of many days, but it might also record the vanishing of every possible emblem for the new birth and Heaven, the evaporation of every intimation of some higher realm. And, although the first four stanzas explicitly grope for a hint of meaning beyond the merely visible, the verse is remarkably prosaic. Nor is this tonality enriched by the poem's conclusion. The "Sacrament" mandated by this season is the Lord's Supper, a celebration of the promise that loss will be repaired. Yet here a "Trade" has taken place: "Trade," the business world of "Clerks in Counting Rooms," has supplanted the noble religious heritage of New England. The altered message is sobering: God has gone, and He will not return.

In this poem, in "My Life had stood—a Loaded Gun—," and in many other Dickinson poems, the meaning must be extracted not merely from the verse's reference to some independent world of myth (here latter-day American Puritanism), but also from Dickinson's own system of encoded meaning. Thus the appearance of parataxis signals the drive toward death, and "Noon" names the magical conflation of zero and infinity that is Heaven. This commingling of archetypal elements and intensely personal symbols suggests several things. As master craftsman, Dickinson was not content to work only with God's symbolic system; one portion of her strength is measured by the ability of her private system of signification to stand coequal with the myths of the Bible in her poetry. Yet this insinuation of the personal, however consistent in its application, can contribute to a reader's feeling that the verse is cryptic. What is more, the very fact that the poet is able to stand thus equal with the Divinity suggests that the force of the old order is passing away, never to be fully recaptured. The symbol system of Christianity can no longer dominate the literature that draws upon it. Thus the ultimate nightmare has become reality: one last time, God has vanished from the world—not because He has withdrawn, but because our art has been "liberated" from His tyranny.

In 1862, all over New England, men and boys had already begun to flood into the cities of the East and into the Midwestern heartland where they could find a prosperity that their own land no longer held. Once the Civil War ended at Appomattox in 1865, the floodgates were opened. Farmhouses in the Pelham Hills to the east of Amherst and in the Berkshire Mountains to its west stood vacant, and Massachusetts would never be the same again.

> *A House upon the Hight—*
> *That Wagon never reached—*
> *No Dead, were ever carried down—*
> *No Peddler's Cart—approached—*
>
> *Whose Chimney never smoked—*
> *Whose Windows—Night and Morn—*
> *Caught Sunrise first—and Sunset—last—*
> *Then—held an Empty Pane—*
>
> *Whose fate—Conjecture knew—*
> *No other neighbor—did—*
> *And what it was—we never lisped—*
> *Because He—never told—*
>
> (#399)

Almost two thousand years before this time, in a far-off foreign land, Jesus Christ had instructed His followers to spread the good news of the Redeemer. "Ye are the light of the world. A city that is set on a hill cannot be hid." (Matthew 5:14.) Two centuries before Emily Dickinson's birth, her English forebears had been part of a holy errand into the wilderness where a New Jerusalem, God's Kingdom on earth, would be established. And a sermon was preached in those earliest days of this land: "For we must consider that we shall be as a city upon a hill, the eyes of all people are upon us."

Now the "House upon the Hight" is empty. Is it the New Jerusalem of America, last outpost of Christ's glorious vision now abandoned, evacuated of meaning and of influence? Is it no more than an empty clapboard farmhouse, with the family gone to richer prospects? Or is the distinction no longer significant?

Part Five ◆ *Adieu*

FROM: *The Man with the Blue Guitar*

XXI

A substitute for all the gods:
This self, not that gold self aloft,

Alone, one's shadow magnified,
Lord of the body, looking down,

As now and called most high,
The shadow of Chocorua

In an immense heaven, aloft,
Alone, lord of the land and lord

Of the men that live in the land, high lord.
One's self and the mountains of one's land,

Without shadows, without magnificence,
The flesh, the bone, the dirt, the stone.

—Wallace Stevens

Therefore have I uttered that I understood not;
things too wonderful for me, which I knew not.
Hear, I beseech thee, and I will speak:
I will demand of thee, and declare thou unto me.
I have heard of thee by the hearing of the ear;
but now mine eyes seeth thee.

—Job 42:3–5

I ◆ The Cosmos as Mirror

It was not a good time to have wrestled so strenuously with the Lord. Deeply buried in Dickinson's mission, beneath the anger and the arrogance, there was profound belief: the confidence that God could wound, but not be wounded; the presumption that the word could be strained to the poet's uttermost and still not relinquish its ghost. In Massachusetts two centuries before Emily Dickinson's birth, such assumptions might have held true. However, even as early as 1862 they did not. All of America was falling away from the faith of the Fathers. The New Jerusalem was a faded memory to most, and the vigor of God's presence was leaving the land. Quite independently of the poet's challenge, words were losing the shadow of supernatural significance.

Even before she was thirty, Dickinson acknowledged the presence of this brooding, demythologizing force. At its simplest level it occurred as a problem of naming. "*'Acturus' is his other name — / I'd rather call him 'Star.' / It's very mean of Science / To go and interfere!*" Yet the consummate wordsmith understood that this problem of language reflected a deeper difficulty. "*What once was 'Heaven' / Is 'Zenith' now — / Where I proposed to go / When Time's brief masquerade was done / Is mapped and charted too*" (#70). Such a meditation is entirely different from poems that act as a verbal assault upon God. Here it is not the speaker who raises doubts, but "Science"; and these doubts deal not with the *nature* of Divinity or of Heaven, but with their very *existence*.

Without a belief in God or in some transcendent realm, every individual loses the possibility of hope for an afterlife. Yet the poet / hero endures a second blow as well, the loss of the ready possibility for epic engagement. Without the God Who wounds, there can be no wrestle for dominion: "*They leave us with the Infinite,*" one speaker muses. "*But He — is not a man —*" (#350). Sometimes the dismissal of the Deity is ascribed to "Science," and the speaker reflects ruefully upon the sterility of such notions as "'Zenith'" or "Infinite." Yet Dickinson could see that the ebbing of belief also affected those indifferent to the immediate claims of science. Thus her strongest poems acknowledge that the drift away from God was generational, the phenomenon of an increasingly secular America.

> *Those — dying then,*
> *Knew where they went —*

> *They went to God's Right Hand—*
> *That Hand is amputated now*
> *And God cannot be found—*
>
> *The abdication of Belief*
> *Makes the Behavior small—*
> *Better an ignis fatuus*
> *Than no illume at all—*
>
> (#*1551*)

The slow passage of time away from that era of ardent faith upon which New England was founded eventually dealt an unthinkable blow: the wounding God was Himself critically wounded—subjected to some species of castration—and an unrelenting night followed. The smothering, unyielding dark is worse than some blinding light of faith. Indeed, the ultimate irony is that even an "ignis fatuus" of false promises to be exposed was better than an existence that has been entirely deprived of heroic possibility.

When she embarked upon her grand mission to speak as "Representative," did Dickinson understand that this bleak prospect would also present itself to challenge her capacities? No one can identify a moment of tragic insight, and thus the question cannot yield a certain answer. Although a great preponderance of the early poetry addresses a world that has been scarred by the God of Jacob, there are a very few poems in the hand of 1862 that address the terrible burdens of the poet in a world without the Divinity altogether—the poet who surveys a landscape without even the illumination of God's will-o'-the-wisp.

> *We grow accustomed to the Dark—*
> *When Light is put away—*
> *As when the Neighbor holds the Lamp*
> *To witness her Goodbye—*
>
> *A Moment—We uncertain step*
> *For newness of the night—*
> *Then—fit our Vision to the Dark—*
> *And meet the Road—erect—*
>
> *And so of larger—Darknesses—*
> *Those Evenings of the Brain—*
> *When not a Moon disclose a sign—*
> *Or Star—come out—within—*
>
> *The B[r]avest—grope a little—*
> *And sometimes hit a Tree*

Directly in the Forehead—
But as they learn to see—

Either the Darkness alters—
Or something in the sight
Adjusts itself to Midnight—
And Life steps almost straight.

(#419)

The darkness of this poem—not the Deity's momentary displeasure, but some perennial condition to which we must "grow accustomed"—portends a new kind of calamity. The "Moon" fails to disclose "a sign" and there is no hint of otherworldly significance in the quotidian. Nor can one discover a "Star," the herald of God's birth as man. Appropriately, then, God is present in this poem only obliquely or by default: although "Goodbye" is colloquial for "God be with you," the wishful sentiment is mordant here, for this invocation of the Deity has been used only to signal departure. No longer blinding, the "Light is put away—": the Father, the Son, and the Holy Ghost have all been driven from the land, and a new kind of wilderness overtakes us.

Before it had been God's demand that we accept *His* vision of nature that had threatened the eye / I; now the speaker confronts an even more insidious danger. She cannot assert the eye as she did before, to see and then to correct God's definitions because God's definitions no longer dominate the collective imagination. At the same time, the fragile membrane that separates self or "I" from the outside world is violated—not by God's assaults or by death, but by the collapse of the categories that moor the components of the external world to some fixed referent outside the self. Thus these are "Evenings of the *Brain*"; the failure of both "sign" and "Star" are *"within."* Self, individual sense impressions, and the meaning of these impressions have all become incoherently fused. As before, there is a wound. Now, however, it is no mark of the wrestle with an adversarial God, just the result of a purely physical, blind encounter with a "Tree / Directly in the Forehead—."

Is there any use for the poet in such a world? With supremely quiet understatement, the verse suggests that someone at least must learn how to use her feet: someone must take an "uncertain step / . . . Then—fit our Vision to the Dark." Still heroic, perhaps (for only the "B[r]avest" dare to move), the poet has a new kind of mission. She must investigate the meaning of God's demise. She must parse the dark to understand the significance of a "sign" that fails in an interior world. Above all, she must confront self in an end-stopped universe.

Perhaps the need for God's power would never be so apparent as in those days of its decline. Dickinson states the general case—that anything shows most poignantly when it must wrestle for survival: *"'tis when / A Value struggle—it exist—* / *A Power—will proclaim* / *Although Annihilation pile* / *Whole Chaoses on Him—*" (#806). So long as God's legend on earth remained strong, Emily Dickinson could forge a poetic Voice of immense power by juxtaposing it against the force of the Divinity: both God and poet could be articulated with the clarity of chiaroscuro in such wrestle for dominion. Not surprisingly, then, this fading of God's presence is a unique impediment to the poet's efforts to assert eye / I.

Thus one response to God's decline is a remarkable effort to revive Him.

> *I rose—because He sank—*
> *I thought it would be opposite—*
> *But when his power dropped—*
> *My Soul stood straight.*
>
> *I cheered my fainting Prince—*
> *I sang firm—even—Chants—*
> *I helped his Film—with Hymn—*
>
> *And when the Dews drew off*
> *That held his Forehead stiff—*
> *I met him—*
> *Balm to Balm—*
>
> *I told him Best—must pass*
> *Through this low Arch of Flesh—*
> *No Casque so brave*
> *It spurn the Grave—*
>
> *I told him Worlds I knew*
> *Where Monarchs—grew—*
> *Who recollected us*
> *If we were true—*
>
> *And so with Thews of Hymn—*
> *And Sinew from within—*
> *And ways I knew not that I knew—till then—*
> *I lifted Him—*
>
> (#616; var. "stood"
> and "Monarchs—")

One strategy of the poem is built upon a series of reversals. Christ is said to have risen from the dead, and by virtue of this miracle the promise of a similar resurrection was offered to all other human beings. He "lifted" us— so the story has been told. Yet eventually the unthinkable occurred: "his power dropped—." And the poet who had hurled herself against God's infinite resources must now create a speaker to reinfuse the waning Son with power.

The strength of such a speaker is manifested in attitudes of phallic rectitude: she stands "straight"; her "Hymn" has the intrinsic muscular potency of "Thews"; and her ultimate achievement is an erection, "I lifted Him—." Indeed, such resources recall the terms of "We grow accustomed to the Dark—," for bravery was begun in that other poem when the speaker could "meet the Road—erect—." Such a maneuver is not unrelated to the stance elsewhere in Dickinson's work: "*A still—Volcano—Life—* / . . . *A quiet— Earthquake Style—*" (#601) constitutes one consistent element of her repertoire. Before, such attitudes had functioned as defenses against the destructive, intrusive habits of the Deity; here, however, the speaker's phallic strength is not a form of defense, but of assistance, and she must draw upon it to prop up the God-man Whose puissance has been drained away. Other elements in the poem reflect an even more poignant reversal of roles. Christ's pledges were supposed to ease humanity's inevitable confrontation with death; here, the speaker "Chants . . . Hymns" to cheer the "fainting Prince" when the film of death beclouds His eyes. In stanzas four and five, she even recites scraps of the New Testament to soothe His pain. Jesus had instructed severely that all who would be saved must pass through the "strait gate" (Matthew 7:13); in the case of the Christ, this narrow path of suffering is an inevitable concomitant of the estate of man into which He has entered. Gently, the speaker echoes His own words to remind this displaced Deity that all men, even the "Best . . . must pass / Through this low Arch of Flesh—." Then, to palliate the hardship of His dual estate, she reminds Him of the promised afterlife, recalling to Him His own generosity upon the cross when the thief asked to be "recollected" after Christ had come into His "kingdom" (Luke 23:42).

Withal, the speaker's resolute strength is insufficient: the terrible specter of a God Whose Right Hand has been "amputated" is embedded in the verse structure of this poem, for virtually every stanza is severely wounded—lacking not a hand, but feet and in one case an entire line, strung with rhyme inconsistent throughout. The poem literally limps toward its conclusion; and if the penultimate line swells in length and tonal density, it still cannot rectify the pervasive sense of injury.

What, then, can one make of the proud assertion with which the poem concludes, "I lifted Him—"? No one can literally restore the vitality of a God-man Who perished centuries ago. Yet Dickinson has a singular claim as a poet: the body of her work, much of it a protracted encounter with the Lord that repeatedly invokes his legend—seemingly the enactment of resolute hostility—has really functioned as a wrestle of parturition. Although the faith of the Fathers was being forgotten at the very time that Emily Dickinson was addressing herself to it—although God's death throes were already apparent in 1862 and subsequent generations would turn away from the rigorous creed of the Congregationalist past altogether—subsequent generations would read the poetry that had been written in Amherst during those several decades of transition. Indeed, the use of the word "Sinews" is an explicit allusion to Jacob's wrestle and the desolation that followed his engagement at Peniel: traditionally, it named the muscle in the thigh that the Hebrews were forbidden to eat, a taboo arising from the fact that it was the *sinew* of Jacob's thigh that had been wounded. Here, the speaker discovers "Sinew from within," a power of the verse to resurrect the God-made-man. One strength of the wordsmith's art is demonstrated tonally by the assonance of "Thews," "Sinew," "knew," and "knew," which literally strings the last stanza together; yet another, much greater strength inheres in the more general power of poetry. Subsequent generations would become engaged in a woman's solitary struggle against a God of power. And for the men and women of those subsequent generations, God's legend would be born again, vigorous and compelling, in the poetry of Emily Dickinson. So long as her work is read, she can deliver an empowered Deity to her readers.

Eventually, Dickinson came to appreciate a paradoxical fact. The relationship between God and His creatures has an essentially reciprocal quality. Perhaps we need Him to provide an heroic dimension to our otherwise entirely banal lives; at the same time, He may need our belief. Perhaps it is not enough for God to exist; perhaps He requires our confidence in Him to suffuse *His* existence with meaning. "*How dare I, therefore, stint a faith / On which so vast depends— / Lest Firmament should fail for me— / The Rivet in the Bands*" (#766). Yet the belief of one cannot sustain an entire culture. Thus when God's legend loses its potency and society is cut loose from that intimate link to the supernatural that had initially seemed to Dickinson little more than tyranny, an entire order of splendor is lost. "*The abdication of Belief / Makes the Behavior small—*"; the dwindling of divine power robs arts as well.

> *One Crucifixion is recorded—only—*
> *How many be*
> *Is not affirmed of Mathematics—*
> *Or History—*
>
> *One Calvary—exhibited to Stranger—*
> *As many be*
> *As Persons—or Peninsulas—*
> *Gethsemane—*
>
> *Is but a Province—in the Being's Centre—*
> *Judea—*

> *For Journey—or Crusade's Achieving—*
> *Too near—*
>
> *Our Lord—indeed—made Compound Witness—*
> *And yet—*
> *There's newer—nearer Crucifixion*
> *Than That—*

(#553)

Quietly, indeed without apparent self-consciousness, this poem assumes a radical reversal.

Elsewhere, "Crucifixion" had stipulated an event of incomparable significance: the "Horror," God's death in agony upon the cross. Yet when the notion of the Divinity loses its hold upon our imagination and Christ seems no longer a murdered God but merely a suffering man, the sacrilegious element of His death dwindles in importance, and the unique essence of the moment is lost. Christ becomes noteworthy not because He was divine, but because He was human; the meaning of Calvary is defined not by transcendent values, but by earthly ones. The Crucifixion becomes a prototype for human misery, and the story of Christ's death—indeed, the entire Christian legend—lays claim to our attention not because it describes a unique happening, but because it can affirm a continuing thread of ordinary experience. There is a subtle argument embedded in such a view, an argument that would ultimately erase the distinct claims of Christianity over all other religions: any mythology that has long standing, any mythology in which many have believed (or to which many have responded empathetically), has a similar claim to our attention. The touchstone of truth is not an unchanging and eternal God, but the reaction of many individual men and women: *human affirmation,* not revealed truth, confers importance upon a "mythic" event.

The location of authority is thus reversed: before it had resided with God; now it resides in human nature. The word "Crucifixion" becomes no more than a trope for extraordinary pain: "As many be / As Persons—or Peninsulas—." The world of legend has no external, independent validity: "Gethsemane— / Is but a Province—in the Being's Centre—." The crucial terms of Christianity, along with those from all other fables of transcendence, are drawn into human consciousness and absorbed into our daily vocabulary to become strategies for describing the terms of our existential condition.

Elsewhere, Dickinson would perceive this transaction as a desolating loss; however, this poem seems to escape such judgment. True, the heroism of the "Crusade's Achieving" is no longer available to us: "Judea" is "Too near—." Yet the materialistic thrust of "Compound Witness—" seems to stand without ironic commentary: Christ's sacrifice was "Compound" because His death was offered in behalf of many; but it is also like compound interest upon a loan, piling up credit upon credit as years pass and increasing numbers of people find it relevant to their own experience.

Inevitably, however, the language of poetry does become diminished. Although Christian terminology can still possesses a *frisson* of implication, the loss of the categories that had seemed so to constrain this language and to fetter human options proves to be at least as desolating as it is liberating. The word's power to name is increasingly limited to the things of this world and the elements of human consciousness.

> *A great Hope fell*
> *You heard no noise*
> *The Ruin was within*
> *Oh cunning wreck that told no tale*
> *And let no Witness in. . .*
>
> (#1123)

Once Christ was deemed our "Hope," but if this poem alludes to Christ, it does so only by affirming that the failure of His experiment has brought disappointment to every one of us, "The Ruin . . . within." Indeed, the Son's hold over the elements of this poem is so feeble that the verse seems more plausibly to refer to some entirely personal disillusionment, a particular "Hope" that was not fulfilled. What is more, this appropriation of transcendent terms is far from an isolated case: attenuated religious language can be found in many other poems written after 1862.

> *Had I not seen the Sun*
> *I could have borne the shade*
> *But Light a newer Wilderness*
> *My Wilderness has made—*
>
> (#1233)

Once the "Sun" and "Light" had signified God, and "Wilderness" was the agony of separation from divine guidance. In this poem, however, the explicitly Biblical connotation has been virtually eliminated: "Sun" and "Light" mean no more than some happiness, glimpsed but never to be possessed; "Wilderness" is but an emphatic form of disappointment.

Poems that are composed of such language are not necessarily bad works of art: "A great Hope fell" has enjoyed the respect of critics; even "Had I not seen the Sun" is a deft formulation. However, the terms of the success to which such work can aspire are limited: since it cannot engage that which surpasses ordinary human experience, it must content itself with articulating the human condition in ways that touch upon the experience of many.

We play at Paste—
Till qualified, for Pearl—
Then, drop the Paste—
And deem ourself a fool—

The Shapes—though—were similar—
And our new Hands
Learned <u>Gem</u>-Tactics—
Practicing <u>Sands</u>—

(#320)

Hovering behind this verse is a traditional religious notion. God's Kingdom was described as the "Pearl of Great Price" for which all of life's limited pleasures ought to be traded; "Paste" might be taken as generic for this world, and "Pearl" for Heaven. Again, however, the force of the legend has become so diluted that the poem might more plausibly be taken as a wry homily concerning our impatience with the earlier stages of our development of any earthly skill. As all three of these poems suggest, one way a de-mythologized vernacular can muster power is by treading the peripheries of belief—using a language that preserves the echo of transcendence. However, when even the echo dies, when the word is restricted entirely to the immanent realm, art may become end-stopped.

Perhaps the ultimate irony is that this demythologized world, now entirely emancipated from the tyranny of God's rule, still bears the mark of wounding. Now, however, there is no antagonist to combat—no locus of intention and intelligence to receive our resentment and anger. Nothing remains except a universe that has been evacuated of meaning and intrinsic relationships.

Four Trees—upon a solitary Acre—
Without Design
Or Order, or Apparent Action—
Maintain—

The Sun—upon a Morning meets them—
The Wind—
No nearer Neighbor—have they—
But God—

The Acre gives them—Place
They—Him—Attention of Passer by—
Of Shadow, or of Squirrel, haply—
Or Boy—

> *What Deed is Their's unto the General Nature—*
> *What Plan*
> *They severally—retard—or further—*
> *Unknown—*

(#742)

The injury is not a presence, but a nullity—not a castrating blow to the groin, but the absence of any consistent force in the cosmos. There is not even the uniformity of systematic destruction. God is gone. Nature is random, "*Without Design.*"

Nothing connects. The poem may seem at first another spare and supple still life. Yet it is radically different from other such poems. Although "The Angle of a Landscape" reveals little more than a concatenation of dismembered parts, a "Pattern" of God's systematic destruction can be discerned in them; thus the components of that "Landscape" combined to spell a destiny of doom. "A Pit—but Heaven over it—" describes a moral universe infected with Gothic horror, and the fixed spatial array of its parts serves to define the shape of our peril. By contrast, no thread of commonality holds the contents of *this* work together—nothing but happenstance seems to justify their inclusion in the same piece of verse.

In fact, the syntax and diction of the poem exert a kind of centrifugal force. "Four Trees" is the subject of the sentence that makes up the first stanza; standing at the beginning of the initial line, the words seem to announce a palpable presence to dominate the visible world. Yet as the stanza dwindles to its scant conclusion, all specific options for connectedness are denied. The "Trees" bear no relation to each other: they embody no "Design," affirm no "Order." But they are not relevant to their surroundings, either, and they engage in no "Action." The residual acknowledgment, that they "Maintain," is simply negation clothed in the superficies of a positive assertion. "Maintain" is a transitive verb that must have some object to complete its meaning; standing as it does here, without any word to fulfill its potential, it is vacuous, and the utterance for which it is the predicate is no more than nonsense. The second stanza seems to begin more positively, with a completed sentence: "The Sun . . . meets them—." Yet the sentence asserts mere juxtaposition, not interaction. And this tentative coherence arouses our expectations only to disappoint them, for the phrase "The Wind—" is introjected immediately afterwards, entirely at random. The verbal formulation "No nearer Neighbor—have they—/ But God" is particularly vexing. It comes so close to being grammatical (and the reader may by this point long so anxiously to discover a coherent, meaningful sentence) that its disruptive elements are elusive. The adjective "nearer" requires the adverb "than" to complete the spatial comparison that it announces; instead, the adverb "but" intrudes. However, the word "but" necessarily introduces an exception; and this word would make syntactic sense only if "nearer" were omitted. Two thoughts seem collapsed, then—they have no neighbor but God; they have no nearer neighbor than God. These thoughts are in no way resolved, however, and the result is little more than elegant gibberish. Even the intrusion of the term "God" is unsettling, for the poem gives us no reason to suppose that He is essentially different from any of the other members of the scene, "Sun . . . Morning . . . Wind." This confusion of status is continued into the next stanza, where the "Acre," which ought to be "it," is designated by the pronoun "Him"; and the disorder is brought to conclusion by a faulty parallel as "Shadow," "Squirrel," and "Boy" are each equally designated as a "Passer by."

Every one of these violations of the rules of ordinary usage is small; perhaps no one of them is sufficient to disrupt an entire poem. However, their effect is cumulative. The coherent relationships that are conventionally stipulated by grammar and diction are repeatedly denied in this poem. In the end, the accrued slippage—the carefully orchestrated series of failed relationships—acquires its own divisive meaning. The same linguistic structures that usually assert order are deployed here to assert separateness. Instead of interacting in harmony, the words militate against one another, each bristling away from the others as if to stand alone. The poem has no centripetal, syntactic design: just as the contents of the scene bear only an accidental relationship to each other, so the most powerfully unifying forces that act upon the verse are the page that holds the poem, and the stanzas and lines that assign the words a place.

Indeed, the most arresting ordered arrangement available to the reader in both printed and manuscript copies of the poem is the series of compellingly shaped stanzas that decrease to but a single foot and conclude with the disyllable "Unknown." Like the "Tree" that is hit by the speaker in "We grow accustomed to the Dark—," these words, lines, and stanzas on the page offer a sensuous reality to the reader. It is not the reality of transcendence, to be sure, but it may be the only reality available. And such limited "reality" must increasingly become the stuff of poetry—isolated objects without any intrinsic relationship to each other; *words* with "design."

The theocentric culture in which Dickinson had been reared stipulated that there was a Force behind the veil of appearance giving order and meaning to the world. Although the poet had started in rebellion against this coercive Power and Its mandated meaning, the structure that could be accepted as a "given" nonetheless provided an armature for art: there was an intrinsically coherent system to correct, and the artist was not constrained to begin *ex nihilo*. Yet as God's power diminished and died, intrinsic order died with it. In "Four Trees—upon a solitary Acre—," the "Acre" and all the elements upon it stand in a perpetual state of existential isolation. If anything at all is to give them significance or relatedness, it must be "Attention of Passer by—." Thus the task of pulling the visible world into some meaningful configuration, once God's right, now falls entirely to human beings. It is an enormous, possibly overwhelming burden.

The unrelenting necessity of sorting the myriad elements of the universe in which we live, of assigning values and establishing useful relationships, has the potential for producing an anxiety that becomes the condition of being. Little wonder, then, that Dickinson's poetry of this epoch sometimes depicts an unsettling reversal of the relationship between human consciousness and that which exists external to it.

> *The Brain—is wider than the Sky—*
> *For—put them side by side—*
> *The one the other will contain*
> *With ease—and You—beside—*
>
> *The Brain is deeper than the sea—*
> *For—hold them—Blue to Blue—*
> *The one the other will absorb—*
> *As Sponges—Buckets—do—*
>
> *The Brain is just the weight of God—*
> *For—Heft them—Pound for Pound—*
> *And they will differ—if they do—*
> *As Syllable from Sound—*

(#632)

In this poem, nothing exists outside of "The Brain," and our capacity for perceiving the world becomes its own desperate maelstrom—a vortex that sucks external reality inward. The twin blots of blue, "Sky" and "sea," are reduced to nothing more than ideas in the human head. Even the Lord is subjected to mutilating reduction. "The Brain" and "God . . . will differ . . . / As Syllable from Sound—": syllables are concocted from sounds and contain them; the brain has been created by God, but nonetheless contains Him.

At first, this sweeping assertion of the "Brain's" capacities may appear an ultimate confirmation of the primacy and authority of self, and in one sense it is. Yet the self that has been thus empowered is paradoxically limited, for every significant other self has been obliterated through absorption. "You" might refer to the reader; it might refer to some beloved. One cannot tell, and it does not matter. The voracious "Brain . . . will contain . . . You" along with everything else; and without another separate and distinct self in either the transcendent or the immanent realm, what is the value of this arrogation of authority?

Moreover, without any external force to regulate it or at least to provide a constant standard, the consciousness that has interiorized everything else is in peril from each minute disruption or conflict; and when consciousness is unsettled, so is poetry. "*The Brain, within it's Groove / Runs evenly—and true— / But let a Splinter swerve— / 'Twere easier for You— / To put a Current back— / When Floods have slit the Hills— / And scooped a Turnpike for Themselves— / And trodden out the Mills—*" (#556). Before, "Floods" had been construed as one extinguishing force in God's experiment with mankind; now they operate within. Before, God had been the hero-poet's adversary; now there is no external foe—just some disorder in the penetralia of the self, a disorder that is rendered by the image of "Mills" that have been "trodden out" by *uncontrolled feet* in the "Brain."

If this inward movement is carried to its logical conclusion, poetry must take the isolated interior world for its subject: the artist has access to nothing else. And when Dickinson's metaphorical notions of "Nature" as a "Haunted House" and "Art" as a "House that tries to be haunted" are adapted to this condition of existential isolation, the result is a Gothic nightmare.

> *One need not be a Chamber—to be Haunted—*
> *One need not be a House—*
> *The Brain has Corridors—surpassing*
> *Material Place—*
>
> *Far safer, of a Midnight Meeting*
> *External Ghost*
> *Than its interior Confronting—*
> *That Cooler Host.*
>
> *Far safer, through an Abbey gallop,*
> *The Stones a'chase—*
> *Than Unarmed, one's a'self encounter—*
> *In lonesome Place—*
>
> *Ourself behind ourself, concealed—*
> *Should startle most—*
> *Assassin hid in our Apartment*
> *Be Horror's least.*
>
> *The Body—borrows a Revolver—*
> *He bolts the Door—*
> *O'erlooking a superior spectre—*
> *Or More—*
>
> (#670)

"Because I could not stop for Death—" makes a useful contrast to this poem. There a literary model, the novel of seduction, stands behind the movement of the verse, for the speaker's triumph over death is mirrored in the poem's refusal to follow the prescribed resolution. Still, the novel of seduction is external to the essential import of that verse, the speaker's refusal to submit to God's demands. It is a pattern to be manipulated, nothing more. Here, however, the literary form of the Gothic novel is literally absorbed into the speaker. Wistfully, she recollects worlds and fictions that can be kept outside of the integral "I": "Far safer, through an Abbey gallop, / The Stones a'chase—." However frightening the specters of actual abbeys or fictional buildings may be, theirs is but an "External Ghost" whom we can banish. The "Haunted" *self* presents a different order of danger, for the latent peril is entirely within. None can elude it, and when truth is revealed, the "concealed . . . Assassin" is no other but "Ourself."

Ironically, this development in the poetry accomplishes almost accidentally the very violation of self that God had so often attempted in vain: the coherence of individual consciousness is disrupted and split in twain. Now self must find its subject by inspecting self. Sometimes there is a faint, ghoulish echo of the Lord's Supper in this process: "*Deprived of other Banquet, / I entertained Myself— / At first—a scant nutrition— / An insufficient Loaf— / But grown by slender addings, / To so esteemed a size / 'Tis sumptuous enough for me— / And almost to suffice / A Robin's famine able— / Red Pilgrim, He and I— / A Berry from our table / Reserve—for charity—*" (#773). Sometimes the trope moves away from these images that contain diluted religious language to tropes that reflect the money and counting rooms of a society increasingly divested of heroism: "*The Heart is the Capital of the Mind—*" (#1354). And sometimes the verse explicitly acknowledges that all of this feeding upon nothing but self devolves into a kind of abhorrent spiritual cannibalism.

> The Mind lives on the Heart
> Like any Parasite—
> If that is full of Meat
> The Mind is fat.
>
> But if the Heart omit
> Emaciate the Wit—
> The Aliment of it
> So absolute.
>
> (#1355)

The lip-smacking, practical, nutritional tone of the first stanza underlines the macabre; and a similar practicality is continued by the musing of the second. If the mind has no food other than the "Heart," sooner or later its stores will be used up, and the "Wit" will become emaciated, too. A variant second stanza suggests Dickinson's explicit preoccupation with the effect of God's waning power upon this process.

> But, if the Heart be lean
> The boldest mind will pine
> Throw not to the divine
> Like Dog a Bone[1]

Even the "boldest" may falter when the heart's supply begins to dwindle. Then even the Mastiff-God may be remembered as a preferable alternative; however, turning to the Divinity under these desperate circumstances is no better than throwing a dog a bone.

Occasionally this narrow focus upon self is vaunted as a strength: "*You cannot take itself / From any Human soul— / That indestructible estate / Enable him to dwell— / Impregnable as Light / That every man behold / But take away as difficult / As undiscovered Gold—*" (#*1351*). Hiding behind the printed words in this poem is the breathless pun for "undiscovered Gold"—Mine! Yet an insistence upon the exclusive claims of self—Mine!—is most acceptable when it is argued against the willfulness of an omnipotent Divinity. The ruthless strength of the opponent justifies and limits the extremity of the speaker's attitude. However, when the Divinity's power vanishes, this exclusive concern of self for self begins to take on the tonalities of an emotional aberration.

The notion of some ultimate face-to-face fulfillment is not relinquished; now, however, the speaker seeks to confront neither the abandoning God nor the lover who might displace Him, but only self. Some portion of consciousness is split off, then, to stand at a hypothetical distance in order to advise, judge, criticize, or do combat; and this profound fissure in the speaker's emotional integrity becomes its own kind of terror. "*The Battle fought between the Soul / And No Man—is the One / Of all the Battles prevalent— / By far the Greater One—*" (#*594*). In the tight little world of self, all significant action is turned inward, and this unrelieved focus is often realized grammatically through reflexive constructions. Sometimes Dickinson undertakes principally to depict the convolutions of such an attitude: "*The Soul unto itself / Is an imperial friend— / Or the most agonizing Spy— / An Enemy—could send— / Secure against it's own— / No treason it can fear— / Itself—it's Sovreign—of itself / The Soul should stand in Awe—*" (#*683*). Sometimes she captures the exquisite precision of pain that is entirely internal, both caused by self and felt by self: "*My Soul—accused me—And I quailed— / As Tongues of Diamond had reviled / ... Her favor—is the best Disdain / Toward Artifice of Time—or Men— / But Her Disdain—'twere lighter bear / A finger of Enamelled*

Fire—" (#753). But the most devastating concomitant of this radical inward-turning motion is a condition of self-enmity: "*Me from Myself—to banish— / Had I Art— / Invincible my Fortress / Unto All Heart— / But since Myself— assault Me— / . . . How this be / Except by Abdication— / Me—of Me?*" (#642) Such anguish cannot be evaded or resolved because the intolerable tension does not result from ambiguous intentions or conflict over some meditated behavior. Instead, it seems an inherent and inevitable component of self-consciousness. The various components of the interior world may begin to seem alien—not part of "me"—and the only escape that can be postulated is some cutting off of one part of self, a mutilating wound. "*To flee from memory / Had we the Wings / Many would fly / Inured to slower things / Birds with dismay / Would scan the mighty van / Of men escaping / From the mind of man*" (#1242).

A wrestle with the Lord may seem a hopeless contest—mere humanity hurling itself against the infinite resources of the Divinity. Yet there were unexpected comforts in such a confrontation. Pain had a cause, and one's anger and resentment at suffering could be directed toward God. When human companionship did not suffice to ease the sense of intractable loneliness, that painful isolation could be construed as a result of God's withdrawal, and some measure of perverse comfort could be drawn from the expectation that if only He would return, the loneliness could be dispelled. Perhaps there are no conditions that can make death entirely tolerable, and the poet who grappled with God surely perceived death as His ultimate weapon. Still, the fact that there was *agency* entailed in this event—that when the "last Onset" arrived, one could expect a "King" to be waiting in the room— lent even death some measure of conviviality. Yet these meager comforts must also be forsaken when a belief in the Deity cannot be sustained. Then the isolated consciousness must confront pain or loneliness or death entirely alone.

> *This Consciousness that is aware*
> *Of Neighbors and the Sun*
> *Will be the one aware of Death*
> *And that itself alone*
>
> *Is traversing the interval*
> *Experience between*
> *And most profound experiment*
> *Appointed unto Men—*
>
> *How adequate unto itself*
> *It's properties shall be*
> *Itself unto itself and none*
> *Shall make discovery.*

> Adventure most unto itself
> The Soul condemned to be —
> Attended by a single Hound
> It's own identity.
>
> (#822)

The ghost of some God lingers here: death seems a "profound experiment" that has been "Appointed unto Men—." Yet these touches are no more than the vestiges of faith: the principal actor is also the principal victim, "Consciousness." Death is an ultimate of anguish, now not because it is God's final affliction, but because it is the moment of supreme seclusion. What may be worse, "Consciousness" can anticipate this last "Adventure" over and over again, each imaginative exploit as horrifying as the finality itself, so that the excruciating awareness of one's own imminent dissolution becomes a constant companion of existence. Inevitably, such a state of mind borders upon derangement. "*I never hear that one is dead* / *Without the chance of Life* / *Afresh annihilating me* / *That mightiest Belief,* / *Too mighty for the Daily mind* / *That tilling it's abyss,* / *Had Madness, had it once or twice* / . . . *I do not know the man so bold* / *He dare in lonely Place* / *That awful stranger Consciousness* / *Deliberately face —* " (#1323).

There is a dreary, gray, dead-end tonality to this poetry—as if language itself had been stripped of its vitality. There is no residue of adventure, and the banishment of an empowered Deity now precludes the possibility of any further epic encounter. Perhaps the principal advantage God had offered was to glorify the poet's mission. However, an unshakable confidence in His existence had served another purpose as well, one not altogether apparent until the demise of His power revealed it. Just as in life the interaction with others confirms our sense of self, so the poet's wrestle with this divine Being had served to articulate identity—paradoxically, even in those cases when identity had seemed the explicit target of His attack. When God's loss of authority leaves self alone to ponder only self, monotony and alienation invade the speaking Voice, and the sense of a strong "I" in the poem is dissipated. One remedy might have been to turn outward, not to God, but to other human beings: in our everyday existence, men and women retain their sense of self by just such social exchanges. Some artists might have written powerful poetry about relationships of this sort, but Dickinson could not. Her original mission had been so exclusively defined in interior, transcendent terms that whenever the world of ordinary human interactions enters the verse, it does so chiefly by way of being unavailable. "*A Door just opened on a street—* / *I—lost—was passing by—* / *An instant's Width of Warmth disclosed—* / *And Wealth—and Company.* / *The Door as instant shut—And I—* / *I—lost—was passing by—* / *Lost doubly—but by contrast—most—* / *Informing misery—* " (#953).

One challenge for the post-Christian poet, then, is to discover an effective mode for mapping the interior wasteland, to invent a verse that can address acute pain that has no transcendent cause.

> *There is a pain — so utter —*
> *It swallows substance up —*
> *Then covers the Abyss with Trance —*
> *So Memory can step*
> *Around — across — upon it —*
> *As one within a Swoon —*
> *Goes safely — where an open eye —*
> *Would drop Him — Bone by Bone.*

> (#*599*)

The "Abyss" is either the chaos that preceded creation or the state of nullity toward which the destructive force of time drives us: traditionally, the term has religious overtones. Here, however, the void is entirely internal, and "Abyss" transforms what ought to be a discrete and limited interior distance into an unfathomable, yawning cavern. Temporal and spatial relationships become utterly disrupted, and "Memory" maneuvers "Around—across—upon" the pain with no more consequent purpose than avoiding danger. The threat offered here is the same offered elsewhere by death, a disintegrating "drop . . . Bone by Bone" whose end cannot be stipulated. Whereas the beginning of death can at least be determined by the cessation of life, however, this unstructured and continuous state of pain is coextensive with life. And the starkest contrast between this poem and some study of imminent death is that here, no eye / I struggles against extinction: it cannot, for "pain . . . swallows substance up—."

Above all, existential anguish disrupts boundaries. The exhausted categories of the Christian myth may seize control of consciousness. Or, alternatively, the membrane between self and outside world may rupture, and elements that ought to be perceived as external to an individual identity flood in to give shape to suffering.

> *After great pain, a formal feeling comes —*
> *The Nerves sit ceremonious, like Tombs —*
> *The stiff Heart questions was it He, that bore,*
> *And Yesterday, or Centuries before?*
>
> *The Feet, mechanical, go round —*
> *A Wooden way*
> *Of Ground, or Air, or Ought —*

> *Regardless grown,*
> *A Quartz contentment, like a stone—*
>
> *This is the Hour of Lead—*
> *Remembered, if outlived,*
> *As Freezing persons, recollect the Snow—*
> *First—Chill—then Stupor—then the letting go—*
>
> (#341)[2]

Similar in essential ways to the other poems upon this subject, "After great pain" is the best of the group, deriving its haunting power from the radical compression of several subjects.

The themes of violation and disorder persist throughout. Yet here, it is not only the integrity of mental processes that suffers, but art as well, and the two are conflated into a single, grotesque trope—a social gathering of some sort that is being held in the speaker's consciousness. The initial guests seem gathered for a funeral: a "formal feeling comes—," and when the speaker's own "Nerves" prepare for the unnamed ritual by sitting "ceremonious, like Tombs," the outside world of disaster and death can be felt in the sanctuary of the brain. Still, a reader can follow the gist of the poem thus far: suffering so profound that the affective self becomes disordered and its components are splintered apart and personified as separate entities. Yet, when the second stanza introduces "Feet" into this array of internal parts, a tone of madness intrudes—as if the speaker's lower extremities had been brutally shoved into the head or as if some of the participants, "Nerves" and "Heart" perhaps, had begun to dance. In fact, the introjected "Feet" announce a second theme—poetry that has been fatally wounded by the pain of its creator.

The "mechanical," circular motion of the "Feet" may recall the ratchet wheel of the clock that ticks us toward doom, but these "Feet" have not even the *click* of metallic precision, and they stagger "A Wooden way," without vitality or purpose. If God's engine were behind this passage toward oblivion, a reader could expect the insistent beat of parataxis or at least the imperative forward movement that time infuses into so many other Dickinson poems. Instead, this speaker declines to orient the motion to any fixed, external entity, "Ground, or Air, or Ought—." As the final stanza pulls away from the increasingly macabre concatenation of images to offer a general conclusion, there is a fatalistic settling into cold, not the frigidity of death, but the atrophy of all mental processes. Elsewhere, cold is one of God's weapons, yet such is not the case here. Now the menace is entirely internal—lassitude, inanition, and finally the utter relinquishment of will.

Dickinson wrote a number of poems that bring the speaker to the verge of madness, poems that deal with the stark reality of death or with the unstructured chaos of some amorphous Heaven. Probably the proleptic meditation "I felt a Funeral, in my Brain" is most similar to "After great pain." Yet in that poem, as in other poems that treat the horrors of "Design," the speaker resists threats to identity that are inflicted from without: "Sense" attempts to break through, and "Reason" endeavors to forge connections. The tension in such works derives precisely from the juxtaposition of two forces: the speaker's determination to understand the outrage, thereby perhaps to subdue it, and the destructive energy of some exterior power, process, or event that defies human comprehension and control. Here, however, the speaker recounts no struggle, there is no external adversary, and the poem records nothing more than a process of yielding. This absence of active volition is mirrored in verse that appears passive despite the summation of the final stanza—vague regarding matters of time; listless in pushing toward resolution, with a last line that merely trails away; inconsistent or careless in matters of syntax, for here there is not even the carefully monitored syntactic slippage that makes every part of "Four Trees—upon a solitary Acre—" push away from every other part. If Dickinson had been an entirely unselfconscious worker, this verse might even invite speculations about her own emotional stability (although creating an *illusion* of incipient madness or profound depression surely requires a relatively sane and disciplined intellect). Yet as always, Dickinson works with spare precision; the conditions under which emotions become destabilized is precisely the issue in this poem.

When God had seemed the Author of human misery, the speaker could sustain coherence by resisting Him. However, when pain has no identifiable external cause—when it becomes no more than an existential fact—it can contaminate the very sensibility that experiences it. There is a slow paralysis of will as "I" becomes the thrall of "pain." And this is truly madness—not the bottomless chasm of actual death into which God would "drop" us, but the surrender to a living death, "the letting go—." Alienation and ennui, the quintessential maladies of the modern world.

Such misery has no structure and goes nowhere.

> *Pain—has an Element of Blank—*
> *It cannot recollect*
> *When it begun—or if there were*
> *A time when it was not—*
>
> *It has no Future—but itself—*
> *It's Infinite contain*
> *It's Past—enlightened to perceive*
> *New Periods—of Pain.*

(#650)

The poem is circular, concluding exactly where it began, with "Pain." Here, "Pain" has usurped many of the processes that would usually fall to the speaker: it is "Pain" that "cannot recollect"; it is "Pain" that looks in vain toward some "Future." "Pain" has replaced consciousness with "Blank"; and as the contorted, ultimately meaningless statements concerning "Future," "Infinite," and "Past" suggest, it has exploded the usual boundaries of space and time. Indeed, the effect of this kind of pain upon time is a wry irony. So long as it was the Clock of Design that spelled our doom, the poet's capacity to evade time and the lovers' ability to redesign temporal relationships could be forms of personal triumph. Now, however, time seems not an enemy to individual coherence, but a friend—some fixed system within which individual experience can be ordered. Part of pain's nightmarish power, then, resides in its capacity to destroy that orderly system. "*Pain—expands the Time—* / *Ages coil within* / *The minute Circumference* / *Of a single Brain—*" (#967).

Ultimately, free-floating pain and the consequent temporal disruption produce a condition in which art is impossible.

> *I felt a Cleaving in my Mind—*
> *As if my Brain had split—*
> *I tried to match it—Seam by Seam—*
> *But could not make them fit.*
>
> *The thought behind, I strove to join*
> *Unto the thought before—*
> *But Sequence ravelled out of Sound*
> *Like Balls—upon a Floor.*
>
> (#937)

The fair copy of this poem dates from 1864, and it is reasonable to suppose not only that it was composed after "I felt a Funeral, in my Brain," but also that the explicit echoing of the first line signals an intended contrast. In the earlier poem, death invades consciousness, and the speaker struggles unsuccessfully to withstand it and retain coherence; now, the speaker is being assailed by no external force, and the "Cleaving" that splits consciousness is entirely self-contained. A residual echo of heroic wrestling is summoned by the language; however, because the contest has become internalized. Instead of striving with an opponent, the speaker strives pitifully "to join" the fractured portions of her own "thought." The desire to understand this paralyzing state sets the poem in motion, but this becomes a dead-end effort, for the last two lines affirm that speech and poetry are no longer possible. "Sound" in "Sequence" is a grammatical term: it identifies an utterance that has logical and syntactic order and that thereby conveys meaning. When "Sequence" is "*ravelled out of Sound,*" this coherence is lost. What is left is babble, the negation of art.

There is a linguistic countermovement to this descent into gibberish, a thread of tangible, domestic terms that suggest a speaker straining toward the Voice of the "Wife." A cleaver was a kitchen tool in Dickinson's day; women made things "fit" when they were sewing, "Seam by Seam—." These concretizing words affix the poem to some external, material reality; however, neither the words nor the objects they name have any intrinsic order beyond their inclusion in the domestic realm. Hence while such diction may steady the poem by lending an illusion of location, it can never give an explanation for the disjunction in the speaker's "Mind," and it can never repair the fatal break. Indeed, there is a particular hopelessness to the final image, where the domestic, the emotional, and the artistic are all brought to conclusion. The "Balls—upon a Floor" are balls of *yarn,* and this unvoiced term is punned to mean story or narrative. When the yarn ravels out, emotions are spent, the housewife's needlework is undone, and the coherent myth that had permitted a poet to address the transcendent has died.

There is telling evidence of craftsmanship throughout this bleak poetry: the control over the sound "I" in "I felt a Cleaving in my Mind—" and in "Pain—has an Element of Blank—"; the careful dislocation of both cause and sequence in many such poems; the keening, empty "o" that so thoroughly permeates "After great pain" that the poem acquires almost the texture of a ritual lamentation. Nonetheless, this verse of isolated despair is thin. It has none of the density that characterizes such poems as "'Twas like a Maelstrom, with a notch" or "I cannot live with You—." One source of this decline in artistic complexity, perhaps the principal source, is precisely the capacity of the pain it treats to nullify the force of time: this kind of pain "has no Future—but itself / . . . It's Past—enlightened to perceive / New periods—of Pain"; thus poetry that addresses this form of suffering can exist only in the present. Its anguish is exclusively *now.* By contrast, the wound at Peniel describes a beginning of agony, and the landmarks in the Old and New Testaments amplify our comprehension of human tragedy: so long as the Christian myth held sway, no person's pain could exist only in the present. It bore a necessary and significant relationship to the sweeping Design of pain inherent in creation. The complex array of signs and emblems and valenced language that devolved from Christianity could dignify every sorrow, however small or personal. Yet once God's Right Hand had been "amputated," this expressive accumulation from the past was lost, and much of the meaning of present life was lost with it.

To be sure, the principal message of this poetry of existential pain is readily available to the reader. But while it lacks much of the frustratingly cryptic quality of Dickinson's God-centered verse, it also lacks the mysterious, haunting power. Once heroic, the poet now stands in danger of becoming a species of factory worker who confronts not some Supreme Power, but merely the many engines of the modern world.

> *From Blank to Blank —*
> *A Threadless Way*
> *I pushed Mechanic feet —*
> *To stop — or perish — or advance —*
> *Alike indifferent —*
>
> *If end I gained*
> *It ends beyond*
> *Indefinite disclosed —*
> *I shut my eyes — and groped as well*
> *'Twas lighter — to be Blind —*

(#761)

"Blank" is almost a totemic word in Dickinson's work to identify a course of human affairs that has been stripped of larger significance. Now the "thread" of meaningful narrative sequence is gone, and there are no defined beginnings or endings to be acknowledged or rejected. Even the structure that the drive toward death had imposed has been lost, and poetry bears a commensurate wound: "To stop—or perish—or advance— / Alike indifferent—." What now can dictate the shape of art? Nothing waits ahead except the "Indefinite," and the poet who had battled with such tenacity to retain autonomy and the right to her own integral vision of the world deliberately shuts her eyes. Does she seek to recall the blinding faith of her grandfather's day? Was it easier before? Was it, paradoxically, less dark? Were troubles less weighty to bear? How was it "lighter—to be Blind—"?

Possibly in 1850 when she first embarked upon her defiant mission, Emily Dickinson did not recognize the deep belief that led her to suppose the combat could be forever sustained; probably it did not occur to her to wonder what would happen if she won her wrestle with the Lord. Yet somehow during the course of her career His light flickered, and then it was extinguished. She found herself in a silent, dark world whose spiritual poverty and isolation she had perhaps never fully anticipated: "*That polar privacy / A soul admitted to itself— / Finite infinity*" (#1695). Without companion, without a reigning Deity—with language not reaching ever outward toward an immensity of meaning, but curling back reflexively upon the speaker—with an earth as devoid of intrinsic significance as some barren lunar wasteland, the poet was forced to seek a new way for art.

II ✦ *Can You Make a World Anew with Words?*

Eventually, Emily Dickinson came to understand that there was an inescapable destructive element in all acts of creation.

> *The Opening and the Close*
> *Of Being, are alike*
> *Or differ, if they do,*
> *As Bloom upon a Stalk.*
>
> *That from an equal Seed*
> *Unto an equal Bud*
> *Go parallel, perfected*
> *In that they have decayed.*
>
> (#1047)

A "Bloom upon a Stalk" is no end in itself, but one part of a complex process; "Seed" and "Bud" are other parts of "equal" importance; and paradoxically, each stage can be "perfected" only insofar as it has "decayed" and permitted the next stage to come into being. Sometimes, like a patriotically American poet, Dickinson put this notion into political terms.

> *Revolution is the Pod*
> *Systems rattle from*
> *When the Winds of Will are stirred*
> *Excellent is bloom*
>
> *But except it's Russet Base*
> *Every Summer be*
> *The Entomber of itself,*
> *So of Liberty —*
>
> *Left inactive on the Stalk*
> *All it's Purple fled*
> *Revolution shakes it for*
> *Test if it be dead.*
>
> (#1082)

The "Bloom" is "Excellent ... *except*" for the fact that fulfillment requires it to be "The Entomber of itself" by developing into the next pod and waiting for the winds of "Revolution" to rattle another cycle of systems loose.

Nothing is final; not even gold can stay; and poetry, too, must pass like all these other things, leaving destruction in its wake.

> To pile like Thunder to it's close
> Then crumble grand away
> While Everything created hid
> This — would be Poetry —
>
> Or Love — the two coeval come —
> We both and neither prove —
> Experience either and consume —
> For None see God and live —
>
> (#1247)

It is not difficult to apprehend the general notion of a force that spends its power and finishes with some grand annihilation. However, the precise terms in this verse are strangely cryptic, perhaps intentionally so.

The first stanza seems to address the purely aesthetic component of verse: the gathering of linguistic strength, the verbal climax, and the falling away. The introduction of "Love" in the second stanza is puzzling: carnal love surely has its own climax and falling away, but the use of the word "prove" locates this "Love" at a different level, with the divine love that is supposed to have given rise to creation. The primary definition of "prove" in Dickinson's dictionary is suggestive: "to ascertain some unknown quality or truth by an *experiment*" (italics mine). In the poem, we "prove" the "Love" embedded in creation by the course of our lives—conception, birth, life, and death. Thus do we "consume" the "Experience" of personal existence. Indeed, without life's interment there could be no Paradise, "For None see God and live—." Elsewhere in Dickinson's poetry this process of life which leads inevitably and inexorably toward death is viewed pejoratively as *God's* experiment; in this poem, however, it seems to be *our* experiment—not a sadistic infliction, merely a fact. As the pod inheres in the flower, so death inheres in life.

Although the precise nature of poetry's destructive power is not described in this poem, a reader who is conversant with Dickinson's work can infer a plausible case. The hero-poet had usurped God's power over language and expelled the mythic realm from art. As a consequence, words are limited to naming objects that have no element of transcendence and thus no "Design" of intrinsic relationship to one another; or even worse, words bounce from the external world back in upon the speaker, reflexively, limiting art to the interior world of a nightmare consciousness. Confronted with such a situation, the poet must begin again and attempt to rebuild the temple of art—not as an arrogant, adversarial hero now, but as a bereft orphan, shaping the ashes of self.

One such effort to rebuild can be found in Dickinson's poems of definition. Almost entirely absent from all the verse inscribed before 1863, by the late 1860s this form of verse had become a commonplace in Dickinson's work, and it continued to appear with regularity until the poet's death. Often the definition is of a word that names an abstract entity that might be construed as one component of the speaker's intellectual or affective self. Such poems, applying as they do to the lonely inner realm, sometimes bear a striking resemblance to the poems of existential anguish.

> *Hope is a subtle Glutton—*
> *He feeds upon the Fair—*
> *And yet—inspected closely*
> *What Abstinence is there—*
>
> *His is the Halcyon Table—*
> *That never seats but One—*
> *And whatsoever is consumed*
> *The same amount remain—*
>
> (#1547)

This utterance rebounds among the confines of the brain like light traveling the distance between the walls of a mirrored room, little more than a bulletin issued from one mind to another. It illuminates a truth, but an exceedingly limited one: that "Hope" by its nature presumes an absence of fulfillment. Still, its speaker is reaching toward something or someone beyond self, for a homily is a more sociable utterance than the self-centered cry of anguish. Moreover, it is difficult, perhaps impossible to make any definition entirely interior: even if "Glutton" calls no precise image to mind, the word identifies a class of creatures in the external world, not an emotion or a thought or an abstraction of the claustral mind. Thus although the thrust of the poem is centripetal, pulling "Glutton" inward to clarify the import of "Hope," a faint connection is made between the inner and the outer worlds through this defining process.

Other poems of definition further exploit the possibility for making a connection between an insular self and the world of objects that exist outside of self, and they do so by finding what might loosely be termed an "objective correlative" for one or another element of human consciousness.

> *Presentiment—is that long Shadow—on the Lawn—*
> *Indicative that Suns go down—*
>
> *The Notice to the startled Grass*
> *That Darkness—is about to pass—*
>
> (#764)

What dominates this poem is not the internal concèption, "Presentiment," but the extended description of the natural world that has been invoked as a kind of definition. Even though God's transcendence has been banished, once again nature has begun to acquire meaning. Indeed, the verse invokes at least two different kinds of possible significance.

One is defined by the speaker's capacity first to locate some configuration in nature that possesses an integral order or design and then to grasp the essential import of this order as it would be understood by other human beings. Here a "long Shadow—on the Lawn—" constitutes the spare configuration. A scientist could explain that the length of the shadow cast by the sun is in direct ratio to the obliquity of the angle made by the sun's rays; however, such understanding does not require a scientist's training. The most untutored, primitive peoples understood this way of telling time. Yet this is not intuitive knowledge, not the apprehension of some eternal verity shimmering through the veil of a material world. It is nothing more than a rudimentary lesson of experience, and it requires only the knowledge that in life and in the world there are invariable events and conjunctions: "Suns" always "go down"; a "long Shadow" always acts as prelude to that event. Does the phrase "Suns go down—" invoke the fallen Christian legend? Possibly. However, it is much more likely to invoke the realization that just as days end, so do seasons, years, and lives: nothing on earth can endure forever.

The second level of import is more elusive and suggestive. The "long Shadow" evidently serves "Notice" to the "Grass," too. That is, nature seems almost self-conscious, coming to some awareness of its own habits and meaningful configurations. The implication is faint here; however, in other late poems about nature, it is developed somewhat more fully.

Just as the ghost of Christ's legend lingers in "Presentiment—," the pale shades of Jacob at Peniel and revivals in mid-nineteenth-century Amherst can be discovered in another poem that approximates definition.

> *Longing is like the Seed*
> *That wrestles in the Ground,*
> *Believing if it intercede*
> *It shall at length be found.*
>
> *The Hour, and the Clime—*
> *Each Circumstance unknown,*

> *What Constancy must be achieved*
> *Before it see the Sun!*
>
> (#1255)

The verse purports to limn "Longing"; a convert of 1850 might hear a faint echo of faith as well. As before, nature seems to be in the process of coming to know itself (here, the "Seed" is construed as "Believing" in a "Sun" it has never known); even more than before, the spent terminology of the Christian myth permeates this generally secular verse. Indeed, one of Dickinson's best-loved poems of definition has many of these same traits.

> *"Hope" is the thing with feathers—*
> *That perches in the soul—*
> *And sings the tune without the words—*
> *And never stops—at all—* . . .
>
> (#254)

Christ and the "Hope" that He gave to the world were repeatedly figured in traditional emblems as a bird—"the thing with feathers—." Yet most modern readers do not feel the presence of Christ in this poem, nor does any other element of the verse suggest His legend. "The thing with feathers—" is the source of unseen song, perhaps choristers in treetops whistling against the gale. Perhaps it is even every human's potential for music and poetry, brave stays against the brooding dark.

Repeatedly, then, the speaker communicates a truth about human consciousness by means of some perception of a natural entity or event that can be shared with the reader: the speaker's isolation is thus relieved, and the reader is simultaneously enlightened. Sometimes the poem takes the frank form of definition; sometimes another linguistic trope serves a quasi-defining function. "*Remembrance has a Rear and Front— / 'Tis something like a House —*" (#1182); "*Exhiliration is the Breeze / That lifts us from the Ground / And leaves us in another place*" (#1118); "*Surprise is like a thrilling—pungent— / Upon a tasteless meat / Alone—too acrid—but combined / An edible Delight*" (#1306). Little by little as these poems accrete (and there are scores of them), a kind of mapping process is revealed: the contours of consciousness take shape and become coherent, and the outside world once again becomes relevant to human consciousness.

Occasionally, the linguistic patterns in one of these poems so clearly echo Dickinson's earlier works that they reveal her keen awareness of the poetic transformation that is taking place.

> *I stepped from Plank to Plank*
> *A slow and cautious way*

> *The Stars about my Head I felt*
> *About my Feet the Sea.*
>
> *I knew not but the next*
> *Would be my final inch —*
> *This gave me that precarious Gait*
> *Some call Experience.*
>
> (*#875*)

The last line of this poem of 1864 explicitly repudiates religious or transcendent implication and converts the verse into no more than an aphoristic definition. Yet it is difficult to believe that a poet who is elsewhere so aware of her own methods (and who here writes about "Feet") has forgotten the potent emblematic image of the "*Plank in Reason*" (*#280*) that failed to serve as transport from earth to Heaven; nor can she have forgotten the voracious role of the "Sea"—seat of divine "Maelstrom" in the God-centered verse (see Nos. *414, 502, 721*). Indeed, "Plank to Plank" may even be intended as an acceptable alternative to the "Blank to Blank" of "Mechanic feet" that go nowhere in the end-stopped verse of existential despair (*#761*). For one thoroughly conversant with the body of this poetry, as the poet herself seems supremely to have been, these associations converge to fortify the implication of the poem in question. All of the pain and danger that have been uncompromisingly met by the "Feet" of this sobered hero-poet treading above the "Sea"—the chance of Heaven relinquished and the stagnation of pain without cause or end—have conferred a real-world benefit: "Experience."

Without a doubt, a new Voice emerges in the poetry after 1862 or 1863. Perhaps it grows out of the "Wife's" Voice, for it recognizes the needs of others as sensitively as the "Wife" had; yet this Voice seldom has explicitly feminine attributes, and it eschews the exclusively domestic realm. Instead, it reveals a philosophical turn of mind, bringing to fulfillment the sententious strain in much of the poetry of definition. Most of all, it speaks with the authority of one who can comprehend extremities of suffering: it has "Experience."

> *There is a strength in knowing that it can be borne*
> *Although it tear—*
> *What are the sinews of such cordage for*
> *Except to bear*
> *The ship might be of satin had it not to fight—*
> *To walk on seas requires cedar Feet*
>
> (*#1113; var. "knowing"*)

Again the speaker returns to Jacob's struggle in the allusion to "sinews" of strength: at long last, experience has provided the healing power to repair that wound of primal separation that we suffered so many generations ago, and the poet's "Feet" have acquired the immense force of those fabled "cedars" of Lebanon from which Solomon's temple in ancient Jerusalem had been built.

Ironically, the very authority that had been conferred by Dickinson's complex "Experience" as poet carried its own requirement for courage. Not irretrievably trapped within self, the poet was nonetheless forced to acknowledge the loneliness and separateness of this demythologized world. Sometimes the consequent limitation is expressed in self-consciously Emersonian terms.

> *Light is sufficient to itself—*
> *If Others want to see*
> *It can be had on Window Panes*
> *Some Hours in the Day.*
>
> *But not for Compensation—*
> *It holds as large a Glow*
> *To Squirrel in the Himmaleh*
> *Precisely, as to you.*
>
> (#862)

No universal sign, "Light" exists entirely in its own right. It came into being for no purpose. It *is*. Nothing more. It gives no "Compensation," for it *is* in equal measure to a human observer in New England and to an unreflective rodent a hemisphere away. Animals and mankind can make equal use of it. Indeed, the speaker even avoids assigning a shape to "Light's" extent. No noon is here, no sunrise—only a casual combination, "Some Hours in the Day." Sometimes Dickinson states the loss in explicitly religious terms.

> *The fascinating chill that music leaves*
> *Is Earth's corroboration*
> *Of Ecstasy's impediment—*
> *'Tis Rapture's germination*
> *In timid and tumultuous soil*
> *A fine—estranging creature—*
> *To something upper wooing us*
> *But not to our Creator—*
>
> (#1480)

Ironically, under these circumstances, the song itself becomes a kind of wounding: although it beckons toward "something upper," it cannot lead to the Divinity that resides behind the material world, and therefore it is never more than "Earth's corroboration / Of Ecstasy's impediment." Art has become foreshortened because nature is neutral and indifferent. We may long to discern the Divinity in the outlines of this world, but they limn no supernatural power. "*We can but follow to the Sun— / As oft as He go down / He leave Ourselves a Sphere behind— / 'Tis mostly—following— / We go no further with the Dust / Than to the Earthen Door— / And then the Panels are reversed— / And we behold—no more*" (#920). This poem focuses not upon the legend that has been lost, but upon the flat, residual fact: despite the poet's deft success in using nature to *define* elements of the self, human beings and nature have no more than an accidental relationship.

The poet may well be able to work her way out of the nightmare consciousness and into a world of comforting, tangible, separate entities. Yet insofar as she has no God-given relationship with nature, she has become a disenfranchised singer.

> *It is a lonesome Glee—*
> *Yet sanctifies the Mind—*
> *With fair association—*
> *Afar upon the Wind*
>
> *A Bird to overhear*
> *Delight without a Cause—*
> *Arrestless as invisible—*
> *A matter of the Skies.*
>
> (#774)

Whether the poet-speaker's "Glee" is song or joy seems not to matter, for it appears entrapped in its own isolation. The human never sees the warbling creature, nor does the bird sing for the purpose of allowing anyone "to overhear." This juxtaposition is no more than chance. Nor can the poet imitate the essence of the singer's "Delight," for that is "A matter of the Skies"— essentially outside of mankind's province. Validation comes only through the poet's own awareness of "association," human and bird each making music. In what, then, can the poet's particular mission consist? She cannot spell the terms of the Supernatural, for glory has departed from the world. She cannot muse upon the merely interior world of self, for such reflection produces a monotone of existential alienation and despair. She cannot spend her genius upon poems of definition, for their range is too limited. One answer lies in her capacity to celebrate these external entities in themselves, to "Delight" in mere existence as the bird does.

Nature may be utterly indifferent to any mortal quandary; still, the poet can wring art from such a world, not by seeking transcendent truth in nature, but by capturing the play of brilliant surfaces that constitute its everything for us. A poet can arrest the vigor of life itself; verse can become "being" that has been confirmed through words and images and rhythms. Nature and its manifold components *exist:* that is their sufficient miracle. A poet can formulate a figment of the imagination that will validate this unfolding existence and communicate it vitally to generations of readers: that is her unique triumph as artist.

The notion that it is the poet's imagination, not God, that can give meaning to the natural world lies behind some of the very earliest of Dickinson's works. "*I'll tell you how the Sun rose— / A Ribbon at a time— / The Steeples swam in Amethyst— / The news, like Squirrels, ran—* " (#318); "*She sweeps with many-colored Brooms— / And leaves the Shreds behind— / Oh Housewife in the Evening West— / Come back, and dust the Pond!*" (#219); "*Blazing in Gold and quenching in Purple / Leaping like Leopards to the Sky / ... And the Juggler of Day is gone*" (#228). Yet the most powerful poetry written before 1863 generally addressed the problems inherent in a nature suffused with God's meaning; indeed, the writer's capacity to assemble a striking series of images was sometimes even a hindrance to the more important work of exposing the Deity's compulsion to annihilate. However, once God had been expelled, this capacity became not an impediment, but a strength, and the poet could turn with a different kind of interest to the use of the creating imagination.

A further examination of the revised portion of "It sifts from Leaden Sieves—" (see pp. 437–38) provides a good example of Dickinson's method.

> *It scatters like the Birds—*
> *Condenses like a Flock—*
> *Like a Juggler's Figures situates*
> *Upon a baseless Arc—*
>
> *It traverses yet halts—*
> *Disperses as it stays—*
> *Then curls itself in Capricorn,*
> *Denying that it was—*

> (#311)

The first version of this poem focused upon the snow's muffling, suffocating force: the action moved relentlessly forward, and the snow was a tangible object, named variously as "Fleeces" or "Celestial Vail"; little by little, it obscured and buried the world. This second version focuses not upon the snow—not even upon the snow's effect—but upon movement itself, the life inherent in the snow. The artistry of the work, then, consists of a series of rapid shifts that make the snow itself unavailable as a fixed entity. The collective nouns "Birds" and "Flock" identify nothing but an ever-swirling, amorphous cloud that "scatters" and "Condenses." Although a juggler in fact usually has his or her hands on two of the objects that are being spun in the air, the *illusion* conveyed by any "Juggler's Figures" is of objects always in motion, always suspended in the air—an illusion that gives meaning, perhaps, to the paradox of a "baseless Arc—." When the poem concludes with denial, the snow itself has not vanished; only the restless, dancing movement that gave it life has gone. In the real world, such motion cannot be started up again at will. The artistic achievement here is to hold the momentary vigor of this flurried activity in suspension indefinitely, perpetually available to generations of readers.

The best of these later poems about nature operate with a brilliant economy: they shun the merely decorative and summon up some essence of color or movement or resonance—the dynamic interplay of objects, air, and light that seems vitality itself. Probably the most famous of these poems takes a hummingbird as its subject.

> *A Route of Evanescence*
> *With a revolving Wheel—*
> *A Resonance of Emerald—*
> *A Rush of Cochineal—*
> *And every Blossom on the Bush*
> *Adjusts it's tumbled Head—*
> *The mail from Tunis, probably,*
> *An easy Morning's Ride—*
>
> (#1463)

Only the last two lines tend to curtail the seamless fluidity of the verse. Throughout most of it the tangible world trails into a rush of vapor, color is tousled by sound, and the whirring bird is known solely because of its streaming tour through the sunlit garden. Words are used here almost as pigments, glinting to reflect a passage of light, and Art becomes something very close to Life.

To be sure, the craft at work sometimes intrudes self-consciously into such poems. "*There came a Wind like a Bugle—* / *It quivered through the Grass*" (#1593); the simile here violates the integrity of the scene—not enlivening, but overshadowing it. Yet at her best Dickinson was able to render the external world in the process of being itself without any felt strain of artistry. Another poem about the wind has two variant openings: "*The Wind begun to knead the Grass—* / *As Women do a Dough—*" and "*The Wind begun to rock the Grass* / *With threatening Tunes and low—*" (#824). Both capturing the intimacy of a stroking, ceaseless, shifting breeze. More effective yet is this short and deceptively simple statement:

> *I think that the Root of the Wind is Water—*
> *It would not sound so deep*
> *Were it a Firmamental Product—...*
>
> (#1302)

Here the deep organ-tone of a sighing atmosphere is conjured by a blurring of blues, the verse blowing with the sound of "w" and groaning with "o."

It is perhaps a characteristic problem with this class of Dickinson's work that a poem may begin strongly and conclude weakly because a striking trope can neither be sustained nor brought to succinct and effective conclusion.

> *A soft Sea washed around the House*
> *A Sea of Summer Air*
> *And rose and fell the magic Planks*
> *That sailed without a care—*
> *For Captain was the Butterfly*
> *For Helmsman was the Bee*
> *And an entire universe*
> *For the delighted crew.*
>
> (#1198)

The first three or four lines conjure the peculiar, humid density of hot, mid-summer air—the garden undulating like some vast green aquarium whose occupants appear to swim and float rather than to walk or fly—time imperceptibly slowed as the sun hovers still overhead. Yet when this image is elaborated, as it is in the concluding four lines, "Butterfly" and "Bee" becoming "Captain" and "Helmsman," the tone of mysterious, quiet viscidity is dissipated into a cloying cuteness.

At best, of course, such poetry allows for a brevity of immense expanse.

> *The Bustle in a House*
> *The Morning after Death*
> *Is solemnest of industries*
> *Enacted upon Earth—*
>
> *The Sweeping up the Heart*
> *And putting Love away*
> *We shall not want to use again*
> *Until Eternity.*
>
> (#1078)

Perhaps this insight could issue only from a "Wife": so many small, unobtrusive homely acts are recollected here. To an outsider, the juxtaposition of "Bustle" and "The Morning after Death" might seem macabre; mourning, weeping, fainting into prostration—surely these attitudes would be more suitable to the occasion. Yet the outsider's notions of propriety indulge the luxury of a lethal sensibility. Every mother knows that even "after Death" those who have been left must eat and wear clothes that are mended; more, she knows that *especially* "after Death," the business of living must be expedited, lest those who sorrow grieve too strenuously. Thus such "Bustle" becomes a way of "Sweeping up the Heart," not denying unhappiness or bereavement, but learning to contain them by expressing affection for the family that remains. Taken as a whole, the poem addresses not so much a phenomenon of dying as a process of living: it venerates the incalculable value of quotidian domestic activities—continuous forms of affirming life that may become noticeable only in such moments of crisis.

This well-known and much-admired poem about death and the salvific force of domestic order is an unusual use of the creating imagination: most often Dickinson applies it not to the world of men and women, but to nature. *"The Leaves like Women, interchange / Sagacious Confidence— / Somewhat of nods and somewhat / Portentous inference"* (#987); or *"An Everywhere of Silver / With Ropes of Sand / To keep it from effacing / The Track called Land"* (#884); or *"This slow Day moved along— / I heard it's axles go / As if they could not hoist themselves / They hated motion so—"* (#1120). Almost invariably, such poems stand as testament to the poet's ability to create an aesthetic formulation that celebrates not nature's significance, but its very being. However, there are striking exceptions.

Sometimes poetry of this sort seems to go one step further by affirming that nature itself has inherent aesthetic configurations, mysteries, or secrets that cry out for poetic representation.

> The Road was lit with Moon and star—
> The Trees were bright and still—
> Descried I—by the distant Light
> A Traveller on a Hill—
> To magic Perpendiculars
> Ascending, though Terrene—
> Unknown his shimmering ultimate—
> But he indorsed the sheen—
>
> (#1450)

God and *His* Design play no role here; nonetheless, it would seem that a design of some sort can be discovered by the artist—and it is not a design that has been imposed primarily by the felicitous use of language. Thus this almost translucent poem begins with a simple descriptive statement, not with a striking linguistic figure. What emerges from the careful unfolding of the scene is a pattern of upright geometrical lines that becomes a visual schematic for art: the "Trees," the ascending "Traveller," and all the other portentous shadows and dim figures that seem "magic Perpendiculars." The poem makes no claim for an otherworldly influence or end; quite the contrary, it seems patently intended as no more than a beautifully suggestive moonscape. Still, while the "Traveller's" "shimmering ultimate" is less than spiritual, it appears to be somewhat more than mundane; the verse hangs poised forever between hints of mystery and inescapable moorings to the merely quotidian. Although the inherent aesthetic shapeliness of the scene calls out for some artistic response, it is nature itself, not some force behind it, that has issued the request. Thus one justification for writing post-Christian poetry might be that there are such privileged moments as these, permitting insight of a sort and requiring some artistic response to fulfill their potential. Just as the "Traveller" has "indorsed the sheen," the poem validates the entire assemblage.

The configuration that lurks in nature to provide a necessary occasion for art is not always essentially aesthetic: it may entice in another way, by promising a secret.

> *What mystery pervades a well!*
> *The water lives so far—*
> *A neighbor from another world*
> *Residing in a jar*
>
> *Whose limit none have ever seen,*
> *But just his lid of glass—*
> *Like looking every time you please*
> *In an abyss's face!*
>
> *The grass does not appear afraid,*
> *I often wonder he*
> *Can stand so close and look so bold*
> *At what is awe to me.*
>
> *Related somehow they may be,*
> *The sedge stands next the sea—*
> *Where he is floorless*
> *And does no timidity betray*
>
> *But nature is a stranger yet;*
> *The ones that cite her most*
> *Have never passed her haunted house,*
> *Nor simplified her ghost.*

> *To pity those that know her not*
> *Is helped by the regret*
> *That those who know her, know her less*
> *The nearer her they get.*
>
> (#*1400*)

Familiar words appear here; yet "abyss" and "awe" have become detached from any connection with God, now signifying no more than that which appears bottomless and that which inspires terror and respect. Not even a tunnel to transcendence, the well is a kind of magical telescope that while it peers into the ground simultaneously reflects the sky—yoking the ethereal stratosphere with subterranean secrets, probing into some forgotten past, perhaps, even as it remains firmly and unmovingly at our feet. The temptation to peer within is almost irresistible, and the interior provides a perversely celestial face-to-face, self viewing self against a background of sky. The paradoxes of the thing seem inexhaustible: water surrounded by "grass" is inversely "Related" to "the sea," which is water surrounding grass. Symbol of nothing in particular, the "well" nonetheless stands as general representative of nature's "haunted house," and thus, like the "magic Perpendiculars" of the previous poem, seems to demand the kind of inquiry that becomes poetry. Dickinson makes this all-but-explicit claim, even though the poem's penultimate stanza firmly dismisses both a Trinitarian reading of nature and Emersonian transcendentalism. If nature's "mystery" is to be revealed, some new process of aesthetic investigation must be invented.

Whereas the well's secret is so deep that a reader cannot even hazard a guess whether it be benign or malevolent, other portentous elements of nature leak more of their hidden meaning to us. There is still savagery in the garden, even when God has been entirely forsworn, and the most unprepossessing creatures of the air display at least enough ruthlessness to reveal a small corner of some frightful and ultimately incomprehensible truth.

> *A Bird came down the Walk—*
> *He did not know I saw—*
> *He bit an Angleworm in halves*
> *And ate the fellow, raw,*
>
> *And then he drank a Dew*
> *From a convenient Grass—*
> *And then hopped sidewise to the Wall*
> *To let a Beetle pass—*
>
> *He glanced with rapid eyes*
> *That hurried all around—*

> They looked like frightened Beads, I thought —
> He stirred his Velvet Head
>
> Like one in danger, Cautious,
> I offered him a Crumb
> And he unrolled his feathers
> And rowed him softer home —
>
> Than Oars divide the Ocean,
> Too silver for a seam —
> Or Butterflies, off Banks of Noon
> Leap, plashless as they swim.

(#328)

The central concern of this little drama is a misfit between the categories available to the speaker and those that appear to be relevant to the "Bird." Here is something that bears relation only to itself, and humans have been relegated to the status of onlookers. At the same time, however, the speaker seems compelled to observe the miniature spectacle—determined to watch minutely and offer a description, however inadequate it may be.

The speaker's choice of words embodies the attitudes of polite society. Her almost trivial variation of the idiom to bite in half—"bit . . . in halves"—is painstakingly literal, and it anticipates the well-bred shock that is expressed by "ate the fellow, raw." The notion of drinking "Dew" from a "Grass" comes so close to drinking from a *glass* that the deviation calls attention to itself; eyes "like frightened Beads" and a "Velvet Head" complete the speaker's civilizing efforts. Yet these tropes are most noteworthy here for their failure to capture and organize the essence of the event, their inability to contain the sense of "danger" that finally intrudes into the speaker's consciousness. When the bird departs, every crude or menacing aspect of his behavior ought to dictate some uncouth, primitive home to receive him; instead, the tone of the verse alters drastically, and the speaker allows herself to suppose that plush realms of fantasy land await. Oddly, although the speaker fails in her attempt to comprehend and describe the bird's nature, the poem itself does not fail to the same degree, for the use of these inadequate social categories to deal with the activities of an essentially unknowable bird serves nicely to highlight nature's impenetrable enigma. Thus the verse may fill the reader not with frustration, but with a heightened appetite to seek out the "ghost" of this "haunted house."

Perhaps the most nearly perfect poem addressing a nature possessed of some compelling mystery is a piece of verse that was much admired in Dickinson's own lifetime.

A narrow Fellow in the Grass
Occasionally rides —
You may have met Him — did you not
His notice sudden is —

The Grass divides as with a Comb —
A spotted shaft is seen —
And then it closes at your feet
And opens further on —

He likes a Boggy Acre
A Floor too cool for Corn —
Yet when a Boy, and Barefoot —
I more than once at Noon
Have passed, I thought, a Whip lash
Unbraiding in the Sun
When stooping to secure it
It wrinkled, and was gone —

Several of Nature's People
I know, and they know me —
I feel for them a transport
Of cordiality —

But never met this Fellow
Attended, or alone
Without a tighter breathing
And Zero at the Bone —

(#986)

Written in about 1865, this poem was published in the Springfield *Daily Republican* on February 14, 1866; Sam Bowles, noting its verisimilitude, remarked to Sue Dickinson, "How did that girl ever know that a boggy field wasn't good for corn?"[1] Perhaps he forgot that Emily Dickinson's family engaged in extensive farming; certainly he seems to have underestimated the care with which she observed the world around her.

The insistent "thingness" of the snake itself is everywhere present in this poem: if the first line is said aloud, for example, the tongue is forced to flicker almost obscenely in the mouth just to render the sound; and sinuous, serpentine movement is sustained for many lines by the insistent reiteration of the sound "s." The progress of the poem moves the snake into some undefined psychological relationship with the speaker, a move away from simple realism toward a portent of danger. In the first two stanzas the speaker has recourse to civilizing images: the snake "rides" as if there were a carriage; the

"Grass" is divided as if by a "Comb." Yet the long middle stanza relinquishes civilization and moves beyond the boundaries of arable land, into the swamp where not even corn can grow; it leaves the present behind as well, recollecting the more vulnerable time of childhood when opinions have not yet become fully formed and primitive fears and thought patterns still lurk very close to consciousness. Insofar as "Barefoot" alludes to poetry, it may identify a time when verse was in its infancy, a dawning time when symbols had not yet been articulated and the figurative implications of the serpent were latent, but not realized. Interestingly, Dickinson stipulates a man-and-boy for speaker, perhaps to emphasize the implications of male sexuality or even phallic brutality that the notion of a snake so often carries—implications that are reinforced here in part by the exposed feet and toes and in part by the "Whip lash" whose leather is quietly "Unbraiding in the Sun" like a bundle of worms. All such implications hover invitingly in the poem. However, they are by no means firmly fixed in it; indeed, they are as elusive as the snake itself that "wrinkled, and was gone."

In the penultimate stanza, the reflective adult returns to the poem to offer a summation that is not religious, not moral, not even aphoristic. The use of the word "transport" is especially interesting: in the theocentric poetry, it always carried the implication of a passage from earth to Heaven. Yet here God's realm is not invoked, nor is any other comprehensive form of transcendence: the poem resolutely declines to identify the snake with Satan or with evil, the standard Christian "meanings" of snake. Instead, the speaker voices his inclination to establish connections between humanity and nature. Usually, he muses, this desire holds no threat, for the affinities seem generally benign. The case of the snake is different; whatever the unspeakable tie may be, it is fearsome and chill, and its terror is reinforced by a reduction to "Zero" within the verse. The rhyme scheme is exquisitely modulated: beginning at first almost with consonance alone (the pattern of "s" that weaves throughout the first stanza), this dissonance of rhyme is gradually reduced to nothing by the perfect chiming of "alone" and "Bone" in the final stanza. Such forceful pulling together is emphasized by the general prevalence of the long "o" sound at the conclusion—an empty, forlorn sound that affirms the word "Zero."

These poems suggest that building a world with words that have lost the shadow of transcendence is an effort that can yield but limited success. Individual poems may be effective, sometimes remarkably so; yet they lack the force of verse that can reach beyond earthly experience into some eternal realm. Even though Dickinson occasionally postulates that some inherent property in nature calls out to be completed through artistic expression—or, alternatively, that some natural objects seem innately suitable to be used symbolically (like the snake in this last poem)—she never assumes the existence of any coherent system of symbols; nor does she undertake to invent such a system. Thus each poem stands alone, an isolated glimpse into an earthbound secret whose full extent cannot be charted and whose particulars emerge at such rare intervals that the essence of nature must remain forever hidden.

Unlike the theocentric poetry or even the love poetry, verse of this sort cannot build upon itself, cannot show progress save in technical mastery, cannot refer to any complex structure whose parts might be gradually investigated. In the God-centered work, the brevity of each poem did not detract from its power, for each poem bore a quite specific relationship to the immense architectonic it excoriated—and thus by indirection, each such poem partook of transcendence in concert with all the others. However, when the semiotic system of latter-day American Puritanism finally lost its hold over the creative imagination, only the broken shards of magnificence remained. Grandeur had gone. Under these diminished circumstances, even Emily Dickinson's best work could be no more than elegant, isolated gems.

III ✦ Requiem

For many years the private life that Emily Dickinson led in the Brick House on Main Street remained essentially unaltered. Austin and Sue settled into the Evergreens next door; the birth of their son, Edward (Ned) Dickinson, in June 1861, was followed five years later by the birth of a daughter on November 29, 1866; she was named Martha after Susan's sister, and the family called her Mattie. Aunt Lavinia Norcross died in Boston in April 1860, and her husband, Loring, died in January 1863; Emily Dickinson felt these losses acutely, and her comradeship with the surviving children, her younger cousins Fannie and Loo Norcross, was undoubtedly in part a compensation to her for the death of their parents. There were always deaths to contend with (Frazer Stearns, the son of the president of Amherst College, and a friend of Austin's, was killed in action fighting for the Union cause in March 1862); however, during this period those nearest and dearest to Dickinson were for the most part spared. Emily and Vinnie lived with Mother and Father; Austin and Sue lived next door with their two children. There were family squabbles: as we have seen, Austin's relationship with Sue was far from idyllic, and periods of strain characterized Emily's friendship with her sister-in-law. Nonetheless, the Dickinsons formed an unbroken, close-knit little community until 1874.

It is difficult to chart the course of Emily Dickinson's social life: although an exchange of letters gives unambiguous evidence of separation, there are no similarly reliable records for visits and attendance at parties. Dickinson seems to have been a more or less regular visitor at the Evergreens until about 1860, popular at dinner parties and known for her sprightly wit. After that time she began to withdraw, principally because of her increasingly severe eye trouble. Her last two long visits away from Amherst were occasioned by this illness: seven months in the Boston area in 1864 and a shorter period in 1865. Accounts of her sociability after the second Boston trip vary. Mattie would later claim that her aunt Emily continued to visit the Hollands in Springfield even after 1865.[1] Perhaps she also continued to make the short journey down to Middletown, Connecticut, with Vinnie to visit Eliza Coleman Dudley, whose husband was a minister in that town until 1868, when he accepted a pulpit in Milwaukee. If it is true (and undoubtedly it is) that she played with Mattie and her friends by lowering gingerbread and cookies in a basket from her second-story bedroom window, it is also true that she made less spectral appearances to her friends and family. For many years she continued to be on hand to receive guests at Father's gala party during commencement week. She had never enjoyed entertainments like the Ladies' Sewing Circle, and gradually she stopped attending Austin and Sue's ever more elegant social gatherings next door; yet she saw those with whom she wished to visit: Sam Bowles (according to her whim), Judge Lord and his wife, the Norcross cousins, Mr. and Mrs. Holland, and a considerable number of local friends and neighbors.

Although the appearance of Amherst changed, alterations came to the town with exceeding slowness. Austin was much involved in these improvements. For example, he promoted and supervised the erection of a new building for the First Congregational Church in 1867–68. The stately stone church could be viewed easily from Father's property, for it stood almost across the street from the Evergreens on land that had been purchased from the Montagues, distant cousins of the Dickinson family. Emily, no longer a regular churchgoer by this time, is said to have been given an official view of the edifice by moonlight one night with Austin while both stood on the corner of Father's land. Edward Dickinson delivered the dedicatory speech on September 23, 1868, to an overflowing crowd. The new church was planned along grand lines; indeed, its explicitly prepossessing appearance reflected the way in which intensely personal religious fervor had yielded to civic pride. Other elements in the township manifested this change as well; over the course of the three decades from 1855 to 1885, the muddy farm village became a gracious New England jewel whose amenities did justice to the increasingly distinguished alumni of Amherst College who returned for commencement celebrations each year. Austin was a charter member of the Ornamental Tree Association, which was founded in 1860, and he was one of those who put pressure on the township to fill in the frog-infested, swampy sections of the Common. In 1875, at Austin's request, Frederick Law Olmsted (the visionary genius who had designed Central Park) put together a plan for the comprehensive redevelopment of the Common—sketching traffic patterns and sidewalks and recommending landscaping. Although the design was implemented only in bits and pieces, what had once been a boggy eyesore eventually grew into a tree-lined centerpiece for the town.

Before 1873 there was no system of public street-lighting, and the darkness of long winter nights was virtually as impenetrable as it had been in Emily Dickinson's girlhood. In September 1873, however, the selectmen were entrusted with two hundred dollars for the purpose of purchasing lamps and lampposts and having them erected in the central portions of the town. By March 1874 ten had been installed. In August of the following year, Austin convened a meeting in his offices to consider the introduction of gas lines into the township (of course, electricity was not introduced until many more years had passed); by late summer 1877 the Amherst Gas Company had been formed, and planning was at least begun to install a system of piped gas in the township. The first concrete sidewalks were laid in 1876; during the year ending March 1, 1878, twenty-four hundred yards of concrete walkways had been put down, and many more were added in the years following.

Perhaps the most significant improvement was the introduction of running water, an innovation prompted by two quite separate requirements. On a daily basis, household needs were always pressing. Well water was in constant peril of contamination, and as the population of the central portions of the town grew denser, this danger was an increasing worry. A less daily concern, but perhaps a more serious one, was the threat of fire. The Dickinsons' Brick House was an exception: most homes in New England villages were built of wood, as were many public structures. A major fire in a town with no water save from wells could sweep away whole blocks at a time. The first great fire in Amherst occurred in 1838, a blaze that began under the druggist's shop in an uncovered chimney flue; it destroyed an enormous amount of valuable property in the middle of town, including the Mansion House that had belonged to Noah Webster. After that time, serious fires occurred about every seven years. Among the notable conflagrations: in the winter of 1857 the North dormitory of Amherst College burned to the ground; in 1872 a sweeping fire destroyed the buildings to the rear of Phoenix Row. However, not until the great fire of 1879 leveled Merchant's Row did the need for water power seem overwhelming. The blaze broke out in the early morning of July 4, and its lurid light was clearly visible from Emily Dickinson's bedroom, which faced west, toward the town. "We were waked by the ticking of the bells,—the bells tick in Amherst for a fire, to tell the fireman," she wrote to Fanny and Loo Norcross.

I sprang to the window, and each side of the curtain saw that awful sun. The moon was shining high at the time, and the birds singing like trumpets.

Vinnie came soft as a moccasin, "Don't be afraid, Emily, it is only the fourth of July."

I did not tell that I saw it, for I thought if she felt it best to deceive, it must be that it was. . . .

. . . I could hear buildings falling, and oil exploding, and people walking and talking gayly, and cannon soft as velvet from parishes that did not know that we were burning up.

And so much lighter than day was it, that I saw a caterpillar measure a leaf far down the orchard; and Vinnie kept saying bravely, "It's only the fourth of July." . . .

Vinnie's "only fourth of July" I shall always remember. I think she will tell us so when we die, to keep us from being afraid.[2]

Sparks could carry over considerable distances in the warm night breezes, and the Dickinsons counted themselves lucky to have been spared. Many other townspeople felt similarly, and by the summer of 1880 water had been piped into town from the Pelham hills.

Only a few events, like the death of Frazer Stearns and this spectacular fire, made a dramatic impression on Emily Dickinson. She did not belong to public-improvement organizations as Austin did; she did not visit abroad with Vinnie's enthusiastic sociability; for many years, except for the trouble with her eyes, her usual daily routine was punctuated by no major changes.

When significant changes came, as inevitably they did, it was the oldest, most persistent, and most intimate enemy whose power was felt: death. There were several warnings. In the early spring of 1871, Father became seriously ill. Sam Bowles wrote his son that the elder Mr. Dickinson had "been quite feeble all winter, a sort of breaking-down with dyspepsia, & it shames him that he is hardly to be recognized in his old character."[3] Edward Dickinson had turned sixty-eight on New Year's Day of 1871; however, until now his health had proved remarkably durable. Others in the family were also sick that winter (only Vinnie retained the full vigor of her health), but Emily feared principally for her father. In the early spring, when Father was finally out of danger, she wrote to Loo Norcross:

The will is always near, dear, though the feet vary. The terror of the winter has made a little creature of me, who thought myself so bold.

Father was very sick. I presumed he would die, and the sight of his lonesome face all day was harder than personal trouble. He is growing better, though physically reluctantly. I hope I am mistaken, but I think his physical life don't want to live any longer. You know he never played, and the straightest engine has its leaning hour. . . . Now we will turn the corner. All this while I was with you all, much of every hour, wishing we were near enough to assist each other. Would you have felt more at home, to know we were both in extremity? That would be my only regret that I had not told you.[4]

Loo Norcross was bearing her own cross, for she was taking care of Eliza Coleman and Eliza's mother in what proved to be their final bout with the disease that had plagued the family for so many decades.

Eliza Coleman Dudley had removed to Milwaukee with her husband in 1868. By the spring of 1870, consumption had eroded her strength, and the Norcross sisters, who were distant cousins, went out to help with domestic chores and attempt to nurse her back to some semblance of health. In November 1870 Dr. and Mrs. Coleman journeyed to the Midwest to join their only remaining child, doubtless fearful that she would die before they could see her one more time. Yet Mrs. Coleman also suffered from tuberculosis, and there were now two patients to take care of. In mid-December 1870, at about the same time that Edward Dickinson fell so ill, Mrs. Coleman's condition took an abrupt turn for the worse; on January 11, 1871, she died.

The mother was scarcely gone before the daughter lapsed into her own final decline. In January 1871 Loo Norcross wrote Mrs. Eudocia Flynt of Monson, Massachusetts, Mrs. Coleman's sister-in-law:

Of Eliza's feebleness—you probably have heard—She does not leave her room sometimes not her bed—We—all realize that a day may bring the most extreme conditions.

. . . The process of tubercular formation and—hemorrhage has been rapid and frequent and you can readily understand how frail she is.[5]

The specter that had haunted the Norcross family even before Emily Dickinson's birth was still plying its quiet destruction. By the end, Eliza Coleman Dudley had lost even the sad, haunting beauty that had graced her face from girlhood: pitifully wasted, she expired on June 3, 1871, at the age of thirty-nine.

Perhaps because of the distant family connection, Emily Dickinson had kept up her intimate friendship with Eliza Coleman—the only one of her girlhood companions with whom she remained in more or less continuous communication. Thus she was much affected by this ongoing tragedy in the Midwest. She identified with the Norcross cousins, who were nursing these invalids at the same time that she was so anxiously concerned about Father's health; perhaps even more, she identified with lovely Eliza, the first of her playmates to die. The reaction to Eliza's death that is revealed in Dickinson's correspondence is one of anger: "Oh! Cruel Paradise," she wrote to Loo after hearing the news.[6] Yet her verse records a more complex reaction, for at about this time, Dickinson wrote one of her first great elegiac poems, almost certainly to mark Eliza Coleman's passage into the unknown.

> *Whatever it is — she has tried it —*
> *Awful Father of Love —*
> *Is not Our's the chastising —*
> *Do not chastise the Dove —*
>
> *Not for Ourselves, petition —*
> *Nothing is left to pray —*
> *When a subject is finished —*
> *Words are handed away —*
>
> *Only lest she be lonely*
> *In thy beautiful House*
> *Give her for her Transgression*
> *License to think of us —*

(#1204)

Elsewhere depicted with excruciating horror—as the *rictus sardonicus* in a "Face of Steel" (#*286*) or as the persistent, "supple Suitor" (#*1445*)—here unknowable, unavoidable death is greeted with the dignity of supreme resignation. "Whatever it is—she has tried it—": such language moves beyond even the poetic. Not precisely the diction of prose or of everyday discourse, it nonetheless almost entirely discards the density of figurative language to speak with an eloquent, matter-of-fact directness. Perhaps Christ's own prayer, the "Our Father," lies behind this verse; yet Dickinson's elegy recurs but softly to that prayer, primarily to forswear any personal demand. No longer disposed to "petition" for self (by requesting daily bread or by begging to be forgiven of trespasses), no longer defiantly determined to wrestle for dominion, this speaker is willing to accord final authority to the Lord. It is to *His* "beautiful House" that the young woman has repaired. Even the dispute over language itself seems to be concluded: "Words are handed away—." The woman's life has been curtailed; one more "subject" of God's royal power "is finished." Yet the "subject" of some long disagreement may be ended as well. There comes a time, perhaps, when protest seems trivial: outrage over the fact that death will claim everyone yields to understanding, acceptance, and wonder at the heroic courage all must discover in themselves when the final trial is at hand. If the language of the elegy for fragile Eliza Coleman seems to exceed the poetic, the Voice in which it is spoken seems almost to transcend the human. It is a Voice of experience and wisdom, one well acquainted with the deep night of anguish and despair. A Voice whose time of war has passed.

Though much more frequent in the poetry written after 1870, this tonality very occasionally found expression in Dickinson's earlier work. Perhaps the most famous instance is another elegy. Evidently not written in response to some particular death, this poem seems to have been composed in the mid-1860s, and four copies of it exist. Dickinson clearly thought well of it herself, and she dispatched it to several different correspondents: in 1866 she sent a copy to Higginson, and in 1883 she enclosed a copy with the title "Country Burial" in a letter to the publisher Thomas Niles.

> *Ample make this Bed—*
> *Make this Bed with Awe—*
> *In it wait till Judgment break*
> *Excellent and Fair.*
>
> *Be it's Mattress straight—*
> *Be it's Pillow round—*
>
> *Let no Sunrise' yellow noise*
> *Interrupt this Ground—*

(#*829*)

There is evidence of a sublime transaction in this poem: the superb simplicity of its address has been purchased by acceptance. Without a volley, without the sound of any victory or loss, peace comes to the verse; and as the enmity toward God drains away, a gentle rush of compassion and respect for our merely mortal condition flows into Dickinson's work. Ordinary humanity becomes as worthy of attention and respect as God in all His glory. Thus whereas in the theocentric poetry "Awe" had named our response when confronted with the Divinity or the poet, here it is the appropriate attitude toward any mortal who has experienced life and passed into death. Elsewhere the term "Ample" is bitterly ironic (the "ample Crack," for example, that discloses the meager configuration of God's "Landscape"). Here there is paradox, but not bitterness. No grave's bed is ample in the usual sense; however, every grave is large enough: it is the equal portion to which all are ultimately brought. Yet in the final analysis, "Ample" is meant to apply to a mind that is sufficiently open to appreciate the worth of even the least among us. One need not become heroic by besting the Divinity: anonymous humanity confers superlative enough.

Perhaps these changes in the informing mission of Dickinson's work were the result of some conscious strategy; perhaps they were the consequence of personal development, of a greater capacity for tolerance, or of the matured vision that occasionally accompanies age. Whatever the cause, Dickinson's increasing willingness to relinquish the militancy that had marked her initial quest was to stand her in good stead as time passed.

For a little while, Emily Dickinson's life returned to a smooth course; after the exhausting winter and spring of 1870–71, Father rallied and then seemed entirely to recover his former vigor. The *Amherst Record* sketched a suitably respectful likeness of him in its October 11, 1871, edition:

HONORABLE EDWARD DICKINSON. If there is a native of Amherst to whom the name at the head of this article is a stranger, he must indeed be a curiosity. . . . The name of Dickinson . . . is so identified with everything that belongs to Amherst, that any attempt to speak of town history in which that name should not appear the most prominent would be impossible. . . . A gentleman of the elder school, he is by no means a fogy. . . . We believe we trangress no law of propriety in claiming him to be the most prominent of the living men in Amherst. . . .[7]

Father's continued public prominence was due in part to the fact that he had been throwing his energies once more into local railroad issues. Indeed, his near-collapse may well have resulted from this activity.

Construction of another east-west railroad line through Massachusetts had been authorized by the legislature in the spring of 1864. The Massachusetts Central was incorporated on May 10, 1869, and Edward Dickinson immediately undertook to secure sufficient financial backing for the enterprise. After earnest political dealing and persuasion, the citizens of Amherst voted a commitment to buy a thousand shares of stock on October 4, 1870 (just before Edward fell ill). Construction began shortly thereafter in Boston, and the line through Amherst to Northampton and beyond seemed assured. In 1872, however, work was abruptly halted: the contractor had not completed the necessary railroad bridge over the Connecticut River between Hadley and Northampton, and once again the entire scheme was in jeopardy. For more than a quarter-century, Father had held no public office in the state. Now, however, in his seventieth year, he began to contemplate a return to the Massachusetts legislature: his presence in Boston would put him in contact with the big-business men of New England, and he would be in an ideal position to urge the state's financial support. Thus like his father before him (though the comparison would doubtless have been anathema), he spent his declining years petitioning the Massachusetts General Court for money to support the public cause that had dominated his imagination throughout his adult life. On July 10, 1872, he presented his resignation as treasurer of Amherst College to the Board of Trustees; Henry Ward Beecher, chairman of the Board, issued a statement thanking him for his devoted service of thirty-seven years. There was quite a flurry over the succession, but when it died down, leaving Austin in possession of the office his father had just quit, Edward could turn his full attention to politics and the cause of the railroad, secure in the knowledge that a direct male descendant of Samuel Fowler Dickinson would still preside over Amherst College's financial affairs.

In November 1873 he was elected to the Massachusetts House of Representatives: to the end he had remained faithful to the Whigs, and he stood for office as an independent. Well into his seventieth year, Edward Dickinson was something of a political anachronism now, and the Boston *Journal* published a biographical sketch of him that was reprinted in the Springfield *Republican*. It was titled "TRIBUTE TO A VETERAN": One of the old "River Gods."

Hon. Edward Dickinson of Amherst, member-elect of the House of Representatives, was a member of the House in 1838 and 1839, nearly as long ago as Mr. Gilbert of Gloucester. . . . He is a man of sterling personal character and integrity, always manifesting the keenest interest in public affairs, especially in town affairs. He is a type of the men once known as the "River Gods," and, although slow and conservative, will prove a valuable man in the House. As far as railroad matters are concerned, he is largely interested, in behalf of his section of the state, in the success of the Massachusetts Central.[8]

A few months earlier, W. S. Tyler's *History of Amherst College During Its First*

Half Century had been published, and it contained an even more Roman account of the old warrior.

> At the age of threescore years and ten Mr. Dickinson still stands erect, perpendicular, with his sense of seeing and hearing unimpaired, with his natural force and fire chastened and subdued but scarcely abated, one of the firmest pillars of society, education, order, morality and every good cause in our community.[9]

The legislature was convened on January 7, 1874, and Edward Dickinson, who had celebrated his seventy-first birthday on New Year's Day, was in Boston again.

Once more he entered vigorously into the political fray, as always promoting the interests of Amherst, the College, and the railroad. By now, however, age had begun to take its toll, and he returned home for a week at the end of February, physically run-down from the exertion. As luck would have it, the session that he returned to in the first week of March was unusually protracted. Charles Sumner, the senior United States senator from Massachusetts, died without warning on March 11; the Massachusetts legislature was charged with the responsibility of appointing his successor, and the contentious debate was carried for more than three weeks before Governor Washburn was selected. All other business of the General Court had been delayed by this unexpected diversion, and the legislature was forced to extend its term until the end of June. Edward Dickinson was not pleased to be away so long, but railroad affairs were on the docket for late spring, and he could not afford to return permanently to Amherst before the session ended. Like a ghostly echo of the letters he had written almost forty years earlier to his tearful young wife, the correspondence with Austin affirms his intention to relinquish public life forever: "I shouldn't be here much longer," he wrote on June 5, "& never again, so we must put up with inconvenience."[10] This time, he wrote the truth.

On Thursday, June 11, he returned to Amherst during a short recess; he spent long hours catching up on the work in his own legal practice—remaining in his office until nine that Saturday night. On Sunday he spent a quiet day at home, passing an hour or so alone with his daughter Emily in the garden, and then he returned to Boston that evening. Monday, June 15, was cruelly hot and humid in Boston, but the legislature was scheduled to debate the completion of the Troy and Greenfield railroad, and Edward Dickinson had to be in attendance throughout. At midday, in the midst of a speech, he was overcome with dizziness and forced to take his seat. The House adjourned, and a friend went with him to the Tremont House, where he was staying. They summoned a doctor who administered a sedative, but Edward Dickinson died almost at once.

His colleagues wired Amherst, first of the illness and immediately afterward of the death, and it became Austin's duty to tell his unsuspecting family of Father's plight. "We were eating our supper the fifteenth of June," Emily later wrote the Norcross sisters,

and Austin came in. He had a despatch in his hand, and I saw by his face we were all lost, though I didn't know how. He said that father was very sick, and he and Vinnie must go. The train had already gone. While horses were dressing, news came he was dead.

Father does not live with us now—he lives in a new house. Though it was built in an hour it is better than this. He hasn't any garden because he moved after gardens were made, so we take him the best flowers, and if we only knew he knew, perhaps we could stop crying. . . .

I cannot write any more, dears. Though it is many nights, my mind never comes home.[11]

For years afterward, the family angrily debated the cause of death. Though the attending physician had diagnosed an attack of apoplexy, the Dickinsons contended that Father had died as a result of the medicine he had been given—opium or morphine, to which, they claimed, he always had an adverse reaction. Actually, the immediate occasion for his demise matters little. Edward Dickinson had already evinced many symptoms of age and physical debilitation; his death at seventy-one should have surprised no one. In fact, despite Emily's explicit forebodings three and a half years earlier, no one seems to have been in the least prepared for it. He was their "River God" and thus beyond the perils of mortality.

Mrs. Edward Dickinson responded with such consistent self-effacement that her shock and grief are scarcely mentioned in any accounts of the family's history. It is the children who stand out in vivid relief—anguished, inconsolable, sometimes heroic. Surprisingly, it was Vinnie who rose to the occasion. Throughout the days and weeks that followed Father's death—during the funeral preparations, the burial, the greetings of mourners, who continued to come for many days—Vinnie's consideration and gentle kindness were always available. She greeted everyone who called, and she remembered to extend the usual courtesies of refreshment and comfort because, as she claimed, it was what Father would have wished. Thus those who visited the Homestead could be assured of seeing only Vinnie, who glided among friends and dignitaries with uncharacteristic, low-voiced solemnity. Her sister and brother indulged in extravagant grief.

Emily took to her room. She was willing to talk with Sam Bowles; other than that she saw no one. Later, her niece, Mattie, recollected a frightening phrase that her aunt Emily repeated over and over again: "Where is he? I can't find him!" However, her own father's overwhelming reaction seems to have been even more impressive—an unforgettable deviation from the norm for this genial, easygoing, reliable man. When Edward Dickinson's body was first brought from the station, Austin leaned over and kissed the forehead, saying, "There, father, I never dared do that while you were living." But this final, belated gesture was a mark of despair more than of love, for it was at last too late to hope for an affectionate response. As the days passed, Austin fell into despondency. Truly the fabric of the family was rent. "I remember my grandfather's funeral by the odor of syringa," Mattie wrote later, "and the excitement of settees from College Hall placed in rows on the front lawn to accommodate those the house could not hold, but most of all by my terror at my father's grief. The world seemed coming to an end. And where was Aunt Emily? Why did she not sit in the library with the family if he could?"[12]

Edward Dickinson was accorded every honor: the Reverend Jonathan Jenkins preached a laudatory sermon limning the deceased as a latter-day Samuel (and he may have chosen this Old Testament prophet with no ironic parallel to Samuel Fowler Dickinson in mind); the stores in the village were closed, and all business was suspended during the ceremony; the body was carried to its final resting place by local professional men, merchants, and Amherst College professors all walking together. Edward Dickinson was laid to rest in the same small plot as his own father's grave, and the stern, powerful face that had dominated the lives of all three Dickinson children vanished below ground forever.

Emily responded through her poetry. She cut a flyleaf from a book, bearing Father's autograph with the date 1824, and she inscribed on it: "*The most pathetic thing I do / Is play I hear from you— / I make believe until my Heart / Almost believes it too / But when I break it with the news / You knew it was not true / I wish I had not broken it— / Goliah—so would you—*" (#1290).[13] After that terrible June day, many of the frankly elegiac poems addressed Father's death explicitly; indeed, sometimes there is an almost frighteningly literal intent, as if one might send a message by mail to the afterworld. The following poem is written on the back of a piece of notepaper: at the top are the words "Dear Father—"; the rest of the page is empty, save for the signature, "Emily." On the verso these lines appear:

> *Knock with tremor—*
> *These are Caesars—*
> *Should they be at Home*
> *Flee as if you trod unthinking*
> *On the Foot of Doom—*
>
> *These seceded from your summons*
> *Centuries ago—*

> *Should they rend you with "How are you"*
> *What have you to show?*

(#*1325*)

The group of lines beginning "The most pathetic thing I do" is, self-avowedly, a tearful and pleading effort. But "Knock with tremor" has an element of dignity that surpasses the personal intent implied by the letter format.

The unique event of *Father's* death is not the ultimate subject (though the timing of the poem and the full evidence of the holograph copy leave little doubt that it was the occasion for this poem); instead, the poet's acute bereavement is transformed, and Father becomes a "Representative" of all the dead. Like "Ample make this Bed—," this elegy celebrates the dignity and heroism of every mortal who has passed into that unknown beyond: "Caesars—" all, heroes and conquerors of realms that the living can conjure only by reputation. It is clear that the ranks of these victors contain even the humblest, for their new kingdom is a domestic realm like the most common cottage in any New England village. Elsewhere the identification of the grave as some new house has a relatively literal implication; here, however, "Home" suggests a state of being, not that unvarying location the grave, a condition that converts the merest " 'How are you' " into some blaze of Titanic roar. Humanity passing through life into death defines a form of heroism that is integral to our very nature. One need not subdue nations or kings or Divinities: the full extent of life itself is challenge enough. Indeed, perhaps the most noteworthy fact about this poem is God's absence: death is no longer construed as His ravishment. Death seems to have very little to do with God at all here: it has become an entirely human affair, the final exploration of our birthright as men and women.

Emily Dickinson wrote several elegiac poems of lesser quality for Father's death. In January of the following year, she was still painfully conscious of her loss: "Thank you for Affection," she wrote Mrs. Holland, "It helps me up the Stairs at Night, where as I passed my Father's Door—I used to think was safety." She concluded by thanking her friend for the gift of clover plucked from Father's grave, which, as tradition has it, she never once visited, even though it was less than a five-minute walk from her back door. "Home is so far from Home, since my father died," she wrote Higginson shortly after the first anniversary of his death; two years afterward, she celebrated the third anniversary of Father's passing by enclosing a four-line elegy in a letter to Higginson and questioning his opinion about the existence of some afterlife. "Since my Father's dying, everything sacred enlarged so," she explained.[14]

Austin, without his sister's recourse of creating art, fell into a state of deep despondency. Sam Bowles, who departed for Europe in mid-July 1874, wrote Susan Dickinson with great concern in early August: "I hope Austin is taking care of himself, with your help. He has great need of husbanding of life now."[15] Sometime that fall Susan became pregnant with her third child, a boy born in August 1875—just two months after the first anniversary of Edward Dickinson's death. Susan was far from young for childbearing, forty-four when the infant was delivered, and the baby may simply have been an entirely unexpected and coincidental compensation for Austin's loss. Unexpected or not, the entire family rejoiced in the child, whom they named Gilbert and called "Gib" for short. Ned, Austin's older son, suffered from severe epilepsy and had always been sickly; Edward Dickinson had fretted over the male succession because of his only grandson's weak physical condition, and had he still been alive, this second grandson would have pleased him mightily. Indeed, fortune seemed to smile in every way for this boy; he was beautiful to look at, and he grew into a charming and intelligent toddler. Both parents doted upon him, and his precocity delighted Aunt Emily: "Austin's Baby says when surprised by statements—'There's—sum*th*n—else—there's Bum*bul* Beese,' " she wrote to Mrs. Holland when Gilbert was two and a half.[16] And if the blond little boy recompensed his parents for the loss of Father, the late-blooming love of Phil Lord surely consoled Emily Dickinson, for their affection finally found open expression in 1878, about four years after Edward Dickinson's demise. Yet one further consolation came to the poet that may have surpassed all the others.

It is a paradoxical fact that any authentic conversion is an unstable state: Puritan doctrine had always taught that the Christian who did not question his or her belief continually was in unsuspecting peril of complacency, that as soon as any human being became confident of having the gift of faith, this confidence was a certain sign of sinfulness. Thus uncertainty and conflict were the essential ingredients of any vital spiritual life, and every true follower of Christ necessarily possessed some constantly shifting mixture of belief and skepticism or doubt. In the days of her youth, Emily Dickinson's religious attitudes were surely dominated by defiance and anger, yet even in those early days there had been pensive moments of hope and trust in the Lord—never enough to suffuse her with faith or to persuade her to submit to conversion, but enough to find some expression in the poetry. In those early years the Voice of faith was faint in both religious and aesthetic terms: prayerful utterances were few in number and poetically weak by comparison with the great verse of challenge and rage. As the years passed, however, the balance shifted, at first only slightly, but more and more as time went by. By the mid-1860s or early 1870s, well before Father's death, a new poetry of faith had emerged.

At about the same time as the elegy "Ample make this Bed—," the same Voice of transcending simplicity can be found in prayerful poetry that has a fresh quality, tones of faith that do not follow traditional modes of ornate worship, but achieve strength by means of unaffected sincerity. Dickinson was deeply moved by the fact that God in apparent humility had elected to become one of us, and this late religious poetry often has an air of domestic familiarity that befits one awaiting a guest.

> *The Soul should always stand ajar*
> *That if the Heaven inquire*
> *He will not be obliged to wait*
> *Or shy of troubling Her*
>
> *Depart, before the Host have slid*
> *The Bolt unto the Door —*
> *To search for the accomplished Guest,*
> *Her Visitor, no more —*
>
> (#*1055*)

Christ offered us a Heavenly House in which there were many mansions: here, in a poem that explicitly repudiates "*The Soul selects her own Society*" (#*303*), Dickinson reciprocates the invitation, suggesting that each human "Soul" might open its door to become a lodging for the Lord. Almost certainly she had Paul's epistolary injunction in mind: "Be not forgetful to entertain strangers: for thereby some have entertained angels unawares" (Hebrews 13:2). Yet the attitude of the verse invokes not some land of ancient Biblical splendor, but the township of Amherst in the year of our Lord 1865. Moreover, the informing image has a special significance in the context of her own work: before, death (at worse) or sexual fulfillment (at best) had been "behind a door." Now the trope is permitted a less heightened, melodramatic interpretation that makes the notion of opening the door to God an everyday courtesy and delight. The Divinity is available in the familiar surroundings of one's own home.

The year before Father died, Dickinson wrote to the Norcross cousins: "The loveliest sermon I ever heard was the disappointment of Jesus in Judas. It was told like a mortal story of intimate young men. I suppose no surprise we can ever have will be so sick as that. The last 'I never knew you' may resemble it." It is an insight like this one that informs the elegies with power—the realization that there is an unspeakable expanse of heroism within the full course of every life. Jesus displayed the quality of His love not by forsaking the grandeur of Heaven for the lowly station of earth and humanity (that was the standard view of Dickinson's culture), but rather, by becoming heroic in this quintessentially human way—by accepting series of disillusionments and pains that make up a usual life. In the end, the Crucifixion seemed not a horror, but a supreme glory: death is implicit in the fact of every life, and in every life death is the ultimate fulfillment of minor griefs. As it is for all of us, unrecognized heroes alike, so was it for the Christ: "When . . . he confides to us that he is 'acquainted with Grief,' we listen, for that also is an Acquaintance of our own."[17] Prayerful poetry, then, might even be a dialogue like familiar earthly conversations.

> *"Unto Me?" I do not know you —*
> *Where may be your House?*
>
> *"I am Jesus — Late of Judea —*
> *Now — of Paradise" —*
>
> *Wagons — have you — to convey me?*
> *This is far from Thence —*
>
> *"Arms of Mine — sufficient Phaeton —*
> *Trust Omnipotence" —*
>
> *I am spotted — "I am Pardon" —*
> *I am small — "The Least*
> *Is esteemed in Heaven the Chiefest —*
> *Occupy my House" —*
>
> (#964)

Over and over again the motif of the "House" appears throughout this verse, but now Dickinson has become willing to accept the blissful expectation of this future estate without also possessing the certainty that could come only with seeing God on earth. And repeatedly it is the innate mystery and wonder of the human condition that facilitates this acceptance. "*I cannot see my soul but know 'tis there / Nor ever saw his house nor furniture, / Who has invited me with him to dwell; / But a confiding guest consult as well, / What raiment honor him the most, / That I be adequately dressed*" (#1262). Faith is no longer a question of submitting to God's power; instead, it has become a matter of accepting His generous invitation, and the persistent legend of the thief's request enters into her formulations of this transaction, too.

> *"Remember me" implored the Thief!*
> *Oh Hospitality!*
> *My Guest "Today in Paradise"*
> *I give thee guaranty.*
>
> *That Courtesy will fair remain*
> *When the Delight is Dust*
> *With which we cite this mightiest case*
> *Of compensated Trust.*

Of all we are allowed to hope
But Affidavit stands
That this was due where most we fear
Be unexpected Friends.

(#1180)

These poems of simple faith were composed in the late 1860s and early 1870s—before that day in June 1874 when Father left for Boston and never returned alive. Thus Emily Dickinson's belief was born not from extremity of need or weakness in the aftermath of supreme loss but, rather, from the considerations of an examined life. Yet there is little doubt that her hard-won faith offered solace in the hours and days of crisis that followed Father's death. It was a solace she would need: the easy years were behind her now.

On June 15, 1875, exactly one year after Father's death, Mother suffered a disabling stroke. "Mother was very ill, but is now easier, and the Doctor thinks that in more Days she may partly improve," Dickinson wrote Higginson several weeks after the event.

She was ignorant at the time and Her Hand and Foot left her, and when she asked me the name of her sickness—I deceive for the first time. She asks for my Father, constantly, and thinks it rude he does not come—begging me not to retire at night, lest no one receive him. I am pleased that what grieves ourself so much—can no more grieve him.

Although Mrs. Dickinson's condition fluctuated, she never regained anything resembling a normal state; Emily Dickinson's long period of service had begun. She had taken to wearing white exclusively after Father's death: always one of her favorite colors (perhaps because it was flattering to her fair complexion and vivid chestnut-red hair), it became a visible sign of perpetual mourning. After Mother's stroke, visits of any length outside the house seemed impossible: Mother could do nothing for herself, and one of the daughters was required in constant attendance. Since Vinnie thrived on her socializing and gossiping, it appeared only natural to both daughters that Emily should become Mother's attendant. Nor did Emily Dickinson resent this burden; in fact, as Mother's condition grew steadily worse, her daughter's devotion became ever more patient. "I have only a moment," Dickinson wrote the Norcross cousins.

Mother's dear little wants so engross the time—to read to her, to fan her, to tell her health will come tomorrow, to explain to her *why* the grasshopper is a burden, because he is not so new a grasshopper as he was,—this is so ensuing, I hardly have said "Good-morning, mother," when I hear myself saying "Mother, good-night."

And to Mrs. Holland she wrote:

The responsibility of Pathos is almost more than the responsibility of Care. Mother will never walk. . . .

Her poor Patience loses it's way and we lead it back. . . .

Time is short and full, like an outgrown Frock—[18]

Perhaps the saddest fact was that the elder Mrs. Dickinson suffered her stroke several months before Gilbert was born; although she certainly knew him and appreciated the joy he gave his parents, she was never in a condition to delight in him herself, for the lively, talkative boy could enter his grandmother's hushed room for only brief, quiet visits.

In October 1877 Sam Bowles fell desperately ill; in January 1878 he died, at the age of fifty-one, a bright star in Emily Dickinson's firmament falling below the horizon into the black void of death. "It is a little more than three years since you tried to help us bid Father Good-Night, which was so impossible that it has never become less so—," Dickinson wrote to her neighbors the Hills. "Now we have given our Mr Bowles—to the deep Stranger—."[19] Dickinson wrote many notes of condolence to Sam Bowles's wife, Mary, and to his beloved friend Maria Whitney. In fact, the correspondence with Maria Whitney seems to have become intimate only after their mutual friend had left the world so prematurely, for each woman could understand the other's grief with sympathy and affection.

As the years ticked slowly by, it is difficult to know what life became in the big Brick House, now so still and filled with shadows, a big house occupied by two spinsters and their crippled mother. Neither Emily nor Vinnie was very old when Sam Bowles died in 1878: Vinnie was forty-four, and Emily was forty-seven. Yet Vinnie was the only one of the three to go regularly into society, and her elder sister had surely begun to live more in current books and newspapers and in memories from the past than in the world that buzzed outside. Even the Heaven Emily Dickinson had come to accept may now have seemed more immediate to her than the Amherst that was busily modernizing itself just beyond her garden. Father and Mr. Sam were not really gone: they were merely waiting. Two years after Bowles's death, Emily Dickinson wrote to Maria Whitney:

I am constantly more astonished that the Body contains the Spirit—Except for overmastering work it could not be borne. . . .

> Could that sweet Darkness where they dwell
> Be once disclosed to us
> The clamor for their loveliness
> Would burst the Loneliness—

I trust you may have the dearest summer possible to Loss—.

And three years later she wrote, "The past is not a package one can lay away. I see my father's eyes, and those of Mr. Bowles—those isolated comets. If the future is mighty as the past, what may vista be?"[20]

There was still happiness to balance against the increasing loneliness. Helen Hunt Jackson had recognized the genius of Dickinson's work very soon after becoming acquainted with it. In 1876 she wrote the poet what may be the most accurate and heartening assessment of her verse that was ever given during her lifetime.

I hope someday, somewhere I shall find you in a spot where we can know each other. I wish very much that you would write to me now and then, when it did not bore you. I have a little manuscript volume with a few of your verses in it—and I read them very often—You are a great poet—and it is a wrong to the day you live in, that you will not sing aloud. When you are what men call dead, you will be sorry you were so stingy.

Widely published herself, perhaps Jackson could not comprehend the mixed feelings that had contributed to the reticence her friend had developed by then with regard to publication. Nonetheless, this praise encouraged Dickinson to pursue the relationship, and it was in 1878, only three months after Sam Bowles's death, that Jackson begged permission to have "*Success is counted sweetest*" (#67) published anonymously. October of that year brought one of her rare visits to Amherst. Afterward Dickinson wrote Maria Whitney:

I had within a few days a lovely hour with Mr and Mrs Jackson of Colorado, who told me that love of Mr Bowles and longing for some trace of him, led them to his house, and to seek his wife. They found her, they said, a stricken woman, though not so ruthless as they feared. That of ties remaining, she spoke with peculiar love of a Miss Whitney of Northampton, whom she would soon visit, and almost thought of accompanying them as far as yourself. . . .

I hope that you are well, and in full receipt of the Great Spirit whose leaving life was leaving you.[21]

None of Sam Bowles's friends ceased to long for his vital presence.

The years between 1878 and 1882 passed with few major events: there was the great fire on July 4, 1879, that lit up Emily Dickinson's orchard and caused the birds to carol as if the sun had shone. Judge Lord was sick enough in March 1881 to fall behind in his judicial work; however, he soon recovered and went back to the bench. Mother's condition remained much the same: "Mother is lying changeless on her changeless Bed," Dickinson wrote to Mrs. Holland in the spring of 1881, "hoping a little, and fearing much."[22] If life was diminished, at least it was relatively stable, composed chiefly of the endless series of small tasks that went into nursing Mother and punctuated by the visits of those whom Emily Dickinson still saw with regularity—Phil Lord, some of her Amherst neighbors, Austin and his family, occasionally a friend of many years' standing who was making a visit to Amherst.

Almost immediately after Mabel Loomis Todd moved to town with her husband in August 1881, the brilliant young faculty wife was "taken up" by Susan Dickinson; she met Vinnie at the Evergreens that November and began visiting the Homestead very soon afterward. She often played the piano and sang, and Emily Dickinson would listen appreciatively—but always out of sight. It is a striking fact that this woman who was so crucial to the process that eventually caused Dickinson's poetry to be published never once met the author face to face. Evidently the time when Dickinson was willing to make new acquaintances had finally passed. There were few buttresses in her usual routines to protect against disaster.

The quick succession of tragedies that beset her final years began on April 1, 1882, when Charles Wadsworth died. He had made a surprise visit to Amherst and Northampton in the late summer of 1880. "He rang one summer evening to my glad surprise," Dickinson wrote shortly after his death:

"Why did you not tell me you were coming so I could have it to hope for," I said—"Because I did not know it myself. I stepped from my Pulpit to the Train," was his quiet reply. He once remarked in talking "I am liable at any time to die," but I thought it no omen.

Neither side of the correspondence between them has survived, but Dickinson's reaction to Wadsworth's death reveals the extent to which she relied on this mentor who had advised her soul. "My closest earthly friend died in April," she wrote Higginson that summer. "He was my Shepherd from 'Little Girl'hood and I cannot conjecture a world without him." In December, still grieving, she wrote Phil Lord: "My Clergyman passed from Earth in spring, but sorrow brings it's own chill." And in mid-April 1886, only one month before her own death, her vivid regret over the loss of him was unabated. Thus she wrote to Charles Clark:

"Going Home," was he not an Aborigine of the sky? The last time he came in Life, I was with my Lilies and Heliotropes, said my sister to me, "the Gentleman with the deep voice wants to see you, Emily," hearing him ask of the servant. "Where did you come from," I said, for he spoke like an Apparition.[23]

Even so early as 1882, Heaven as Home may have seemed nearer than next door.

Wadsworth's death in April was followed by Judge Lord's falling critically ill during the first days of May. The Springfield *Republican* reported on May 3: "Judge Lord of the supreme court, sick at Salem, was delirious last night, his mind dwelling on cases in court, and his condition gave little hope of recovery."[24] Yet by May 8 he was out of danger, and Dickinson wrote him on the 14th:

To remind you of my own rapture at your return, and of the loved steps, retraced almost from the "Undiscovered Country," I enclose the Note I was fast writing, when the fear that your Life had ceased, came, fresh, yet dim, like the horrid Monsters fled from in a Dream.

. . . Vinnie came in from a word with Austin, passing to the Train. "Emily, did you see anything in the Paper that concerned us"? "Why no, Vinnie, what"? "Mr Lord is very sick." I grasped at a passing Chair. My sight slipped and I thought I was freezing.[25]

Though Phil Lord recovered this time, sorrows kept coming. In July, Higginson was sick enough for his illness to be reported in the newspapers (though he, too, recovered). And in November, Mother died.

Emily Norcross Dickinson, who had come to Amherst as a quiet, homesick bride more than half a century earlier, was seventy-eight when she slipped away. She was hopelessly invalided, and by ordinary standards her death might even have been termed a blessing. Yet it was a deep loss to the daughter whose life had come to be centered around Mother's care. Emily Dickinson knew that Mother's passage was no tragedy, that time had run its course for the shy little woman: thus loss was expressed chiefly in terms of awe that even this timid spirit had embarked upon the great adventure from which none return. "The dear Mother that could not walk, has *flown*," Dickinson wrote Mrs. Holland.

It never occurred to us that though she had not Limbs, she had *Wings*—and she soared from us unexpectedly as a summoned Bird—She had a few weeks since a violent cold, but . . . she seemed entirely better that last Day of her Life and took Lemonade—Beef Tea and Custard with a pretty ravenousness that delighted us. After a restless Night, complaining of great weariness, she was lifted earlier than usual from her Bed to her Chair, when a few quick breaths and a "Dont leave me, Vinnie" and her sweet being closed—That the one we have cherished so softly so long, should be in that great Eternity without our simple Counsels, seems frightened and foreign.

The letter to Maria Whitney that conveyed the news of Mother's death also carried one of Dickinson's most tender elegies.

All is faint indeed without our vanished mother, who achieved in sweetness what she lost in strength, though grief of wonder at her fate made the winter short, and each night I reach finds my lungs more breathless, seeking what it means.

> *To the bright east she flies*
> *Brothers of Paradise*
> *Remit her home,*
> *Without a change of wings,*
> *Or Love's convenient things,*
> *Enticed to come.*
>
> *Fashioning what she is,*
> *Fathoming what she was,*
> *We deem we dream —*
> *And that dissolves the days*
> *Through which existence strays*
> *Homeless at home.*

The sunshine almost speaks, this morning, redoubling the division, and Paul's remark grows graphic, "the weight of glory."[26]

The conclusion of this reflection echoes Paul's second epistle to the Corinthians: "Though our outward man perish, yet the inward man is renewed day by day. For our light affliction, which is but for a moment, worketh for us a far more exceeding and eternal weight of glory." (II Corinthians 4:16–17.)

Dickinson meditated at length upon these deaths—Father's suggesting that *all* are "Caesars" who have moved into the unknown province beyond the grave and Mother's demonstrating that even the most self-effacing and humble among us will probe the secrets of "that great Eternity." Certainly the intensity of Emily Dickinson's reaction was heightened by her secluded way of life and by the fact that she had never married and had children of her own, so that her ties of affection with the younger generation were at one remove, lodged chiefly with Austin's children. Yet there were spiritual and intellectual reasons as well for this preoccupation: she had spent most of her life "seeking what it means." Little by little as she moved through the years following Father's death, maturity enriched her understanding in several ways.

Long ago, confronting the demands for conversion in her late teens and early twenties, Emily Dickinson had fashioned an image of the self as a relatively fixed entity that was defined chiefly through the combat with the Divinity that repulsed His menaces and asserted personal autonomy. Now, at long last, she could begin to understand that individual identity is a miracle of constant change and development. Each successive "self" must incorporate some form of its earlier stages as the prerequisite for growth; once passed, however, these former epochs are gone forever and can never be relived. Perhaps, then, death is not a unique loss, but merely one additional stage of growth—both for the deceased and for those left behind who are forced to parse the implications of this passage. When Mrs. Holland's husband died in 1881, one of the several condolence letters Dickinson sent took the form of a poem.

Dear Sister.

> The Things that never can come back, are several—
> Childhood—some forms of Hope—the Dead—
> Though Joys—like Men—may sometimes make a Journey—
> And still abide—
> We do not mourn for Traveler, or Sailor,
> Their Routes are fair—
> But think enlarged of all that they will tell us
> Returning here—
> "Here!" There are typic "Heres"—
> Foretold Locations—
> The Spirit does not stand—
> Himself—at whatsoever Fathom
> His Native Land—

Emily, in love—[27]

"Childhood—some forms of Hope—the Dead—": this line describes the shape of the life cycle; it suggests that death is no different from the other stages and that each in turn passes even as it is experienced. The "Joys" that both "make a Journey—" and "abide" are people, with us as the objects of our sustained affection even though they may be separated by distance or death. Thus far the verse is relatively accessible. However, the last five lines present an audacious claim for the existence of some transcendent meaning in the merely immanent.

According to Dickinson's dictionary (which presents the standard Puritan definition), a *type*—something that is "typic"—is an event that is "a figure of something to come." The dictionary continues by giving an example: "Abraham's sacrifice and the paschal lamb, were *types* of Christ"—that is, they presaged His coming. The culture in which Dickinson was reared always understood the word in this context, as a way of identifying privileged moments in history that articulate the shape and meaning of the Judaeo-Christian myth. Yet Dickinson's usage in this poem transforms the term. The assertion " 'Here!' There are typic 'Heres' " removes the notion of "typic" from its usual *historical* and *mythic* context and applies it to ordinary, *quoti-*

dian existence, claiming that each life, here and now, has its own privileged moments of insight—even, perhaps, of foreknowledge, "Foretold locations." One's self is not constant and unchanging: "The Spirit does not stand." It moves through many "Fathoms" of time and eternity, always changing and always, nonetheless, "Himself"—regardless of the distance from "His Native Land—."

Primarily, the poem offered reassurance that Dr. Holland's death was but another kind of journey, not one from which travelers return to "tell us" of foreign lands, but one that foretells our own journey to join them. Thus might death become a "typic 'Here.'" Yet as both the plural "Heres" and the formula "Childhood—some forms of Hope—the Dead—" imply, there might be other privileged moments as well. *Life itself* is pregnant with meaning, even without an empowered Christian legend to stamp it with the pattern of transcendence.

This lonely, rigorous process of "seeking what it means" brought forth a second complex insight. If there is an inescapable destructive element in all acts of creation—if *"The Opening and the Close / Of Being, are alike"* (#1047)—then death may be not the ultimate loss of self, but some final confirmation of self. Probably no one of us can *know* "what it means" while still alive; perhaps none but the Deity Himself can understand the paradox that might make death some form of new life. Perhaps if God is really divine, no mere earthly creature could have the capacity to comprehend Him. In March 1883 Dickinson wrote Mrs. Holland a note:

I have seen one Bird and part of another—probably the last, for Gibralter's Feathers would be dismayed by this savage Air—beautiful, too, ensnaring—as Spring always is.

"Though he slay me, yet will I trust him"—[28]

The concluding quotation, from the Book of Job, suggests that Emily Dickinson finally came to faith as Job did, by accepting the fact that as the Great Creator of a world whose secrets we can only imperfectly grasp, God is intrinsically unknowable to man. We must accept all, even suffering and apparent destruction, because our limitations leave us unqualified to comprehend the Divinity.

This attitude of compliance sometimes infused the late poems of faith with a tone of submissive wonder.

> *The Thrill came slowly like a Light for*
> *Centuries delayed*
> *It's fitness growing like the Flood*
> *In sumptuous solitude—*
> *The desolation only missed*

While Rapture changed it's Dress
And stood amazed before the Morns
In ravished Holiness—

(#1495; var. *"Light"* and *"Morns"*)

There is an astonishing pace here, almost like orgastic release. Elements that had been treated as abhorrent in earlier work—the "ravishing" method of God's love, the doom that is implied by "Flood"—are here integrated into an experience of "Rapture." Indeed, the poem is centered around a paradox. Although these annihilating forces suffuse the verse, "desolation" is specified as the "only" missing element: the speaker's integrity is left intact, and the experience of conversion (or perhaps even of death itself) is rendered as no more than a change of "Dress."

The kind of acceptance that is reflected in this poem and in the March 1883 letter to Mrs. Holland suggests a quality of fortitude that is won chiefly by travail and loss. Although Emily Dickinson was slow to recover from her mother's death, her increased willingness to view death as part of the continuum of existence ultimately led her to appreciate life's mysteries all the more intensely. During the summer of 1883 she wrote to Maria Whitney with a rich savor—both for the season and for vitality itself. What vivid contrast this letter offers to the vision of a springtime "crumbling," "fading," and "flying" that had been the burden of Emily Dickinson's letter to her cousin, John Grave, written almost three decades earlier.

Men are picking the grass from father's meadow to lay it away for winter, and it takes them a long time. They bring three horses of their own, but Dick, ever gallant, offers to help, and bears a little machine like a top, which spins the grass away.

It seems very much like a gentleman getting his own supper—for what is his supper winter nights but tumblers of clover?

You speak of "disillusion." That is one of the few subjects on which I am an infidel. Life is so strong a vision, not one of it shall fail. . . .

. . . To have been made alive is so chief a thing, all else inevitably adds. Were it not riddled by partings, it were too divine.[29]

In August 1883 there was a Dickinson family reunion, and scores of relations came to Amherst. William Dickinson, Samuel Fowler Dickinson's second son, took the occasion to move his father's and mother's graves to a plot almost adjacent to the one in which Mr. and Mrs. Edward Dickinson were buried. When Edward had buried his own father almost a half-century earlier, he had purchased a plot with only four places: two for his parents and two for his wife and himself. His son would marry and form a new family with its own plot, and his daughters would be buried in their husbands' plots, so Edward Dickinson had supposed those many years ago. Now, however, it was clear that Emily and Lavinia would want to be laid to rest beside their parents, and Uncle William thoughtfully relocated their paternal grandparents so that their wishes might be honored. Yet to everyone's horror, it was not one of the elder Dickinsons who next journeyed graveward, but the little boy who had gladdened their hearts during the darkness following Edward Dickinson's death.

Gib attended school on Thursday, September 27, 1883. On the way home (so the story has been told), he played in the mud with some friends; on Friday he was sick and did not go to school. As the weekend progressed, his illness grew worse: he had dysentery and ran a high fever. "Gib had a pretty sick night, last," Austin wrote in his diary on Sunday, September 30. "Sue and I were up with him most of the time."[30] Gilbert had contracted typhoid. Still, the family had yearning hopes for his recovery; such cases were sometimes pulled through if the patient could be prevented from becoming too dehydrated, but it required strenuous around-the-clock nursing. For five days Austin and Sue were with the child continuously; neither parent slept very much, and both were frantic with anxiety and grief. On October 4, a Thursday, the illness reached its crisis: his aunt Emily, who seldom ventured even so far as the Evergreens now, took the pathway across only to be confronted by a nightmarish scene (described in a letter to Mrs. Holland several months later):

"Open the Door, open the Door, they are waiting for me," was Gilbert's sweet command in delirium. *Who* were waiting for him, all we possess we would give to know—Anguish at last opened it, and he ran to the little Grave at his grandparent's feet—All this and more, though *is* there more? More than Love and Death? Then tell me it's name![31]

Although Gib held on to life for almost one more day, Emily was nauseated by the smell of disinfectants and after lingering a while, returned to the Homestead—violently sick to her stomach, with a raging headache, and unable to wait through the "watch." At a quarter to five on the afternoon of Friday, October 5, the boy died.

The entire family was changed by the tragedy. Austin fell into deep despondency; Sue, unable by now to bear more children, was both grieved and hardened; Emily became bedridden. Although the physicians called it "nervous prostration," she was almost certainly already in the early stages of Bright's disease, which claimed her life less than three years later.

Bright's disease is a relatively painless way to die: a slow failure of the kidneys that sometimes comes as the consequence of a strep infection, it is almost without symptoms at the onset. The victim slowly weakens, eventually expires; the duration of the sickness is between three and four years.

Emily Dickinson had written of having a severe bout of flu in the fall of 1882, shortly before her mother's death, and this may well have been the infection that precipitated her fatal disease. In any case, she was not physically well in 1883, and her debilitation was only made worse by grief over Gib's death. Doubts about the existence of an afterlife surely remained: she gives voice to them in the letter to Mrs. Holland. Although she was shocked and greatly saddened by Gilbert's untimely end, however, there is no evidence that she was in the least embittered. She wrote several touching elegies for this child, whose plea in those last hours came to seem almost a proof of something "more."

> The Heart has many Doors—
> I can but knock—
> For any sweet "Come in"
> Impelled to hark—
> Not saddened by repulse,
> Repast to me
> That somewhere, there exists,
> Supremacy—
>
> (#1567)

Gilbert's "Open the Door . . . they are waiting for me" had become a talisman of passage into God's House.

Early in the following year, on March 13, 1884, Otis Phillips Lord died, and the cycle of pain was complete.

> Quite empty, quite at rest,
> The Robin locks her Nest, and tries her Wings.
> She does not know a Route
> But puts her Craft about
> For <u>rumored</u> Springs—
> She does not ask for Noon—
> She does not ask for Boon,
> Crumbless and homeless, of but one request—
> The Birds she lost—
>
> (#1606)

The girl who had demanded so stridently to see Heaven so that she might glimpse the face of the Godhead has at length matured into a woman who values "The Birds she lost" above all other things: now Dickinson demands to see Heaven only for the *humans* who now live there. "I thought the Churchyard Tarrytown, when I was a Child," she wrote her aunt Kate Sweetser, "but now I trust 'tis Trans."[32]

Most of her time was spent resting; often in bed, Emily Dickinson had ample time to review her life and the product of her vocation. Posthumous fame tantalized her imagination, but even more tantalizing was the notion of this God Who had chosen to become man. "Contention 'loves a shining Mark,'" she wrote to Mrs. Holland in the spring of 1885.

Only *fight* about me, said the dying King, and my Crown is sure—
   It is only the Moss upon my Throne that impairs my Dying.
   . . . Saul criticized his Savior till he became enamored of him—then he was less loquacious—. . . .
   But you must go to Sleep. I, who sleep always, need no bed.
   Foxes have Tenements, and remember, the Speaker was a Carpenter—[33]

Perhaps there was self-conscious roguery in leaving the poetry in such a mysterious condition, as if to ensure the contention that would make her "Crown . . . sure." Of her "Throne" she seems to have been casually certain. Lying upon her pillow, she could recall the Saviour Who had voiced a very human cavil: "The foxes have holes, and the birds of the air have nests; but the Son of man hath not where to lay his head" (Matthew 8:20). And she concludes this missive with an admonition that verges upon prayer: "remember, the Speaker was a Carpenter."

The clergymen of Emily Dickinson's youth had focused their hopes upon the Resurrection: a God-man had risen from the grave and had pledged to ransom all the faithful from death; the "signs" of this promise were to be found scattered throughout nature as the Lord's reassurance to mankind. Even in her later years Dickinson was not persuaded by this phenomenon. If anything, she lost much of her fascination with flourishes of heroism and drama; instead, she turned her attention increasingly to the commonplace. "To be human is more than to be divine," she wrote Higginson three years after Father's death; "when Christ was divine, he was uncontented till he had been human."[34] Little by little, as she moved toward her own death, it was God's yearning to partake of humanity that moved her inclination toward belief, and the paradox of a second birth from death was replaced by a new set of paradoxes that took precedence in her imagination.

God had willingly abandoned the splendor of Heaven and come to earth. Moreover, He had not come as a prince or a potentate; instead, He came as the son of a common carpenter. His birth was so lowly that it ought to have passed without notice—cradled in the straw of a barn in the small town of Bethlehem. Although a choir of angels sang the anthem of his coming, they had appeared neither to emperors nor to wisemen in the temple, only to shepherds in the fields who were grazing their flocks. The Babe grew to adulthood with little visible sign of His unique nature; and when He finally took His place as a public Man, He chose neither sword nor scepter, but accepted the role of a simple teacher. The Bible speaks of "multitudes" that sometimes congregated to hear Him speak. In truth, these occasional crowds were not so large as those that gathered regularly to watch the Roman spectacles. And His time to preach was brief and sequestered: three years in an obscure province at the outer reaches of the mighty Roman Empire. By all logic, He should have been overlooked, or if noticed, soon forgotten. How was it, then, that 1886 years after the birth of Jesus, His legend had become venerated all over the earth? Could one believe better for having seen Him, touched His garments, even witnessed the Resurrection? Or is not the persistence of His message an even more persuasive miracle?

Jesus, the Christ, had been a sublime impossibility: the intersection of the finite and the infinite, of the historical and the eternal. The condition of commonplace reality was forever altered by this miraculous union: Emily Dickinson did not have to go to Heaven if she wished to see God; she could discover the lineaments of the Divinity merely by looking into a mirror, for God had become human. That was one miracle. The second miracle was that this good news came to us all, despite its humble and obscure origins. Kierkegaard has remarked this paradoxical conflation of the sublime and the ordinary: "The news of the day the beginning of eternity! If God had permitted himself to be born in an inn, wrapped in swaddling-clothes and laid in a manger, could the contradiction have been greater than that the news of the day should be the swaddling-clothes of eternity."[35] What seems no more than some extraordinary coincidence—accident, gossip, the spread of rumor—must surely be divine Providence at work, uncounted generations of God bestowing belief!

Thus it was that Emily Dickinson finally came into an estate of faith, not by virtue of the Resurrection, but of the Incarnation. A Child Who was God and a message, passed by word of mouth, that nonetheless spanned centuries.

> *"And with what body do they come?"*—
> *Then they do come—Rejoice!*
> *What Door—What Hour—Run—run—My Soul!*
> *Illuminate the House!*
>
> *"Body!" Then real—a Face and Eyes—*
> *To know that it is them!—*
> *Paul knew the Man that knew the News—*
> *He passed through Bethlehem—*
>
> (#1492)

Part Six ◆ "One of the Ones
That Midas Touched"

A Field of Stubble, lying sere
Beneath the second Sun—
It's Toils to Brindled People thrust—
It's Triumphs—to the Bin—
Accosted by a timid Bird
Irresolute of Alms—
Is often seen—but seldom felt,
On our New England Farms—

(#1407)

At the end there were birds. Birds had never been merely neutral in Dickinson's work, and the poet who had watched them swoop through the family's orchard pursuing flies and mosquitoes had always been inclined to construe these soaring songsters as personae for the poet. At the beginning, when she determined self-consciously to sing "New Englandly," she had asserted, "*The Robin's my Criterion for Tune*" (#285). When there was some injury to the power of writing poetry, this too was expressed in the familiar ways: "*Not dumb—I had a sort that moved— / A Sense that smote and stirred— / Instincts for Dance—a caper part— / An Aptitude for Bird—*" (#1046). And even when an impassable barrier seemed to exist between the poet-observer and nature, the terror of the consequent isolation was conveyed in part by a disruption of this usual identification—as when in "*A Bird came down the Walk—*" (#328), the essence and mission of the winged creature utterly eludes the speaker. Just as throughout the verse Dickinson plays with the notions of feet and their usual activities as a way of alluding to poetry, so over and over again, she employs the figure of the bird to represent the poet. Yet the identification was never more poignant or powerful than in those years following Father's death when Emily Dickinson reviewed her life and work in order to make some final assessment. "What sort of bird have I been?" she seems to ask. Or "What does it mean to have been a *bird*?"—a poet instead of merely a person, an unchanging Voice instead of a woman, wife, mother, grandmother. "A Field of Stubble, lying sere" is one such meditation.

Entirely intelligible standing alone, the poem is even more interesting when it is put into the context of its inception. In mid-February 1877, fifteen-year-old Ned Dickinson suffered his first serious bout of epilepsy; the boy had always had a frail constitution, and now the family genuinely feared for his life. He took more than a month to recuperate, and during this period his aunt Emily sent him a letter that included this piece of verse: "Dear Ned—I send you a Portrait of the Parish [her title for the poem], and the first sugar— Dont bite the Parish, by mistake, though you may be tempted—."[1] Possibly the adolescent did not discern all of the wry nuances in this communication; still, the missive is laden with implication. The poet seems to have had eschatological musings, a preoccupation with first and last things. Ned was no longer Austin's only male heir, for Gilbert had been born a year and a half earlier; nonetheless, he was Edward Dickinson's namesake and the only male grandchild Edward had known—the heir apparent of the House whose reputation had been rescued by Emily Dickinson's father. This purely family concern with beginnings and endings is echoed thematically in the two gifts. In New England the season of maple sugaring is universally recognized as the beginning of warmth. When it comes early (in the first week of March), knowledgeable natives conclude that winter will be curtailed that year; hence the "first sugar—" is spring's talisman. Yet the *poem* is an autumnal scene, a verse not of sowing, but of reaping. In the Christian emblem tradition, both spring with its signs of the promised resurrection and autumn with its emblems of the great harvest of souls could be read as foreshadowing the reward for every good Christian, and in this way *both* gifts could be construed as a "Portrait of the Parish" and its notions of the afterlife to follow. All of these implications might readily have been meaningful to Ned.

There is one further nest of meanings that were of especial concern to the poet, however. Dickinson had styled herself "Uncle Emily" to Ned when he was younger; indeed, long before Ned's birth she had determined to usurp her brother's birthright and become the one true inheritor of the "Dickinson honor" that had so obsessed her father. Now in 1877, nearly three years after Father's death, Emily Dickinson had already written the greater part of the poetry that would become her claim to pre-eminence. Thus "A Field of Stubble, lying sere" addresses certain private preoccupations with ultimates and endings. What would be the final judgment of her work? Would the ages to follow be ones in which a poet, however great, could command acclamation? What in general would be the lot of the post-Christian artist?

The scene that the poem examines is an aftermath. In its most literal sense, "the second Sun" is the day after the harvesting of some grain: the "timid Bird" hops among the rows of "Stubble," pecking at the ground for gleanings. In the immediate wake of the reaping, there will be sustenance enough, sufficient "Alms"; however, winter will inevitably come, and then aliment will be rare indeed. Such is the surface story of the verse. Yet, as the speaker notes, this spectacle "*Is often seen—but seldom felt,* / *On our New England Farms—*": it is not the scene itself, but its import that the poem seeks to explore. By 1877 the last major revival had come and gone in Amherst, and the last great harvest of souls had been gathered in. The heroic age of New England, the rigorous culture of the Puritan Fathers upon which this country was founded, had finally passed. Two generations later, Robert Frost would write of an "Oven Bird" singing a twentieth-century song that describes this autumnal season: "*And comes that other fall we name the fall.* / *He says the highway dust is over all.*" Although Emily Dickinson did not know that America's bleak future would be of billboards and motorcars, she did know that even as the second millennium after Christ was drawing to its conclusion, the poet was compelled to feast upon lean subject matter, the meager leavings of a great tradition. The harvesters of the first sun had been a "Brindled People," tawny and burned by the bright light of faith. But "Brindled" is an archaic word, and theirs is a conviction whose shining time has passed. Can poetry of consequence still be created? Will the men and women of succeeding generations comprehend the glory of the quest that had fired Dickinson's creative imagination? This poem cannot answer such questions. Still, it raises them—obliquely, but with plaintive insistence.

Emily Dickinson wrote many eloquent elegies for those who passed from life while she still lingered, and her later years gave occasion for elegiac musings upon her own poetic work as well. Sometimes these are almost private, poems whose full poignancy cannot be appreciated without the recollection of some earlier verse. "*A Drunkard cannot meet a Cork / Without a Revery— / And so encountering a Fly / This January Day / Jamaicas of Remembrance stir / That send me reeling in— / The moderate drinker of Delight / Does not deserve the spring—*" (#1628): this midwinter verse of 1884 requires the echo of a springtime poem composed twenty-four years earlier for the full amplitude of its cadences to be heard. "*I taste a liquor never brewed— / From Tankards scooped in Pearl— / Not all the Frankfort Berries / Yield such an Alcohol! / Inebriate of Air—am I / And Debauchee of Dew— / Reeling—thro endless summer days— / From inns of Molten Blue—*" (#214). The early poem is invigorated by limitless optimism: the "summer days" will be "endless"; and the dancing delight can go "reeling" out into the "Molten Blue" of open skies. The seasoned poet's vision is literally sobered by 1884. The merest aromatic "Cork" of warm "January" sunlight will stir the sharp "Revery" of those bygone days. Now, however it is only poignant recollection and not hopeful ambition that has been roused; thus the dancing movement still stirs, but only so that it may come "reeling *in*" to "Jamaicas of Remembrance." Although the past is heady, rich, and vivid, it is gone, available only in momentary, unconnected fragments. Outgoing optimism has been replaced by inward-looking retrospection, and what had once been a brazen clarion of challenge has become no more than a nostalgic souvenir.

Similarly, in 1885, lying upon her bed in the corner room, Dickinson wrote about the sky swimming in carmine, and the verse recalls those many early poems that had inquired about God's presence in nature: "*Is it, or is it not, Marine— / Is it, or not, divine— / The Eye inquires with a sigh / That Earth sh'd be so big— / What Exultation in the Woe— / What Wine in the fatigue!*" (#1642) At length, even the creative, questioning "Eye" has become tired. There is still "Exultation" in the "Woe," for it recalls those heroic battles with the Divinity. There is even a hint of sacramental "Wine" as "fatigue" becomes its own emblem, not a portent of the future, but the reminder of a vanished past when the cosmos, perhaps Heaven itself, had seemed ripe for conquest and a glorious weariness had come from wrestling with the Lord.

In those days, thirty years and more in the past, integrity and autonomy had seemed all-important—a more than sufficient stake upon which to wager both life and vocation. Yet in her later years, the poet began to wonder whether the sustaining of integrity and autonomy were enough to make a life complete and worth living. One of the first poems to touch upon this quandary was included in a letter of 1873. Vinnie had just returned from New York, where she had been visiting the Hollands, and after her sister's return the poet wrote to Mrs. Holland.

Vinnie says you are most illustrious and dwell in Paradise. I have never believed the latter to be a superhuman site.

Eden, always eligible, is peculiarly so this noon. It would please you to see how intimate the Meadows are with the Sun. Besides—

> The most triumphant Bird I ever knew or met
> Embarked upon a twig today
> And till Dominion set
> I famish to behold so eminent a sight
> And sang for nothing scrutable
> But intimate Delight.
> Retired, and resumed his transitive Estate—
> To what delicious Accident
> Does finest Glory fit!

While the Clergyman tells Father and Vinnie that "this Corruptible shall put on Incorruption"—it has already done so and they go defrauded.

Emily—[2]

On the one hand, the "Bird" is "triumphant," and its song seems clearly to have made God and His legend entirely superfluous; on the other, the tract offered by this earthly singer is but a "transitive Estate—." It exists only as a "delicious Accident," not susceptible of control or even prediction, and it is essentially impermanent. What is more, although the *"Bird"* may be "triumphant," the poem that proclaims this victory is curiously flat: it captures no rich, sonorous sensuosity, and it conveys no significant message. Thus the speaker employs transitive verbs to convey the process by which she apprehends the singer; however, the verbs that name the bird's activities are all intransitive save the last ("resumed"), which signals departure. The bird *is;* it states its own independent, "intimate Delight." Then it leaves. That is all. Dickinson's letter may claim that both Eden and Paradise have been contained in this event, but the quality of the verse itself belies the assertion. There is no felt victory. Nor can the speaker follow the bird to experience its triumph more fully. Thus the residual import of the poem is a sense of felt loss, a falling away. An artist who has concocted all of being from enacting the role of hero-poet may *require* combat to sustain elation. Once the days of battle have ceased, existence itself may seem hollow and drained of meaning—and like some aged Ulysses who longs to go to sea again, the poet may feel useless, outdated, out of place, or ultimately unfulfilled.

Three years later, Dickinson enclosed a poem tentatively entitled "Blue Bird" in a letter to Higginson. It returns to a similar situation, treating it with an even more somber tone.

> *After all Birds have been investigated and laid aside—*
> *Nature imparts the little Blue-Bird—assured*
> *Her conscientious Voice will soar unmoved*
> *Above ostensible Vicissitude.*
>
> *First at the March—competing with the Wind—*
> *Her panting note exalts us—like a friend—*
> *Last to adhere when Summer cleaves away—*
> *Elegy of Integrity.*
>
> (#1395)

Superbly simple in its rendering of the singer, this poem may be like so much of the other late verse, aiming to deliver nothing more than nature in the state of being itself. Still, the activities of this "Blue-Bird" are reminiscent of the course of Emily Dickinson's own "conscientious" creative life. And what remains is neither sensuous sound nor portentous message, but only an "Elegy of Integrity." Can this be the residual reward of a career spent in combat with the Lord?

In 1879 Dickinson wrote a second poem about a bluebird. It returns with an almost obsessive concern to the condition of the isolated singer, as if Dickinson were manipulating the terms of some equation and seeking a solution. The skeletal story of the verse tells much the same tale as the two earlier poems. Here it is the bird's gaiety and "joy" that are emphasized, not his "triumph," yet the verse takes the form of a declarative observation and does not attempt to replicate the exultant cry of ecstasy. Thus the poem seems almost prosaic when measured against Dickinson's best work, even though the reader is expected to believe that the bird's song is rapturous.

> *Before you thought of Spring*
> *Except as a Surmise*
> *You see—God bless his suddenness—*
> *A Fellow in the Skies*
> *Of independent Hues*
> *A little weather worn*

> *Inspiriting habiliments*
> *Of Indigo and Brown—*
> *With specimens of Song*
> *As if for you to choose—*
> *Discretion in the interval*
> *With gay delays he goes*
> *To some superior Tree*
> *Without a single Leaf*
> *And shouts for joy to Nobody*
> *But his seraphic self—*
>
> (#1465)

Dickinson mailed a copy of this poem to her friend and fellow poet, Helen Hunt Jackson, who was living in Colorado at the time. Jackson's response was more than enthusiastic; it was collegial.

My dear friend,

I know your "Blue bird" by heart—and that is more than I do any of my own verses.—

I also want your permission to send it to Col. Higginson to read. These two things are my testimonial to its merit.

We have blue birds here—I might have had the sense to write something about one myself, but I never did: and now I never can. For which I am inclined to envy, and perhaps hate you. . . .

What should you think of trying your hand on the oriole? He will be along presently.

Yours ever—
Helen Jackson[3]

Jackson was a close personal friend of Thomas Wentworth Higginson, who had pronounced her America's finest woman poet. Her acquaintance with Dickinson's work, though probably not extensive, was at least sufficient to convince her that his accolade had been misplaced; and her request to pass the poem along to Higginson, coupled with her half-playful, half-rueful assertion of "envy" and "hate," was explicitly intended to communicate her own generous admiration for Dickinson's poetry. Although it was late for Emily Dickinson to have discovered such an encouraging reader, she seems to have been touched by this gesture.

In the earliest days of her vocation, Emily Dickinson had found a responsive and appreciative audience in Sue; however, as Sue became increasingly preoccupied with her children and her busy social life, the two women drifted apart. By the late 1870s Emily Dickinson had no reliable confidante with whom to discuss her work and the problems attendant upon the twilight of her vocation. Now Helen Hunt Jackson, a sympathetic woman who was also a fellow artist, offered such companionship. Indeed, for a number of reasons Jackson may have been the best reader Dickinson could have found at this point. Jackson had spent her girlhood in Amherst, had played with Emily Dickinson during those long, somnolent summer afternoons of the past, could recollect the quiet, parochial, church-centered New England village of bygone days. Thus she could comprehend the many nuances of Dickinson's poetic journey. Yet unlike Emily Dickinson, Jackson had chosen to embrace the full range of usual women's roles: she had married and borne a son, though her first husband had died in a wartime accident in 1863, and her son had died in 1865. Writing had not been her calling, then—not a mission in life burning so ardently that it consumed all the energies that might have been apportioned elsewhere. Instead, writing had offered a refuge after these personal tragedies, in part assuaging her grief, in part giving her a career that enabled her to earn a living. Thus she brought a different perspective from Dickinson's to the writing of poetry. She had managed to achieve immense popular success as an author during her own lifetime, but she was by no means a great artist, and her letters to Dickinson suggest that her judgment was balanced enough for her to recognize the disparity between them. Therefore, when Dickinson responded to Jackson's request, she did so by posing a set of subtle questions concerning the relationship between life and art, questions that lie behind this entire series of poems about a solitary singer. "To the Oriole you suggested," she wrote, "I add a Humming Bird and hope they are not untrue—."[4]

Although it is much more complex than the earlier poems about an isolated singer, the "Oriole" offers a culmination of one theme that had run through them. Now the bird has become an almost Godlike embodiment of the poet and the process of isolated artistic creativity. The songster's brief, glorious flight through the orchard has very much the quality of a poet's life, entirely spent in spinning shimmering threads of song—all the bird's beating, furious energy expended in flying, alighting ever so briefly, then restlessly springing into the air again. Elsewhere Dickinson asked what a career of wrestling with the Divinity's control had done to the language from which poetry can be made. Here, however, the focus of inquiry is intensely personal. What does it mean to have given one's entire existence to art? What has it all been worth? Has it been a life well spent?

Emily Dickinson's long quest had begun when she disobeyed the injunction to submit to the golden crown of faith. Unwilling to concede this metal of dominion to the lord, she had *"dealt a word of Gold"* to verse and strung the wilderness with *"Golden lines"* (#430). In those days, she had acquired a Midas touch: thus this oriole is the bird who spells her particular fate.

One of the ones that Midas touched
Who failed to touch us all
Was that confiding Prodigal
The reeling Oriole—

So drunk he disavows it
With badinage divine—
So dazzling we mistake him
For an alighting Mine—

A Pleader—a Dissembler—
An Epicure—a Thief—
Betimes an Oratorio—
An Ecstasy in chief—

The Jesuit of Orchards
He cheats as he enchants
Of an entire Attar
For his decamping wants—

The splendor of a Burmah
The Meteor of Birds,
Departing like a Pageant
Of Ballads and of Bards—

I never thought that Jason sought
For any Golden Fleece
But then I am a rural man
With thoughts that make for Peace—

But if there were a Jason,
Tradition bear with me
Behold his lost Aggrandizement
Upon the Apple Tree—

(#1466)

When Midas first acquired his golden touch, he thought it a prize beyond estimation. Soon, however, he discovered that all the staples of existence— bread and fruit, water and wine—were transformed into gold before he could take the nourishment he needed. Life itself became inconsistent with the possession of this rare gift, and in the end, Midas begged the gods to take back their endowment so that he might become an ordinary mortal once again. These are the principal elements of the legend that Emily Dickinson chose for the "Oriole" she conjured at Helen Hunt Jackson's invitation, elements that resound with poignancy now, in the concluding years of Dickinson's creative life.

Other legends also infuse this bird's flight with significance: one of them is the parable of the prodigal son (see Luke 15:11–32). Christ tells the story of a man who had two sons. The younger demanded his entire birthright immediately; when the father complied, the prodigal son took every bit of his wealth and squandered it upon rich living, heedless of the quotidian needs that might arise in times to come. After he had spent all his resources, a great famine arose in the land, and he began to think, "How many hired servants of my father's have bread enough and to spare, and I perish with hunger!" He returned repentant to his father's house, where he was lovingly received. By 1879 Emily Dickinson was already well along in the acceptance of faith that marked her last years: she had begun the arduous return to the Father in Heaven above, confident of the same loving reception that had greeted the young man of the Gospel. Yet this poem focuses not upon her faith, but upon her art. The "Prodigal" bird of the verse is a reckless spendthrift, similar to the son in the Gospel. Indeed, the legends of Midas and of the prodigal son reinforce each other here: the central figures in both were brought by pain and adversity to appreciate the components of everyday reality, the joys of their appointed rounds as opposed to some extravagant and unusual way of life. This "Prodigal" bird, then, becomes the poet who has exchanged all the rewards of ordinary existence for the single golden purpose of creating verse; such is the premise that attends his dancing entrance into the orchard.

Because there is no way of knowing how much of Emily Dickinson's poetry Helen Hunt Jackson had seen, no one can guess how many allusions to it she was able to discern in this poem. Nonetheless, the oriole's bibulous pillage of the orchard is described here in terms that echo several of the most significant metapoetic verses in Dickinson's corpus. The "reeling" circuit of the poet-bird, "drunk" with power, reiterates the flight in "*I taste a liquor never brewed,*" a soaring toward the sun, "*Reeling—thro endless summer days—.*" (And it anticipates that other echo, the bittersweet "Jamaicas of Remembrance" that would come "reeling in.") The "dazzling" quality of his trill recollects one of Dickinson's homilies concerning poetry: "*Tell all the Truth but tell it slant— / . . . The Truth must dazzle gradually / Or every man be blind—*" (#1129). The "mistake" of supposing the bird to be a "Mine" has several implications. At the simplest level, it punningly suggests that the speaker expects the bird to stay—that he would claim it as "Mine"—and that he thinks it to be a veritable "Mine" of gold whose ore can never be played out. And these recall the assertions of earlier speaker-poets. In "*Some—Work for Immortality—,*" the haughty speaker distinguishes between her own exalted state and that of an artist who sells his wares: "*One's—Money—One's—the Mine—*" (#406). Here "Mine" does stipulate an inexhaustible vein of golden creativity. And in "*Mine—by the Right of the White Election!*" (#528) the speaker vaunts the value of her own vision, the poet's eye / I, above all other things. Finally, the stolen "Attar" echoes what may be Dickinson's most famous poem about the poet: "*This was a Poet—It is That* / *Distills amazing sense* / *From ordinary Meanings—and* <u>*Attar*</u> *so immense* / *From the familiar species* / *That perished by the Door—*" (#448, *my emphasis*). The oriole may be "The Meteor of Birds," but he travels through the orchard of this poem like a comet trailing Emily Dickinson's songs.

The speaker seems at a loss to define the kaleidoscopic creature: sometimes the epithets that come to mind sound positive—"Epicure" and "Oratorio." Yet negative judgments overbalance in the end. The bird is a "Dissembler" and "a Thief"; "He cheats as he enchants." Worst of all, what he swindles from us is any possibility of real-world fulfillment. "Departing like a Pageant / Of Ballads and of Bards—" in the fifth stanza, he takes the "entire Attar" of the orchard with him. Attar is a fragrant substance that is concocted from the petals of flowers. No prudent New England housewife would ever make her attar from the flowers of an orchard, for the effect would be much like that of some fatal frost: the trees would bear no apples at all. Insofar as the bird represents the poet, he has sacrificed normal fruition for an exotic, fragrant song. Has the exchange proved worthwhile? The overwhelming air of loss suggests it has not.

Who can know whether the bird itself was happy? In fact, who would even think to inquire whether the bird's life had been one of fulfillment? Perhaps it was. Wheeling and swooping drunkenly to seize the necessity of the moment, the *bird* may have been well pleased with its own brief, ardent span of existence. It is in the nature of things that birds have but a limited horizon of twig and seed and sky, with superfluous song as accompaniment. Sad to say, the human speaker has a broader, more comprehensive vision of life's possibilities than the spendthrift, passionate bird: he has a sense of history—the capacity to conjure recollections of a mythic past and hopes for "Peace" that look toward the future. And at the conclusion of this verse, the speaker's somber tone suggests the attitude of one who has been defrauded.

Dickinson deliberately identifies this speaker as "a rural *man*": it is a striking juxtaposition to the explicitly feminine claim at the outset of her career, "*The Queen, discerns like me—* / *Provincially*" (#285). After so many years, there is nothing at all of the woman left in "One of the ones that Midas touched"; perhaps full confirmation as a woman has been sacrificed along with the orchard's possibility for bearing fruit, both compounded into the "Attar" of poetry. Jacob is gone, too, although his name is cunningly recalled by Jason, whose "Golden Fleece" echoes the "silver fleeces" that dawned upon the Peniel Hills of Dickinson's early poem (#59). Indeed, the two legends flow together here. Jacob had fleeced Esau of his rightful inheritance, had wrestled with the Lord and won; Jason, too, had been involved in a contest about his birthright, and only the quest of capturing the golden fleece had ensured him his rightful claim. Yet these apparent triumphs had been accompanied by terrible loss for both heroes: God had withdrawn His face from Jacob forever; Jason's wife, Medea, had turned upon him and murdered their sons. What had seemed great victories for these ancient warriors had spelled tragedy instead. So it may be with the poet.

This speaker does not long for heroic combat, but for "Peace" in a quiet country setting; yet he cannot be certain of gaining even this modest end, for some whirligig bird, touched by "Midas," has spoiled his crop and left nothing but a resonance of song in its wake. Thus the poem ends with puzzlement. How can the plundering bird be adequately described? With what element of grandeur and what element of desolation? Of course, the bird as sentient, living creature has left. Thus the "Apple Tree" is empty. The fruit it would have borne is quintessentially New England's; ineluctably, it recalls Eden as well. But both Eden and New England have been made barren by the thievery. Agonizingly, the several stories reinforce one another—the pagan, the Biblical, and the New World tale all tell of sterility and loss and the residual, golden memory of alluring heroic possibility.

The only remnant of "lost Aggrandizement" is the superb poem itself, in which there is not a live bird, but an unchanging golden bird; not a live woman, but the poet's creation—an unfailing Voice that still issues vibrantly from the page. These achieve a kind of immortality, a triumph of sorts. But is it life? Or has life been as ruthlessly consumed by the imperative to create art as the orchard's "Attar" was consumed by the robber-bird? Has the golden prize been worth the forfeit? Is it better to have been a poet—even a very great poet—than merely to have lived a full life in the ordinary way?

The second poem that Emily Dickinson included in her letter to Helen Hunt Jackson, the "Humming Bird," merely makes the implicit query of this "Oriole" poem more pointed: it is the verse beginning "*A Route of Evanescence*" (see p. 483), and it presents a totally different alternative for the bird. Not the vandal who steals being in order to sustain song, the "Humming Bird" is a vibrant affirmation of vitality. One of Dickinson's finest renditions of nature captured in the process of dynamic existence, this poem celebrates the beauty of movement, light, and color in the everyday world. If the "Oriole" is Art, the "Humming Bird" is Life. Poet to fellow poet, Dickinson offers the two options to Helen Hunt Jackson as if to ask, "Must one choose? If one must, which is best?"

Some decisions are not irrevocable. Dickinson had refused faith in her youth, but when at length she began to believe, God was there, unchanged and ready to accept her. Yet other decisions cannot be retrieved. Time as we know it moves only forward, and the woman who had poured all of her passions into shaping the Word could never return to the past and begin again, selecting Life over Art. Emily Dickinson's final years gave her ample time to ponder the choices she had made. Sometimes there were moments of surpassing satisfaction. "The sweet Acclamation of Death," she wrote of

George Eliot; "There is no Trumpet like the Tomb."[5] Yet since the English novelist had died in 1880 and the note to Higginson that contains this sentiment was written in April 1886, Emily Dickinson probably had her own impending death in mind—death and the posthumous fame she seems confidently to have expected.

Although she never lost her faculties, she was weak at the end, and many thoughts crowded in upon her. God was much in her mind. She recollected her time of wrestling with the Lord. "Audacity of Bliss," she wrote to Higginson in the spring of 1886 when she knew that she was dying; "said Jacob to the Angel, 'I will not let thee go except I bless thee'—Pugilist and Poet, Jacob was correct—."[6] In May 1886, when Higginson himself was briefly ill, Dickinson wrote a cryptic note: "Deity—does he live now? / My friend— does he breathe?" Did she mean to inquire after Higginson's health? His faith? His confidence in her poetry? None can know, for it was her last letter to him. But the very last letter she wrote was addressed to the Norcross cousins, and its meaning is entirely clear. Dickinson had read Hugh Conway's sentimental, spiritual novel, *Called Back,* and this note was an expression of confidence about the realm that awaited her.

May, 1886

Little Cousins,

    Called back.

      Emily.[7]

———————

The end came swiftly and with little pain. On Thursday, May 13, Vinnie sent for Austin; Emily had slipped into unconsciousness at ten in the morning, and Dr. Bigelow spent most of the day with her because she was suffering convulsions. By Friday, still unconscious, she had lapsed into the death rattle that signaled doom. On Saturday, May 15, Austin wrote in his diary:

It was settled before morning broke that Emily would not wake again this side.

The day was awful. She ceased to breathe that terrible breathing just before the whistles sounded for six.

Mrs Montague and Mrs Jameson were sitting with Vin.

I was near by.[8]

As she had when Father died, Vinnie acted with composure despite her profound grief. Austin was more visibly shaken. On Tuesday, May 18, an obituary appeared on the editorial page of the Springfield *Republican.* Though it was not signed, it had been composed by Susan Dickinson.

The death of Miss Emily Dickinson, daughter of the late Edward Dickinson, at Amherst on Saturday, makes another sad inroad on the small circle so long occupying the old family mansion. . . . Very few in the village, except among the older inhabitants, knew Miss Emily personally, although the facts of her seclusion and her intellectual brilliancy were familiar Amherst traditions. . . . As she passed on in life, her sensitive nature shrank from much personal contact with the world, and more and more turned to her own large wealth of individual resources for companionship. . . . Not disappointed with the world, not an invalid until within the past two years, not from any lack of sympathy, not because she was insufficient for any mental work or social career—her endowments being so exceptional—but the "mesh of her soul," . . . was too rare, and the sacred quiet of her own home proved the fit atmosphere for her worth and work. . . .

. . . To her life was rich, and all aglow with God and immortality. With no creed, no formulated faith, hardly knowing the names of dogmas, she walked this life with the gentleness and reverence of old saints, with the firm step of martyrs who sing while they suffer.[9]

Already, a gentle myth-making had begun.

Emily Dickinson was buried on Wednesday, May 19, 1886. Thomas Wentworth Higginson came to Amherst for the funeral; it was but the third time he had ever seen his long-time correspondent. Her body, dressed in white, was laid in a white casket, with violets and ground pine over it. "The grass of the lawn was full of buttercups and violet & wild geranium," Higginson noted in his diary. The poet was fifty-five when she died, but the rich auburn hair and creamy skin had changed very little since her girlhood days. "She . . . looked 30," Higginson wrote with some astonishment, "not a gray hair or wrinkle, & perfect peace on the beautiful brow."[10] Higginson read aloud from the poems of Emily Brontë: "Last Lines." Emily Dickinson's casket was carried out the back door, through the yard and between the hedges, and across the meadow to the graveyard. On a bright May day filled with so strong a scent of apple blossoms that many mourners remarked it, she was laid to rest next to Mother and Father.

Except for the housekeeper Maggie Maher, Vinnie was alone now in the big house. Emily had always liked dogs and for a while had owned an enormous dog named Carlo; however, to her sister's distress, Vinnie loved cats. After Emily's death, Vinnie's cat population could be allowed to grow at its leisure, and little by little the number increased to perhaps thirty who padded through the darkened rooms. Always something of an eccentric in her later years, Vinnie became fanatic once her sister had died. She was obsessed to see that the poetry was printed, turning first to Sue and then to Mabel Loomis Todd for assistance. She grew quarrelsome, petty over matters of money and property, and eventually litigious. Millicent Todd Bingham later recollected childhood visits to the old Dickinson Homestead after Emily Dickinson's death. Lavinia could not have been very elderly, perhaps not yet sixty, yet she had become a frightful parody of the pretty, plump, flirtatious, affectionate girl who had sat on Joseph Lyman's lap and taken the combs out of her hair.

There she sat in her apple-green kitchen, or on the sheltered back porch, an uncompromising, slender little figure in a black cashmere dress made in the style of the sixties. The knife-pleatings which adorned it fascinated me. Her sour, shriveled face with its long nose was wrinkled like a witch of the fairytale, her hands twisted and knotted like the faggots in the wood box. But her hair, her marvelous dark hair streaked with gray, seemed to concentrate all the juices of her wizened body—heavy, luxuriant, the focus of interest in her person. Sometimes it was tied in a sort of bow-knot on the back of her head, held fast by two large pins shoved in from either side. But often she sat there with it hanging, while with her gnarled hands, outspread fingers rigidly extended, she thrust through it slowly, caressing it from root to farthest tip. Pussy sat near by washing her face, and fat Maggie billowed about the kitchen as Miss Vinnie sat slowly combing her hair with her knotty fingers. . . .

Sometimes she would open the door into the dining-room, windows always shut, inner blinds so nearly closed that the pattern of the dark-blue china on the sideboard could hardly be distinguished—the design an old-fashioned ship in a strange harbor, called "The Landing of Lafayette."[11]

At first friendly to Mabel Loomis Todd, Vinnie gradually allied herself with Sue and turned against the young woman who had become Austin's mistress. Vinnie was a bitter old woman; Sue was strong-willed and persuasive; and the Dickinsons' first loyalty had always been to the family.

After Emily, Austin was the next to die. A tall man, impeccably dressed, still wearing a startling shock of copper-red hair, he was a dignified and imposing presence to the end. Yet he did not have the will to seize happiness. The marriage to Sue had grown steadily more strained, and his affair with Mabel Loomis Todd, begun in 1882, continued until his death. Much of Amherst seems to have known about it, and it became a source of profound humiliation for Sue. Mabel seems to have been willing to go away with him. She even demanded some sort of resolution in the summer of 1892, and Austin wrote the draft of a letter to a friend in Omaha, inquiring about the possibility of establishing himself there. But there is no way of knowing even so much as whether the letter was written in final form and sent off. Infected with the familial reluctance to leave this little New England village, Austin juggled his relationships until death made the decision for him in August 1895.

Vinnie lived in the Brick House until her death in 1899, and Sue lived with her grown children just next door. Ned became engaged, but died in 1898 before marrying. With Austin dead, Gilbert dead in childhood, and Ned dead without issue, the House founded by Edward Dickinson was left without a male heir to carry its name forward. Martha Dickinson married, but she bore no children; when she died in 1943, all of Edward's descendants were gone, and the line was ended.

The first volume of Emily Dickinson's *Poems,* edited jointly by Mabel Loomis Todd and T. W. Higginson, was published in November 1890; it had gone through eleven printings by the end of 1892. In November 1891 a second volume of *Poems* was published, and by 1893 this had gone into its own fifth printing. Well before the third volume of *Poems* came out in 1896, Emily Dickinson and her poetry had received worldwide attention. The stories told by the good citizens of Amherst who claimed to have "known the truth" about her had already become fabulous. More than one person was willing to divulge the name of the man for whom she had renounced the world and turned to poetry; the problem was that several *different* names were whispered confidentially in this context. More than a decade after Vinnie's death, the Brick House was purchased by the Parke family, and the daughters can still remember childhood dinners that were interrupted by people peering into the windows—wanting to know what Emily Dickinson's home was like.

In the hundredth year after Dickinson's death, Amherst College graduated no more than one or two students who went into the ministry. No longer an outpost of latter-day Puritanism, Amherst College trains young men and young women who will take their places in law, business, medicine, and teaching. Though it is still situated upon a hill, it has become a thoroughly secular institution. Dickinson's poetry is sometimes perceived as an echo of New England's religious past; yet it is often hailed as the first example of "modernism," too, for poetry in America had already begun to change by 1886, and the great poets who came after Emily Dickinson were forced to create their art in a world where God no longer held sway. Amherst College owns the Brick House and allows visitors to be guided through it once or twice a week. The townspeople all refer to it as "the Dickinson House"— "the *Emily* Dickinson House"—and almost no one remembers the role that Samuel Fowler Dickinson played in the founding of the College, or the energy and diligence with which Edward Dickinson set about restoring his father's good name.

Did Emily Dickinson glimpse fame and her own surpassing Power as she lay on the bed facing west and sundown in those last days during the spring of 1886? Did she know that the House would be securely her own? Or were her thoughts entirely upon our Father in Heaven, preparing to receive this prodigal daughter who had expended her whole life upon the poetry that described a long pilgrimage to faith?

Notes

PART ONE ‖ I · Samuel and Edward

1 Emily Dickinson, *The Letters of Emily Dickinson,* ed. Thomas Johnson and Theodora Ward, 3 vols. (Cambridge, Mass.: Harvard University Press, 1958), vol. II, p. 460 (June 1869).

2 Martha Dickinson Bianchi, *Emily Dickinson Face to Face: Unpublished Letters with Notes and Reminiscences* (Hamden, Conn.: Archon Books, 1970), p. 71.

3 Ibid., p. 75.

4 The Brick House on Main Street has been the focus of a good deal of attention, and as with so many other aspects of the Dickinson legend, the discussion has inevitably produced a number of confusions. Richard Sewall reproduces a charcoal sketch in his biography of Emily Dickinson, which is labeled "'The birthplace of Samuel Fowler Dickinson Esq. Amherst Mass.' Charcoal drawing, date and artist unknown" (see Richard B. Sewall, *The Life of Emily Dickinson* [New York: Farrar, Straus and Giroux, 1974], vol. I, opposite p. 34). However, the authoritative history of Amherst offers a different attribution for this farmhouse. On p. 44 of Carpenter and Morehouse, *The History of the Town of Amherst, Massachusetts* (Amherst: Press of Carpenter & Morehouse, 1896), pictures of five houses all appear together. The charcoal sketch, which Sewall identifies as Samuel Fowler Dickinson's birthplace, is here identified as "L. D. Cowles' Old House," and a very modest frame house just above is identified as "Old Dickinson House—(Capt. Daniel's)." W. S. Tyler follows Austin Dickinson's story: "When Esq. Dickinson erected his brick house, he removed the wood house which he had previously occupied on the same site to Pleasant Street where it still stands, a small old-fashioned two-story house a little north of the blacksmith shop." The picture in Carpenter and Morehouse may be of this frame house *after* the move. See W. S. Tyler, *History of Amherst College During Its First Half Century* (Springfield, Mass.: Clark W. Bryan and Company, 1873), p. 31.

When the Brick House was first built, it had only three chimneys and no cupola; in 1855 two additional chimneys and the cupola were added as part of Edward's extensive renovation. During the time between 1813 and 1855, the house went through a number of metamorphoses, but the description given in the text is of the basic home—the house more or less as it exists today and as it probably was originally. At some time the basic brick house had a substantial clapboard wing on the western side; a sketch of the house on the letterhead used by D. Mack, Jr., and Son (who purchased the building in 1833) shows the center of Amherst and, in the distance, the Dickinson home with this wing. In 1855, the wing was removed. A reproduction of the sketch on the letterhead can be found in *Essays on Amherst's History,* ed. Theodore P. Greene (Amherst: The Vista Trust, 1978), p. 62.

5 *Reunion of the Dickinson Family at Amherst, Massachusetts, August 8th and 9th, 1883* (Binghamton, N.Y.: Binghamton Press, 1884), p. 174. See n. 42 to Part Three, Section I, below.

6 Tyler, *History,* p. 119. For a similar account, see Edward Hitchcock, *Reminiscences of Amherst College* (Northampton, Mass.: Bridgman & Childs, 1863), p. 5.

7 Heman Humphrey, *Revival: Sketches and Manual* (New York: American Tract Society, 1859), p. 114.

8 Bianchi, *Face,* pp. 76–77.

9 Tyler, *History,* p. 120.

10 His Latin oration at Dartmouth had been titled *De administrationis civilis et morum natura: Atque momento eorum mutae relationis* (The Nature of Civil Government and Manners: Their Mutual Relationship and Influence). Two years later, in 1797, he delivered a reworked version of this address at the Fourth of July celebrations in Belchertown. Here his evocation of America's birth suggests something of the speaker's own sense of melodrama: "This is the day, which calls forth the sublime feelings of independence, and the congenial flow of American souls. We do not celebrate the romance of departed heroes, but the atchievements [*sic*] of our fathers. We do not celebrate the feasts of heathen Gods, but the anniversary of reason. We do not commemorate the building of thrones, or the coronation of Kings; but, we commemorate *the nativity of a nation,* that memorable day, on which three million people were born to freedom! Let us remember, we are no longer subjects of ghastly tyranny; but the citizens of an unalienable [*sic*] commonwealth!" (Samuel Fowler Dickinson, *An Oration in Celebration of American Independence* [Northampton, Mass.: William Butler, 1797], p. 18. A copy of this address may be found in the Dickinson Collection of the Jones Library in Amherst.)

11 The record of Samuel Fowler Dickinson's tenure in office can be found in Carpenter & Morehouse, *Town of Amherst.* Records of the Temperance Society, of the local Whigs, and of the Amherst town meetings can be found in the Boltwood Collection of the Jones Library (although Carpenter & Morehouse print minutes of the town meetings as an appendix, the minutes in the Boltwood Collection are more complete). It is probably impossible at so late a date to reconstruct the activities of this tireless man. Greene notes some activities; Martha Dickinson Bianchi notes others; and the records of the societies to which he belonged mention others.

12 See Frederick Tuckerman, *Amherst Academy* (Amherst: Printed for the Trustees, 1929), p. 10. Actually, scholars disagree about just who originated the idea for the Amherst Academy. All agree that Samuel Fowler Dickinson was among the originators; Tuckerman (the most reliable on this count) asserts, "The original subscription was started, it appears, by Samuel Fowler Dickinson and Hezekiah Wright Strong" (p. 11). He then quotes a letter from Strong, however, asserting that he and he alone had begun the subscription for the Academy.

13 Ibid., pp. 64, 104.

14 Tyler, *History,* pp. 40, 41.

15 Ibid. Tyler is quoting from Noah Webster's notes of the proceedings. Italics mine.

16 Ibid., p. 42. Hitchcock claims that the transformation of the original plan was hatched by Colonel Graves and Samuel Fowler Dickinson together, and that of the two, Dickinson was the more moderate: "Col. Graves was ardent and impulsive, and thought to be visionary, so that it needed the cooler and more practical judgment of Mr. Dickinson to prevent extravagance in opinion and give confidence to the public" (*Reminiscences,* p. 6). Tyler, however, gives a different account: "The enlargement of the plan from a mere Professorship in Amherst Academy into a separate Collegiate Institution was expressly owing to Mr. Dickinson's suggestion and influence" (*History,* p. 120).

17 Tyler, *History,* p. 49. See pp. 47–49.

18 Ibid., p. 43. Writing in 1873, Tyler recognizes the audacity involved in such a commitment. "In reviewing this document, we can not but be impressed with the conviction that its authors were men not only of warm hearts and high religious aims, but of large views. . . . That they were also men of fervid zeal, strong faith, moral courage and holy boldness, no one has ever denied. If any proof were necessary, it would be found even to demonstration in the very fact that they dared to undertake such an enterprise in that age, and not only undertook, but achieved it. It was another thing to raise a permanent fund of fifty thousands dollars for a literary institution in that day from what it is in our day. It would be easier to raise half a million or a million now. It is a common affair now. Then, nothing of the kind had ever been attempted. It was an original idea, and a grand one, and a bold one." (Ibid., pp. 45–46.) Our

judgment today must be sharpened by considering (again) that *Tyler* was writing in 1873. It would be difficult to define an equivalent project today!

19 All of the several historians of Amherst College make it clear that the Trustees in Amherst made every effort to cooperate with Williams, that they informed the Williams College Trustees of their intentions and offered to merge with that college should a merger prove more feasible than the maintenance of two separate colleges. See Heman Humphrey, *Sketches of the Early History of Amherst College* (Northampton, Mass.: At the request of the Trustees of Amherst College, 1905), p. 10 ff. See also Tyler, pp. 51–61.

20 See Thomas Le Duc, *Piety and Intellect at Amherst College* (New York: Columbia University Press, 1946). See also Early Historical Miscellany, "Papers of J. Leland," bound manuscripts for Amherst College.

21 Tyler, *History,* p. 63.

22 Theodore Baird in Greene, *Essays,* p. 114.

23 The legislature questioned the validity of the pledges, and at the same time the Trustees of Williams College urged subscribers to withdraw their money. Donors began to come forward to retract their promises, claiming that they had been led to believe that the new college intended incorporation with Williams. Suddenly, the entire fifty-thousand-dollar pledge was cast into doubt. It is unlikely that any of these recanters believed that they had actually received such assurances. What happened was simply that Williams College had put pressure on Trinitarians loyal to its cause, arguing that the establishment of Amherst College would spell the doom of Williams College. In fact, the president and Trustees of Williams had been considering a relocation almost from the time the College opened, and the Amherst / Northampton area was one likely spot for migration. If Amherst College were to become well established in this region, Williams College could no longer relocate within Massachusetts: the Unitarians dominated in the east; Amherst College would dominate in the central area. This opposition from Williams College was, in the long run, probably even more firmly entrenched than Unitarian opposition, and Edward Dickinson would still encounter it during the late 1830s when he attempted to obtain funds from the commonwealth of Massachusetts for Amherst College.

24 Baird in Greene, *Essays,* p. 117. See also Humphrey, *Sketches;* Bianchi, *Face,* p. 77.

25 Tyler, *History,* p. 121. In the first of these two citations, Tyler is quoting from one of the ministers who regularly came together in Amherst during this period to pray for the success of the new college.

What Samuel Dickinson did was systematically to mortgage his own property against the possibility that a donor would be found. Over and over again, no donor *was* found. Little by little, then, all his possessions were forfeited. Many men contributed time and money to the new college, but Tyler makes it clear that this continued willingness on Samuel Dickinson's part to sacrifice all his worldly possessions made a crucial, perhaps necessary difference. "With all the zeal and efforts of numerous friends and benefactors, the work would often have stopped, had [Squire Dickinson] not pledged his property till the money could be raised" (Ibid., p. 121).

26 February 9, 1821, the Dickinson family correspondence, Houghton Library, Harvard University. Hereafter, documents from this archive will be identified as "Dickinson Papers, HCL."

27 Dickinson Papers, HCL. Sewall asserts that Edward Dickinson spent his first year of college at Amherst and then went down to Yale (*Life,* vol. I, p. 45). The chronology is confusing, and Sewall fails to note the discontinuities. However, if the dates of Samuel Fowler Dickinson, Sr.'s letters to Edward are correlated with those of the letters between Edward and his brothers and sisters, it is possible to piece together the dates of a rather more interrupted college career with some precision.

28 July 22, 1821; Sept. 4, 1821, Dickinson Papers, HCL.

29 Tyler, *History*, p. 121.

30 February 10, 1823, Dickinson Papers, HCL.

31 Millicent Todd Bingham, *Emily Dickinson's Home* (New York: Dover Publications, 1967), p. 492. In September 1821, William was in Edward's corner in the dispute over Father's wish that the older brother return to Amherst. "I know how it is *exactly,*" he wrote on September 25; "you have no need to tell me. It is just like this. I'm Mad to think of it. In the first place Col. Graves [a friend of Samuel Fowler Dickinson's and another of the founders of Amherst College] comes in Good Morning Mr. Dickinson. Very fine morning Sir. (Sir very plain) Well Sir" (Dickinson Papers, HCL).

32 February 23, 1831, Dickinson Papers, HCL. Still, the pull of the Homestead on Main Street was great, even for this angry young man. Four years later, after the Brick House had been sold, the boys' sister Catherine Dickinson Sweetser wrote Edward that Samuel Fowler, Jr., had sounded General Mack out about the possibility of buying it back. The bargain was never struck, but Samuel Dickinson, Sr., evidently heard of the proposal and rejected it. Father felt, Catherine says, that "there would be nothing for him to do in Amherst—he would find his place occupied by others—& if he had nothing to do—he would be unhappy as ever" (letter from Catherine Dickinson to Edward, May 12, 1835, Dickinson Papers, HCL). Samuel Fowler, Jr.'s wife, Susan, spent some time in Amherst in the spring of 1852, and he may have vacationed there himself, although if he did, there is no record of it.

33 On August 28, 1834, Joseph A. Sweetser (soon to become the husband of Edward's sister Catherine) wrote to Edward: "I asked [Timothy Dickinson, Edward's brother] if the hope of a good situation in New York next spring would be any inducement for him to return and spend the winter with Mr. Pitkin. He replied that he should be laughed at for returning now, and *he had rather die than be laughed at.* . . . You may judge from this that I have exerted influence to induce him to return. It can do no good he is determined and you know enough of your own family to know what that word means with them." (Dickinson Papers, HCL.) Edward kept in touch with these brothers through J. A. Sweetser, who saw them from time to time—and through Catherine, who seems to have made a point of keeping communications open. The youngest brother, Frederick, did not follow his father west; instead, he became Edward's charge and completed his education at Amherst College. (Jay Leyda, *The Years and Hours of Emily Dickinson,* 2 vols. [New Haven: Yale University Press, 1960], vol. I, p. 36.)

34 Letters Concerning the Postmaster Dispute, Dickinson Papers, HCL.

35 A copy of this document may be found in the Boltwood Collection of the Jones Library.

36 Dickinson Papers, HCL.

37 Dickinson Papers, HCL.

38 In Edward Dickinson's letter to Emily Norcross of December 19, 1827, he gives a rather complete description of the house: "Front room below, 17 ft. long, & 15 ft. 2 inches wide—4 windows & blinds. 2 Front chambers—17 ft. long—15 ft. & 4 inches wide—4 windows in each. Dining room, about the same size—2 windows. The bed-room chambers, large enough." (Dickinson Papers, HCL.) In a later letter (March 19, 1828), he described the color scheme as well. The Bible inscriptions are in the Dickinson Papers, HCL.

39 An account of the complicated division of the house may be found in book 63 (1830) in the Hampshire County Registry of Deeds (in Northampton, Mass.). In 1830 Edward Dickinson purchased, then immediately sold back, the western portion of the Homestead. In 1831, he purchased the western acre of the home lot (see book 67) but immediately sold it to Solomon and Almira Eastman (book 67). Evidently this western lot was held for Edward Dickinson, who bought it again sometime during June 1834. An account of these transactions may also be found in the archives of the Jones Library.

40 W. A. Dickinson, "Representative Men of the Parish," in *An Historical Review: 150th Anni-*

versary of the First Church of Christ in Amherst, Massachusetts, August 8th and 9th, 1889 (Amherst: Press of the *Amherst Record,* 1890), see p. 63. Tyler says that Samuel Fowler Dickinson was offered a job as "Steward with the oversight and general management of the grounds" (*History,* p. 212), a description vague enough to cover either sort of work. Sewall describes him as having "the direction of the manual labor required of the students" (*Life,* vol. I, p. 37). Leyda records that on January 5, 1833, Samuel Fowler Dickinson came to Cincinnati "to take charge of the Manual Labour Seminary" (vol. I, p. 19), and goes on to quote from a Cincinnati paper that was reprinted in the *Hampshire Gazette* on June 6, 1838: "About five years ago, at the request of the Trustees of the Lane Seminary [Samuel Fowler Dickinson] removed to Walnut Hills, near Cincinnati, and took charge of the financial concerns of that institution" (Leyda, *Years and Hours,* vol. I, p. 20). Lane was not a very big operation when Samuel Dickinson went out there with the Beechers; probably a lot of people did several jobs at once, so that Dickinson might have supervised the manual labor *and* taken care of the books.

41 In March 1833 Lavinia Norcross (Emily Norcross Dickinson's sister) wrote, "I wish very much to hear what your arrangements are for the Spring—what part of the house you occupy" (Dickinson Papers, HCL). That they did make the move is indisputable. Leyda quotes from *Colton's Reminiscences:* "Called, as by direction, on Edward Dickinson, Esq., then occupying the east part of Gen Mack's house" (Leyda, *Years and Hours,* vol. I, p. 60). Colton was not likely to be mistaken; he was pastor of the First Church from 1840 to 1851.

42 Stanley King, *A History of the Endowment of Amherst College* (Amherst: Amherst College, 1950), p. 35. It was during Edward's term as treasurer of Amherst College that the College went through its most arduous financial period after obtaining its charter. When he took office, the College was deeply in debt. His services were many: he went to the Massachusetts state legislature and eventually obtained financial aid there, and Tyler calls him "the best financier in the corporation" (*History,* p. 540). The account in King, pp. 35–66, is usefully circumstantial.

43 Dickinson Papers, HCL.

44 January 5, 1838; January 9, 1838; February 16, 1838. Dickinson Papers, HCL.

45 Edward Dickinson had a much more active public life than his father. A complete account of his activities does not exist, and a definitive compilation would be difficult to put together. He held public office many times. Town-meeting records indicate that he ran for this office or some other, such as the U.S. Congress, virtually every time an opportunity presented itself, sometimes getting only one vote—presumably his own. In 1838, 1839, and 1873 he was a member of the Massachusetts House of Representatives; he served in the state Senate in 1842 and 1843; he was a member of the Massachusetts governor's council in 1846 and 1847. He was elected as a Whig to the thirty-third United States Congress (March 4, 1853, to March 3, 1855); and because of his loyalties to the Whig Party he declined to be a candidate for the Republican nomination as lieutenant governor in 1861. His political fortunes would undoubtedly have been better if he had consented, as he did not, to make his peace with the new Republican Party. He was Whig at a time when that old-fashioned party was in its final hours as a force in American politics; but it was the party of his father, and he never deserted it. (When he went to the Massachusetts legislature in 1873, he went as an Independent.) Millicent Todd Bingham, in *Emily Dickinson's Home,* provides a full account of his one term in Congress. Although this narrative of his activities in Washington makes for surprisingly slow reading, it is useful, for it captures something of the nature of Edward Dickinson's limitations, his unwillingness or his inability to throw himself into the center of political activity, and his failure to emerge as a leader among strong men.

In Amherst, he was in the Temperance League and held a number of local offices. A partial list includes: justice of the peace, fire warden, town-meeting moderator, member of the Town

Tomb Committee, Town Hall Committee, High School Committee, and a committee to consider annexations of Pelham, highway surveyor, representative to the Massachusetts General Court. He held many of these offices for several years—some for decades.

As stated earlier, he was treasurer of Amherst College from 1835 to 1873, during its more difficult financial crisis. He was also a Trustee of Amherst Academy from 1835 until his death, an office that included supervision of financial matters, hiring and firing of faculty, even supervision of curriculum.

He was, in addition, an immensely active (and financially successful) lawyer, often taking his cases before the county seat in Northampton or traveling to Greenfield, Pelham, Holyoke, and Springfield on legal business. On January 27, 1854, he was admitted to practice before the Supreme Court of the United States.

In sum, it is not surprising to discover that the only day of the week that Edward Dickinson could be assured of spending at home was Sunday; perhaps it is surprising that he could afford even that day.

46 Quoted by Bingham, *Home*, p. 329.

47 *The Lyman Letters: New Light on Emily Dickinson and Her Family,* ed. Richard B. Sewall (Amherst: University of Massachusetts Press, 1965), pp. 70–71. According to Sewall, this letter dates from the mid-1860s.

48 August 18, 1870, Dickinson, *Letters,* vol. II., p. 473.

49 June 20, 1852; ibid., vol. I, p. 213; Spring, 1876; vol. II, p. 551.

50 May 1838, Dickinson Papers, HCL.

51 Samuel Fowler Dickinson (Chairman), Report of Committee on the Burying Ground (December 10, 1832), unpublished manuscript, Amherst Town Engineer's Office.

P A R T   O N E ‖ *II · Mother and Father*

1 April 10, 1826, Dickinson Papers, HCL. This itemized description of "womanly qualities" had a flattering tone that echoed, loosely and imperfectly, some of the notions of femininity inherent in "The Cult of True Womanhood."

During the nineteenth century, as men's and women's worlds grew increasingly separated and isolated from each other, a myth grew about "Woman's Nature" and "Woman's Role." Nancy F. Cott summarizes the essential elements of this notion: according to the "'cult' (it might almost be called a social ethic), mother, father, and children grouped together in the private household ruled the transmission of culture, the maintenance of social stability, and the pursuit of happiness. . . . The importance given to women's roles as wives, mothers, and mistresses of household was unprecedented." (Nancy F. Cott, *The Bonds of Womanhood* [New Haven: Yale University Press, 1977], pp. 1–2.) One can see how Edward's image of the "selfless wife" would comport with this notion, and Cott quotes several sources (an excerpt from *Godey's Lady's Book* on page 73, for example) that depict women in ways that seem similar to Edward's fantasies. However, several things must be said to clarify this issue, for the image of marriage Edward elaborated in his courtship of Emily Norcross bears little *real* relationship to the "Cult."

"The Cult of True Womanhood" did not portray women as nonentities whose emotions were simply vacuous. Quite the contrary, it described a world of *balanced but opposite powers:* men would move in the harsh, often corrupt world of business, and their power would be located there; women's power, which was primarily in the realm of emotions or sentiment, would be exercised within the home, but it would not be limited to the home. Naturally, the husband's *emotional* center would be in the domestic world (which was dominated by the values of his wife); insofar as the wife's emotions exercised an effect upon her husband, the values she cherished might be passed, through him, into the external world of society at large. The wife's power was, therefore, postulated as very great, and no prospective husband who grasped the notions of "The Cult of True Womanhood" and believed them could ever say, as Edward did, that his "whole soul [would be engaged] in [his] business"! Such a statement would be sacrilege. There are several excellent discussions of the "Cult"; I will mention only two. The full, classic statement is in Barbara Welter, *Dimity Convictions: The American Woman in the Nineteenth Century* (Athens, Ohio: Ohio University Press, 1976). A brilliant elaboration may be found in Ann Douglas, *The Feminization of American Culture* (New York: Alfred A. Knopf, 1977).

After all this has been said, it seems clear that rural Amherst in the 1820s was not yet under the full sway of the "Cult," perhaps because men's and women's spheres were not entirely separated there. In any case, to get some balance of the picture Edward gives of his "requirements" for marriage, one might look at two other marriages, that of Emily Norcross's beloved sister, Lavinia, and that of Edward's friend Edward Hitchcock. Lavinia (after whom the second Dickinson daughter was named) fell deeply in love with her first cousin, Loring Norcross. The family all disapproved of their marriage—Edward Dickinson was among those who most strongly disapproved. Nonetheless, the couple married, had three children (only two of whom survived to adulthood), and lived very happily together. The letters from both Loring and Lavinia to the Edward Dickinsons reveal a kind of easy emotional closeness which was very different from Edward and Emily's relationship. Nor was a wife always excluded from a husband's work. The distinguished scientist Edward Hitchcock, who had come as professor to Amherst College in 1825 and was its president from 1845 to 1854, worked closely with his wife throughout his career. She was a superb draftsman, and "her pencil illustrated all his books, and hung the walls of his lecture-rooms with diagrams" (W. S. Tyler, *History of Amherst College During Its First Half Century* [Springfield, Mass.: Clark W. Bryan and Company, 1873], p. 364). These examples prove nothing in general, but they do suggest that if Edward Dickinson had chosen to establish a more intimate, more comradely relationship with a wife, he would at the very least not have been remarkable for doing so in the Amherst to which Emily Norcross moved in 1828.

2 June 4, 1826, Dickinson Papers, HCL.

3 March 19, 1828, Dickinson Papers, HCL.

4 Ellen K. Rothman, *Hands and Hearts* (New York: Basic Books, 1984), p. 43. This work is useful throughout. It corroborates the findings of Carl N. Degler, *At Odds: Women and the Family in America from the Revolution to the Present* (New York: Oxford University Press, 1980). So, for example, Degler cites several correspondences between young women and young men contemplating marriage: "the references to personal happiness [in their letters] are significant, for they reveal the goal behind the couple's freedom of choice. Southgate put the matter quite baldly, she thought her suitor 'better calculated to promote my happiness than any person I have yet seen'" (p. 13). And "Contrary to what is sometimes thought about the Victorian years, courtship did not have to be formal, excessively restricted, or even chaperoned. Not until late in the 19th century and then only among the urban upper classes was the European practice of chaperoning at all well known. . . . If we leave aside premarital sexual experience as a measure of the freedom of courtship, then the Victorian courtship is far from staid. . . . Middle- and lower-class women moved about not only without chaperones, but also with a certain amount of abandon. . . . It was not unusual for a young woman to accompany a young man on fishing trips, with no one else along, or to accept invitations for walks together, discussing personal matters" (p. 20). James Reed, *From Private Vice to Public Virtue* (New York: Basic Books, 1978), confirms these "liberal" views of sexual intimacy. Citing a diary from 1860 (as revealing typical sexual mores between courting couples),

Reed says that Ward's "diary reveals that they were allowed a surprising amount of time alone together. Heavy letter writing was followed by heavy petting." After Ward had been going steady with Miss Vought for about six months, he noted: "Friday evening the girl and I had a very sweet time. I kissed her on her soft breasts, and took many liberties with her sweet person, and we are going to stop" (p. 30). This information is useful not only for evaluating the courtship between Edward Dickinson and Emily Norcross, but also as a measure of the freedom their daughters probably had (for a chief occupation among courting couples in mid-nineteenth-century Amherst was walking or riding through the Pelham Hills, a private enough activity).

5 Dickinson Papers, HCL.

6 April 18, 1828, ibid.

7 Alfred Ely in the *Hampden Journal and Advertizer,* September 16, 1829, quoted by Jay Leyda, *The Years and Hours of Emily Dickinson* (New Haven: Yale University Press, 1960), p. 11.

8 In her last letters, Emily Norcross's anger at Edward is quite palpable, though never directly expressed as such. She taunts him with her excursions to lectures and concerts, and she especially nettles him by telling him about the attentions paid to her by "Mr. Chapman": "I conclude you do wish me to cultivate my musical powers," she writes on December 25, 1827, "but I have as yet [not] attended the Society to which you refered [*sic*]. . . . I will observe to you that I last evening commenced a course of lectures on American History—anything for a variety I suppose you admit[.] Mr. Woodbridge is our Lecturer from Ware. . . . Mr. Chapman was so polite as to call upon us with the honourable gentleman after the lecture last evening. And do you not suppose that I was quite captivated with him, but no more of this." (Dickinson Papers, HCL.) To the enraged letter Edward writes back, she replies on February 5, 1828 (only three months before their wedding), "I think your sentiments correct and I would hope not to deviate from them *should I become a subject to your authority*" (Dickinson Papers, HCL; italics mine). Although Edward's letters during the last eight or nine months of the courtship are filled with anger at Emily Norcross's behavior, it is also the case that he voices a certain concern for her—most often expressed as anxiety lest she catch cold (while going out in the evening to attend these various lectures and parties). The anxiety has a formulaic quality ("you know I have the right to be concerned for your welfare, now"), and it is difficult to tell by this point in the exchange how much Edward was authentically worried and how much his worry was an indirect expression of *his* anger (i.e., really meaning, "If you don't stop this unsuitable behavior you'll catch your death of cold, and that's what you deserve"). But he often chides her—usually without humor and almost always without affection.

The failures of communication in their letters are so many that they are difficult to disentangle. One clarification can be made by comparing Edward's *statements* with his *actions.* By the late 1820s, it had become clear that Amherst was not a place where an ambitious man would readily make a fortune: its water power could not support the factories that grew up in New England mill towns, and without even a railroad spur until the middle 1850s, it was isolated from the great urban areas. Men who were impatient with the relatively slow pace of rural business life did not remain in Amherst: they moved to Boston, New York, or some other large Eastern city, or they moved west. The 1820s and 1830s witnessed a vast migration out of Amherst—floods of sons and young married couples, spurred by tales of opportunities elsewhere, left parents and friends behind in a rush toward prosperity and success. Edward's decision to remain in Amherst seemed to give one kind of clear signal: that his commitment to business was not so complete that it really would engross all of his time and attention. If his rhetoric strongly articulated the opposite, a prospective wife might easily make the mistake of failing to comprehend the extent to which his life would be different from that of other Amherst men. Carpenter and Morehouse, *The History of the Town of Amherst, Massachusetts* (Amherst: Press of Carpenter & Morehouse, 1896), give an account of the shifts in Amherst business, but perhaps the best account is given in an unpublished Amherst College honors thesis, "The Minds of Hands: Working People of Amherst in the Mid-Nineteenth Century," by Stephen Aron (April 1982).

9 Dickinson Papers, HCL.

10 Ibid.

11 Ibid.

12 Ibid.

13 Millicent Todd Bingham, *Emily Dickinson's Home* (New York: Dover Publications, 1967), p. 4.

14 Millicent Todd Bingham, *Ancestors' Brocedes: The Literary Debut of Emily Dickinson* (New York and London: Harper Brothers, 1945), p. 232.

15 John Cody, *After Great Pain* (Cambridge, Mass.: Harvard University Press, 1971), p. 51. Cody's work is, of course, of great interest to any biographer-critic. Many of his insights seem quite valid. To take the case in point, there certainly was a disruption of *some* sort between Emily Dickinson and her mother. My own reaction to Cody's work is complicated. Many of his insights strike me as valid—even if his elaboration of these insights does not. More important, however, he seems not at all to understand that Emily Dickinson's poetry is a highly complex, tightly controlled work of art that operates within finely tuned conventions common to her time and place. Cody sees Emily Dickinson as a "patient"—and all of her poetry becomes evidence for a diagnosis of her "illness." I would prefer to see her as an artist (like many artists, one with a complicated and often uneasy inner life)—and the various components of her life become relevant insofar as they help us to understand and appreciate her art.

16 Emily Dickinson, *The Letters of Emily Dickinson,* ed. Thomas Johnson and Theodora Ward (Cambridge, Mass.: Harvard University Press, 1958), vol. I, pp. 55, 150–51 (October 25, 1851), 244 (April 21, 1853), 161 (December 15, 1851), 203 (late April 1852), vol. II, p. 604 (early 1878).

17 Bingham, *Home,* pp. 413, 5.

18 Dickinson, *Letters,* vol. II, pp. 404 (April 25, 1862), 475, 517–18 (January 1874).

19 Richard W. Wertz and Dorothy C. Wertz, *Lying-In: A History of Childbirth in America* (New York: Schocken Books, 1977), p. 34.

20 Ibid., p. 37.

21 Ibid., p. 66.

22 Ibid., pp. 68–69.

23 George Frisbie Whicher, *This Was a Poet* (New York: Charles Scribner's Sons, 1938), p. 28.

24 See Lewis O. Saum, "Death in the Popular Mind of Pre–Civil War America," *American Quarterly,* vol. XXVI, no. 5 (December 1974), p. 485. "Very frequently the family list that ran from husband and wife through the children in order of age would end with 'anonymous,' and 'not named' or 'unnamed.' Infants so designated often had attained several months, sometimes over a year of age. In keeping with this practice J. S. Brown of Phillips, Maine, concluded a letter-listing of the names and ages of his seven children [in 1850] with one who was 'a year old has no name yet.' . . . George and Fidelia Baldwin . . . indulged in the happiness that came with their healthy new baby; 'but how long we shal be allowed to keep him is inknown to us.' This same letter referred to a previous child they had lost, and that fact as well as the general mood probably accounts for their use of a fairly common designation for the new arrival—the 'little stranger.'" This entire special issue of *American Quarterly* ("Death in America") is very useful in understanding Dickinson's world.

25 Frederick C. Warner, "List of Births Attended, 1805–1833, by Dr. Isaac G. Cutler of Amherst," *Detroit Society for Genealogical Research Magazine,* vol. 35, no. 1 (Fall 1971), p. 29. But the fact was that in the early nineteenth century in America a woman and her baby were safer with a midwife than with a doctor. Because modesty forbade a man's looking upon a

woman's genitals, there was no obstetrical training until late in the century. The first birth a
doctor might witness was likely to be the first he had been called upon to assist. During most
of the early nineteenth century, the doctors who gradually replaced midwives gave inferior
service to the women they tended. "At mid-century modesty and fear of patients' disapproval
blocked clinical training in midwifery even in hospitals. In Boston in 1845 Doctors John C.
Warren and Jacob Bigelow of the Massachusetts General Hospital requested a committee to
consider adding a maternity wing to the hospital so that medical students might no longer be
deprived of clinical training and thus 'be called to their first case without ever having seen a
delivery or possessing more knowledge of the science than can be gathered from books.' The
committee agreed to the wisdom of the proposal but rejected it. . . . The committee explained
why clinical training was impossible and in doing so revealed a clear sense that the hospital
could not change the society's classificatory scheme for women since its status came from
patronage by the respectable." (Wertz and Wertz, *Lying-In,* p. 87.)

26 Wertz and Wertz, *Lying-In,* pp. 79–80.
27 February 12, 1829, Dickinson Papers, HCL.
28 Dickinson Papers, HCL.
29 June 7, 1829, ibid.
30 Dickinson Papers, HCL.
31 Lavinia Norcross describes the night watches over Amanda in 1833; many years afterward,
Susan Dickinson, Austin's wife, gives a humorous but telling account from her own youth:
"Watching the sick would hardly be included in nocturnal pleasures, but it was considered,
as I look back upon it, too natural a duty to even speak of, much less question as a suitable
dissipation. Young and old took the place of night watchers in all emergencies. Quite early in
life I showed a knack with the sick and tried my powers somewhat enthusiastically. A night
of length and stillness passed in the sick room of Mrs. Moore, the widow of the first President
of the college, is cut upon my memory like a steel engraving. She lived in what came to be
known as the Bentley house. . . . In the manner of the time, the plan of it was four square
rooms and a wide, long hall, unwarmed and uncarpeted. As my vigil began at eight o'clock
and 'the hired girl' was entirely banished at that early hour, the solitude of the lonely May
night, both within and without, began to tell upon my nerves before midnight. My patient
was comfortably convalescent so that I was not braced by anxiety for her case. I will own I
was habitually called a 'fraid cat' by my own family. . . . Such being my temperament, I was
chilled to the marrow to find I must go down to the kitchen for broth for my patient. . . . I
somehow lived through this, and reached my sick woman's bed with the broth. . . . A narrow
waspish figure, bent and cracked, she did not, to my sixteen-year-old soul, radiate any atmosphere that I loved. But I softened in every emotion when she spoke of her possible demise.
As I heard her say, 'My dear girl, the habiliments of the grave assume an aspect of terror to
me,' I rallied, out of sheer girlish pity, and talked glibly of the joys and certainty of heaven,
and her own personal crown, quoting the scriptures to the point, until I was so fascinated
with my theme I felt ready to fly away to the better world myself. . . . Only once more I
watched and was so scared I withdrew from the ministering angels of that day, forever. . . .
My charge was a very old woman slowly recovering from a long illness, whom I had never
seen before, who was comfortably fixed in one of the bed rooms. . . . The steady talk of the
clock of time and eternity, the wild scramble of the rats in the wall, the cracking and snapping
of the old house itself, the soft scurry in the grass outside the open window of things I could
not name but worse did imagine. And in between, such stillness! Suddenly a series of curdling
shrieks pierced the darkness and filled the house. It was murder of course, and frozen with
terror I stiffened. But the sick woman faintly whispered, 'It is my daughter. She is subject to
nightmare. You must wake her quickly.' There was only a thin partition between me and those
hellish yells. I could not do it—but I must! My reputation as a watcher was at stake. Shaking
with fright I grasped the iron candlestick—the tallow dripping over my fingers—and fled to

clutch the poor victim, who with wide staring eyes was fast in the grip of her horror. She blessed me for delivering her, but alas! nobody saved me from the most awful night of my life! I never watched again." (Susan G. Dickinson, "Two Generations of Society," in *Essays on Amherst's History*, ed. Theodore P. Greene [Amherst: The Vista Trust, 1978], pp. 179–81.) It is important to note that the account given here is (deliberately) amusing. Watches were seldom funny—even when seen retrospectively.

32 Bingham, *Home*, p. 118.

33 June 7, 1829, Dickinson Papers, HCL.

34 She was so disagreeable that her name eventually became synonymous with displays of ill humor in the family. In later years she "was often referred to in moments of bad temper as 'coming out' in her high-strung grandchildren. If a door was banged—'It's not me—it's my Grandmother Gunn!' was an excuse glibly offered." (Martha Dickinson Bianchi, *Emily Dickinson Face to Face: Unpublished Letters with Notes and Reminiscences* [Hamden, Conn.: Archon Books, 1970], pp. 87–88.) Lucretia Gunn Dickinson's nomadic life after her husband's death is the strongest testimony one could want of her disposition. The children's letters after Samuel Fowler Dickinson's death reflect their sorrow and even more their guilt. Under such circumstances, it would be only natural for me—or several—to welcome the widowed mother. The fact was that no one wanted her. In late September 1839 she wrote querulously to Edward: "I have been hoping to get along without troubling you with my situation but have at last made up my mind[;] it would be best I do not ask to go to your house for I know it is not convenient but perhaps I can stay at your Aunt Irenes. . . . I know my complaints trouble you but what can I do[?] I have no one to look to *but* my Children." In December of the same year she wrote even more piteously: "I am a frail tenement. When I have turns which I frequently do that my life is in iminent [*sic*] danger although it would not prolong my life a moment, yet it would be a satisfaction to be with some of my Children when these seasons occur. . . . I know I am made up of imperfections." (Both letters are in the Dickinson Papers, HCL.) Only after Lucretia Gunn Dickinson died in May 1840 did she cease to be a trial to her children.

Perhaps the oddest thing in this account is Edward's failure to step forward and take her into his family. When other crises arose, he played such a role (when his sister Mary's children were orphaned, for instance, he took responsibility for their welfare, bringing them to Amherst and seeing that they were well taken care of). But in the case of his own mother, this most dutiful of sons silently declined to offer her a home with his family; the animosities were too entrenched, as she herself acknowledged.

35 December 6, 1830, Dickinson Papers, HCL.

36 Richard B. Sewall, *The Life of Emily Dickinson* (New York: Farrar, Straus and Giroux, 1974), vol. I, p. 74.

37 Leyda, *Years and Hours*, vol. I, p. 16.

38 Bingham, *Home*, p. 4. Sewall, following Bingham, makes much the same assertion: "In character and temperament, Emily was a Dickinson; it has been said that all she inherited from her mother was her first name" (*Life*, vol. I, p. 74).

39 June 1, 1831, Dickinson Papers, HCL.

40 See Kenneth S. Robson, "The Role of Eye-to-Eye Contact in Maternal-Infant Attachment," *Journal of Child Psychology and Psychiatry*, vol. 8 (1967), pp. 13–14. See also Daniel Stern, *The First Relationship* (Cambridge, Mass.: Harvard University Press, 1977), p. 109. Stern gives an extended description of such interaction on pp. 2–5. The reader is urged to compare his description with the description on p. 58 of Emily Norcross Dickinson's nervous, ineffectual, hovering attempts at nonverbal "nurturing" behavior. The comparison is necessarily inexact, since Mrs. Dickinson was not ministering to an infant; it is nonetheless suggestive.

41 See Margaret S. Mahler, Fred Pine, and Anni Bergman, *The Psychological Birth of the Human*

Infant (New York: Basic Books, 1975), p. 3. This book is a classic in the field and contains a great deal of useful information for anyone wishing to understand the development of "object relations" more fully. Also of seminal importance is the work of René Spitz, *The First Year of Life* (New York: International Universities Press, 1965). Mahler's work and, to an even greater extent, that of Spitz have been refined by recent clinical studies: hours and hours of mother-infant interaction have been filmed and studied frame by frame. Thus, while Mahler places the beginning of the separation-individuation phase at about the third month, more recent work establishes the inception of this activity much earlier in the infant's life. See also T. Berry Brazelton, "Evidence of Communication During Neonatal Behavioral Assessment," in *Before Speech,* ed. Margaret Bullowa (New York: Cambridge University Press, 1979). This entire collection of essays is also an excellent introduction to the field.

42 Anneliese Riess, "The Mother's Eye," *Psychoanalytic Study of the Child,* vol. XXXIII (1978), p. 382. See also Annemarie P. Weil, "The Basic Core," *Psychoanalytic Study of the Child,* vol. XXV (1970). Virtually everyone who has studied early interactions between mother and child agrees that unusual difficulty always occurs for a mother who would be quite adequate under normal circumstances but who is confronted with an unusually *gifted* child—a proto-artist, perhaps. Weil remarks: "Unusual sensitivities may be the forerunner of psychosis and severe failure of ego development in some children, while in others the same handicaps, under adequate maternal protection—substitution for the deficient protective barrier—may become unusual advantages" (p. 449). Phyllis Greenacre has paid considerable attention to the special needs (and atypical development) of the artistically gifted child; see her *Emotional Growth* (New York: International Universities Press, 1971), vol. 2.

43 See Erik H. Erikson, *Childhood and Society* (New York: W. W. Norton Co., 1963), p. 250. Erikson discusses this same period from a slightly different point of view: "The parental faith which supports the trust emerging in the newborn, has throughout history sought its institutional safeguard (and, on occasion, found its greatest enemy) in organized religion. . . . All religions have in common the periodic childlike surrender to a Provider or providers who dispense earthly fortune as well as spiritual health; some demonstration of man's smallness by way of reduced posture and humble gesture; the admission in prayer and song of misdeeds, of misthoughts, and of evil intentions; fervent appeal for inner unification by divine guidance; and finally, the insight that individual trust must become a common faith, individual mistrust a commonly formulated evil."

44 September 19, 1826; June 1, 1831, Dickinson Papers, HCL.

45 Dickinson, *Letters,* vol. I, pp. 17, 19, 26, 71, 116, 154, 215. Of course, Dickinson *sometimes* thought of letters as a form of "speech"; however, she did not usually construe them in this way (as her parents did), and the language of "seeing" is strikingly more common than that of "saying." As she grew more self-conscious artistically, she seems to have been entirely aware of her habit and to have intended all of the visual imagery to be infused with the associations more commonly attached to speech. "The Ear is the last Face," she asserted in 1874. "We hear after we see." (Ibid., vol. II, p. 518.)

46 This unusual pattern runs throughout the letters. There is food imagery, too, but not in such profusion as in the poetry (and most often when food *is* mentioned in the correspondence, Dickinson is referring quite literally to her own cooking, the family's farm produce, and so on). When food / starvation imagery does occur in the letters, there is frequently a *link* between the notion of starvation and the inability to see someone. So, in writing to Louise Norcross in late 1872, Dickinson says (just after they have recently parted): "How short it takes to go, dear, but afterward to come so many weary years—and yet—'tis done as cool as a general trifle. Affection is like bread, unnoticed till we starve, and then we dream of it, and sing of it, and paint it, when every urchin in the street has more than he can eat. We turn not older with years, but newer everyday. Of all these things we tried to talk, but the time refused us. Longing, it may be, is the gift no other gift supplies. Do you remember what you said the

night you came to me? I secure that sentence. If I should see your face no more it will be your portrait, and if I should, more vivid than your mortal face." (Ibid., p. 499.) The preceding example has often been quoted (in part) for the food imagery; the following example (less often quoted) demonstrates the extent to which this food imagery is subsumed into the larger pattern of visual imagery. "It was so delicious to see you—a Peach before the time, it makes all seasons possible and Zones—a caprice" (ibid., p. 540; about 1875). There is also, of course, extensive use of the "eye," "face," "see" imagery in the poetry, but Dickinson's use of it there is too complex to treat at this point.

47 Ibid., pp. 361–62, 406–7, 469, 792.

48 Ibid., pp. 406 (Spring 1862); 601 (early 1878); vol. III, pp. 780 (late June 1883); 811 (early 1884); vol. II, p. 389 (January 2, 1862); vol. III, p. 745 (late 1882); vol. I, p. 220 (February 24, 1853); vol. II, pp. 572 (early 1877), 610 (early June 1878).

49 Ibid., vol. I, pp. 95 (April 3, 1850), 211–12 (June 11, 1852).

50 Ibid., p. 86 (January 1850); vol. III, p. 774 (spring 1883).

51 Ibid., p. 748 (November 1882).

52 Bingham, *Brocades,* pp. 8–9. One must compare this fussing, ineffectual behavior with the successfully flexible and responsive mother that Stern describes.

53 Dickinson, *Letters,* vol. III, p. 754 (mid-December 1882).

54 Leyda, *Years and Hours,* vol. I, p. 19.

55 See Reed, *Vice to Virtue.* It is impossible to know which methods of birth control would have been known to Edward and Emily Dickinson in the 1830s and after. Charles Knowlton, a New Englander who came from Berkshire County, Massachusetts (adjacent to Hampshire County), published the first American tract on birth control in 1832, *Fruits of Philosophy; or, The Private Companion of Young Married People.* Six months after the publication of this book, he settled in Ashfield in the Berkshires—not a neighbor to Amherst by any measure, but near enough to influence thinking there. His speaking engagements took him all over western Massachusetts, evidently, and though Reed does not locate him in Amherst, Knowlton was in Greenfield, where Edward often went on business. Knowlton recommended douching with an antisperm ingredient added to water (perhaps vinegar or lemon juice). While not a perfect form of birth control, the practice of douching if followed regularly certainly reduced pregnancies. (See Reed, *Vice to Virtue,* pp. 6–10.) At the same time that Knowlton was promoting this form of controlling conceptions, however, there was a strong movement, with essentially religious or moral roots, that argued that sexuality, even in marriage, ought to be used only for the purpose of procreation. The control of intercourse was viewed by enthusiasts as one way for a wife to assert moral influence within the family (see ibid., pp. 19–28). One piece of Dickinson lore complicates the issue. "By the 1850s all the basic processes of rubber manufacturing had been worked out, and the business of manufacturing 'questionable rubber goods' was booming in the United States" (ibid., p. 15). Austin and Sue, however, seem not to have had the success in limiting their family that would come with the regular use of condoms: "Ned, the first child, was born a full five years after the wedding and only after Sue (according to [Mabel Loomis Todd's journal] entry) had 'caused three or four to be artificially removed' and had failed in repeated attempts to prevent his birth" (Sewall, *Life,* vol. I, pp. 188–89). One might suppose that if Edward and Emily Dickinson had been in the position of having birth control so efficient that they limited their own family after the birth of Lavinia, the same information (plus condoms, after 1850) would have been available to Austin and Sue. The most conservative conclusion is still interesting: Edward and Emily did *something* to limit the number of children Emily had to bear; whatever they did would have been fraught with anxiety and uncertainty, and probably only a sense of real fear and / or urgency would have produced the pattern of children in their family.

56 Dickinson Papers, HCL.

57 Ibid.

58 Dickinson, *Letters,* vol. III, p. 751 (late 1882).

59 Tyler gives a complete account of this period. See *History,* pp. 242–72.

60 Emily Norcross Dickinson never overcame her fears of separation, and she was surely the primary model for all three children, who stayed in Amherst and lived within a stone's throw of one another. Father contributed his measure: he was gratified by a prosperous son who lived in the house built by Father and given "magnanimously" as a wedding present—and bribe—and two grown daughters who never had to marry for financial reasons and who could live well, even elegantly, forever in the Homestead; the children's decisions not to separate from the parents contributed to the reclamation of the Dickinson name in Amherst, which was Edward Dickinson's obsession. But without Mother's early and continuing example, Father might have maintained this *status quo* with considerably greater difficulty. Years after the mid-1830s, Emily Norcross Dickinson's granddaughter recollects her: "I see her still in a dainty lavender morning dress with the sunshine on her curling white hair, standing at the end of the piazza to watch my grandfather drive away to Court at Northampton. She would be a little anxious about him until he was safely back, as she could never help being when any of her loved ones were ever so briefly away from her care. Her face was a little clouded as she turned away. . . . Up to [the moment of her disabling stroke] she kept a firm hand on her household, always anxious for untoward events that might bear down on those she loved from any unknown quarter when they were out of her actual sight." (Bianchi, *Face,* pp. 13–14, 88.) It is noteworthy that Emily Norcross regarded the *sight* of her loved ones as the only reliable reassurance of their welfare.

61 January 12, 1838, Dickinson Papers, HCL.

62 Dickinson Papers, HCL.

63 Late March 1838; January 17, 1838, Dickinson Papers, HCL. It is gratuitous to argue the "Oedipal phase," so widely has this act of the family drama been accepted. One fact about Emily Dickinson's "falling in love with her father" between the ages of perhaps four and seven must be observed, however. If any girl experiences her mother's love as insufficient (for whatever reason), she will come to this period of intense, passionate feeling for her father with a residue of unfinished business: more will be at stake because the need for love will be augmented by the unfulfilled needs of that earlier period. And then, there are innate differences of affect: some children experience their feelings more intensely and acutely than others. For whatever combination of reasons, all of the evidence in Emily Dickinson's letters and poetry suggests that she turned to Edward Dickinson with tremendous needs, passions, and expectations, and that *in reality* (as opposed to her idealizations of him) he was utterly unable to rise to these needs.

64 March 13, 1838, Dickinson Papers, HCL.

65 Edward's letters from Boston during this period are not devoid of conventional expression of affection. January 9, 1838: "My wife & children are very dear and whatever affects [*sic*] *them,* affects me. . . . Whatever help you want, you must have—James or Daniel Barnard must be employed to assist & I will pay them when I come home." February 22, 1838: "I might say with you, that the reading of your letter produced a tear in my eye—my feelings were deeply affected, and I felt as you say you did that I must go immediately to my dear family." March 18, 1838: "It continues to storm, and I can not help thinking how much the wind will disturb you, nights, driving as it does, agst. your chamber window. Most glad should I be if I could be with you to quiet you, at such a time." (Dickinson Papers, HCL.) Despite these expressions, however (some of which, like that of March 18, 1838, seem authentically tender), Edward continued to spend most of his time away and to be emotionally unavailable to his children.

66 Dickinson, *Letters,* vol. II, p. 528 (to Higginson, July 1874).

67 A good deal of study has been done on the various ways a child facilitates the separation-individuation process. D. W. Winnicott discovered the child's use of a "transitional object"—

that is, a "thing" (usually a blanket or a teddy bear, or some other soft toy that can be carried around) that serves the dual function of being "sometimes 'me' and sometimes 'not-me.'" In countless hours of play with such a toy, the child *practices* the process of learning to disengage the sense of "self" from the sense of "other." See D. W. Winnicott, "Transitional Objects and Transitional Phenomena," in *Collected Papers* (New York: Basic Books, 1958), pp. 229–42.

Once Winnicott published his discovery, psychologists and psychiatrists who worked with small children and studied the emergence of the "self" began to question whether "things" other than blankets, bears, and the like might be used in a similar way. Not surprisingly, they discovered a relatively large repertoire of modes by which different babies used "transitional objects" (now that the term had been so much more broadly defined) to practice separation-individuation. These become especially crucial when circumstances have suddenly *forced* the child to experience extended separation. One such "transitional object" is the word. "Language provides one mode of keeping contact with the other as separation-individuation proceeds. Consistently produced noises associatively linked with wishes, experiences, etc., become available to the infant very early, so that separation occurs from an object *with whom there is already shared language*." (Rose M. Edgcumbe, "Developmental Line for Language Acquisition," *Psychoanalytic Study of the Child*, vol. XXXVI [1981], pp. 79–80.) Of course, since the development of language had already played so disproportionately large a role in Emily Dickinson's early communication with her mother, language—Words—would be the most logical choice for handling this rather traumatic experience of sudden separation. Edgcumbe goes on to say that by the age of two or two and a half, "the child begins to take over familiar phrases of his mother as part of the process of internalizing her caring as well as controlling functions. . . . Internalized concepts help to sustain the relationship during separation, and words may help the child to recall the image of the absent object. The child begins to use words learned from the object as a means of reassuring and explaining to [himself] and as a means of reinforcing demands and prohibitions taken over from the object in the beginning of superego formation." (Ibid., pp. 91–92.) Speaking, then, of a particular child, "Charlotte," Edgcumbe goes on: "Charlotte was able to separate easily from mother, and used speech to maintain contact. She would say 'mummy' and, once she was shown where her mother was, she could go on playing. . . . Language enabled them to have 'a long-distance relationship.'" (Ibid., pp. 97–98.) Other investigators have discovered that musically gifted infants will deploy familiar snatches of melody as a "transitional object" to evoke the presence of Mother—even a sense of merging with her—during separations. See D. Viscott, "A Musical Idiot Savant: A Psychodynamic Study, and Some Speculations on the Creative Process," *Psychiatry*, vol. XXXIII (1971), pp. 494–515.

68 *The Lyman Letters: New Light on Emily Dickinson and Her Family*, ed. Richard B. Sewall (Amherst: University of Massachusetts Press, 1965), p. 78. Sewall's comment here is apt: "It has often been pointed out by analysts of her stylistic development that for her the Word was, in sober truth, the beginning. Here, in a notable autobiographic comment, she signalizes her passage from 'unsifted' girlhood to maturity by the degree of her awareness of the power of words. Joseph knew her when she thought words were 'cheap & weak.' Now she does not 'know anything so mighty.' Echoes of the next sentence are frequent in her writings; and, again, she never put the idea better. For her, words had an existence, a power, an autonomy of their own. 'I have no grace to talk,' she once wrote, 'my own words so chill and burn me.' She feared 'a word left careless on a page.' When she read of the death of George Eliot, she said, 'The look of the words as they lay in the print I shall never forget.' 'You need the balsam word,' she wrote to her cousins in bereavement. Again: 'A word is inundation when it comes from the sea.' And, happiest of all, 'How lovely are the wiles of Words!' When she says in her final sentence in the excerpt, 'Sometimes I write one . . . ,' she is surely making a vast understatement as her remark to Higginson in 1862 that 'I made no verse—but one or two—until

this winter—' We know she had written hundreds, and always with her extraordinary attention to the Word." (Ibid., pp. 77–78.) My own point is that such attention to the individual "word" does not begin in maturity (though Dickinson may have become aware of it in maturity, may even, as her remarks suggest, have dated her maturity from the moment when she did become self-conscious about the degree to which she "cathected" words). Human beings establish their notions of language simultaneously with the early acquisition of language and first implementations of it, even though they will probably discover these notions much later in life.

69 Dickinson, *Letters,* vol. II, pp. 404 (April 25, 1862), 588, 612, 618, 670, 752.

Eventually, Dickinson converted a loss into a great gain for us—to a lesser extent for herself as well. These early dilemmas of communication (both the initial problems with non-verbal communication and the subsequent need to rely to an inordinate degree on *language* to aid in the process of separation-individuation and to sustain her through periods of separation) led to an appreciation of the "Power of the Word" which formed the basis of her art. Many students of the creative process now believe that creativity in the adult is usually a re-enacting of the separation-individuation processes.

Greenacre, in her study "Woman as Artist," sees creativity as sometimes rooted in disruptions of object relation. "When the relationship to the personal object is disturbed, the young child may turn away to the collective substitute object and there gratify [her] wishes in actuality or in fantasy." (Phyllis Greenacre, "Woman as Artist," *Psychoanalytic Quarterly,* vol. XXIX, no. 2 [1960], p. 211.) Indeed, many who are interested in studying the root sources of creativity (not merely verbal creativity) believe that the adult "artist" has her roots in that state of development when the child learns separation-individuation. Muensterberger quotes a famous anecdote and then draws certain inferences: "'At the beginning of each picture,' [Picasso said,] 'there is someone who works with me. Towards the end I have the impression of having worked without a collaborator.' Following Picasso's self-observation . . . we can perhaps assume that the painter's collaborator and the imaginary ancestor or the mythological spirit to whom preliterate man surrenders part of his ego, in a more or less unreflected discharge of energy, are the same person: it is the preoedipal mother imago. . . . It seems that the oscillation back and forth of the adult ego is significantly connected with that period when, as Piaget has shown, the child reaches out for the vanished object." (Warner Muensterberger, "The Creative Process," *Psychoanalytic Study of Society,* vol. II [1962], pp. 168–69. See also David Beres, "Psychoanalytic Psychology of Imagination," *Journal of the American Psychoanalytic Association,* vol. VIII, no. 2 [April 1960], pp. 252–69.)

Winnicott's own comments are particularly useful, for they allow us to see that the great *achievement* of art (as it is viewed by the audience) may be an expression of failure by the artist. "In search for the self the person concerned may have produced something valuable in terms of art, but a successful artist may be universally acclaimed and yet have failed to find the self that he or she is looking for. The self is not really to be found in what is made out of products of body or mind, however valuable these constructs may be in terms of beauty, skill, and impact. If the artist (in whatever medium) is searching for the self, then it can be said that in all probability there is already some failure for that artist in the field of general creative living. The finished creation never heals the underlying lack of sense of self." (D. W. Winnicott, *Playing and Reality* [New York: Basic Books, 1970], pp. 54–55.) Not at the beginning, but at the end, the very end, of Emily Dickinson's life, she realized this failure. And the poignancy, even tragedy, of that realization permeated her last letters and poems. The "loss" that seems to have been converted into a great "gain" was probably a "gain" more for us than for her. Dickinson was severely limited in the choices available to her for remedying her problems, and poetry was, then, a gain for her, too, if it is understood in this context. But there is no denying her own sense of regret toward the conclusion of her life. The flesh made word is cold comfort in the end.

PART ONE ‖ III · School

1 Paul Boyer, *Urban Masses and Moral Order in America: 1820–1920* (Cambridge, Mass.: Harvard University Press, 1978), p. 10.

2 Ibid., p. 183.

3 In 1830, when Emily Dickinson was born, "the Church meant the Orthodox Trinitarian Congregational Church. In Emily's girlhood, the total population of all the villages within the town limits was about three thousand. These people supported five Congregational Churches, all trinitarian, all orthodox." See Millicent Todd Bingham, *Emily Dickinson's Home* (New York: Dover Publications, 1967), p. 35 ff.

Daily life was remarkably stable. Neighboring Northampton, which boasted a number of local industries and factories, nearly doubled in size between 1830 and 1860, expanding from 3,613 to 6,788; at the same time, the population of Amherst increased by only 575 persons, from 2,631 to 3,206 (see U.S. Census, 1810–1860). Other facts also attest to the relative stability of the Amherst community. In 1860 almost half the craftsmen in Amherst had resided in that town for at least ten years; by 1870 almost half of the local craftsmen owned their own homes. In 1860 more than half of Amherst's nonagricultural laborers were New England–born.

Even so close a city as Northampton was more "cosmopolitan." Stylish women bought their dresses at Stoddard and Lathrops in Northampton when they did not have them made by a local dressmaker, and they bought their bonnets at Mrs. Osborne's shop in the same city. The "Puritanic" code of Trinitarian living prohibited even apparently harmless amusements: "cards and dancing, common [in Northampton] were not even so much as mentioned in Amherst as suitable, nay possible occupations for immortal beings" (Susan G. Dickinson, "Two Generations of Society," in *Essays on Amherst's History,* ed. Theodore P. Greene [Amherst: The Vista Trust, 1978], p. 169). In some measure, the relatively heterogeneous society of Northampton (and such other nearby towns as Holyoke and Springfield) was due to the the influx of Europeans who came to work in New England factories. This influx scarcely touched Amherst.

The most complete study of the poet's reading has been done by Jack Lee Capps, *Emily Dickinson's Reading 1836–1886* (Cambridge, Mass.: Harvard University Press, 1966). The Bible was the book Emily Dickinson read most frequently and alluded to most often; Shakespeare, too, was a great favorite. But she also read with enormous delight the novels of the Brontës, Dickens, and George Eliot, and she read newspapers and journals which kept her informed about current events.

4 Emily Dickinson, *The Letters of Emily Dickinson,* ed. Thomas Johnson and Theodora Ward (Cambridge, Mass.: Harvard University Press, 1958), vol. I, p. 84 (January 23, 1850).

5 *New England Primer* (Hartford, 1842), p. 22.

6 Mrs. Jane Taylor, *Physiology for Children* (n.p., 1847), p. 89.

7 Peter Benes, *The Masks of Orthodoxy* (Amherst: University of Massachusetts Press, 1977), p. 45. Other useful works on this subject are: Allan I. Ludwig, *Graven Images* (Middletown, Conn.: Wesleyan University Press, 1966); Dickran and Ann Tashjian, *Memorials for Children of Change* (Middletown, Conn.: Wesleyan University Press, 1973).

8 Thomas Bridgman, *Inscription on the Grave Stones . . . of Northampton* (Northampton, 1850), p. 134.

9 Dickinson, *Letters,* vol. I, p. 36 (September 1846).

10 Ibid., vol. II, p. 537 (late January 1875).

11 In response to these recurrent episodes of revival in New England, an abridged version of Samuel Mather's classic work, *The Figures and Types of the Old Testament* (originally printed in Dublin in 1683), was reissued in 1834. Mather's treatise had been a standard reference

work for earlier generations of conservative ministers—Increase Mather, Edward Taylor, Cotton Mather. Now his most influential work was again available to the ministers and faithful of Dickinson's day. Mather writes:

> A type is some outward or sensible thing ordained of God under the Old Testament, to represent and hold forth something of Christ in the New.
>
> It may be otherwise worded. But the Description, if it be true, must be to this effect; as if we say, that a Type is an institute resemblance of Gospel-Truths and Mysteries; or that it is a Sign holding forth Christ, or something of Christ in the New Testament. [Samuel Mather, The Figures and Types of the Old Testament, ed. Mason I. Lowance (New York: Johnson Reprint Corporation, 1969), p. 52.]

Such a definition establishes a strict and quite literal historical correspondence: some actual person, event, or object in the Old Testament points toward and is fulfilled by Christ and His covenant of the New Testament; the "type" is the precursor, and Christ as fulfillment is the "antitype." Mather's book was evidently not a part of the Dickinson library (although it would certainly have been read by the ministers who preached to them and by the students at Amherst College who were preparing themselves for the ministry). However, the enormous *Companion to the Bible* that belonged to the family (showing evidence of much use) has a long section on typology that is so conventional it might have come directly from Mather. Indeed, this work—by Henry Matthew, edited and revised by William Jenks—has a publishing history similar to that of Mather's *Figures and Types:* Matthew lived from 1662 to 1714, and his *Companion* was originally published at about the same time as Mather's *Figures and Types;* in response to the renewed fervor of revivalism, the book was edited by Jenks and reprinted in 1838. Speaking of types, Jenks says: "The term is usually employed to denote a prefigurative action or occurrence, in which one event, person, circumstance, is intended to represent another, similar to it in certain respects, but future and distant. . . . Whatever persons or things, therefore, recorded in the *Old* Test. were expressly declared by Christ, or by his apostles, to have been designed as *prefigurations* of persons or things relating to the *New* Test., such persons or things, so recorded in the *former,* are types of the persons or things with which they are compared in the *latter.*" (Henry Matthew, *A Companion to the Bible,* ed. William Jenks [Brattleboro, Vt., 1838], pp. 52–53.)

Barbara Lewalski describes the notion of the correlative types (and its relationship to more historical typology) excellently well. "In the private sphere the same two formulas were available for relating the contemporary Christian to the Biblical type. When the emphasis is upon the great benefits and advantages the Christian enjoys in his religious life, the ease and comfort of the Gospel in comparison to the Law, the Christian may see himself (through Christ) as an antitype of the Israelite of old. But when on the other hand he concentrates upon his essential spiritual vision in this life, he is more likely to view himself as a correlative type with the Old Testament Israelites, located on the same spiritual plane and waiting like them for the fulfillment of all signs in Christ at the end of time. The two approaches were not incompatible." (Barbara Kiefer Lewalski, *Protestant Poetics and the Seventeenth-Century Religious Lyric* [Princeton, N.J.: Princeton University Press, 1979], p. 132.)

Several other works are of great use in examining this material. See Ursula Brumm, *American Thought and Religious Typology,* trans. John Hoaglund (New Brunswick, N.J.: Rutgers University Press, 1970); Sacvan Bercovitch, *Typology and Early American Literature* (Amherst: University of Massachusetts Press, 1972); Mason Lowance, *The Language of Canaan* (Cambridge, Mass.: Harvard University Press, 1980). Bercovitch's book has a superb bibliography.

12 Dickinson, *Letters,* vol. I, p. 52 (November 2, 1847).

13 *New England Primer* (1842), p. 22.

As it happens Foster's discussion of Noah touched an issue that dominated Dickinson's imagination throughout her life: the necessity of dealing with separation and loss, of extending faith to "the things unseen." The essay begins:

> *"By faith Noah, being warned of God of things not seen as yet, moved with fear, prepared an ark to the saving of his house; by which he condemned the world, and become heir of the righteousness which is by faith."*

—The Apostle was to inculcate the importance and necessity of faith, that is, the assured and efficacious belief of things on the divine testimony, these things not being themselves present, in their own evidence, either to the senses or to reason.

Things unseen . . . So wide a sphere must that faith extend to which is yet absolutely essential to religion. . . . This is the required faith; this, from the beginning of the world to the end, is essential to the character of the children of God; a most noble, a sublime power in the human soul,—if it can exist there.

But if there were not examples, it would seem difficult to conceive that such a power can be there. . . . It would seem as if such a faith as that required were something quite beyond the capacity of our nature. It was well therefore for the Apostle to bring in view a splendid assemblage of examples of this faith; real instances in which faith has been embodied as a living spectacle; showing its possibility, its power, its manner of operation, its worthiness, and its great reward. This assemblage contains . . . the prime of the ancient world. [It invites] comparison between them and the heroes and demigods of mythology; the heroes, the sages, and the men celebrated for virtue, in the ancient and heathen history.

Very early in the series appears the patriarch Noah, the second grand progenitor of the human race, a preeminently conspicuous object,—inasmuch as the whole human world is seen reduced and contracted down to him and his small family; a very narrow isthmus between a world of men before, and a world after. If but *there* a fatal breach had been made! . . . There, as in a cradle surrounded with perils, was the infancy of the immense population that has spread over the world.

In this great crisis man was preserved. [John Foster, *Miscellaneous Essays on Christian Morals* (New York: D. Appleton and Co., 1844), pp. 195–97.]

14 Dickinson, *Letters,* vol. I, p. 32 (March 28, 1846).
15 Ibid., p. 7 (May 12, 1842).
16 Ibid., pp. 14 (May 7, 1845), 6 (May 12, 1842), 9 (February 23, 1845), 13 (May 1845).
17 Ibid., pp. 31–32 (March 28, 1846).
18 Ibid., p. 13 (May 7, 1845).
19 W. S. Tyler, *History of Amherst College During Its First Half Century* (Springfield, Mass.: Clark W. Bryan and Company, 1873), pp. 282–84.
20 Edward Hitchcock, *The Highest Use of Learning: An Address Delivered at His Inauguration to the Presidency of Amherst College* (Amherst: J. S. & C. Adams, Printers, 1845), pp. 4–36 passim.

It is relatively unimportant precisely *who* taught Dickinson her natural theology: in this town, the line would have been pure Hitchcock (as, of course, it would be later at Mount Holyoke). Natural theology was an ancient and honorable field whose purpose was to "read" the "transcendent meaning of the natural world." Many times before the mid-nineteenth century, scientists and natural theologians had split in conflict. Darwin's discoveries would drive the final wedge between them, and by the twentieth century, philosophers and scientists would come to a sort of agreement: philosophers and theologians would retain authority over the transcendent realm; scientists would be given free rein to describe the immanent world—and on the whole, the conflict between them was resolved by this division. "Natural theology," however, was mortally wounded.

Hitchcock was probably the most interesting professor at the College during Dickinson's youth and young womanhood; his younger daughter, Jane, was Lavinia Dickinson's best friend. Edward Hitchcock was in and out of Amherst Academy throughout Dickinson's school years. As Tuckerman points out, "the teachers in the scientific branches were second to none in New England" (Frederick Tuckerman, *Amherst Academy* [Amherst: Printed for the Trustees, 1929], p. 87. It is difficult to determine how often Hitchcock strolled over to the Academy during Emily Dickinson's time there (it was but three blocks from the College); however, he had been the principal organizer of the science program at an earlier date, and during the years 1840–48 the students at the Academy were welcome at his lectures at the College (see ibid., pp. 96–142). His talented wife, Orra White, had been second preceptress at the Academy, and Mary Lyon, the head of the Mount Holyoke Female Seminary during Dickinson's years there, had been his especial protégée. Surely no thinker in her environment influenced her so much as Hitchcock. He was far from provincial. He often took a term off to go abroad, and he was as much in touch with the massive pre-Darwinian discoveries and controversies as his more famous colleague at Harvard, Louis Agassiz. Indeed, in this relatively obscure New England hamlet, Emily Dickinson had the rare luck of being directly in touch with the breaking discoveries that were eventually to revise the accumulation of nineteen centuries of Christian belief; and Edward Hitchcock himself made this possible.

Hitchcock had been born at Deerfield, Massachusetts, in 1793. He had taken geology as his primary field of scientific interest from the beginning of his study (though, the sciences being less completely divided at that time, he was an authority on botany, physics, and chemistry as well, and taught all of these). Before Agassiz propounded the theory of glacier movement in 1838, Hitchcock had noted massive evidences of what he termed "diluvial elements and depressions" which he thought to be the result of the action of the moving waters of ancient seas. Once the glacier theory was fully propounded, he accepted it readily (and did not find that it conflicted with his reading of the Bible). It was he who proved the existence of large fauna, giant bipeds and quadrupeds, in the Trias in New England from their fossilized footprints. He was internationally active. In 1840 he founded the American Association of Geologists (and was its first president). In 1848 this organization expanded to include physicists, and it was renamed at that time as the American Association for the Advancement of Science. Hitchcock published very prolifically, both in science and theology.

21 William Paley, *Works,* 2 vols. (London: Henry Fisher, Son, and P. Jackson, 1828), vol. II, pp. 1, 3–7.

22 Edward Hitchcock, *Religious Lectures on Peculiar Phenomena* (Amherst: J. S. & C. Adams, 1850), p. 55. This collection of four essays or "sermons" was delivered at Amherst College (in 1845, 1846, 1848, 1849) and at the Mount Holyoke Seminary as well. It was put into book form and the volume was reissued twice. The Dickinsons owned the book and almost certainly heard all of the talks given at Amherst as well (Emily Dickinson may have heard the 1848 talk twice). Of all Hitchcock's publications, this is the one most certain to have been read by Dickinson. In truth, a perusal of Hitchcock's sermons (a great number of which have been collected in the Amherst College Archives) reveals that his natural theology was basically quite simple and unchanging. He worked many variations of *example,* but the tenets remained the same. I have endeavored here to be as representative as possible of his general beliefs (as well as to use the material in the *Religious Lectures*). The general theories and these examples both find their way into Dickinson's poetry.

Much of this talk about "natural symbols" sounds Emersonian. Eventually, of course, Dickinson read Emerson—both his essays (or some of them) and his poetry. However, long, long before that time, she was exposed to this Trinitarian belief in natural theology and natural signs. The crucial difference is this: Hitchcock and his fellow scientist / theologians believed that certain facts of nature represented *particular* and *doctrinally limited* spiritual facts—sunrise, for example, was the "promise" or "sign" or "analogy" of Christ's resurrection and the expiation therein which allows each Christian to hope to be "born again." According to this Trinitarian view, *nature was not endlessly malleable:* natural signs could not mean just anything at all, depending on the disposition and imaginative or intuitive insight of any given individual. Thus, although Trinitarians believed that nature was "signed," they also believed that the "vocabulary" or "range" of these signs was *expressly limited* to the *truths of revealed religion.* Emerson did not.

23 Ibid., p. 56.

24 Ibid., pp. 57–58. Hitchcock is skirting trouble here, for although he repeatedly asserts that these "signs" must be read according to the "Book of Revelation," that is, the Bible, he is taking a line (citing heathens' worship of the rainbow and presuming some "reading" of it) that tends toward Emersonianism.

25 Dickinson, *Letters,* vol. I, pp. 21 (September 25, 1845), 37 (September 8, 1846), 9 (February 23, 1845).

26 Ibid., pp. 66 (May 16, 1848), 9 (February 23, 1845), 23 (January 12, 1846), 37–38 (September 8, 1846).

27 Ibid., vol. II, p. 475 (August 16, 1870).

28 Ibid., vol. I, p. 17 (August 3, 1845).

29 Hitchcock, *Religious Lectures,* pp. 9, 67, 70. It is of some worth to note, perhaps, how very different the Trinitarian position in the 1840s and 1850s was from that taken a century earlier in New England, during the time of Jonathan Edwards and the "Great Awakening." In the eighteenth century the clergy had been bitterly divided over many issues: they had disagreed about the roles played by reason and faith (Chauncy and Edwards had been at swords' points over this matter); they had split over the requirement for admission into a congregation; and they had been in disagreement about the role women might play in religion. By Emily Dickinson's school days, none of these issues was subject to debate. Probably Trinitarians had grown less ready to wrangle with one another because they were subject to attack from without and were forced to close ranks for protection. Whatever the reason, by 1840 the battles of Jonathan Edwards's day were long past. It was desirable for members of the congregation to enter the church by a profession of faith, but it was no longer necessary; and, far from being excluded from religious matters, women were urged to use all their influence to bring the unconverted to God's way. (Hitchcock's unfailing support of Mary Lyon's "missionary" work at Mount Holyoke is a striking contrast to the ways of the past.) Most striking, however, was the easy and companionable relationship assigned to reason and the irrational faculties: although they had once been deemed such enemies, it was now thought that under ideal circumstances, they would work together harmoniously toward the same end. An excellent account of that earlier period in New England can be found in *The Great Awakening,* ed. Alan Heimart and Perry Miller (Indianapolis and New York: The Bobbs-Merrill Co., 1967). The introduction to this book is useful, as are the readings from Edwards, particularly "'Justification by Faith Alone'" and "Thoughts on the Revival of Religion," and from Chauncy, especially "Enthusiasm Described and Caution'd Against" and "Seasonable Thoughts on the State of Religion."

30 Emerson's name is not mentioned in the sermons that remain from the days of Dickinson's Amherst, nor is there any mention of him in the curricula of her schools. Nonetheless, it seems clear that the "heresy" of supposing that there are "natural symbols" in the created world that could be interpreted by anyone according to his or her own powers of insight was anathema to these Trinitarians. There is no evidence that Dickinson read Emerson until her friend and "preceptor" Ben Newton gave her a copy of Emerson's *Poems* in 1850. Thus Dickinson probably did not become much acquainted with Emerson's theories of man's relationship to nature until well after she left school. Nevertheless, her ministers and teachers were certainly aware of them, and the clear and urgent message that the Scriptures are our *only* guide to natural signs and emblems seems a calculated response to the persuasive former Unitarian from Boston.

31 Dickinson Papers, HCL.

32 Dickinson, *Letters,* vol. I, pp. 27–29.

33 Quoted in Heman Humphrey, *Revival: Sketches and Manual* (New York: American Tract Society, 1859), p. 341. This long publication of the Tractarian Society is the single best guide to mid-nineteenth-century American revivals that I have found. There is voluminous firsthand testimony by ministers and parishioners, and the book is all the more valuable to a twentieth-century reader for Humphrey's relative lack of an imposed "style" or "design." Its very simplicity and literalness make the book immensely useful.

Perhaps the most interesting thing about Humphrey's description of nineteenth-century revivals (something that entirely accords with Hitchcock's tone and line of argument) is a shift of emphasis: ministers seldom if ever appeal to the doctrine of innate depravity. Humphrey does occasionally; Hitchcock virtually never. Rather, their tone is stern (especially Humphrey's), but persuasive rather than condemning. THE PRIMARY ISSUE IN CONVERSION HERE IS ACKNOWLEDGING GOD'S *AUTHORITY.* True, an individual had to acknowledge his or her sin and unworthiness, but this seems to have become, if not secondary, at least much toned down from Jonathan Edwards's day. This element of the revival in the nineteenth century was probably a reflection of the more general weakness of the Trinitarians' hold on their congregations as cities expanded, patterns of human life changed, and moral values became increasingly instrumental. Humphrey offers an interesting suggestion (which was followed dramatically in Edward Dickinson's case): "The meeting should always be opened with a short prayer, and all should be requested to *kneel.* Some may regard posture as a matter of very little consequence; but it is 'much every way.' It brings down stiff knees, that perhaps have never kneeled before; begets a sacred awe and reverence which pertains to no other posture; and no other posture should be encouraged at such a meeting, where there is room to kneel." (Ibid., p. 347.)

34 It was Whicher who first asserted that Emily Dickinson used Webster's 1847 *American Dictionary* (see George Frisbie Whicher, *This Was a Poet* [New York: Charles Scribner's Sons, 1938], p. 232). It is inconceivable that the Dickinson family would have used any dictionary other than Webster's—although until the Lyman letters came to light, no one could know with certainty which edition they possessed (and Whicher cited no authority for his assertion). However, Joseph Lyman's remarks make it almost certain that the Dickinsons owned the 1828 edition, and I have uniformly used this text when defining words in Dickinson's poetry.

35 Richard M. Rollins, "Words as Social Control: Noah Webster and the Creation of the *American Dictionary,*" *American Quarterly,* vol. XXVIII, no. 4 (Fall 1976), p. 427.

36 Noah Webster, *An American Dictionary of the English Language* (New York: S. Converse, 1828). Although the dictionary is not paginated, the words and their definitions are easily found, listed in alphabetical order.

37 Webster, *Dictionary,* preface.

His granddaughter Emily Fowler Ford has given the best account. See *Notes on the Life of Noah Webster,* ed. Emily Ellsworth Ford Skeel, 2 vols. (New York: privately printed, 1912), vol. I, pp. 35–36: "In the winter of 1807 Rev. Moses Stuart, who was pastor of the First Congregational Church of New Haven, a man of larger scholarship, fervent imagination, and deep personal piety, so wrought upon his congregation that a season of especial religious interest developed into a general revival as it was then called. The young Webster daughters were solemnly impressed with a new sense of their relations to God, and of the value of personal consecration to a devout life. They went to their father for counsel and he, under this stimulus, took up the study of the Bible anew, with a special view toward comprehending certain of the doctrines which he had felt when urged upon him were against reason. He spent some weeks in this review of his former opinions and objections, but as he advanced in his studies, his doubts rolled away, and he accepted humbly and enthusiastically the doctrine of the atonement, or redemption by Christ. When he arrived at this conclusion he lost no time in announcing it. He called his family together, and told them with much emotion of his new convictions, and that while he had aimed at the faithful discharge of parental duty, there was one sign and token of headship which he had neglected—the duty of family prayer. He commenced at once to read the Scriptures, and led his household in prayer. From that time he continued the practice until his death. He, with his two elder daughters, Emily and Julia, made a public profession of their faith in April, 1808." This account is particularly interesting if compared with Edward Dickinson's behavior: what an unusual mixture of piety and defiance Edward Dickinson gave his children, ritually observing daily prayers and a reading of the Bible, attending church regularly on the Sabbath, and yet withholding his submission to God until he was almost fifty and his children were adults!

38 Tyler, *History,* pp. 109 (italics mine). Webster lived almost in the middle of the village, near the site where Kellogg's Block was later constructed. He was a prominent and active member of the First Church (was a member of the committee that issued the call to Dr. Clark), and he served as representative to the Massachusetts legislature in 1814, 1815, and 1819. He "was a favorite with the intelligent farmers of Amherst and the vicinity, with whom he conversed familiarly on subjects pertaining to their occupation. . . . He opened his house often—every term it is said—to students as well as residents of the town. The influence of so genial and so accomplished a family was as great as it was happy in the Academy, in the College, and in the community." (Ibid., p. 108.) Noah Webster was president of the Board of Trustees that elected Zephaniah Moore first president of Amherst College, and was still president of the Board on September 19, 1821, when the initial class of forty-seven young men began their studies at the College.

Philip F. Gura, whose principal interest is the Unitarian use of language, begins his study— *The Wisdom of Words: Language, Theology, and Literature in the New England Renaissance* (Middletown, Conn.: Wesleyan University Press, 1982)—with an evocation of Noah Webster in 1839, addressing the members of the New York Lyceum: "He stood before them as the acknowledged dean of American language study. . . . His address to the Lyceum is most interesting because of his emphasis on the peculiar religious nature of his life-long interest in words. In eloquent phrases he explained how he had always 'attempted to correct the obvious inaccuracies of language,' not just to make the English tongue more civil but, more importantly, to aid the cause of the Christian religion, because 'the sacred scriptures, containing all the true knowledge of the Supreme Being . . . ought to be explained in plain, intelligible language.' His long attempt to codify the American dialect was only what he believed it was, 'the duty of Christians to countenance,' for his work allowed people to learn as much as possible of the Supreme Being and his demands through the proper understanding of his revelations to men" (p. 15). Gura's discussion of Emerson (pp. 75–105) makes for an especially interesting contrast with Dickinson. One must suppose that Emerson was able to accept the proposition that "nature, more than the Bible, displayed the revealed will of God and that . . . man had to respond to nature, as well as to Scripture, with his intuitive faculty" (p. 75) principally because he was not convinced that man's interpretation of nature had to submit to Scriptural orthodoxy and because "reason" did not convince him of God's existence. Emerson's views were radical for their time, but little by little Emerson himself became the "dean of American language study" in areas that were no longer dominated by Trinitarian orthodoxy. Until well after the Civil War, however, Amherst was relatively insulated from such heterodoxy (both religious and linguistic), even though Emerson and others like him came through to give lectures: Hitchcock himself reasserted the duty to submit our observations of nature to the discipline of Scriptural revelation in no uncertain terms. To do otherwise (as Dickinson eventually did) was to be isolated from received opinion in Amherst: more, it was an act of defiance that was explicitly defined as heresy.

39 Hitchcock, *Religious Lectures,* p. 112. Hitchcock wrote often in the same vein. His *Discourse: The Religious Bearing of Man's Creation* (Albany: Van Benthuysen, Printer, 1856) is especially useful. Although it offers no additional arguments to those found in the *Religious Lectures,* it

does offer new examples from recent geological finds and from work in comparative anatomy—and references to both of these find their way into Dickinson's poetry. Also, it gives Hitchcock's position quite concisely.

40 During the time Emily Dickinson was a student there, the Amherst Academy made no distinction between the education given to male and female students; both took the same courses, were instructed together in the same classrooms, were allowed to attend classes at Amherst College. (Visitors to the College at that time often remarked the unusual presence of young women in the lecture rooms.) The texts used at the Academy give some idea of the intellectual rigor that characterized its education. See Tuckerman, *Academy,* pp. 99–100.

CLASSICAL DEPARTMENT

SECOND DIVISION

Andrews and Stoddard's Latin textbooks.
Goodrich's Greek Grammar and Lessons, Cornelius Nepos, Caesar's Commentaries.
Geography, Ancient History, and English Grammar.

FIRST DIVISION

Cooper's Virgil, Folsom's Cicero, Jacob's Greek Reader, Anthon's Sallust, Andrews's Latin Exercises, Knapp's Greek Testament, Arithmetic, Algebra, written translations and compositions.

REFERENCE BOOKS

Leverett's Latin Lexicon, Ramshorn's Latin Synonyms, Donnegan's Greek Lexicon, Worcester's Ancient Atlas, Lempriere's Classical Dictionary, Eschenburg-Fiske's Manual of Classical Literature.

ENGLISH DEPARTMENT

SECOND DIVISION

Malte-Brun's Geography, Worcester's Elements of History, Goldsmith's History of England, Pond-Murray's Grammar, Watts on the Mind, Mrs. Lincoln's Familiar Lectures on Botany, Adams' Arithmetic, Sullivan's Political Class Book, Smellie's Philosophy of Natural History, Hayward's Physiology, Analysis of Cooper's Task, Parker's Exercises in Composition.

FIRST DIVISION

Day's Algebra, Playfair's Euclid, Olmsted's Natural Philosophy, Gale's Chemistry, Abercrombie on the Intellectual Powers, Upham's Intellectual Philosophy, Newman's Rhetoric, Paley's Natural Theology, Goodrich's Ecclesiastical History, Alexander's Evidences of Christianity, Smith's Anatomy, Wilkins's Astronomy, Hedge's Logic, Kames' Elements of Criticism, Wayland's Moral Science, Butler's Analogy, Analysis of Paradise Lost, and compositions.

Yet no mere list of texts can communicate the pervasive religious tone. Joseph E. Worcester's *Elements of History* (Boston: Wm. J. Reynolds & Co., 1826) begins with a section entitled "Uses of History": "True history has numberless relations and uses as an exhibition of the conduct of Divine Providence; and it presents numerous instances in which events, important to the welfare of the human race, have been brought about by inconsiderable means, contrary to the intentions of those who were the principal agents in them" (p. 2). Mrs. Almira H. Lincoln's *Familiar Lectures on Botany* (Hartford, Conn.: F. J. Huntington, 1835) has a similarly providential view of human life in the world: "The Deity has not only placed before us an almost infinite variety of objects, but has given to our minds the power of reducing them into classes, so as to form beautiful and regular systems, by which we can comprehend, under a few terms, the vast number of individual things, which would, otherwise, present to our bewildered minds a confused and indiscriminate mass. This power of the mind, so important in classification, is that of *discovering resemblances*. . . . The study of Botany naturally leads to greater love and reverence for the Deity. . . . Those who feel in their hearts a love to God, and who see in the natural world the workings of His power, can look abroad, and adopting the language of a Christian poet, exclaim 'My Father made them all'" (pp. 2, 15). (Mrs. Lincoln also asserts, "The study of Botany seems peculiarly adapted to females" [p. 14].) Religious instruction insinuated itself into every portion of the curriculum. Worcester's pronouncements and Mrs. Lincoln's pious claims are intellectually tame. Paley's works and Butler's were a sterner matter; however, perhaps even these would not have so influenced Dickinson if the religious element in her texts had not been buttressed by a coherent, consistent, and unrelenting conviction in both the Academy and the larger community that to "learn" necessarily implied to "learn about God." Thus all of the students at the Academy were required regularly to attend morning and evening prayers five days a week in the Academy Hall; on Saturday evening there was a Bible class that all the students were required to attend; and everyone was expected to be present at public worship (both morning and afternoon) on the Sabbath.

No one could spend any considerable time as a student at the Amherst Academy without formulating some conclusions respecting his or her relationship to God; similarly, no one who intended to pass his or her life as an educated member of the Amherst community could evade a confrontation with a demand for the submission of "reason" to "faith." (Any time spent at the Mount Holyoke Seminary during the reign of Mary Lyon would only intensify the terms of this confrontation.)

41 Humphrey, *Revival*, p. 432.
42 Ibid., p. 446. The convert expatiates at length upon this theme: "[The Bible appears to me] quite like a new book. I have read it more or less from my childhood; so that in one sense it has been familiar to me, but in another sense it has been a sealed book. Every chapter I read strikes me as it never did before. The words are the same, but the sense is different. The psalms and the gospels, especially, open new fields of contemplation which I never thought of. I used, when my mother required me to read a given number of chapters every Sabbath-day, to be tired of it; but now I should be glad to read it all the time."
43 Dickinson, *Letters*, vol. I, p. 104 (late 1850).
44 Ibid., pp. 30 (March 28, 1846), 27 (January 31, 1846).
45 Repeatedly, conversion is referred to as "golden": for example, Humphrey says, "Many have [run from a revival], and thus lost their golden opportunity; and where are they?" (*Revival*, p. 450). Since the texts cited are so universally the same (and are so often those referring to Jerusalem the Golden City or to a Heavenly Gold) one must presume that the theme of "gold" was not limited to revivals in the Amherst area. Humphrey's voice would have been particularly strong in these, nonetheless; he preached widely in the region, frequently at the Mount Holyoke Seminary.
46 Dickinson, *Letters*, vol. I, p. 30 (March 28, 1846).
47 Ibid., p. 94 (April 3, 1850).
48 Tyler, *History*, p. 345.

49 Ibid., p. 347.

50 Dickinson, *Letters,* vol. I, pp. 27–28 (January 31, 1846), 31 (March 28, 1846). It is tempting to suppose that Dickinson derived this visual image (clearly in "emblem" form) from Holmes and Barber's *Emblems and Allegories,* which includes several pictures of a boat teetering on the edge of a waterfall or seeming to be hurtling ahead in the rapids toward some fearful, annihilating descent. See William Holmes and John W. Barber, *Emblems and Allegories* (Cincinnati, Ohio: John H. Johnson, 1851), two volumes in one, separately paginated, containing *Religious Emblems* (first pub. 1846) and *Religious Allegories* (first pub. 1848). However, since the first volume of *Religious Emblems* was not published until 1846, and Dickinson's letter is from so early in that year that it is difficult to believe she had Holmes and Barber's emblems explicitly in mind. Humphrey delivers himself of a fearful threat in *Revival:* damnation as endlessly falling. "You shrink back from the bottomless gulf, upon the brink of which you are standing." (Humphrey, *Revival,* p. 434.)

The image of endlessly falling occurs often in Dickinson's poetry (and doubtless has personal emotional significance there as well as, perhaps, a religious origin). Probably it is impossible to know *exactly* where she derived the notion, but it seems to have been a commonplace among Puritanical Americans in mid-century. The "Fall" was as old as the Bible.

51 Dickinson, *Letters,* vol. I, p. 36 (September 8, 1846).

52 Tyler, *History,* pp. 37–38, quoting an unnamed teacher of that era. There is disagreement about the date of Mary Lyon's stay at the Amherst Academy. Tyler places it in 1821, Tuckerman in 1818. The earlier date seems more accurate when taken in conjunction with Hitchcock's biographical information—which does not give a date for her education at the Academy (Edward Hitchcock, *The Power of Christian Benevolence Illustrated in the Life and Labors of Mary Lyon* [Northampton: Hopkins, Bridgman, and Company, 1852], pp. 23, 324).

53 The Mount Holyoke Journal Letter, Williston Memorial Library, Mount Holyoke College, pp. 3–4. This document, a diary of the institution's progress throughout the year, was kept in 1847 and 1848 by Susan L. Tolman (September to November 16), Rebecca Fiske (November 23–27), Susan L. Tolman (December 3 to April 26), and Rebecca Fiske (May 12 to August 3). I have used a typescript copy of a handwritten copy in the Archives marked "for Miss Lyon." Doubtless Mary Lyon wished to have a history of the Seminary; however, this journal was kept also for the women who traveled with missionary husbands to foreign lands. Information about them (when received) was recorded along with daily happenings. Hereafter, I will cite this source as JL.

54 Dickinson, *Letters,* vol. I, p. 59 (January 17, 1848). Dickinson gives an account of a typical day for her at Mount Holyoke in a letter to Abiah, November 6, 1847: "I will tell you my order of time for the day, as you were so kind as to give me your's. At 6. o'clock, we all rise. We breakfast at 7. Our study hours begin at 8. At 9. we all meet in Seminary Hall, for devotions. At .11. I recite a lesson in 'Pope's Essay on Man' which is merely transposition. At .12. I practice Calisthenics & at 12 1 / 4 read until dinner, which is at 12 1 / 2 & after dinner, from 1 1 / 2 until 2 I sing in Seminary Hall. From 2 3 / 4 until 3 3 / 4. I practise upon the Piano. At 3 3 / 4 I go to Sections, where we give in all our accounts for the day, including Absence,—Tardiness—Communications—Breaking Silent Study hours—Receiving Company in our rooms & ten thousand other things, which I will not take time or place to mention. At 4 1 / 2. we go into Seminary Hall, & receive advice from Miss Lyon in the form of a lecture. We have Supper at 6. & silent-study hours from then until the retiring bell, which rings at 8 3 / 4, but the tardy bell does not ring until 9 3 / 4, so that we dont often obey the first warning to retire." See Dickinson, *Letters,* vol. I, pp. 54–55. A twentieth-century reader might remark the long hours of devotion (which continued in more strenuous form from the habits of the Amherst Academy). Miss Lyon met alone once a week with each group, "Hop-

ers," "Christians," and "No-Hopers"; she talked quietly (persuasively, perhaps) but never harshly.

Dickinson entered as a "junior"; the curriculum at all levels continued (sometimes repeated) the robust intellectual fare of the Amherst Academy. In *Lyon,* Hitchcock gives the following reading list from the twelfth annual catalogue (1848–49):

STUDIES OF THE JUNIOR CLASS

Review of English Grammar; Latin, (Cornelius Nepos;) History, (Worcester's Elements, Goldsmith's Greece, Rome, and England, and Grimshaw's France;) Day's Algebra; Playfair's Euclid and Wood's Botany commenced; also Smellie's Philosophy of Natural History and Marsh's Ecclesiastical History.

STUDIES OF THE MIDDLE CLASS

Latin; Cutler's Physiology; Silliman's Chemistry; Olmsted's Natural Philosophy; Olmsted's Astronomy; Wood's Botany continued; Newman's Rhetoric; also Alexander's Evidences of Christianity.

STUDIES OF THE SENIOR CLASS

Playfair's Euclid finished; Wood's Botany continued; Hitchcock's Geology; Paley's Natural Theology; Upham's Mental Philosophy, in two volumes; Whately's Logic; Wayland's Moral Philosophy; Butler's Analogy; and Milton's Paradise Lost.

All the members of the school attend regularly to composition, reading, and calisthenics. Instruction is given in vocal music, in linear and perspective drawing, and in French. Those who have attended to instrumental music can have the use of the piano a few hours each week.

Certain incidents in Dickinson's life have been elaborated fancifully by her sister, Lavinia, or her niece, Martha Dickinson Bianchi. Dickinson's relationship with Mary Lyon is one. In *The Life and Letters of Emily Dickinson* (Boston and New York: Houghton Mifflin, 1924, reissued 1930) Bianchi gives the following account: "But if Thanksgiving was radiant, Christmas was gloom in comparison, and the legend of Emily Dickinson's insurrection is one of the best in the family archives. It was only a day in advance that Miss Lyon announced, at morning devotion, that Christmas would be recognized as a fast. The girls were not to leave their rooms through long, definite hours and were to meditate to order. After laying down this unseductive programme she added that the school might rise in token of responsive observation. The school did rise—all except Emily and her roommate. The school sat down and Miss Lyon, appalled by such flagrant disregard of the decent required pieties, enlarged upon her programme. At the end of which she added that if there were any so lost to a sense of the meaning of the day as to wish to spend it otherwise, they might stand that the whole school might observe them. And be it said to her glory, of the two terrified objects of her anathema Emily stood alone" (pp. 25–26).

That Dickinson did not take happily and docilely to the rigidly ordered routine at Mount Holyoke is scarcely surprising, but there is no record of this incident in the Journal Letter. (Bianchi has undoubtedly conflated Dickinson's reaction to a prayer meeting she attended on January 17 [see n. 57] with what may have been her disappointment at not being able to come home. It was not unusual that she did not come home for Christmas: Christ's birthday was a holy day for Trinitarians, not a "pagan" festival.)

One of the most offensive facts about the romanticizing of certain "events" in Dickinson's life is that, in the end, it trivializes them. Brash defiance over going home for vacation is childish: genuine concern about faith and conversion is not. Sydney R. McLean was the first to correct Madame Bianchi, in the graduate paper on the subject he wrote at Yale in 1933 and published in revised form as "Emily Dickinson at Mount Holyoke," *New England Quarterly,* March 1935, pp. 25–42.

55 JL, p. 6.

56 Jay Leyda, *The Years and Hours of Emily Dickinson* (New Haven: Yale University Press, 1960), vol. I, pp. 133, 135.

57 Dickinson, *Letters,* vol. I, p. 60 (January 17, 1848). Leyda records Clara Newman Turner's account, as it was recalled many years later: "To illustrate the independence and honesty of her convictions,—Miss Lyon, during a time of religious interest in the school, asked all those who wanted to be Christians to rise. The wording of the request was not such as Emily could honestly accede to and she remained seated—the only one who did not rise. In relating the incident to me, she said, 'They thought it queer I didn't rise'—adding with a twinkle in her eye, 'I thought a lie would be queerer.' " (*Years and Hours,* p. 136.) Probably Clara Newman is giving a "truthful" report (though Dickinson grew a good deal easier about revivals and conversion in her later life than she was *in situ*). Two facts seem clear: (1) Emily Dickinson felt deeply about the matter of conversion—did so over a period of years—was conflicted and at the last unconverted; and (2) at the Mount Holyoke Seminary (as at Amherst College later, during the revival of 1850) there were *many* students who remained unconverted, despite the constant, quiet pressure. What was felt most powerfully by Dickinson was the pressure to submit reason to faith.

58 Dickinson, *Letters,* vol. I, p. 67 (May 16, 1848).

59 Leyda, *Years and Hours,* vol. I, pp. 170, 170–71.

60 Tyler, *History,* p. 351.

61 Dickinson, *Letters,* vol. I, p. 94 (April 3, 1850).

62 Ibid., p. 98 (May 7, 17, 1850).

63 Leyda, *Years and Hours,* vol. I, p. 173. I have quoted Leyda here over Johnson because Leyda's transcription, "I have builded beautiful temples," looks correct to me; Johnson read for this, "I have heeded beautiful tempters" (Dickinson, *Letters,* vol. I, p. 95).

64 Dickinson, *Letters,* vol. I, p. 99 (May 7, 17, 1850).

65 Tyler, *History,* pp. 352–53.

66 Leyda, *Years and Hours,* vol. I, p. 178. Austin Dickinson was admitted to the First Church by profession on January 6, 1856.

67 Dickinson, *Letters,* vol. I, p. 104 (late 1850).

PART ONE ‖ *IV · The 1850s*

1 Emily Dickinson, *The Letters of Emily Dickinson,* ed. Thomas Johnson and Theodora Ward (Cambridge, Mass.: Harvard University Press, 1958), vol. I, pp. 80 (January 11, 1850), 83–84 (January 23, 1850).

2 Jay Leyda, *The Years and Hours of Emily Dickinson* (New Haven: Yale University Press, 1960), vol. II, p. 478.

3 *The Lyman Letters: New Light on Emily Dickinson and Her Family,* ed. Richard B. Sewall (Amherst: University of Massachusetts Press, 1965), p. 58. Joseph Lyman knew all three Dickinson children as intimate friends and was accepted generously into the family. After he left Amherst, he continued to correspond with Emily and Lavinia, probably with Austin as

well. None of Lyman's letters in this correspondence remain; fortunately, however, he copied long passages from the Dickinson letters into letters of his own or onto loose-leaf sheets (the latter mostly about Emily). His descriptions of the encounters with Lavinia were included in letters to Laura Baker, the woman he subsequently married. A short chronology of Lyman's life:

JOSEPH BARDWELL LYMAN

Born: October 6, 1829 (in Chester, Mass.)
At Williston Seminary with Austin: 1844–46
Guest at Dickinson House: 1846
Becomes a student at Yale: 1846
Graduates from Yale: 1850
Leaves New England: spring 1851
Marries (Laura Baker): July 1858
In Confederate Army: March 1862–September 1863
Visits Cambridge: fall 1863
Visits Easthampton: 1864
Dies: January 28, 1872

(A more complete account may be found in *Lyman Letters;* I am indebted to Sewall for the above chronology.)

4 One thing must be stressed in the account of Joseph Lyman's relationship with the Dickinson family, especially with Lavinia. It is unmistakably clear that the intimacy the couple enjoyed was not unusual: Joseph's letters to his fiancée assume certain norms for premarital behavior that are consistent with the findings in Ellen K. Rothman, *Hands and Hearts* (New York: Basic Books, 1984). Moreover, Lavinia's sexual responsiveness and Joseph Lyman's sexual interest in her (along with his willingness to discuss with Laura Baker this earlier relationship) provide a stark contrast to the stilted absence of candor and sexual affection that had characterized every stage of the courtship between Emily Norcross and Edward Dickinson. To cite a specific example: no one could know whether Edward Dickinson had ever kissed *anyone* (including Emily Norcross) from reading the entire array of long letters he wrote over the two and a half years of their premarital acquaintance; moreover, although Vinnie's manner and physical appearance come through quite directly and touchingly in these short sketches from the Lyman letters, nothing circumstantial whatsoever about Emily Norcross can be inferred from Edward's epistles—neither about her physical appearance nor about her manner when she was with him.

Social historians have been readjusting our notion of "Victorian" sexual practices in America for some time now. Carl Degler's excellent essay "What Ought to Be and What Was: Women's Sexuality in the Nineteenth Century," *American Historical Review,* vol. 79 (December 1974), pp. 1467–90 offers a corrective view. One simple fact—that Amherst was a little village where couples could easily find ways to be alone—would contribute to the possibility of physical intimacy during courtship. When Lavinia Norcross married her cousin Loring suddenly (the family generally opposed the marriage because of the close kinship), there were scarcely disguised speculations in family letters that she might be pregnant.

That having been said, however, one should attempt to define the Dickinson family's deviation from the norm. Mother and Father seem to have given their children a good deal of objective freedom: Joseph and Vinnie did their caressing in the comfort of the Dickinson parlor. However, the attitude that Mother and Father took toward their own marriage and the relationship between the sexes—most important, the example they gave in their own home—was not encouraging. Although Mother and Father may not have argued, they were

anything but emotionally spontaneous with each other, and there is no record of loving intimacy between them at all.

5 *Lyman Letters,* pp. 17–18.

6 Leyda, *Years and Hours,* vol. I, p. 196.

7 Ibid.

8 Ibid., pp. 209, 216. The young man who was suing for Vinnie's hand was probably William
Howland, who had attended Williston Academy and Amherst College (graduating in 1846)
and then remained in Amherst to be a tutor at Amherst College while studying law with
Edward Dickinson. In 1852 he moved to Springfield to practice, and one of Emily Dickinson's
earliest verses ("'Sic transit gloria mundi'") was probably intended for him. It was one of the
very few poems published in her lifetime, appearing in the Springfield *Republican* on February
20, 1852.

It is worth mentioning that Vinnie's diary (many entries of which can be found in Leyda)
indicates that Howland often came to the Dickinson home for dinner and that Edward Dickinson seems to have enjoyed his company. Thus the existing record of events is widely at
variance with Vinnie's senescent memories and lingering angers toward her father, whom she
afterward construed as having driven her suitors away.

9 *Lyman Letters,* p. 14.

10 Ibid., p. 60.

11 Dickinson, *Letters,* vol. I, p. 127 (July 27, 1851).

12 Millicent Todd Bingham, *Emily Dickinson's Home* (New York: Dover Publications, 1967),
pp. 89, 297.

13 Ibid., p. 248.

14 *Lyman Letters,* p. 70.

15 Dickinson, *Letters,* vol. I, p. 118 (June 29, 1851).

16 Bingham, *Home,* pp. 148–49, 174.

17 The context of this often quoted sentiment makes it clear that Dickinson had the three children principally in mind: Edward's sister and brother-in-law, Mary and Mark Newman, had
both died, leaving their children orphaned; the two daughters came to live in Amherst under
Edward's protection, and Emily and Lavinia perforce came to know them very well, even
though these cousins lived separately from the Edward Dickinson family. It is the inability of
the Newman girls to fit into the fairly closed circle of Austin, Emily, and Vinnie that the
remark notes. See Dickinson, *Letters,* vol. I, p. 245 (April 21, 1853).

18 Leyda, *Years and Hours,* vol. I, p. 81.

19 Bingham, *Home,* pp. 238–39.

20 Dickinson, *Letters,* vol. I, p. 239 (April 8, 1853).

21 Ibid, pp. 233 (March 24, 1853), 241 (April 12, 1853), 249 (May 16, 1853), 274 (December
13, 1853).

22 An invaluable guide to interpreting Dickinson's tone in these letters is the work of Carroll
Smith-Rosenberg—I am thinking especially of "The Female World of Love and Ritual," in *A
Heritage of Her Own,* ed. Nancy F. Cott and Elizabeth H. Pleck (New York: Simon and
Schuster, 1979), pp. 311–42. In analyzing correspondences between women friends during
the nineteenth century, Smith-Rosenberg has found precisely the kind of emotional intensity
in these letters that can be found in Dickinson's letters to Abiah Root or Jane Humphrey or
Susan Gilbert. As Smith-Rosenberg observes: "These relationships ranged from the supportive
love of sisters, through the enthusiasm of adolescent girls, to sensual avowals of love by
mature women" (p. 312). What is striking and unusual about Dickinson's letters to these
friends is not the gushy, "romantic" tone, but the inability to tolerate separation. As Smith-
Rosenberg observes, "Young girls helped each other overcome homesickness and endure the
crises of adolescence" (p. 324). Dickinson never managed to accept separation, nor did she
employ her friendships with other young women to aid in the process of becoming indepen-

dent of her own family. Especially in the case of Susan, Emily Dickinson's inclination goes in quite the other direction: she looks forward to the time when Sue can be *absorbed into the family* so that there will ultimately be four children instead of only three.

23 A letter from Edward Dickinson, February 16, 1838, gives the usual pattern: "Don't forget, My Dear Emily, to ask morning & evening, for the protection of that kind Providence which takes care of us all, and that we may be preserved to enjoy not only the society of each other, but of the happy & unnumbered host, whose employment will be to increase in knowledge & happiness forever. Would to heaven that I could rightly appreciate the value of this preparation for futurity. I have not room to express my feeling on this subject." (Dickinson Papers, HCL.)

24 Dickinson, *Letters*, vol. I, pp. 82–83 (January 23, 1850).

25 Ibid., pp. 166–67 (about January 1852).

26 Ibid., p. 82 (January 23, 1850).

27 Ibid., p. 109 (about 1851).

28 Richard B. Sewall gives an excellent account of the Gilbert sisters' background: see *The Life of Emily Dickinson* (New York: Farrar, Straus and Giroux, 1974), vol. I, pp. 186–205. It is interesting that Emily Dickinson elected to play such an active role in Austin's courtship. She campaigned for the Gilbert girls in turn (Mattie first and then Sue, as Austin's own affections wavered between them). There is no evidence that she played a similar role in any of his *other* romances, and her desire to have one or the other of these girls for a sister-in-law seems to have been based as much on her own need for companionship now that the friends of her girlhood had begun to drift away from Amherst as it was on Austin's romantic inclinations. That she may have felt instrumental in Austin's choice helps to explain her rage and misery at the "betrayal" implicit in Sue's urging Austin to consider relocation in the Midwest. See text p. 115.

29 Ibid., p. 104.

30 Dickinson, *Letters*, vol. I, p. 114 (June 15, 1851).

31 Ibid., pp. 168–69 (January 21, 1852), 182 (about February 1852).

32 Ibid., pp. 209–10 (early June 1852).

33 Sewall gives a masterful account of the vicissitudes of the relationship during Austin's engagement to Sue. Austin, too, seems to have had a fatal inability to "love" a woman who was emotionally available: Mattie Gilbert, for instance, seems not to have had Sue's many emotional conflicts, and might well have proved a loving wife (her subsequent marriage seems to have been happy enough). Austin's letter to Mattie informing her of the engagement between himself and Sue is strangely tormented in tone:

> Heaven bless you—Mattie for those kind . . . words that told me you were glad I loved Sue—& she loves me— Yes—Mattie— We *do* love—each other—with a strength & a passion—unless you have sometime felt it's power—mightier than you can guess. . . .
>
> It seems strange to me, too—does[nt] it to you, Mattie—that just such characters should have chosen each other to love, that two so tall, proud, stiff people, so easily miffed,—so apt to be pert, two that could . . . stand under the "oak tree" just at the setting of a glorious Sunday's sun—& speak words,—& look, look, so cold,—so bitter, as hardly the deepest hatred could have prompted a pair as would the guiltiest wretch—& his most wronged victim—that two who could love so well, or hate so well—that two just such *could* not choose but love each other!—but we *could not*, Mattie—
>
> We have loved each other a *long time*—longer than either has guessed, but we were too proud to confess it— How we at *last* broke down—I hardly know. [Leyda, *Years and Hours*, vol. I, p. 266]

Later on, Austin came to understand the extent to which Father's distant and unaffectionate nature had affected his own life. Even during the courtship, Austin lamented to Sue that he had never known real affection from the members of his family (and here, given Emily's affection for him, the claim seems a bit too absolute). However, the inescapable inference from the behavior of all three children is that "love" had been given by the parents only in distorted ways—on Mother's side, genuine affection, but ineptly offered; on Father's side, a consuming passion for the Dickinson Family Name that precluded personal kindness, even to his son, and that required Father's principal emotional investment to be given to life *outside* the home, thus mutilating his capacity to lodge emotions in personal relationships.

34 Dickinson, *Letters,* vol. I, pp. 304–6. It is worth remarking that Vinnie also found it difficult to be separated from those she loved. Bingham quotes a letter of hers written in May 1853:

> I've just heard of that frightful rail road accident on the New York way & it makes me feel so sad that I want to sit right down & ask if you are safe. When I hear of such things I feel a desire to cling closer, closer, to my dear friends lest I should lose some of them, & you know I've none to spare. I feel to night as I think over my friends scattered over the earth, & some so far away, if I could once gather them together they should never stray again. . . .
>
> We are lonely with out you Austin, though we are very busy gardening, sewing, cleaning & Mother says it seems as though you had been struck out of existance. [Bingham, *Home,* p. 282.]

35 Dickinson, *Letters,* vol. I, pp. 306, 307 (about 1854). The poem that concludes this letter articulates an "answer" to the blow Dickinson anticipated at the double loss that might be inflicted by Sue and Austin's move to the Midwest—and the answer is poetry. To put the matter prosaically: insofar as Dickinson could embed the emotions involved in her *relationship* with Austin and Sue (or with any other beloved individual from whom she was separated) in a poem, thus retaining access to these emotions even though the other member of the relationship was gone, then she could repair the wound of loss—or, if not repair it, minimize it. This is not a crazy solution (though Dickinson herself seems to have recognized, at least in the case of Austin and Sue, that it was more satisfactory to have the people themselves to relate to). Indeed, this power of poetry has been a commonplace of *love* poetry for many centuries—the lover's passion forever "alive" in his / her verse even when the living bodies of the lovers are long dead. Nonetheless, the decision to define self in terms of a work of art is perhaps the confession of some degree of emotional failure, even when the work of art is supremely successful.

36 Part of Vinnie's bitter recollections about the way she and Emily were treated by Father had to do with Father's preference for Austin. "He became quite admiring of Austin and said he would give him a house and anything he wanted if he would only stay in Amherst," Bingham transcribes from her mother's notes of Vinnie's remarks (Millicent Todd Bingham, *Ancestors' Brocades: The Literary Debut of Emily Dickinson* [New York and London: Harper Brothers, 1945], p. 232).

37 Leyda, *Years and Hours,* vol. I, p. 332. Eventually, Austin repaid his father for the house (named "the Evergreens"). In fact, the financial manipulations by which Edward Dickinson obtained enough money for his real-estate investments in the mid-1850s are complex (and present a not altogether pleasing picture of him). Barton Levi St. Armand has put the story together excellently well; see *Emily Dickinson and Her Culture* (London: Cambridge University Press, 1984), pp. 307–10.

38 Whicher was one of the first to put Dickinson's retirement from the world into a proper New England context: just as there were precedents for Vinnie's "village-gossip" role (one has only to consult the fictions of Jewett or Freeman to find them), there were precedents for Emily's reclusiveness. "Emily Dickinson's retirement from the world had, of course, a tradition behind it. For it has always been a possible way of life for New England spinsters and widows, among them Hawthorne's mother and Alice James herself. Yet this is not the only sense in which she

belonged to New England. For however much of the particularity of her New England circumstances Emily Dickinson transcended to make her great impression upon us, she remains profoundly a poet of her milieu. No one was more conscious than she herself that the consequences of having lived at a certain time in a certain place and in a certain way may be all but absolutely decisive. We must begin, at least, with New England if we hope to gain a true perspective of the myth, the poet, and the poems." (George Frisbie Whicher, *This Was a Poet* [New York: Charles Scribner's Sons, 1938], p. 8.)

One must also take into account the fact that the daughters of Edward Dickinson could *afford* not to marry (as, for example, Susan Gilbert could not!). They would be maintained in great comfort for their entire lives under Father's roof. Also, if they did not marry, they would not have to confront the rigors of childbirth. Certainly Mother's experiences (in whatever form they were conveyed to her daughters) would not have been reassuring about the bearing of children. Susan Gilbert also had a morbid fear of the dangers of birthing. Such fears were not, as we have already seen, unjustified by fact, but Emily Dickinson lived in a family where they were likely to be unusually intense.

39 Bingham, *Home,* pp. 413–14.

40 Ibid., p. 451.

41 Mary's fear lest her writing prove insufficiently elevated for so intellectual a young man as "Coelebs" is humorous, but not without its barb: "It seems so strange to direct to one of my Brothers, that I am quite at a loss how to begin; & the difficulty is not in the least removed, when I consider, that *you* belong to that class of people called *sentimental,* but as I promised myself I would write to you this week, shall do it—& notwithstanding I cannot equal 'Coelebs' in elegance of style. . . ." (January 25, 1828, Dickinson Papers, HCL.)

Edward's tendency to regard women as a different breed from men, despite his claims at the beginning of these essays, is evident from his earliest writing. One can only guess at the variety of ways—from subtle to blatant—that his dismissive, perhaps even contemptuous manner was conveyed to his daughters. One is noted in Bingham: "Edward Dickinson's final letter from Washington [in 1854] is addressed to his daughter Emily. He refers to none of the affairs of state with which his mind was filled. Such matters were discussed with Austin. But in writing to his daughter he appears to have assumed that family and church activities, Sue Gilbert's attack of fever, the weather, the date of his homecoming and his living accommodations for the following session would pretty well cover the topics in which she would be interested, preoccupied as she was with domestic duties. Although from time to time he gave her books, which may or may not have been those she would have chosen, an exchange of ideas was not the plane on which they met." (Bingham, *Home,* p. 386.)

The few remaining references to Edward's mother—the notorious Grandmother Gunn, whose shade was invoked to explain violent fits of temper—are perhaps the only clue we have to the sources for Edward's feelings about women. He was not simply misogynistic: Susan Gilbert managed to charm him well enough. But he seems to have had no notion of his daughter Emily's intelligence or creative capacities; she existed for him as someone who helped to provide a sufficiency of creature comforts when he was at home. Although many people were given the opportunity to read Dickinson's poetry—Sue, Austin, Sam Bowles, Higginson, many diverse friends—there is no indication that *Father* ever read any.

42 These essays were published in the *New England Inquire* on December 22, 1826, and January 5, January 26, February 23, and April 20, 1827. The *Inquire* was published in Amherst for about two years; it ceased publication because it was not a financial success. Edward may have written other articles for the paper (one suspects that he did); however, the only solid evidence of his publication is the fact that holographs of six essays on "Female Education" (five of which were published) still exist in the Dickinson archives at Houghton. The quotation in the text is taken from the essays of December 22, 1826, and January 5, 1827.

43 Dickinson, *Letters,* vol. I, p. 84 (January 23, 1850).

44 Edward Dickinson, "Female Education," *New England Inquire,* January 5, 1827.

45 Dickinson, *Letters,* vol. I, pp. 100–101 (October 27, 1850).

46 Ibid., p. 115 (June 22, 1851).

47 Ibid., p. 127 (July 27, 1851).

48 Ibid., p. 231 (March 18, 1853).

49 Ibid., pp. 242–43 (April 16, 1853).

50 Ibid., p. 212 (June 11, 1852).

51 Leyda, *Years and Hours,* vol. I, p. 232. Bingham prints a letter from Edward to Austin that was written, if not on this day, then very close to it.

> Austin. You will see by the Editor's glorification article in to-day's "Express.," that the Am. & Bel. r.road is "a fixed fact." The contract is made—the workman will be digging, in "Logtown", next week—& we shall see those animating shantees, smoking through an old flour barrel, for a chimney, before many days. The boys fired a few guns—old folks looked on, approvingly—and the whole thing seems as much like a dream, as if we had waked up in the "Mariposa tract", of Col. Fremont, surrounded by the pure "rocks".
> The two great eras in the history of Amherst, are
> 1. The founding of the College.
> 2. The building of the rail road.
> We here "set up our Ebenezer."
> HaHa!!! [Bingham, *Home,* p. 219.]

The document is revealing on several counts. First, it suggests how potently and persistently Edward's identification with his own father's schemes shaped his life. Second, there is a note of pitiful shallowness in this gloating: the vision of an evangelical college (tuition-free to indigent young men of virtue) is scarcely matched by the installation of a railroad spur. Edward wanted—perhaps needed—to view himself not just as having reclaimed the Dickinson honor, but as having surpassed his own father.

52 Dickinson, *Letters,* vol. I, p. 257 (June 19, 1853). The Dickinsons did a great deal of entertaining during these months. The festivities concerning the railroad had begun by May 16 (as Dickinson notes in a letter to Austin on that day). In July the commotion was still keeping the Dickinson girls busy attending to guests: "We have'nt written you oftener, because we've had so much company, and so many things to do," Emily apologizes to Austin (ibid., p. 261 [July 8, 1853]).

53 Ibid., p. 252 (June 5, 1853).

54 The Amherst *Express* occasionally noted that Edward Dickinson, M.C., had returned home to attend to this or that item of private business. After he failed to be re-elected to office, something of a small quarrel arose in the local paper. It is interesting only because it shows the lack of imagination in a man who had direct access to the world-shaking events of his day and who repeatedly chose to return to the little village in New England to attend to "private business" instead of becoming an actor in the great American drama that preceded the Civil War. See Leyda, *Years and Hours,* vol. I, pp. 297, 323.

55 Dickinson Papers, HCL.

56 Dickinson, *Letters,* vol. I, p. 161 (December 15, 1851).

57 See Bingham, *Home,* pp. 179–80. A modern reader looking at Bingham's list may be inclined to dismiss the record, supposing that Emily Dickinson was not personally affected by the deaths of those whose names have failed to turn up regularly in letters. The fact was that most of her letters to Austin concluded with a list of the sick and dying in Amherst; this is not an indication of her morbidity (or if it is, it is the indication of a morbid tendency that afflicted the entire society of which she was a part). The following excerpt from a letter of November 16, 1851, is typical, and it also demonstrates her tendency to construe "house" in terms other than those of brick and mortar:

Col' Kingman's other daughter died yesterday—her funeral is tomorrow. Oh what a house of grief must be their's today—the grass not growing green above the grave of Martha, before little Ellen is laid close beside. I don't know but they are the happier, and we who longer stay the more to be sorrowed for.

Mr. [William] Tyler preached this PM—a sermon concerning Spencer, of which you heard us speak when you were here. A beautiful memorial of his life and character, and preached by the request of Spencer's friends in the village. . . . Susie is lonely, and Martha, and I am lonely too, and this is a lonely world, in the cheerfullest aspects of it. We will not live here always—but [?] will dwell together beyond the bright blue sky, where "they live whom we call dear." [Dickinson, *Letters*, vol. I, pp. 157–58.]

58 Leyda, *Years and Hours*, vol. I, p. 252.

59 Quoted in Sewall, *The Life of Emily Dickinson*, vol. I, p. 106.

60 Of the three children, Vinnie was perhaps the most bitter when death overtook her, and only she among the three had failed to forge some token of "self" that would withstand time and death. Austin's marriage was not happy when he died; however, he had sired children. Vinnie had neither poetry nor children; her propensity for inventing stories of lovers turned away by Father may have spoken rather precisely to the disappointments (but not to the facts) of her *own* life. Emily seems at the end of her life to have been the most serene of the three. She had loved Otis Lord deeply, and her love had been returned. And of course, she understood the quality of her work and reposed in it an unshakable trust in a "birth" after death, the "I" of the poetry to live forever and be forever the same.

61 Dickinson, *Letters*, vol. II, pp. 315, 330. In early June 1854 Dickinson wrote a hasty letter to Austin containing this apology: "This is truly extempore, Austin—I have no notes in my pocket" (ibid., vol. I, p. 296). A few *drafts* of letters were preserved when, after Emily Dickinson's death, Lavinia burned all of her sister's correspondence—drafts of letters to the "Master" and to Judge Otis Lord. That is, there seems good reason to take Dickinson at her word here and to assume that she was making first drafts of much of her correspondence (hence her repetition of the effective phrase in the letters to Susan and to John Graves). This is a significant fact principally because it suggests that far from working haphazardly, Dickinson had begun to keep some sort of file or record of her work—first drafts or letters or phrases copied into a notebook. She seems also to have begun looking over her own work to choose effective turns of language for further use.

62 The most obvious of these are:

Letters, vol. II, p. 324 (about January 20, 1856): "I often wish I was a grass, or a toddling daisy, whom all of these problems of the dust might not terrify"; *The Poems of Emily Dickinson in Three Volumes*, ed. Thomas Johnson (Cambridge, Mass.: Harvard University Press, 1951, 1955), vol. I, p. 265 (#333): "*The Grass so little has to do—/. . . I wish I were a Hay—.*" Johnson ascribes this poem to 1862. The clear echo of the phrase in the letter, however, suggests either that the poem existed in an earlier draft (and that Dickinson was already writing mature verse by 1856 or earlier) or that having kept a file of the letters, Dickinson plucked the felicitous phrase out of an earlier letter to use a variant of it in this poem. The same speculation can be advanced for other letter/verse correlations.

Letters, vol. I, p. 155 (November 11, 1851): "It seemed to me I could pack this little earthly bundle, and bidding the world Goodbye, fly away"; *Poems*, (#527): "*To put this World down, like a Bundle —/And walk steady, away,*" (Johnson date, 1862).

And the following, which—though the correspondence is less exact—is more tantalizing because more lengthy: *Letters*, vol. I, p. 304 (late August 1854): "I rise, because the sun shines, and sleep has done with me, and I brush my hair, and dress me, and wonder what I am and who has made me so, and then I wash the dishes, and anon, wash them again, and then 'tis afternoon, and Ladies call, and evening, and some members of another sex come in to spend the hours, and then that day is done. And, prithee, what is Life?" *Poems*, (#443): "I *tie my Hat — I crease my Shawl — / Life's little duties do — precisely —As the very least / Were infinite — to me — / I put new Blossoms in the Glass — / And throw the old — away — / I push a petal from my Gown / That anchored there — I weigh / The time 'twill be till six o'clock / I have so much to do — / And yet — Existence — some way back — / Stopped — / struck — my ticking — through —"* (Johnson date, 1862).

These are but three examples; there are others throughout the letters of this period. My own conjecture is that sometime around 1850 Dickinson began to keep rather methodical records of her various forms of writing. On January 23, 1850, she wrote to Jane Humphrey, "I have written you a great many letters since you left me—not the kind of letters that go in post-offices—and rise in mail-bags—but queer—little silent ones —. . . but wanting in proof to you—therefore not valid—somehow you will not answer them—and you *would* paper, and ink letters—I will try one of those—tho' not half so precious as the other kind. I have written *those* at night—when the rest of the world were at sleep." (*Letters,* vol. I, p. 81.) This account sounds very much like later accounts of her work on poetry; on October 17, 1851, Dickinson includes a poem (Johnson #2) written in prose form as the last lines of a letter to Austin.

All of this points to the beginning of a disciplined apprenticeship to a *craft* or *vocation* of poetry. I make this point emphatically because Dickinson has sometimes been construed as a kind of naïve, unthinking, spontaneous, possibly hysterical writer.

The composition of a very large number of poems has been assigned to the years around 1862 because of correlations between the handwriting of the poems and the handwriting in the letters of that year. Once the assumption has been made that an extraordinary number of superb poems were *written* in a surprisingly short time, some commensurate explanation for this prodigious production has been sought (the kind most usually advanced has been a "blighted romance"). All such speculation suggests the kind of magical thinking that has so often been applied to Dickinson and her work. There is a much simpler and more probable explanation.

Let us suppose that Dickinson began a process of consolidation in 1858 or so and intensified it—the consolidation, not the *pace* of writing poems—in 1862, the year when she first wrote Higginson, hoping perhaps for encouragement that might lead to publication. I have no wish to dispute the convincing case for dating the *existing copies* of poems by analyzing the handwriting, and I am quite prepared to accept Johnson's findings. However, if we assume that Dickinson began trying her hand at poetry in about 1850, that both her commitment to writing and her application to this work intensified as the years went on, and that this culminated in periods of consolidation, then we find a more believable pattern of production and one that corresponds much more nearly to that of other poets. Furthermore, we are no longer in the position of having to discover some major, real-life crisis that could do two things simultaneously: disrupt the woman's life sufficiently to make her abruptly renounce the world for her art, and at the same time allow her sufficient wit and emotional stamina to produce a prodigious amount of excellent poetry in a very short time (all the while carrying a full load of household duties). Hereafter, poems quoted in the text will follow the Johnson edition unless otherwise indicated and will simply be cited by number.

63 Dickinson, *Letters,* vol. I, p. 236 (March 27, 1853); vol. II, p. 316.
64 Dickinson, *Poems,* #842. Johnson dates this poem in 1864; here again, however, the fair copy may have been made long after the poem was written. The pattern of the fox / hound metaphor in the letters and the poem is striking.
65 D. W. Winnicott, *The Maturational Processes and the Facilitating Environment* (New York: International Universities Press, Inc. 1965), pp. 186, 185, 186, 187.
66 Dickinson, *Letters,* vol. I, pp. 117–18 (June 29, 1851).
67 Ibid., p. 235 (March 27, 1853). The theme of competition with Austin and the notion of Austin's "birthright" run throughout this correspondence. For example: on July 20, 1851

(vol. I, p. 125), Dickinson writes to Austin in Boston, "Oh how I wish I could see your world and it's little kingdoms, and I wish I could see the King—Stranger—he was my *Brother*"; on October 1, 1851 (vol. I, p. 137), she writes, "You say we must'nt trouble to send you any fruit, also your clothes must give us no uneasiness. . . . If you'd only *teased* us for it, and declared that you *would* have it, I should'nt have cared so much that we could find no way to send you any, but you resign so cheerfully your birthright of purple grapes, and do not so much as *murmur* at the departing peaches, that I hardly can taste the one or drink the juice of the other"; on April 12, 1853 (vol. I, p. 241), she ventures, "I have taken *your place* Saturday evening, since you have been away, but I will give it back to you as soon as you get home."

68 Ibid., vol. II, p. 631 (about 1878).

69 Ibid., p. 432 (Cambridge, June 1864). This remark was especially poignant during this period of Dickinson's life, because she was in Cambridge being treated for some sort of eye disorder and was under doctor's instructions not to use her eyes for reading or to subject her sight to bright light. The power of the Word was especially meaningful now.

70 Ibid., vol. II, p. 345 (about January 4, 1859).

71 Ibid., vol. I, pp. 303 (August 18, 1854), 144 (October 9, 1851).

72 Ibid., p. 95 (April 3, 1850).

73 Leyda, *Years and Hours,* vol. I, p. 331.

74 Bingham, *Home,* p. 409.

75 Dickinson, *Letters,* vol. II, pp. 323–24 (about January 20, 1856). It is not difficult to detect some of the subtle implications of this letter. The move, which served to culminate Edward's long quest, was a kind of "death" for other members of the family. Mother's illness was the most obvious sign of a casualty. However, Austin's subservience may also have clouded Emily Dickinson's happiness (even though she actively urged him to stay); she was not without ambivalence in her relationship to Austin. The "gone-to-Kansas" feeling is most immediately a reference to the forlornness of moving (even a block and a half), but there is another implication here: people who moved to Kansas were "go-getters" who had seized the opportunity to better themselves financially; the migration west was the visible sign of America's abandonment of transcendent values for materialistic ones. Dickinson did not take readily to the submission of self demanded by Amherst's version of the transcendent; but she condemned mere materialism and a seeking after "the world" throughout her poetry. Perhaps she thought Father's worldly ambitions shabby; surely this move to the new house was the apotheosis of Father's brick-and-mortar notion of "honor."

76 The occupation of "watching" had many variants. Usually one watched with a feverish patient, with someone who was dying, or with the newborn. Many homes had a bedroom especially for such purposes: in the Evergreens even today (in 1986) there is a first-floor bedroom—a warm room near both the kitchen and the house's only full bathroom—where the mortally ill and the newly born were always taken. It was this sort of "watch" that Vinnie kept for Aunt Lavinia during 1859 and 1860, in the many months preceding her death.

The "watch" kept over Mother during these years of nameless lassitude was of a different kind. For one thing, Mother's condition varied: sometimes she appears to have been incapacitated for long periods; at other times she was up and around (on August 20, 1859, she was part of an outing to Mount Holyoke, for example). However, the housekeeping could not be left in her hands, and when Vinnie left for Boston in February 1859 to spend what would prove an interrupted but lengthy stay with her aunt, housekeeping chores and Mother's care were both left to Emily. The first certain report of Mrs. Dickinson's recovery came in 1860. Mary Shepard wrote to L. M. Boltwood on February 9, "Among the callers, we have had— was *Mrs.* Edward Dickinson, last Thursday P.M. appearing as well as *4 years* ago—when last she was here" (Leyda, *Years and Hours,* vol. II, p. 7). The emphasis suggests that Mrs. Dickinson's recovery was noteworthy.

No easy explanation can be given for Mother's illness (which sounds very much like depression). She may have gone through a menopausal depression. Yet two things argue against this: her long history of withdrawal and sadness, and the fact that the onset of *this episode* of depression coincided so exactly with the move back to the Homestead. Perhaps, for Emily Norcross, Edward's victory was a bringing to fulfillment of all those elements in the marriage that had caused her emotional pain and had fostered her innate inclination to reticence and depression. It is ironic that some have supposed that *Emily Dickinson* went through a severe emotional crisis in 1857 (a year from which there is almost no direct evidence of her activities and which thus permits of virtually unlimited speculation) when it was her *mother* who was actually going through a documented illness.

77 Dickinson, *Letters,* vol. II, p. 321 (October 16, 1855).

78 Ibid., p. 341 (about November 6, 1858).

79 Ibid., pp. 327, 329, 335.

PART TWO ‖ Interlude

1 Theodora Ward, *A Capsule of the Mind* (Cambridge, Mass.: Harvard University Press, 1961), p. 47.

2 Emily Dickinson, *The Letters of Emily Dickinson,* ed. Thomas Johnson and Theodora Ward (Cambridge, Mass.: Harvard University Press, 1958), vol. II, p. 412 (July 1862).

3 So often Dickinson's procedures look as if they might have been derived from Emerson that it is well to make the distinction again. Sewall, in discussing Tyler's funeral sermon for Edward Hitchcock (1864), quotes Tyler, "There is also a language of plants and animals, and it is the language of God," and then goes on to observe, "Were it not for Hitchcock's deeply imbedded Congregational orthodoxy, one might conclude from this passage that he was an Amherst Emerson" (Richard B. Sewall, *The Life of Emily Dickinson* [New York: Farrar, Straus and Giroux, 1974], vol. II, pp. 355–56). The difference is crucial. In the section of *Nature* entitled "Language," Emerson offered his now famous formulation: "1. Words are signs of natural facts. 2. Particular natural facts are symbols of particular spiritual facts. 3. Nature is the symbol of spirit." This is close enough to Hitchcock's view to be confusing, but there are some essential differences. Emerson asserted that man could "see" these spiritual facts with his own power—a power of insight that could be nurtured by a "simplicity" of life. Furthermore, the range of "spiritual truths" a man might "see" was virtually unlimited. By contrast, Hitchcock and the Amherst Trinitarians thought that *no one could, by nature of his or her own powers,* "see" the spiritual facts of nature; only *faith* could adjust the sight to allow human beings to see the "signs" and "emblems" and "symbols" of nature. And the range of what could or would be seen was quite narrowly limited: the professed Christian would "see" confirmation of Christ's promised new birth, and this was the spiritual truth that nature boded forth to the redeemed.

Emily Dickinson's belief differed from both of these standard positions. She began with a view similar to Hitchcock's, not as an article of accepted faith, but as a premise that might be formulated thus: the Maker's nature is inevitably revealed by the nature of His creation; God *wants* and *intends* us to believe that He is good–that He is, in short, what Hitchcock and his fellow Trinitarians make Him out to be. Nor did Dickinson depart from the specifically *religious* reading of nature that the Amherst ministers engaged in. It was *God* and *His ways toward mankind* she sought first to infer; and second she sought to discover man's larger fate—what happened to a human being after death, for example. It was her conclusions that were heresy: God is not good; we can place no confidence in His promises; His "signs" are deceits. Finally, Dickinson would claim (here somewhat closer to Emerson) that one can begin with any thread of the complicated web of creation (Amherst Trinitarianism is as good as anyplace else): all will lead back to the same God and the same sobering truth. Hence, although each man and woman discerns "provincially," each will follow his or her own trail back to the same Creator.

4 Samuel Mather, *The Figures and Types of the Old Testament,* ed. Mason I. Lowance (New York: Johnson Reprint Corporation, 1969), p. 52. A fuller quotation from Mather is revealing: *"In his sojourning and travelling to and fro in an afflicted Condition almost all his Days . . .* he seems to have been the most afflicted Saint that we read of in Scripture, except *Job . . . in regard of his wrestling and prevailing with the Lord. . . .* So Christ often [grappled with agony], and particularly the Night before his Suffering [on the cross]" (pp. 85–86).

5 See Jack Lee Capps, *Emily Dickinson's Readings 1836–1886* (Cambridge, Mass.: Harvard University Press, 1966), pp. 69–71, especially pp. 70–71.

6 See Emily Dickinson, *The Poems of Emily Dickinson,* ed. Thomas Johnson (Cambridge, Mass.: Harvard University Press, 1951, 1955), vol. III, p. 954 (on verso of #*1385*).

7 #*59* ("A little East of Jordan"), #*110* ("Artists wrestled here!"), #*201* ("Two swimmers wrestled on the spar"), #*284* ("The Drop, that wrestles in the Sea—"), #*1255* ("Longing is like the Seed"), #*1724* ("How dare the robins sing"). However, because this story from Genesis had so many significant resonances for Dickinson, based on elements of the text that had been elaborated by the revival preachers and Biblical scholars of her day, it is difficult to know where to leave off in "identifying" Jacob poems in the Dickinson canon. For example, #*190* ("He was weak, and I was strong — then") is undeniably a Jacob poem, even though the verb is "strove" and not "wrestled." Furthermore, there are many other poems in which the verbs "strive," "wrestle," and "grapple" hint—sometimes very strongly, sometimes only in indirect ways—at a recursion to the Jacob struggle. See, for example, #*1724*, which concludes, *"Insulting is the sun / To him whose mortal light / Beguiled of immortality / Bequeaths him to the night. / Extinct be every hum / In deference to him / Whose garden wrestles with the dew, / At daybreak overcome!"*

8 Ward's comments on the poems are often canny. Surprisingly, however, although Ward offers a good account of revivals and conversions (*Capsule,* pp. 14–18), she does not identify the role played in them by the story of Jacob, and thus she is not in a position to identify the underlying source for the struggle described.

9 See (in the Dickinson family library) Charles Simmons, *A Scriptural Manual* (New York, 1845), p. 55. "Wrestling Scripture: Sin and danger of perverting the Bible . . . The long-suffering of our Lord *is* salvation; even as our beloved brother Paul also, according to the wisdom given unto him, hath written unto you; . . . As also in all his epistles, speaking in them of these things; in which are some things hard to be understood, which they that are unlearned and unstable *wrest,* as they do also the other scriptures, unto their own destruction" (italics mine). This short excerpt and the longer passage from which it is taken have very much the tone of Father Mapple's sermon on submission in *Moby Dick.* It seems convincing evidence that Melville had heard such sentiments delivered from the pulpit—as Dickinson had also.

10 Richard P. Blackmur, "Religious Poetry in the United States," in *Religious Perspectives in American Culture,* ed. James Ward Smith and A. Leland Jamison (Princeton, N.J.: Princeton University Press, 1961), pp. 276–78.

11 Dickinson, *Letters,* vol. II, p. 404 (April 25, 1862).

12 See *The Interpreter's Bible* (Nashville, Tenn.: Abingdon, 1952), vol. I, pp. 722–28. See also Charles R. Brown, *What Is Your Name?* (New Haven: Yale University Press, 1924). Actually, the play on words is even more complex. The ancient legend that underlies this episode concerns the primitive belief that every region had an indigenous supernatural being whose name was intricately connected with the place in which he resided; here that being was the "Jab-

bok" (named after a nearby stream). It is the word "Jabbok" on which the word "abhaq" is the most immediate pun. In English, "Jacob" and "Jabbok" are virtually the same word, but turned inside out—that is, they are *mirrors* of each other. Jacob's journey at this point is to a rendezvous with his brother Esau, whom he had cheated of a birthright. Worried about this fraternal face-to-face encounter, Jacob meets God instead—God having assumed the name Jabbok for the purpose of this combat. Thus there are several face-to-face encounters compressed here: (1) the feared encounter with Esau, (2) the actual encounter with God-as-Jabbok, (3) the verbal play of "encountering"—as "Jacob" faces and mirrors "Jabbok." All of this complexity is echoed by additional word play; so (in Genesis 32:20) such words as "appease," "before," and "accept" all have the Hebrew root for "face" as one of their constituents; and the same sort of word play on the Hebrew root for "face" can also be seen in Genesis 33:10. See *Interpreter's Bible* and *What Is Your Name?* for a fuller explanation. Actually, there are conflicting opinions concerning the momentous occasion when God withdrew His face from mankind forever: the Jewish tradition inclines to the belief that *in some sense* the prophet Moses was accorded that final privilege. There are texts from the Bible to support such a view:

> . . . all the people rose up, and stood every man at his tent door, and looked after Moses, until he was gone into the tabernacle. And it came to pass, as Moses entered into the tabernacle, the cloudy pillar descended, and stood at the door of the tabernacle, and the LORD talked with Moses. And all the people saw the cloudy pillar stand at the tabernacle door: . . . And the LORD spake unto Moses face to face, as a man speaketh unto his friend (Exodus 34:8–11).

> And it came to pass, when Moses came down from mount Sinai with the two tables of testimony in Moses' hand, when he came down from the mount, that Moses wist not that the skin of his face shone while he talked with him. And when Aaron and all the children of Israel saw Moses, behold, the skin of his face shone; and they were afraid to come nigh him (Exodus 34:29–30).

> And there arose not a prophet since in Israel like unto Moses, whom the LORD knew face to face, *in all the signs and the wonders which the LORD sent him to do in the land of Egypt, to Pharaoh, and to all his servants, and to all his land* (Deuteronomy 34:10–11, my emphasis).

Not surprisingly, however, the American Puritans traditionally construed Moses as the correlative type for a leader in the wilderness or for a law-giver. Thus *this* series of "face-to-face" confrontations was not between man and God directly, but between man (here the prophet Moses) and a *sign* or *symbol* of God, the pillar of fire that makes Moses' face shine with such frightening radiance. Probably Dickinson knew of the tradition that postulated Moses as the last man to confront God directly; however, when she wrote of Moses' relationship with God, she focused upon a different visual loss—God's forcing Moses to look upon the Promised Land while refusing to allow him to enter it (see the discussion of Poem #597).

13 Dickinson, *Letters,* vol. II, pp. 327–28 (late April 1856).

14 Ibid., p. 356 (December 1859).

15 Ibid., vol. III, p. 903 (spring 1886), italics mine.

PART THREE ‖ I · The Voice

1 Archibald MacLeish, "The Private World," in *Emily Dickinson: Three Views,* by Archibald MacLeish, Louise Bogan, and Richard Wilbur (Amherst: Amherst College Press, 1960), p. 19.

2 The photographs and paintings of the Dickinson family suggest that Emily Norcross Dickinson and both her daughters suffered in varying degrees from "exotropia" or walleye. The onset of symptoms from this congenital disorder is often soon after birth, and characteristic problems are eye strain, blurring of vision, difficulties with prolonged periods of reading, headaches, double vision, and extreme sensitivity to bright light—all of which would probably occur only intermittently. If the inferences made from slender evidence are true and the three women *did* all suffer from this disease, then the physical ailment would have provided yet another explanation for the eye-contact deprivation that seems to have occurred in Emily Dickinson's early life, for both mother and child would have had difficulty of a purely mechanical sort in achieving such contact (although unless the mother already had *other* inadequacies in achieving intimate communication, one would assume that this mechanical defect could be in large measure compensated by, for example, touch). It is evident from Austin's letters home during his Boston days that he, too, suffered from some of these symptoms, yet extant photos and paintings do not suggest that he suffered from exotropia. Moreover, although both Vinnie and Emily had the physical look associated with the disease and Austin had the symptoms—even to the point of having to rest his eyes—only Emily seems to have attached *terror* to the eye disorder. For a complete discussion of the medical problem see Martin Wand and Richard B. Sewall, "'Eyes Be Blind, Heart Be Still': A New Perspective on Emily Dickinson's Eye Problem," *New England Quarterly*, September 1979, pp. 400–406.

3 Emily Dickinson, *The Letters of Emily Dickinson*, ed. Thomas Johnson and Theodora Ward (Cambridge, Mass.: Harvard University Press, 1958), vol. II, p. 404 (April 25, 1862).

4 *The Lyman Letters: New Light on Emily Dickinson and Her Family*, ed. Richard B. Sewall (Amherst: University of Massachusetts Press, 1965), p. 76. Franklin's edition of the Manuscript Books gives further evidence (though indirect) that it was a gathering together and not a great burst of phenomenal creativity that took place in 1862–63. As Franklin asserts: "One motive Emily Dickinson had in constructing these books was to reduce disorder in her manuscripts. As she copied poem after poem onto Uniform sheets of stationery, she destroyed earlier versions, so that today few worksheets survive for poems included in the fascicles." See *The Manuscript Books of Emily Dickinson*, ed. R. W. Franklin (Cambridge, Mass.: The Belknap Press of Harvard University Press, 1981), vol. I, pp. ix–x. As one pursues the Franklin edition, an elegantly simple fact emerges. These must be copies and not pieces of unedited, original poetry all composed in an extraordinarily short period of time: when a poem is long, it consistently begins at the top of a page; when there is sufficient space left on a page after one poem has been inscribed, a brief poem regularly has been chosen to fill in the gap. In short, this is a writer transcribing her work and taking care to be economical with the area of the paper she is using.

5 Dickinson, *Letters*, vol. II, pp. 433–35. The account I have given of her relatively circumscribed life is conservative: that is, I mention only what we *know* she did. It is possible that she visited Springfield more often than the correspondence indicates, for letters can demonstrate only a separation, and letters constitute our evidence.

6 This letter is in manuscript and has been reproduced in Richard B. Sewall, *The Life of Emily Dickinson* (New York: Farrar, Straus and Giroux, 1974), vol. I. pp. 153–54.

7 Adrienne Rich, "Vesuvius at Home: The Power of Emily Dickinson," *Parnassus: Poetry in Review*, vol. V, no. 1 (Fall-Winter 1976), p. 51.

8 Martha Dickinson Bianchi, *Emily Dickinson Face to Face: Unpublished Letters with Notes and Reminiscences* (Hamden, Conn.: Archon Books, 1970), p. 66.

9 Rich, "Vesuvius," pp. 60, 61.

10 Millicent Todd Bingham, *Emily Dickinson's Home* (New York: Dover Publications, 1967), p. 112.

11 Susan P. Conrad, *Perish the Thought: Intellectual Women in Romantic America, 1830–1860* (Secaucus, N.J.: Citadel Press, 1978), pp. 26–27. Barbara Welter's "The Cult of True Wom-

anhood," in her *Dimity Convictions: The American Woman in the Nineteenth Century* (Athens, Ohio: Ohio University Press, 1976), also illuminates this issue—as does Ann Douglas Wood's essay "The 'Scribbling Women' and Fanny Fern: Why Women Wrote," *American Quarterly,* vol. 23 (1971), p. 6.

12 Quoted by Ann Douglas Wood in "'Scribbling Women,'" p. 6.

13 Thomas Wentworth Higginson, "An Open Portfolio," reprinted in *The Recognition of Emily Dickinson,* ed. Caesar R. Blake and Carlton F. Wells (Ann Arbor, Mich.: University of Michigan Press, 1968), p. 3.

14 Dickinson, *Letters,* vol. III, p. 733 (about 1882).

15 Ibid., vol. II, p. 345 (about January 4, 1859).

16 Ibid., p. 376 (1861?).

17 Ibid., vol. III, p. 883 (early August 1885).

18 Thomas Johnson, *Emily Dickinson: An Interpretive Biography* (Cambridge, Mass.: Harvard University Press, 1955), pp. 54–55.

19 Dickinson, *Letters,* vol. II, p. 380 (summer 1861).

20 Ibid., pp. 408–9 (June 7, 1862).

21 Mahler gives a superb description of this period that has vexed so many parents: "In other words, at the time when the junior toddler of 12 to 15 months has grown into the senior toddler of up to 24 months, a most important emotional turning point has been reached. Now the toddler begins to experience, more or less gradually and more or less keenly, the obstacles that lie in the way of what he evidently anticipated at the height of his 'practicing' exhilaration would be his 'conquest of the world.' Concomitant with the acquisition of primitive skills and perceptual cognitive faculties, there has been an increasingly clear differentiation, a separation, between the intrapsychic representation of the object and the self-representation. At the very height of mastery, toward the end of the practicing period, it had already begun to dawn on the junior toddler that the world is *not* his oyster, that he must cope with it more or less 'on his own,' very often as a relatively helpless, small, and separate individual, unable to command relief or assistance merely by feeling the need for it, or even by giving voice to that need." (Margaret S. Mahler, Fred Pine, and Anni Bergman, *The Psychological Birth of the Human Infant* [New York: Basic Books, 1975], p. 78.) See also Anna Freud, "Negativism and Emotional Surrender," *International Journal of Psycho-Analysis,* vol. 33 (1952), p. 265.

22 William Paley, *Works* (London: Henry Fisher, Son, and P. Jackson, 1828), vol. II, p. 3.

23 See poems 195, 197, 415, 517, 776, 828, 1023. In poems 986 and 1104 the word is almost, but not quite, centered.

24 Charles R. Anderson, *Emily Dickinson's Poetry: Stairway of Surprise* (New York: Holt, Rinehart and Winston, 1960), pp. 55, 57.

25 Dickinson, *Letters,* vol. I, p. 9 (February 1845). Italics mine.

26 Bingham, *Home,* p. 409.

27 Jay Leyda, *The Years and Hours of Emily Dickinson* (New Haven: Yale University Press, 1960), vol. II, p. 39.

28 Dickinson, *Letters,* vol. II, p. 449 (early March 1866).

29 Ibid., vol. III, p. 882 (summer 1885).

30 In *The Bonds of Womanhood* (New Haven: Yale University Press, 1977), Nancy Cott gives several descriptions of the changing role of the mother in the nineteenth century. Early in the century, the marked division between men's and women's roles began; "More than ever before in New England history, the care of children appeared to be mothers' sole work and the work of mothers alone" (p. 46). As the century drew on, a mythology of the home arose: "Home was an 'oasis in the desert,' a 'sanctuary' where 'sympathy, honor, virtue are assembled'" (p. 64). Ultimately, this intensely private role was held to have a social virtue: "The purpose of women's vocation was to stabilize society by generating and regenerating moral character.

This goal reflected an awareness, also apparent in other social commentary and reform efforts of the time, that the impersonal world of money-making lacked institutions to effect moral restraint" (p. 97).

31 Bingham, *Home,* p. 113.

32 Critics have often made the claim that this imagery is an unselfconscious, emotive expression of her own emotional hunger. John Cody makes the strongest psychological claim of any of Dickinson's critics: "'Affection is like bread,' wrote Emily Dickinson, 'unnoticed till we starve, and then we dream of it, and sing of it, and paint it.' The observation reflects the profound and primitive identification of food with love and reveals perhaps the most powerful under-current of the poet's personality, a ravenous search for affection. Emily Dickinson seems al-ways to have craved love; indeed she dreamed of it and she sang of it in her poems. Her insatiable love needs and their frustration saturate the poetry and the letters, and one finds her forever deriving new images of emotional want and fulfillment from the basic metaphor of food and drink." (John Cody, *After Great Pain* [Cambridge, Mass.: Harvard University Press, 1971], p. 39.)

Cody's remarks are not altogether off the mark: there *is* a cry for affection in Dickinson's work. However, his unfamiliarity with the symbol system that dominated Dickinson's culture does not allow him to understand the relationship between "food" and *separation,* for he never mentions this imagery in connection with the Lord's Supper at all. Thus he is not equipped to understand the rather explicit desire for a "self" that has been confirmed by interaction with a significant "other." Most important, he perceives Dickinson as a *patient* afflicted with *symptoms,* not as a controlled artist fashioning poetry.

33 John Calvin, *Institutes,* Book IV, Section xvii, 20–21, translated by Henry Beveridge, 2 vols. (London: James Clarke & Co., Limited, 1975), vol. II, pp. 572–75. Lewalski has examined the relationship to the Lord's Supper and the evolution of the Protestant religious lyric:

The Reformation focus upon the literal text led Calvin and his English followers to pay the closest attention to the trope and figures of scripture as the very vehicle of the Holy Ghost. Tropes are now perceived as God's chosen formulations of his revealed truth which man must strive to understand rightly, in themselves, and not as a stimulus to a higher vision.

This attention to figurative language was dictated also by Calvin's doctrine of the sac-raments, especially of the Lord's Supper. . . . Calvin insists over and over again that [the Catholics] are the literalists, unable to recognize Christ's phrase, "This is my Body," as a figurative statement—a metonymy conforming to the common scriptural usage of such figures. [Barbara Kiefer Lewalski, *Protestant Poetics and the Seventeenth-Century Reli-gious Lyric* (Princeton, N.J.: Princeton University Press, 1979), p. 77. See also Lewalski's discussion of sacramental meditation, pp. 147–60.]

Ursula Brumm also discusses the particular importance of the Lord's Supper in American Protestant thought and in formulations of American Protestant poetry. Her discussion of Edward Taylor's Meditations on the Lord's Supper (*American Thought and Religious Typol-ogy,* trans. John Hoaglund [New Brunswick, N.J.: Rutgers University Press, 1970], pp. 56–85) are especially relevant to Dickinson's poetry.

34 Dickinson, *Letters,* vol. II, pp. 454, 600, 614–15 (June 9, 1899; January 1878; about 1878).

35 In this poem it is especially interesting to notice Dickinson's evasiveness about the *gender* of the poet ("This was a Poet — It is That"). "Amazing Grace" is significant in several ways to this poem. "Amazement" in the Protestant tradition is linked to the Fall, the losing of God's purity for a maze of crooked paths: so Milton writes of Eve after the Fall:

Thus Eve with Countenance blithe her storie told;
But in her Cheek distemper flushing glow'd

On th' other side, Adam, soon as he heard
The fatal Trespas done by Eve, *amaz'd,*
Astonied stood and Blank. . . .

(*Paradise Lost,* book IX,
lines 886–90; italics mine)

And throughout Milton's epic poem, sin and "amazement" are conflated. In keeping with this tradition, Christ's redemption becomes a *different kind* of amazement; thus is Paul *blinded* by Grace in his conversion. "Amazing Grace" takes up the complex theme of such Grace and its relationship to eyesight and to the right path for *reward* and *glory.* Its subject was therefore close to Dickinson's own rendering of this long tradition:

Amazing Grace! How sweet the sound,
That saved a wretch like me!
I once was lost, but now I'm found,
Was blind, but now I see. . . .

36 Dickinson, *Letters,* vol. II, p. 415 (August 1862).

37 Ibid., vol. I, pp. 138–39 (October 1, 1851).

38 This is a simplified explanation. Actually, Emerson himself is more ambivalent than the quotation in the text suggests about this yielding up of "self" to "the Universal Being": hence in this famous section of *Nature,* the theme of "*integrity*" and "*integrate*" hammers insistently against the passive receptivity of the dominant image. The conclusion of the essay (chapter VIII, "Prospects") inverts the initial posture of man and the universe: "The invariable mark of wisdom is to see the miraculous in the common. . . . So shall we come to look at the world with new eyes. It shall answer the endless inquiry of the intellect. . . . Know then that the world exists for you. For you is the phenomenon perfect." Not surprisingly, this last section sounds much like Whitman. Emerson is perhaps most optimistic—most capable of creating an integrated and contained speaker—when the force of transcendence is not *immediately* at issue and man can confront the universe unassailed.

39 Dickinson, *Letters,* vol. II, p. 518 (January 1874).

40 Monteiro and St. Armand, quoting William Holmes and John W. Barber, *Religious Allegories,* p. 11. Monteiro and St. Armand make the connection between this emblem plate and the poem "Faith — is the Pierless Bridge" (#915), but not to the poem cited in the text. However, it seems clear that Dickinson had this emblem in mind here, too. See George Monteiro and Barton Levi St. Armand, "The Experienced Emblem: A Study of the Poetry of Emily Dickinson," in *Prospects,* ed. Jack Salzman (New York: Burt Franklin & Co., 1981), p. 256.

41 See Cynthia Griffin Wolff, "Literary Reflections of the Puritan Character," *Journal of the History of Ideas,* vol. XXIX, no. 1 (January-March 1968). I make the point in this essay that the "saint's life," which was typically offered in a funeral sermon, is the most *social* version of self that a Puritan society offered. Ironically, only after death could this summation be possible—and it was the "meaning" of the life-in-the-world (as extracted by the minister who preached the sermon) that allowed for a prediction of the dead person's status in the afterlife. Thus the sermon that dominated the "narrative form" of the funeral functioned to instruct those who were still alive and constrained to practice Christianity within a social context; and *never* did a Puritan's life have so much meaning for others as it did here, *after death!*

42 The account of the family reunion was written by a member of the family who lived in upstate New York, and it was printed there. Such was the usual practice: one had one's work printed in the town where one lived; there were enough job printers to do that. For an account of printers in the Amherst area, see *Amherst Imprints, 1825–1875,* ed. Newton McKeon and Catherine Cowles (Amherst: Amherst College, 1946).

43 Wood, "'Scribbling Women,'" pp. 81–82, 83.

44 Sewall, *Life,* vol. II, pp. 469–70.

45 Leyda, *Years and Hours,* vol. II, p. 122.

46 Sewall, *Life,* vol. II, pp. 473, 471.

47 Leyda, *Years and Hours,* vol. I, p. 355.

48 Dickinson, *Letters,* vol. II, p. 342 (dated about December 1858). I conjecture that this letter was written earlier, for the poem "Nobody knows this little Rose," which was printed in the *Republican* in August 1858, may have been an enclosure in this letter. Certainly the sympathy Emily Dickinson felt for Mary Bowles is patent—not only throughout this period of repeated stillbirths, but later as well.

49 Ibid., p. 361 (Leyda and Johnson differ about the date of this; about 1860).

50 Ibid., p. 354 (September 1859).

51 Ibid., pp. 361–62 (April 1860).

52 Ibid., pp. 363 (about 1860), 364 (about 1860). Although the precise date for *neither* of these is available, I would postulate that p. 364 preceded p. 363. The question of "faith"—the Trinitarian belief that one must experience a conversion experience in order to gain access to Heaven—was especially vexing in the case of the death of babies (who could not, obviously, have experienced a conversion experience), and in some circles was hotly debated at this time. Dickinson may have had the current debate in mind in these letters to Sam Bowles, even though the Bowleses were Unitarians, for the issue was being widely discussed. Harriet Beecher Stowe eventually broke with her staunchly Trinitarian father's position, precisely because she could not assent to the proposition that babies could not be admitted to Heaven. *The Minister's Wooing,* published in 1859 and thus quite current, addresses this quesion.

53 Monteiro and St. Armand, "Emblem," p. 260, commenting on THE PATH OF LIFE, AND WAY OF DEATH (fig. 36) in Holmes and Barber, *Allegories.* The emblem is graphic and might have impressed even as secular a man as Sam Bowles.

54 George S. Merriam, *The Life and Times of Sam Bowles,* 2 vols. (New York: Century Co., 1885), vol. I, pp. 5, 12, 171.

55 I am indebted to Sally Begley for this scrutiny of the attitude of the *Republican* toward the activities of Higginson.

56 Dickinson, *Letters,* vol. II, p. 413 (summer 1862).

57 Merriam, *Sam Bowles,* vol. I, pp. 208, 216.

58 Leyda, *Years and Hours,* vol. I, p. 363.

59 *Atlantic Monthly,* vol. III, #15 (February 1859), pp. 137–50 passim.

60 Ibid., vol. IX, #54 (April 1862), pp. 401–11 passim.

61 R. J. Wilson, "Emily Dickinson and the Problem of Career," *Massachusetts Review,* vol. XX, #3 (Autumn 1979), p. 459.

62 Higginson, "Letter," p. 409.

63 Dickinson, *Letters,* vol. II, p. 403 (April 15, 1862).

64 Ibid., pp. 411–12 (July 1862).

65 Sewall, *Life,* vol. II, p. 538.

66 Karen Dandurand, who discovered five Dickinson poems that were published in 1864 in New York, comes to this decisive conclusion: "The publications and reprints in 1864 make clear that editors were interested in her poems and that more poems would have been published had she offered them" ("New Dickinson Civil War Publications," *American Literature,* vol. 56, no. 1 [March 1984], p. 17).

PART THREE ‖ II · The Wrestle for Dominion

1 W. H. Auden, *Forewords and Afterwords* (New York: Random House, 1973), p. 52. Auden says: "The Christian faith is always a scandal to the imagination and reason of the flesh, but the particular aspect which seems most scandalous depends upon the prevailing mentality of a period or a culture. Thus, to both the gnostics of the fourth century and the liberal humanists of the eighteenth, the Cross was an offense, but for quite different reasons. The gnostic said: 'Christ was the Son of God, therefore He cannot have been physically crucified. The Crucifixion was an illusion.' The liberal humanist said: 'Christ was physically crucified, therefore He cannot have been the Son of God. His claim was a delusion.' In our own day, the stumbling block is again different. I think most Christians will find themselves [sympathetic to Simone Weil's statement], 'If the Gospels omitted all mention of Christ's resurrection, faith would be easier for me. The Cross by itself suffices me.'"

2 Ann Douglas, *The Feminization of American Culture* (New York: Alfred A. Knopf, 1977), p. 218. A reassuring posthumous voice even began to dominate certain sermon patterns. See the entire chapter "The Domestication of Death."

3 The following passage from Ik Marvel's *Dream Life* can demonstrate the sentimental tone in which "religion" was rendered. "But your clergyman will say perhaps, with what seems to you, quite unnecessary coldness, that goodness is not to be reckoned in your chances of safety;—that there is a Higher Goodness, whose merit is All-Sufficient. This puzzles you sadly; nor will you escape the puzzle, until in the presence of the Home altar, which seems to guard you, as the Lares guarded Roman children, you *feel*—you cannot tell how,—that good actions must spring from good sources; and that those sources must lie in that Heaven, toward which your boyish spirit yearns, as you kneel at your mother's side." (Donald G. Mitchell [Ik Marvel], "Boy Religion," in *Dream Life* [New York: Charles Scribner, 1851], p. 77.) Dickinson's own liking for such literature as *Dream Life* is perhaps the most fascinating puzzle. It is clear from the letters that she *did* like it, and not surprisingly, the predilection is sometimes reflected in her work. The following "consolation" poem—scarcely among her best—is treasured by many Dickinson readers even today.

> *I never saw a Moor —*
> *I never saw the Sea —*
> *Yet know I how the Heather looks*
> *And what a Billow be.*
>
> *I never spoke with God*
> *Nor visited in Heaven —*
> *Yet certain am I of the spot*
> *As if the Checks were given —*
>
> *(# 1052)*

Clearly the "wrestle" for faith was always active. Dickinson's best poetry may denounce God, but the dynamic of hope and despair seems always to have been at work within her.

4 Emily Dickinson, *The Letters of Emily Dickinson*, ed. Thomas Johnson and Theodora Ward (Cambridge, Mass.: Harvard University Press, 1958), vol. II, p. 341 (about November 6, 1858).

5 Ibid., pp. 423, 424 (February 1863).

6 Ibid., pp. 425–26 (about 1863). Dickinson signed this letter "'Barabbas' —" after the hardened criminal who was brought before Pilate along with Jesus. When Pilate asked the crowd which to release, the crowd settled upon the unworthy Barabbas. Dickinson almost certainly had in mind that Higginson was facing death in the Civil War and that she had been spared

this mortal confrontation; possibly she felt guilty about her safety and his danger, another example of God's whimsy.

7 There are some poems of conventional faith among even Dickinson's earliest work. Nos. *18, 48, 129, 178, 235, 325, 392,* and *575* are a few of the best of this stamp.

8 It would be interesting to know whether Dickinson was familiar with Donne's "Ecstasy" or with the religious tradition that infused this love poem. Of all the metaphysical poets widely read today, Donne is perhaps the one that she would have been least likely to know. Yet her profane appropriation of religious conventions is very like Donne's.

9 Dickinson, *Letters,* vol. II, p. 514 (1873?). Again, this is a simplification. Both Wordsworth and Emerson moved away from the confident, optimistic postures of the early work to more somber views. Emerson especially fell into extreme dubiety in such essays as "Montaigne; or the Sceptic" (1850), "Illusions" (1857), and "Fate" (1860). Indeed, many of Emerson's observations in "Illusions" coincide with Dickinson's own views about nature.

10 A number of Dickinson's poems render sunrise and sunset as bloody scenes of destruction. See, for example, Nos. *110, 152, 223, 658, 1140, 1174, 1415, 1471, 1593,* and *1764.*

11 Dickinson, *Letters,* vol. II, p. 554 (1876).

12 Ibid., p. 576 (about March 1877).

13 Heman Humphrey, *Revival: Sketches and Manual* (New York: American Tract Society, 1859), p. 337.

14 See Emily Dickinson, *The Poems of Emily Dickinson,* ed. Thomas Johnson (Cambridge, Mass.: Harvard University Press, 1951, 1955), vol. II, pp. 753–54.

15 All versions of this poem come from Johnson #216. That Dickinson did not complain about emendations or about the fact that the poem had been published suggests her willing cooperation in the venture.

16 See R. W. Franklin, ed., *The Manuscript Books of Emily Dickinson,* 2 vol. (Cambridge, Mass.: Belknap Press of Harvard University Press, 1981), vol. I, pp. 537, 555. Franklin finds what he terms a final stanza of this poem (what I would term an alternate stanza) at the end of the packet including the fair copy. The holograph copy of the poem itself has been lost, and the only copies available are two made by Mrs. Todd. The Todd copies (transcribed from an original) differ slightly: in one, the penultimate line was omitted and then inserted (evidently an error in transcribing that was corrected by the insertion); in the other, a fair copy with no corrections, the omitted line in included in its correct place. For reasons I do not understand, Franklin choses to omit this penultimate line, perhaps presuming that Todd added it. Yet all of Todd's transcriptions of the poems are agonizingly accurate; it was the Bianchi batch of poems that were published in "corrected" form. I have cited the poem as Todd copied it in her fair draft.

17 Dickinson, *Letters,* vol. II, p. 559 (August 1876); vol. III, pp. 667 (July 1880), 728 (April 30, 1882), 779 (mid-June 1883).

18 Edward Hitchcock, *Religious Lectures on Peculiar Phenomena* (Amherst: J. S. & C. Adams, 1850), p. 47.

19 See Franklin, *Manuscript Books,* vol. II, p. 851. It is clear in the manuscript copy that Dickinson intended the sixth line to be doubly long. Every printed copy of the poem breaks that line into two, regularizing the second stanza to four lines. In *Poems,* Johnson prints the beginning of the first word of the seventh line with a small letter, not a capital, preserving the practice in Dickinson's fair copy; yet the author also slightly *indented* that word, indicating that if she had had room on the page, the sixth line would have been continued.

20 Dickinson, *Letters,* vol. II, pp. 524 (May 1874), 585 (June 20, 1877).

21 Hitchcock, *Religious Lectures,* pp. 109–10.

22 Dickinson, *Letters,* vol. I, p. 54 (November 6, 1847).

23 Jay Leyda, *The Years and Hours of Emily Dickinson* (New Haven: Yale University Press, 1960), vol. II, p. 80.

PART THREE ‖ *III · Love and the Love Poetry*

1 This reading seems to imply that #577 was written after #510; both are in the handwriting of 1862 and dated as such in the Johnson edition. In fact, it doesn't matter which was written first. It is sufficient to note that both draw upon the same language for the nightmare description of Heaven.

2 Emily Dickinson, *The Letters of Emily Dickinson,* ed. Thomas Johnson and Theodora Ward (Cambridge, Mass.: Harvard University Press, 1958), vol. I, pp. 116 (June 22, 1851), 236 (March 27, 1853), 282–83 (January 13, 1854); vol. II, p. 408 (June 7, 1862).

3 Ibid., pp. 408–9 (June 7, 1862), 415 (August 1862).

4 Ibid., p. 392 (no date).

5 Ibid., vol. III., pp. 737–38 (August 1882).

6 Jay Leyda, *The Years and Hours of Emily Dickinson* (New Haven: Yale University Press, 1960), vol. I, p. 362; vol. II, pp. 28, 75.

7 Ibid., pp. 37, 44–45.

8 Ibid., pp. 125, 129–30.

9 Dickinson, *Letters,* vol. II, pp. 385 (early December 1861), 390 (about January 11, 1861).

10 Ibid., pp. 394–95. The poem is Johnson #792.

11 Ibid., p. 394. The poem is Johnson #1072.

12 Leyda, *Years and Hours,* vol. II, p. 76.

13 Dickinson, *Letters,* vol. II, p. 402 (early April 1862).

14 Ibid., pp. 334 (about June 1858), 382 (October 1861).

15 Ibid., pp. 419 (November 1862), 419–20 (November 1862), 589–90 (about 1877). See Johnson's account of the incident for Bowles's quotation (*Letters,* vol. II, pp. 589–90).

16 Ibid., p. 540 (about 1875).

17 Leyda, *Years and Hours,* vol. I, pp. 267, 285, 288.

18 Dickinson, *Letters,* vol. II, p. 548 (February 1876).

19 Ibid., pp. 614–15 (about 1878).

20 Ibid., vol. III, p. 728 (April 30, 1882); vol. II, p. 616 (about 1878).

21 Ibid., p. 617 (about 1878); vol. III, pp. 663–64 (about 1880), 728 (April 30, 1882).

22 Leyda, *Years and Hours,* vol. II, pp. 375–76. It is always interesting to know where rumors begin. During her lifetime, Dickinson's epistolary friendship with the Reverend Charles Wadsworth was acknowledged by all her family, and no one raised the slightest hint of unrequited love. After her death, however, rumors did linger—not about her relationship with Wadsworth, but about her love for Judge Lord (these fueled by his niece and, perhaps, Sue). To counteract them, Vinnie began to spin a tale of hopeless, but utterly pure and unconsummated love between her deceased sister, Emily, and the Philadelphia minister Charles Wadsworth. Martha Bianchi further amplified the story and gave a heightened account of it in *The Life and Letters* (Boston and New York: Houghton Mifflin, 1924, reissued, 1930). Afterward, the tale became an unsubstantiated staple of the Emily Dickinson legend.

23 Dickinson, *Letters,* vol. III, pp. 747 (November 1882?), 753 (December 3, 1882), 816 (March 1884).

24 Leyda, *Years and Hours,* vol. II, p. 475.

25 *The Lyman Letters; New Light on Emily Dickinson and Her Family,* ed. Richard B. Sewall (Amherst: University of Massachusetts Press, 1965), pp. 34, 36–37.

26 The three "Master" letters are in Dickinson, *Letters,* vol. II, pp. 333 (about 1858), 373–75 (about 1861), 391–92 (early 1862).

27 Millicent Todd Bingham, *Emily Dickinson's Home* (New York: Dover Publications, 1967), p. 374.

PART   FOUR   ‖   The Razor's Edge

1 See Emily Dickinson, *The Poems of Emily Dickinson,* ed. Thomas Johnson (Cambridge, Mass.: Harvard University Press, 1951, 1955), vol. I, pp. 231–34, for an account of these variants.
2 Emily Dickinson, *The Letters of Emily Dickinson,* ed. Thomas Johnson and Theodora Ward (Cambridge, Mass.: Harvard University Press, 1958), vol. III, p. 670 (early September 1880).

PART   FIVE   ‖   I · The Cosmos as Mirror

1 Emily Dickinson, *The Poems of Emily Dickinson,* ed. Thomas Johnson (Cambridge, Mass.: Harvard University Press, 1951, 1955), vol. III, pp. 936–37.
2 There has been some disagreement concerning the order of lines in stanza two of this poem. There is but one copy of the poem—a holograph in which Emily Dickinson numbered the lines of the second stanza in the following way:

[1] The Feet, mechanical, go round —
[3] Of Ground, or Air, or Ought —
[2] A Wooden way
[4] Regardless grown,
   A Quartz contentment, like a stone —

Johnson opines that Dickinson was indicating the correct line order of the stanza by this numbering; and since the verse makes more syntactic sense when it is printed in the order indicated by her numbering, I have reproduced the stanza in that form. See Johnson, *Poems,* pp. 272–73.

PART   FIVE   ‖   II · Can You Make a World Anew...

1 See Emily Dickinson, *The Poems of Emily Dickinson,* ed. Thomas Johnson (Cambridge, Mass.: Harvard University Press, 1951, 1955), vol. II. pp. 711–14, for an account of the reception of this poem.

PART   FIVE   ‖   III · Requiem

1 Martha Dickinson Bianchi, *The Life and Letters of Emily Dickinson* (Boston and New York: Houghton Mifflin, 1924, reissued 1930), p. 68.
2 Emily Dickinson, The *Letters of Emily Dickinson,* ed. Thomas Johnson and Theodora Ward (Cambridge, Mass.: Harvard University Press, 1958), vol. II, pp. 643–44 (early July 1879).
3 Jay Leyda, *The Years and Hours of Emily Dickinson* (New Haven: Yale University Press, 1960), vol. II, p. 172.
4 Dickinson, *Letters,* vol. II, p. 486 (spring 1871).

5 Leyda, *Years and Hours*, vol. II, p. 167.

6 Dickinson, *Letters*, vol. II, p. 488 (mid-July 1871).

7 Leyda, *Years and Hours*, vol. II, p. 179.

8 Ibid., pp. 209–10.

9 W. S. Tyler, *History of Amherst College During Its First Half Century* (Springfield, Mass.: Clark W. Bryan and Company, 1873), p. 540.

10 Millicent Todd Bingham, *Emily Dickinson's Home* (New York: Dover Publications, 1967), p. 446.

11 Dickinson, *Letters*, vol. II, p. 526 (summer 1874).

12 Bianchi, *Life and Letters*, p. 84; Leyda, *Years and Hours*, vol. II, p. 224; Martha Dickinson Bianchi, *Emily Dickinson Face to Face: Unpublished Letters with Notes and Reminiscences* (Hamden, Conn.: Archon Books, 1970), p. 13.

13 Johnson dates this poem as about 1873; however, given both the content of the poem and its format, it is impossible for me to believe that it was written *before* Edward Dickinson's death in 1874. One additional observation might serve to support this view: after Edward's death, his books were apportioned among the family; before that time, it would have been unusual for his daughter to have appropriated the flyleaf in one of *his* books to write a poem on. See Emily Dickinson, *The Poems of Emily Dickinson*, ed. Thomas Johnson (Cambridge, Mass.: Harvard University Press, 1951, 1955), vol. III, p. 895.

14 Dickinson, *Letters*, vol. II, pp. 537 (January 1875); 538 (after Easter 1875?); 583 (June 1877).

15 Leyda, *Years and Hours*, vol. II, p. 229.

16 Dickinson, *Letters*, vol. II, p. 633 (early January 1879).

17 Dickinson, *Letters*, vol. II, pp. 502–3 (early 1873); vol. III, p. 837 (1884?).

18 Ibid., vol. II, p. 542 (July 1875); vol. III, p. 675 (September 1880).

19 Ibid., vol. II, p. 600 (January 1878).

20 Ibid., vol. III, pp. 661–62 (about June 1880), 780 (late June 1883). The poem in the first letter is Johnson #*1493*.

21 Ibid., vol. II, pp. 545 (March 1876), 623 (late 1878).

22 Ibid., vol. III, p. 690 (early spring 1881).

23 Ibid., pp. 738 (August 1882), 737 (Summer 1882; August 1882), 753 (December 3, 1882), 901 (mid-April 1886).

24 Leyda, *Years and Hours*, vol. II, p. 369.

25 Dickinson, *Letters*, vol. III, p. 730 (May 14, 1882).

26 Ibid., pp. 746 (November 1882), 771 (spring 1883). The poem in the second letter is Johnson #*1573*.

27 Ibid., pp. 714–15 (late 1881).

28 Ibid., p. 765 (March 1883).

29 Ibid., p. 794 (summer 1883).

30 Leyda, *Years and Hours*, vol. II, p. 406.

31 Dickinson, *Letters*, vol. III, p. 803 (late 1883).

32 Ibid., p. 818 (early spring 1884).

33 Ibid., p. 871 (spring 1885).

34 Ibid., vol. II, p. 592 (September 1877).

35 Sören Kierkegaard, *Philosophical Fragments*, trans. David F. Swenson (Princeton, N.J.: Princeton University Press, 1936), p. 46

PART SIX ‖ *"One of the Ones That Midas Touched"*

1 Emily Dickinson, *The Letters of Emily Dickinson,* ed. Thomas Johnson and Theodora Ward (Cambridge, Mass.: Harvard University Press, 1958), vol. II, p. 577 (March 1877).

2 Ibid., p. 508 (early summer 1873).

3 Ibid., p. 639 (May 12, 1879).

4 Ibid., p. 639 (1879).

5 Ibid., vol. III, p. 904 (April 1886).

6 Ibid., p. 903 (spring 1886).

7 Ibid., p. 905 (early May 1886), p. 906 (May 1886).

8 Jay Leyda, *The Years and Hours of Emily Dickinson* (New Haven: Yale University Press, 1960), vol. II, p. 471.

9 Ibid., pp. 472–73.

10 Ibid., p. 475.

11 Millicent Todd Bingham, *Ancestors' Brocades: The Literary Debut of Emily Dickinson* (New York and London: Harper Brothers, 1945), p. 14.

BIBLIOGRAPHY

Bibliography

ALLEN, MARY ADELE. *Around a Village Green: Sketches of Life in Amherst.* Northampton, Mass.: Kraushar Press, 1939.

Amherst Imprints, 1825–1875. Ed. Newton McKeon and Catherine Cowles. Amherst, Mass.: Amherst College, 1946.

ANDERSON, CHARLES R. *Emily Dickinson's Poetry: Stairway of Surprise.* New York: Holt, Rinehart and Winston; London: Heinemann, 1960.

ANDERSON, PEGGY. "Emily Dickinson's Least Favorite Biblical Book?" *Dickinson Studies,* 46 (1983), 27–28.

ANDERSON, VINCENT P. "Emily Dickinson and the Disappearance of God." *Christian Scholars Review,* 11, No. 1 (1981), 3–17.

ARON, STEPHEN. "The Minds of Hands: Working People of Amherst in the Mid-Nineteenth Century." Unpublished Amherst College honors thesis, April 1982.

Atlantic Monthly, III, No. 15 (Feb. 1859), 137–50, IX, No. 54 (April 1862), 401–11.

ATTEBERY, BRIAN. "Dickinson, Emerson and the Abstract Concrete." *Dickinson Studies,* 35 (1979), 17–22.

AUDEN, W. H. *Forewords and Afterwords.* New York: Random House, 1973.

BANNING, EVELYN I. *Helen Hunt Jackson.* New York: Vanguard Press, 1973.

BARNES, DANIEL R. "Telling It Slant: Emily Dickinson and the Proverb." *Genre,* 12 (1979), 219–41.

BAYM, NINA. "God, Father, and Lover in Emily Dickinson's Poetry." PMLA, 164 (Fall 1979), 193–209.

BENES, PETER. *The Masks of Orthodoxy.* Amherst, Mass.: University of Massachusetts Press, 1977.

BENFEY, CHRISTOPHER E. G. *Emily Dickinson and the Problem of Others.* Amherst, Mass.: University of Massachusetts Press, 1985.

BENNETT, PAULA. "Emily Dickinson and the Value of Isolation." *Dickinson Studies,* 36 (1979), 40–49.

BENVENUTO, RICHARD. "Words Within Words: Dickinson's Use of the Dictionary." *Journal of the American Renaissance,* 29, No. 1 (1983), 46–55.

BERCOVITCH, SACVAN. *Typology and Early American Literature.* Amherst, Mass.: University of Massachusetts Press, 1972.

BERES, DAVID. "Psychoanalytic Psychology of Imagination." *Journal of the American Psychoanalytic Association,* VIII, No. 2 (April 1960), 252–69.

BERG, BARBARA J. *The Remembered Gate: Origins of American Feminism—The Woman and the City, 1800–1860.* London: Oxford University Press, 1978.

BIANCHI, MARTHA DICKINSON. *Emily Dickinson Face to Face: Unpublished Letters with Notes and Reminiscences.* Boston and New York: Houghton Mifflin, 1932. Reprinted, Hamden, Conn.: Archon Books, 1970.

——. *The Life and Letters of Emily Dickinson.* Boston and New York: Houghton Mifflin; London: Cape, 1924. Reissued in 1930.

——. "My Surviving Aunt: Lavinia Dickinson." *Prairie Schooner,* 51 (1977–78), 325–44.

BINGHAM, MILLICENT TODD. *Ancestors' Brocades: The Literary Debut of Emily Dickinson.* New York and London: Harper Brothers, 1945.

————. *Emily Dickinson: A Revelation.* New York: Harper; Toronto: Musson, 1954.

————. *Emily Dickinson's Home: Letters of Edward Dickinson and His Family.* New York: Harper; Toronto: Musson, 1955. Reprinted, New York: Dover Publications, 1967.

BLACKMUR, RICHARD P. "Religious Poetry in the United States." In *Religious Perspectives in American Culture.* Ed. James Ward Smith and A. Leland Jamison. Princeton, N.J.: Princeton University Press, 1961.

BLAKE, CAESAR R., and WELLS, CARLTON F., eds. *The Recognition of Emily Dickinson: Selected Criticism Since 1890.* Ann Arbor: University of Michigan Press; Toronto: Ambassador Books, 1964.

BLOCK, RUTH H. "American Feminine Ideals in Transition: The Rise of the Moral Mother, 1785–1815." *Feminist Studies,* 1 (Winter-Spring 1973), 58–72.

BODGAN, JANET. "Care or Cure? Childbirth Practices in Nineteenth-Century America." *Feminist Studies,* 4 (June 1978), 21–40.

BOWLES, SAMUEL, or HOLLAND, JOSIAH. "Employment for Women: A Few Words to Those 'Who Write for the Papers.'" *Springfield Republican,* Dec. 6, 1865.

BOYER, PAUL. *Urban Masses and Moral Order in America: 1820–1920.* Cambridge, Mass.: Harvard University Press, 1978.

BRAZELTON, T. BERRY. "Evidence of Communication During Neonatal Behavioral Assessment." In *Before Speech.* Ed. Margaret Bullowa. New York: Cambridge University Press, 1979.

BRIDGMAN, THOMAS. *Inscription on the Grave Stones . . . of Northampton.* Northampton, Mass., 1850.

BROWN, CHARLES R. *What Is Your Name?* New Haven: Yale University Press, 1924.

BRUMM, URSULA. *American Thought and Religious Typology.* Trans. John Hoaglund. New Brunswick, N.J.: Rutgers University Press, 1970.

BUCKINGHAM, WILLIS J., ed. *Emily Dickinson: An Annotated Bibliography—Writings, Scholarship, Criticism, and Ana, 1850–1968.* Bloomington: Indiana University Press, 1970.

————. "Emily Dickinson's Dictionary." *Harvard Library Bulletin,* 25 (1977), 489–92.

BURBICK, JOAN. "'One Unbroken Company': Religion and Emily Dickinson." *New England Quarterly,* 53 (1980), 62–75.

BURKE, SALLY. "A Religion of Poetry: The Prayer Poems of Emily Dickinson." *Dickinson Studies,* 33 (1978), 17–25.

BURROWS, GEORGE. "Impressions of Dr. Wadsworth as a Preacher." San Francisco, Calif., 1863.

CALVIN, JOHN. *Institutes.* Trans. Henry Beveridge. 2 vols. London: James Clarke & Co., Limited, 1975.

CAMBON, GLAUCO. "Emily Dickinson's Circumference." *Sewanee Review,* 84 (1976), 342–50.

CAMERON, SHARON. *Lyric Time: Dickinson and the Limits of Genre.* Baltimore and London: Johns Hopkins University Press, 1979.

————. "Naming as History: Dickinson's Poems of Definition." *Critical Inquiry,* 5 (1978), 223–51.

CAMPBELL, JOSEPH. *The Hero with a Thousand Faces.* Cleveland: World Publishing Co., 1949.

CAPPS, JACK LEE. *Emily Dickinson's Reading 1836–1886.* Cambridge, Mass.: Harvard University Press; London: Oxford University Press, 1966.

CARPENTER AND MOREHOUSE. *The History of the Town of Amherst, Massachusetts.* Amherst, Mass.: Press of Carpenter & Morehouse, 1896.

CARTON, EVAN. "Dickinson and the Divine: The Terror of Integration, the Terror of Detachment." *Journal of the American Renaissance,* 24 (4th Quarter 1978), 242–52.

CHASE, RICHARD VOLNEY. *Emily Dickinson,* American Men of Letters Series. New York: William Sloane Associates, 1951. London: Methuen; Toronto: McLeod, 1952.

CLENDENNING, SHEILA T. *Emily Dickinson, a Bibliography: 1850–1966.* Kent, Ohio: Kent State University Press, 1969.

CODY, JOHN. *After Great Pain: The Inner Life of Emily Dickinson.* Cambridge, Mass.: Belknap Press of Harvard University Press, 1971.

CONRAD, SUSAN P. *Perish the Thought: Intellectual Women in Romantic America, 1830–1860.* Secaucus, N.J.: Citadel Press, 1978.

COTT, NANCY F. *The Bonds of Womanhood.* New Haven: Yale University Press, 1977.

———. "Passionless: An Interpretation of Victorian Sexual Ideology, 1790–1850." *Signs,* 4, No. 2 (1978), 219–36.

———. "Young Women in the Second Great Awakening in New England." *Feminist Studies,* 3 (Fall 1975), 15–29.

———. ed. and intro. *Roots of Bitterness: Documents on the Social History of American Women.* New York: Dutton, 1972.

COWING, CEDRIC B. "Sex and Preaching in the Great Awakening." *American Quarterly,* 20, No. 3 (Fall 1968), 624–44.

CREWS, FREDERICK, ed. *Psychoanalysis and Literary Process.* Cambridge, Mass.: Winthrop Publishers, 1970.

DANDURAND, KAREN. "New Dickinson Civil War Publications." *American Literature,* 56, No. 1 (March 1984), 17–28.

D'AVANZO, MARIO L. "Dickinson's 'The Reticent Volcano' and Emerson." *American Transcendental Quarterly,* No. 14 (Spring 1972), 11–13.

———. "Emily Dickinson's and Emerson's 'Presentiment.'" *Emerson Society Quarterly,* No. 58, Pt. 4 (1970), 157–59.

———. "'Unto the White Creator': The Snow of Dickinson and Emerson." *New England Quarterly,* 45, No. 2 (June 1972), 278–80.

DEGLER, CARL N. *At Odds: Women and the Family in America from the Revolution to the Present.* New York: Oxford University Press, 1980.

———. "What Ought to Be and What Was: Women's Sexuality in the Nineteenth Century." *American Historical Review,* 79 (December 1974), 1467–90.

DEMOS, JOHN. "The American Family in Past Time." *American Scholar,* 43 (1974), 60–84.

———. "Developmental Perspectives on the History of Childhood." *Journal of Interdisciplinary History,* 2, No. 2 (Autumn 1971), 315–27.

DICKINSON, EDWARD. "Female Education." *New England Inquire,* Dec. 22, 1826; Jan. 5, Jan. 26, Feb. 23, and April 20, 1827.

DICKINSON, EMILY. Dickinson Papers. Houghton Library, Harvard University.

———. *The Letters of Emily Dickinson.* Ed. Thomas H. Johnson and Theodora Ward. 3 vols. Cambridge, Mass.: Harvard University Press, 1958.

———. *The Poems of Emily Dickinson.* Ed. Thomas Johnson. 3 vols. Cambridge, Mass.: Harvard University Press, 1951, 1955.

DICKINSON, FREDERICK. *To the Descendants of Thomas Dickinson.* Chicago, 1897.

DICKINSON, SAMUEL FOWLER. *An Oration in Celebration of American Independence.* Northampton, Mass.: William Butler, 1797.

——— (chairman). "Report of the Committee on the Burying Ground (December, 10, 1982)." Unpublished ms., Amherst Town Engineer's Office.

DICKINSON, SUSAN GILBERT. "Annals of the Evergreen." Unpublished ms., Houghton Library, Harvard.

DICKINSON, W. AUSTIN. "Representative Men of the Parish, Church Buildings and Finances." In *An Historical Review: One Hundred and Fiftieth Anniversary of the First Church of Christ in Amherst, Massachusetts, November 7, 1889.* Amherst, Mass.: Press of the Amherst Record, 1890.

DIEHL, JOANNE FEIT. *Dickinson and the Romantic Imagination.* Princeton, N.J.: Princeton University Press, 1981.

DONEGAN, JANE B. "Man-Midwifery and the Delicacy of the Sexes." In *Remember the Ladies*. Ed. Carol V. R. George. Syracuse: Syracuse University Press, 1975.

DONOGHUE, DENIS. *Emily Dickinson*. Pamphlets on American Writers, No. 81. Minneapolis: University of Minnesota Press, 1970.

DOUGLAS, ANN. *The Feminization of American Culture*. New York: Alfred A. Knopf, 1977.

DUCHAC, JOSEPH. *The Poems of Emily Dickinson: An Annotated Guide to Commentary Published in English, 1890–1977*. Boston: G. K. Hall & Co., 1979.

EBERWEIN, JANE DONAHUE. *Dickinson: Strategies of Limitation*. Amherst, Mass.: University of Massachusetts Press, 1985.

EDELSTEIN, TILDEN G. *Strange Enthusiasm: A Life of Thomas Wentworth Higginson*. New Haven and London: Yale University Press, 1968.

EDGCUMBE, ROSE M. "Developmental Line for Language Acquisition." *Psychoanalytic Study of the Child*, XXXVI (1981), 79–80.

ERIKSON, ERIK H. *Childhood and Society*. New York: W. W. Norton Co., 1963.

FABER, M. D. "Psychoanalytic Remarks on a Poem by Emily Dickinson." *Psychoanalytic Review*, 56, No. 2 (1969), 247–64.

FAST, ROBIN RILEY. "'The One Thing Needful': Dickinson's Dilemma of Home and Heaven." *Journal of the American Renaissance*, 27, No. 3 (3rd Quarter 1981), 157–69.

FEIDELSON, CHARLES. *Symbolism and American Literature*. Chicago: University of Chicago Press, 1965.

FERLAZZO, PAUL J., ed. *Critical Essays on Emily Dickinson*. Boston: G. K. Hall & Co., 1984.

———. *Emily Dickinson*. Boston: Twayne Publishers, 1976.

FORD, THOMAS W. *Heaven Beguiles the Tired: Death in the Poetry of Emily Dickinson*. University: University of Alabama Press, 1966.

FOSTER, JOHN. *Miscellaneous Essays on Christian Morals*. New York: D. Appleton and Co., 1844.

FRANKLIN, RALPH W. "Editing Emily Dickinson." *Dissertation Abstracts*, XXVI (1965), 3335 (Northwestern).

———. *The Editing of Emily Dickinson: A Reconsideration*. Madison: University of Wisconsin Press, 1967.

———, ed. *The Manuscript Books of Emily Dickinson*. 2 vols. Cambridge, Mass.: Belknap Press of Harvard University Press, 1981.

FREUD, ANNA. "Negativism and Emotional Surrender." *International Journal of Psycho-Analysis*, 33 (1952), 265.

FRYE, NORTHROP. *Fables of Identity: Studies in Poetic Mythology*. New York: Harcourt, Brace & World, Inc., 1963.

FUESS, CLAUDE M. *Amherst: The Story of a New England College*. Boston: Little, Brown, 1935.

GARBOWSKY, MARYANNE M. "A Maternal Muse for Emily Dickinson." *Dickinson Studies*, 41 (Dec. 1981), 12–17.

GELPI, ALBERT J. *Emily Dickinson: The Mind of the Poet*. Cambridge, Mass.: Harvard University Press, 1966.

———. *The Tenth Muse*. Cambridge, Mass.: Harvard University Press, 1975.

GILBERT, SANDRA M., and GUBAR, SUSAN. *The Madwoman in the Attic: The Woman Writer and the Nineteenth-Century Literary Imagination*. New Haven: Yale University Press, 1979.

———. "Patriarchal Poetry and Women Readers: Reflections on Milton's Bogey." *PMLA*, 93, No. 3 (1979), 247–64.

GILLON, EDMOND VINCENT, JR. *Early New England Gravestone Rubbings*. 2nd ed. New York: Dover Publications, 1981.

GORDON, LINDA. "Voluntary Motherhood: The Beginnings of Feminist Birth Control Ideas in the United States." *Feminist Studies*, 1 (Winter-Spring 1973).

The Great Awakening. Ed. Alan Heimart and Perry Miller. Indianapolis and New York: Bobbs-Merrill Co., 1967.

GREENACRE, PHYLLIS. *Emotional Growth.* Vol. 2. New York: International Universities Press, 1971.

———. "Woman as Artist." *Psychoanalytic Quarterly,* XXIX, No. 2 (1960), 211.

GREENE, THEODORE P., ed. *Essays on Amherst's History.* Amherst, Mass.: Vista Trust, 1978.

GRIFFITH, CLARK. *The Long Shadow: Emily Dickinson's Tragic Poetry.* Princeton, N.J.: Princeton University Press, 1964.

GURA, PHILIP F. *The Wisdom of Words: Language, Theology, and Literature in the New England Renaissance.* Middletown, Conn.: Wesleyan University Press, 1982.

GURKO, MIRIAM. *The Ladies of Seneca Falls: The Birth of the Woman's Rights Movement.* New York: Schocken Books, 1974.

GUTHRIE, JAMES. "'Before I Got My Eye Put Out': Dickinson's Illness and Its Effects on Her Poetry." *Dickinson Studies,* 42 (June 1982), 16–21.

———. "The Modest Poet's Tactics of Concealment and Surprise: Bird Symbolism in Dickinson's Poetry." *Journal of the American Renaissance,* 27, No. 4 (4th Quarter 1981), 230–37.

HAGENBUCHLE, ROLAND. "Sign and Process: The Concept of Language in Emerson and Dickinson." *Journal of the American Renaissance,* 25 (1979), 137–55.

HAMMOND, WILLIAM GARDINER. *Remembrance of Amherst: An Undergraduate's Diary, 1846–1848.* Ed. George Frisbie Whicher. New York: Columbia University Press, 1946.

HANDLIN, OSCAR, and HANDLIN, MARY F. *Facing Life: Youth and Family in American History.* Boston: Little, Brown, 1971.

HECHT, ANTHONY. "The Riddles of Emily Dickinson." *New England Review,* 1 (1978), 1–24.

HIGGINS, DAVID. *Portrait of Emily Dickinson: The Poet and Her Prose.* New Brunswick, N.J.: Rutgers University Press, 1967.

HIGGINSON, THOMAS WENTWORTH. "Emily Dickinson's Letters." *Atlantic Monthly,* LXVIII (Oct. 1891), 444–56.

———. "Letter to a Young Contributor," *Atlantic Monthly,* IX (April 1862), 401–11. Reprinted in *Atlantic Essays,* Boston, 1871.

———. "Ought Women to Learn the Alphabet?" *Atlantic Monthly,* VI (Feb. 1859).

———. *Out-Door Papers.* Boston, 1863.

HITCHCOCK, EDWARD. *Discourse: The Religious Bearing of Man's Creation.* Albany: Van Benthuysen, Printer, 1856.

———. *Elementary Geology.* Amherst, Mass., 1840.

———. *The Highest Use of Learning: An Address Delivered at His Inauguration to the Presidency of Amherst College.* Amherst, Mass.: J. S. & C. Adams, Printers, 1845.

———. *The Power of Christian Benevolence, Illustrated in the Life and Labors of Mary Lyon.* Northampton, Mass.: Hopkins, Bridgman, and Company, 1852; New York, 1858.

———. *The Religion of Geology and Its Connected Sciences.* Boston, 1851.

———. *Religious Lectures on Peculiar Phenomena.* Amherst, Mass.: J. S. & C. Adams, 1850.

———. *Reminiscences of Amherst College.* Northampton, Mass.: Bridgman & Childs, 1863.

HOLMES, WILLIAM, and BARBER, J. W. *Emblems and Allegories.* Cincinnati: J. H. Johnson, 1851. (Two volumes in one, separately paginated. Contains *Religious Emblems,* 1846, and *Religious Allegories,* 1848.)

HUMPHREY, HEMAN. *Revival Conversations.* Boston, 1844.

———. *Revival: Sketches and Manual.* New York: American Tract Society, 1859.

———. *Sketches of the Early History of Amherst College.* Northampton, Mass.: At the request of the Trustees of Amherst College, 1905.

The Interpreter's Bible. Nashville, Tenn.: Abingdon, 1952.

JENKINS, REV. JONATHAN L. "A Sermon Delivered at Edward Dickinson's Funeral." Unpublished ms., Dickinson Collection, Houghton Library, Harvard.

JOHNSON, GREG. "'Broken Mathematics': Emily Dickinson's Concept of Ratio." *Concerning Poetry,* 13 (1980), 21–26.

JOHNSON, THOMAS H. *Emily Dickinson: An Interpretive Biography.* Cambridge, Mass.: Belknap Press of Harvard University Press; London: Oxford University Press; Toronto: S. J. R. Saunders, 1955.

JONES, ROWENA REVIS. "The Preparation of a Poet: Puritan Directions in Emily Dickinson's Education." *Studies in the American Renaissance,* 1982, 285–324.

JUHASZ, SUZANNE. "'But Most, Like Chaos': Emily Dickinson Measures Pain." *American Transcendental Quarterly,* 43 (Summer 1979), 225–41.

———, ed. *Feminist Critics Read Emily Dickinson.* Bloomington: Indiana University Press, 1983.

———. "'I Dwell in Possibility': Emily Dickinson in the Subjunctive Mood." *Dickinson Studies,* 32 (1977), 105–9.

———. "'A Privilege So Awful': Emily Dickinson as Woman Poet." *San Jose Studies,* 2, No. 2 (May 1976), 94–107.

———. "Reading Emily Dickinson's Letters." *Journal of the American Renaissance,* 30, No. 3 (3rd Quarter 1984), 170–92.

———. "The 'Undiscovered Continent': Emily Dickinson and the Space of the Mind." *Missouri Review,* 3, No. 1 (Fall 1979), 86–97.

KEEFER, FREDERICK, and VLAHOS, DEBORAH. "Dickinson's 'If You Were Coming in the Fall.'" *Explicator,* 29, No. 3 (Nov. 1970), Item 23.

KELLER, KARL. *The Only Kangaroo Among the Beauty: Emily Dickinson and America.* Baltimore and London: Johns Hopkins University Press, 1979.

KETT, JOSEPH F. "Adolescence and Youth in Nineteenth-Century America." *Journal of Interdisciplinary History* 2, No. 2 (Autumn 1971), 315–27.

———. "Growing Up in Rural New England, 1800–1840." In *Anonymous Americans.* Ed. Tamara K. Hareven. Englewood Cliffs, N.J.: Prentice-Hall, 1971.

———. *Rites of Passage: Adolescence in America, 1790 to the Present.* New York: Basic Books, Inc., 1977.

KHER, INDER NATH. *The Landscape of Absence: Emily Dickinson's Poetry.* New Haven and London: Yale University Press, 1974.

KIERKEGAARD, SÖREN. *Philosophical Fragments.* Trans. David F. Swenson. Princeton, N.J.: Princeton University Press, 1936.

KING, STANLEY. *A History of the Endowment of Amherst College.* Amherst, Mass.: Amherst College Press, 1950.

KNIGHTS, L. C. "Defining the Self: Poems of Emily Dickinson." *Sewanee Review,* 91, No. 3 (Summer 1983), 357–75.

LAMBERT, ROBERT GRAHAM, JR. "The Prose of a Poet: A Critical Study of Emily Dickinson's Letters." Unpublished ms.

LANTZ, HERMAN R. "Romantic Love in the Pre-Modern Period: A Social Commentary." *Journal of Social History,* 15, No. 3 (Spring 1982), 349–70.

LANYI, RONALD. "'My Faith That Dark Adores—': Calvinist Theology in the Poetry of Emily Dickinson." *Arizona Quarterly,* 32, No. 3 (Autumn 1976), 264–78.

LE DUC, THOMAS. *Piety and Intellect at Amherst College 1865–1912.* New York: Columbia University Press, 1946.

LEITES, EDMUND. "The Duty to Desire: Love, Friendship, and Sexuality in Some Puritan Theories of Marriage." *Journal of Social History,* 15, No. 3 (Spring 1982), 383–408.

LERNER, GERDA. *The Female Experience: An American Documentary.* Indianapolis: Bobbs-Merrill Co., 1977.

LEWALSKI, BARBARA KIEFER. *Protestant Poetics and the Seventeenth-Century Religious Lyric.*

Princeton, N.J.: Princeton University Press, 1979.

LEYDA, JAY. *The Years and Hours of Emily Dickinson.* 2 vols. New Haven: Yale University Press; London: Oxford University Press; Toronto: Burns and MacEachern, 1960.

LINCOLN, ALMIRA H. (MRS.). *Familiar Lectures on Botany.* Hartford, Conn.: F. J. Huntington, 1835.

LINDBERG-SEYERSTED, BRITA. *Emily Dickinson's Punctuation.* Oslo: American Institute, University of Oslo, 1976.

——. *The Voice of the Poet: Aspects of Style in the Poetry of Emily Dickinson.* Cambridge, Mass.: Harvard University Press, 1968.

LOWANCE, MASON. *The Language of Canaan.* Cambridge, Mass.: Harvard University Press, 1980.

LUBBERS, KLAUS. *Emily Dickinson: The Critical Revolution.* Ann Arbor: University of Michigan Press, 1968.

LUCAS, DOLORES DYER. *Emily Dickinson and Riddle.* DeKalb: Northern Illinois Press, 1969.

LUDWIG, ALLAN I. *Graven Images.* Middletown, Conn.: Wesleyan University Press, 1966.

LYON, MARY. "Mount Holyoke Female Seminary." In *Old South Leaflets.* Boston, 1904.

MACHOR, JAMES L. "Emily Dickinson and Feminine Rhetoric." *Arizona Quarterly,* 36 (1980), 131–46.

MACK, ARIEN, ed. *Death in American Experience.* New York: Schocken Books, 1973.

MACLEISH, ARCHIBALD; BOGAN, LOUISE; and WILBUR, RICHARD. *Emily Dickinson: Three Views.* Amherst, Mass.: Amherst College Press, 1960.

MAHLER, MARGARET S.; PINE, FRED; and BERGMAN, ANNI. *The Psychological Birth of the Human Infant.* New York: Basic Books, 1975.

MANN, JOHN S. "Emily Dickinson, Emerson, and the Poet as Namer." *New England Quarterly,* 51 (1978), 467–88.

MARTIN, WENDY. *An American Triptych: Anne Bradstreet, Emily Dickinson, Adrienne Rich.* Chapel Hill: University of North Carolina Press, 1984.

MARVEL, IK. *Reveries of a Bachelor.* New York, 1850.

MATHER, SAMUEL. *The Figures and Types of the Old Testament.* Ed. Mason I. Lowance. New York: Johnson Reprint Corporation, 1969.

MATTHEW, HENRY. *A Companion to the Bible.* Ed. William Jenks. Brattleboro, Vt., 1838.

MATTHIESSEN, FRANCIS OTTO. *American Renaissance: Art and Expression in the Age of Emerson and Whitman.* New York and London: Oxford University Press, 1941.

MCGREGOR, ELIZABETH. "Standing with the Prophets and Martyrs: Emily Dickinson's Scriptural Self-Defense." *Dickinson Studies,* 39 (1981), 18–26.

MCLEAN, SYDNEY R. "Emily Dickinson at Mount Holyoke." *New England Quarterly,* March 1935, 25–42.

MERRIAM, GEORGE S. *The Life and Times of Samuel Bowles.* 2 vols. New York: Century Co., 1885.

MILLER, F. DEWOLFE. "Emily Dickinson: Self-Portrait in the Third Person." *New England Quarterly,* 46, No. 1 (March 1973), 119–24.

MILLER, PERRY. *The American Puritans: Their Prose and Poetry.* New York: Doubleday, 1956.

MILLER, RUTH. "Inner Than the Bone: Emily Dickinson's Third Tribunal." *Proceedings of the Conference of University Teachers of English.* University of the Negev, Beer-Sheva, March 1971, 36–54.

——. "Poetry as a Transitional Object." 25 (Fall 1978), 447–68.

——. *The Poetry of Emily Dickinson.* Middletown, Conn.: Wesleyan University Press, 1968.

MITCHELL, DONALD G. [IK MARVEL]. *Dream Life.* New York: Charles Scribner, 1851.

MOERS, ELLEN. *Literary Women.* New York: Anchor Press, 1977.

MOLSON, FRANCIS J. "Emily Dickinson's Rejection of the Heavenly Father." *New England Quar-*

terly: A Historical Review of New England Life and Letters, 47 (1974), 404–26.

MONTEIRO, GEORGE, and ST. ARMAND, BARTON LEVI. "The Experienced Emblem: A Study of the Poetry of Emily Dickinson." In *Prospects.* Ed. Jack Salzman. New York: Burt Franklin & Co., 1981.

MOREY, FREDERICK L. "Emily Dickinson as a Modern." *Dickinson Studies,* 26 (1974), 83–86.

MOSSBERG, BARBARA ANTONINA CLARKE. *Emily Dickinson: When a Writer Is a Daughter.* Bloomington: Indiana University Press, 1982.

THE MOUNT HOLYOKE JOURNAL LETTER. Unpublished ms., Williston Memorial Library, Mount Holyoke College.

MUDGE, JEAN MCCLURE. *Emily Dickinson and the Image of Home.* Amherst, Mass.: University of Massachusetts Press, 1975.

MUENSTERBERGER, WARNER. "The Creative Process." *Psychoanalytic Study of Society,* II (1962), 168–69.

New England Primer. Hartford, 1841, 1842.

NORTON, MARY BETH. *Liberty's Daughters: The Revolutionary Experience of American Women, 1750–1800.* Boston: Little, Brown, 1980.

Notes on the Life of Noah Webster. Ed. Emily Ellsworth Ford Skeel. 2 vols. New York: Privately printed, 1912.

ODELL, RUTH. *Helen Hunt Jackson.* New York and London: D. Appleton–Century, 1939.

PALEY, WILLIAM. *Works.* 2 vols. London: Henry Fisher, Son, and P. Jackson, 1828.

"PAPERS OF J. LELAND." Unpublished ms., Amherst College Library.

PARKES, HENRY BAMFORD. "Sexual Morals in the Great Awakening." *New England Quarterly,* 3 (1930).

PATTERSON, REBECCA. "Emily Dickinson's 'Double' Tim: Masculine Identification." *American Imago,* 28, No. 4 (Winter 1971), 330–62.

———. *The Riddle of Emily Dickinson.* Boston: Houghton Mifflin; Toronto: Thomas Allen, 1951; London: Gollancz, 1953.

PECKHAM, HARRY HOUSTON. *Josiah Gilbert Holland in Relation to His Times.* Philadelphia: University of Pennsylvania Press; London: H. Milford, Oxford University Press, 1940.

PERLMUTTER, ELIZABETH F. "Hide and Seek: Emily Dickinson's Use of the Existential Sentence." *Language and Style: An International Journal,* 10 (1977), 15–32.

PHELAN, JOAN D. "Puritan Tradition and Emily Dickinson's Poetic Practice." *Dissertation Abstracts International,* 33 (1973), 5136A (Bryn Mawr).

PHELPS, ALMIRA H. LINCOLN. *Familiar Lectures on Botany.* Hartford, Conn., 1829.

PICKARD, JOHN B. *Emily Dickinson: An Introduction and Interpretation.* New York: Holt, Rinehart and Winston, 1967.

PLUNKETT, HARRIETTE MERRICK. *Josiah Gilbert Holland.* New York, 1894.

POLLACK, VIVIAN R. *Dickinson: The Anxiety of Gender.* Ithaca, N.Y.: Cornell University Press, 1984.

POLLITT [POHL], JOSEPHINE. *Emily Dickinson: The Human Background of Her Poetry.* New York: Harper, 1930. Reprinted, New York: Cooper Square, 1970.

PORTER, DAVID T. *The Art of Emily Dickinson's Early Poetry.* Cambridge, Mass.: Harvard University Press, 1966.

———. *Dickinson: The Modern Idiom.* Cambridge, Mass.: Harvard University Press, 1981.

PORTER, EBENEZER. *The Rhetorical Reader.* New York, 1842.

QUARLES, FRANCIS. *Emblems, Divine and Moral.* London, 1824.

The Recognition of Emily Dickinson. Ed. Caesar R. Blake and Carlton F. Wells. Ann Arbor: University of Michigan Press, 1968.

REED, JAMES. *From Private Vice to Public Virtue: The Birth Control Movement and American Society Since 1830.* New York: Basic Books, 1978.

Reunion of the Dickinson Family at Amherst, Massachusetts, August 8th and 9th, 1883. Binghamton, N.Y.: Binghamton Press, 1884.

RICH, ADRIENNE. "Vesuvius at Home: The Power of Emily Dickinson." *Parnassus: Poetry in Review,* V, No. 1 (Fall-Winter 1976), 49–74.

RIESS, ANNELIESE. "The Mother's Eye." *Psychoanalytic Study of the Child,* 33 (1978), 382.

ROBSON, KENNETH S. "The Role of Eye-to-Eye Contact in Maternal-Infant Attachment." *Journal of Child Psychology and Psychiatry,* 8 (1967), 13–14.

ROLLINS, RICHARD M. "Words as Social Control: Noah Webster and the Creation of the *American Dictionary.*" *American Quarterly,* XXVIII, No. 4 (Fall 1976), 427.

ROSENBAUM, S. P., ed. *A Concordance to the Poems of Emily Dickinson.* Ithaca, N.Y.: Cornell University Press, 1964.

ROSENBERG, CHARLES E. "Sexuality, Class and Role in Nineteenth-Century America." *American Quarterly,* 25 (July 1973), 131–53.

ROTHMAN, ELLEN K. *Hands and Hearts.* New York: Basic Books, 1984.

RUPP, RICHARD H., ed. *Critics on Emily Dickinson.* Readings in Literary Criticism, vol. 14. Coral Gables, Fla.: University of Miami Press, 1972.

ST. ARMAND, BARTON LEVI. *Emily Dickinson and Her Culture: The Soul's Society.* London: Cambridge University Press, 1984.

———. "Emily Dickinson's American Grotesque: The Poet as Folk Artist." *Topic: A Journal of the Liberal Arts,* 32 (1977), 3–19.

———. "In the American Manner: An Inquiry into the Aesthetics of Emily Dickinson and Edgar Allan Poe." *Dissertation Abstracts,* 30 (1969), 294A (Brown).

———. "Paradise Deferred: The Image of Heaven in the Work of Emily Dickinson and Elizabeth Stuart Phelps." *American Quarterly,* 29 (1977), 55–78.

SAUM, LEWIS O. "Death in the Popular Mind of Pre–Civil War America." *American Quarterly,* XXVI, No. 5 (Dec. 1974).

SCOTT-SMITH, DANIEL. "Family Limitation, Sexual Control, and Domestic Feminism in Victorian America." In *Clio's Consciousness Raised.* Ed. Hartman and Banner. New York: Harper & Row, 1974. Also in *Feminist Studies,* I (1973).

SEWALL, RICHARD B. *The Life of Emily Dickinson.* 2 vols. New York: Farrar, Straus & Giroux, 1974.

———. *The Lyman Letters: New Light on Emily Dickinson and Her Family.* Amherst, Mass.: University of Massachusetts Press, 1965.

———, ed. *Emily Dickinson: A Collection of Critical Essays.* Englewood Cliffs, N.J.: Prentice-Hall, 1963.

SHELDON, GEORGE. *A History of Deerfield, Massachusetts.* Vol. I. Greenfield, Mass., 1895.

———. *Lucius Manlius Boltwood.* Boston, Mass., 1905.

SHERWOOD, WILLIAM ROBERT. *Circumference and Circumstance: Stages in the Mind and Art of Emily Dickinson.* New York: Columbia University Press, 1968.

SHULLENBERGER, WILLIAM, and WARD, CANDICE, eds. "Special Issue: Emily Dickinson." *Massachusetts Studies in English,* 7–8 (1981).

SHURR, WILLIAM H. *The Marriage of Emily Dickinson: A Study of the Fascicles.* Lexington: University Press of Kentucky, 1983.

SILLIMAN, BENJAMIN. *Geological Lectures.* New Haven, Conn., 1829.

SIMMONS, CHARLES. *A Scriptural Manual.* New York, 1845.

SMITH, ALEXANDER. *Poems.* London, 1853.

SMITH-ROSENBERG, CARROLL. "The Female World of Love and Ritual." In *A Heritage of Her Own.* Ed. Nancy F. Cott and Elizabeth H. Pleck. New York: Simon and Schuster, 1979.

———. "The Hysterical Woman: Sex Roles and Role Conflict in Nineteenth-Century America." *Social Research,* 39 (Winter 1972), 652–78.

———. "Puberty to Menopause: The Cycle of Feminity in Nineteenth-Century America." *Feminist Studies,* 1 (Winter-Spring 1973), 58–72.

SOULE, GEORGE J., JR. "Emily Dickinson and Jacob: 'Pugilist and Poet' Wrestling to the Dawn." *Emily Dickinson Bulletin,* 31 (1977), 50–58.

SPITZ, RENÉ. *The First Year of Life.* New York: International Universities Press, 1965.

SPRAGUE, ROSEMARY. *Imaginary Gardens: A Study of Five American Poets.* Philadelphia: Chilton Book Co., 1969.

STEARNS, ALFRED E. *An Amherst Boyhood.* Amherst, Mass.: Amherst College Press, 1946.

STEINER, DOROTHEA. "Emily Dickinson: Image Patterns and the Female Imagination." *Arbeiten aus Anglistik und Amerikanistik,* 6, No. 1 (1981), 57–71.

STEPHENSON, WILLIAM E. "Emily Dickinson and Watts's Songs for Children." *English Language Notes,* 3, No. 4 (June 1966), 278–81.

STERN, DANIEL. *The First Relationship.* Cambridge, Mass.: Harvard University Press, 1977.

SUDOL, RONALD ALLAN. "Elegy in the Poetry of Emily Dickinson." *Dissertation Abstracts International,* 37 (1976), 1557A–58A.

TAGGARD, GENEVIEVE. *The Life and Mind of Emily Dickinson.* New York: Alfred A. Knopf; don: G. Allen, 1930.

TASHJIAN, DICKRAN, and TASHJIAN, ANN. *Memorials for Children of Change.* Middletown, Conn.: Wesleyan University Press, 1973.

TAYLOR, JANE (MRS.). *Physiology for Children.* n.p., 1847.

THOMAS, OWEN P. "Father and Daughter: Edward and Emily Dickinson." *American Literature,* 40, No. 4 (Jan. 1969), 510–23.

TODD, JOHN EMERSON. *Emily Dickinson's Use of the Persona.* The Hague: Mouton & Co., 1973.

———. "The Persona in Emily Dickinson's Love Poems." *Michigan Academician,* 1, No. 12 (Winter 1969), 197–207.

TUCKERMAN, FREDERICK. *Amherst Academy: A New England School of the Past, 1814–1861.* Amherst, Mass.: Printed for the Trustees, 1929.

TYLER, WILLIAM S. *History of Amherst College During Its First Half Century, 1821–1871.* Springfield Mass.: Clark W. Bryan and Company, 1873. A new edition extending the history appeared in 1895, published in New York.

———. *The Wise Man of the Scriptures; or Science and Religion. A Discourse delivered in the Village Church in Amherst March 2d, 1864, at the Funeral of Rev. Prof. Edward Hitchcock, DD., LL.D.* Springfield, Mass., 1864.

VISCOTT, D. "A Musical Idiot Savant: A Psychodynamic Study, and Some Speculations on the Creative Process." *Psychiatry,* XXXIII (1971), 494–515.

WALSH, JOHN EVANGELIST. *The Hidden Life of Emily Dickinson.* New York: Simon and Schuster, 1971.

WAND, MARTIN, and SEWALL, RICHARD B. "'Eyes Be Blind, Heart Be Still': A New Perspective on Emily Dickinson's Eye Problem." *New England Quarterly* (Sept. 1979), 400–406.

WARD, THEODORA VAN WAGENEN. *The Capsule of the Mind: Chapters in the Life of Emily Dickinson.* Cambridge, Mass.: Harvard University Press; London: Oxford University Press, 1961.

WARNER, FREDERICK C. "List of Births Attended, 1805–1833, by Dr. Isaac G. Cutler of Amherst." *Detroit Society for Genealogical Research Magazine,* 35, No. 1 (Fall 1971), 29.

WEBSTER, NOAH. *An American Dictionary of the English Language.* New York: S. Converse, 1828.

WEIL, ANNEMARIE P. "The Basic Core." *Psychoanalytic Study of the Child,* XXV (1970).

WEISBUCH, ROBERT. *Emily Dickinson's Poetry.* Chicago: University of Chicago Press, 1975.

WELLS, ANNA MARY. *Dear Preceptor: The Life and Times of Thomas Wentworth Higginson.* Boston: Houghton Mifflin, 1963.

WELTER, BARBARA. *Dimity Convictions: The American Woman in the Nineteenth Century.* Athens, Ohio: Ohio University Press, 1976.

WERTZ, RICHARD W., and WERTZ, DOROTHY C. *Lying-In: A History of Childbirth in America.* New York: Schocken Books, 1977.

WHICHER, GEORGE FRISBIE. *This Was a Poet: A Critical Biography of Emily Dickinson.* New York: Charles Scribner's Sons, 1938.

WILSON, R. J. "Intellectuals and Society in Western Massachusetts: Emily Dickinson and the Problem of Career." *Massachusetts Review,* XX, No. 3 (Autumn 1979), 451–61.

WINNICOTT, D. W. *The Maturation Processes and the Facilitating Environment.* New York: Interternational Universities Press, Inc., 1965.

———. "Transitional Objects and Transitional Phenomena." In *Collected Papers.* New York: Basic Books, 1958.

WOLFF, CYNTHIA GRIFFIN. "Literary Reflections of the Puritan Character." *Journal of the History of Ideas,* XXIX, No. 1 (Jan.—March 1968).

WOLOSKY, SHIRA. *Emily Dickinson: A Voice of War.* New Haven, Conn.: Yale University Press, 1984.

WOOD, ANN DOUGLAS. "The 'Scribbling Women' and Fanny Fern: Why Women Wrote." *American Quarterly,* 23 (1971), 6.

WOODRESS, JAMES. "Emily Dickinson." In *Fifteen American Authors Before 1900: Biographical Essays on Research and Criticism.* Ed. Earl N. Harbert and Robert A. Rees. Madison: University of Wisconsin Press, 1984.

WORCESTER, JOSEPH E. *Elements of History, Ancient and Modern.* Boston: Wm. J. Reynolds & Co., 1826.

WYLDER, EDITH P. "The Voice of the Poet: Selected Poems of Emily Dickinson with an Introduction to the Rhetorical Punctuation of the Manuscripts." *Dissertation Abstracts,* 28 (1968), 4194A–95A (University of New Mexico).

INDEX OF FIRST LINES

Index of First Lines

The Johnson number of the poem is given in parentheses. An asterisk indicates that the poem is quoted in full; other page numbers indicate where the poem is quoted in part or mentioned.

Index

A Note on the Type

The text of this book was set in Sabon, a type face designed by Jan Tschichold (1902–1974), the well-known German typographer. Because it was designed in Frankfurt, Sabon was named for the famous Frankfurt type founder Jacques Sabon, who died in 1580 while manager of the Egenolff foundry.
Based loosely on the original designs of Claude Garamond (c. 1480–1561), Sabon is unique in that it was explicitly designed for hot-metal composition on both the Monotype and Linotype machines as well as for film composition.

Composed by Graphic Composition, Inc., Athens, Georgia
Printed and bound by Murray Printing, Westford, Massachusetts
Book designed by Betty Anderson
Picture inserts designed by Anthea Lingeman

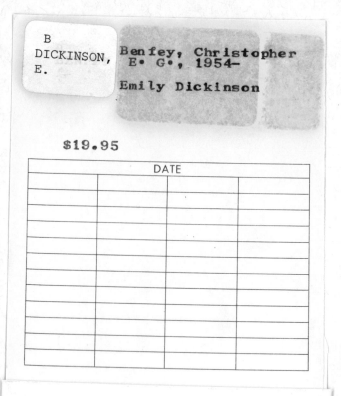